ETHICS AND CRIMINAL LAW

SECOND EDITION

Other books in the *Essentials of Canadian Law* Series

Immigration Law

International Trade Law

Family Law

Copyright Law

The Law of Sentencing

Administrative Law

Securities Law

Computer Law 2/e

Maritime Law

Insurance Law

International Human Rights Law

Franchise Law

Legal Ethics and Professional
Responsibility 2/e

Refugee Law

Statutory Interpretation 2/e

National Security Law: Canadian
Practice in International Perspective

Public International Law 2/e

Individual Employment Law 2/e

Bankruptcy and Insolvency Law

The Law of Partnerships and
Corporations 3/e

Civil Litigation

Conflict of Laws

Legal Research and Writing 3/e

Religious Institutions and the Law
in Canada 3/e

Detention and Arrest

Canadian Telecommunications Law

The Law of Torts 4/e

Intellectual Property Law 2/e

Animals and the Law

Income Tax Law 2/e

Fundamental Justice

Mergers, Acquisitions, and Other
Changes of Corporate Control 2/e

Criminal Procedure 2/e

Criminal Law 5/e

Personal Property Security Law 2/e

The Law of Contracts 2/e

Youth Criminal Justice Law 3/e

Constitutional Law 4/e

Bank and Customer Law in Canada 2/e

The Law of Equitable Remedies 2/e

The Charter of Rights and
Freedoms 5/e

Environmental Law 4/e

Pension Law 2/e

International and Transnational
Criminal Law 2/e

Remedies: The Law of Damages 3/e

Freedom of Conscience and Religion

The Law of Trusts 3/e

The Law of Evidence 7/e

ETHICS AND CRIMINAL LAW

SECOND EDITION

DAVID LAYTON
of the British Columbia bar

HON. MICHEL PROULX (DECEASED)
formerly of the Quebec Court of Appeal

Ethics and Criminal Law, second edition
© Irwin Law Inc., 2015

Published in 2015 by

Irwin Law Inc.
14 Duncan Street
Suite 206
Toronto, ON
M5H 3G8

www.irwinlaw.com

ISBN: 978-1-55221-378-0
e-book ISBN: 978-1-55221-379-7

Library and Archives Canada Cataloguing in Publication

Proulx, Michel, 1939–2007
[Ethics and Canadian criminal law]
        Ethics and criminal law / David Layton of the British Columbia
bar, Hon. Michel Proulx, Quebec Court of Appeal. — Second edition.

(Essentials of Canadian law)
Previously published under title: Ethics and Canadian criminal law
    / Michel Proulx, David Layton.
Issued in print and electronic formats.
ISBN 978-1-55221-378-0 (pbk.).—ISBN 978-1-55221-379-7 (pdf)

        1. Criminal law—Moral and ethical aspects—Canada. 2. Legal
ethics—Canada. I. Layton, David (David M.), author II. Title.
III. Series: Essentials of Canadian law

KE339.P76 2015   174'.30971   C2014-908430-7
KF306.P76 2015   C2014-908431-5

The publisher acknowledges the financial support of the Government of Canada
through the Canada Book Fund for its publishing activities.

We acknowledge the assistance of the OMDC Book Fund, an initiative of
Ontario Media Development Corporation.

Printed and bound in Canada.

1 2 3 4 5   19 18 17 16 15

SUMMARY
TABLE OF CONTENTS

DETAILED
TABLE OF CONTENTS

CHAPTER 4:
CONFIDENTIALITY 157

ACKNOWLEDGEMENTS AND DEDICATION

Thanks to the colleagues and friends I have practised criminal law with over the past twenty years in Toronto and Vancouver, most recently at the firm of Ritchie Sandford, for making the work so stimulating and enjoyable. I will always hold a special flame for my friends at Shiller Layton Arbuck in Toronto. And so too for my companions in the Law Geeks Supreme Court of Canada reading group — Kim Eldred, Kevin Drolet, and Nikos Harris — who have allowed me to combine a love for the law, ethics, food, and drink.

Over the last decade, I have spoken about legal ethics with many Canadian lawyers and judges, and I am grateful to them for sharing their views. I have also learned much from the law students I have taught at the University of British Columbia and the University of Victoria. The listservs of the Trial Lawyers Association of British Columbia and the Canadian Association for Legal Ethics have also been great sources of information and knowledge about common problems and current trends in legal ethics.

I owe a substantial debt to the growing number of academics who, since the first edition of this book was published, have made legal ethics a truly exciting topic of study and debate in this country. Particular thanks goes to Adam Dodek, a leader in the field whom I met when we were both becoming interested in the topic and who has produced stellar work ever since; David Tanovich, with whom I have exchanged many emails about the proper role of defence counsel over the years; Michael Code, who as a professor at the University of Toronto Faculty of Law repeatedly included me in the professional responsibility bridge week put on for first-year students at that institution; Alice Woolley, a prolific and sage commentator who kindly reviewed a draft chapter of this book; and Brent Cotter, a professor of mine at Dalhousie Law School who was one of the few academics then dedicated to the notion that professional responsibility should be a core subject in the law school curriculum and who remains an important force in Canadian legal ethics today.

My wonderful partner, Zoe Druick, has supported and nurtured me through two editions of this book and much else besides. My parents, Norman and Mary Layton, have also been unstinting in their help and encouragement.

It has been a pleasure working again with Jeff Miller at Irwin Law, and my editors, Alisa Posesorski and John Sawicki, have done much to improve the book. Thanks to all of them.

Although the manuscript for this edition was submitted before I began working as Crown counsel, I should say that the opinions expressed are mine personally and do not necessarily reflect the views of the prosecution service in British Columbia.

Finally, I remain in awe of and ever grateful to my co-author, Michel Proulx, who died in early 2007. Michel invited me to work with him on the first edition of this book when I was still new to the profession. He supported and encouraged me not only in my career but personally as well. His energy and enthusiasm for the law, and for life, was infectious and invigorating, and he took my career to places that would not have been possible without him. Michel's moral sense remains at the heart of this edition, and I am proud to dedicate it to him, my mentor, colleague, and friend.

David Layton

ACKNOWLEDGEMENTS
from the First Edition

I should underline, at the outset, that the offer from the publishers to write this book came as a result of a suggestion to them by my colleague Louise Otis, following a panel on ethics in criminal law which was held in Montreal a few years ago and had a great success among the practitioners.

The realization of a lifetime project of this magnitude could not have been achieved without the contribution and support of so many great scholars and friends.

I am particularly indebted to my co-author who made this book possible. His passion for the subject and his dedication to quality in research were truly remarkable.

I would also like to thank the following, throughout Canada, for their comments on the text and their valuable time. My colleagues Melvin Rothman, Morris Fish and Joseph Nuss, the Honourable Michael Moldaver, J.A., The Honourable Fred Kaufman, Bruno Pateras, Q.C., Richard Shadley, Q.C., Frangois Daviault, Raphael Schachter, Q.C., Richard Masson, Lori Weitzman, Guy Cournoyer, Marc David, Suzanne Costom; Clayton Ruby, Q.C.; Alan D. Gold; Richard C.C. Peck, Q.C.; Joel E. Pink, Q.C.; Fred Ferguson, Q.C.; Daniel A. Bellemare, Q.C.

Special thanks are expressed to Daniel A. Bellemare, Q.C., Assistant Deputy Attorney General of Canada, who was intrumental in obtaining financial assistance extended by the Department of Justice for the publication of this book.

I appreciated, throughout the life of this project, the moral support of a great friend and colleague, Pierre A. Michaud, Chief Justice of the Quebec Court of Appeal.

I am also grateful to many other prominent jurists, too numerous to mention, who were a source of inspiration and guidance in my professional life as a defence attorney and a judge of the Quebec Court of Appeal. I would be happy if somehow, 1 were able to reflect their collective wisdom in this treatise.

I also wish to express my sincere gratitude to Micheline Mongeau, my administrative assistant, and my law clerk Marie-Lise Dufort. Their daily assistance was invaluable.

Finally, a special word for Brenda, my formidable partner in life. She has shown unconditional support as well as extraordinary patience and encouragement for this project. Along with our six daughters, and often our sons-in-law, she reminded me that no challenge can be met without special commitment and perseverance.

Michel Proulx, J.A.

ABBREVIATIONS

Canada

CBA Code	Canadian Bar Association, *Code of Professional Conduct* (Ottawa: CBA, 2009)
FLSC Code	Federation of Law Societies of Canada, *Amended Model Code of Professional Conduct* (Ottawa: FLSC, 2014)
Alta	Law Society of Alberta, *Code of Conduct* (Calgary: LSA, 2013)
BC	Law Society of British Columbia, *Code of Professional Conduct for British Columbia* (Vancouver: LSBC, 2014)
Man	Law Society of Manitoba, *Code of Professional Conduct* (Winnipeg: LSM, 2014)
NB	Law Society of New Brunswick, *Code of Professional Conduct* (Fredericton: LSNB, 2004)
NL	Law Society of Newfoundland and Labrador, *Code of Professional Conduct* (St John's: LSNL, 2013)

NS	Nova Scotia Barristers' Society, *Code of Professional Conduct* (Halifax: NSBS, 2014)
Ont	Law Society of Upper Canada, *Rules of Professional Conduct* (Toronto: LSUC, 2014)
Que	*Code of Ethics of Advocates*, CQLR c B-1, r 3 as it appeared on August 2014.
Sask	Law Society of Saskatchewan, *Code of Professional Conduct* (Regina: LSS, 2014)

United States

ABA Model Rule(s)	American Bar Association, *Model Rules of Professional Conduct* (Chicago: ABA, 1983)
ABA Defense Standard(s)	American Bar Association, *ABA Standards for Criminal Justice: Prosecution and Defense Function*, 3d ed (Washington, DC: ABA, 1993) standards 4-1.1 to 4-8.6
ABA Prosecution Standard(s)	American Bar Association, *ABA Standards for Criminal Justice: Prosecution and Defense Function*, 3d ed (Washington, DC: ABA, 1993) standards 3-1.1 to 3-6.2
Third Restatement	American Law Institute, *Restatement of the Law: The Law Governing Lawyers*, revised ed (St Paul, MN: ALI, 2000)

INTRODUCTION

A. DIFFICULT QUESTIONS

What should criminal defence counsel do when a client wants her to take possession of a thumb drive containing documents that are related to the charged crime but might help in mounting a defence? Can a lawyer refuse to negotiate a plea deal for a client who wants to cooperate with the prosecution, on the ground that "snitches" sometimes fabricate evidence to save their own skin, and helping one might be bad for business? When, if ever, can a lawyer jointly act for multiple accused in the same case? Can defence counsel override a client's instructions regarding which witnesses to call at trial? To what extent can a prosecutor get involved in a police service's pre-charge investigation of a criminal matter? In preparing a witness to testify, can Crown counsel draw the witness's attention to other evidence in the case that appears inconsistent with the witness's testimony, and ask for an explanation?

These difficult questions offer just a smattering of the broad range of ethical issues that lawyers face in the practice of criminal law. They engage a complex range of duties, sometimes seemingly inconsonant, that a lawyer owes to the client and the administration of justice. Such duties are closely connected to the lawyer's special role in the criminal justice system, a role reflected in ethical standards adopted by the legal profession. At the same time, lawyers often bring to bear personal conceptions of justice that help to shape their singular role as advocates. To make matters more complicated still, lawyers are commonly called on to make hard decisions in difficult circumstances, often with limited time for careful consideration. Frequently, there is no "right" answer to a particular ethical problem, although there may be many obviously bad ones.

The primary goal of this book is to help lawyers who practise criminal law identify and follow standards of conduct most acceptable to clients, the courts, the public, the profession, and the individual practitioner. We also believe that the book will be of use to civil lawyers, judges, educators, students, and anyone else with an interest in law and ethics. The remainder of this introduction sets out a road map outlining how we have approached our task.

B. THE STUDY OF ETHICS AND CRIMINAL LAW

We use the term "legal ethics" to encompass the study of lawyers' professional duties and thus the principles and standards that should guide lawyers in conducting a morally sound practice of law. Using this brief definition, we can move on to examine the factors influencing an ethics of law and the hallmarks of our own perspective on what it means to be an ethical lawyer.

1) The Components of an Ethics of Law

The components that contribute to an ethics of professional conduct are diverse and fluid. A number of sources, taken together, serve to develop and reflect the general principles that shape lawyers' actions and ideals, including formal codes of professional responsibility, the views and writings of lawyers, events actually occurring in the courtroom, the demands and needs of clients, disciplinary decisions by governing bodies, judicial pronouncements, the expectations of the public, and the teachings and reflections that occur in law schools. These and other sources come together to constitute the legal culture that frames and influences ethical debate and are discussed throughout this introduction.

Our legal culture undergoes constant and inevitable change, and so too, then, do expectations and standards pertaining to lawyers' behaviour. What was contentious fifty years ago may seem totally unproblematic today, and vice versa. Or the preferred method of approaching an issue may change dramatically over time. Ideas about legal ethics by no means mutate daily, yet there is an undeniable malleability of emphasis regarding principles, concepts, and concerns. This topic, and hence its study, is definitely not static. Moreover, while certain ethical issues yield to reasonably clear answers, on many occasions identifying or applying the proper standards can be a maddeningly challenging exercise. Reasonable people sometimes differ as to the proper ethical approach to apply in a given situation. Legal ethics is not an exact science, with every problem amenable to a set and indisputable resolution. What can be most engaging, if a little frustrating, about the study of lawyers' ethics is the elusiveness of a widespread consensus on many important issues.

2) Our Approach

Our book is aimed at practitioners who require immediate guidance applicable to the legal system as it currently operates. The lawyer today whose client is, for example, about to commit perjury is working within a rights-based adversarial process and a particular ethical framework provided by, among other sources, the governing body's rules of professional conduct and the *Criminal Code*. Lawyers undoubtedly take on a role morality that demands and justifies actions that might seem wrong or unpalatable in another context. In this respect, our approach to resolving ethical problems is not terribly daring and leans only tentatively towards the prescriptive. Nonetheless, within a traditional framework we have tried to re-emphasize attributes of lawyering that sometimes get lost in the adversarial, rights-focused world of criminal trial practice.

In particular, lawyers must constantly reflect on what they are doing, and why, and appreciate how their actions affect the client, the legal system, and the public at large. Ethical lawyering requires assessment and reassessment at many stages, not an unthinking acceptance of neutral partisanship or the rote application of a written rule of professional conduct. Lawyers should also recognize that harm to the public is not automatically justified by dint of the function that they perform as criminal counsel. Whether harm might occur, and whether it can be tolerated, is part of the individual lawyer's assessment. Furthermore and accordingly, lawyers *do* exercise personal conceptions of justice in approaching ethical issues, and so they must be prepared to accept responsibility for the decisions made. Accepting the legitimacy of a systemic role morality does not erase the fact that lawyers are moral agents whose actions have real repercussions.

As a last point, one often encounters lists of ethical duties owed by lawyers to clients, the courts, the profession, and the public. Zeal, candour, diligence, competency, integrity, confidentiality, independence, fairness, honesty, dignity, avoidance of conflict, and other concepts are often mentioned, and rightly so. But making lists of ethical duties can be a bit numbing and, without more, of questionable utility. At the risk of unduly simplifying matters, we group a lawyer's duties to the client under a single overarching principle, namely, that of loyalty owed by a fiduciary. Similarly, duties owed to everyone else can be traced to a fundamental obligation to uphold the integrity of the legal system employed to determine criminal matters.

Expressed at such a level of generality, these two guiding principles are extremely malleable and provide little more than a beginning in discussing ethical issues. However, we must start somewhere, and concomitant fidelity to the client and the legal system is the almost universally accepted point that we have chosen. In fact, many of the chapters in this book illustrate a common theme in most contemporary discussions of ethics and criminal law: the challenge to accommodate the duty of loyalty to the client with the obligation to maintain the integrity of our justice system. As if arriving at an acceptable balance between these responsibilities were not difficult enough, there is also the constant need to incorporate the lawyer's own considered sense of justice into the mix.

C. CANADIAN WRITINGS

Not so long ago, scant attention was paid to ethical matters in Canadian texts and law journals. The paucity of writing was positively embarrassing, especially when compared to the reams of information available in the United States. Lawyers in Canada seemed largely content to leave the discussion of ethics to the occasional article in a trade newspaper, the after-dinner speech, and war stories told in the robing room or pub. The great majority of academics paid the subject no attention at all. When the first edition of this book was published, this sorry state of affairs had begun to change with the emergence of several new texts and a smattering of law journal articles on law and ethics. But, as doctoral student Adam Dodek observed at the time, legal ethics could still be described as "a subject in search of scholarship."[1]

Thankfully, since then we have seen something approaching a "big bang" in the study of legal ethics in this country. The number of books and articles has exploded, at least comparatively speaking, and a strong group of academics have dedicated themselves to teaching and writing

---

1   Adam Dodek, "Canadian Legal Ethics: A Subject in Search of Scholarship" (2000) 50 UTLJ 115.

about a multitude of diverse topics concerning professional responsibility. In 2008, Adam Dodek, by then a professor at the University of Ottawa and a leader in the field, could therefore say that as a subject of scholarship, Canadian legal ethics was "ready for the twenty-first century at last."[2] While much work remains to be done, the progress continues at a rapid pace today. It is truly an exciting time to be working and writing in this field.

D. CANADIAN GOVERNING BODIES AND RULES OF PROFESSIONAL CONDUCT

Lawyers in Canada are substantially self-regulated, and governing bodies for the profession exist in each provincial and territorial jurisdiction. These bodies enjoy significant control over many aspects of lawyering, including admission to the bar, training, continuing education, discipline, and competency standards. Also deserving mention is the Canadian Bar Association (CBA), a national organization of lawyers. In contrast to the law societies, membership in the CBA is voluntary, and the group does not regulate the profession. However, the *de facto* influence of the CBA in many areas, including professional standards, has been considerable. The CBA has membership exceeding 37,000, including approximately two-thirds of all lawyers practising in Canada, and boasts resources that rival those of the larger law societies. It is active in many issues affecting lawyers and the public and provides important links for Canadian lawyers that cross provincial boundaries.

Codes of professional conduct are primarily a phenomenon of the twentieth century, and the first prominent effort to produce a code in Canada was the CBA's 1920 Canons of Legal Ethics. The current CBA Code of Professional Conduct (CBA Code) was initially approved by the organization's national council in 1974, then substantially revised in 1987 and again in 2004 and 2009. It used to be that most law societies adopted the CBA Code holus-bolus, while others used it as a basic template and made modest alterations or additions. In the late 1980s and the 1990s, several governing bodies moved towards bespoke code making, which tended to create a more comprehensive and contemporary product. This trend translated into rules that bore diminishing resemblance to the CBA Code, the prime example being the particularly impressive ethical code employed by the Law Society of Alberta.

---

2   Adam Dodek, "Canadian Legal Ethics: Ready for the Twenty-First Century at Last" (2008) 46 Osgoode Hall LJ 1.

However, in 2009 the Federation of Law Societies of Canada (FLSC), an organization comprising all of the national governing bodies, released a model code, the aim being to have the same set of professional conduct rules apply across the country. The model code clearly takes much from the CBA Code but represents a significant change insofar as the law societies have collectively taken over primary responsibility for promulgating rules that will, it appears, eventually apply uniformly in all or much of Canada. At the time of writing, the model code has been adopted in most provinces, usually with minor changes, the only exceptions being Quebec, New Brunswick, and Prince Edward Island. In light of this trend, in early 2014 the CBA announced plans to discontinue the CBA Code once no Canadian law society used it or incorporated it by reference as the ethical rules for the jurisdiction.

Whether based on the FLSC's model code or not, the written codes promulgated by Canadian law societies offer a formal expression of standards of conduct expected of lawyers. The codes say a lot about the role that lawyers play in the legal system and about the profession's collective beliefs and expectations as to appropriate behaviour. There is a constant tension between the desire to articulate lofty ideals in a hortatory code and providing specific and practical guidance to lawyers who encounter ethical problems. All Canadian codes on some level try to accomplish both tasks. In every jurisdiction, violation of a governing body's ethical code may lead to disciplinary proceedings and attendant punitive consequences. It used to be that the behaviour mostly targeted by a governing body for investigation and disciplinary proceedings was fraud on a client or failure to respond to requests for information. But more and more disciplinary decisions concern other alleged infractions, such as misleading a court, failing to avoid a conflict of interest, breaching a client's confidences, or acting discourteously to a fellow lawyer or member of the public.

While important in the context of self-regulation by the profession, the codes do not carry the force of law in civil or criminal litigation. In other words, courts are by no means bound by the provisions of the rules of professional responsibility adopted by a particular law society. Nevertheless, a court often considers the governing body's code of conduct where relevant to an issue at hand. As stated by the Supreme Court of Canada, "an expression of a professional standard in a code of ethics relating to a matter before the court should be considered an important statement of public policy."[3] The rules of professional conduct

---

3   *MacDonald Estate v Martin*, [1990] 3 SCR 1235 at 1246. To the same effect, see *Canadian National Railway Co v McKercher LLP*, 2013 SCC 39 at para 16.

promulgated by a law society can therefore influence decision making in the courts.

E. COMMON LAW AND STATUTORY AND CONSTITUTIONAL PRINCIPLES

Questions of legal ethics are frequently the subject of pronouncement from the courts. A dissatisfied client may sue a lawyer for negligence, violation of fiduciary duty, breach of contract, and so on, requiring an assessment of the propriety of the lawyer's actions. More commonly, in the criminal sphere convicted clients are increasingly likely to ground an appeal on an allegation that trial counsel was ineffective or on a claim that Crown counsel acted unfairly in prosecuting the case. There may also be many occasions during a trial where the presiding judge is required to make a ruling that includes an assessment of a lawyer's conduct, for example the decision whether counsel has a proper basis to put a question to a witness in cross-examination or whether to strike an accused's guilty plea because he has received inadequate advice from counsel. Finally, lawyers who push the envelope regarding acceptable ethical behaviour may be subject, rightly or wrongly, to criminal charges that fall to be determined in a court of law.

These sorts of judicial rulings involve diverse areas of substantive law, spanning the gamut from torts to equity to criminal law to constitutional principles. And such rulings themselves contribute to the development of an ethics of professional conduct for lawyers. What a judge has to say about counsel's actions, while not necessarily tantamount to a binding standard, will frequently influence debate and practice in the area. In the realm of ethics and criminal law, constitutional principles as interpreted by the courts are especially important. The client-lawyer relationship is closely entwined with a multitude of constitutional guarantees, including solicitor-client confidentiality and privilege, the right to the effective assistance of counsel, the ability to choose one's lawyer, control of the conduct of the defence, and many others. Thus, while we have not endeavoured to write a text on constitutional law or criminal procedure, these subjects are important to understanding ethics in the criminal law context.

Finally, just as the number of texts and articles on legal ethics has greatly increased in the last decade, we are seeing many more judgments that comment on issues of professional conduct. There seems to be a snowball effect in this regard, courts' being more and more likely to address ethical issues as judges become more familiar with the academic literature and the burgeoning jurisprudence. The caselaw addressing matters of criminal law and ethics is much richer and more extensive than when we completed our first edition.

F. A COMPARATIVE APPROACH

The first edition of this book took a comparative approach to ethics and criminal law in large part because so little was written on the topic in this country. But, as noted in sections C and E, above, this is no longer the case. We have therefore cut back on our examination of materials from other jurisdictions. These sources can nonetheless offer illuminating discussions of ethical problems that confront criminal lawyers, and in particular we have continued to reference material available in the United States. After all, we share with that country a common law legal system based on adversarial principles, a constitutionally entrenched bill of rights, and a unified profession. On the other hand, the American context is not perfectly replicated in Canada.[4] To pick one example, professional organizations in the United States often do not regulate attorneys, the courts frequently bearing responsibility for adopting and enforcing standards of professional conduct. Solutions to ethical issues that may be perfectly acceptable in the United States are thus not necessarily appropriate for use here, depending on the context. Nonetheless, our somewhat *ad hoc* review of what is happening in the United States is hopefully useful in providing a taste of different perspectives from a similar legal system.

G. AMERICAN PUBLISHED STANDARDS OF PROFESSIONAL CONDUCT

American codes of professional conduct are particularly numerous and comprehensive. It is thus worth reviewing the main standards of professional responsibility used by lawyers in our neighbour to the south, especially since we refer to these standards quite often in the text.

In the United States, the leading professional organization for lawyers is the American Bar Association (ABA), more or less the counterpart of the CBA. The ABA promulgated a set of ethical canons in 1908,

---

4   Alice Woolley, "Integrity in Zealousness: Comparing the Standard Conceptions of the Canadian and American Lawyer" (1996) 9 Can JL & Jur 61.

representing one of the earliest Anglo-American attempts at providing lawyers with a broad set of guidelines. These Canons of Professional Ethics were based on a similar document produced by the Alabama Bar Association in 1887, which in turn was substantially influenced by the lectures of Judge George Sharswood. The canons later influenced the form and content of the CBA's 1920 Canons of Legal Ethics.

However, the ABA's canons were criticized by some as being unduly vague and hence of not much use to practitioners.[5] Others have argued that the canons were irredeemably tainted because they aimed to exclude people from the legal profession on the basis of gender, class, and race.[6] In any event, the ABA has subsequently produced three major documents of interest to the criminal lawyer: the Model Code of Professional Responsibility, the Model Rules of Professional Conduct (ABA Model Rules), and the Standards for Criminal Justice. Also of prime importance, though not produced by the ABA, is the American Law Institute's (ALI) Restatement of the Law Governing Lawyers. We will briefly discuss each of these four documents in a little more detail.

1) ABA Model Code of Professional Responsibility

In 1969 the Model Code of Professional Responsibility was introduced by the ABA, replacing the canons. Most state and federal jurisdictions in the United States adopted the model code, albeit sometimes in revised form. An interesting component of the model code is the distinction drawn between "disciplinary rules" and "ethical considerations." Disciplinary rules set out minimum standards of behaviour, the violation of which can warrant formal investigation and censure. In contrast, ethical considerations are of an aspirational nature, providing ideals for which lawyers are encouraged but not required to strive. The ABA model code also includes "canons," which are axiomatic norms intended to express in general terms the standards applicable to lawyers' behaviour.

As noted immediately below, the model code was superseded by the ABA's Model Rules in the early 1980s. While many American jurisdictions were slow to switch over to the model rules, the great majority have now done so. The influence of the model code being much reduced compared to fifteen years ago, references to it have been removed from the current edition of our text.

---

5   See Charles W Wolfram, *Modern Legal Ethics* (St Paul: West, 1986) at 53–56.

6   Monroe Freedman & Abbe Smith, *Understanding Lawyers' Ethics*, 4th ed (New Providence, NJ: LexisNexis, 2010).

2) ABA Model Rules of Professional Conduct

In 1983 the ABA's House of Delegates approved the Model Rules of Professional Conduct. These written standards jettisoned the distinction between disciplinary rules and ethical considerations used in the model code, instead utilizing the "rules and commentary" approach familiar to Canadian lawyers. Since their initial inception, the model rules have been amended many times, and most American jurisdictions have adopted ethical codes based on the model rules. The application and interpretation of the model rules is subject to consideration by formal and informal opinions issued by the ABA Committee on Ethics and Professional Responsibility. We make frequent reference to the model rules in this book and have also cited certain opinions of the aforementioned ABA committee.

3) ABA Criminal Justice Section's Standards for Criminal Justice

In 1968 the ABA Criminal Justice Section published standards for the practice of law by criminal lawyers, which were approved by the House of Delegates in 1971. Chief Justice Warren Burger called the standards "the single most comprehensive and probably the most monumental undertaking in the field of criminal justice ever attempted by the American legal profession in our national history."[7] The standards cover a wide range of topics including the defense function and the prosecution function and are organized somewhat like the ABA Model Rules, with black-letter rules followed by commentaries.

The standards are not enforceable codes, rather being intended as a guide to professional conduct and performance. Unlike the ABA's model code and rules, they have not been taken up for use in regulating attorneys at the state and federal levels. Nonetheless, American courts have often looked to the standards in assessing the propriety of impugned lawyer conduct. We make frequent reference to the standards (as ABA Defense Standards or ABA Prosecution Standards), given that they provide a valuable assessment of many ethical issues pertaining to the practice of criminal law.

The standards are currently in their third edition, although a fourth edition is in the works and will likely be adopted in the next couple of years.

---

7   Quoted in American Bar Association, Criminal Justice Standards Home, online: www.americanbar.org/groups/criminal_justice/pages/CriminalJusticeStandardsHome.html.

4) The ALI's Restatement of the Law Governing Lawyers

The American Law Institute drafts and publishes restatements of law, model codes, and other proposals for legal reform. In 2000 the ALI released its eagerly anticipated Restatement of the Law Governing Lawyers, often called the "Third Restatement."[8] This massive two-volume effort comprises an exhaustive review of the law pertaining to the work of lawyers and includes extensive material pertaining to lawyers' ethics. The work is organized in the form of black-letter standards followed by commentaries and examples that tend to be more discursive than those provided in the ABA Model Rules. The Third Restatement also includes "Reporter's Notes" for each rule, which focus on caselaw and other references pertinent to the topic at hand. The Third Restatement thus offers a helpful perspective on many ethics issues, compiled by leading experts, and a handy overview of the statutory landscape, caselaw, and academic commentary in the United States. It has had considerable influence in Canada, most notably by supplying the definition of conflict of interest adopted by the Supreme Court of Canada and in most Canadian ethical codes.

H. TOPICS COVERED

In this book, we have directed our attention to subject areas that reflect many of the most common and demanding ethical issues confronting criminal lawyers. A brief synopsis of these subject areas, organized on a chapter-by-chapter basis, follows:

Chapter 1 — Defending the Guilty: The defence of an accused individual often involves working towards the acquittal of the guilty. Sometimes a defence lawyer has irresistible knowledge that the client is in fact guilty. This chapter examines the restrictions on the conduct of the case where a lawyer possesses such knowledge. More fundamentally, however, we introduce the notion that a defence lawyer plays a special role in the system, a role based largely upon a duty of loyalty owed to the client. The question becomes the extent to which this role is necessarily tempered by fidelity to the truth-finding function of the criminal justice system.

---

8   Somewhat confusingly, there were no previous restatements covering the law governing lawyers.

Chapter 2 — Choosing and Refusing Clients: The discussion of role morality for lawyers continues in this chapter, where we try to determine when, if ever, a lawyer can refuse the case of a prospective client. Social opprobrium and personal distaste for a client or cause can work against accepting a retainer, yet refusal to take on a matter can restrict an individual's access to justice.

Chapter 3 — Decision Making: Who controls the conduct of a case? The traditional view in Canada is that criminal lawyers reign supreme in deciding how to carry out the litigation. On this view, the client holds ultimate authority with respect to only a few especially important matters, such as the decisions how to plead and whether to testify. However, a different approach, which gives credence to the client's right to control the conduct of the case, is gaining support in Canada of late. We adopt this newer model and examine how it might apply in especially difficult circumstances, such as where the client demands that counsel conduct litigation in an unethical manner or is incapable of providing rational instructions regarding the conduct of the case because of mental health problems.

Chapter 4 — Confidentiality: One of the central aspects of a lawyer's duty of loyalty to the client is the concomitant obligation to keep confidential all information obtained as a result of the retainer. The duty of confidentiality infuses pretty much every aspect of a lawyer's work. In this chapter, we examine its justification, breadth, and operation. We also discuss the important distinction between the ethical duty of confidentiality and the evidentiary and substantive rule of solicitor-client privilege. And we look at the lawyer's special duties not to misuse disclosure materials so as to harm the client, witnesses or other third parties, and the public interest in the proper administration of justice.

Chapter 5 — Confidentiality Exceptions: While confidentiality is a mainstay of the client-lawyer relationship, competing societal values often push for the disclosure of confidences. Public safety may be in jeopardy, or the court may have been misled. The exact nature of permissible derogations from the duty of confidentiality is often contentious and unclear. We review the instances where confidential information can be revealed absent the client's consent, and we also argue against excessively wide exceptions to the basic rule of non-disclosure.

Chapter 6 — Conflict of Interest: A conflict of interest occurs whenever a lawyer's duty of loyalty to a client is compromised by a competing interest. A threat to the client's confidences is often, though not always, implicated. Perhaps more than with any other ethical issue, principles concerning conflict of interest are frequently the subject of judicial application. This chapter therefore contains an extensive discussion of relevant caselaw. Principal topics include the pitfalls and benefits of multiple representation, the problems that can arise in relation to former clients, and the efficacy of client waivers.

Chapter 7 — Client Perjury: The lawyer faced with anticipated or completed client perjury must wend her way through an ethical minefield. There is no shortage of opinion on offer from commentators as to the proper course of action, yet consensus is elusive on many points. The discussion in this chapter provides, in a fashion that will by now be familiar to the reader, an example of the tension between a lawyer's duty of loyalty to the client and adherence to the integrity of the truth-finding function of the criminal justice process.

Chapter 8 — Witnesses: The testimony of witnesses is crucial to the outcome of most criminal trials. Lawyers often have contact with witnesses outside of the courtroom, for example in conducting initial interviews and preparing witnesses to testify at trial. In this chapter, we explore how the ethical principles governing out-of-court contact seek to balance counsel's obligation to advance resolutely the client's best interests with the duty to avoid conduct that creates an unacceptable risk of misleading the court or treating a witness unfairly.

Chapter 9 — Plea Discussions: A substantial majority of criminal cases end in a guilty plea. It is thus crucial for criminal lawyers to pursue an ethical course of action even where the issue of guilt may ultimately not be disputed. Many of the elements of the client-lawyer relationship discussed in Chapter 3 are elaborated on at this juncture, including the need for full consultation with the client and respect for the client's goals and desires. A particularly thorny problem concerns the client who maintains innocence yet insists on pleading guilty.

Chapter 10 — Physical Evidence Relevant to a Crime: Client perjury is probably the paradigmatic topic of discussion regarding lawyers' ethics in the United States. In Canada, the debacle involving serial rapist and murderer Paul Bernardo, his lawyer Ken Murray, and the famously concealed videotapes has made the proper handling of incriminating physical evidence a hot ethical issue for criminal defence counsel. We attempt to provide guidance as to how this vexing problem can be approached.

Chapter 11 — Termination of the Client-Lawyer Relationship: Client-lawyer relationships usually start with fond hopes for a happy partnership that achieves the best possible result. For a variety of reasons, not always within the control of the parties, the relationship may end sooner than expected. This chapter reviews some of the circumstances where a lawyer can or must end the representation, the manner by which this step should be taken, and the duties attendant upon termination.

Chapter 12 — The Prosecutor: Many of the principles discussed above are relevant to lawyers who prosecute criminal offences. But the special role of the prosecutor demands the refinement of these principles, often very substantially. Most notably, Crown counsel acts as a "minister of justice" in the public interest and accordingly must temper or control zealous advocacy in a way not required of defence counsel. This chapter examines the nature of the prosecutor's function, as well as the way in which this function operates in the particular circumstances of a criminal case.

I. SCOPE OF THE BOOK AND RECOMMENDATIONS MADE

This book does not attempt to cover every ethical dilemma that a criminal lawyer may encounter. Instead, we have aimed to draw out general principles from the problems that are canvassed and to provide concrete suggestions for a great many instances where the proper course of action for the criminal lawyer is not immediately clear. In doing so, we have made use of examples in the text, in many instances employing scenarios borrowed from actual cases, as a means of illustrating relevant principles and warning of dangerous ethical snares. Additionally, special emphasis is given to certain points through the use of bold type and headings such as "caveat," "caution," "recommendation," and so on. There is no magic in these particular terms, other than to make sure that the point in question does not escape the reader's attention.

CHAPTER 1

DEFENDING
THE GUILTY

A. INTRODUCTION

Almost every defence lawyer has been asked, whether by family, friends, or strangers, "How can you defend a guilty person?" The typical member of the public probably has no problem with counsel representing a culpable accused on a guilty plea. What may raise her ire is counsel who helps the guilty client try to avoid conviction. In response to this challenge, the lawyer can often deflect the inquiry by posing other questions in reply, such as, "How can you say that a person is guilty before the verdict?" "But guilty of what?" or "How do you know the person is guilty?" But the persistent interlocutor, not satisfied with these partial answers, may push further and say, "What I mean is, how can you defend an accused person who you know is guilty?" It is this issue — how can counsel ethically fight against the conviction of a client he knows to be guilty — that is the focus of this chapter.

Defending an accused who has confessed guilt to counsel or whom counsel otherwise knows to be guilty has been described as "the supreme test problem in the ethics of advocacy."[1] It encapsulates an existential question that goes to the very core of a defence lawyer's mission. Academics who study the adversarial, rights-based nature of our criminal justice system have long grappled with issues surrounding

---

1   Hugh Macmillan, "The Ethics of Advocacy" in James Ames, *Jurisprudence in Action: A Pleader's Anthology* (New York: Baker, Voorhis, 1953) at 307.

the defence of the guilty client, and, if anything, the debate has grown more intense of late. As we will see, controversy prevails among many commentators regarding how best to handle the difficult problems related to this issue. Of course, it is practising lawyers and their clients who are most immediately affected by the issue, which engages diverse ethical duties — to the client, the administration of justice, and the profession — and implicates counsel's own conscience and sense of morality. On a broader scale still, this issue foments public debate and, sometimes, misunderstanding as to the fundamental rights of the accused and the aims of the criminal justice system. Some members of the public will always be galled by defence counsel's zealous and aggressive representation of a client who is "obviously" guilty.

B. RELATED RULES OF PROFESSIONAL CONDUCT

Most Canadian rules of professional conduct contain identical or very similar standards addressing the role of lawyer as advocate.[2] These standards are important in ascertaining the proper approach to the defence of an accused who is known to be guilty. They seek to promote the need for zealous representation of the client but without countenancing the improper subversion of the truth. The rules collected in most of the codes, under the heading "The Lawyer as Advocate," begin with the following general provision: "[W]hen acting as an advocate, a lawyer must represent the client resolutely and honourably within the limits of the law, while treating the tribunal with candour, fairness, courtesy, and respect."[3] The commentaries to this provision continue the theme:

> [1] Role in adversarial proceedings: In adversarial proceedings, the lawyer has a duty to the client to raise fearlessly every issue, advance every argument and ask every question, however distasteful, that the lawyer thinks will help the client's case and to endeavour to obtain for the client the benefit of every remedy and defence authorized by law. The lawyer must discharge this duty by fair and honourable means, without illegality and in a manner that is consistent with the lawyer's duty to treat the tribunal with candour, fairness, courtesy

---

2   Alta, Sask r 4.01; BC, Man, Ont, NS, NL r 5.1; NB ch 8; CBA Code ch IX.
3   Alta, Sask r 4.01(1); BC, Man, Ont, NS, NL r 5.1-1. Very similar are NB ch 8 and CBA Code ch IX.

and respect and in a way that promotes the parties' rights to a fair hearing in which justice can be done . . . .[4]

[3] The lawyer's function as advocate is openly and necessarily partisan. Accordingly, the lawyer is not obliged (except as required by law or under these rules and subject to the duties of a prosecutor set out below) to assist an adversary or advance matters harmful to the client's case.[5]

[5] A lawyer should refrain from expressing the lawyer's personal opinions on the merits of a client's case to the court or tribunal.[6]

These commentaries are useful in ascertaining the ethical duties and limits imposed on counsel who represents a client known to be guilty. But, in addition, most Canadian codes contain two further commentaries that offer still greater specificity with respect to the role of criminal defence counsel:

[9] Duty as defence counsel: When defending an accused person, a lawyer's duty is to protect the client as far as possible from being convicted except by a court of competent jurisdiction and upon legal evidence sufficient to support a conviction for the offence with which the client is charged. Accordingly, and notwithstanding the lawyer's private opinion on credibility or the merits, a lawyer may properly rely on any evidence or defences including so-called technicalities, not known to be false or fraudulent.[7]

[10] Admissions made by the accused to a lawyer may impose strict limitations on the conduct of the defence, and the accused should be made aware of this. For example, if the accused clearly admits to the lawyer the factual and mental elements necessary to constitute the offence, the lawyer, if convinced that the admissions are true and voluntary,

4   Alta, Sask r 4.01(1) (commentary); BC, Man, Ont, NS, NL r 5.1-1, commentary 1. NB ch 8, commentary 14(b) & (c) and CBA Code ch IX, commentary 1 use very similar language.
5   Alta, Sask r 4.01(1) (commentary); BC, Man, Ont, NS, NL r 5.1-1, commentary 3. Similar too is the wording used in NB ch 8, commentary 3(a) and CBA Code ch IX, commentary 17.
6   Sask r 4.01(1) (commentary); BC, Ont, NS, NL r 5.1-1, commentary 5. Man r 4.01(1) (commentary) uses the same wording but adds the following sentence: "A lawyer's role is to present the evidence on behalf of a client fairly without assertion of any personal knowledge of the facts at issue." Similar wording is found in Alta r 4.01(1) (commentary) and CBA Code ch XVIII, commentary 3.
7   Alta, Sask r 4.01 (commentary); BC, Man, Ont, NS, NL r 5.1-1, commentary 9. NB ch 8, commentary 14(b) & (c) and CBA Code ch IX, commentary 10 use almost identical wording.

may properly take objection to the jurisdiction of the court, the form of the indictment or the admissibility or sufficiency of the evidence, but must not suggest that some other person committed the offence or call any evidence that, by reason of the admissions, the lawyer believes to be false. Nor may the lawyer set up an affirmative case inconsistent with such admissions, for example, by calling evidence in support of an alibi intended to show that the accused could not have done or, in fact, has not done the act. Such admissions will also impose a limit on the extent to which the lawyer may attack the evidence for the prosecution. The lawyer is entitled to test the evidence given by each individual witness for the prosecution and argue that the evidence taken as a whole is insufficient to amount to proof that the accused is guilty of the offence charged, but the lawyer should go no further than that.[8]

Also relevant are several other provisions contained in the advocacy chapter of most Canadian codes, which state that a lawyer shall or must not

- knowingly assist or permit a client to do anything that the lawyer considers to be dishonest or dishonourable;[9]
- knowingly attempt to deceive a tribunal or influence the course of justice by offering false evidence, misstating facts or law, presenting or relying upon a false or deceptive affidavit, suppressing what ought to be disclosed or otherwise assisting in any fraud, crime or illegal conduct;[10]
- knowingly assert as true a fact when its truth cannot reasonably be supported by the evidence or as a matter of which notice may be taken by the tribunal;[11] or
- make suggestions to a witness recklessly or knowing them to be false.[12]

---

8   Alta, Sask r 4.01 (commentary); BC, Man, Ont, NS, NL r 5.1-1, commentary 10. CBA Code ch IX, commentary 11 uses almost identical language. NB ch 8, commentary 4(d) does too but only includes the first and last sentences of the commentary.

9   Alta r 4.01(2)(d); Sask r 4.01(2)(b); BC, Man, Ont, NS, NL r 5.1-2(b); NB ch 8, commentary 10(ii); CBA Code ch IX, commentary 2(b).

10   Alta r 4.01(2)(g); Sask r 4.01(2)(e); BC, Man, Ont, NS, NL r 5.1-2(e); NB ch 8, commentary 10(v); CBA Code ch IX, commentary 2(e).

11   Alta r 4.01(2)(i), Sask r 4.01(2)(g); BC, Man, Ont, NS, NL r 5.1-2(g); NB ch 8, commentary 10(vii).

12   Alta r 4.01(2)(k); Sask r 4.01(2)(h); BC, Man, Ont, NS, NL r 5.1-2(h). CBA Code ch IX, commentary 2(g) adds the following sentence: "This does not prevent a cross-examiner from pursuing any hypothesis that is honestly advanced on the strength of reasonable inference, experience or intuition."

C. GENESIS OF THE PRESENT RULES

Nineteenth-century philosopher Jeremy Bentham famously went so far as to argue that a lawyer who receives a confession of guilt becomes an accessory after the fact if he undertakes a defence at trial.[13] Yet Bentham's view was by no means common currency among his contemporaries who practised criminal law. As early as 1840, the profession in England was forced to grapple with the issue of defending the client who is known to be guilty in the celebrated *Courvoisier* case.[14] Courvoisier was charged with the murder of his aristocratic employer, Lord Russell, and was defended by Charles Phillips, a leading counsel of the day. After the trial, which ended with the conviction and eventually the hanging of the accused, it was publicly revealed that on the second day of the proceedings, Courvoisier had confessed his guilt to Phillips. Phillips then consulted with Baron Parke, who, according to the English practice at the time, was assisting Tindal LCJ in the case. Though reportedly "much annoyed" with Phillips's initiative,[15] Baron Parke inquired as to whether Courvoisier still wished to be defended by Phillips. On receiving an affirmative answer, Baron Parke told Phillips that he "was bound to do so, and to use all fair arguments arising on the evidence."[16]

The *Courvoisier* case not only generated much controversy at the time[17] but ultimately influenced the "ethical canons of lawyers in England,

---

13   Jeremy Bentham, *Rationale of Judicial Evidence: Specially Applied to English Practice*, vol 7, book 9 in John Bowring, ed, *The Works of Jeremy Bentham* (Edinburgh: W Tait, 1838–43) at 474.

14   *R v Courvoisier* (1840), 9 C & P 362, 173 ER 869 (NP) [*Courvoisier*]. The ethical issues thrown up by *Courvoisier* are not discussed in the case report but were well publicized at the time and have been canvassed by many commentators. A particularly thorough and entertaining discussion of *Courvoisier* is provided by David Mellinkoff, *The Conscience of a Lawyer* (St Paul, MN: West, 1973). For a more recent examination of the case and its ethical implications, see Michael Asimow & Richard Weisberg, "When the Lawyer Knows the Client is Guilty: Client Confessions in Legal Ethics, Popular Culture, and Literature" (2009) 18 S Cal Interdisciplinary LJ 229 at 230–32, 244–45, 248, and 257.

15   See Mellinkoff, above note 14 at 138.

16   Phillips's recounting of the story was eventually published in *The Times*, 20 November 1849, in the form of his correspondence with Samuel Warren. The letters exchanged between Phillips and Warren are reprinted by George Sharswood, *An Essay on Professional Ethics*, 4th ed (Philadelphia: T & JW Johnson, 1876) Appendix 1 at 183ff.

17   For a more recent case involving public controversy about defence counsel's trial tactics, given the high likelihood that he had received a confession from his client, see note 146, below in this chapter, and the associated example.

America, and wherever the Anglo-American system of legal representation has taken hold."[18] By the early twentieth century, the idea that a lawyer has a duty to defend vigorously a client known to be guilty was fairly well-established. In England, this duty was affirmed in an extremely influential report released by the General Council of the English Bar in 1915.[19] The council had been asked by the Bar Committee of Shanghai "to advise on the propriety of Counsel defending on a plea of 'Not guilty' a prisoner charged with an offence, capital or otherwise, when the latter has confessed to Counsel himself the fact that he did commit the offence charged."[20] In its report, the council answered by confirming that in such circumstances a lawyer often has a duty to continue with the defence,[21] but nonetheless set out certain limitations aimed at preventing counsel from misleading the court. The influence of the council's report in Canada can hardly be overemphasized: its text was reproduced almost verbatim in the 1974 CBA Code,[22] and today forms the vast bulk of the commentary found in most Canadian ethical codes on admissions received from a criminal client.[23]

By the 1930s, the notion that a lawyer could represent a client known to be guilty was sufficiently well-established, at least among practitioners, that the High Court of Australia could state, in response to the assertion by counsel that receiving a client's confession represented the worst predicament he had ever encountered as a lawyer, "Why he should have conceived himself to have been in so great a predicament, it is not easy for those experienced in advocacy to understand."[24]

This chiding comment was made in a leading Commonwealth case on the subject, *Tuckiar v R*.[25] During the trial, the accused admitted to

---

18   Mellinkoff, above note 14 at 131. See also Walter F Schroeder, "Some Ethical Problems in Criminal Law" in Law Society of Upper Canada, *Representing an Arrested Client and Police Interrogation* (Toronto: R De Boo, 1963) 87 at 94; Robert P Lawry, "Cross-Examining the Truthful Witness: The Ideal Within the Central Moral Tradition of Lawyering" (1996) 100 Dick L Rev 563 at 569 and 572.

19   The report is reproduced in UK, Supreme Court of Judicature, *The Annual Practice* (London: Sweet & Maxwell, 1917) at 2433–434 [*The Annual Practice*].

20   *The Annual Practice*, ibid at 2433. It is Macmillan, in "The Ethics of Advocacy," above note 1 at 321–22, who reports that the request for advice came from the Bar Committee of Shanghai.

21   However, in the council's view the duty usually did *not* apply where the confession came before trial: see Section G, below in this chapter.

22   Interestingly, the 1920 CBA Canons of Legal Ethics did not include language from the 1915 report, even though they addressed the defence of the client known to be guilty at §§ 2(5) & (6).

23   See the commentaries cited at note 8, above in this chapter.

24   *Tuckiar v R* (1934), 52 CLR 335 at 346 (HCA) [*Tuckiar*].

25   *Ibid*.

his lawyer that he had committed the crime. Counsel conveyed this information to the judge and opposing counsel during a meeting in chambers, and did so again in open court following the jury's verdict of guilt.[26] The High Court strongly disagreed with counsel's actions and, in a statement that has become a classic description of a criminal defence lawyer's duty, noted that

> [w]hether he be in fact guilty or not, a prisoner is, in point of law, entitled to acquittal from any charge which the evidence fails to establish that he committed, and it is not incumbent on his counsel by abandoning his defence to deprive him of the benefit of such rational arguments as fairly arise on the proofs submitted.[27]

These sentiments remain valid in Canada, not to mention much of the Commonwealth and the United States. The hard question, about which there is no unanimous consensus, concerns how far defence counsel can go in defending the guilty client.

D. RATIONALE FOR DEFENDING ONE SUSPECTED OR KNOWN TO BE GUILTY

The rationale that permits a lawyer to defend a client she suspects or even knows to be guilty is inextricably linked to the nature of our criminal justice system, including the special role the system assigns to defence counsel. Crucially, the criminal justice process is adversarial. The opposing sides are responsible for presenting their own cases by bringing forward evidence, cross-examining the opponent's witnesses, presenting argument, and utilizing other available forensic methods. Partisanship is an integral part of this process. The decision as to guilt is made, not by the parties themselves, but by a neutral trier of fact.

The state employs a powerful and comparatively well-financed apparatus of professionals — police and prosecutors — to investigate and prosecute crime. Yet the workings of the criminal justice system are complex, unfamiliar, and often intimidating to laypeople. Many if not most self-represented accused are at a tremendous disadvantage in terms of putting forward their best defence.[28] The justice system thus relies on defence counsel to represent accused persons and so to ensure their substantive and procedural rights are protected. And defence

---

26   *Ibid* at 343–44.
27   *Ibid* at 346.
28   *R v Martin*, 2010 BCCA 526 at para 16.

counsel's proper and necessary role, given the system is adversarial, is to put forward the *client's* position in the litigation, as opposed to counsel's own view of the facts or law.

Acting as the client's advocate — as an unabashed partisan — is thus central to the defence lawyer's function. In taking on this role, and thereby helping to ensure the client's effective representation, counsel gives both accused persons and the public confidence the adversarial system is functioning accurately and fairly.[29] Counsel's adversarial role also promotes the autonomy and dignity of the accused by facilitating his control over the conduct of the defence.[30] The partisan criminal defence lawyer thus "does good simply by fighting for his or her clients. The virtues of their causes are usually of little significance because it is the responsibility of others in the system to present opposing views and to decide the case on the merits."[31]

The view that litigating lawyers must be loyal and zealous advocates for their clients is strongly reflected in the ethical code provisions reproduced in Section B above. Representative is the commentary stating that "[t]he lawyer's function as advocate is openly and necessarily partisan," and as such "the lawyer is not obliged . . . to assist an adversary or advance matters harmful to the client's case."[32] But the notion that a lawyer's proper role is necessarily partisan is *especially* pervasive and powerful in the context of defending in the criminal justice system, for three reasons.

First, few litigants have as much at stake as do criminal defendants. If convicted, they face the powerful stigma of being branded criminals, possible or certain loss of liberty, and a cavalcade of other potential adverse consequences such as loss of employment, damage to family and other personal relationships, forfeiture of property, and restrictions on international travel. Sometimes, many of these deleterious consequences arise immediately on being charged. What is more, accused persons are typically poor and disadvantaged, and virtually friendless within the justice system. By helping and listening to them, and acting

---

29   *R v Neil*, 2002 SCC 70 at para 12 [*Neil*]; *R v Sinclair*, 2010 SCC 35 at para 163, Fish and LeBel JJ, dissenting but not on this point; *R v Joanisse* (1995), 102 CCC (3d) 35 at 57 [para 64] (Ont CA), leave to appeal to SCC refused (1996), 111 CCC (3d) vi (SCC) [*Joanisse*]; *R v Vachon*, 2011 QCCA 2103 at para 63 [*Vachon*].

30   The importance of autonomy and dignity in terms of controlling a criminal defence is recognized in *R v Swain* (1991), 63 CCC (3d) 481 at 505–6 [paras 35–36] (SCC) [*Swain*].

31   David Layton, "The Criminal Defence Lawyer's Role" (2004) 27 Dal LJ 379 at 381.

32   See the commentaries cited at note 5, above in this chapter.

as their storytellers in response to a state narrative of criminality, defence lawyers affirm their humanity and worth as members of society.[33]

Second, defence counsel's assigned role in the criminal justice system is inextricably entwined with several constitutional rights afforded every accused person in connection with her legal representation. To begin with, the adversarial system, from which counsel's role as partisan advocate arises, is *itself* a principle of fundamental justice protected by the *Charter of Rights and Freedoms*.[34] Furthermore, the accused enjoys other *Charter* rights that are largely based on the notion that criminal counsel must act as a partisan in resolutely advancing the client's defence. These include the right to counsel,[35] the right to choice of counsel,[36] the right to conflict-free counsel,[37] the right to the effective assistance of counsel,[38] and the steadfast protection of solicitor-client privilege.[39] It is not going too far to say that defence counsel's role as zealous advocate for the accused in a criminal case is a principle of fundamental justice enshrined in the *Charter*.[40] Defence counsel's

33   This proposition flows somewhat from the point made in the text associated with note 30 and is elaborated on in David Luban, *Legal Ethics and Human Dignity* (Cambridge University Press, 2007) at 68–73, and Alice Woolley, "To What Should Lawyers Be Faithful?" (2012) 31 Criminal Justice Ethics 124 at 128–32. For powerful first-person accounts of defence counsel playing this role, see Abbe Smith, "Defending Those People" (2012) 10 Ohio State J of Criminal L 277; Stanley Goldman, "In Defense of the Damned" (2008) 5 Ohio State J of Criminal L 611; Barbara Allen Babcock, "Defending the Guilty" (1983–84) 32 Clev St L Rev 175.

34   *Canadian Charter of Rights and Freedoms*, Part I of the *Constitution Act, 1982*, being Schedule B to the *Canada Act 1982* (UK), 1982, c 11 [*Charter*]; *Swain*, above note 30 at 505–6 [paras 35–36]; *R v Mian*, 2014 SCC 54 at para 37.

35   *Smith v Jones* (1999), 132 CCC (3d) 225 at para 5 (SCC), Major J, dissenting but not on this point; *R v Bhandher*, 2012 BCCA 441 at para 50; *R v Rejzek*, 2009 ABCA 393 at para 15, leave to appeal to SCC refused, [2010] SCCA No 39; *R v Okafor*, 2009 ONCA 672 at para 12; *R v Al-Enzi*, 2014 ONCA 569 at paras 79 and 82, leave to appeal to SCC refused, [2014] SCCA No 405.

36   *R v McCallen* (1999), 131 CCC (3d) 518 [para 35] (Ont CA).

37   For examples of courts using counsel's necessarily partisan role to justify the principles underlying conflict of interest rules, see *Neil*, above note 29 at paras 12–13, 16–17, and 19(ii); *Canadian National Railway Co v McKercher LLP*, 2013 SCC 39 at paras 25–26 [*McKercher*]; *R v MQ*, 2012 ONCA 224 at para 30.

38   *Joanisse*, above note 29 at 57 [paras 63–64]; *R v GDB*, 2000 SCC 22 at paras 24–25; *Vachon*, above note 29 at para 63.

39   *R v McClure*, 2001 SCC 14 at paras 2 and 31–33.

40   See *British Columbia (AG) v Christie*, 2007 SCC 21 at para 22, which although not mentioning criminal defence counsel, recognizes that the role lawyers play has in some situations been granted constitutional status. See also *Law Society of British Columbia v Mangat*, 2001 SCC 67 at paras 43–45; *Lavallee, Rackel & Heintz v Canada (AG)*, 2002 SCC 61 at paras 52 and 65–68, LeBel J, dissenting

partisan garb in the criminal justice system is thus spun from constitutional cloth.

The third reason why defence counsel's role as zealous advocate holds such strength in the criminal law realm has to do with the more general due process rights enjoyed by accused persons at common law and under the *Charter*. Each accused has the right to be presumed innocent until proven guilty according to law after a fair and public hearing by an independent and impartial tribunal.[41] Most crucially for our discussion, this means the Crown bears the onus of making out its case on the high evidentiary standard of proof beyond a reasonable doubt.[42] An accused also has the right to make full answer and defence,[43] which includes the ability to test the prosecution case at trial by cross-examining Crown witnesses.[44] Accused persons are further protected by the principle against self-incrimination, the central tenet of which is that they cannot be conscripted to assist in building the prosecution case.[45] Among other things, this means the defence has no general duty to disclose information bearing on guilt or innocence to the Crown.[46] Finally, an accused will sometimes have the right to exclude evidence under section 24(2) of the *Charter* as a remedy for a breach of another *Charter* guarantee, for instance the section 8 right against unreasonable search and seizure, this even though the excluded evidence is reliable and incriminating.[47]

---

but not on this point [*Lavallee, Rackel & Heintz*]; *Federation of Law Societies of Canada v Canada (AG)*, 2013 BCCA 147 at paras 105–14, leave to appeal to SCC granted, [2013] SCCA No 235. Justice Rosenberg has aptly recognized criminal defence counsel's role as zealous advocate as "a cornerstone of our adversary system": *R v Felderhof* (2003), 180 CCC (3d) 498 at para 85 (Ont CA) [*Felderhof*].

41   *Charter*, above note 34, s 11(d); *R v St-Onge Lamoureux*, 2012 SCC 57 at para 24 [*St-Onge Lamoureux*].

42   *R v Starr*, 2000 SCC 40 at paras 230–37; *R v JHS*, 2008 SCC 30 at para 13; *R v Griffin*, 2009 SCC 28 at para 33.

43   *R v Bjelland*, 2009 SCC 38 at para 20; *R v NS*, 2012 SCC 72 at para 15 [*NS*]; *Criminal Code*, RSC 1985, c C-46, s 650(3).

44   *R v Seaboyer* (1991), 66 CCC (3d) 321 at 388–89 [paras 29–34] (SCC); *R v Osolin* (1993), 86 CCC (3d) 481 at 516–18 [paras 157–60] (SCC) [*Osolin*]; *R v Lyttle*, 2004 SCC 5 at para 41 [*Lyttle*]; *R v Pires*, 2005 SCC 66 at paras 3 and 29 [*Pires*]; *NS*, above note 43 at para 24.

45   *R v White*, [1999] 2 SCR 417 at paras 40–44; *R v Brown*, 2002 SCC 32 at paras 91–104. Examples of the principle against self-incrimination in action include the s 7 *Charter* right to silence (*R v Singh*, 2007 SCC 48 at para 21) and the ss 11(c) and 13 *Charter* rights against testimonial compulsion (*R v Nedelcu*, 2012 SCC 59 at paras 44 and 74–75, LeBel J, dissenting but not on this point).

46   *R v S(RJ)* (1995), 96 CCC (3d) 1 at para 88 (SCC). See also Chapter 10, Section D.

47   The s 24(2) test is set out in *R v Grant*, 2009 SCC 32 at paras 59–128. Cases where incriminating physical evidence has been excluded include *R v Harrison*,

These due process rights are animated by an unremitting desire to protect individuals from a powerful and sometimes overweening state, by a grave concern that absent such protection, the agents of the state, most particularly the police but also Crown prosecutors, may abuse their powers and so cause serious harm to society and its members. The fear of convicting an innocent person is especially strong, and this is why the *Charter* can in some respects be said to overprotect accused persons, for instance by placing the onus on the Crown to make its case on the high standard of proof beyond a reasonable doubt and by preventing the accused from being compelled to provide the state with information regarding the charged offence. Ultimately, the goal of the criminal justice system is not only to ascertain the truth but also to keep the state in check.[48]

In sum, not only do criminal defence lawyers play an adversarial role that is constitutionally enshrined in the *Charter*, but they do so in a system that seeks to balance the search for truth with the protection of individual rights. Defence counsel's zealous advocacy is consequently often directed not so much at truth finding as it is at advancing the accused's constitutional guarantees, including the right to test and resist Crown evidence and to not be compelled to assist in building the prosecution case.[49] Ethical defence lawyering thus flows from a concept of justice that includes due process rights and their underlying values.[50]

For all of these reasons, defence counsel who vigorously defends a client knowing he is guilty sends a message to police and prosecutors alike that fair and complete evidence will be needed to secure a conviction, which benefits not only the client in question but also the entire justice system. This zealous lawyer also recognizes an inherent dignity and autonomy in even the culpable accused, who is deserving of due process rights and fair procedures as she navigates the complex and often daunting criminal justice process. The result may be the acquittal of persons who have committed criminal offences — in a sense, the overprotection of the guilty — but society has deemed this to be a necessary price to pay for the proper protection of individual rights. The principle that a guilty person must be defended preserves the integrity of

---

2009 SCC 34 at paras 20–42; *R v Morelli*, 2010 SCC 8 at paras 98–113; *R v Côté*, 2011 SCC 46 at paras 45–48.

48   Layton, above note 31 at 383; Luban, above note 33 at 30–31 and 62.
49   In other words, "while lawyers must *tell* the truth, they are not required to *seek* the truth or to aid in the search": W William Hodes, "Seeking the Truth versus Telling the Truth at the Boundaries of the Law: Misdirection, Lying and 'Lying with an Explanation'" (2002) 44 S Tex L Rev 53 at 60–61 [emphasis in original].
50   Layton, above note 31 at 383.

the criminal justice system and, more generally, benefits society itself. Ultimately, the lawyer's actions in defending the guilty client are justified by the particular role that counsel plays in an adversarial, rights-based legal system.

E. RATIONALE FOR RESTRICTING COUNSEL IN THE CONDUCT OF THE CASE

While strong advocacy in the cause of a client is ethically desirable, regardless of whether the client is known to be guilty, a lawyer's loyalty to the client is subject to constraints. The law permits an accused to insist that the Crown prove its case according to the justice system's applicable standards and rules and to challenge and test the Crown case within an adversarial setting. But the law does not allow an accused, nor counsel acting on his behalf, to act dishonestly or fraudulently in conducting the defence. We therefore see a balance, or perhaps a tension, between the legitimate pursuit of an accused's rights in conducting a defence and the need to ensure lawyers do not knowingly mislead the court and hence unacceptably subvert the truth-finding function of the criminal justice process.

The need for a balance is nicely articulated by Reid LJ in his oft-quoted comments in *Rondel v Worsley*:

> Every counsel has a duty to his client fearlessly to raise every issue, advance every argument, and ask every question, however distasteful, which he thinks will help his client's case. But, as an officer of the court concerned in the administration of justice, he has an overriding duty to the court, to the standards of his profession, and to the public, which may and often does lead to a conflict with his client's wishes or with what the client thinks are his personal interests. Counsel must not mislead the court, he must not lend himself to casting aspersions on the other party or witnesses for which there is no sufficient basis in the information in his possession, he must not withhold authorities or documents which may tell against his clients but which the law or the standards of his profession require him to produce.[51]

Canadian jurisprudence strongly affirms Reid LJ's sentiments with respect to the limits on counsel's duty to fearlessly raise every issue and

---

51   [1969] 1 AC 191 at 227–28 [*Rondel*]. See also *Meek v Fleming*, [1961] 2 QB 366 at 379–80 (CA). The first sentence of this quotation is included in the ethical code commentaries cited at note 4, above in this chapter.

advance every argument for the client.[52] Our courts have made clear that criminal defence counsel does not have *carte blanche* to do whatever she chooses in conducting a client's case, and in particular must not knowingly act so as to mislead the court.[53] All Canadian ethical codes repeatedly express this same restriction.[54]

Counsel who exceeds the proper bounds of partisanship risks attracting not only disciplinary action but criminal prosecution.[55] Delineating the boundaries of ethical partisanship is thus an important consideration for the lawyer who represents a client known to be guilty. Counsel who has irresistible knowledge of a client's guilt is necessarily limited in conducting the defence, for he knows that evidence or assertions to the contrary are false and may mislead the court. To take an easy example, counsel who has received a clear, unequivocal, and reliable confession from the accused cannot call a false alibi.[56] As we shall see, however, the line between advocacy that merely forces the Crown to prove its case and that which serves to mislead the court is not always easy to discern.

F. ACQUIRING KNOWLEDGE THAT THE CLIENT IS GUILTY

Given that counsel faces restrictions in acting for a client known to be guilty, a preliminary but crucial issue is when counsel can be said to have obtained such knowledge.

---

52 Criminal cases quoting Reid LJ's comments with approval include *R v Samra* (1998), 129 CCC (3d) 144 at paras 64–65 (Ont CA); *R v Dunbar*, 2003 BCCA 667 at para 336; *Felderhof*, above note 40 at para 95; *Lyttle*, above note 44 at para 66.

53 See the cases *ibid* plus *R v SGT*, 2011 SKCA 4 at para 60; *R v Tshiamala*, 2011 QCCA 439 at paras 152–54, leave to appeal to SCC refused, [2011] SCCA No 220; *R v Legato* (2002), 172 CCC (3d) 415 at paras 83–88 (Que CA) [*Legato*]; *R v Ford* (1993), 78 CCC (3d) 481 at 498 [paras 63–64] (BCCA).

54 See the ethical code provisions cited at notes 7–12, above in this chapter.

55 Actions that mislead the court may constitute crimes under the *Criminal Code*, above note 43, such as being a party to perjury (ss 21 and 131), counselling perjury (ss 22, 131, and 464), fabricating evidence (s 137), and obstructing justice (s 139). See, for example, *R v Sweezey* (1987), 39 CCC (3d) 182 at 188 (NLCA); *R v Dorion*, 2007 NBCA 41, leave to appeal to SCC refused, [2007] SCCA No 413.

56 This interdiction is expressly set out in the ethical rules cited at notes 7 & 8, above in this chapter.

1) The Basic Presumption against Judging the Client's Culpability

Counsel's role in the criminal justice system is neither to judge the client nor to arrive at a personal determination as to the client's guilt. The expressions of this sentiment by distinguished lawyers and commentators are legion. "A client is entitled to say to his counsel, I want your advocacy, not your judgment; I prefer that of the Court," stated Baron Bramwell in a much-repeated quotation from *Johnson v Emerson and Sparrow*.[57] Just as famous are the comments of defence lawyer Thomas Erskine in *R v Paine*:

> If the advocate refuses to defend, from what he may think of the charge or of the defence, he assumes the character of the judge; nay, he assumes it before the hour of judgment; and in proportion to his rank and reputation, puts the heavy influence of perhaps a mistaken opinion into the scale against the accused, in whose favour the benevolent principle of the English law makes all presumptions, and which commands the very judge to be his counsel.[58]

Daniel Soulez-Larivière, in his excellent book on the ethics of advocacy, says, "À . . . chacun son métier. Aux juges de juger, aux avocats de défendre. Un avocat qui veut se faire juge de son client se trompe de métier, mélange les fonctions, affaiblit la sienne pour le plus grand mal de toute l'institution judiciaire."[59] To the same effect, David Mellinkoff has advised that a lawyer should never let his "own conscientious scruples stand in the way of a proper defence for his client."[60]

That a lawyer reasonably believes the client to be guilty is thus largely irrelevant to the conduct of the defence at trial.[61] Certainly, such a belief does not, without more, preclude counsel from calling evidence

---

57   (1871), LR 6 Ex 329 at 367.
58   (1792), 22 Howell's St Tr 358 at 412.
59   Daniel Soulez-Larivière, *L'Avocature* (Paris: Éditions du Seuil, 1995) at 245. His words can be translated as "[t]o each their role. To judges to judge, to lawyers to defend. A lawyer who wants to judge her own client is mistaken as to her profession, mixes up respective functions, and weakens her own function to the detriment of the entire judicial system."
60   Mellinkoff, above note 14 at 191.
61   See the ethical code commentaries cited at note 7, above in this chapter, which state "notwithstanding the lawyer's private opinion on credibility or the merits, a lawyer may properly rely on any evidence or defences including so-called technicalities, not known to be false or fraudulent." See too Que s 2.04: "The advocate may undertake the defence of the client no matter what his personal opinion may be on the latter's guilt or liability."

that suggests the client's innocence or from making submissions to the same effect before a jury. Counsel who limits a defence based on no more than a personal suspicion the client is guilty may be denying the client access to constitutional rights.[62] Moreover, the lawyer's belief may be wrong. As G Arthur Martin said, "I have heard many unlikely stories in my time from defendants; some surprisingly, turned out to be true. Some cases look impossible; intensive preparation indicates that they are not really so."[63] A lawyer who rejects partisanship and instead plays the role of judge risks contributing to a wrongful conviction, something that has occurred all too often in Anglo-American criminal justice systems.[64]

The substantial damage that a lawyer can cause by too quickly judging a client is illustrated by the decision of the Quebec Court of Appeal in *R v Delisle*.[65] There, the victim of a serious assault identified the accused as one of several assailants. The accused insisted to counsel that this identification was erroneous, and that a man named Kevin Carl was the person who, in the others' company, participated in the assault. The lawyer disregarded the accused's story, based on his own evaluation of the case, and did not investigate the possibility that Carl was the real culprit. Counsel did not call his client at trial, thinking he could win the case by attacking the sufficiency of the identification evidence. The accused was nonetheless convicted.

Following the conviction but before sentencing, Carl contacted the lawyer, confiding that he was the person responsible for the acts attributed to the accused. Counsel was unsuccessful in an attempt to reopen the case based on this new information. On appeal, however, the information was introduced as fresh evidence, and the conviction was quashed based on a breach of the right to the effective assistance of counsel.[66] As the court observed:

---

62 Many of these rights are discussed in Section D, above in this chapter.

63 G Arthur Martin, "The Role and Responsibility of the Defence Advocate" (1970) 12 Crim LQ 376 at 387.

64 For a tragic case where shoddy defence work likely contributed to a wrongful conviction, see Nova Scotia, *Royal Commission on the Donald Marshall, Jr, Prosecution: Findings and Recommendations* (Halifax: The Commission, 1989) vol 1 at 72–77. Regarding the importance of the defence function in avoiding wrongful convictions, see Bruce MacFarlane, "Convicting the Innocent: A Triple Failure of the Justice System" (2006) 31 Man LJ 403 at 470–72, and Manitoba, *The Inquiry Regarding Thomas Sophonow: The Investigation, Prosecution and Consideration of Entitlement to Compensation* (Winnipeg: Manitoba Justice, 2001) at 53.

65 (1999), 133 CCC (3d) 541 (Que CA) [*Delisle*].

66 *Ibid* at 558 [para 59].

In the case at bar, counsel for the appellant totally misunderstood the role which was his, by setting himself up as the judge of his client instead of respecting his client's instructions and truly defending his client's interests. Taking into account what we know now as a result of fresh evidence, this demonstrates even more the danger for counsel of relying upon his impressions.[67]

A similar problem arose in *R v Moore*, where counsel told his client that he was ethically precluded from calling the client to testify in a sexual assault case because the client had failed a defence-administered polygraph test.[68] The client did not take the stand and was convicted based on the complainant's evidence. In overturning the conviction on the ground of ineffective assistance of counsel, the Saskatchewan Court of Appeal recognized that this was not a case where the client had sought counsel's help to present false evidence.[69] Rather, counsel appeared to have formed the belief that the client was guilty based on the polygraph results and felt ethically constrained from presenting the client's evidence as a result.[70] But, as the court noted, polygraph results are "far from infallible" and are inadmissible in evidence at trial.[71] They are certainly *not* conclusive and irresistible proof a client is lying. Consequently, whatever the lawyer's *belief*, he could not be said to have *known* his client was lying, and so the rules of professional conduct that prohibit knowingly calling false evidence were not engaged. Counsel was not ethically precluded from calling his client as a witness, and was wrong to advise the client otherwise.[72]

Delisle and *Moore* demonstrate how a client's constitutional rights can be undermined by counsel who takes on the role of judge and unjustifiably limits the conduct of the defence. On the other hand, counsel's opinion regarding the nature and strength of the Crown case will almost certainly influence the advice given to the client, and properly so. A lawyer should always advise the client regarding the prospects of success at trial.[73] A considered view of the prosecution evidence may

---

67   *Ibid.* See also *Vachon*, above note 29 at paras 50 and 57–78; *R v Fraser*, 2011 NSCA 70 at paras 83–93 and 97–104.

68   2002 SKCA 30 at paras 20–25 [*Moore*].

69   *Ibid* at para 45.

70   The judgment never expressly states that this was so, but it is hard to come to any other conclusion based on the facts set out therein.

71   Above note 68 at paras 26–35. See also *R v Oickle*, 2000 SCC 38 at para 95 [*Oickle*].

72   *Moore*, above note 68 at paras 47–55.

73   See Alan D Gold, "Abuse of Power by the Defence Bar" in Law Society of Upper Canada, *The Abuse of Power and the Role of an Independent Judicial System in its*

lead counsel, with the client's consent, to adopt the defence most consistent with the anticipated evidence, the idea being to avoid undermining the integrity of the defence position by fruitlessly attacking unassailable evidence. Obviously, there is a distinction between providing the client with informed, candid, and reasonable advice, which is ethically permissible, and rushing to judgment against the client so as to limit the defence unduly, which is not.

2) The Exception: Irresistible Knowledge of Guilt

In the very great majority of cases, a lawyer is not justified in restricting the conduct of the defence based merely on a personal view of a client's guilt. Occasionally, however, after careful investigation and thorough assessment, a lawyer may reach such a level of certainty with respect to the client's culpability that she "will have as much reason to feel confidence in concluding that a client is guilty as charged as to feel confidence about anything else."[74] Indeed, we sometimes forget that the lawyer's special position as a recipient of confidential information that must not be shared with third parties may make her *better* able to determine what is true or false than is the prosecutor, judge, or jury.[75] In these unusual cases, the lawyer is surely restricted in the conduct of the defence by the ethical codes' prohibition against *knowingly* assisting in dishonest action, presenting false evidence, or otherwise misleading the court.[76]

Little has been written in Canada regarding the factual basis necessary to justify the conclusion that a lawyer is knowingly misleading the court. Canadian ethical codes typically place express restrictions on criminal defence counsel who has received a "clear" confession from his client.[77] These rules also state that the lawyer must be "convinced" the admissions are true, and they prohibit the lawyer from calling evidence he "believes to be false."[78] The question arises as to precisely when counsel for an accused can be said to *know* his client is guilty

---

Regulation and Control (Toronto: R De Boo, 1979) 617 at 632; Martin, above note 63 at 396. See also Chapter 3, Section E.

74 Charles W Wolfram, *Modern Legal Ethics* (St Paul: West, 1986) at 586.

75 See Deborah Rhode, "Ethical Perspectives on Legal Practice" (1985) 37 Stan L Rev 589 at 618–20. *Contra* Jay Silver, "Truth, Justice, and the American Way: The Case *against* the Client Perjury Rules" (1994) 47 Vand L Rev 339 at 383: arguing defence counsel are often biased against their clients and have access to unreliable evidence.

76 See the provisions cited at notes 7–12, above in this chapter.

77 See the commentaries cited at note 8, above in this chapter.

78 *Ibid.*

and whether this standard may be satisfied by information received from *any* source, and not only by an admission received from the client.

In the United States, the matter of knowledge has received more attention, usually in the closely related context of client perjury, and a variety of tests have been suggested by courts and commentators.[79] A "firm factual basis" is perhaps the most widely endorsed test, at least in the jurisprudence.[80] It requires more than just the lawyer's belief and is not satisfied merely because counsel is faced with inconsistencies in the accused's statements; rather, a firm factual basis "mandates that a lawyer act in good faith based on objective circumstances firmly rooted in fact."[81] Other suggested standards include "good faith determination,"[82] "good cause to believe,"[83] "compelling support,"[84] "beyond a reasonable doubt,"[85] "clear and convincing evidence,"[86] "an undeniable conclusion,"[87] and "absolutely no doubt."[88]

---

79   For a review of some of the relevant caselaw and commentary, see Monroe Freedman, "Getting Honest about Client Perjury" (2008) 21 Georgetown J Legal Ethics 133 at 142–48; Monroe Freedman, "But Only If You Know" in Rodney Uphoff, ed, *Ethical Problems Facing the Criminal Lawyer: Practical Answers to Tough Questions* (Chicago: American Bar Association, 1995) at 138–39; Edward L Wilkinson, "'That's a Damn Lie!': Ethical Obligations of Counsel When a Witness Offers False Testimony in a Criminal Trial" (2000) 31 St Mary's LJ 407 at 411–15; Nathan Crystal, "False Testimony by Criminal Defendants: Still Unanswered Ethical and Constitutional Questions" [2003] U Ill L Rev 1529 at 1534–37 and 1553–56; Raymond McKoski, "Prospective Perjury by a Criminal Defendant: It's All about the Lawyer" (2012) 44 Ariz St LJ 1575 at 1614–17.

80   *United States ex rel Wilcox v Johnson*, 555 F2d 115 at 122 (3d Cir 1977); *United States v Long*, 857 F2d 436 at 444–45 (8th Cir 1988), cert denied 502 US 828 (1991) [*Long*]; *State v Berrysmith*, 944 P2d 397 at 401 (Wash App 1997); *Commonwealth v Mitchell*, 781 NE2d 1237 at 1246–47 (Mass 2003) [*Mitchell*]; *Brown v Commonwealth*, 226 SW3d 74 at 84 (Ky 2007); *State v Chambers*, 994 A2d 1248 at 1260–64, n 13–16 (Conn 2010). See also Third Restatement § 120, comment "c."

81   *Mitchell*, above note 80 at 1247.

82   *People v Bartee*, 566 NE2d 855 at 856 (Ill App 1991), cert denied, 502 US 1014 (1991). But see *People v Calhoun*, 815 NE2d 492 at 499–504 (Ill App 4th Dist 2004) [*Calhoun*], suggesting that this standard is too low and that the "firm factual basis" standard is superior.

83   *State v Hischke*, 639 NW2d 6 at 10 (Iowa 2002).

84   *Sanborn v State*, 474 So2d 309 at 313, n 2 (Fla Dist Ct App 1985).

85   *United States v Del Carpio-Cotrina*, 733 F Supp 95 (SD Fla 1990); *Shockley v State*, 565 A2d 1373 at 1379–80 (Del Super Ct 1989); *Commonwealth v Alderman*, 437 A2d 36 at 39 (Pa Super 1981) [*Alderman*].

86   Third Restatement § 120, comment "c" (Reporter's Note).

87   Wayne Brazil, "Unanticipated Client Perjury and the Collision of Rules of Ethics, Evidence, and Constitutional Law" (1979) 44 Mo L Rev 601 at 608–09.

88   Norman Lefstein, "Client Perjury in Criminal Cases: Still in Search of an Answer" (1988) 1 Geo J Legal Ethics 521 at 528.

Although Canadian ethical codes tend to focus on instances where a criminal defence lawyer has received an admission from the client, we believe the general prohibition against knowingly misleading the court can sometimes be engaged based on knowledge emanating from other sources.[89] The standard that must be met before counsel can be said to have knowledge of guilt must be very demanding, however, given the lawyer's special role as partisan in an adversarial system that seeks not only the truth but also to protect the client's constitutional rights. In our view, knowledge of guilt within the meaning of the ethical rules can only be said to exist where counsel reaches an *irresistible conclusion* that the client is culpable on the criminal standard, by which we mean a conclusion that not even a zealous but honest partisan could deny.[90] Our standard, which has been endorsed by the Supreme Court of Canada,[91] will be easy to meet where the client provides counsel with a clear and convincing admission that fully jibes with the rest of the evidence in the case. But it will be very difficult to satisfy, and only rarely be met, where the client has not admitted guilt.[92] Absent such an admission, it will not be enough for the lawyer simply to conclude that he would find the client guilty beyond a reasonable doubt if deciding the case as a judge or jury member.[93] Rather, the lawyer must irresistibly

---

89 Our view is shared by Michael Code, "Ethics and Criminal Law Practice" in Alice Woolley et al, *Lawyers' Ethics and Professional Regulation*, 2d ed (Markham, ON: LexisNexis, 2012) 435 at 463; Alice Woolley, *Understanding Lawyers' Ethics in Canada* (Markham, ON: LexisNexis, 2011) at 303–4; David Tanovich, "The Ethical Limits of Defence Lawyering in Sexual Assault Cases" Ottawa Law Rev [forthcoming]; Gregory Lafontaine, "Client Perjury and the Criminal Defence Lawyer as Lie Detector" (2006) 27:1 For the Defence 6 at 6. See also ABA r 3.3, comment 8; Third Restatement § 120, comment "c."

90 Layton, above note 31 at 397–98.

91 *R v Youvarajah*, 2013 SCC 41 at para 61, citing the first edition of our text. The standard is also supported by Woolley, above note 89 at 167, and is mentioned with apparent approval in *Legato*, above note 53 at para 86.

92 Sensible examples as to when a lawyer might truly *know* the client is guilty despite the absence of an admission are provided by Lefstein, above note 88 at 529; Edward Kimball, "When Does a Lawyer 'Know' Her Client Will Commit Perjury?" (1988) 2 Geo J Legal Ethics 579 at 583–84. See also *State v McDowell*, 681 NW2d 500 at 509–14 (Wis 2004), cert denied, 543 US 938 (2004), holding that absent "the most extraordinary circumstances," knowledge that a client intends to commit perjury must be based on an admission from the client. A proffered example is where the accused is conclusively shown committing the crime on surveillance video and apprehended at the scene but insists he is innocent (*ibid* at 511, n 10). However, the standard adopted in *McDowell* is criticized as too demanding in *Calhoun*, above note 82 at 502.

93 See *United States v Midgett*, 342 F3d 321 at 326–27 (4th Cir 2003): a lawyer cannot be said to have knowledge even where the client's version of events is

come to this conclusion while adopting a very different mindset — that of the zealous but honest partisan.

Some defence lawyers may view the position that a lawyer can ethically "know" the client is guilty in the absence of a confession as a heresy.[94] Yet in our view it is unacceptable for counsel to put up a defence she irresistibly concludes is false, for instance by calling evidence that someone else committed the crime, regardless of how she comes to know the client is undoubtedly the culprit. The justification for prohibiting a lawyer from knowingly misleading the court should apply whether the knowledge of falsity originates from the client's confession or from other reliable sources of information. Consequently, although a lawyer must in the vast majority of cases resist passing judgment on a client, there will be exceptional situations where he cannot escape the irresistible conclusion and where the attendant ethical constraints will therefore apply. Counsel is precluded from reaching such a conclusion, however, absent a careful investigation of all relevant aspects of the case.

3) The Most Likely Instance of Irresistible Knowledge of Guilt: The Confession

The most likely manner by which a lawyer will come to an irresistible conclusion that the client is guilty is by a reliable, unequivocal, and unrecanted confession.[95] As the ethical rules emphasize, before imposing any restrictions on the conduct of the defence, the lawyer must be "convinced" the client's admission is "true and voluntary."[96] The most sincere sounding confession of guilt can, on further examination, turn out to be false. People occasionally confess to crimes they have

---

"far-fetched" and "dramatically outweighed by other evidence."

94   See John B Mitchell, "The Ethics of the Criminal Defense Attorney — New Answers to Old Questions" (1980) 32 Stan L Rev 293 at 296–98, n 12; Silver, above note 75 at 358–92; Meredith Blake & Andrew Ashworth, "Ethics and the Criminal Defence Lawyer" (2004) 7 Legal Ethics 167 at 176 [Blake & Ashworth, "Ethics"]; Monroe Freedman & Abbe Smith, *Understanding Lawyers' Ethics*, 4th ed (New Providence, NJ: LexisNexis, 2010) at 182–83. See also *Long*, above note 80 at 445: court appears to hold that "firm factual basis" standard only met where counsel has received explicit admission from client.

95   It must be said, however, that in most cases clients do not admit guilt to their lawyers unless and until they decide to plead guilty: see Layton, above note 31 at 397; Goldman, above note 33 at 616; Robert P Mosteller, "Why Defense Attorneys Cannot, but Do, Care about Innocence" (2010) 50 Santa Clara L Rev 1 at 9 and 37–38.

96   See the commentaries cited at note 8, above in this chapter.

not committed.[97] The admission may be made in an attempt to protect the true culprit. Or the client may be suffering under a mental affliction that causes delusions. Some clients falsely confess in the belief the admission will put an early end to the unpleasant stress and strain of the criminal process. To guard against these false confessions, counsel must ask probing questions of the client who has made an admission of guilt, review the Crown case, and, where warranted, undertake independent investigation.[98]

Counsel must also determine whether the accused's admission clearly covers the factual and mental elements necessary to constitute the offence charged.[99] It is essential that the lawyer be thoroughly familiar with the legal delineation of the offence and clarify the facts to which the client admits. Sometimes the law is not clear as to the ambit of a criminal offence, in which case any non-frivolous legal issue should be resolved in favour of the client. A general admission may be made as a means of expressing moral guilt, despite the absence of legal liability. Some clients may wrongly assume they are guilty, being unfamiliar with available defences such as self-defence, intoxication, or lack of criminal responsibility.[100] Additionally, a client may make an admission, whether or not during a confidential conversation with counsel, that is inconsistent or vague to the extent that no certainty as to guilt can be established. It is also possible that the client makes inconsistent statements to counsel, some suggesting or admitting guilt and others not.[101]

In all of these examples, counsel must do whatever she can to reduce the uncertainty. As the ABA Defense Standards recognize, a lawyer

---

97 See *Oickle*, above note 71 at paras 34–45; J Vincent Aprile II, "Client Perjury: When Do You Know the Defendant Is Lying?" (2004) 19:3 Crim Just 14 at 15; Mellinkoff, above note 14 at 149–50; James M Pool, "Defending the 'Guilty' Client" (1979) 64 Mass L Rev 11 at 15; Kathy Swedlow, "Pleading Guilty v. Being Guilty: A Case for Broader Access to Post-conviction DNA Testing" (2005) 41 Criminal L Bull 575 at 589–91; Christopher Sherrin, "Guilty Pleas from the Innocent" (2011) 30 Windsor Rev Legal Soc Issues 1 at 3–7.

98 See ABA Defense Standard 4-4.1.

99 See the commentaries cited at note 8, above in this chapter.

100 See the example given by J Sedgwick in "Panel Discussion: Problems in Ethics and Advocacy" in Law Society of Upper Canada, *Defending a Criminal Case* (Toronto: R De Boo, 1969) 279 at 287–88: client admits bigamy to his lawyer, but a statutory defence nonetheless applies.

101 Inconsistency does not, of itself, lead to knowledge that a client is guilty: *Alderman*, above note 85 at 42; *Mitchell*, above note 80 at 1247; *Johnson v United States*, 404 A2d 162 at 164 (DC 1979); *Nix v Whiteside*, 475 US 157 at 190–91 (1986), White J, concurring; Aprile, above note 97 at 16; Crystal, above note 79 at 1535–36.

has a duty to investigate the facts and law relevant to a case, a duty that persists even where the client has admitted guilt.[102] The irony in this approach may be that counsel secures information that serves to limit the conduct of the defence.[103] However, this price is worth paying to ensure counsel is thoroughly prepared to conduct the case.

Sometimes the client makes a confession in a non-confidential setting, where the prosecutor and presiding judge know of its existence. For instance, the client may admit guilt in a statement made to police or during testimony on a *voir dire* or in a prior proceeding in which he is a witness but not an accused.

Example 1: An accused is charged with first-degree murder. She has confessed to police and seeks to exclude the confession during a pretrial *voir dire*. During the *voir dire*, the accused testifies and concedes the truth of her incriminating statement, though not its voluntariness. The confession is ruled inadmissible, following which the accused pleads not guilty. Assuming counsel is satisfied the client told the truth on the *voir dire*, the confession will restrict the conduct of the defence. Moreover, because the Crown and judge were privy to the confession, either may object if counsel makes an assertion or calls evidence inconsistent with the confession during the trial.

Another possibility is that the client has confessed to the police or a third party yet in speaking to counsel denies the confession is true, in which case counsel is faced with conflicting versions. This, without more, does not constitute irresistible knowledge of guilt.

Example 2: At a trial for the murder of a nine-year-old boy, the Crown calls the accused's brother CN as a prosecution witness. CN previously made a series of statements to police at first denying involvement but eventually admitting to being his brother's accomplice in the killing. After claiming protection under section 5 of the *Canada Evidence Act*,[104] CN denies any involvement in the crime. The Crown cross-examines CN as an adverse witness, and he eventually admits that his incriminating statements to police were true. The accused is nonetheless acquitted. The Crown next prosecutes CN for the murder based on the incriminating statements to police and the evidence of eyewitnesses who saw the brothers near where the deceased went missing. In speaking to his lawyer, CN denies guilt and says he only helped his brother

---

102 ABA Defense Standard 4-4.1. See also *Sankar v State of Trinidad and Tobago*,
       [1995] 1 All ER 236 at 241 (PC) [*Sankar*].
103 Silver, above note 75 at 388.
104 RSC 1985, c C-5.

dispose of the body. Defence counsel retains several experts who opine that CN has a low intellectual capacity, a subnormal IQ, and difficulty understanding questions. In our view, CN's earlier admissions do not fix defence counsel with irresistible knowledge of CN's guilt. This is especially so given CN's various exculpatory statements and testimony, the expert opinions as to his intellectual deficiencies, and his insistence to counsel that the admissions are untrue.[105]

A particularly difficult application of these principles arises where a client admits the elements of the charged offence to counsel, or expresses a willingness to do so in court, in anticipation of a plea resolution, but for whatever reason the resolution agreement is not consummated or is repudiated, and the matter proceeds to a contested trial. In many such cases, the client-lawyer relationship will have broken down along with the prospect of a resolution agreement, and counsel will be discharged or withdraw as a result.[106] But where the client and counsel are otherwise content to continue with the retainer, an issue arises as to whether the admissions received by counsel will restrict the conduct of the defence at trial. If counsel is convinced the client's admissions are true and voluntary, and they are not retracted, counsel knows the client is guilty within the meaning of the ethical rules, and the defence will be limited.[107] If, on the other hand, the client's admissions in anticipation of the guilty plea were partial or equivocal,[108] or are satisfactorily retracted following derailment of the resolution agreement, the lawyer may be able to mount a defence free of the limitations that come from irresistible knowledge of guilt.

The prospect of counsel remaining on the case after a plea resolution falls apart is especially tenuous where she has repeated the client's unequivocal admissions in open court or conveyed them to the Crown in circumstances that do not attract the protection of plea negotiation privilege. In addition to the ethical restrictions that will arise if counsel

---

105 This example is based on the facts in R v Noël, 2002 SCC 67, where the accused testified in his own defence and denied guilt. The Court did not comment on the propriety of calling the accused as a witness, but presumably did not view counsel as having been ethically precluded from doing so.

106 The conditions under which the client-lawyer relationship may be terminated are canvassed in Chapter 11.

107 The potential for this problem was raised but not addressed in any direct way in R v Nixon, 2011 SCC 34 at para 58. See also the discussion at note 146, below in this chapter, and the associated text.

108 Vachon, above note 29 at para 57, appears to support the common-sense view that admissions to some facts in anticipation of a guilty plea do not limit the defence in respect of facts that were not the subject of admissions.

can be said to have knowledge of guilt, counsel may be a witness for the Crown and may in any event legitimately feel that her credibility as zealous advocate for the client has been publicly undermined in a way that requires withdrawal from the retainer.[109]

4) Avoidance Techniques: Restricting Client-Lawyer Communications, Wilful Blindness, "Woodshedding," and Viewing Guilt as Completely Irrelevant

Some lawyers skirt the ethical limitations imposed where there is irresistible knowledge of a client's guilt by strenuously avoiding any such knowledge. One strategy is to refrain from discussing the facts of the case with the client.[110] A related tack is to avoid acquiring any knowledge from outside sources that might threaten counsel's carefully cultivated ignorance. Another approach is to encourage the client to develop an exculpatory version of events, without regard for the version's validity. This latter method is known by the colloquial terms "woodshedding" or "horseshedding" and is sometimes also referred to as "the lesson."[111] Still other lawyers may choose to view a clear and unequivocal confession as absolutely irrelevant, on the theory that guilt is a legal concept never knowable before the final verdict and thus plays no part in the role of the advocate.[112]

The above methods of avoiding or ignoring knowledge of the client's guilt are problematic. Let us start with the lawyer who refuses to discuss the facts of the case with her client. A lawyer requires full information to provide competent and useful legal advice. To restrict artificially the flow of information between client and lawyer thus clashes

---

109 See, for example, *R v Adamson* (1991), 3 OR (3d) 272 at 275 (Gen Div), aff'd (1991), 65 CCC (3d) 159 (Ont CA): counsel removed from record after client retracts admission of identity made by counsel in open court.

110 See *R v IBB*, 2009 SKPC 76 at paras 20–44, where counsel refused to hear his client's version of events until minutes before the trial was to commence, as apparently was his usual practice; this even though the Crown's identification case was weak, the client had strenuously denied guilt in a statement to police, and the co-accused in confessing to police had asserted the client's innocence. Counsel's approach was criticized by the court (*ibid* at paras 64–67, 73, and 81) and resulted in the client's guilty plea being struck.

111 The approach is famously illustrated in Otto Preminger's film *Anatomy of a Murder*, adapted from John Voelker's 1958 novel of the same name (written under the pseudonym Robert Traver). This example is cited, and presumably seen to demonstrate improper behaviour, in the comment to ABA Defense Standard 4-3.2.

112 Blake & Ashworth "Ethics," above note 94 at 176: only the "legal fact of guilt" can limit the lawyer's duty of full and fearless representation.

with the proper role of counsel and may serve to harm the client. For instance, the client may be prevented from revealing exculpatory information that *helps* his cause. Being deprived of inculpatory information may also lead to counsel's being surprised or unprepared at trial, with resultant damage to the defence cause. As the commentary to ABA Defense Standard 4-3.2 states:

> The client is usually the lawyer's primary source of information for an effective defense. An adequate defense cannot be framed if the lawyer does not know what is likely to develop at trial. The lawyer needs to know essential facts, including the events surrounding the act charged, information concerning the defendant's background, and the defendant's record of prior convictions, if any. In criminal litigation, as in other matters, information is the key guide to decisions and action. The lawyer who is ignorant of the facts of the case cannot serve the client effectively.[113]

Complete candour and honesty between client and lawyer can serve only to improve the strength of any legitimate defence. Deliberate ignorance fostered by restricting the normal flow of communication, though it may be the practice of some defence counsel, is therefore not recommended.[114] A middle ground is to wait until disclosure is obtained and reviewed with the client before soliciting a version of events. This approach can have merit in that the disclosure will often help to refresh the client's memory on relevant matters and will usually assist counsel and client in ascertaining what facts will be material in defending the case. Yet postponing a discussion of the facts while counsel waits to receive and review the disclosure creates a risk that valuable evidence will be lost or its probative value reduced in the meantime.[115]

---

113 ABA Defense Standard 4-3.2, comment [note omitted]. See also Freedman & Smith, above note 94 at 152–53; Stephen Gillers, "Monroe Freedman's Solution to the Criminal Defense Lawyer's Trilemma Is Wrong as a Matter of Policy and Constitutional Law" (2006) 34 Hofstra L Rev 821 at 828; Woolley, above note 89 at 177–79.

114 See ABA Defense Standard 4-3.2(b): "Defense counsel should not instruct the client or intimate to the client in any way that the client should not be candid in revealing facts so as to afford defense counsel free rein to take action which would be precluded by counsel's knowing of such facts." But see Adam Dodek, "Reconceiving Solicitor-Client Privilege" (2010) 35 Queen's LJ 493 at 512, n 69, suggesting our view is controversial within the criminal bar.

115 See ABA Defense Standard 4-3.2(a): "*As soon as practicable*, defense counsel should seek to determine all relevant facts known to the accused" [emphasis added]. See also John Wesley Hall, Jr, *Professional Responsibility in Criminal Defense Practice* (St Paul, MN: Clark Boardman Callaghan, 2005) (loose-leaf

Of course, it is entirely possible that the client decides of her own accord not to discuss the facts of the case with counsel. In such an event, counsel should carefully explain the advantages of making full disclosure in a confidential setting. If the client persists in refusing to provide any information, counsel has not received an inculpatory admission and will probably have greater latitude in mounting a defence. At the same time, counsel has made a valid effort to inform himself for the purpose of providing complete and competent legal advice and cannot be faulted if the defence suffers because of the client's decision.

The problems presented by other avoidance techniques are generally even more glaring. Counsel who woodsheds a client with the aim of encouraging a particular version of events runs the risk of complicity in manufacturing false evidence. It is one thing to make sure the client understands her position based on the law but quite another to encourage and then rely on a fabricated version of events.[116] As for the lawyer who ignores a clear and truthful confession based on the view that knowledge of guilt is irrelevant, he is placing excessive emphasis on the need for zealous advocacy and concomitantly risks acting unethically and illegally by consciously misleading the court. The argument that the truth is never known until a legal determination of guilt is made suffers from a confusion of concepts. Legal guilt is not the equivalent of factual truth, but we can surely say that counsel knows something to be true before the trier of fact's final determination. Finally, a lawyer whose suspicions are reasonably aroused should never intentionally avoid acquiring information for the purpose of remaining ignorant of facts that, if known, would limit her conduct of the defence. The deliberate ignorance of such facts can be equated with actual knowledge, according to the doctrine of wilful blindness.[117]

As a last point, counsel who is tempted to employ some or all of the above techniques to avoid acquiring knowledge of a client's guilt risks public exposure, which in turn may lead to disciplinary action or criminal charges. For instance, the client may bring an ineffective assistance of counsel claim on appeal, leading to the introduction of fresh evidence that alerts the court and Crown to the fact that counsel received a confidential confession. Another possibility is that the

---

September 2012 supplement) § 9.16 at 359: client should be encouraged to convey all potentially relevant information at the first interview.

116 The ethical principles applicable to discussing the facts and law with a client are discussed more generally in Chapter 8, Section G(5).

117 For discussions of the concept of wilful blindness in criminal law, though not in relation to the conduct of lawyers, see *R v Spencer*, 2011 SKCA 144 at paras 83–86; *R v Briscoe*, 2010 SCC 13 at paras 21–24.

client discharges counsel and retains a new lawyer who on learning of shameless woodshedding, reports former counsel to his governing body. Or perhaps the client decides to co-operate with the police and, while providing a sworn, videotaped statement or testifying in court for the prosecution, reveals counsel's impropriety. The lesson is simple. Counsel can never safely assume that unethical behaviour will be shielded by solicitor-client privilege.

G. ACCEPTING OR CONTINUING WITH THE RETAINER OF A CLIENT KNOWN TO BE GUILTY

In its 1915 report, the General Council of the English Bar addressed the issue of whether counsel should accept or continue with a retainer on receiving a confession from the client. The proper course of action, according to the council, depended on the timing of the confession in relation to the commencement of the trial:

> Different considerations apply to cases in which the confession has been made before the advocate has undertaken the defence and to those in which the confession is made subsequently during the course of the proceedings.
>
> If the confession has been made before the proceedings have been commenced, it is most undesirable that an advocate to whom the confession has been made should undertake the defence, as he would most certainly be seriously embarrassed in the conduct of the case, and no harm can be done to the accused by requesting him to retain another advocate.
>
> Other considerations apply in cases in which the confession has been made during the proceedings, or in such circumstances that the advocate retained for the defence cannot retire from the case without seriously compromising the position of the accused.[118]

The council thus determined that a lawyer receiving a confession before trial was not only justified in rejecting or ending the retainer but, absent serious compromise to the defence case, was obligated to do so.

A very few commentators have shared the council's view.[119] Their argument is that the client will suffer harm if counsel stays on the case,

---

118 *The Annual Practice*, above note 19 at 2433.

119 See Schroeder, above note 18 at 92; Justice DA Ipp, "Lawyers' Duties to the Court" (1998) 114 Law Q Rev 63 at 87; Carleton Kemp Allen, "*R. v Dean*" (1941) 57 Law Q Rev 85 at 103–4 and 106–7.

for "having been apprised of his client's guilt or the untruthfulness of certain vital testimony, it is highly doubtful if he could plead the case effectively and affect 'warmth for his client' without his being plagued by conscience that he was acting as a false dissembler."[120] Yet the idea that a lawyer must reject a retainer on receiving a confession of guilt from a client or prospective client seems strange from a contemporary Anglo-American perspective. The theoretical underpinnings that justify counsel acting for the client who is known to be guilty apply equally at *all* stages of the process, whether before, during, or after the trial. Once one accepts the rationale behind the defence of the guilty, there is no reason why counsel must refuse to undertake the case simply because the confession is made before trial.

There are also practical problems associated with the notion that counsel cannot accept a retainer on receiving a confession before the start of trial. Where a lawyer follows the General Council's dictate, and refuses to take on a case because she has received a confession from the prospective client, the problem will likely be transferred to another counsel. If the client persists in being completely candid, and repeats the confession to other lawyers, he will never be able to acquire counsel to act at a contested trial.[121] If the client decides to withhold the confession from subsequent counsel, the system has worked to discourage the very openness and free flow of information that is necessary for a successful client-lawyer relationship.

Today, the ethical rules guiding English barristers contain no prohibition against taking on or keeping a case where counsel has received a confession before trial.[122] As for Canadian ethical codes, they typically espouse the general view that defence counsel is justified in undertaking the defence of the client who is known to be guilty.[123] None prohibits counsel from accepting or continuing with a retainer where knowledge of guilt is acquired before the start of trial. It is thus clear that the General Council's position carries no credence in this country. There may be a debate as to whether a lawyer who receives a confession

---

120 Schroeder, above note 18 at 92.
121 See "Panel Discussion: Problems in Advocacy and Ethics," above note 100 at 292–94.
122 See Bar Standards Board, *The Bar Standards Board Handbook*, 1st ed (London: BSB, 2014) Guidance C9 at 24–25.
123 See the commentaries cited at note 8, above in this chapter.

before trial has a *discretion* to terminate the relationship,[124] but there is no doubt whatsoever that she is not obligated to do so.[125]

H. THE NEED TO MAINTAIN CONFIDENTIALITY

Counsel's knowledge concerning the guilt of the client frequently comes from confidential information, most often in the form of a client confession. In such a case, counsel is bound by the duty of confidentiality owed to the client and is prohibited from sharing the information with anyone else.[126] Sadly, this duty has not always been honoured. The lawyers in the *Courvoisier* and *Tuckiar* cases acted improperly by sharing information of their clients' guilt with the presiding judge and others.[127] Taking such action not only violates the client's confidence but may compromise the fact-finder's ability to try the case fairly.[128]

It is equally unacceptable to reveal a client's incriminating confidences by way of suggestive comment or to make statements that imply impropriety on the part of the client. The resulting harm to the client can be seen in the Supreme Court of Canada case *R v Colpitts*.[129] There, the accused had made inculpatory statements to the police in relation to a charge of murdering a prison guard. At trial, he testified that these statements to police were untrue, explaining that he had been trying to protect the real killer, who was a friend at the time. The accused's testimony was likely sabotaged in advance, however, by defence counsel's damning pronouncement to the judge and jury, made just before calling his client to the stand:

> My Lord, yes, I am going to call one witness for the defence, and that will be Reginald Colpitts, the accused. And, Sir, I must — as a matter of professional ethics — do assert that this is going to happen against

---

124 See Allan C Hutchinson, *Legal Ethics and Professional Responsibility*, 2d ed (Toronto: Irwin Law, 2006) at 169: advocating a discretion. In our view, a lawyer usually has a duty to provide a vigorous defence even where a confession has been received from the client and cannot unilaterally end the retainer on this basis alone.

125 *R v Li* (1993), 36 BCAC 181 at para 64 (CA), leave to appeal to SCC refused, [1994] SCCA No 209 [*Li*]; Sedgwick, above note 100 at 292–94.

126 See *Tuckiar*, above note 24 at 346–47. Also see, generally, Chapter 4.

127 The facts of these cases, and the nature of defence counsels' respective breaches of confidentiality, are set out in Section C, above in this chapter.

128 See Mellinkoff, above note 14 at 136.

129 [1966] 1 CCC 146 (SCC) [*Colpitts*].

my better judgment and counsel. But Mr. Colpitts has decided to take the stand and I — of course — will act as examiner.[130]

This pronouncement was ill-advised, raising the real possibility that the client had admitted guilt to counsel but was nonetheless insistent on taking the stand and committing perjury. Justice Spence, who penned the majority reasons in *Colpitts*, stated that these remarks, in conjunction with the trial judge's charge, "could only suggest, and strongly suggest, to the jury that they could place no reliance upon the evidence given by the appellant in his defence."[131]

I. THE NEED FOR FULL AND PROMPT CONSULTATION WITH THE CLIENT

Regardless of when counsel obtains irresistible knowledge the client is guilty, it is imperative that the client be fully informed in advance as to the impact such knowledge may have on the retainer, especially regarding any restrictions on the conduct of the defence.[132] In this vein, most Canadian ethical codes direct, in the context of client confessions to counsel, that "admissions made by the accused to the lawyer may impose strict limitations on the conduct of the defence, *and the accused should be made aware of this.*"[133] Moreover, counsel must inform the client of any limitations on the defence as soon as reasonably possible so that the client's option of discharging counsel and retaining another lawyer is not unduly restricted.

J. PRELIMINARY ADVICE FOR COUNSEL WHO LEARNS OF A CLIENT'S GUILT ONLY AT TRIAL

A lawyer who receives a confidential confession from the accused during the course of a trial is placed in a particularly difficult predicament. Time constraints and the pressures of the trial make it hard to engage

---

130   *Ibid* at 156.
131   *Ibid* at 157. Also telling was defence counsel's address to the jury, in which he made exceedingly little reference to his client's testimony (*ibid* at 155).
132   See *Li*, above note 125 at para 64. More generally, see *McKercher*, above note 37 at paras 45 and 58: lawyer has duty to disclose to client any factors relevant to lawyer's ability to provide effective representation.
133   See the commentaries cited at note 8, above in this chapter [emphasis added].

in careful consideration of the available options. Yet, to the fullest extent possible, such consideration is demanded of counsel.

There are several steps a lawyer should take or consider in reacting to the mid-trial confession. First, the impact of counsel's knowledge on the trial process must be determined in the context of the case at hand and then discussed with the client.[134] Second, if the client refuses to accept any applicable restrictions, she may decide to discharge counsel.[135] Where the client does not discharge the lawyer but nonetheless persists in refusing to accept any necessary limitations on the defence, counsel must seek the court's permission to withdraw from the case for "ethical reasons."[136] Continuing to act but ignoring the client's instructions is prohibited, as is carrying out those instructions in breach of the ethical rules.[137] Third, counsel remains bound by duties of confidence and loyalty to the client and should not divulge any client-lawyer communications.[138] These duties apply even where counsel is discharged or attempts to get off the record. Fourth, it may be appropriate, if not obligatory, for counsel to consult independent counsel in an attempt to resolve the problem, and concomitantly to minimize the possibility of later complaints by the client.[139] Fifth, and finally, some of these steps may require a short break in the trial proceedings. To this end, counsel should request an adjournment, though in doing so, no confidential information can be released.

Example: S is charged with murder. He gives a statement to police that, while largely incriminating, opens up the possibility of several defences, including provocation, mistake, and self-defence. S tells counsel that the statement made to police is true, and counsel cross-examines several Crown witnesses with the aim of raising one of these defences. Counsel intends to call S as a witness to provide further evidence in support of the defence. However, just as counsel is poised to start the defence case, S confidentially confesses that the exculpatory portions of the statement to police are untrue and that the killing was intentional and unprovoked. Counsel immediately decides to abandon any defence based on these portions of the statement and unilaterally chooses not to call the accused to the stand. He delivers a curt jury address, in which he states only that the jury is justified in convicting the accused

---

134 See Section I, above in this chapter.
135 See *Li*, above note 125 at para 64.
136 See Chapter 11, Section L(4)(a).
137 See Chapter 11, Section F.
138 See Section H, above in this chapter.
139 See Chapter 5, Section G.

if satisfied the Crown has met its burden of proof. This response to the client's confession is inadequate and represents a breach of counsel's duty to keep the client informed. The lawyer should have followed the steps recommended above, starting with an adjournment request to permit consultation with the client and independent counsel.[140]

K. LIMITATIONS ON THE CONDUCT OF THE DEFENCE

We have discussed the rationale behind limiting counsel's conduct of the defence where she knows the client is guilty. The question becomes, once defence counsel obtains such knowledge, what is permissible and what is precluded? The general limitation is simply stated: the lawyer may not conduct the defence so as to mislead the court knowingly. Narrowing our focus, the propriety, or impropriety, of certain specific defence tactics is made fairly clear in a commentary found in most Canadian ethical codes.[141] To recap the substance of this commentary, counsel who has received a clear and unequivocal confession from the accused

- "may properly take objection to the jurisdiction of the court, the form of the indictment or the admissibility or sufficiency of the evidence";
- "must not suggest that some other person committed the offence";
- "must not . . . call any evidence that, by reason of the [client's] admissions, the lawyer believes to be false";
- "[must not] set up an affirmative case inconsistent with such admissions, for example by calling evidence in support of an alibi intended to show that the accused could not have done or, in fact, has not done the act"; and
- "is entitled to test the evidence given by each individual witness for the prosecution and argue that the evidence taken as a whole is insufficient to amount to proof that the accused is guilty of the offence charged, but the lawyer should go no further than that."[142]

---

140 This example is adapted from *Sankar*, above note 102. There, it was not totally clear that the accused had confessed to counsel, though the inference he had done so was strong. The Privy Council ruled that counsel had failed to investigate the issue fully with the client and explain any available options, and added that if necessary, an adjournment should have been sought for this purpose (*ibid* at 241).

141 Reproduced above in the text associated with note 8.

142 *Ibid*.

The limits established by this commentary are consistent with the basic notion that a lawyer who has received a confession from the client can utilize defences that are not reliant on information or submissions known to be false.[143] Because of the case-to-meet theory of our criminal justice system, and as the commentary makes clear, counsel can therefore raise a jurisdictional issue, challenge the validity of the indictment, oppose the admissibility of evidence, or argue that the Crown has failed to prove its case beyond a reasonable doubt. As long as the particular defence does not mislead the court, counsel's conduct is legitimate. By the same token, counsel is prohibited from running any defence that involves knowingly misleading the court. As the commentary states, it is improper to call evidence counsel knows to be false, such as a bogus alibi, or to assert that another party committed the offence.

The prohibition against knowingly calling false evidence extends to evidence that counsel knows to be false but that the witness wrongfully believes to be true.[144]

Example: W is charged with murdering a young girl, whose body has not been found. His lawyer, F, is minutes away from finalizing a plea deal, under which the prosecution will forgo seeking the death penalty in return for disclosure of the location of the girl's remains, when the body is discovered by a volunteer searcher. The prosecution is no longer interested in the plea deal. Yet, in working towards the deal, F received a clear and unequivocal confession of guilt from W, which he knows is true because W precisely described the body's location. At trial, F calls opinion evidence from several entomologists, which if reliable would establish a timeline of events excluding W as the killer. The experts honestly believe their opinions are reliable, but F knows otherwise. Applying Canadian ethical principles, F should not have called the experts as witnesses, because the codes prohibit lawyers from leading evidence that "*the lawyer* believes to be false."[145] It matters not that the experts believed their evidence to be accurate.[146]

---

143 See the commentaries cited at note 7, above in this chapter.

144 Third Restatement § 120, comment "d"; Geoffrey Hazard & W William Hodes, *The Law of Lawyering*, 3d ed (Gaithersburg, MD: Aspen Law & Business, 2001) (loose-leaf 2013 supplement) § 29.12 at 29-20–29-22.

145 See the commentary cited at note 8, above in this chapter [emphasis added].

146 This example is based on the 2002 murder trial of David Westerfield, although we have inferred the existence of an express confession. Lawyer Steven Feldman's defence tactics, in particular his calling of the expert evidence and cross-examination of the victim's parents to suggest another perpetrator, attracted criticism when, following the trial, the media revealed the gist of the plea discussions, and many assumed that Feldman must have known of his client's

In many respects, the commentary addressing admissions from one's client provides lawyers with relatively straightforward and uncontentious guidance. There are few who would contend, for example, that defence counsel is ethically justified in calling alibi witnesses she knows to be part of a criminal conspiracy to exonerate a guilty client. But the propriety of other courses of conduct is not so obvious and is not expressly addressed by the commentary. The truly difficult scenarios create controversy because they seem to fall within a grey area where testing the Crown case, which the commentary says is permissible, could be seen to risk misleading the court, which the commentary says is impermissible. The following are four provocative and interrelated scenarios often raised in ethical debates:

1) How far can counsel go in testing the reliability of a truthful witness?
2) Can counsel cross-examine a witness to attack the reliability of testimony he knows or suspects to be inaccurate, even though counsel also knows the accused is guilty?
3) Can defence counsel call truthful evidence as part of the defence case and then use the evidence to suggest the client did not commit the crime?
4) Can counsel make final submissions that suggest a possible defence, based on evidence led by the Crown, even though the defence is inconsistent with counsel's knowledge of the client's guilt?

Examining these scenarios allows us to delve into some of the most controversial issues concerning the ethical limits applicable where defence counsel knows the client is guilty.

1) Cross-examining the Truthful Witness

The possibility that defence counsel may be ethically limited in cross-examining the truthful witness has been the subject of much discussion by commentators. A helpful starting point in examining this issue is the Supreme Court of Canada's 2004 decision in *R v Lyttle*.[147] *Lyttle* describes the legal and ethical threshold that must be met before coun-

---

guilt. Hodes, above note 49 at 70–71, agrees with our analysis of the expert evidence issue. Contrast Asimow & Weisberg, above note 14 at 247–48 and 257, who argue that Feldman had a discretion whether to call the expert evidence. For a discussion of Feldman's attempt to shift the blame to another suspect, see Peter Joy & Kevin McMunigal, *Do No Wrong: Ethics for Prosecutors and Defenders* (Chicago: American Bar Association, 2009) ch 21.

147 *Lyttle*, above note 44.

sel can put a suggestion to a witness in cross-examination.[148] In doing so, the case sets out some important ground rules and thus helps frame the analysis as to whether a defence lawyer can seek to impeach a witness she knows is telling the truth.

a) The Decision in *R v Lyttle*

In *Lyttle*, defence counsel sought to cross-examine several prosecution witnesses to suggest the complainant in a robbery case had falsely identified the accused as his attacker to avoid exposing the real culprits, who were his co-conspirators in a drug-dealing organization. The trial judge prohibited counsel from cross-examining on this point unless she undertook to call defence evidence to support the allegation. While there is no suggestion that defence counsel knew her client was guilty, *Lyttle* bears on the issue of whether counsel can impeach a truthful witness, insofar as the decision sets out the level of knowledge defence counsel must have to put a suggestion to a witness in cross-examination.

Lyttle holds that defence counsel can cross-examine a witness on a point provided counsel has a "good faith basis" for asking the question. A good faith basis does not require that the defence be able to prove the suggested facts otherwise than by cross-examination.[149] Rather,

> a good faith basis is a function of the information available to the cross-examiner, his or her belief in its likely accuracy, and the purpose for which it is used. Information falling short of admissible evidence may be put to the witness. In fact, the information may be incomplete or uncertain, provided the cross-examiner does not put suggestions to the witness recklessly or that he or she knows to be false. The cross-examiner may pursue any hypothesis that is honestly advanced on the strength of reasonable inference, experience or intuition. The purpose of the question must be consistent with the lawyer's role as an officer of the court: to suggest what counsel genuinely thinks possible on known facts or reasonable assumptions is in our view permissible; to assert or to imply in a manner that is calculated to mislead is in our view improper and prohibited.[150]

As this quotation makes clear, counsel is prohibited from putting a suggestion to a witness recklessly or knowing it to be false, a restriction that has since been included in many Canadian ethical codes.[151] Counsel

---

148 The judgment makes clear that the threshold is both legal *and* ethical in nature (*ibid* at paras 46, 51, and 66).

149 *Ibid* at paras 47 and 53–63.

150 *Ibid* at para 48.

151 See the commentaries cited at note 12, above in this chapter.

who knows a particular fact is true cannot assert the contrary to a witness in cross-examination. Counsel is presumably permitted simply to ask the witness whether the fact is true or not, but this unassertive style of cross-examination will usually carry much less force with the trier of fact in terms of undermining the prosecution case.

Example: A woman calls 911 to report that a strange man has broken into her house and sexually assaulted her. Police have no suspects, and the investigation goes cold. Five years later, a DNA profile obtained from semen collected from the woman's pyjamas matches that of B, who is charged with the crime. B admits guilt privately to his lawyer. In cross-examining the complainant, counsel puts to her that she met B at a bar and took him home, where they had consensual sex. Counsel further suggests that she fabricated the sexual assault story to cover up a one-night stand of casual sex. B does not testify, and counsel relies on the consensual sex defence in his closing submissions to the jury. On this scenario, counsel has contravened the "good faith basis" test in *Lyttle* and acted unethically, by putting assertions to the complainant that he knew to be false.[152]

Lyttle does not go so far as to prohibit *any* attack on the reliability of a witness known by counsel to be truthful. Importantly, the judgment does *not* stop defence counsel from putting suggestions to the witness that counsel *knows or suspects to be true* and then using the witness's answers to argue that the Crown has not met its onus of proving guilt beyond a reasonable doubt. Counsel never claims the witness is lying, only that the fact-finder cannot be sure the witness is telling the truth. In taking this tack, counsel does not "assert or . . . imply in a manner that is calculated to mislead," to quote the interdiction in *Lyttle*.[153] Whether a good faith basis exists to pose a question "is a function of the information available to the cross-examiner, his or her belief in its likely accuracy, and the purpose for which it is used."[154] Asking a question in an attempt to elicit evidence counsel knows or suspects may be true, for the purpose of putting the Crown to its proof in a criminal trial, fits within this definition and so is entirely proper.

---

152 This example is based on a real case, but the element of a confession to the lawyer has been added (see Christie Blatchford, "The Still, Sad Music of Humanity" *The Globe & Mail* (6 November 2004) A21). David Tanovich, in "Law's Ambition and the Reconstruction of Role Morality in Canada" (2005) 28 Dal LJ 267 at 295, speculates that B may in fact have confessed to his lawyer.

153 *Lyttle*, above note 44 at para 48.

154 *Ibid.*

Lyttle nonetheless represents a significant limit on counsel's ability to impeach the truthful witness, especially when viewed in conjunction with other rules of evidence. We say this partly because of tactical considerations but also because counsel has an ethical and legal duty not to undertake a cross-examination that seeks to elicit inadmissible evidence.[155] A number of evidentiary rules, in addition to the good faith requirement in *Lyttle*, are especially worthy of note in this regard.

First, the rule in *Browne v Dunn* permits the trier of fact to draw an adverse inference against a party regarding a material point on which a witness is not challenged in cross-examination.[156] *Lyttle*'s prohibition against counsel putting to a witness a fact counsel knows to be false may well work to trigger *Browne v Dunn*[157] and so create a real possibility that the judge or jury will draw an inference favouring the witness's reliability on that fact.

Second, defence counsel may be unable to advance a theory of the defence that contradicts the truthful witness's testimony — even as a mere possibility that the Crown must disprove to establish guilt — because there is no evidentiary foundation to support the theory. Absent a sufficient evidentiary basis, counsel will be prevented from floating any specific non-guilt scenarios in closing submissions.[158]

Third, although counsel can quite properly put a suggestion to the truthful witness that counsel suspects might be true, where the witness rejects the suggestion and where there is no other evidence in support, counsel will have no evidentiary basis on which to argue in favour of the factual proposition in closing. In other words, a suggestion put by counsel in cross-examination does not constitute evidence if rejected by the witness.[159]

---

155 See Chapter 8, Section H(2).
156 *Lyttle*, above note 44 at para 64; *R v McNeill* (2000), 144 CCC (3d) 551 at para 43 (Ont CA); *R v Dexter*, 2013 ONCA 744 at para 21; *R v Ali*, 2009 BCCA 464 at para 26.
157 *R v Chertin*, 2006 ONCJ 19 at para 13 (counsel's knowledge that witness is truthful may lead to *Browne v Dunn* problems).
158 *R v Pappas*, 2013 SCC 56 at para 21. For example, the defence can only argue that the Crown has failed to disprove that an alternative suspect committed the offence if the evidence establishes a sufficient nexus between the suspect and the offence. Absent an evidentiary nexus, there is no air of reality to the possibility, and so it need not be disproved by the Crown: *R v Grandinetti*, 2005 SCC 5 at paras 47–48 [*Grandinetti*]. However, the defence need not meet the "air of reality" threshold simply to argue that the Crown has failed to prove each element of the offence: *R v Gunning*, 2005 SCC 27 at para 30.
159 *R v Ejiofor* (2002), 5 CR (6th) 197 at paras 15–17 (Ont CA); *R v Smith*, 2007 NSCA 19 at paras 124–28, aff'd without reference to this point 2009 SCC 5.

Finally, the Supreme Court of Canada has held that defence counsel cannot attack the credibility of a complainant through a cross-examination that relies on myths and stereotypes regarding victims of sexual assault.[160] To put it another way, counsel cannot subvert rules of evidence that prohibit certain lines of cross-examination, such as questioning that attempts to show a complainant's prior sexual activity makes it more likely she consented to the charged sexual activity, or is otherwise less worthy of belief.[161]

Example: Counsel has received a reliable confession from his client in a murder case. The Crown disclosure reveals a modicum of information regarding another suspect, X, who was briefly investigated by police shortly after the murder. But this information, if elicited from the investigating officers, is insufficient to give an air of reality to the possibility X committed the crime. The rules of evidence thus preclude counsel from cross-examining the officers to bring out the evidence,[162] altogether apart from the fact counsel knows his client is guilty.

In sum, the decision in *Lyttle*, viewed together with various rules of evidence, may make it very difficult for counsel who has received an admission of guilt from the client to put forward a viable argument that the Crown has failed to meet the burden of establishing guilt on the criminal standard. With this point firmly in mind, we are ready to examine the arguments for and against cross-examining to impeach a witness known by counsel to be truthful. By way of prelude, however, a caveat is necessary. The vast preponderance of literature in this area — and there is a lot of it — comes from academics and lawyers in the United States. In discussing whether it is ethical to impeach the truthful witness, American commentators on both sides of the debate typically assume an aggressive, all-out attack in which cross-examining counsel expressly puts to the witness that she is lying or mistaken and directly asserts that core elements of the witness's version of events are

---

160 *R v Mills* (1999), 139 CCC (3d) 321 at para 90 (SCC) [*Mills*]. See also *R v Quesnelle*, 2014 SCC 46 at para 17.

161 Such questioning would contravene s 276 of the *Criminal Code*, above note 43. The issue of lawyers' breaching evidentiary rules in the sexual assault context is addressed in Elaine Craig, "The Ethical Obligations of Defence Counsel in Cases of Sexual Assault" (2014) 51:2 Osgoode Hall LJ 426.

162 *Grandinetti*, above note 158 at paras 47–48; *R v Pickton*, 2007 BCSC 799 at paras 68–85; *R v Scotland*, [2007] OJ No 5302 at paras 19–26 (SCJ); *R v Tehrankari*, [2008] OJ No 5651 at paras 68–85 (SCJ), aff'd 2012 ONCA 718 at paras 34–48, leave to appeal to SCC refused, [2012] SCCA No 547; *R v Masterson*, [2009] OJ No 2867 at para 19 (SCJ). A similar restriction applies in many American states: see Joy & McMunigal, above note 146 at 180–82.

false.[163] Yet as we have just seen, the decision in *Lyttle* and commentaries in many Canadian ethical codes expressly prohibit suggesting a known falsehood to a witness in cross-examination. The particularly aggressive version of cross-examination debated in the United States is thus off-limits in Canada.[164]

b) Arguments against Impeaching the Witness Known to Be Truthful

There are several arguments presented against permitting a lawyer to attack the reliability of the truthful witness.[165] First, such action is akin to calling false evidence, for the cross-examination may serve to convince the judge and jury that certain facts known to be false by counsel are true. Indeed, it has been noted that defence counsel who uses cross-examination to attack the truthful witness's reliability has arguably gone further than counsel who knowingly calls a false alibi. The latter counsel merely brings out the alibi with non-leading

---

163 See, for example, Freedman & Smith, above note 94 at 209; Asimow & Weisberg, above note 14 at 244–45; Hodes, above note 49 at 70; Richard Zitrin & Carol Langford, *The Moral Compass of the American Lawyer: Truth, Justice, Power and Greed* (New York: Ballantine, 1999) at 42–47; Eleanor Myers & Edward Ohlbaum, "Discrediting the Truthful Witness: Demonstrating the Reality of Adversary Advocacy" (2000) 69 Fordham L Rev 1055 at 1065–72, all of which take the position that the lawyer is permitted, or even required, to cross-examine the witness as if the lawyer does not know the client is guilty or the witness is truthful. David Luban, "Partisanship, Betrayal and Autonomy in the Lawyer-Client Relationship: A Reply to Stephen Ellmann" (1990) 90 Colum L Rev 1004 at 1027–28 [Luban, "Partisanship"], assumes the same type of cross-examination in arguing against impeaching a sexual assault complainant the lawyer knows to be truthful.

164 Interestingly, a common source of support for proponents of aggressive cross-examination is ABA Defense Standard 4-7.6(b), which allows counsel to cross-examine to undermine the truthful witness. Yet standard 4-7.6(d), which is rarely mentioned, prohibits counsel "from asking a question which implies the existence of a factual predicate for which a good faith basis is lacking." This latter standard arguably mirrors the prohibition in *Lyttle*, above note 44 at para 68.

165 Commentators who advance some or all of these arguments include Harry I Subin, "The Criminal Lawyer's 'Different Mission': Reflections on the 'Right' to Present a False Case" (1987) 1 Geo J Leg Ethics 125; Harry I Subin, "Is This Lie Necessary? Further Reflections on the Right to Present a False Defense" (1988) 1 Geo J Legal Ethics 689; Lawry, above note 18; William H Simon, *The Practice of Justice: A Theory of Lawyers' Ethics* (Cambridge, MA: Harvard University Press, 1998) ch 7 [Simon, *Practice*]; William H Simon, "The Ethics of Criminal Defense" (1993) 91 Mich L Rev 1703 [Simon, "Ethics"]; Deborah L Rhode, *In the Interests of Justice — Reforming the Legal Profession* (Oxford: Oxford University Press, 2000) at 103; Tanovich, above note 152 at 295–96.

questions, while the usual cross-examination technique is more aggressive and most likely involves counsel expressly suggesting falsehoods to a witness.[166] Second, the great importance our justice system ascribes to cross-examination as an engine for uncovering the truth does not justify permitting counsel to mislead the judicial process. Third, cross-examining the truthful witness to suggest his evidence is unreliable may cause the witness harm, an unfair result given that he has testified truthfully. This harm seems especially egregious where the attack focuses on the witness's sincerity, for defence counsel's aim is to suggest the witness is a liar. Fourth, given that counsel will only rarely *know* that a witness is truthful, the actual impact of precluding cross-examination to impeach will be limited. Finally, the need to protect individual autonomy and dignity against the power of the state does not justify impeaching the truthful witness where to the lawyer's knowledge the accused is indisputably guilty. Truth as a systemic goal should not be completely ignored in pursuit of rights-based concerns, especially where there is absolutely no risk an innocent person will be convicted.[167]

c) Arguments for Impeaching the Witness Known to Be Truthful

The arguments for the other side, that is to say in support of permitting defence counsel to attack the reliability of the truthful witness, appear to be dominant in the United States and Canada, at least among lawyers and commentators.[168] They should be familiar to the reader by

---

166 For the reasons explained in the paragraph associated with notes 163–64, above in this chapter, this argument would not apply in Canada because the cross-examination described is prohibited.

167 Indeed, it has been argued that defending the accused who admits guilt to counsel harms the system by wasting resources, including defence counsel's, which could be better devoted to protecting accused persons who may be innocent: Randolph Braccialarghe, "Why Were Perry Mason's Clients Always Innocent? The Criminal Lawyer's Moral Dilemma — The Criminal Defendant Who Tells His Lawyer He Is Guilty" (2004) 39 Val U L Rev 65 at 77–80.

168 See, for example, Wolfram, above note 74 at 650–51; Kenneth Pye, "The Role of Counsel in the Suppression of Truth" [1978] Duke LJ 921 at 945; John B Mitchell, "Reasonable Doubts Are Where You Find Them: A Response to Professor Subin's Position on the Criminal Lawyer's 'Different Mission'" (1987) 1 Geo J Legal Ethics 339; Myers & Ohlbaum, above note 163; David N Yellen, "'Thinking Like a Lawyer' or Acting Like a Judge?: A Response to Professor Simon" (1998) 27 Hofstra L Rev 13; Lee E Teitelbaum, "Ethics, Morality, and Truth-Telling" [2006] Utah L Rev 157 at 171–72; Peter J Henning, "Lawyers, Truth, and Honesty in Representing Clients" (2006) 20 Notre Dame JL Ethics & Pub Pol'y 209 at 271–73; Aviva Orenstein, "Special Issues Raised by Rape Trials" (2007) 76 Fordham L Rev 1585 at 1603–4; Hall, above note 115, at § 19.9; Hutchin-

this point.[169] The central tenet in favour of allowing such conduct is the nature of the defence advocate's role in our criminal justice system. A primary function of the system, and the lawyer's role in it, is to ensure the Crown proves its case on a standard of proof beyond a reasonable doubt. It is therefore legitimate for counsel to test the strength of the prosecution case, including by cross-examination that questions the reliability of the truthful witness. In the United States, the influential ABA Defense Standards thus state that the defence lawyer's knowledge a witness is telling the truth does not preclude cross-examination.[170]

Perhaps the most quoted expression of this position in the American literature comes from White J of the Supreme Court of the United States, who in the 1967 decision of *United States v Wade* stated:

> Absent a voluntary plea of guilty, we . . . insist that [defense counsel] defend his client whether he is innocent or guilty. The State has the obligation to present the evidence. Defense counsel need present nothing, even if he knows what the truth is. He need not furnish any witnesses to the police, or reveal any confidences of his client, or furnish other information to help the prosecution's case. If he can confuse a witness, even a truthful one, or make him appear at a disadvantage, unsure or indecisive, that will be his normal course. Our interest in not convicting the innocent permits counsel to put the State to its proof, to put the State's case in the worst possible light, regardless of what he thinks or knows to be the truth. Undoubtedly, there are some limits which defense counsel must observe but more often than not, defense counsel will cross-examine a prosecution witness, and impeach him if he can, even if he thinks the witness is telling the truth, just as he will attempt to destroy a witness whom he thinks is lying. In this respect, as part of our modified adversary system and as part of the duty imposed on the most honorable defense counsel, we countenance or require conduct which in many instances has little, if any, relation to the search for truth.[171]

---

son, above note 124 at 168; Gold, above note 73 at 637–39; Gavin Mackenzie, *Lawyers & Ethics: Professional Responsibility and Discipline* (Scarborough, ON: Carswell, 1993) (loose-leaf March 2013 supplement) at § 7.4; Woolley, above note 89 at 211–13; Layton, above note 31 at 389–400.

169 They largely mirror the arguments set out in Section D, above in this chapter.
170 See ABA Defense Standard 4-7.6(b). The first edition of the ABA Defense Standards, released in 1971, took the opposite view: "[A lawyer] should not misuse the power of cross-examination or impeachment by employing it to discredit or undermine a witness if he knows the witness is testifying truthfully."
171 388 US 218 at 257–58 (1967).

Another argument in favour of giving defence counsel significant latitude in cross-examining the truthful witness comes from Professors Monroe Freedman and Abbe Smith, who stress the harm that a limited cross-examination would cause to the client-lawyer relationship.[172] If the candid client informs the lawyer of her guilt, but the lawyer responds by restricting the conduct of the defence to the client's detriment, the duty of confidentiality has been compromised, and the promotion of unrestricted communication between lawyer and client dealt a serious blow. The lawyer's failure to cross-examine the truthful witness or the insistence on placing substantial restrictions on the cross-examination can be seen to further violate confidentiality by signalling to judge and jury that the lawyer believes the witness to be reliable. In the longer term, as clients learn to keep certain information secret from lawyers to avoid a restricted defence, lawyers will unwittingly engage in the vigorous and attacking cross-examination of truthful witnesses. A rule that forbids counsel from knowingly undertaking such a cross-examination thus arguably carries the seeds for its own undermining.

d) The Approaches Suggested by Professors Luban and Simon

Professors David Luban and William Simon are American academics who have advanced particularly thoughtful and nuanced views on the problem of cross-examining the truthful witness. Although not widely endorsed in the criminal defence bar, their views are worth considering.

Professor Luban appears to accept, albeit reluctantly, that defence counsel can cross-examine to attack the reliability of the truthful witness in the ordinary course, as part of counsel's necessary function of preventing abuse of state power.[173] But Luban would prohibit such an attack if the result would be to further an institution that "poses chronic and persistent threats to individual well-being, threats that are an inherent part of the institutional culture and not just an accident of human wickedness."[174] The main instance where Luban contends this restriction on impeaching the truthful witness should apply is in the

---

172 Freedman & Smith, above note 94 at 211–12.
173 Luban, "Partisanship," above note 163 at 1031. This reluctance is even more evident in Luban's subsequent article, "Are Criminal Defenders Different?" (1993) 91 Mich L Rev 1729 at 1762 [Luban, "Criminal Defenders"], where he expresses significant ambivalence about the impeachment of truthful witnesses, especially when done in a way "calculated to damage or humiliate them."
174 Luban, "Partisanship," above note 163 at 1029, n 90, developing the argument made earlier in David Luban, *Lawyers and Justice: An Ethical Study* (Princeton, NJ: Princeton University Press, 1988) at 150–52.

case of the sexual assault victim. Luban argues that in cross-examining such a victim, the lawyer's duty to defend the accused against the powerful state must succumb to a countervailing duty, namely, to avoid furthering the patriarchal "network of cultural expectations and practices that engenders and encourages male sexual violence."[175] Defence counsel must not attack the reliability of the sexual assault victim he knows is truthful, because to do so would deter women from reporting rapes and perpetuate the myth that women frequently invite sexual advances or lie about them occurring.

Luban's view has been criticized on the basis that the lawyer is effectively restricting the client's defence based on his own moral or political views.[176] After all, many lawyers will hold very different views as to what institutions pose chronic and persistent threats to individual well-being. This concern has led some critics to argue that defence counsel must reject Luban's approach and attack the reliability of a witness known to be truthful whenever doing so will advance the client's interests.[177] Others would reject Luban's approach but nonetheless allow lawyers to refuse to accept sexual assault cases out of discomfort or concern about the potential for adverse impact flowing from zealous advocacy.[178]

Yet another approach is offered by Professor Simon.[179] Simon rejects Luban's proposal, for the reasons just mentioned.[180] But he would only allow counsel to attack the reliability of a witness known to be truthful where to do so would "subvert punishment that, though required

---

175 Luban, "Partisanship," above note 163 at 1028–29. The special considerations applicable in the sexual-assault context are also discussed in Tanovich, above note 89.

176 Simon, "Ethics," above note 165 at 1710; Abbe Smith, "Rosie O'Neill Goes to Law School: The Clinical Education of a Sensitive New Age Public Defender" (1993) 28 Harv CR-CLL Rev 1 at 42–45; Stephen Ellmann, "Lawyering for Justice in a Flawed Democracy" (1990) 90 Colum L Rev 116 at 155–56; Layton, above note 31 at 395–96.

177 See, for example, Smith, above note 176 at 42–45, and Orenstein, above note 168 at 1603–4, both addressing the issue of cross-examination to impeach the truthful sexual assault complainant.

178 See Freedman & Smith, above note 94 at 210–11, referring to Professor Freedman's decision to stop accepting rape cases.

179 Simon's approach to this issue is endorsed by Tanovich, above note 152 at 302–6, whose analysis is in turn adopted by Jeremy Tatum, "Navigating the Fine Line of Criminal Advocacy: Using Truthful Evidence to Discredit Truthful Testimony," online: (2012) 2:2 UWO J Leg Stud 2 http://ir.lib.uwo.ca/uwojls/vol2/iss2/2.

180 Simon, *Practice*, above note 165 at 176–77. Simon's views are also canvassed in his earlier article, "Ethics," above note 165.

by law, is unjustly harsh and discriminatory in terms of more general norms of legal culture."[181] On this view, the impeachment of a truthful witness is sometimes permitted, not because it jibes with a lawyer's personal morality or politics, but because the lawyer has drawn on fundamental precepts of justice, particularly in the realms of sentencing and anti-discrimination, to conclude that impeachment is required to nullify the effect of an unjust law.[182] Simon would not countenance attacking the reliability of the sexual assault victim known by counsel to be truthful, at least not in the ordinary course, because in most cases there is nothing unjust about the punishment of sexual offenders.

Simon recognizes that under his approach different lawyers may come to different decisions as to whether impeachment is permissible in a particular case but argues that the justice system by no means requires universality of result in determining whether a particular action is proper or improper.[183] Police officers, Crown counsel, and judges and juries all have varying degrees of discretion in carrying out their tasks.[184] Why, asks Simon, should defence counsel be any different? What is important, he says, is that on the whole, lawyers' decisions regarding whether to impeach make a positive contribution in terms of the legal values we believe are relevant.[185] Certainly, it cannot be said that the ethical rules as they now stand always provide a clear answer as to whether or how counsel can attack the reliability of a witness known to be truthful. Simon's approach is thus arguably no worse than the present system in terms of permitting diversity within the defence bar and has the benefit of anchoring each lawyer's decision whether to impeach in well-accepted principles of substantive justice.[186]

---

181 Simon, *Practice*, above note 165 at 189–90.
182 Luban's response is that under his approach the lawyer's personal morality is guided extensively by basic principles grounding the justice system and that personal morality is surely not irrelevant to the process under Simon's analysis: see David Luban, "Reason and Passion in Legal Ethics" (1999) 51 Stan L Rev 873.
183 Simon, *Practice*, above note 165 at 191.
184 Police officers have discretion in deciding whether to proceed with an investigation: Chapter 12, Section E(1). Crown counsel exercise significant discretion regarding decisions such as whether to stay a charge: Chapter 12, Section D(1). Somewhat similarly, a judge's or jury's decision to convict is not subject to review provided it is reasonable on the facts (*R v RP*, 2012 SCC 22 at para 9), and an unreasonable acquittal can never be appealed by the Crown (*R v Powell*, 2010 ONCA 105 at para 26). Indeed, a jury has the power as a matter of conscience to refuse to follow the law in acquitting the accused (*R v Krieger*, 2006 SCC 47 at paras 27–28).
185 Simon, *Practice*, above note 165 at 191.
186 *Ibid* at 192.

e) Recommended Guidelines for Cross-examining to Impeach the Truthful Witness

Luban rightly describes the question whether counsel should be permitted to cross-examine to impeach a witness he knows to be truthful as "perhaps the most difficult of all dilemmas of advocacy."[187] There will probably always be disagreement among thoughtful counsel and commentators as to where the line should be drawn. Yet in Canada, the ethical codes expressly permit counsel who knows his client is guilty to "test the evidence given by each individual witness for the prosecution" and then to argue the evidence as a whole is insufficient to justify a conviction. As Gavin MacKenzie argues, "clearer language would be required to alter the traditional view that it is entirely proper for criminal counsel to discredit or impeach the evidence of witnesses whom they know are testifying truthfully."[188] *Lyttle* limits but does not extinguish counsel's ability to impeach a truthful witness through cross-examination. Accordingly, we believe criminal defence lawyers in Canada should be permitted to impeach the truthful witness subject to some important restrictions and guidelines.

First, *Lyttle* precludes counsel from seeking to impeach the truthful witness by putting to her an assertion counsel knows to be false.[189] Depending on the circumstances, this restriction may constitute a very significant limit on counsel's ability to impeach the witness's reliability. Together with other rules of evidence,[190] the holding in *Lyttle* may make it difficult if not impossible to effectively impeach a witness known by counsel to be truthful.

Second, counsel with irresistible knowledge of guilt must always consider whether the best course of action is for the client to plead guilty. This is especially so where the Crown case is strong and where the restrictions imposed by *Lyttle* and other evidentiary rules make it highly unlikely that the reliability of a witness or witnesses can be successfully impeached so as to raise a reasonable doubt. Though the decision whether to plead guilty belongs solely to the accused, counsel is justified in forcefully advising a client to do so in such circumstances.[191]

---

187 Luban, "Criminal Defenders," above note 173 at 1762. Professor Smith, who rejects Luban's view that counsel should never cross-examine to impeach a truthful sexual assault victim, nonetheless says that coming to the right answer on this difficult and charged scenario is not merely "a close call," as Luban contends, but is "a painfully close call" (Smith, above note 176 at 43).

188 MacKenzie, above note 168 at § 7.4.

189 See Section K(1)(a), above in this chapter.

190 See the discussion in the text associated with notes 155–62, above in this chapter.

191 See Chapter 9, Section L(3).

Third, a lawyer should refuse to impeach the truthful witness where there is absolutely no possibility of success and where the exercise can only inure to the client's detriment. If the client nonetheless insists on impeachment, counsel should withdraw based on a breakdown in the client-lawyer relationship,[192] seeking leave of the court if necessary.[193] It is true that, by withdrawing, counsel is refusing to assist in advancing the client's constitutional right to test the Crown case. Yet a lawyer should be permitted to decline to conduct a case in a manner that runs contrary to the client's best interests, especially if doing so will create a real risk of causing harm to the witness.[194]

Fourth, counsel never acts unethically in impeaching the reliability of a truthful witness within the constraints set out in *Lyttle*, that is, by putting questions to the witness in an attempt to elicit evidence counsel knows or suspects might be true, for the purpose of arguing that the Crown has failed to prove its case on the criminal standard.[195] In fact, we believe there is a *duty* to do so where the aim is to raise a reasonable doubt as to whether the witness is mistaken (unreliable), as opposed to whether he is lying (insincere). Imposing this duty is justified given counsel's role as zealous advocate in a rights-based criminal justice system combined with the reality that impeachment focusing only on reliability, and not sincerity, will almost always cause less harm to the witness and any other societal interests that may be implicated by the case.

Exemplary in this regard is the decision of the British Columbia Court of Appeal in *R v Li*,[196] a robbery case in which the Crown relied on the eyewitness evidence of two jewellery store clerks. Both clerks identified the accused as their assailant from a photo lineup within hours of the offence. Defence counsel received a confession from his client before trial. The court recognized that the confession prevented counsel from setting up an affirmative defence to the charges but held that counsel nonetheless had a duty to test the proof of the case in every proper way, including by cross-examining the clerks to show they were not entirely sure in their identifications and to bring out the aspects of their descriptions that were inconsistent with the accused's characteristics.[197]

---

192 See Chapter 11, Section G.
193 See Chapter 11, Section L(4)(a).
194 Layton, above note 31 at 398.
195 See the text in the paragraph associated with notes 153–54, above in this chapter.
196 Above note 125.
197 *Ibid* at paras 66–68.

f) Cross-examining to Impeach Character

What if the truthful witness can be impeached by casting aspersions on her character? Perhaps the witness, though truthful, has a motive to fabricate, has given substantially inconsistent statements to the police, and has criminal antecedents for offences of dishonesty. These points can be brought out in cross-examination and then used in counsel's closing to suggest that a reasonable doubt exists as to whether the witness is being truthful. The potential for harm to the witness's reputation, and to broader societal interests as well, is greater where impeachment is directed at sincerity in this manner, as opposed to factors bearing on whether the witness is mistaken. For this reason, some commentators, though generally comfortable with defence counsel cross-examining to impeach a truthful witness, draw the line at an attack directed at character.[198] Others, while perhaps less troubled by the "attack on character" scenario, nonetheless find the issue particularly difficult and offer no firm opinion as to whether such conduct is permissible.[199] And some would prohibit an attack on sincerity in certain specific circumstances. Thus, Professor Luban is against impeaching the sincerity of a truthful sexual assault complainant because of special concerns about personal and systemic harm that can flow from an aggressive cross-examination, a position that has been developed in Canada by Professor David Tanovich.[200]

In our view, there is no need to adopt a bright-line rule on the issue of whether a truthful witness can be cross-examined to attack her sincerity. Rather, defence counsel should be afforded a broad discretion in deciding whether to do so. This is the position adopted by the Third Restatement,[201] and it is supported by several arguments.

---

198 Macmillan, above note 1 at 325; Sedgwick, above note 100 at 319; Meredith Blake & Andrew Ashworth, "Some Ethical Issues in Prosecuting and Defending Criminal Cases" [1998] Crim L Rev 16 at 20 and 30 [Blake & Ashworth, "Some Ethical Issues"]; Blake & Ashworth, "Ethics," above note 94 at 173.

199 G Arthur Martin, "Panel Discussion: Problems in Advocacy and Ethics," above note 100 at 320; Teitelbaum, above note 168 at 171–72.

200 Tanovich, above note 152 at 295–96. While there is much overlap between the approaches taken by Professors Tanovich and Luban, Professor Tanovich's theoretical framework ultimately draws much more on the ideas of Professor Simon.

201 Third Restatement § 106, comment "c," states that a lawyer is "never required" to cross-examine a truthful witness to impeach credibility, for instance by attacking the witness's character or capacity for truth-telling. Also favouring a discretion are Layton, above note 31 at 298–99, and Asimow & Weisberg, above note 14 at 234–38 and 246–47. *Contra* Tanovich, above note 89 and above note 152, arguing that a lawyer can *never* ethically cross-examine a truthful witness to suggest she is lying, at least in the context of sexual assaults; and Freedman & Smith, above note 94 at 212–13, and Woolley, above note 89 at 212–13, contending

First, there is nothing in the wording of the ethical codes or the judgment in *Lyttle* to suggest that counsel should be denied the proposed discretion. Indeed, the language in the code commentary dealing with admissions received from the client is uniformly permissive.[202]

Second, the Canadian criminal justice system recognizes that the right to full answer and defence does not always trump other legal interests, such as the privacy and security of witnesses,[203] equality rights,[204] and freedom of religion.[205] And while the accused's right to a fair trial must always be protected,[206] cross-examination will be curtailed where its probative value is substantially outweighed by any attendant prejudicial impact, including harm to the countervailing legal interests just mentioned.[207] Indeed, these same legal interests are espoused in anti-discrimination provisions found in most ethical codes.[208] Defence counsel should thus be permitted to take these interests into account in deciding whether to cross-examine a truthful witness to impeach sincerity.[209]

Third, for the reasons provided by Professor Simon, there is nothing inherently problematic about allowing different lawyers to reach different conclusions in deciding how to handle this ethical dilemma based on their application of prevailing legal norms.[210]

Finally, recognizing a discretion for defence lawyers in this area is *not* tantamount to counsel adopting the guise of judge. It is merely to

that a lawyer must *always* conduct such a cross-examination if it will inure to the client's benefit.

202 See the commentaries cited at note 8, above in this chapter, which for instance state that counsel in receipt of a confession from the client is nonetheless "entitled" to test each witness's evidence and to argue that the Crown case as a whole is insufficient to establish guilt.

203 *Mills*, above note 160 at paras 61 and 72–94.

204 *Ibid*. For an extensive discussion of equality and non-discrimination principles in the context of cross-examining a sexual-assault complainant, see Tanovich, above note 89.

205 *NS*, above note 43 at paras 2 and 31–32.

206 *Osolin*, above note 44 at 520–21 [paras 164 and 166]; *NS*, above note 43 at paras 24 and 38.

207 *Osolin*, above note 44 at 518–23 [paras 161–70]; *R v Shearing*, 2002 SCC 5 at paras 76 and 107–9 [*Shearing*]; *Pires*, above note 44 at para 29; *St-Onge Lamoureux*, above note 41 at para 128. *Osolin* and *Shearing* make this point in the context of sexual assault charges and reference the importance of taking equality interests into account in determining whether the probative value of the proposed cross-examination is substantially outweighed by its adverse impact.

208 See Chapter 2, Section D.

209 Layton, above note 31 at 398–99.

210 See the text associated with notes 183–86, above in this chapter.

say that in determining how best to fulfill the role of partisan advocate in the criminal justice system, defence lawyers can legitimately take into account the impact cross-examining to impeach might have on other juridical interests that are engaged on the facts, including any harm that may be occasioned to the witness.

In deciding how to exercise the discretion whether to cross-examine to impeach the sincerity of a witness known to be truthful, counsel should take into account a variety of factors including

- the criminal defence lawyer's proper role as a zealous advocate charged with protecting the client's constitutional guarantees, including the right to test the Crown case and the right not to be convicted unless the prosecution can establish guilt beyond a reasonable doubt;
- the degree to which impeachment can be carried out without contravening evidentiary rules (*Lyttle*'s "good faith" requirement, the "air of reality" test, limitations on cross-examining a sexual assault complainant, and so on);
- the extent to which impeaching the witness's credibility as permitted by the evidentiary rules will advance a viable defence;
- any adverse impact on the defence that might flow from attempting to impeach the witness;
- any harm to the witness that might reasonably be expected to arise from the contemplated cross-examination;
- the possible application of other legal principles recognized by the criminal justice system and ethics codes, such as gender and racial equality or freedom of religion; and
- whether counsel views the contemplated cross-examination with such repugnance that he would be materially hampered in carrying it out in an effective manner.[211]

As explained in Section I, above, counsel must provide the client with timely and full disclosure of any restrictions that irresistible knowledge of guilt may impose on the representation. Where a restriction is not mandated by the legal or ethical rules, but rather flows from the exercise of counsel's discretion — for instance, not to impeach a truthful witness's sincerity — the client must be told that other lawyers may be willing to conduct the cross-examination in question. Armed with this knowledge, the client can either accept the restrictions or

---

211 If repugnance precludes counsel from conducting a competent defence on behalf of the client, he must withdraw: see Chapter 2, Section I(1), and Chapter 11, Section F.

seek to retain a new lawyer to conduct the desired defence.[212] Where the lawyer foresees from the start that the client will insist on cross-examining a truthful witness in a particular manner, and the lawyer is not prepared to do so for ethical reasons, the retainer should be refused outright.[213]

2) Cross-examining the Perjurious or Mistaken Witness

Perjury must be exposed and rejected whenever possible, even perjury directed at convicting the obviously guilty client.[214] The same applies where counsel is confronted with testimony that while not perjurious, is nonetheless inaccurate. Counsel is therefore completely justified in using cross-examination to challenge testimony that is known to be perjurious, mistaken, or exaggerated, this even though the client has confessed his guilt.[215] Counsel should also be able to attack a witness where there is uncertainty as to whether the witness is telling the truth, once again regardless of the fact that counsel has received a confession from the accused. On this scenario, the known information — that the client is guilty — is not inconsistent with the possibility that the witness is lying or mistaken.

Example: The accused is charged with murder and in confidence confesses his guilt to counsel. Just before trial, the Crown discloses a witness who claims to have received a jailhouse confession from the accused. The accused vehemently denies having admitted guilt to the witness. Counsel is perfectly justified in vigorously attacking the credibility of the witness and alleging he is a liar, all the while knowing that the client is guilty.

---

212 In doing so, the client may decide not to disclose his guilt to the new lawyer so as to escape entirely any limitations on the conduct of the defence, including those imposed by *Lyttle*.

213 See Third Restatement § 106, comment "c," read in conjunction with § 32, comment "j."

214 Even commentators who strongly insist that counsel can never impeach a truthful witness are willing to accept that false portions of the testimony are properly subject to challenge: see, for example, Subin, above note 165 at 150.

215 This scenario arose with respect to mistaken testimony in *Li*, above note 125, as described in the text associated with notes 196–7, above in this chapter.

3) Presenting Truthful Evidence as Part of the Defence, Knowing the Trier of Fact May Use the Evidence to Arrive at a False Conclusion

We have seen that the rules of professional responsibility preclude counsel who has received a confession from setting up "an affirmative case" inconsistent with the client's admission.[216] In this regard, the rules specify that counsel cannot call any evidence she knows to be false, such as an alibi intended to show the accused did not commit the offence.[217] But what about calling witnesses who testify to facts counsel believes to be true, or at least does not believe to be false, in an effort to raise a reasonable doubt? Suppose counsel has received a confession, and the Crown calls an eyewitness who truthfully identifies the accused but inaccurately describes some material aspect of the accused's physical characteristics, say height or weight. Can defence counsel call a witness to challenge the inaccuracies, despite being saddled with the knowledge that the client is indeed guilty?

This very scenario was considered in *R v Li*, the eyewitness robbery case discussed in Section K(1)(e), above in this chapter.[218] To recap, defence counsel had received a confession of guilt from his client but nonetheless cross-examined a number of witnesses to bring out discrepancies between the accused's true attributes and the perpetrator as described by the eyewitness complainants. Counsel then called two defence witnesses, who gave evidence as to these attributes, namely, the accused's hairstyle at the time in question and his proficiency in English. The aim of this evidence was to undermine the witnesses' identification testimony, although this defence failed and the accused was convicted. On appeal, the court held that defence counsel had acted ethically in calling the two witnesses, because their testimony was not contrary to the facts counsel knew to be true and was used for the limited purpose of arguing that the eyewitness complainants were not sufficiently reliable to support a finding of guilt.[219]

The scholars Meredith Blake and Andrew Ashworth have argued that the conduct of the defence in *Li* may come close to setting up an affirmative defence that counsel knows to be false,[220] and may therefore

---

216 See the commentaries cited at note 8, above in this chapter.
217 *Ibid.*
218 *Li*, above note 125.
219 *Ibid* at paras 66–68.
220 Blake & Ashworth, "Some Ethical Issues," above note 198 at 20. For a more forceful condemnation of the type of defence advanced in *Li*, see Subin, above note 165 at 126.

extend beyond a mere testing of the prosecution case. Yet we believe there is nothing to recommend drawing a bright line between defence counsel cross-examining to elicit truthful evidence ("legitimate") and defence counsel calling witnesses to do the same thing as part of the defence case ("illegitimate"). Indeed, both methods may be used to bring out exactly the same type of truthful evidence in the same case, as no doubt occurred in Li itself.[221] Such evidence may also come out during examination-in-chief, without any active involvement by defence counsel. The ethical propriety of eliciting evidence in the cause of obtaining an acquittal should depend not on distinguishing between forensic techniques but rather on the potential truthfulness of the evidence and the purpose to which it is put.

This brings us to the more general point, which is that forbidding counsel from calling truthful defence evidence as a means of attacking the prosecution case where counsel knows of the client's guilt may lead to unpalatable results. Let us assume for the moment that a lawyer confronted with the fact pattern from Li decides not to call defence evidence that would successfully challenge the inaccurate part of the identification testimony. Despite cross-examination on the point, the eyewitnesses hold convincingly firm in their inaccuracies. The result might be that the trier of fact accepts the identification evidence and convicts the accused, based in part on evidence known by defence counsel to be false. In a system where the prosecution bears the onus of proving guilt beyond a reasonable doubt, this result is unacceptable. For the reasons already outlined regarding the related issue of cross-examining a truthful witness, counsel should be permitted to call *any* truthful evidence as part of the defence case for the purpose of arguing that the Crown has failed to meet its heavy burden of proof. What counsel cannot do is rely on truthful evidence to assert that the accused is innocent, which is something counsel knows to be false.[222]

a) Presenting an Alternative Suspect Defence

The same approach should apply where counsel is able to elicit truthful evidence, whether through cross-examination or as part of the defence case, that points to another identifiable individual as being a possible perpetrator. As noted earlier, in Canada there is an evidentiary hurdle — the "air of reality" threshold — that must be crossed before coun-

---

221 Li, above note 125 at para 68, noting that the witnesses were cross-examined to raise a reasonable doubt on the issue of identification.
222 See R v Brager, [1965] 4 CCC 251 at 253 [para 9] (BCCA): counsel must not knowingly "invite the jury to draw a false inference from the evidence."

sel can run an alternative suspect defence.[223] Assuming this hurdle is met, the defence will cause harm to the alternative suspect, not only by raising the possibility that he is the perpetrator, but in many cases because counsel will also elicit bad character evidence such as the suspect's disposition for violence. Counsel who knows of the client's guilt should therefore have a discretion to refuse to pursue an alternative suspect defence, after weighing the potential for harm to the alternative suspect against the importance of asserting the accused's right to test the Crown case at trial.[224]

We expect that most defence lawyers would usually choose to exercise their discretion to pursue a viable alternative suspect defence. Regardless, where the defence is mounted, counsel cannot suggest that the alternative suspect is in fact the perpetrator,[225] or that the accused is innocent. Counsel's knowledge of the truth allows only the argument that the prosecution has not met its onus of disproving the possibility that the alternative suspect committed the crime.

Sometimes an alternative suspect defence is run without reference to an *identifiable* person, in which case counsel merely points to the possibility that an unknown perpetrator committed the crime. Given the absence of any harm to third parties in mounting this "soft" alternative suspect defence,[226] counsel should not be afforded a discretion to refuse to do so. Provided it is in the best interests of the client, the lawyer should cross-examine prosecution witnesses to elicit any alternative suspect evidence that is known or suspected to be truthful and call any other such evidence as part of the defence case, for the purpose of arguing that the Crown has failed to prove guilt on the criminal standard.

---

223 See note 162, above in this chapter, and the associated text.

224 The arguments in favour of affording counsel a discretion and the sorts of factors counsel may wish to consider in its exercise are set out in Section K(1)(e), above in this chapter. For further discussion of advancing an alternative suspect defence for a client who is known to be guilty, see Joy & McMunigal, above note 146, ch 21; Ellen Y Suni, "Who Stole the Cookie from the Cookie Jar?: The Law and Ethics of Shifting Blame in Criminal Cases" (2000) 68 Fordham L Rev 1643.

225 The ethical rules cited at note 8, above in this chapter, state that on receiving an admission of guilt, counsel "may properly take objection to the . . . sufficiency of the evidence, *but must not suggest that some other person committed the offence*" [emphasis added].

226 See Joy & McMunigal, above note 146 at 176: a "hard" alternative suspect defence focuses on an identifiable individual, while a "soft" version raises the possibility of an unknown culprit.

b) Calling Truthful Alibi Witnesses in response to Inaccurate Prosecution Evidence

An often-discussed hypothetical that engages many of the issues we have been discussing asks whether defence counsel can call truthful alibi witnesses in response to erroneous time-of-the-offence evidence unwittingly led by the prosecution. Assume, for example, that the accused is charged with robbery. The victim identifies the accused as the robber but mistakenly tells police that the robbery occurred at 10:30pm, when it actually took place at 10:00pm. There is no way for either the victim or the police to know the time is wrong. Meanwhile, the accused, seeing the wrong time in the police report, admits to his lawyer that he committed the robbery but at 10:00pm, not 10:30pm. The accused went directly from the robbery to a bar he frequents. Several bar patrons and employees can provide him with a firm alibi for any time after 10:15pm, thus covering the period during which the victim believes the robbery took place. When the victim testifies to the wrong time at trial, what should the lawyer do about presenting the alibi?[227]

We have already established that counsel can properly call truthful evidence for the limited purpose of arguing that the Crown has failed to establish guilt on the criminal standard. However, the commentary in most ethical codes that addresses the defence of a client who has confessed guilt expressly prohibits counsel from raising an affirmative defence, such as "by calling evidence in support of an alibi."[228] Does this commentary preclude defence counsel from calling the alibi evidence in the example given above?

No, for the simple reason that the commentary does not prohibit counsel from calling evidence that is true.[229] Its precise wording only proscribes counsel who has received admissions from the client from "set[ting] up an affirmative case *inconsistent with such admissions*, for example, by calling evidence in support of an alibi intended to show that the accused could not have done or, in fact, has not done the act."[230] On the hypothetical described above, the alibi evidence is true, and is not inconsistent with the client's admissions. It is led to rebut evidence that is clearly false — that the accused committed the robbery at 10:30pm — and is relied on for the narrow, and true, proposition that

---

227 This example comes from a 1987 Michigan State Bar Committee ethics opinion, reported in (1987) 3 Laws Man on Prof Conduct (ABA/BNA) 44. The bar committee concluded that "it is perfectly proper to call to the witness stand those witnesses on behalf of the client who will present truthful testimony."

228 See the commentaries cited at note 8, above in this chapter.

229 *Contra* Henning, above note 168 at 275–76, including at n 235.

230 See the commentaries cited at note 8, above [emphasis added].

the accused did not commit a robbery at this particular time. There is nothing improper in defence counsel calling this evidence, provided counsel's closing submissions are carefully framed to assert only that the prosecution has not proven its case, because the accused was elsewhere at 10:30pm, and do not suggest that someone else must have committed the robbery and hence that the client is innocent.

4) Submissions That Rely upon Truthful Evidence to Suggest a False Conclusion

It has always been accepted that, to quote the words of Baron Parke in the *Courvoisier* case, counsel can "use all fair arguments arising from the evidence."[231] Is it "fair," however, to make submissions based on truthful evidence where the practical result may be to mislead the trier of fact? In the alibi problem discussed immediately above, for instance, we have maintained that the defence lawyer breaches no ethical rules by suggesting that the prosecution has not proven its case and by relying on truthful witnesses in support of the claim. Yet it has been argued, not unreasonably, that the trier of fact may view counsel's submission as an assertion that a factual possibility, known by counsel to be false, is actually true.[232] The risk of deception is arguably greatest where the submission is made to a jury, which is less likely than a judge to appreciate the precise meaning of the qualified, "case not proven" language used by defence counsel.

Take the hypothetical discussed by several American commentators involving an accused who is charged with receiving stolen property. Irrefutable evidence shows that he was observed loading stolen electronic equipment into the back seat of a car. The accused's mental state becomes crucial — did he know that the property was stolen? An argument in support of the defence is that the actions of the accused, in placing the property in the back seat of the car instead of using the trunk, are consistent with a belief that the property was not stolen. But suppose the accused tells counsel that he knew the property to be stolen and used the back seat only because the trunk was stuck shut. Can counsel nonetheless argue to the jury, based on the evidence presented by the Crown, that "the accused obviously had no idea that the equipment was stolen, otherwise he would have hidden it in the trunk"?

This hypothetical demonstrates that putting the prosecution to its proof can simultaneously work to deceive the trier of fact. Certainly,

231 See note 16, above in this chapter, and accompanying text.
232 Simon, "Ethics," above note 165 at 1718.

the language used by defence counsel in the above example seems calculated to suggest forcefully that the accused is factually innocent. But if counsel chooses not to raise the weakness in the Crown case, the mistaken inference may nonetheless be made by the trial judge in the charge or by some of the jurors during the deliberations. Once again, the best answer to this troubling dilemma is for counsel to put the possibility to the jury, despite knowing it to be false, but in doing so not to assert the possibility is in fact true.[233] This approach, though it permits a certain amount of zealousness, undoubtedly limits counsel's options in presenting the defence during submissions to the trier of fact. It may also be that counsel's careful balancing of the sometimes conflicting ethical dictates — allegiance to the client and honesty in dealing with the court — alerts the judge and prosecutor to the possibility the client has confessed. Nevertheless, this compromise provides the maximum protection that our adversarial criminal justice system can offer to one who despite his confession to counsel wishes to contest guilt.[234]

The Ontario Court of Appeal has given credence to this approach in *R v Young*.[235] There, the accused was charged in connection with controlled substances found in the apartment where he was staying. Evidence located during the police search allowed for the inference that a man named McPherson lived there too. Defence counsel knew that McPherson had been in jail for many months, so the drugs were not his, but believed the Crown to be unaware of this fact. Counsel's strategy was thus to defend the case on the basis that the Crown could not prove beyond a reasonable doubt that the accused, as opposed to McPherson, had possession of the drugs. Mounting such a defence would necessarily involve counsel's eliciting evidence from police witnesses as to any items from the apartment connected to McPherson and then relying on this evidence to make the onus argument. As it happened, the prosecutor learned of the true state of affairs before trial, and so defence counsel abandoned this plan. But in recounting the history of the case, the court expressly commented that there was nothing to suggest that counsel's initial strategy was inappropriate.[236]

---

233   The last sentence of the commentary cited at note 8, above in this chapter, implicitly endorses this approach, for it permits counsel who has received an admission of guilt from the client to "argue that the evidence taken as a whole is insufficient to amount to proof that the accused is guilty of the offence charged . . . ."

234   Our view of this problem is shared by Woolley, above note 89 at 306–7, and Luban, above note 33 at 72–73.

235   2007 ONCA 714.

236   *Ibid* at paras 8–9.

CHOOSING AND REFUSING CLIENTS

A. INTRODUCTION

There are several distinct aspects to the question of lawyers' choosing and refusing clients. First, there are those facets of client selection that should normally raise no substantial ethical dilemmas. For example, it may be that refusing a prospective client is completely uncontroversial because the suggested retainer would manifestly involve a breach of the rules of professional conduct. Second, and more contentious and difficult, is the issue as to whether a lawyer enjoys a general discretion to reject a potential client. The classic presentation of the problem lies in the case of the unpopular or repugnant client. As we will see, Canadian rules of professional conduct do not preclude a lawyer from exercising some discretion in deciding whether to accept a case. However, it remains to determine exactly how this discretion should be exercised. Third, where a lawyer properly decides not to accept a retainer, certain duties are nevertheless owed to the individual whose matter has not been taken on. Prime among these are the duties to assist in finding counsel and to maintain the prospective client's confidentiality.

B. INSTANCES WHERE COUNSEL CANNOT ACT

On occasion, a lawyer must reject an available retainer, usually because the representation would effectively undermine the proper basis of a client-lawyer relationship or otherwise require the lawyer to engage in unethical conduct. Accordingly, a lawyer is required to refuse a case in the following circumstances:

1) *Conflict of interest:* A lawyer cannot act if the brief would involve labouring under an irresolvable conflict of interest.[1]
2) *Potential to be a witness:* Though this falls within the prohibition against conflict of interest, it is worth emphasizing that a lawyer should reject a retainer that raises a real spectre of him becoming a witness.[2]
3) *Lack of competence:* It is unacceptable for a lawyer to act in a case where she is unable to provide competent representation.[3]
4) *Continuing retainer with another lawyer:* A client may approach counsel asking for representation while already represented by another lawyer in the same matter. The new client cannot be accepted unless the pre-existing retainer has been terminated.[4]
5) *Illegal purpose:* The rules of professional conduct prohibit a lawyer from taking on any case that would require a breach of the law.[5]

1) Due Diligence to Ensure Retainer Does Not Involve Illegality

A lawyer must not knowingly assist a client, or anyone else for that matter, in dishonesty, crime, fraud, or illegality.[6] "Knowledge," in this context, means not only actual awareness of wrongdoing but wilful blindness and recklessness as well.[7] Furthermore, a lawyer must be alert not to become the unwitting dupe of an unscrupulous client and must if harbouring a suspicion as to whether the retainer involves any impropriety make reasonable inquiries to obtain information about the

---

1   See, generally, Chapter 6.
2   See Chapter 6, Section L.
3   Alta, Sask r 2.01(2) (commentary); Que s 3.01.01; BC, Man, Ont, NS, NL r 3.1-2, commentaries 5–6; NB ch 2, commentaries 3 and 6; CBA Code ch II, commentaries 3 and 6.
4   See Chapter 11, Section O(1).
5   Alta r 2.02(10); Sask r 2.02(7); BC, Man, Ont, NS, NL r 3.2-7; Que s 4.02.01(g); CBA Code ch III, commentary 7.
6   See rules cited, *ibid.* See also *Wood v Schaeffer*, 2013 SCC 71 at para 109, LeBel & Cromwell JJ, dissenting but not on this point [*Wood*].
7   Ont r 3.2-7, commentary 1.

client and the subject matter and objectives of the mandate so as to verify that nothing improper is involved.[8]

Example: X is charged under a false name. Counsel cannot reveal X's true identity to the court against X's will without impermissibly breaching the duty of confidentiality.[9] But knowingly representing X under a false name at any appearance will likely constitute the offence of attempting to obstruct justice.[10] It will also necessarily mislead the court. For this reason, most Canadian codes specifically prohibit counsel from misrepresenting a client's identity to the court,[11] but the basic prohibition against misleading the court would apply in any event.[12] Counsel must therefore refuse the retainer unless X agrees to reveal his true identity to the authorities. Helping X to find new counsel in the knowledge that he intends to persist in using the false identity is probably also improper.[13]

2) Impropriety of a Retainer to Defend Client regarding a Future Crime

A prospective client may ask a lawyer to act if he is arrested at some future point regarding a crime that has not yet occurred but rather is in the planning stages. The prospective client may offer to pay in advance to ensure the lawyer is available to conduct bail hearings if the individual or any associates are arrested. This proposed retainer gives the client some assurance that legal representation from a preferred lawyer will be available if the client is caught.

By agreeing to such an arrangement, a lawyer is breaching his duty to the administration of justice by assisting, encouraging, or at the very least acquiescing in the client's commission of a crime. Not only must

---

8   Alta r 2.02(10) (commentary); Sask r 2.02(7) (commentary); Ont r 3.2-7–3.2-7.2, commentaries 1–3.1; BC, Man, NS, NL r 3.2-7, commentaries 1–3; CBA Code ch III, commentary 7.

9   The answer may be different, however, in the few provinces having a confidentiality exception broad enough to cover disclosure where necessary to prevent any future crime: see the analogous discussion in Chapter 7, Section F(4)(f).

10   The danger of a lawyer's being charged for playing fast and loose with the court regarding a client's identity is demonstrated by *R v Guttman* (1992), 73 CCC (3d) 62 (Man CA), leave to appeal to SCC refused, [1992] SCCA No 372; *R v Doz* (1984), 12 CCC (3d) 200 (Alta CA), leave to appeal to SCC refused, [1984] SCCA No 84; *Law Society of Upper Canada v Brown*, [1997] LSDD No 93.

11   Alta r 4.01(2)(p); Sask r 4.01(2)(k); BC, Man, Ont, NS, NL r 5.1-2(k).

12   See Chapter 1, Section E.

13   See Section J, below in this chapter.

the lawyer refuse to accept the retainer,[14] but he should advise the potential client not to commit the planned crime.[15]

Example: X asks a lawyer to represent individuals who he says may be arrested from time to time for trafficking controlled substances. Either X will call when assistance is needed or the individuals will call the lawyer directly and mention X's name. Agreeing to this arrangement is improper because it encourages the commission of criminal acts, and perhaps even constitutes the criminal offence of knowingly contributing to the activities of a criminal organization.[16]

It is nonetheless acceptable to agree to act for a client who, in good faith and on reasonable grounds, wishes to challenge or test a law, provided that no injury to person or violence is done and that the test can most effectively be made with a technical breach.[17] It is also permissible to agree in advance with an organization engaged in legitimate activity to be available to act for employees who might be charged with a criminal offence.[18] Nor is there anything improper about agreeing to act in the future regarding a crime that has already occurred, such as where a client is under police investigation and seeks an assurance that the lawyer will be available to start work immediately if charges are laid.

Example: A lawyer is approached by an anti-poverty organization to provide legal assistance if demonstrators are arrested while protesting during an upcoming G20 conference. Accepting the retainer is unproblematic provided the lawyer has no reason to believe the organization plans anything other than legal protest. This is so even if there is a possibility that some of the organization's members or followers might become overzealous in the course of their legitimate protest and break the law.

---

14   ABA Defense Standard 4-3.7(c) & comment.

15   *Wood*, above note 6 at para 109, LeBel & Cromwell JJ, dissenting but not on this point; ABA Defense Standard 4-3.7(a): counsel has duty to encourage clients to comply with law.

16   See *Criminal Code*, RSC 1985, c C-46, s 467.11. For a case where a lawyer was convicted of this offence for assisting a criminal organization in various ways, see *R v Mastop*, 2013 BCCA 494, leave to appeal to SCC refused, [2014] SCCA No 23. See also Chapter 6, Section K(4).

17   Alta r 2.02(10); Sask r 2.02(7) (commentary); BC, Man, Ont, NS, NL r 3.2-7, commentary 4; CBA Code ch III, commentary 8.

18   ABA Defense Standard 4-3.7(c) & comment; ABA Model Rules r 1.2(e), comment 12; Charles Wolfram, *Modern Legal Ethics* (St Paul, MN: West Publishing, 1986) at 698 (text associated with note 53).

Finally, there is nothing unethical about criminal defence counsel's representing a client repeatedly as and when the client is charged with criminal offences or in need of advice regarding arrests, search warrants, or other interactions with police. Counsel is acting only in relation to existing matters with respect to which legal advice is legitimately needed, and in so doing is not encouraging future criminal conduct.

C. ACCEPTING A COURT-ORDERED RETAINER

Most Canadian rules of professional conduct suggest that a lawyer must accept a court-ordered retainer.[19] These rules provide no general discretion to refuse a potential client where counsel is mandated to take the case by judicial order. Nonetheless, before accepting such a retainer, counsel has a duty to alert the court to any ethical concern that poses a realistic risk of impacting adversely on the quality of the representation, such as lack of competence or an irresolvable conflict of interest.[20] To remain silent in the face of such an impediment would be to countenance a flawed client-lawyer relationship in circumstances where the client and/or the administration of justice would suffer attendant harm. In reviewing ethical concerns with the court, counsel must honour any restrictions imposed by a duty of confidentiality. If counsel's ethical concern cannot be alleviated, the court's permission to decline the retainer will ordinarily be obtained.[21]

Less clear, in terms of a valid ground to refuse a court-ordered retainer, is the case in which the court requires counsel to undertake an extremely lengthy matter for meagre compensation. In the United States, where court appointments are common, the ABA Model Rules expressly permit a lawyer to refuse an appointment where representing the client will likely result in an unreasonable financial burden on the lawyer.[22] Canadian ethical rules do not follow suit and arguably preclude counsel from refusing to act in the face of such an order, even though the result might be to destroy a legal practice and drive the lawyer into bankruptcy. However, given the existence of legal aid programs, court-mandated representation in criminal cases virtually never occurs in

---

19   BC 2.1-1(c); Alta, Sask r 3.01(1) (commentary); Man, Ont, NS, NL r 4.1-1, commentary 4; CBA Code ch XIV, commentary 6.

20   Or any of the factors set out in Section B, above in this chapter.

21   An analogy can be drawn to the situation where counsel seeks a court's leave to withdraw from a case due to "ethical reasons." In such a case, the court is required to grant leave: see Chapter 11, Section L(4)(a).

22   ABA Model Rule 6.2(b).

Canada. Indeed, much more likely is a request by defence counsel for judicial assistance in obtaining funding where a legal aid plan has refused coverage[23] or is seen to provide inadequate compensation.[24]

D. PROHIBITING DISCRIMINATION

As we will shortly discuss, a Canadian lawyer is normally not ethically obligated to accept any client with the means to pay the required fee. Yet there is one area where lawyers are prohibited from declining a retainer. Most rules of professional conduct forbid discrimination on the same grounds generally prohibited by human rights legislation.[25] These rules are drafted broadly enough to encompass the decision whether or not to provide legal services. The result is that a lawyer cannot refuse a case on grounds such as the prospective client's race, ancestry, place of origin, colour, ethnic origin, citizenship, creed, sex, sexual orientation, age, marital or family status, or disability.[26] It is also improper for a lawyer to provide an inferior quality of service based on discriminatory grounds.[27] Discrimination can occur when a decision to refuse a client is made on a prohibited ground or where a decision to refuse though not intended to be discriminatory nonetheless results in a discriminatory adverse effect.[28]

Breaching the rules of professional conduct pertaining to improper discrimination risks a human rights complaint and constitutes unethical conduct that could lead to disciplinary action by the governing body. In several American jurisdictions that employ comparable anti-discrimination provisions, a finding of professional misconduct cannot be made without a prior judicial determination of discrimination.[29]

---

23   See, for example, *R v Rushlow*, 2009 ONCA 461; *R v Dew*, 2009 MBCA 101; *R v Williams*, 2011 BCCA 85.

24   These applications will be granted only exceptionally, in particular where an accused cannot find competent counsel to act at legal aid rates: see *R v Peterman* (2004), 185 CCC (3d) 352 (Ont CA).

25   Alta, Sask r 5.03(5); BC, Man, NS, NL r 6.3-5; Ont r 6.3.1-1 & 6.3.1-2; Quebec *Professional Code*, CQLR c C-26, s 57; NB ch 21; CBA Code ch XX.

26   This list of prohibited grounds largely tracks Ont r 6.3.1-1. To similar effect, see Man r 6.3-5; NB ch 21; CBA Code ch XX. The other codes mentioned in note 25, above in this chapter, simply prohibit discrimination as defined in the applicable human rights legislation.

27   See, for example, Ont r 6.3.1-2; NB ch 21, commentary 1(i).

28   See the discussion in Ont r 6.3.1-1, commentary 11.

29   See, for example, New York, *Rules of Professional Conduct*, r 8.4(g); California, *Rules of Professional Conduct*, r 2-400(C).

This precondition does not apply in Canada, meaning a governing body can initiate a disciplinary proceeding without the need for a pre-existing adverse finding from a court or human rights tribunal.

It might be argued that distaste for a client or his views based on a prohibited ground should excuse a lawyer from accepting the retainer if acting on the case would undermine the quality of representation.[30] Granted, permitting the lawyer to refuse the case in these circumstances holds the potential to render the anti-discrimination rule patently ineffective. Yet the alternative may leave the client with such poor-quality representation that the lawyer is violating the ethical rule requiring competent service.[31]

On the other hand, attenuating the lawyer's choice is arguably justified because the alternative may unfairly limit access to the legal system, cause substantial emotional and psychological damage to the rejected client, and result in attendant harm to the image of the profession and the justice system. This is especially so where the lawyer finds the client repugnant for reasons unrelated to the subject matter of the retainer. Ultimately, the message that most governing bodies send by virtue of anti-discrimination rules may therefore be that lawyers who are unable to set aside repugnance for the client or the client's views on certain specific grounds should not be practising law.[32]

E. THE UNPOPULAR OR REPUGNANT CLIENT: SETTING UP THE PROBLEM

Perhaps the most difficult problem associated with the decision to accept or reject a case arises from the example of the unpopular or repugnant client.[33] Taking on a notoriously abhorrent case can cause the

---

30 See Man r 6.3-5, commentary 6, stating that the anti-discrimination rule does not affect a lawyer's right to refuse a retainer where she is unable to represent the client competently and to the best of her ability.

31 See Chapter 3, Section K(1).

32 For a good discussion of this issue, arguing for a nuanced view of the rules, see Alice Woolley, *Understanding Lawyers' Ethics in Canada* (Markham, ON: Lexis-Nexis, 2011) at 48–49.

33 An indication of the dilemma facing the profession in this regard is reflected in the changing position of Monroe Freedman. In his first book, *Lawyers' Ethics in an Adversary System* (New York: Bobbs-Merrill, 1975) at 11, Freedman argued that lawyers must accept any prospective client. Shortly thereafter, he performed a *volte-face*, arguing that lawyers should be morally accountable for the clients they choose to represent (Monroe Freedman, *Understanding Lawyers' Ethics* (New York: Matthew Bender, 1990) at 66–70), a position maintained to

lawyer considerable personal risk and discomfort. She may be subject to intense criticism in the media and from family and friends. Other clients, both potential and existing, may decide they are uncomfortable with the lawyer's decision to act, with the result that business suffers. Colleagues may shun the lawyer, not wanting to court societal displeasure by any sort of association. Caution may lead the lawyer to perpetual inaction, as the following comment, written in the mid-1960s, laments:

> The average lawyer hesitates to participate in the controversial issues of his time. He wonders what his other clients might think. He wonders about the social consequences to himself, his wife, and his family. And he listens to the enemy within. This enemy speaks in a thousand voices, now whispering caution and then whining fear, now pleading in reasonable accents for practicality and self-interests, and then shouting direful predictions of disaster. But above all the voice says wait: wait until your prestige is secure, your voice more powerful; wait for the right time, for the right case. But the right case at the right time seldom comes. And while the lawyer waits, the voice of the demagogue is unanswered and the unpopular client's right to counsel goes by default.[34]

The lawyer may also encounter very real difficulties in undertaking the representation in a competent manner, struggling to overcome strongly held personal views in an effort to provide the client with zealous advocacy. The lawyer's individual autonomy and dignity, as reflected in her personal morality, is thus not always easily sublimated to the role of advancing a client's case.[35]

And yet, by virtue of their daily work, criminal lawyers have made basic choices about the propriety of representing accused persons, and they are comfortable with and even champion such representation based on the singular role that a defence lawyer plays in the justice system.[36] We have examined this role and its justifications in the previ-

---

this day (Monroe Freedman & Abbe Smith, *Understanding Lawyers' Ethics*, 4th ed (New Providence, NJ: LexisNexis, 2010) at 69–72).

34 Daniel Pollitt, "Counsel for the Unpopular Cause: The 'Hazard' of Being Undone" (1964–65) 43 NCL Rev 9 at 17–18.

35 It has been observed that "[t]he decision to act for a particular client is always a moral choice, implicating the lawyer's personal views of whether or not a 'moral lawyer' can assist a particular client in pursuit of a given goal" (Randal Graham, "Moral Contexts" (2001) 50 UNBLJ 77 at 104).

36 See Margareth Etienne, "The Ethics of Cause Lawyering: An Empirical Examination of Criminal Defense Lawyers as Cause Lawyers" (2005) 95 J Crim L & Criminology 1195, arguing that in a broad sense many defence counsel can be

ous chapter.[37] If one accepts that the justice system is a necessary and good institution and that the lawyer must undertake special duties to ensure the system operates properly, then such duties, to the extent they may superficially clash with common or non-legal morality, are justified. The lawyer thus acts pursuant to a role morality that requires actions and attitudes not demanded of, and perhaps even shunned by, other members of society. Indeed, it is not going too far to suggest that a community consensus exists to the effect that defence lawyers play an important function that justifies representing individuals who may well be guilty.[38] Consequently, in the overwhelming majority of cases, representing an accused is completely unproblematic for the lawyer whose practice is devoted to criminal law.

On the other hand, the problem of whether a criminal lawyer should accept a repellent client is not purely hypothetical. In recent times we have seen controversy caused by criminal lawyers who decide to accept, or reject, the case of an unpopular client. In the leading child-pornography case of *R v Sharpe*,[39] the accused was for a time unable to obtain representation, at least in part because of the unpalatable nature of the charges.[40] Or consider the decision made by Phil Rankin, a Jewish lawyer involved in human rights issues, who was approached to take the case of an accused charged with a murder having significant racist overtones. Mr Rankin decided not to accept the retainer, on the basis that he was unable to guarantee that his legal work would not be adversely affected by his personal views.[41] In 2001, politician Stockwell Day ignited a firestorm of controversy, and attracted a defamation suit, by accusing a criminal lawyer of promoting the possession of child pornography by launching a constitutional challenge on behalf of an individual accused of such a crime.[42]

Moreover, and more commonly, some criminal advocates — not a lot, but some — adopt policies that shun representation for certain categories

---

viewed as "cause lawyers," for example in the sense that they are motivated by a desire to assist the disadvantaged or prevent the abuse of police power.

37 See Chapter 1, Section D.

38 See *Goddard v Day*, 2000 ABQB 820 at paras 22–24 [*Day*].

39 2001 SCC 2.

40 He ultimately retained one of British Columbia's leading criminal counsel to handle the appeals.

41 See Robert Matas, "Murder Case Tests Lawyer's Beliefs" *The Globe and Mail* (25 April 1998) A5; "Lawyer Declines Murder Case" *The Globe and Mail* (27 April 1998) A3.

42 See Jill Mahoney, "Is It the End of Day?" *The Globe and Mail* (13 January 2001). The lawsuit was eventually settled, with Mr Day's paying $60,000 in damages and very substantial legal costs to the plaintiff.

of client or operate to restrict a client's representation so that a position the lawyer finds distasteful is not advanced. Examples include refusing to defend an accused charged with any sex-related offence,[43] declining to represent anyone facing charges in a racist crime,[44] or rejecting cases where the potential client wishes to testify against a co-accused in return for a more lenient sentence.[45] Or a defence lawyer might choose never to represent a police officer charged with an on-duty crime of violence[46] or avoid acting for alleged members of organized crime groups.[47]

Lawyers who restrict their practice in this manner are allowing strongly held personal views about morality to guide their work, something that we usually do not begrudge members of society. The problem is that if enough criminal lawyers restrict their practice in these ways, some accused persons may have trouble finding a competent lawyer. The issue thus becomes whether to accommodate a lawyer's morality, which may reflect views held by the populace at large, at the risk of limiting access to the legal system for certain accused persons. One approach to this problem, called the cab-rank rule, absolutely precludes a lawyer from bringing to bear personal moral views in deciding whether to accept a proffered retainer. We now turn to look at the cab-rank rule and some of the arguments made by its proponents and detractors.

F. THE CAB-RANK RULE

In England and Australia, barristers have long espoused the cab-rank rule of accepting clients.[48] This rule is held up as an exemplar of the profession's unremitting dedication to ensure access to justice for all

---

43 See, for example, Freedman & Smith, above note 33 at 71; Andrew Hall, "We Say No and We Mean No!" (1990) 140 New LJ 284; Brian Raymond, "The Profession's Duty to Provide; A Solicitor's Right to Choose" (1990) 140 New LJ 285.

44 See, for example, "Lawyer Declines Murder Case," above note 41.

45 Ethical issues associated with taking this position are discussed in Chapter 9, Section I.

46 Freedman & Smith, above note 33 at 71.

47 Prominent American defense lawyer Joseph Tacopina has said he does not accept organized crime cases (Mark Leibovich, "A-Rod's Defender Knows How to Tap Dance," interview of Joseph Tacopina in *The New York Times Magazine* (20 September 2013), online: www.nytimes.com/2013/09/22/magazine/a-rods-defender-knows-how-to-tap-dance.html?_r=0).

48 For England and Wales, see Bar Standards Board, *The Bar Standards Board Handbook* (London: Bar Standards Board, 2014) r C29 at 43–44. For Australia, see, for example, The New South Wales Bar Association, *The New South Wales Barristers' Rules* (Sydney: New South Wales Bar Association, 2014) r 21–24B; Bar

members of society. Reviewing the nature of the cab-rank rule, as well as its justifications, will help us to determine whether the rule delivers on this lofty promise.

1) The Cab-Rank Rule and Its Justification

The cab-rank rule, as its name implies, requires a barrister to accept any client who requests legal representation provided that a proper fee is paid and that the lawyer is available and competent to take on the work. The central feature of the rule is that barristers do not choose clients based on the nature of the case or the individual. Consequently, an invidious cause or an odious individual will not be denied access to legal representation. Indeed, abnegating choice in client selection is said to insulate lawyers from public criticism for accepting an unpopular client: the lawyer elides personal responsibility by pointing to the rule's noble mandate. As explained by Lord Reid in *Rondel v Worsley*, the cab-rank rule thus helps to promote justice, for no one is forced to go without counsel or to settle for a second-rate lawyer because leading counsel is unwilling to risk social opprobrium by taking on the case:

> It has long been recognised that no counsel is entitled to refuse to act in a sphere in which he practices, and on being tendered a proper fee, for any person however unpopular or even offensive he or his opinions may be, and it is essential that that duty must continue: justice cannot be done and certainly cannot be seen to be done otherwise. If counsel is bound to act for such a person, no reasonable man could think the less of any counsel because of his association with such a client, but, if counsel could pick and choose, his reputation might suffer if he chose to act for such a client, and the client might have great difficulty in obtaining proper legal assistance.[49]

A secondary justification for the cab-rank rule is that a lawyer who assesses the viability or propriety of a potential client's case as a precursor to accepting or declining the retainer may be in error.[50] A valid cause, and the assertion of a legitimate legal right, could be rashly spurned in

---

Association of Queensland, *Bar Association of Queensland Barristers' Conduct Rules* (Brisbane: Bar Association of Queensland, 2011) r 21–24B.

49 [1967] 3 All ER 993 at 998. See also the comments by Lord Pearce, *ibid* at 1029–030, and by Lord Upjohn, *ibid* at 1033. See also *Giannarelli v Wraith* (1988), 165 CLR 543 at 580 (HCA), Brennan J, but contrast the tepid support for the rule offered by Dawson J, *ibid* at 594 [*Giannarelli*].

50 See Richard Wasserstrom, "Lawyers as Professionals: Some Moral Issues" (1975) 5 Hum RQ 1 at 9–10 (though not endorsing the cab-rank rule).

the result. On this view, lawyers who choose their clients are usurping the role of a judge or jury. It is better to leave the final decision making function to the court and to accept that zealous argument by a non-judgmental advocate is the best means of achieving justice.

In Canada, the cab-rank rule, if utilized, would arguably promote not only access to justice but also the accused's constitutional rights to legal representation, counsel of choice, and control over decisions of fundamental importance to her criminal defence.[51] Granted, lawyers are not state actors who are bound by the constitution in their daily activities. Yet the notion that lawyers should have some obligation to advance these constitutional rights can be seen as emblematic of their crucial role in the justice system and a fair exchange for the valuable monopoly granted to the profession by the state.[52]

2) An Example: The Case of *Goddard v Day*

The purported utility of the cab-rank rule can be illustrated by looking at the facts in the case of *Goddard v Day*.[53] Mr Day, at that time a member of Alberta's legislative assembly, wrote a letter to a Red Deer newspaper criticizing criminal lawyer and school trustee Lorne Goddard for his role in defending a man charged with possessing child pornography. The letter appeared to use the mere act of representation, which included a constitutional challenge to provisions of the *Criminal Code*,[54] as a basis for suggesting that Mr Goddard personally supported the possession, and even the production, of child pornography.[55] Mr Goddard responded by launching a defamation suit against Mr Day.

One of the defences attempted by Mr Day in the defamation litigation asserted that Mr Goddard by virtue of the role played by lawyers in advancing their clients' causes must have personally endorsed his client's legal arguments. For example, an amended Statement of Defence filed by Mr Day stated that Mr Goddard,

> as a member of the Law Society of Alberta, made certain legal representations as to the rights of individuals in Canada to possess child pornography and as to the unconstitutionality of s. 163.1(4) of the Criminal Code of Canada, which representations were made

---

51 These rights are discussed in Chapter 1, Section D.

52 Anthony Thornton, "The Professional Responsibility and Ethics of the English Bar" in Ross Cranston, ed, *Legal Ethics and Professional Responsibility* (Oxford: Clarendon Press, 1995) 53 at 68.

53 Above note 38.

54 See *R v KLV*, [1999] AJ No 350 (QB).

55 The text of the letter is reprinted in the article by Mahoney, above note 42.

on March 26, 1999 in the Court of Queen's Bench of Alberta in the case of *R. v. Valley*. As such, the Plaintiff must, in accordance with the obligations of a Barrister being a member of the Law Society of Alberta, have actually believed or alternatively did in fact believe that those said representations as to the rights of individuals and as to the unconstitutionality of s. 163.1(4) of the Criminal Code of Canada fairly and accurately represented the law in Canada at the time the Plaintiff made the representations on behalf of his client, Kevin Valley.[56]

Mr Day then argued that the public so despises child pornography that a lawyer who makes constitutional arguments in support of an accused charged with possession of such material would as a matter of course be hated and despised, be the subject of ridicule, be shunned or avoided, and be adversely affected in the estimation of others.[57]

This brazen association of a defence lawyer's personal beliefs with the actions of a client and the conduct of the defence represents exactly the sort of problem supporters of the cab-rank rule seek to avert. If Mr Goddard had had absolutely no choice but to accept the accused as a client, it would have been less likely that the public would conclude that he endorsed the actions of his client and subject him to ridicule and hatred. On the other hand, we will revisit the *Goddard v Day* decision below to show how an interlocutory ruling in the case is not especially supportive of the cab-rank rule.[58]

3) Room for a Lawyer's Personal Viewpoint

Embracing the cab-rank rule does not preclude a lawyer from exercising moral persuasion upon the client.[59] A cab-rank adherent can quite properly advise the client not only regarding the legal pitfalls and weaknesses in a case but also with respect to the morality of achieving the client's desired goal. Of course, counsel who finds a potential client's cause to be highly unpalatable and candidly says as much will often not be hired in the first place. Alternatively, through dialogue with the client, a lawyer may come to accept that the retainer's objectives are not repugnant after all.

---

56   *Day*, above note 38 at para 4.
57   *Ibid* at para 21.
58   See the discussion in Section G(2), below in this chapter.
59   See David Pannick, *Advocates* (Oxford: Oxford University Press, 1992) at 153.

4) Criticism of the Cab-Rank Rule

The cab-rank rule asserts an impressive vision of the legal profession's role in ensuring that all accused persons have access to justice. There is a substantial question, however, as to whether the rule truly operates in accord with its supporting theory. Consider, for instance, that a great many exceptions are permitted under the cab-rank rule. A lawyer can legitimately reject a case for many reasons, including incompetence to act, conflict of interest, inability of the client to pay the required fees, and a busy schedule that does not permit counsel to take on the case.[60] These and other exceptions to the cab-rank rule effectively provide lawyers with considerable discretion in deciding whether to accept a client. It has thus been persuasively argued that the rule is largely a myth or fiction and that lawyers who purport to follow it in fact are able to pick and choose clients with relative freedom, rejecting cases they find distasteful by imposing stringent fee requirements or claiming a busy schedule.[61]

While there is still support for the cab-rank rule in England and Wales, the panegyric testimonials traditionally surrounding the rule have been tempered of late, no doubt in part because of the honest recognition that it is open to easy avoidance. Contrast the staunch defence of the rule by Lord Reid in *Rondel v Worsley*, quoted above,[62] with the equivocal and tepid support offered by Lord Steyn in the more recent House of Lords decision in *Arthur JS Hall & Co v Simons*.[63] Though referring to the cab-rank rule as "a valuable professional rule," Lord Steyn observed that "its impact on the administration of justice in England is not great. In real life a barrister has a clerk whose enthusiasm for the unwanted brief may not be great, and he is free to raise the fee within limits. It is not likely that the rule often obliges barristers to undertake work which they would not otherwise accept."[64]

---

60 See, for example, the many exceptions countenanced by *The Bar Standards Board Handbook*, above note 48, r C29 & C30 at 43–45. In Australia, some rules of professional conduct attempt to restrict the discretion by expressly forbidding lawyers from setting an inordinately high fee for the purpose of avoiding a case: see, for example, *The New South Wales Barristers' Rules*, above note 48, r 22; *Bar Association of Queensland Barristers' Conduct Rules*, above note 48, r 22.

61 John Flood & Morten Hviid, *The Cab Rank Rule: Its Meaning and Purpose in the New Legal Services Market; Report for the Legal Services Board* (London: Legal Services Board, 2013).

62 See the text accompanying note 49, above in this chapter.

63 [2000] 3 All ER 673 (HL).

64 *Ibid* at 680. To similar effect, see the comments of Lord Hope, *ibid* at 714. More solicitous of the rule's continuing role in the administration of justice is Lord Hobhouse, *ibid* at 738.

Perhaps the cab-rank rule is better seen as an aspirational principle, intended to promote access to justice for all those in need of legal representation, no matter how unpopular or controversial their cause. But if this is true, it seems disingenuous to maintain the conceit that barristers are truly bound by a rule requiring them to take every client who requests their services. Does the public really need fooling on this point? A decent argument can also be made that contemporary public criticism of criminal defence lawyers focuses not so much on choice of client as on perceived deficiencies regarding the manner of representation, such as mounting frivolous defences or attacking vulnerable complainants in cross-examination. In other words, the public-perception problem the cab-rank rule is meant to address appears largely overstated, at least in the criminal law context.[65]

G. THE AMERICAN POSITION: A GREATER FREEDOM OF CHOICE FOR THE LAWYER

In the United States, the major professional governing bodies have never mandated the cab-rank rule, although some lawyers have chosen to follow its precepts. The American approach instead overtly affords the lawyer significant choice on the matter of client selection, in stark contrast to the theory behind the cab-rank rule.

1) Rules of Professional Conduct in the United States

Most jurisdictions in the United States do not employ a cab-rank rule, rather permitting a lawyer substantial freedom in deciding whether to take on a case. The Third Restatement goes the furthest of the major ethical codes in this regard, stating that "[l]awyers are generally as free as other persons to decide with whom to deal, subject to generally applicable statutes such as those prohibiting certain kinds of discrimination. A lawyer, for example, may decline to undertake a representation that the lawyer finds inconvenient or repugnant."[66] The ABA Model Rules and Defense Standards, while less strident, are generally to the same effect.[67]

---

65   W Bradley Wendel, "Institutional and Individual Justification in Legal Ethics: The Problem of Client Selection" (2006) 34 Hofstra L Rev 987 at 995–96.
66   Third Restatement § 14, comment "b." To similar effect, see *ibid* § 16, comment "b," and § 32, comment "j."
67   ABA Model Rules 1.2(b) and 6.2, comment 1; ABA Defense Standard 4-1.6.

The American position is not without certain significant exceptions, however, and also must be viewed in light of aspirational precepts contained in most rules of professional conduct. For instance, counsel must take on a case absent "good cause" to refuse where representation of a client is mandated by court order.[68] "Good cause" is not exhaustively defined in the rules but, among other things, is said to include circumstances where "the client or the cause is so repugnant to the lawyer as to be likely to impair the client-lawyer relationship or the lawyer's ability to represent the client."[69] Unless this standard is met, mere distaste for the client, or a desire to avoid public opprobrium, does not excuse counsel from the court appointment. It is also worth mentioning that, despite the general freedom given to American lawyers to accept or reject a proffered retainer, the rules of professional conduct urge lawyers not to shun a prospective client. The ABA Model Rules are among the clearest in this regard, stating that "[l]egal representation should not be denied to people who are unable to afford legal services, or whose cause is controversial or the subject of popular disapproval."[70]

2) Justification for the American Position

Several arguments are forwarded to support the American position that a lawyer should have a general discretion to refuse a prospective client. First, the duties associated with a retainer, once assumed, are onerous, and counsel is restricted in the ability to withdraw from the case. The legal system should therefore not lightly impose on lawyers the fiduciary obligations associated with legal representation. Second, the quality of legal representation may actually suffer if counsel is forced to accept cases in which she does not wish to act. The cab-rank rule, on this view, can actually harm the client, who is not assured of counsel who can zealously act in the cause at hand. Third, the client-lawyer relationship is by its very nature a contractual arrangement based on the consent of both parties. Forcing a lawyer to accept a client impinges on the freedom to contract. Fourth, it does not necessarily follow that providing a lawyer with discretion in selecting clients invariably results in the lawyer's being associated with the views and positions of those individuals whose cases are accepted. A legal system can endeavour to divorce a lawyer's personal views from those of the client even where some choice in accepting a case is permitted. Indeed, ABA Model Rule

---

68   ABA Model Rule 6.2.
69   ABA Model Rule 6.2(c); ABA Defense Standard 4-1.6(d).
70   ABA Model Rule 1.2, comment 5. See also ABA Defense Standard 4-1.6(b).

1.2(b) directly addresses this point, providing that a "lawyer's representation of a client, including representation by appointment, does not constitute an endorsement of the client's political, economic, social or moral views or activities."

The notion that a lawyer's perceived independence — and personal reputation — can survive acceptance of a retainer for an unpopular client, despite the absence of the cab-rank rule, was accepted in an interlocutory ruling rendered in *Goddard v Day*.[71] Though a Canadian case, the court's ruling nicely articulates a justification for the American approach, along the lines espoused by ABA Model Rule 1.2(b). Remember that Mr Day contended that a criminal lawyer is personally associated with the cause of any client he chooses to represent. This contention was rejected as part of a ruling striking a portion of the Statement of Defence. Rather, the court accepted that criminal lawyers carry out an important function in the legal system, one that permits advocacy on behalf of an accused without leading to a personal association with the client's impugned actions. In this regard, the court stated:

> I do not doubt that there are some people who would follow the path suggested by the Defence in terms of their estimation of the Plaintiff. However, that is not the test. The test is whether or not it is plain and obvious that the Defence discloses no reasonable defence. I am satisfied that the allegation that someone is a criminal lawyer, or a politician would tend to adversely affect that person in the estimation of some other people. The same might be said of practically every appellation which describes a position or occupation taken by a person. Those other people would not be reasonable people.
>
> I am satisfied that reasonable people would not hate, or despise, or subject a person to ridicule, shun or avoid that person, or consider that person to be a lesser person in their estimation because that person has made a Constitutional argument in a criminal court.
>
> Reasonable people are concerned about the constitutional liberties of fellow citizens. Reasonable people support the Constitution of Canada or at the very least, support the right of other citizens to rely upon the protection afforded by that Constitution.[72]

The court thus accepted that the public understands the role of an advocate in an adversarial, rights-based legal system and does not think less highly of a criminal lawyer based on the clients he chooses to represent.

---

71 *Day*, above note 38.
72 *Ibid* at paras 22–24.

On the other hand, supporters of the cab-rank rule have little faith that a provision like ABA Model Rule 1.2(b), or justifications of the sort offered in *Goddard v Day*, can shield lawyers from public criticism for choosing particular clients and thus promote access to justice.[73] The fact of the matter, according to these commentators, is that affording lawyers any discretion in choosing clients invariably compromises counsel's neutrality within the legal system. If a lawyer has decided to represent a client when he is free to decline the retainer, then it is fair game to attack the lawyer for manifesting an allegiance to the client's cause. In this context, the bald statement that a lawyer does not endorse a client's position, so the argument goes, is ineffective and unconvincing. Moreover, there have been periods in the history of American lawyering where the reluctance of the profession to provide representation for unpopular clients or causes has made access to justice truly difficult.[74]

3) "The Last Lawyer in Town"

One suggestion sometimes made to reduce the possibility that legal services will be denied a deserving individual under the American approach is to encourage lawyers to act for the repugnant client where to refuse representation would leave the individual without a lawyer. Thus, the lawyer should take on a case where she is notionally "the last lawyer in town." The ABA Model Rules evince an attraction to this approach, albeit without imposing an affirmative ethical duty on the lawyer.[75] Limiting the lawyer's choice to refuse a client in the last-lawyer-in-town scenario helps somewhat to address the legitimate concern that freedom of choice in selecting clients might serve to leave some individuals without any legal representation.

A criticism of the last-lawyer-in-town approach, however, is that the lawyer still exercises choice respecting the vast majority of clients, who do not fall within the exception. This is a problem for those who believe that any significant amount of choice leaves lawyers open to being identified with their clients' causes. Plus, the approach tends to place the burden of representation on the few lawyers who do not hesitate

---

73   See Pannick, above note 59 at 140.
74   See Pollitt, above note 34, focusing on the refusal of many lawyers to act in civil rights cases and matters involving communism; David Goldberger, "The 'Right to Counsel' in Political Cases: The Bar's Failure" (1979) 43 Law & Contemp Probs 321, discussing the famous *Skokie* case.
75   See ABA Model Rules 1.2, comment 3, and 6.2, comment 1.

before taking on unpopular cases.[76] Indeed, if all lawyers exercised the discretion not to accept an unpopular client or cause, relying on professional colleagues to act in troublesome cases, individuals might frequently be left without any lawyer. It can also be persuasively argued that the client is left with a restricted choice of counsel and may be forced to accept representation by a lawyer who, though competent, is not particularly well suited to conduct the case.

H. CANADIAN RULES OF PROFESSIONAL CONDUCT

With a general understanding of two distinct ethical models regarding client selection, we can turn to look at the position in Canada.

1) The Text of the Rules

Most Canadian rules of professional conduct emphasize the importance of access to legal services and explicitly require lawyers to "make legal services available to the public efficiently and conveniently."[77] "It is essential," adds the CBA Code, "that a person requiring legal services be able to find a qualified lawyer with a minimum of difficulty or delay."[78] These statements of principle might lead one to conclude that a lawyer must take on any case, regardless of the unpopularity of the cause. However, the rules clearly do not go this far, the position adopted by the decided preponderance of law societies being that

[a] lawyer has a general right to decline a particular representation (except when assigned as counsel by a tribunal), but it is a right to be exercised prudently, particularly if the probable result would be to make it difficult for a person to obtain legal advice or representation. Generally, a lawyer should not exercise the right merely because a person seeking legal services or that person's cause is unpopular or notorious, or because powerful interests or allegations of misconduct or malfeasance are involved, or because of the lawyer's private opinion

---

76 Or, to put it another way, only the lawyer unlucky enough to be asked last will be left without a choice: see William Hodes, "Accepting and Rejecting Clients — The Moral Autonomy of the Second-to-the-Last Lawyer in Town" (2000) 48 U Kan L Rev 977 at 985.

77 BC r 2.1-5(c); Alta, Sask r 3.01(1); Man, Ont, NS, NL r 4.1-1; NB ch 16, commentary 1; CBA Code ch XIV, rule.

78 CBA Code ch XIV, commentary 1.

about the guilt of the accused. A lawyer declining representation should assist in obtaining the services of another lawyer qualified in the particular filed and able to act. When a lawyer offers assistance to a client or prospective client in finding another lawyer, the assistance should be given willingly and, except where a referral fee is permitted by [the rule governing such fees], without charge.[79]

A less nuanced approach is taken in the Quebec *Code of Ethics of Advocates*, which simply states, "The advocate may accept or refuse a mandate."[80] The Quebec Code also provides that a lawyer "shall respect the right of the client to choose his advocate."[81] This latter provision could perhaps be interpreted as restricting a lawyer's ability to reject a client, for doing so arguably interferes with the right of choice regarding legal counsel. The more convincing interpretation, however, is that lawyers in Quebec enjoy considerable discretion in deciding whether to decline a prospective client's request for representation.

Clearer still is the New Brunswick *Code of Professional Conduct*, which provides, "Save where the court orders otherwise, the lawyer may decline to act for a person requesting legal advice or any other professional service."[82] There is no exhortation to be slow to refuse a proffered retainer where the client or cause is unpopular or where refusal will make it difficult for the individual to obtain representation.

Finally, the *Code of Professional Conduct for British Columbia* makes no express reference to the issue. Lawyers in the province thus appear to have free rein to accept or reject prospective clients, apart from where representation is assigned by the court.[83] Granted, the British Columbia Code states that the oaths taken by lawyers on admission to the bar are "solemn undertakings to be strictly observed."[84] Yet the oath currently taken on admittance to the bar in the province does not include an obligation to accept all cases.[85]

Contrast the oath in Ontario, which states, "I shall neglect no one's interest . . . I shall not refuse cases of complaint reasonably found-

---

79   Alta, Sask r 3.01(1) (commentary); Man, Ont, NS, NL r 4.1-1. To similar effect, see CBA Code ch XIV, commentary 6.
80   Que s 3.05.01.
81   Que s 3.05.02.
82   NB ch 4, commentary 17.
83   BC r 2.1-1(c).
84   BC r 2.1-5(e).
85   The same goes for several other Canadian jurisdictions, including Alberta and Nova Scotia.

ed . . . ."[86] This wording on its face mandates that a lawyer accept any non-frivolous case and can be seen to equate with the cab-rank rule ostensibly favoured by barristers in England and Wales. Yet the client-selection provision in the Ontario *Rules of Professional Conduct* is clearly inconsistent with the cab-rank approach,[87] as is the province's jurisprudence.[88]

2) Discerning What the Canadian Rules Mean for Criminal Defence Counsel

The Canadian rules of professional conduct do not impose a cab-rank rule. They have more in common with the American approach, especially the rules in British Columbia, New Brunswick, and Quebec. What little caselaw exists in this area further supports the view that Canadian lawyers have substantial freedom of choice when it comes to client selection.[89] Nonetheless, the ethical rules in Canada caution lawyers to be slow to refuse a retainer where a client will probably face difficulty in securing other legal representation and admonish them to avoid refusing a brief merely because the client or cause is unpopular.

We accept the justification behind affording the lawyer some discretion in choosing or refusing clients. There are commentators, including Professors Alice Woolley, Allan Hutchinson, David Luban, and Monroe Freedman, who to varying extents promote the idea that lawyers have a moral obligation to choose clients carefully, with an eye to the larger social good.[90] This approach jettisons much of the rhetoric surrounding the cab-rank rule, while at the same time refusing to embrace uncritically all justifications for the traditional American position. It also admits that barriers to access to justice relate much more to a client's ability to pay fees than to a lawyer's freedom to decline a case based on the nature of the client's cause.[91] In fact, in the criminal law context it is exceptionally rare for an accused to want for competent counsel

---

86   Bylaw 4 at para 21(1), passed pursuant to the *Law Society Act*, RSO 1990, c L.8, ss 62(0.1) & (1).

87   See the text associated with note 79, above in this chapter.

88   *Demarco v Ungaro* (1979), 21 OR (2d) 673 at 694–695 (HCJ): cab-rank rule does not apply in civil cases.

89   *Ibid.*

90   See Woolley, above note 32 at 50–52; Allan C Hutchinson, *Legal Ethics and Professional Responsibility*, 2d ed (Toronto: Irwin Law, 2006) at 76–79; David Luban, *Lawyers and Justice: An Ethical Study* (Princeton, NJ: Princeton University Press, 1988) ch 8; Freedman & Smith, above note 33 at 69–72.

91   See Mr Justice JC Major, "Lawyers' Obligation to Provide Legal Services" (1995) 33 Alta L Rev 719.

because she is reviled or the charged crime notorious. Lawyers of the highest calibre are eager to take on such briefs for reasons that include a desire for challenging and interesting work, and the attractiveness of an increased profile within the bar and with the public more generally.

The argument endorsing a degree of freedom of choice also rejects, or at least tempers, the Diceyan notion that lawyers are morally neutral providers of access to justice. Decisions regarding what type of law to practise, fees to be charged, and arguments to be placed before the court all have an impact on the greater administration of justice. In these and many other respects, lawyers shape the structure and process of the system within which they work. On this view, permitting lawyers a limited ability to reject certain clients, and thereby to shape the larger legal system, is not especially startling or out of character with their actual role.

Yet this does not mean that lawyers should be viewed as supporters of their clients' causes. True, a lawyer will sometimes take on a case *because* he favours the client's position, or a broader principle at stake such as freedom of speech, and there is nothing wrong with doing so. And all lawyers take on work to earn a living — in other words, partly for the money. But in almost every criminal matter, it can also be said that defence counsel accepts the brief based on an abiding commitment to the fundamental systemic principle that everyone accused of a crime is entitled to a lawyer's help and that the state's case must be tested to ensure no one is convicted absent proof beyond a reasonable doubt.[92] Ultimately, this systemic justification for representing individuals accused of crimes, perhaps as much as any other, means that defence lawyers *generally* should not, and in practice do not, exercise their discretion under the ethical codes to refuse a retainer on the basis that a client or cause is unpopular.

We therefore take the position that allowing lawyers a discretion to decline a case based on heartfelt moral grounds, as the ethical rules in Canada appear to do, is a tenable proposition but that for criminal defence counsel the scope of the discretion will be narrow. The question becomes, what guidelines should a lawyer follow in exercising the discretion to refuse a case?

---

92   See the discussion in the paragraph associated with notes 36–38, above in this chapter. See also Alice Woolley, "Not Only in America: The Necessities of Representing 'Those People' in a Free and Democratic Society" in Abbe Smith & Monroe H Freedman, *How Can You Represent Those People?* (New York: Palgrave MacMillan, 2013) 199 at 206–8.

I. SUGGESTIONS FOR EXERCISING THE DISCRETION TO ACCEPT OR REJECT A CLIENT

In our view, and consistent with the Canadian rules of professional conduct, there are different ways in which a lawyer's personal views can legitimately influence the decision whether to accept a client.

1) Refusal Where the Quality of Representation Would Suffer

A lawyer must reject a retainer where personal distaste concerning the potential client or cause is so severe that the lawyer can reasonably conclude that the quality of legal representation would suffer as a result. This sort of situation is really tantamount to the problem of incompetence.[93] If the lawyer cannot provide competent representation because of her personal beliefs, the brief should not be accepted. The same conclusion follows where the potential client's personality is so abrasive to the lawyer as to impede fatally the duties demanded of any competent advocate. In either case, acceptance of the retainer, followed by compromised representation, would constitute a breach of the lawyer's duties of loyalty and competence to the client. There is no room for the exercise of discretion in such an event, and the lawyer must reject the proffered employment.[94]

2) Responsible Exercise of the Discretion to Accept or Refuse a Case

Leaving the issue of competence aside, what factors can be taken into account in choosing or refusing a particular client? The aim is to recognize some room for a lawyer's legitimate exercise of personal morality without undermining the potential client's right to access justice or the principles that underlie criminal defence counsel's special role in the legal system. In this regard, primary considerations include the following:

---

93 See Charles W Wolfram, "A Lawyer's Duty to Represent Clients Repugnant and Otherwise" in David Luban, ed, *The Good Lawyer: Lawyers' Roles and Lawyers' Ethics* (Totowa NJ: Rowman & Allanheld, 1983) 214 at 224.

94 The one possible exception to this basic proposition may come when a lawyer's distaste arises out of a prohibited ground of discrimination: see Section D, above in this chapter.

1) In most criminal law matters, the client will be facing possible stigma from a conviction, and perhaps also a serious impingement upon liberty. Access to the protections offered by the legal system through the help of counsel will thus constitute a valuable, perhaps even essential, interest. The strength of this interest must not be ignored or unreasonably discounted. Indeed, defence counsel who accepts this rationale — and virtually all of them do — will be exceedingly slow to reject a client simply because he is the subject of public opprobrium.

2) On a somewhat similar note, most Canadian codes state that a lawyer's private opinion about the guilt of an accused person should not constitute the basis to decline employment.[95] Utilizing this rationale for refusing a client would be at odds with a central tenet of the criminal defence lawyer's role. Once a lawyer decides to practise criminal law, choosing a client based on the likelihood he is guilty or not guilty is unacceptable.

3) A lawyer's strong and genuine belief that the representation is repugnant is a legitimate consideration in deciding whether to accept a client, although as noted such a belief will usually be eclipsed by the superordinate principle that all individuals charged with a crime are entitled to a defence.

4) The repugnance felt by the lawyer should relate to concerns intimately connected to the representation at hand and not merely to the personality of the client. Provided a personality clash does not irreparably cripple the client-lawyer relationship, a client should not be rejected merely because he rubs the lawyer the wrong way.

5) A desire to avoid public condemnation for taking on a case and to skirt a real possibility of resulting economic harm to a lawyer's practice are factors that some counsel may take into account. But counsel should be slow to allow public opinion to shape her decision. In any event, lawyers whose practices are dedicated to defence work are unlikely to suffer widespread public disfavour or any consequential business loss by taking on any particular case.

6) The lawyer can take into account the likelihood that the prospective client can obtain competent representation from other counsel; that is the last-lawyer-in-town factor. This consideration is expressly mentioned in many Canadian ethical codes, which state that a lawyer should be cautious in exercising the right to decline employment if the probable result would be to make it difficult for a person to obtain legal advice or representation and should gener-

---

95   See the codes cited at note 79, above in this chapter.

ally refrain from doing so merely because the client or cause is unpopular or notorious.[96]

7) A client cannot be turned away based on a prohibited ground of discrimination.[97]

8) As already mentioned, some criminal defence lawyers refuse to take on entire categories of representation, for example, all individuals facing sex-related charges or all individuals who wish to co-operate with the prosecution.[98] While somewhat uncomfortable with uncompromising refusals to represent clients who fall within a particular category of case, we accept that a dedicated and highly competent criminal lawyer can have a profound moral objection to taking on certain types of representation, in which case it is acceptable to reject such briefs.

J. DUTIES ARISING ONCE A RETAINER IS REFUSED

Where a lawyer decides not to accept a retainer, for whatever legitimate reason, it is advisable to take certain measures designed to protect the interests of both the lawyer and the individual whose case has been declined. A primary duty owed to the rejected individual is to help in finding a suitable lawyer.[99] Subject to the rules pertaining to referrals,[100] the lawyer should generally not charge for providing assistance in this regard. Reasonable assistance will typically involve referring the individual to a firm colleague, a lawyer referral service or legal aid society, or providing him with the names of two or three lawyers who are competent to take on the matter. However, no such duty arises where the individual seeks to implement an illegal scheme, because to assist in locating a lawyer would be to flirt with becoming a party to the illegality.[101]

There are other steps that can or must be taken by a lawyer in conjunction with a decision not to accept the case of a prospective client. First, the lawyer should be very clear with the individual that the case is not being accepted, to prevent any misunderstandings. The safest

---

96 *Ibid.*

97 See Section D, above in this chapter.

98 See the paragraph associated with notes 43–47, above in this chapter.

99 Alta, Sask r 3.01(1) (commentary); Man, Ont, NS, NL r 4.1-1, commentary 4; CBA Code ch XIV, commentary 4.

100 Alta, Sask r 2.06(6); Man, Ont, NS, NL r 3.6-6.

101 In this respect, see the paragraph associated with notes 6–8, above in this chapter. See also Chapter 11, Section N.

course is to set out in writing a quick review of the meetings or contacts leading up to the final decision to reject the retainer. Second, where the case demands that the individual take prompt legal action, for instance, where a trial is quickly approaching, the lawyer should stress the importance of retaining counsel immediately. Third, any documents or other property that has come into the lawyer's possession should be returned to the individual, although the lawyer may wish to make a copy for her own records. Fourth, counsel owes the individual whose case is not accepted a duty of confidentiality that precludes release of secrets to third parties unless authorized by the individual.[102]

---

102 See Chapter 4, Section H(6).

CHAPTER 3

DECISION MAKING

A. INTRODUCTION

A principal function of the client-lawyer relationship is to arrive at decisions regarding the conduct of the case. The client and lawyer have distinct roles and bring different strengths and interests to the process. The client, charged with a criminal offence, faces social stigma and serious restrictions on liberty if convicted. He may have a number of objectives that relate to the legal representation, going beyond the obvious goal of escaping conviction if possible. The client will also often possess information that can be instrumental in identifying and carrying out these objectives. As for the lawyer, she possesses experience and knowledge with respect to the legal system, to a degree the client can never hope to match. The lawyer also has professional obligations, not to mention personal principles and preferences, which shape the way that the defence is conducted. These and other attributes of the client and the lawyer have the potential to influence the decision making process of the professional relationship. The question becomes, how are decisions to be made?

Criminal defence practitioners in Canada have traditionally favoured granting the lawyer near absolute control over the conduct of the defence, allowing the client final say only regarding the decisions how to plead, whether to have a jury, and whether to testify. This conventional approach is variously described as the lawyer-control, lawyer-centred, or lawyer-autonomy model. However, contemporary jurisprudence and commentary is increasingly inclined to reject an un-refined lawyer-control model as overpaternalistic. This is especially so given two developments. First, Canadian courts have recognized that the client has a constitutional right to control aspects of the defence beyond the few exceptions recognized under the lawyer-control model. Second, the problem of how to resolve an intractable disagreement regarding the conduct of the defence has been made less difficult by caselaw affirming a lawyer's ability to withdraw from the representation where the client rejects advice regarding an important matter of trial strategy.

We are thus witnessing a shift in perspective concerning the allocation of decision making authority in criminal cases. A more co-operative or client-centred model, which encourages mutual decision making involving the client and lawyer, is starting to gain traction as the preferable template for structuring the professional relationship.

B. DECISION MAKING AND THE RULES OF PROFESSIONAL CONDUCT

Most Canadian rules of professional conduct contain no direct reference to the locus of general decision making authority in the client-lawyer relationship. But many address the subject tangentially in dealing with other topics. The British Columbia rule setting out criminal defence counsel's obligation to put forward all available defences provides that this duty must be carried out "by all fair and honourable means and *in a manner consistent with the client's instructions.*"[1] A footnote to the New Brunswick rule on competence quotes an English text to the effect that incompetence may arise through "sheer disobedience to the client's instructions."[2] Many codes state that a lawyer should not waive a client's legal rights without the client's informed consent.[3] And several provide that a lawyer can only enter into an agreement with the prosecutor about a guilty plea where, among other things, the client has instructed him to do so.[4]

---

1   BC r 2.1-3(f) [emphasis added].
2   NB ch 2, commentary 1, n 1.
3   Alta, Sask 4.01(1) (commentary); BC, Man, Ont, NS, NL 5.1-1, commentary 7; CBA Code ch IX, commentary 7. To similar effect, see NB ch 8, commentary 8.
4   Alta, Sask 4.01(8); BC, Man, Ont, NS, NL 5.1-8; NB ch 8, commentary 15(a); CBA Code ch IX, commentary 13.

The Alberta code touches on the issue of decision making somewhat more directly in addressing the closely associated duty to obtain instructions from a client. Its basic rule states that "a lawyer must obtain instructions from the client on all matters not falling within the express or implied authority of the lawyer."[5] The commentary, while not particularly clear in defining which matters fall within counsel's express or implied authority, does shed some light on this difficult issue, stating in part:

> Assuming that there are no practical exigencies requiring a lawyer to act for a client without prior consultation, the lawyer must consider before each decision in a matter whether and to what extent the client should be consulted or informed. Even an apparently routine step that clearly falls within the lawyer's authority may warrant prior consultation, depending on circumstances such as a particular client's desire to be involved in the day to day conduct of a matter.
>
> . . . . In addition, certain decisions in litigation, such as how a criminal defendant will plead, whether a client will testify, whether to waive a jury trial and whether to appeal, require prior discussion with the client. As to other, less fundamental decisions, if there is any doubt in the lawyer's mind as to whether the client should be consulted, it is most prudent to do so.[6]

Similar to its Alberta counterpart, the Manitoba code provides that a lawyer must obtain the client's instructions based on informed and independent advice.[7] But its associated commentary arguably comes even closer to recognizing that it is the client, not the lawyer, who generally has the final say in determining how the matter is conducted:

> Lawyers provide legal services based upon the client's instructions. In order to provide appropriate instructions, the client should be fully and fairly informed. There may not be a need for the lawyer to obtain explicit instructions for every single step on a matter. Before taking steps, a lawyer should consider whether and to what extent the client should be consulted or informed. Fundamental decisions such as how to plead and what witnesses to call almost always require prior consultations. The same may not be so with less fundamental decisions. When in doubt, the lawyer should consult with the client.

---

5   Alta r 2.02(3).

6   Alta r 2.02(3) (commentary).

7   Man r 3.2-2A.

A lawyer should obtain instructions from the client on all matters not falling within the express or implied authority of the lawyer.[8]

In the United States, the major ethical codes devote more attention to the issue of decision making authority and offer several different approaches. The ABA Model Rules provide that a normal client-lawyer relationship is based on the assumption that the client, when properly advised and assisted, is capable of making decisions about important matters.[9] The model rules also state that the lawyer shall abide by the client's decisions concerning the *objectives* of the representation, provided the lawyer is not required to commit an illegal or unethical act.[10] The lawyer shall consult with the client regarding the *means* employed to achieve the desired objectives and may take such action as is impliedly authorized by the client.[11] Furthermore, in a criminal case the lawyer must honour the client's decision, after consultation with the lawyer, as to the plea to be entered, whether to waive a jury trial, and whether the client will testify.[12] The comments to the model rules do not prescribe how disputes between the client and lawyer are to be resolved but observe that where there is a fundamental disagreement, the lawyer may withdraw or be discharged.[13]

The ABA Defense Standards illustrate a different approach to the question, one that appears more robust in allocating decision making power to the lawyer:

Standard 4-5.2 Control and Direction of the Case

(a) Certain decisions relating to the conduct of the case are ultimately for the accused and others are ultimately for defense counsel. The decisions which are to be made by the accused after full consultation with counsel include:
   (i)   what pleas to enter;
   (ii)   whether to accept a plea agreement;
   (iii) whether to waive a jury trial;
   (iv)   whether to testify in his or her own behalf; and
   (v)   whether to appeal.
(b) Strategic and tactical decisions should be made by defense counsel after consultation with the client where feasible and appropriate. Such decisions include what witnesses to call, whether

8   Man r 3.2-2A, commentary 1.
9   ABA Model Rule 1.14, comment 1.
10   ABA Model Rule 1.2(a).
11   *Ibid.*
12   *Ibid.*
13   ABA Model Rule 1.2, comment 2.

and how to conduct cross-examination, what jurors to accept or strike, what trial motions should be made, and what evidence should be introduced.

(c) If a disagreement on significant matters of tactics or strategy arises between defense counsel and the client, defence counsel should make a record of the circumstances, counsel's advice and reasons, and the conclusion reached. The record should be made in a manner which protects the confidentiality of the lawyer-client relationship.

The ABA Defense Standards can be read as providing the lawyer with final say over all matters of strategy and tactics, while confining the client's decision making authority to the five areas listed in standard 4-5.2(a).

The Third Restatement shows less affinity for the lawyer-control model. After one works through the meaning of several interlocking provisions, there remains little doubt that, in the case of disagreement, the client has the final say on almost all matters concerning the representation, and the lawyer must follow the client's instructions.[14] Only where the instructions require conduct that counsel reasonably believes to be illegal or unethical, or would intrude on counsel's ability to make immediate decisions during the course of a trial where there is no time for consultation, can a lawyer refuse to comply with a client's wishes.[15] The Third Restatement also promotes the idea that a client and lawyer can agree on the division of decision making responsibility best suited to the circumstances of the case[16] and recognizes that there are some matters on which the lawyer has implied decision making authority, absent instructions to the contrary from the client.[17]

C. CANADIAN CASELAW AND COMMENTARY ON DECISION MAKING AUTHORITY

Just as the various ethical codes reveal diverse approaches to the decision making process, so have Canadian judges and commentators endorsed a range of options. But the dominant view, at least where the representation of a criminal accused is concerned, flows primarily from the opinions of the late G Arthur Martin. Forty-five years ago,

---

14   Third Restatement § 20–24.
15   Third Restatement § 23.
16   Third Restatement § 21(1).
17   Third Restatement § 21, comment "e."

this distinguished criminal practitioner, and soon to be court of appeal judge, endorsed a staunch lawyer-control model, ascribing to the lawyer a very substantial licence to conduct the client's defence as she sees fit.[18] Martin's handling of the issue has had a profound influence on subsequent commentators and the caselaw, especially in Ontario. It is thus apposite to look at his position more closely.

1) Martin's Lawyer-Control Model

To begin with, Martin set out the sensible proposition that a lawyer's function extends far beyond the simplistic role of unquestioningly carrying out all of the client's wishes. Rather, he stated, in a much-quoted passage, that "defence counsel is not the *alter ego* of the client. The function of defence counsel is to provide professional assistance and advice. He must, accordingly, exercise his professional skill and judgment in the conduct of the case and not allow himself to be a mere mouthpiece for the client."[19] Among other things, rejecting the "mere mouthpiece" role requires that a lawyer become fully familiar with the law and facts pertaining to the case and advise the client accordingly as to the best course of action. It also supports the notion that a lawyer cannot justify illegal or otherwise unethical conduct on the fallacious reasoning that she is acting pursuant to the client's instructions.

Yet Martin went considerably beyond a simple rejection of the "mere mouthpiece" role for defence counsel. He additionally stipulated that a lawyer must have absolute control over the conduct of the case, with quite limited exceptions, and believed that the lawyer should be permitted to override the client's express instructions on almost any matter. For support, he drew on an analogy with a surgeon and patient: the surgeon cannot possibly take instructions from a patient as to how an operation should be performed, and so the lawyer must similarly be able to reject the client's directions in conducting a criminal defence.[20]

---

18   G Arthur Martin, "The Role and Responsibility of the Defence Advocate" (1969) 12 Crim LQ 376 [Martin, "Role and Responsibility"]. Martin expressed similar views in "Panel Discussion: Problems in Advocacy and Ethics" in Law Society of Upper Canada, *Defending a Criminal Case* (Toronto: R De Boo, 1969) 279 at 282–86 [Martin, "Panel Discussion"].

19   Martin, "Role and Responsibility," above note 18 at 382.

20   *Ibid* at 383, borrowing in part from American Bar Association, Advisory Committee on the Prosecution and Defense Functions, *Tentative Draft Standards Relating to the Prosecution Function and the Defense Function* (Chicago: ABA, 1970) [ABA, *Tentative Draft Standards*].

This analogy holds an easy charm, but its potency evaporates once one considers several counter-arguments. First, a surgeon surely has no right to proceed with an operation against the patient's wishes, even if those wishes relate to the mechanics of the procedure and are clearly ill-advised. Current ethical rules for doctors preclude imposing treatment against a patient's wishes, full stop, and draw no exception for cases where the patient disagrees only as to how the operation should be performed.[21] Second, the patient may desire treatment options that while reasonable, are not favoured by the surgeon. Should the patient's wishes be ignored? Once again, the medical profession has adopted guidelines that generally defer to the patient's wishes.[22] While a surgeon cannot conduct an operation in an incompetent manner simply because the patient has so instructed, the surgeon-patient analogy falls short of persuasively advancing Martin's lawyer-control model.

Martin also relied on legal precedent for his position, in particular the decision of the House of Lords in *Rondel v Worsley*.[23] In that famous case, the plaintiff sued his criminal counsel for negligence arising out of the conduct of the defence to a charge of grievous bodily harm. The impugned actions included failing to re-examine a defence witness, to cross-examine two prosecution witnesses regarding the nature of the injury, and to call certain defence witnesses. The House of Lords ruled that a barrister has absolute immunity from an action for negligence arising out of the conduct of a case at trial. In coming to this conclusion, several of the judges endorsed the view that a barrister must be accorded total control in the conduct of the defence. To a certain extent, this endorsement represented the uncontroversial recognition that counsel cannot violate the rules of professional conduct at the client's behest.[24] However, at other points in the judgment, the law lords left no doubt that the barrister who acts in the good-faith belief that the client's best interests require certain actions is under no duty to follow his client's instructions to the contrary.[25] The only exceptions to this

---

21 Canadian Medical Association, *Code of Ethics* (Ottawa: Canadian Medical Association, 2004) at para 24: "Respect the right of a competent patient to accept or reject any medical care recommended."

22 *Ibid.*

23 [1967] 3 All ER 993 (HL) [*Rondel*].

24 *Ibid* at 998 ("G"–"H"), Lord Reid; 1011 ("E"), Lord Morris; 1027 ("I"), Lord Pearce; and 1034–35, Lord Upjohn.

25 *Ibid* at 999 ("C"–"D"), Lord Reid; 1011 ("F"–"G"); 1013 ("H"), Lord Morris; 1016 and 1027–28, Lord Pearce; 1034, Lord Upjohn; and 1039–41, Lord Pearson.

general rule appeared to be that the client had the final say in deciding how to plead[26] and whether to testify in his defence.[27]

Martin seized on the sentiments expressed in *Rondel v Worsley* to conclude that "a Canadian lawyer has the same right and duty to exercise his or her own judgment and discretion as the English barrister with respect to his conduct of a case in court."[28] Indeed, Martin went so far as to approve the view, expressed in an older Scottish case, that an advocate's "legal right is to conduct the cause without any regard to the wishes of the client, so long as his mandate is unrecalled."[29]

This perspective leads, not surprisingly, to the conclusion that the lawyer, not the client, makes virtually all decisions concerning the case, including what witnesses to call, whether a witness should be cross-examined, and if so how.[30] Martin left the client with the final say regarding only the decisions how to plead, whether to have a jury trial, and whether to testify, ostensibly because these areas involve fundamental rights.[31] He nonetheless recognized that the client could always fire a lawyer who refused to accept instructions on any matter and that the lawyer could withdraw from the case where disagreement led to a complete breakdown in the professional relationship.[32]

2) Canadian Commentary and Caselaw Supporting Martin's Model

Martin's views were by no means novel at the time he expressed them.[33] The same points were to be found in the proposed first edition of the ABA Defense Standards.[34] As we move ahead four decades, Martin's lawyer-control approach remains fashionable in Canada. Several text writers generally adhere to his position, or at least reiterate it without

---

26   *Ibid* at 1033 ("F"), Lord Upjohn.
27   *Ibid* at 1013 ("D"), Lord Morris.
28   Martin, "Role and Responsibility," above note 18 at 385.
29   *Batchelor v Pattison and Mackersy* (1876), 3 R 914 at 918 (Sess).
30   Martin, "Role and Responsibility," above note 18 at 386.
31   *Ibid* at 386–88. On an earlier occasion, Martin allocated final decision making power to counsel on all matters except how to plead: see Martin, "Panel Discussion," above note 18 at 283.
32   Martin, "Role and Responsibility," above note 18 at 384 and 387.
33   See, for example, *R v MacTemple* (1935), 64 CCC 11 (Ont CA); *Judson v McQuain* (1923), 53 OLR 348 (CA); *Wilson v Huron & Bruce (United Counties)* (1861), 11 UCCP 548.
34   See ABA, *Tentative Draft Standards*, above note 20 at 174, referred to by Martin, "Role and Responsibility," above note 18 at 382–83.

adverse comment.[35] The bulk of judicial authority embraces the idea that defence counsel, and not the accused, controls most aspects of the case, and sometimes even suggests, as did Martin, that counsel can override a client's instructions on most matters without violating any ethical principles.[36] And the main exceptions to this general rule are seen to be those areas identified by Martin as fundamental to the client's defence, namely, whether to plead guilty, whether to have a jury trial, and whether to testify.[37] The dominant view is thus as described in 2006 by the Ontario Chief Justice's Advisory Committee

35 Allan Hutchinson, *Legal Ethics and Professional Responsibility*, 2d ed (Toronto: Irwin Law, 2006) at 102; Gavin MacKenzie, *Lawyers and Ethics: Professional Responsibility and Discipline*, loose-leaf (Scarborough, ON: Carswell, 1993) (March 2013 supplement) §§ 4.11 and 4-23–24; Beverley G Smith, *Professional Conduct for Lawyers and Judges*, 4th ed (Fredericton, NB: Maritime Law Book, 2011) ch 7 at para 15. *Contra* Alice Woolley, *Understanding Lawyers' Ethics in Canada* (Markham, ON: LexisNexis, 2011) at 54–59; Frank Hoskins, "The Players of a Criminal Trial" in Joel Pink & David Perrier, eds, *From Crime to Punishment: An Introduction to the Criminal Justice System*, 7th ed (Toronto: Thomson Carswell, 2010) 197 at 205; Mark M Orkin, *Legal Ethics*, 2d ed (Toronto: Canada Law Book, 2011) at 95.

36 *Sherman v Manley* (1978), 19 OR (2d) 531 at 534 [para 12] (Ont CA) [*Sherman*], leave to appeal to SCC refused (1978), 19 OR (2d) 531n (SCC); *R v R(AJ)* (1994), 94 CCC (3d) 168 at 180 [para 38] (Ont CA); *R v White* (1997), 114 CCC (3d) 225 at 253 [para 90] (Ont CA) [*White*], leave to appeal to SCC refused, [1997] SCCA No 248; *R v Samra* (1998), 129 CCC (3d) 144 at paras 31–33 (Ont CA) [*Samra*], leave to appeal to SCC refused, [1998] SCCA No 558; *R v DiPalma*, [2002] OJ No 2684 at para 38 (CA) [*DiPalma*]; *Stewart v Canadian Broadcasting Corp* (1997), 150 DLR (4th) 24 at 83–88 [paras 139–51] (Ont Ct Gen Div) [*Stewart*]; *R v Downey*, [2002] OJ No 1524 at para 89 (SCJ) [*Downey*]; *R v Furtado* (2006), 43 CR (6th) 305 at para 74(25) (Ont SCJ); *Law Society of Upper Canada v De Teresi*, [2009] OJ No 582 at para 26 (SCJ); *R v Curnew*, 2010 ONCA 764 at para 25; *R v Faulkner*, 2013 ONSC 2373 at paras 39–47 [*Faulkner*]; *R v Moore*, 2002 SKCA 30 at para 48 [*Moore*]; *R v Strauss* (1995), 100 CCC (3d) 303 at para 48 (BCCA); *Wenn v Goyer*, [1986] BCJ No 822 at para 20 (SC) [*Wenn*]; *R v Blair*, 2001 BCCA 441 at para 8.

37 Regarding the decision how to plead, see *R v Lamoureux* (1984), 13 CCC (3d) 101 at 105 [para 24] (Que CA); *R v Prosser*, [1980] 3 WWR 499 at 501 [paras 5–7] (Sask Dist Ct); *R v GDB*, 2000 SCC 22 at para 34 [*GDB*]; *R v DMG*, 2011 ONCA 343 at para 109 [*DMG*]. Also of interest is *R v Loi*, 2013 ONSC 1202 at para 72: a decision to concede criminal liability is akin to a guilty plea and so must be made by the client. Regarding the decision whether to testify, see *R v Smith* (1997), 120 CCC (3d) 500 at paras 13–16 and 26 (Ont CA) [*Smith*]; *R v Archer* (2005), 202 CCC (3d) 60 at para 139 (Ont CA) [*Archer*]; *R v Eroma*, 2013 ONCA 194 at para 8; *GDB*, above in this note at para 34; *R v Dunbar*, 2003 BCCA 667 at para 126 [*Dunbar*]; *R v Brigham* (1992), 79 CCC (3d) 365 at 380"f"–83"g" (Que CA) [*Brigham*]; *R v Delisle* (1999), 133 CCC (3d) 541 at 555–57 [paras 47–55] (Que CA) [*Delisle*]; *Moore*, above note 36 at para 48.

on Criminal Trials: "Defence counsel must control the conduct of the defence, and must not cede that obligation to the accused. With the exceptions of the matters listed above [i.e., how to plead, whether to have a jury trial, and whether to testify], it is for defence counsel to determine how the defence is conducted."[38]

Practice pointer: In closing to the jury, defence counsel have been known to suggest that they and not the client made the decision not to testify, in an attempt to foreclose the jury from drawing an adverse inference from the client's failure to take the stand.[39] Such a comment is improper for two reasons.[40] First, the decision to testify belongs to the client, not counsel. Second, the basis for the decision is irrelevant to the trier of fact's deliberations and, in any event, is not before the jury in the form of admissible evidence.[41]

3) Different Lines of Canadian Judicial Authority

As we have just seen, Martin's decision making model finds support in the jurisprudence and commentary in this country. A similar model appears to dominate in America.[42] Yet several lines of Canadian legal authority run counter to the notion that a lawyer's control over the case extends so far as to permit her to ignore and override a client's instructions in conducting the defence.

To begin with, cases addressing an accused's constitutional right to the effective assistance of counsel recognize, whether explicitly or implicitly, that in conducting a case, defence counsel must conform to

---

38   Ontario, Chief Justice's Advisory Committee on Criminal Trials in the Superior Court of Justice, *New Approaches to Criminal Trials* (Toronto: Superior Court of Justice, 2006) at para 136, online: www.ontariocourts.ca/scj/news/publications/ctr/.

39   The jury is of course precluded from drawing this inference: see *R v Noble* (1997), 114 CCC (3d) 385 (SCC).

40   *Smith*, above note 37 at paras 13–16 and 26; *Archer*, above note 37 at paras 91–99 and 150.

41   Regarding this latter point, see also *R v Tomlinson*, 2014 ONCA 158 at paras 85–103.

42   See the cases cited in Erica Hashimoto, "Resurrecting Autonomy: The Criminal Defendant's Right to Control the Case" (2010) 90 BU L Rev 1147 at 1158–62; Anne Poulin, "Strengthening the Criminal Defendant's Right to Counsel" (2006–7) 28 Cardozo L Rev 1213 at 1239–46; Rodney Uphoff, "Who Should Control the Decision to Call a Witness: Respecting a Criminal Defendant's Tactical Choices?" (1999) 68 U Cin L Rev 763 at 778–95. However, as all three articles note, a number of American cases have taken a view more in line with the co-operative or client-centred model of decision making.

reasonable professional standards, including the exercise of reasonable skill and judgment in the best interests of the client.[43] It follows that overriding a client's instructions so as to conduct the case in an unreasonable manner can never be countenanced and will lead to a conviction's being overturned where the client suffers prejudice as a result. This is so regardless of whether counsel's incompetence relates to the fundamental decisions of how to plead, whether to have a jury trial, and whether to testify.

Somewhat similarly, Canadian law permits a client to sue his lawyer civilly for the negligent conduct of a criminal defence.[44] Our courts have never endorsed the rule of absolute immunity from civil suit that until relatively recently protected criminal barristers in England.[45] Granted, there are significant potential obstacles on the plaintiff's road to success, including the reluctance of courts to find a lawyer liable for "a mere error in judgment."[46] Nonetheless, the existence of a standard of negligence against which the conduct of a criminal trial lawyer can be measured provides some support for the argument that ethical rules should not accord a lawyer absolute power over most decisions made while conducting the defence.

Of course, a contemporary proponent of the lawyer-control model would readily accept that counsel must never conduct the case incompetently or negligently. But there is a further line of authority that clashes more directly with Martin's approach to decision making. It begins with the 1991 decision of *R v Swain*, in which the Supreme Court of Canada held that the Crown should not be permitted to raise the defence of not criminally responsible by reason of mental disorder (NCRMD) against the accused's wishes at the conviction stage of a criminal proceeding.[47] While not directly addressing the issue of whether defence counsel can ever override a client's instructions, *Swain* emphasizes the fundamental

---

43   See, for example, *Stewart*, above note 36 at 87–88 [paras 149–51]; *White*, above note 36 at 247 [para 64]. See also Section K(1), below in this chapter.

44   *Folland v Reardon* (2005), 74 OR (3d) 688 (CA) [*Folland*]; *Fischer v Halyk*, 2003 SKCA 71, leave to appeal to SCC refused, [2003] SCCA No 421 [*Fischer*]; *Michaud v Brodsky*, 2008 MBCA 67; *Meister v Coyle*, 2011 NSCA 119; *Lawrence v Banks*, 2002 BCSC 547; *Paquet v Getty*, 2002 NBQB 272.

45   *Demarco v Ungaro* (1979), 21 OR (2d) 673 (HCJ) [*Demarco*]; *Amato v Welsh*, 2013 ONCA 258 at para 49; *Fischer*, above note 44 at para 19. This English rule was abolished in *Arthur JS Hall & Co v Simons*, [2000] 3 All ER 673 (HL).

46   *Demarco*, above note 45 at 693. Rather, a plaintiff must show that counsel failed to live up to the standard of a reasonably competent lawyer in a criminal proceeding: *Folland*, above note 44 at paras 35–45.

47   (1991), 63 CCC (3d) 481 (SCC) [*Swain*].

importance of allowing an accused control over her own defence.[48] The reasoning in *Swain*, based on respect for the autonomy, dignity, and intrinsic value of all individuals, including those charged with crimes, seems at odds with a decision making model under which the lawyer can reject the client's instructions regarding most aspects of the defence.

What is more, *Swain* specifies that the accused's right to control the conduct of the defence includes not only the decisions whether to have counsel and whether to testify but also the determination as to what witnesses to call.[49] Extending the right of control to decisions whether to call witnesses goes further than the traditional lawyer-control approach. So too does *Swain*'s holding that an accused must have control over the decision whether a certain defence should be relied on.[50] Indeed, the year after *Swain* was decided, the Ontario Court of Appeal relied on it to affirm "the fundamental principle that an accused is entitled to choose his own defence and to present it as he chooses . . . even if this means that the accused may act to his own detriment in doing so."[51] The accused's autonomy in the adversarial justice system, said the court, requires that he be permitted to make such fundamental decisions and assume the risks involved.[52]

Also important in supporting a less paternalistic model of decision making is the Quebec Court of Appeal's decision in *R v Delisle*.[53] There, defence counsel refused to investigate or call as a witness an individual regarded by the accused as the true culprit in a serious assault and also declined to call the accused in his own defence. Simply put, the lawyer did not believe his client and conducted the case accordingly, albeit contrary to the client's instructions. The accused was convicted. On appeal, information from the individual allegedly responsible for the assault was introduced as fresh evidence.

Justice Proulx agreed that a lawyer is not the mere mouthpiece of the client.[54] But he was unprepared to grant defence lawyers the power to run cases in defiance of their clients' instructions. He instead held that a lawyer, while under a duty to provide competent advice, including a duty to attempt to dissuade a client from making a rash decision,

---

48   *Ibid* at 505–6 [paras 33–36].
49   *Ibid* at 505–6 [para 36]. See also Man r 3.2-2A, commentary 1: lawyers provide legal services based on instructions from client, and fundamental decisions such as what witnesses to call will almost always require prior consultation.
50   *Swain*, above note 47 at 505–6 [para 36].
51   *R v Taylor* (1992), 77 CCC (3d) 551 at 567 [para 51] (Ont CA) [*Taylor*].
52   *Ibid*.
53   Above note 37.
54   *Ibid* at 555 [para 47].

must not disregard the client's instructions on an important matter.[55] Where the disagreement is irresolvable, the lawyer must withdraw from the case, not ignore the client's wishes and proceed as the lawyer thinks best.[56] Not surprisingly, the appeal was allowed on the grounds that trial counsel failed to provide effective legal assistance, to the appellant's prejudice, by neglecting to investigate the potential witness and refusing to call the client to the stand.[57]

A final judgment of note on this topic is *R v Szostak*,[58] in which the appellant complained that his counsel raised the NCRMD defence without first obtaining instructions. Relying on *Swain*, the Ontario Court of Appeal held that an accused's right to control his own defence precluded counsel from raising NCRMD without the client's consent or, worse yet, over the client's objections.[59] *Szostak* accepts that the autonomy and dignity of the accused in the adversarial justice system require that he, not counsel, have final say over decisions that are fundamental to the conduct of the case, including not only how to plead or whether to testify but also whether to rely on a particular defence or excuse. The fact that some clients may make poor choices, despite the advice of counsel, does not justify arrogating the decision making power to the lawyer. To paraphrase Rosenberg J, writing for the court, accused persons have the right to act against their best interests in determining how the defence should be conducted, and it is not for defence counsel, no matter how well intentioned, to pursue a course of action regarding a matter fundamental to the defence without proper instructions.[60]

Example 1: Trial counsel overrides his client's instructions that two defence witnesses be called in the belief that he, and not the client, has the ultimate power to decide whether to call a witness. Defence counsel's tactical decision is not unreasonable. Neither, however, is the client's view. Applying a co-operative model of decision making derived from the principles in *Swain*, counsel has acted unethically in overriding his client's instructions. Having failed to convince his client of the

---

55 *Ibid* at 555 [para 48].
56 *Ibid*. A similar approach is taken in *R v McLoughlin*, [1985] 1 NZLR 106 (CA) [*McLoughlin*], and *R v Walling*, [2006] NZCA 39. See also *Brigham*, above note 37 at 380"h"–83"g"; *Downey*, above note 36 at para 89; *R v West*, 2010 NSCA 16 at para 281 [*West*].
57 *Delisle*, above note 37 at 557 [para 55].
58 2012 ONCA 503 [*Szostak*].
59 *Ibid* at paras 77–78 (citing the first edition of this book).
60 *Ibid* at paras 78 and 80.

merits of not calling the witnesses, counsel should have either carried out the client's instructions or applied to withdraw from the record.[61]

Example 2: A client charged with a bank robbery proffers various inconsistent and fanciful explanations to counsel as to why blood with a DNA profile matching his own was found beside a hole that the perpetrators had cut in the wall to enter the bank. Counsel refuses to investigate these theories and strongly and repeatedly advises the client as to the follies of his theories of the case. Once it becomes clear the client will not abandon his theories, counsel has no choice but to withdraw from the representation. To continue with the defence in defiance of the client's instructions, though undoubtedly in the client's best interests, is not an ethical option.[62]

4) Withdrawal and the Decision in *R v Cunningham*

The co-operative model of decision making stipulates that in the event of an irreconcilable disagreement between client and counsel as to the conduct of the defence, the proper course for counsel is to withdraw, not to override the client's instructions. Getting off the record in such circumstances finds support in the Supreme Court of Canada's decision in *R v Cunningham*, which provides that counsel can apply to withdraw for "ethical reasons" where, among other things, a client refuses to accept counsel's advice on an important trial matter.[63] *Cunningham* further holds that the trial judge must grant a request to withdraw for ethical reasons and is precluded from making further inquires into the basis for such a request.[64]

5) The Decision in *R v GDB*

Another important contribution to the debate regarding counsel's decision making authority comes from the Supreme Court of Canada's judgment in *R v GDB*.[65] The appellant had been charged with committing sexual and indecent assaults on his adopted daughter. Before the trial he provided his lawyer with a taped recording of the complainant in which she denied the allegations during a conversation with her

---

61   The facts and analysis come from *R v Abada*, 2011 ONSC 2803 [*Abada*].
62   The facts and, for the most part, the analysis come from *West*, above note 56 at paras 262–81.
63   2010 SCC 10 at para 48 [*Cunningham*].
64   *Ibid* at paras 48–49. For more detail, see Chapter 11, Section L(4)(a).
65   Above note 37.

mother, the appellant's wife. However, for tactical reasons counsel decided not to play the tape in cross-examining the complainant. The appellant was convicted on two of three counts. On appeal he alleged that counsel's decision not to utilize the tape was made contrary to his express instructions and represented a denial of the effective assistance of counsel.

In dismissing the appeal, Major J made several points that relate to our discussion. First, he noted that the constitutional standard for the effective assistance of counsel is not the exact equivalent of a lawyer's ethical obligations. Rather, "the question of the competence of counsel is usually a matter of professional ethics and is not a question for the appellate courts to consider."[66] In particular, if the client suffers no prejudice, the performance of counsel becomes irrelevant on appeal, and any concerns are left to the profession's self-governing body.[67] Second, Major J felt that the lawyer's decision not to use the tape was reasonable. In fact, counsel had probably taken the best course of action, because aspects of the tape potentially undermined the credibility of the appellant's wife, who was the key defence witness, and because the complainant's denial of abuse was arguably coerced.[68]

Third, the appellant posited that even if the decision of trial counsel was entirely reasonable, there was nonetheless an obligation to inform the appellant of the decision not to use the tape and accord him an opportunity to take part in the decision. However, Major J expressly refused to determine whether defence counsel had such a duty. Instead, the finding that the lawyer's decision was tactically sound meant the appellant had not been denied the effective assistance of counsel. If any issue regarding the need to obtain the client's consent arose, it properly fell within the realm of professional conduct governed by the Law Society of Alberta based on prevailing ethical standards.[69] Justice Major nonetheless went on to observe:

> While it is not the case that defence lawyers must always obtain express approval for each and every decision made by them in relation to the conduct of the defence, there are decisions such as whether or not to plead guilty, or whether or not to testify that defence counsel are ethically bound to discuss with the client and regarding which they must obtain instructions. The failure to do so may in some cir-

---

66   *Ibid* at para 5.
67   *Ibid* at paras 28–29.
68   *Ibid* at paras 31–32 and 39–40.
69   *Ibid* at para 33.

cumstances raise questions of procedural fairness and the reliability of the result leading to a miscarriage of justice.

On the facts of this case, I conclude that counsel had the carriage of the defence and the implied authority to make tactical decisions, as the ones made here, in the best interests of the client. In any event, the failure to obtain specific instructions did not affect the outcome of the trial. There was no miscarriage of justice.[70]

GDB thus directly comments on the substance of a lawyer's ethical obligations, albeit in *obiter*. In particular, the decision recognizes that counsel has the implied authority to make tactical decisions, but not decisions on certain issues such as how to plead and whether to testify. The judgment does not, however, hold that counsel's implied authority in the tactical realm allows her to override a client's express instructions on a so-called tactical matter. Indeed, Major J's comment in the penultimate sentence of the quotation above suggests that the appellant while uncomfortable with not using the tape to cross-examine did not specifically instruct counsel to do so.[71] Accordingly, *GDB* should not be read as giving lawyers ethical licence to conduct the defence in contravention of the client's express instructions on tactical matters.

D. RE-EVALUATING THE TRADITIONAL LAWYER-CONTROL APPROACH

Given that the conventional lawyer-control model, as described by G Arthur Martin, still holds considerable sway within the culture of Canadian criminal lawyers, it is worth examining the underlying justifications for this approach.

1) Justifications for the Traditional Lawyer-Control Approach

Many arguments have been put forth to justify allocating an untrammelled decision making power to the lawyer on most strategic and tactical matters involving the conduct of the defence. First, it is sometimes said that the lawyer's experience and learning in the complexities of the

---

70   *Ibid* at paras 34–35.
71   Compare *Florida v Nixon*, 543 US 175 at 193 (2004): client unresponsive when consulted about an important trial matter; right to effective assistance not undermined by counsel pursuing a best-interests strategy despite lack of express client consent.

law and the procedures of a criminal trial are all but incomprehensible to the average accused person, at least absent an impractical amount of study and learning.[72] Allowing a lawyer the freedom to conduct the case as he thinks fit thus results in a better defence and promotes a fair and just result,[73] which not only inures to the benefit of the accused but furthers society's interest in avoiding wrongful convictions.[74] Second, decisions must frequently be made on the spur of the moment during a trial, without time for the niceties of consultation with the client.[75] Counsel is well equipped to make such snap decisions, and her performance will be hampered if client input is constantly required. Third, some contend that the lawyer is more objective and less emotionally involved than the client, and hence better able to arrive at the best decision respecting the means of conducting the case. Fourth, it is said that carrying out an unsound tactical or strategic course of action at the client's insistence may leave the lawyer open to a later claim in negligence[76] or provide the basis for an allegation of ineffective assistance from counsel on appeal.[77] Fifth, acceding to the client's wishes may prolong the trial process unnecessarily, and hence prove costly and time-consuming, to the detriment of the administration of justice.[78] Sixth, the lawyer owes duties to the administration of justice that prohibit the use of certain tactics in conducting the case, despite the instructions of the client to the contrary.[79] For instance, the lawyer cannot accept a client's direction to mislead the court. Seventh, the lawyer-control model obligates the lawyer to provide the client with information and advice, provided circumstances reasonably permit the time to do so.[80] Accordingly, although the lawyer holds the ultimate decision making authority on most matters, it would be wrong to suggest that the client's views are totally ignored or that the client is not informed about material developments. As noted by the Ontario Chief Justice's Advisory Committee on Criminal Trials, after setting out the general proposition

---

72 *United States v Boyd*, 86 F3d 719 at 723 (7th Cir 1996); ABA Defense Standard 4-5.2, comment.

73 *Rondel*, above note 23 at 1028, Lord Pearce.

74 Christopher Johnson, "The Law's Hard Choice: Self-Inflicted Injustice or Lawyer-Inflicted Indignity" (2004-5) 93 Ky LJ 39 at 132–39.

75 *Stewart*, above note 36 at 87 [para 149]; *Faulkner*, above note 36 at para 47.

76 *Rondel*, above note 23 at 1013, Lord Morris; Hutchinson, above note 35 at 102.

77 See Section K, below in this chapter.

78 *Rondel*, above note 23 at 1028, Lord Pearce. This concern is central to the analysis in *New Approaches to Criminal Trials*, above note 38 at paras 35, 62–63, and 118–40.

79 See Section J, below in this chapter.

80 Martin, "Panel Discussion," above note 18 at 284.

of lawyer-control, "This is not to suggest that the accused is to be kept in the dark regarding trial tactics. There is a fundamental distinction between abdicating the role of counsel to the accused on one hand, and on the other hand receiving input from the client and telling him or her about tactical decisions counsel have made."[81] Counsel who combines the lawyer-control model with timely and clear communication with the client and a real respect for the client's opinion will thus minimize the possibility of substantial disagreement concerning the conduct of the defence.

A final point to make in support of the lawyer-control model is that the client is far from helpless if truly dead set against counsel's proposed conduct of the case. The client can always discharge counsel and either retain a new lawyer or proceed with the trial as a self-represented accused.[82]

2) Questioning the Justifications

Some of the justifications for a lawyer-control model are unconvincing or at least overstated. In particular, the notion that a client can never hope to understand the basic process of a criminal matter is suspect. It is more likely that some lawyers do not take the proper time to explain the workings of the system, or care little for the client's views. In any event, in the huge preponderance of cases, the client trusts criminal counsel's expertise and judgment and so accepts his advice. There is no reason to believe that assigning final decision making authority to clients on a broader range of matters will lead them to adopt imprudent strategies that increase the risk of unreliable results and unduly strain scarce systemic resources.

If we are to take seriously the principles of individual autonomy and dignity articulated in *Swain* and its progeny, affording the client considerable decision making power is paramount.[83] After all, it is the

---

81   *New Approaches to Criminal Trials*, above note 38 at para 137. See also ABA Defense Standard 4-5.2(b): counsel should make decisions "after consultation with the client where feasible and appropriate."

82   See, for example, *R v LRF*, 2007 NSCA 32 at paras 137–41: lawyers were discharged after refusing to raise futile and improper matters at clients' insistence. See also Chapter 11, Section D.

83   This position is strongly argued by Monroe Freedman & Abbe Smith, *Understanding Lawyers' Ethics*, 4th ed (New Providence, NJ: LexisNexis, 2010) at § 3.07; and Hashimoto, above note 42; and it is also generally supported by Uphoff, above note 42. Uphoff nonetheless accepts overriding a client's decision as a last resort in limited circumstances, such as where a client of low intelligence insists on a foolhardy approach that will do her serious harm.

client who risks stigma and punishment if convicted. To withhold decision making authority from the client thus represents misguided paternalism. In this vein, one wonders whether the continued persistence of the traditional lawyer-control model today is attributable as much as anything to the relative powerlessness of most criminal accused.

There are other reasons to look askance at the traditional lawyer-control model. Consider, for instance, that where the lawyer conducts a defence contrary to the client's instructions, the result may be to disclose confidential information. Calling a witness against the client's wishes where the existence of the witness comes to the lawyer's attention only because of the professional relationship breaches the duty of confidentiality. Cross-examining a Crown witness on a sensitive matter contrary to the client's wishes will have the same effect. There is no recognized exception to the rule of confidentiality that applies merely because the lawyer in good faith believes disclosure is in the best interests of the client. Accordingly, the duty of confidentiality militates against an unrefined lawyer-control model of representation.

Additionally, a client may have broad and diverse objectives that go beyond simply avoiding a conviction or minimizing a court-imposed punishment. Maybe the client has political aims that would benefit from a full-blown trial and is not interested in bringing a pre-trial motion that might circumvent the entire process. Or perhaps the client desires to bring a non-frivolous pre-trial motion to exclude evidence partly as a means of exposing police misconduct even though the chances of success are modest. Consider also the client who refuses to call a helpful witness because he wishes to spare that individual's privacy or who declines to attack a third party as a possible culprit out of a sense of loyalty to that person. From the lawyer's perspective, implementing these objectives may be misguided or harm the prospects of an acquittal. Yet are such goals improper or totally irrelevant to the representation? Not, we believe, if one takes the autonomy and dignity of the client seriously.

Of course, many of the concerns used to justify a lawyer-control model are far from specious. Yet, as described immediately below, they can be accommodated without ascribing final and overriding decision making power to the lawyer in the realm of strategy and tactics.

3) Updating the Traditional Approach: Increasing Client Involvement

We believe that the lawyer-control model as traditionally envisaged should be updated to reflect the fiduciary nature of the professional relationship and to give greater credence to the client's autonomy, free will, and decision making abilities. A more nuanced approach is required, what we have called a co-operative or client-centred model. A central feature of this model is the unimpeded exchange of information between client and lawyer, and a mutual trust and joint responsibility for a great deal of the decision making. The lawyer, having arrived at a complete understanding of the facts and law, must provide the client with competent advice. Counsel can recommend that the client make a particular decision, provided she does not overwhelm the client's freedom of choice. Approaching decision making in this manner empowers the autonomy and dignity of both client and lawyer and promotes a full and free exchange of information and dialogue that leads to decisions most favourable to the client's goals.

Adopting a co-operative model is not always easy. Lawyers may have difficulty communicating technical information to clients in simple, easily understood language. The lawyer's patience may be tested on occasion. Lawyers must also resist the temptation to frame issues or disclose information in a way that unfairly presents their preferred option in the best light. Problems can also arise where a client feels paralyzed by the predicament of criminal charges and seeks comfort by abdicating responsibility for making important decisions. Finally, the co-operative model can be time-consuming on occasion, given its strong emphasis on informing and consulting with the client.

These potential difficulties cannot be ignored. Yet the current trend among proponents of the lawyer-control model is to accept that counsel must communicate with the client and seek his input regarding many matters material to the conduct of the defence.[84] Much if not most of the client-lawyer interaction will thus be the same under both models. Moreover, the co-operative model recognizes that a normal client-lawyer relationship will provide the lawyer with implied authority to make many decisions[85] and permits clients and lawyers to allocate decision making responsibility regarding many matters by agreement.[86] The model also allows that in some instances the flow of a trial mandates that the lawyer make snap decisions without first consulting with the client.[87] Furthermore, co-operative lawyering supports counsel's advising a client in strong terms as to the best course of action regarding a particular decision.[88] As Professors Freedman and Smith sagely note,

---

84   See the text associated with notes 80–81, above in this chapter.
85   See Section H, below in this chapter.
86   See Section G, below in this chapter.
87   See Section I, below in this chapter.
88   See Section E(1), below in this chapter.

"being client-centered does not mean meekly deferring to a client's initial wishes. Forceful and sometimes psychologically sophisticated counseling is part of client-centered representation, at least when the client seems determined to take a ruinous path."[89]

Of course, no amount of good-faith communication and comprehensive preparation by the lawyer can avoid the occasional dispute with a client as to the proper conduct of a defence. Where the disagreement is intractable, the following guidelines may be helpful:

1) The client can terminate the retainer at any time, and if this step is taken, the lawyer has no choice but to get off the record.[90]

2) The lawyer must never accept instructions that require illegal or unethical action,[91] for example to mount a frivolous argument[92] or to conduct an incompetent defence.[93]

3) Counsel must not conduct the defence contrary to the client's instructions. If counsel is unable or unwilling to comply with those instructions, the proper course is to withdraw from the retainer,[94] applying to the court for permission where appropriate.[95] A court will always grant leave where the application is made for "ethical reasons," which include situations where the client insists that counsel act unethically or has rejected counsel's advice on an important matter of trial strategy.[96]

4) Counsel should be slow to withdraw where the client's instructions are not unreasonable. In such cases, counsel should carefully consider whether the disagreement truly concerns a matter of importance and should keep in mind that withdrawal may cause the client serious harm where the trial is imminent or ongoing.

5) If the relationship is not irreparably ruptured because of the dispute, the client should make the final determination regarding the course of action to be taken. That is to say, in the ordinary course the lawyer should carry out any reasonable and ethical course of action that is desired by the client.

No matter which model of decision making one adopts, treating the client with dignity and respect, receiving the client's input, and keeping

---

89   Freedman & Smith, above note 83 at 59.
90   See Chapter 11, Section D.
91   See Section J, below in this chapter.
92   See Section L, below in this chapter.
93   See Section K, below in this chapter.
94   See, for example, the cases cited at note 56, above in this chapter.
95   See Chapter 11, Section L.
96   See Section C(4), above in this chapter.

her well-informed in a timely way as to the progress of the case and any anticipated issues of substance, goes far to minimize the possibility of an irresolvable dispute arising. The remainder of this chapter focuses in more detail on particular issues regarding decision making in the legal-professional relationship and fleshes out how the lawyer-control and co-operative models operate in particular instances.

E. INFORMING AND ADVISING THE CLIENT

A co-operative model of lawyering demands a high level of trust and communication between client and counsel. So too does the contemporary version of the lawyer-control model. Such an approach dovetails neatly with the lawyer's duties to keep the client informed[97] and advised[98] on all matters relevant to the representation, and to do so promptly. After all, a key purpose of these duties is to enable the client to make effective decisions concerning the conduct of the defence. Absent proper information and advice from the lawyer, the client's ability to do so will be seriously hampered, and his right to the effective assistance of counsel may be violated.[99] As a comment to ABA Model Rule 1.4 states, "The client should have sufficient information to participate intelligently in decisions concerning the objectives of the representation and the means by which they are to be pursued, to the extent the client is willing and able to do so."[100]

Canadian ethical codes contain many provisions underscoring a lawyer's obligation to adequately inform and advise the client, including

- the duty to keep the client reasonably informed;[101]
- the duty to communicate effectively with the client;[102]

---

97 *R v Neil*, 2002 SCC 70 at para 19(iii) [*Neil*]; *Strother v 3464920 Canada Inc*, 2007 SCC 24 at para 55; *Canadian National Railway Co v McKercher LLP*, 2013 SCC 39 at paras 10, 45, and 58.

98 *Côté v Rancourt*, 2004 SCC 58 at para 6 [*Côté*]; FLSC r 3.4-1, commentary 8.

99 See, for example, *R v Ross*, 2012 NSCA 56 at para 40 (NSCA) [*Ross*]; *R v Thibeault*, 2014 CMAC 2 at paras 37–47; *R v Qiu*, 2010 ONCA 736 at para 9; *Moore*, above note 36 at paras 48 and 51; FLSC r 3.4-1, commentary 8.

100 ABA Model Rule 1.4, comment 5.

101 Alta, Sask r 2.02(1) (commentary); BC, Man, NS, NL r 3.2-1, commentary 5(a); CBA Code ch II, commentary 7(a); NB ch 3, commentary 4(a).

102 Alta, Sask r 2.02(1) (commentary); BC, NS, NL r 3.2-1, commentary 3. To similar effect, see Alta, Sask r 2.01(d); BC, Man, Ont, NS, NL r 3.1-1(d); NB ch 2, commentary 5(d) and ch 3, commentary 2.

- the duty to develop and advise the client on appropriate courses of action;[103]
- the duty to provide a client with complete and accurate relevant information about the matter;[104]
- the duty to report developments to the client or, in the absence of any developments, to maintain contact to the extent reasonably expected by the client;[105]
- the duty when providing advice to be candid and honest and to inform the client of all information known to the lawyer that may affect the client's interests;[106]
- the duty to clarify and explain where it becomes apparent that the client has misunderstood or misconceived the lawyer's legal advice;[107]
- the duty to inform the client of a settlement proposal and to explain it properly;[108]
- the duty to inform the client of any reasonably foreseeable undue delay in providing advice or services;[109]
- the duty to answer reasonable requests from the client for information;[110]
- the duty to respond to the client's telephone calls;[111]
- the duty to keep appointments with the client or provide a timely explanation or apology when unable to do so;[112] and
- the duty to answer within a reasonable time any communication requiring a reply.[113]

---

103 Alta, Sask r 2.01(b); BC, Man, Ont, NS, NL r 3.1-1(b); NB ch 2, commentary 5(b).

104 Alta, Sask r 2.02(1) (commentary); BC, Man, NS, NL r 3.2-1, commentary 5(k); CBA Code ch II, commentary 7(k); NB ch 3, commentary 4(k).

105 Alta, Sask r 2.02(1) (commentary); BC, Man, Ont, NS, NL r 3.2-1, commentary 6.

106 Alta, Sask r 2.02(2); BC, Man, Ont, NS, NL r 3.2-2. See also Ont r 3.2-1, commentary 1.1.

107 CBA Code ch III, commentary 2; NB ch 4, commentary 3.

108 Alta, Sask r 2.02(1) (commentary); BC, Man, NS, NL r 3.2-1, commentary 5(j); CBA Code ch II, commentary 7(j); NB ch 3, commentary 4(j).

109 Alta, Sask r 2.02(1) (commentary); BC, Man, NS, NL r 3.2-1, commentary 4; CBA Code ch II, commentary 8; NB ch 3, commentary 2.

110 Alta, Sask r 2.02(1) (commentary); BC, Man, NS, NL r 3.2-1, commentary 5(b); CBA Code ch II, commentary 7(b); NB ch 3, commentary 4(a).

111 Alta, Sask r 2.02(1) (commentary); BC, Man, NS, NL r 3.2-1, commentary 5(c); CBA Code ch II, commentary 7(c); NB ch 3, commentary 4(c).

112 Alta, Sask r 2.02(1) (commentary); BC, Man, NS, NL r 3.2-1, commentary 5(d); CBA Code ch II, commentary 7(d); NB ch 3, commentary 4(d).

113 Alta, Sask r 2.02(1) (commentary); BC, Man, NS, NL r 3.2-1, commentary 5(f); CBA Code ch II, commentary 7(f); NB ch 3, commentary 4(e).

Example 1: Counsel represents a black teacher charged with sexual interference on a white student, in a jurisdiction with a history of racial discrimination and several recent high-profile incidents of race-based violence. The client repeatedly expresses concern about the possibility the jury will be all white and biased against him because of race. Counsel tells the client not to worry but fails to mention the option of applying to bring a race-based challenge for cause, which in the circumstances would undoubtedly be granted by the trial judge. Not informing the client of this important option represents a breach of counsel's ethical duty to develop and advise the client of appropriate courses of action in conducting the defence.[114]

Example 2: An eighteen-year-old accused is charged with sexual interference on a thirteen-year-old girl. His defence is that he mistakenly believed the girl to be fourteen years of age. Defence counsel fails to give the accused any advice as to whether he should take the stand to give evidence as to his belief and its basis, even though the defence stands a markedly lesser chance of succeeding if he does not testify. This failure constitutes a breach of counsel's duty to properly advise the client, leaving the client unable to make an informed decision regarding a fundamental aspect of the defence.[115]

1) Strong Advice and the Lawyer's Personal Morality

The lawyer's advice to the client will often include the exercise of persuasion based on competent strategic and tactical judgment. As several Canadian codes state, "Occasionally, a lawyer must be firm with a client. Firmness, without rudeness, is not a violation of the rule. In communicating with the client, the lawyer may disagree with the client's perspective, or may have concerns about the client's position on a matter, and may give advice that will not please the client. This may legitimately require firm and animated discussion with the client."[116]

More than this, we believe that a lawyer is permitted to bring her personal morality to bear in offering advice to the client. By doing so, the lawyer may alert the client to factors not previously considered. Providing the lawyer with such latitude, albeit short of allowing veto

---

114   This example is based on *R v Fraser*, 2011 NSCA 70, discussed in Richard Devlin & David Layton, "Culturally Incompetent Counsel and the Trial Level Judge: A Legal and Ethical Analysis" (2014) 60 Crim LQ 360.

115   This example is based on *Ross*, above note 99.

116   Alta, Sask r 2.02(2) (commentary); BC, Man, NS, NL r 3.2-2, commentary 3. See also the text associated with note 89, above in this chapter; *R v SGT*, 2011 SKCA 4 at paras 60–61.

power over the client's final decision, recognizes that lawyers are human beings with individual and often valuable conceptions of good. In this respect, the lawyer's role in the decision making process is not amoral or concerned solely with obtaining for the client all that the law can offer.

2) Factors Bearing on the Nature of the Information and Advice Required

The provision of information and advice necessary to meet a lawyer's ethical obligations is contextual,[117] and varies with a number of factors including the nature of the charges, the stage and complexity of the proceedings, the importance of the decision to be made, the client's express or implied objectives in the litigation, and his level of sophistication and experience.[118] An intelligent client who has had many brushes with the criminal justice system may require only brief contact for the purpose of providing advice. A client who is entirely new to the process, suffers from a mental impairment, or has difficulty speaking the court's language may require much more attention and effort from the lawyer to meet this ethical imperative. The time available for consultation is also a factor to consider, although the lawyer should not unfairly pressure the client by neglecting to discuss an important issue until the eleventh hour.

3) A Possible Exception: Keeping Information from a Client

As a general principle, withholding relevant information breaches the duty to keep the client informed and is thus improper. However, in rare instances such action may be acceptable. For instance, a court may order counsel not to pass information on to the client, in which case the duty to keep the client reasonably informed must be curtailed. Provided the client consents, a lawyer may also be justified in giving an express undertaking not to share specified portions of disclosure materials with the client absent permission of the Crown or leave of the court.[119]

In a very different scenario, the lawyer may harbour a legitimate and reasonable fear that disclosure to the client will lead to the death of, or serious bodily harm to, a third party or result in substantial harm to

---

117 *Côté*, above note 98 at para 6.
118 Some of these factors are mentioned in Alta, Sask r 2.02(1) (commentary); BC, Man, NS, NL r 3.2-1, commentary 3.
119 See Chapter 4, Section R(3). See also Ont r 3.2-2, commentary 1.2.

the client. In such circumstances, the lawyer may be justified in at least delaying release of the information to the client.[120]

Another possibility is that the lawyer receives information from a third party that is covered by privilege and so cannot be shared with the client. For example, the lawyer may obtain privileged information from Client A that is relevant to a discrete legal matter involving Client B, in which case disclosure to Client B is *prima facie* prohibited, and the lawyer is faced with a conflict-of-interest problem.[121] Or, privileged information may come from a non-client, such as a document inadvertently disclosed by the Crown that reveals the identity of a confidential informant. Given that inadvertent disclosure is highly unlikely to be interpreted as a waiver of informant privilege, neither the document nor its contents can be passed on to counsel's client.[122]

F. DECISIONS FUNDAMENTAL TO THE CONDUCT OF THE DEFENCE

Many commentators and some ethical codes reserve for the client the ultimate say regarding decisions on matters seen to be particularly fundamental to the conduct of the defence, most notably the decisions how to plead and whether to testify. A representative list of such fundamental matters is set out in ABA Defense Standard 4-5.2(a).[123] In Canada, the Alberta code states that the decisions how to plead, whether to testify, whether to waive a jury trial, and whether to appeal all "require prior discussion with the client."[124] The Manitoba code is somewhat similar, providing that "fundamental decisions such as how to plead and what witnesses to call will almost always require prior consultations."[125] Most other codes make no comment as to whether certain decisions must be made by the client in a criminal matter, apart from stipulating

---

120   See ABA Model Rule 1.4, comment 4; Third Restatement § 20, comment "b," § 24, comment "c," and § 46, comment "c." This justification is analogous to the future-harm exception to the duty of confidentiality, discussed in Chapter 5, Section I.
121   See Chapter 6, Section F(3).
122   See Chapter 4, Section Q.
123   Reproduced in Section B, above in this chapter. See also the Third Restatement § 22(1); ABA Model Rule 1.2(a); *Jones v Barnes*, 463 US 745 at 751 (1983) [*Jones*].
124   Alta r 2.02(3) (commentary).
125   Man r 3.2-2A, commentary 1.

that a lawyer must not enter into a plea agreement without the client's instructions.[126]

For supporters of the co-operative model of lawyering, leaving decisions such as how to plead or whether to testify to the client is simply an especially significant application of the broad principle that decision making power generally rests with the client. But for writers, judges, and practitioners who believe that the lawyer should have completely free rein in conducting most aspects of the defence, these select fundamental decisions are, by their very nature, so important that exceptions to the usual principle of lawyer-control must be made.[127] The exceptions are justified because these decisions for the most part involve the exercise of constitutional rights and in addition must, according to the jurisprudence, be made by the client personally to have effect.[128] It has also been pointed out that society has an interest in ensuring a degree of personal confrontation between the accused and the state at certain key junctures in the criminal trial process, an interest that is bolstered by reserving decision making power to the client in these particular areas.[129]

Given that decisions regarding the plea and whether to testify usually play a central role in the conduct and resolution of a criminal case, we wholeheartedly agree that the client is best suited to make the final call. Yet, consistent with our co-operative view of decision making, we do not restrict the client's power to decide to these limited areas. Nor do we agree that these specific decisions will always be more important than any others in a criminal case. In fact, neatly isolating those decisions that are fundamental to a client's representation can be difficult. Consider, for instance, that proponents of the lawyer-control model have not traditionally viewed the calling of defence witnesses other than the accused or the scope of cross-examination as falling within the client's decision making authority. Yet calling a particular witness or pursuing a line of inquiry in cross-examination can be absolutely crucial to the prospects of success for a particular defence. It is certainly easy to envision circumstances where impeding the defence in either respect would constitute a constitutional violation.[130]

---

126 See the rules cited at note 4, above in this chapter.
127 Hutchinson, above note 35 at 102; MacKenzie, above note 35, § 4.11 at 4–24.
128 See, for example, the cases cited at note 37, above in this chapter.
129 Third Restatement § 22, comment "b."
130 The constitutional right to make full answer and defence includes the rights to cross-examine Crown witnesses and to call defence evidence: *R v Seaboyer* (1991), 66 CCC (3d) 321 at 388–89 [paras 29–34] (SCC); *R v NS*, 2012 SCC 72

It may also transpire that refusing to follow a client's instructions on a matter not traditionally seen as "fundamental" will substantially affect a decision that falls within the realm of the client's absolute decision making power. For instance, a client may wish to advance an alibi defence but not want to testify. If the lawyer refuses to call the alibi witnesses, the client is forced onto the stand because there is no other way to advance the defence. Or suppose that a client is charged with a sexual assault and wants to testify that he never had sex with the complainant. If the lawyer's cross-examination of the complainant focuses on the issue of consent and effectively concedes identity, the client's decision to take the stand has been sabotaged.[131] As these scenarios show, many decisions made concerning the conduct of a trial are interrelated. It is not always easy to isolate the client's decisions regarding how to plead or whether to testify from the lawyer's decisions pertaining to other aspects of the litigation.

There is thus real merit in widening the scope of the client's powers and placing within her control any decision that has a substantial impact on the outcome of the case.[132] This approach finds support in *Szostak*, insofar as the Ontario Court of Appeal concluded that the client's constitutional right to control the conduct of the defence requires that counsel obtain instructions from the client regarding "decisions fundamental to the defence of the case," defined to include "possible pleas, possible defences and possible excuses, including NCRMD."[133] In other words, *Szostak* clearly gives the client the last word on important decisions beyond the few usually identified by proponents of the lawyer-control model.[134]

In determining whether a decision will have a substantial impact on the outcome of the case, a lawyer should consider factors that include its potential influence on the result at the conviction or sentencing phases, the importance ascribed by the client to the decision, whether

---

at paras 15 and 24. Some aspects of cross-examination must nonetheless always be within the sole control of counsel: see Section I, below in this chapter.

131 This is what happened in *McLoughlin*, above note 56.

132 The Third Restatement § 22(1) takes a somewhat analogous approach, insofar as authority is ordinarily irrevocably reserved to the client regarding enumerated fundamental *and comparable* decisions. See also Uphoff, above note 42 at 797: accused should have final say on any trial-related decision that is reasonably likely to affect the outcome of the case.

133 *Szostak*, above note 58 at para 78. *Szostak* is discussed in more detail in Section C(3), above in this chapter.

134 See also Man r 3.2-2A, commentary 1: lawyers provide legal services based on instructions from the client, and fundamental decisions, such as how to plead and what witnesses to call, almost always require prior consultation.

the lawyer's interests conflict with those of the client, whether reasonable persons would disagree as to how the decision should be made, and whether the trial process can feasibly be halted to permit the client to participate in making the decision.[135] Of course, utilizing the cooperative model would be a simpler approach, for the client would have the final say on most matters connected with the case.

G. USING THE RETAINER TO DEFINE THE DECISION MAKING AUTHORITY

The client and lawyer may for perfectly good reasons wish to adopt a specific allocation of decision making authority and accordingly provide for their preferred version in the retainer agreement. Consequently, the terms of a retainer may relegate certain decisions to the lawyer, to be made in the ordinary course without the need for consultation with the client. In effect, the client is giving the lawyer the express authority to act within a defined realm.[136] The Third Restatement has taken this concept the furthest of the major Anglo-American ethical codes. Subject to certain restrictions, it allows the client and lawyer to agree who will make specified decisions, and also stipulates that the allocation of decision making authority can be amended by mutual agreement as the representation progresses.[137]

It is nonetheless fair to say that certain crucial steps taken as part of the conduct of the defence always require specific consultation with the client and clear instructions at the time the decision is made. Such crucial steps include the decisions regarding how the client should plead and whether he should testify.[138] These decisions can never be left to counsel because they are the sole preserve of the client by reason of the law governing the criminal trial.[139] Additionally, there is a decent argument that the client should be permitted to revoke unilaterally at

---

135 These factors are borrowed almost verbatim from the Third Restatement § 22, comment "e."

136 See, for example, the retainer discussed in *Stewart*, above note 36 at 47–48 and 83 [paras 43 and 139].

137 Third Restatement § 21(1). Also favouring this approach is H Richard Uviller, "Calling the Shots: The Allocation of Choice between the Accused and Counsel in the Defense of a Criminal Case" (2000) 52 Rutgers L Rev 719 at 776.

138 See Section F, above in this chapter.

139 See the text associated with note 37, above in this chapter.

any time an agreement to delegate decision making authority to the lawyer regarding other matters of comparable importance.[140]

Where a written retainer does not address the division of decision making authority, it is prudent for counsel to describe for the client at the initial interview those decisions over which the client will always have final say (how to plead, whether to testify, and so on) and to propose in a general way the sorts of decisions that the lawyer can make without necessarily seeking specific instructions. The client and lawyer can thereby arrive at a general understanding regarding the decision making prerogative, subject always to the lawyer's ongoing duty to keep the client informed and advised.[141] Most clients will be quite content to give counsel decision making power regarding a significant preponderance of tactical decisions provided they are kept informed and consulted in advance regarding decisions that may have a substantial impact on the outcome of the case.

H. IMPLIED AUTHORITY

Subject to any agreement between the client and lawyer or contrary instructions from the client, and apart from the fundamental decisions described in Section F, above, the lawyer should have the implied authority to make decisions within the scope of the representation that can reasonably be seen to advance the client's objectives.[142] A sensible guideline for determining whether implied authority exists is to ask whether the client would approve of the contemplated action if fully informed and consulted in advance.[143] If the lawyer is unsure whether implied authority exists, the proper course is to consult with the client before making the decision.[144]

Regardless of the scope of counsel's implied decision making authority, the broad and ongoing duty to inform and consult means the client will usually be kept sufficiently aware of matters so as to be able to intervene with express instructions regarding important deci-

---

140   Third Restatement § 22(3).

141   See Section E, above in this chapter.

142   Third Restatement § 21(3); ABA Model Rule 1.2(a). See also *GDB*, above note 37 at para 34: counsel need not obtain approval for each and every decision made in conducting an accused's defence; *DMG*, above note 37 at para 108 (same).

143   Geoffrey Hazard & W William Hodes, *The Law of Lawyering*, 3d ed (Englewood Cliffs, NJ: Prentice Hall, 1985) (loose-leaf 2013 supplement) § 5.5 at 5–13.

144   Alta r 2.02(3) (commentary); Man r 3.2-2A, commentary 1.

sions.[145] The duty to keep the client reasonably informed also means that the client should generally be appraised after the fact of material steps taken pursuant to the lawyer's implied authority.[146]

I. DECISIONS THAT MUST BE MADE QUICKLY DURING THE COURSE OF A TRIAL

Once a trial is under way, lawyers are required to make a bevy of decisions in conducting the defence. Some decisions are crucial to the outcome of the case while others may be less significant. The need to make certain decisions can be predicted far in advance, yet many issues arise without warning and require an immediate response. The criminal justice system insists on a degree of consistent momentum during the trial process. If proceedings were adjourned every time action had to be taken, so counsel could obtain the client's considered input, the process would bog down, and the quality of justice would suffer. So it makes sense for the lawyer to possess the authority to render those decisions that must be made immediately in response to sudden developments, and without time for consultation,[147] such as whether to object to a question posed to a witness by Crown counsel in chief.

Example: A client insists on approving in advance every question counsel intends to put to the complainant in a criminal harassment case. Counsel must refuse such a request. While arriving at the proper cross-examination strategy requires consultation with the client, it is not feasible to have the client control the entire questioning process. Effective cross-examination, though carefully planned, must also be fluid and spontaneous, permitting counsel to adjust and extemporize in response to the witness's answers and demeanour and any interventions by opposing counsel or perceived reaction on the part of the fact-finder.[148]

This approach to decision making does not mean a lawyer should leave the client ignorant regarding the events that will occur at trial. The trial process, and the roles to be played by client and lawyer, should

---

145 Third Restatement § 21(3), comment "e."

146 See Section E, above in this chapter.

147 Third Restatement § 23, comment "d"; *Jones*, above note 123 at 760, Brennan J, dissenting but not on this narrow point.

148 The facts and analysis come from the decision in *Faulkner*, above note 36 at paras 35–47.

be explained to the client in advance. Moreover, while a lawyer will be unable to predict every instance where an immediate decision is required, she can generally describe the types of decisions that may be made during the trial. It is certainly possible and appropriate to obtain advance instructions or input from the client with respect to some such matters.[149] And if a decision is suddenly and unexpectedly required on a significant matter, there is nothing to stop counsel from requesting a brief adjournment to obtain the client's informed input.

J. INSTRUCTIONS THAT REQUIRE UNETHICAL CONDUCT FROM THE LAWYER

A lawyer cannot accept a retainer involving unethical conduct, which includes any action that facilitates an illegality.[150] Nor can a lawyer who has properly accepted a retainer carry out subsequently revealed instructions that require a breach of the rules of professional conduct. For example, a lawyer cannot accede to a client's insistence that a witness be called for the purpose of giving false exculpatory testimony[151] and must reject instructions that involve taking frivolous steps in the litigation.[152]

If a client refuses to revoke instructions that demand unethical conduct, the lawyer faces a dilemma. Disclosing the improper instructions to the court or Crown counsel is usually not an option, because the duty of confidentiality will be breached.[153] But rejecting the instructions and continuing with the defence is no better a solution. Granted, this course of action has the advantage of avoiding the unethical conduct. Yet it undermines the client's decision making authority and will often cause a total breakdown in the professional relationship. The only acceptable option is thus to withdraw from the representation. Not surprisingly, Canadian codes mandate exactly this response where the client persists in instructing the lawyer to act contrary to professional ethics.[154]

---

149 See, for example, the comments in *Faulkner, ibid* at para 45.
150 See Chapter 2, Section B.
151 Alta r 4.01(2)(g); Sask r 4.01(2)(e); Que s 3.02(01)(c); BC, Man, Ont, NS, NL r 5.1-2(e); NB ch 8, commentary 10(v); CBA Code ch IX, commentary 2(e).
152 See Section L, below in this chapter.
153 It is unlikely that any of the exceptions to the duty of confidentiality set out in Chapter 5 will apply.
154 See Chapter 11, Section F. See also the rules regarding the lawyer as advocate: Alta r 4.01(5) (commentary); Sask r 4.01(4) (commentary); BC, Man, Ont, NS,

K. A CLIENT'S INSISTENCE THAT THE LAWYER ACT INCOMPETENTLY

In rare instances a client will insist on mounting the defence in a manner that any sensible and objective person knowledgeable in the law would view as wholly unreasonable. In other words, were the lawyer to pursue such a course of action of his own accord to the client's prejudice, an appeal court would conclude the client was denied the assistance of effective counsel and order a new trial. Is the lawyer obligated to follow ill-advised instructions that hold the potential to bring disaster for the defence, and perhaps additionally to support a successful appeal ground of ineffective assistance of counsel?

1) Competence and the Rules of Professional Conduct

Canadian rules of professional conduct typically state that "a lawyer must perform all legal services undertaken on a client's behalf to the standard of a competent lawyer."[155] For the purposes of our discussion, performing competently requires three things. First, the lawyer must maintain, on an ongoing basis, an acceptable degree of knowledge in her area of practice.[156] Second, the lawyer must exercise sound judgment and skill in providing representation in a particular case, including adequate preparation, implementation of strategies, and communication with the client.[157] Third, the lawyer must abide by all of the rules governing appropriate conduct in the profession.[158]

Most Canadian codes expressly state that the duty of competence does not require perfection and that an error or omission, though actionable for damages in negligence or contract, does not necessarily reflect a breach of the ethical duty.[159] Conversely, these codes go on to

---

NL r 5.1-4, commentary 1; NB ch 8, commentary 12(b); CBA Code ch IX, commentary 4.

155 Alta, Sask r 2.01(2); BC, Man, Ont, NS, NL r 3.1-2. To similar effect, see Que s 3.01.01; NB ch 2, rule; CBA Code ch II, rule.

156 Alta, Sask r 2.01(a), (i), (j), (k), and 2.01(2) (commentary); BC, Man, Ont, NS, NL r 3.1(a), (i), (j), (k), and 3.1-2(2); Que s 3.01.01; NB ch 2, commentary 5(a), (i), (j), (k); CBA Code ch II, commentaries 1–2 and 5.

157 Alta, Sask r 2.01(b)–(f); BC, Man, Ont, NS, NL r 3.1(a); Que s 3.01.01; NB ch 2, commentary 5(a); CBA Code ch II, commentary 5(a).

158 Alta, Sask r 2.01(g); BC, Man, NS, NL r 3.1(g); NB ch 2, commentary 5(g). Ont r 3.1(g) is framed more narrowly, requiring compliance with "all requirements pursuant to the *Law Society Act*."

159 Alta, Sask r 2.01(2) (commentary); BC, Man, Ont, NS, NL r 3.1-2, commentary 15; NB ch 2, commentary 8; CBA Code ch II, commentary 9.

say that evidence of gross neglect in a particular case or a pattern of neglect or mistakes in several cases may be evidence that the ethical duty of competence has been breached, regardless of tort liability.[160]

Example: Appellate counsel acts in four different appeals alleging that the same trial lawyer breached his clients' rights to the effective assistance of counsel. Appellate counsel files affidavits from the appellants stating that they believe their trial lawyer was using cocaine, but the affidavits contain only hearsay and speculation on the point, and are replete with other inadmissible material including argument, opinion, and irrelevant information. Appellate counsel's factums are rambling, disorganized, and cite almost no legal authority. What legal authority is mentioned is irrelevant to the appeal issues. Appellate counsel's oral submissions exhibit the same flaws. On these facts, counsel has breached the duty of competence owed to his appeal clients.[161]

The rationale behind an ethical rule mandating competency is that a high quality of service best promotes the legal rights and interests of the client and, by extension, bolsters society's interest in a reliable and fair criminal justice system.[162] A competent lawyer will also find that her reputation benefits from providing a high quality of service. There is thus no doubt that a lawyer is ordinarily obligated, and also has a strong personal incentive, to conduct a defence in a manner best calculated to yield a favourable result for the client. The dilemma arises when a client desires representation that runs counter to the lawyer's competent judgment. Canadian rules of professional conduct do not provide the lawyer with express guidance on this point.

2) The Constitutional Right to Effective Assistance of Counsel

It is well-established that an accused person enjoys a constitutional right to the effective assistance of counsel.[163] The logic behind this

---

160 Alta, Sask r 2.01(2) (commentary); BC, Man, NS, NL r 3.1-2, commentary 15; Ont r 3.1-2, commentary 15; NB ch 2, commentary 8; CBA Code ch II, commentary 9. To similar effect, see *Neil*, above note 97 at para 37: breach of ethical rules does not necessarily provide the basis to establish negligence or justify a constitutional remedy.

161 The facts and analysis come from the decision in *Goldberg v Law Society of British Columbia*, 2009 BCCA 147.

162 Alta, Sask r 2.01(2) (commentary); BC, Man, Ont, NS, NL r 3.1-2, commentary 14; NB ch 2, commentary 9; CBA Code ch II, commentary 10.

163 The leading case is *GDB*, above note 37.

right is essentially the same as the primary justifications for an ethical duty of competence: the client's systemic rights and the reliability and justness of the outcome are best promoted by effective advocacy.[164]

The right to the effective assistance of counsel is most often raised on appeal, after the accused has been convicted.[165] The approach favoured by Canadian courts in assessing whether the right has been infringed is derived from the leading American case of *Strickland v Washington*.[166] The *Strickland* standard will be met where the appellant establishes two things: first, that counsel's acts or omissions constituted incompetence and, second, that a miscarriage of justice resulted.[167] The Supreme Court of Canada has described the nature of this two-prong test in *R v GDB*, stating:

> Incompetence is determined by a reasonableness standard. The analysis proceeds upon a strong presumption that counsel's conduct fell within the wide range of reasonable professional assistance. The onus is on the appellant to establish the acts or omissions of counsel that are alleged not to have been the result of reasonable professional judgment. The wisdom of hindsight has no place in this assessment.
>
> Miscarriages of justice may take many forms in this context. In some instances, counsel's performance may have resulted in procedural unfairness. In others, the reliability of the trial's result may have been compromised.
>
> In those cases where it is apparent that no prejudice has occurred, it will usually be undesirable for appellate courts to consider the performance component of the analysis. The object of an ineffectiveness claim is not to grade counsel's performance or professional conduct. The latter is left to the profession's self-governing body. If it is appropriate to dispose of an ineffectiveness claim on the ground of no prejudice having occurred, that is the course to follow.[168]

---

164 See *R v Joanisse* (1995), 102 CCC (3d) 35 at 57 [paras 64–65] (Ont CA), Doherty JA in dissent but not on this point [*Joanisse*], leave to appeal to SCC refused, [1996] SCCA No 347.

165 It should be available to trial judges as well in certain circumstances: see Patrick J LeSage & Michael Code, *Report of the Review of Large and Complex Criminal Case Procedures* (Toronto: Ontario Ministry of the Attorney General, 2008) at 146–50 [*LeSage-Code Report*], online: www.attorneygeneral.jus.gov. on.ca/english/about/pubs/lesage_code/default.asp.

166 466 US 668 (1984) [*Strickland*]. The *Strickland* test is adopted in *GDB*, above note 37 at paras 26–29.

167 *GDB*, above note 37 at para 26.

168 *Ibid* at paras 27–29 [citation omitted].

This quotation emphasizes one respect in which the ethical standards of competence do not equate exactly with the constitutional guarantee of the effective assistance of counsel, namely, that no matter how deficient counsel's performance, the constitutional right will not be violated absent prejudice to the client. A further distinction between the two concepts arises because, as we have seen, most Canadian codes state that a single instance of negligence does not necessarily constitute a breach of the ethical duty of competence.[169] By parity of reasoning, a single instance of counsel's breaching the performance prong of the constitutional test for ineffective assistance does not necessarily constitute incompetence within the meaning of the ethical codes.

3) Decision Making That Accommodates Ethical and Constitutional Concerns

Under Martin's conception of the lawyer-control model, the lawyer has total freedom, and probably an affirmative duty, to reject a client's imprudent instructions. Even where the decision relates to a fundamental matter such as how to plead, said Martin, counsel "is not bound to follow instructions which are *unreasonable* and in proper cases is entitled to refuse to act for a client who rejects his advice."[170]

The co-operative approach is less susceptible to a clear-cut answer where the client's instructions are unreasonable. Provided the client has been fully and competently advised as to the pitfalls of the desired action,[171] there is an argument that a lawyer ascribing to the co-operative method should comply with the client's final decision. For one thing, it does not follow that an appeal court would later find that counsel was ineffective on this scenario, at least not within the meaning of the constitutional law on this point. To the contrary, the client has made an informed decision, against counsel's advice, regarding the conduct of the case and cannot be heard to complain that her lawyer refused to override the strenuously desired course of action.[172] On this view, the lawyer who carries out the instructions is *not* constitutionally ineffective.

---

169   See the rules and text associated with note 159, above in this chapter.
170   Martin, "Role and Responsibility," above note 18 at 387.
171   There is almost certainly a positive duty to attempt to dissuade the client from embarking on a terribly unwise course of action: see *Joanisse*, above note 164 at 72 [para 107].
172   See *Joanisse, ibid* at 77 [para 121]; *R v Elliott* (2003), 181 CCC (3d) 118 at para 181 (Ont CA) [*Elliott*]; *Faulkner*, above note 36 at para 65. This same view is taken in many American cases: see, for example, *People v Galan*, 261 Cal Rptr 834 at 835–36 (Ct App 1989); *People v Colville*, 79 AD3d 189 at 201–2 (NY 2010).

Moreover, in many instances where the client has pushed trial counsel to take a highly ill-advised course of action, the court of appeal will not need to examine the propriety of counsel's conduct in assessing a lack of effective assistance argument. This is so because if no resulting prejudice is apparent, the appeal will usually be resolved on this basis alone, without the need to examine the competency prong of the ineffective assistance test.[173] Accordingly, if the client was destined to lose the case regardless, there is a good possibility the lawyer's conduct will not lead to a finding of ineffective assistance.

Nonetheless, in our view counsel is never mandated to accept instructions that would require the defence to be conducted in an unreasonable manner, especially where likely to result in serious harm to the client's best interests. Doing so may constitute incompetence within the meaning of the rules of professional conduct. Moreover, while client-directed incompetence may not result in a finding of ineffective assistance on appeal, counsel may not be in a position to know this at the time the instructions are given. Rather than being forced to accept unreasonable instructions from a client, counsel should be permitted to withdraw from the representation, either because the client is asking counsel to act incompetently and thus in breach of the ethical rules[174] or because the client has rejected counsel's advice on a matter of important trial strategy.[175]

L. FRIVOLOUS TACTICS

Most Canadian codes of professional conduct preclude counsel in a *civil* matter from making frivolous objections or using tactics that merely delay or harass, stating:

> In civil proceedings, a lawyer should avoid and discourage the client from resorting to frivolous or vexatious objections, attempts to gain advantage from slips or oversights not going to the real merits or tactics that will merely delay or harass the other side. Such practices can readily bring the administration of justice and the legal profession into disrepute.[176]

---

173 *GDB*, above note 37 at para 29.
174 See Section J, above in this chapter.
175 See Section C(4), above in this chapter.
176 Alta, Sask r 4.01(1) (commentary); BC, Man, Ont, NS, NL r 5.1-1, commentary 8. See also CBA Code ch IX, commentary 7.

These rules leave criminal counsel without much guidance because they are expressly said to pertain to civil matters.[177]

Yet there are compelling reasons for prohibiting frivolous arguments in criminal matters too.[178] Meritless tactics waste valuable time and resources and delay the system in reaching a just and final outcome. Mounting a frivolous argument can also harm the client. The judge or jury may become frustrated with defence counsel, and by association the accused, and begin to look askance at entirely valid aspects of the defence case. Putting forth a completely groundless argument may also alienate Crown counsel so that he is less likely to exercise discretion in favour of the accused regarding other, more important, aspects of the case. More generally, advancing hopeless arguments damages counsel's reputation with the judiciary and prosecution service, to the detriment of clients in other cases. Counsel's standing may also suffer within the defence bar.

On the other hand, the client is presumed innocent until proven guilty and has a constitutional right to require the Crown to prove the charge beyond a reasonable doubt. In light of these fundamental constitutional rights, it is crucial that any ethical rule against frivolous arguments contain an exception permitting defence counsel to require that the Crown prove all essential elements of the offence. To this end, the prohibition against taking frivolous steps found in major ethical codes in the United States expressly allows the defence in a criminal matter to require that the prosecution establish every necessary element of the offence.[179] This sort of exception should apply in Canada as well.

Allowing the defence to require that the prosecution prove every element of the case does not, however, give counsel carte blanche to mount hopeless arguments regarding other matters. For instance, the accused usually bears the onus of excluding otherwise relevant evi-

---

177 By contrast, the similarly worded NB ch 8, commentary 7 is not restricted to civil matters, and no distinction is made between civil and criminal matters in Alta r 4.01(2)(b), which provides that when acting as an advocate, a lawyer must not "take any step in the representation of the client that is clearly without merit." See also Que s 3.03.04(d), which provides that a lawyer — presumably including criminal counsel — can generally withdraw where the client insists on a futile or vexatious proceeding.

178 *LeSage-Code Report*, above note 165 at 84–85; Michael Code, "Law Reform Initiatives Relating to the Mega Trial Phenomenon" (2008) 53 Crim LQ 421 at 463–67; David Layton, "Defence Counsel's Ethical Duties and Frivolous Charter Applications" (2006) 110 The Verdict 25. See also the sources mentioned at note 181, below in this chapter.

179 See ABA Model Rule 3.1; Third Restatement § 110(b).

dence under the *Canadian Charter of Rights and Freedoms*[180] and at common law.[181] The issue of whether and when defence counsel is ethically precluded from bringing such an application because of a low prospect of success has been the subject of considerable debate. The concern that meritless pre-trial applications are bogging down the criminal justice system has been expressed most notably by Moldaver J, in a 2005 speech to the Criminal Lawyers' Association,[182] but is also evident in the caselaw,[183] as well as reports commissioned by government and the judiciary.[184]

A modest amount of Canadian jurisprudence touches on defence counsel's professional obligation not to make frivolous arguments. In *R v Samra*, the Ontario Court of Appeal raised the hypothetical case of a lawyer who is asked by the client to make submissions that are "foolish or ill-advised or contrary to established legal principle and doctrine."[185] The court offered the view that defence counsel, not being the alter ego of the client, is not required to make such submissions.[186] No opinion was provided as to whether counsel owes a duty to the court *not* to

---

180 Part I of the *Constitution Act, 1982*, being Schedule B to the *Canada Act 1982* (UK), 1982, c 11 [*Charter*].

181 A significant exception is a statement made to a person in authority, and it has been argued that the prohibition against frivolous tactics should therefore not extend to voluntariness *voir dires*: John Wesley Hall Jr, *Professional Responsibility in Criminal Defense Practice* (St Paul, MN: Thomson/West, 2005) (loose-leaf 2012 supplement) § 3:11.50 at 22 supplement.

182 Michael Moldaver, "Long Criminal Trials: Masters of a System They Are Meant to Serve" (2005) 32 CR (6th) 316. Justice Moldaver's position has attracted some thoughtful academic rebuttals: see Don Stuart, "The *Charter* Is a Living Tree and Not a Weed to Be Stymied — Justice Moldaver Has Overstated" (2006) 40 CR (6th) 280; James Stribopoulos, "Has Everything Been Decided? Certainty, the *Charter* and Criminal Justice" (2006) 34 Sup Ct L Rev (2d) 381. These rebuttals nonetheless appear to accept that frivolous tactics are improper or problematic (Stuart, above in this note at 280–81; Stribopoulos, above in this note at 383).

183 *R v Nixon*, 2011 SCC 34 at para 61 [*Nixon*]; *R v Pires*, 2005 SCC 66 at paras 34–35; *R v Felderhof* (2003), 180 CCC (3d) 498 at paras 40, 45, and 56–57 (Ont CA) [*Felderhof*]; *Dunbar*, above note 37 at paras 330–43.

184 *New Approaches to Criminal Trials*, above note 38 at paras 1–8, 36–44, 59–65, 118–40, 232–36, 270–75, and 308–28; *LeSage-Code Report*, above note 165 at 69.

185 *Samra*, above note 36 at para 30.

186 *Ibid.* See also *R v Beauchamp*, 2005 QCCA 580 at paras 92–93, leave to appeal to SCC refused, [2005] CSCR No 355: accused has the right to raise all points of fact and law provided they are not frivolous; *R v Girimonte* (1997), 121 CCC (3d) 33 at paras 11–12 (Ont CA): responsible counsel will not make unreasonable and frivolous disclosure requests.

make such submissions, although the tenor of the judgment is inclined in this direction.

Another Ontario decision of note is *R v Elliott*.[187] Defence counsel in a murder case had brought a bevy of meritless mid-trial applications, which were heard during a nineteen-month *voir dire*. Rather shockingly, the trial judge granted the applications and stayed the charge.[188] On the Crown appeal, the respondent accepted that the applications were without merit. She nonetheless sought a stay under section 11(b) of the *Charter*[189] on the basis that the Crown and trial court had failed to put a stop to her counsel's trial tactics, the responsibility for which could not be attributed to her, because he was acting incompetently, and so her right to the effective assistance of counsel was breached.[190]

It is not necessary to explain why the Court of Appeal rejected this argument. What is important for our purposes is that, in doing so, the court noted that trial counsel's tactics, though devoid of merit, held a prospect of reaping collateral advantages such as providing leverage in plea negotiations and producing *voir dire* testimony that could be used to cross-examine Crown witnesses in front of the jury. The court nonetheless condemned the strategy of launching frivolous applications to obtain such advantages as "deplorable."[191] This holding is wholly justified: counsel must not misuse the legal process by bringing a hopeless application as a tool to extort or otherwise obtain undeserved collateral benefits for a client.

Contrast the Ontario Court of Appeal's earlier decision in *R v White*, where the appellant argued that trial counsel was ineffective as illustrated in part by the decision to launch a hopeless interlocutory proceeding in the appeal court. The court agreed that this proceeding "had virtually no chance of succeeding" and yet was not prepared to say that counsel was unquestionably wrong to launch it:

> Branding as incompetent the bringing of an application that admittedly had previously met with judicial disapproval and had almost no chance of succeeding but that could not harm the interests of the client, flies in the face of the advocate's professional duty "fearlessly to raise every issue, advance every argument, and ask every question,

---

187 *Elliott*, above note 172.
188 The attorney general of Ontario complained to the Canadian Judicial Council regarding the judge's conduct during the proceedings. On 30 March 2009, the council recommended the judge be removed from office, and he resigned from the bench two days later.
189 Above note 180.
190 *Elliott*, above note 172 at paras 171–74.
191 *Ibid* at para 180.

however distasteful, which he thinks will help his client's case": see The Code of Professional Conduct of the Canadian Bar Association (1988), ch. IX.[192]

These comments suggest that counsel can properly bring an application that verges on the frivolous and somewhat startlingly hint that there may be a positive duty to so do. The better view, however, is that an application with respect to which counsel's client bears the burden and which has no chance of succeeding should not be brought. Fearless advocacy "does not mean that counsel should advance every argument that pops into his or her head, no matter how implausible or lacking in probative value. Having a high tolerance for making unsupportable arguments is not 'fearlessness', it just shows a lack of judgment."[193] As aptly put by Rosenberg J, criminal defence counsel's duty is "to fearlessly raise every *legitimate* issue."[194] Making arguments that are obviously and completely without merit is a different thing altogether and constitutes unethical conduct. Along the same lines, the Supreme Court of Canada has observed that the right to make full answer and defence is not a right to pursue every conceivable tactic in defending against criminal prosecution.[195]

The question becomes, how best to determine whether a *Charter* or comparable common law application is frivolous? It has been suggested that defence counsel should bring a pre-trial *Charter* application only where there is a "reasonable likelihood of success" in obtaining the sought-after remedy or a suitable alternative.[196] This standard may be unduly restrictive and could operate to deny a client the benefit of a legal remedy that he is entitled to, which is of particular concern in the criminal context because a conviction is usually accompanied by significant adverse impact, including loss of liberty and societal stigma.[197] We therefore prefer a more nuanced approach to determining whether

---

192 *White*, above note 36 at 259 [para 112].

193 *Robertson v Edmonton (City) Police Service*, 2005 ABQB 499 at para 25. See also *MD v Windsor-Essex Children's Aid Society*, 2010 ONSC 2831 at paras 79–88: counsel must not engage in frivolous tactics even if so instructed by the client.

194 *Felderhof*, above note 183 at para 94 [emphasis added]. In *Felderhof*, defence counsel was criticized for repeatedly making baseless allegations against Crown counsel (*ibid* at paras 70–79 and 91–97).

195 *R v Quesnelle*, 2014 SCC 46 at para 64.

196 Moldaver, above note 182 at 323. Contrast Hall, above note 181, § 3:11.50 at 20 supplement: arguing that it is ethical to bring a remotely colourable motion to exclude evidence provided there is a possible benefit for the client.

197 See *In re Becraft*, 885 F2d 547 at 550 (9th Cir 1989) [*Becraft*]; *United States v Figueroa-Arenas*, 292 F3d 276 at 281, n 5 (1st Cir 2002) [*Figueroa-Arenas*]; *United States v Aleo*, 681 F3d 290 at 308 (6th Cir 2012), Sutton J concurring.

counsel is ethically precluded from bringing an application based on the following factors and principles:

1) An application should never be brought if it would be against the client's best interests.

2) An application that has no prospect of success in terms of affording the client a useful remedy should never be launched, not even if doing so might glean a collateral benefit. This prohibition applies even if the client insists that the application be brought.

3) In deciding whether there is merit to an application, counsel must master the facts of the case as revealed in the disclosure and by any defence investigations. However, some pertinent facts may be unavailable or lack clarity until evidence is called on a *voir dire*. A lawyer is not acting unethically merely because she reasonably believes that important evidence may well emerge during the application process.[198]

4) Counsel must also master the relevant jurisprudence. Despite the existence of unfavourable precedent, there may be a legitimate basis for putting forth a novel or innovative argument or for asking the court to revisit an earlier ruling, in which case proceeding with the argument will not be unethical.[199] The ethical rule against frivolous applications should not be so broad as to squelch counsel's ability to pursue valid progressions in the law.[200]

5) Reasonable lawyers may hold different views as to the merits of a particular application. Counsel should therefore enjoy some leeway in determining whether there is a prospect of success.

6) It is valid to take into account the availability of other applications or defences. A weak application should probably be jettisoned where there are other more fruitful avenues to an acquittal. Counsel must always remember that "good advocacy requires courage of selection."[201]

7) It may also be acceptable to take into account the degree of jeopardy faced by the client if convicted.

8) Regardless of the merits, if the real purpose of an application is not to obtain a remedy but rather to harass a third party or delay the trial, the application should not be brought.

---

198 ABA Model Rule 3.1, comment 2.

199 ABA Model Rule 3.1 and comment 2: a position is not frivolous if there exists a good-faith basis for arguing for an extension, modification, or reversal of existing law; Monroe Freedman, "The Professional Obligation to Raise Frivolous Issues in Death Penalty Cases" (2003) 31 Hofstra L Rev 1167 at 1175–76.

200 *Becraft*, above note 197 at 550.

201 Moldaver, above note 182 at 322, quoting Laskin J of the Ontario Court of Appeal.

9) The client should be appraised of the prospects of success. He may prefer to focus resources on other trial strategies if the merits of the proposed application are weak.

10) Finally, and importantly, the decision whether to bring an application is made within the context of an adversarial system. Defence counsel must not make the decision based simply on whether she would grant the desired remedy if sitting as judge.[202] Moreover, the judge can nip a meritless application in the bud where the anticipated evidence reveals no basis upon which the sought-after remedy could be obtained, whether on her own instance or at the request of the Crown.[203] This is not to say that defence counsel faces no ethical constraints in deciding whether to bring an application. Rather, it is to acknowledge that counsel is not always obligated to screen out applications simply because they stand a less than stellar chance of success.

M. THE LAWYER IS UNABLE TO OBTAIN INSTRUCTIONS

A lawyer is sometimes unable to obtain instructions from the client. A prime example is the case of the client who disappears and cannot be located. Or a lawyer may be unable to acquire instructions because the client refuses to provide any direction on a key aspect of the conduct of the defence. In any situation where the lawyer, despite reasonable efforts, cannot obtain instructions, it is probable that he will eventually have to withdraw.[204] Continuing with the representation is not a viable option, because the lawyer is left without the client's direction and input in conducting the defence.

It may be, however, that certain uncontroversial interim steps can be taken without express instructions. Thus, where a client disappears, counsel may decide to order disclosure and review the materials, in the hope that the client will reappear before any substantial action is required with respect to the case. Such steps are proper only if reasonably

---

202 *Figueroa-Arenas*, above note 197 at 281: when criminal defence counsel is preparing motions, it is not his responsibility to perform the role of the court.

203 *Nixon*, above note 183 at para 61; *R v Kutynec* (1992), 70 CCC (3d) 289 at 301 [para 31] (Ont CA); *Felderhof*, above note 183 at para 95; *R v Vukelich* (1996), 108 CCC (3d) 193 at para 26 (BCCA); *New Approaches to Criminal Trials*, above note 38 at para 311.

204 See Alta r 2.02(4) (commentary); Man r 3.2-2A, commentary 6. See also Chapter 11, Section G, Example 1.

viewed as falling within the express or implied authority provided to the lawyer by the client. It may also be that the client has a routine court date yet does not appear as required. Counsel may not have had sufficient time to attempt to locate the client and may be unsure as to the cause of the absence. There is nothing wrong with informing the court of the dilemma and asking for time — even up to a few days — to make inquiries.[205] If the client is located, the lawyer's request has avoided a possible arrest and charge for failure to appear at court.

A further question arises as to what steps a lawyer should take in attempting to locate the missing client and how long she should wait before withdrawing. The Alberta code provides helpful guidance in this regard, stating:

> Circumstances dictating the extent of a lawyer's efforts to locate a missing client include the facts giving rise to the inability to contact the client and importance of the issue on which instructions are sought. A wilful disappearance may mandate a less strenuous attempt at location, while the potential loss of a significant right or remedy will require greater efforts. In the latter case, the lawyer should take such steps as are reasonably necessary and in accordance with the lawyer's implied authority to preserve the right or remedy in the meantime. Once a matter moves beyond the implied authority of the lawyer and all attempts to locate the client have been unsuccessful, the lawyer may be compelled to withdraw since a representation may not be continued in the absence of proper instructions.[206]

N. CLIENT WITH DIMINISHED CAPACITY TO PROVIDE INSTRUCTIONS

Representing a client whose ability to make decisions is diminished, whether because of age, physical disability, mental problems, substance abuse, or any other characteristic, presents unique and challenging problems. Our favoured model for decision making in the professional relationship, in which the client enjoys substantial control subject to a few carefully circumscribed limits, requires re-evaluation in circum-

---

205 An appearance as agent may be possible in a summary matter, or counsel may be able to act as a designate for the accused on certain appearances under s 650.01 of the *Criminal Code*, RSC 1985, c C-46.

206 Alta r 2.02(4) (commentary). See also Man r 3.2-2A, commentary 6: a lawyer ought to take reasonable steps to locate the client, but if efforts fail, he should consider withdrawing.

stances where the client has difficulty participating meaningfully in the process. As a general rule, the lawyer's primary aim should be, as far as reasonably possible, to maintain a normal relationship with the client. Establishing normality and ensuring competency in the professional relationship may require taking extraordinary and innovative steps that would be unnecessary, and perhaps even inappropriate, with other clients.

1) Canadian Rules of Professional Conduct

Most Canadian governing bodies have adopted the following basic rule regarding the proper role of counsel who represents a client with a diminished capacity to provide instructions: "When a client's ability to make decisions is impaired because of minority or mental disability, or for some other reason, the lawyer must, as far as reasonably possible, maintain a normal lawyer and client relationship."[207] The commentary to this rule begins with the fundamental proposition that a client-lawyer relationship presupposes the client has the mental ability required to make decisions and provide instructions regarding the conduct of the matter.[208] In determining whether the client meets this standard, counsel should consider factors such as the client's age, intelligence, experience, and mental and physical health, as well as the availability of support and guidance from others.[209] Counsel must then ascertain whether the client can understand the information relative to the decision to be made and is able to appreciate the reasonably foreseeable consequences of the decision.[210]

Where a prospective client is unable to provide instructions, most Canadian codes state that a lawyer should not accept the retainer. The lawyer can nonetheless take action on behalf of the individual to prevent imminent and irreparable harm until a legal representative can

---

207 Alta r 2.02(12); Sask r 2.02(10); BC, Man, NS, NL r 3.2-9. Ont r 3.2-9 uses the word "shall" instead of "must." This same hortatory goal is set out in ABA Model Rule 1.14(a) and comment 1, and is elaborated upon in American Bar Association, Standing Committee on Ethics and Professional Responsibility, Formal Opinion 404 (1996) [ABA, Opinion 404].

208 Alta r 2.02(12) (commentary); Sask r 2.02(10) (commentary); BC, Man, Ont, NS, NL r 3.2-9, commentary 1.

209 Alta r 2.02(12) (commentary); Sask r 2.02(10) (commentary); BC, Man, Ont, NS, NL r 3.2-9, commentary 1.

210 Alta r 2.02(12) (commentary); Sask r 2.02(10) (commentary); BC, Man, NS, NL r 3.2-9, commentary 1.

be appointed. In taking such action, the lawyer is subject to the same duties as would apply in acting for any client.[211]

Where an existing client is unable to provide instructions, the rules provide that the lawyer should consider taking steps to facilitate the appointment of a legal representative to protect the client's interests.[212] Whether doing so is advisable depends on the circumstances, including the importance and urgency of the matter with respect to which instructions are required. In the period before an appointment is made, the lawyer should act to preserve and protect the client's interests. In considering whether such action is needed, and if so in what form, counsel should keep in mind whether the client's inability to provide instructions puts her at risk of substantial physical, financial, or other harm.[213]

The ethical codes further state that a lawyer who takes protective action on behalf of a person or client lacking in capacity may have the implied authority to release confidential information for this purpose.[214] The rule on confidentiality found in these codes provides that such authority will be implied if fairly viewed as necessary to protect a prospective or existing client's interests in all the circumstances, including the reasonableness of the lawyer's belief that the person lacks capacity, the risk of harm to the person if confidential information is not used, and any instructions the person may have provided with respect to the use of confidential information before becoming incapacitated.[215] The codes further provide that where the court or another counsel becomes involved, the lawyer should inform the court or other counsel of the nature of his relationship with the person lacking capacity.[216]

---

211 Alta r 2.02(12) (commentary); Sask r 2.02(10) (commentary); BC, Man, NS, NL r 3.2-9, commentary 2; NB ch 4, commentary 10(a) and (c). See also ABA Model Rule 1.14, comments 9 & 10.

212 Alta r 2.02(12) (commentary); Sask r 2.02(10) (commentary); BC, Man, Ont, NS, NL r 3.2-9, commentary 3; NB ch 4, commentary 10(b). Most of these codes go on to address counsel's obligations in taking instructions from a legal representative, a topic not canvassed here for the reasons given in the text associated with notes 223–57, below in this chapter.

213 These factors are mentioned in ABA Model Rule 1.14(b).

214 Alta r 2.02(12) (commentary); Sask r 2.02(10) (commentary); BC, Man, Ont, NS, NL r 3.2-9, commentary 5.

215 Alta, Sask r 2.03(1) (commentary); BC, Man, Ont, NS, NL r 3.3-1, commentary 10. See also ABA Model Rule 1.14(c) and comment 8.

216 See the rules cited at note 212, above in this chapter, as well as ABA Model Rule 1.14, comment 10.

2) General Guidelines for the Criminal Context

A lawyer should not ignore the possibility that a criminal client's capacity to provide instructions is diminished. But neither should counsel rashly conclude that a client harbours a serious inability to understand the trial process and make decisions pertaining to the case. A lawyer should therefore generally assume the client is able to fulfill her proper role in the retainer, while remaining attuned to potential problems in this regard.

The following guidelines may assist in dealing with the criminal client who appears to exhibit some level of diminished capacity:

1) In ascertaining the degree to which a client's capacity to provide instructions might be diminished, counsel should consider the factors mentioned in the Canadian ethical codes, namely, the client's age, intelligence, experience, and mental and physical health, as well as the availability of support and guidance from others.[217] Also helpful are the more general considerations mentioned in the ABA Model Rules, which advise counsel to consider and balance such factors as the client's ability to articulate a basis for making a decision, the variability of the client's state of mind, the extent to which the client appreciates the consequences of a decision, the substantive fairness of the client's decision, and the consistency of the decision with the client's long-term commitments and values.[218]

2) Counsel should undertake all reasonable efforts to ascertain the client's wishes and otherwise carry on a functional client-lawyer relationship, which will probably require specially tailoring communications to best overcome obstacles created by a disability.[219]

3) Where the disability is likely temporary, as is usually the case where a client is under the influence of alcohol or other drugs, counsel should if feasible postpone taking any important steps in the representation until the problem has dissipated.[220]

4) A client who is fit for trial may nonetheless benefit from the assistance of a family member, close friend, or caregiver in making and communicating decisions about the case. Counsel must not shy

---

217 See the rules cited at note 209, above in this chapter.

218 See ABA Model Rule 1.14, comment 6.

219 See the basic rule regarding the proper role of counsel who represents a client with a diminished capacity to provide instructions, set out in the text associated with note 207, above in this chapter. See also Third Restatement § 24(1).

220 For a review of the ethical issues that can arise in representing addicted clients, see Erin Sparks, "Attorney-Client Relationships: Ethical Dilemmas with Clients Battling Addictions" (2011) 36 J Leg Prof 255.

away from such supportive measures,[221] especially given that interactions with third parties necessary to facilitate proper communication with a client will be covered by solicitor-client privilege.[222]
Family, friends, or health-care or mental health professionals may
also be able to give counsel advice as to the preferable manner of
communicating with the client and interpreting his wishes.

5) If the client cannot provide the lawyer with instructions on important aspects of the case, the ethical rules state that the lawyer may
need to seek the appointment of a legal representative.[223] In the
criminal context, however, the only real option is to raise the issue
of the client's fitness to stand trial.[224] This is so because if the client
is found unfit, a criminal prosecution remains in abeyance until the
client's mental state has improved — the defence does not continue
under the direction of a legal representative.[225] If, by contrast, the
client is found fit for trial, counsel has obtained a judicial endorsement of the client's ability to provide sufficient instructions[226] and
so can continue with the case as long as she is neither discharged
nor required to withdraw for "ethical reasons."[227]

6) It has been suggested that withdrawal is a valid option where a
client becomes unable to provide instructions.[228] We disagree, at

---

221 See ABA Model Rule 1.14, comment 3. This approach also finds some implicit
support in the rules cited at note 208, above in this chapter, in the reference to
"advice, guidance and support of others."

222 See *General Accident Assurance Co v Chrusz* (1999), 45 OR (3d) 321 at 352–55
[paras 104–17] (CA) [*Chrusz*]; ABA Model Rule 1.14, comment 3.

223 See the rules cited at note 212, above in this chapter.

224 See Section N(3), below in this chapter. We have found one case where an application was made to appoint a legal representative for an adult in a criminal
matter: *R v Hart*, 2011 NLCA 64. The court did not decide whether it had jurisdiction to grant the request but observed that the application was "certainly
unusual and may well be unique" (*ibid* at para 3).

225 Another bar to appointing a legal representative is the legal requirement that
certain decisions regarding the conduct of the defence be made personally by
the accused: see note 129, above in this chapter, and the associated text.

226 "An accused who has not been found unfit to stand trial must be considered capable of conducting his or her own defence": *Swain*, above note 47 at 505 [para
35]. See also *Taylor*, above note 51 at 567 [para 51]; *Szostak*, above note 58 at
paras 77–80. Counsel may find that this "judicial endorsement" does not make
the job any easier: see the comment regarding criticism of this threshold at note
235, above in this chapter.

227 See Section C(4), above in this chapter.

228 See *Green v Livermore* (1940), 74 CCC 240 at 242 [para 7] (Ont HCJ).

least absent extraordinary circumstances, given counsel's duty to preserve and protect the interests of such a client.[229]

7) Where the lawyer is unable to obtain instructions and is required to take action to preserve the client's interests, the lawyer should make the decision he reasonably believes the client would make if competent.[230]

8) If a client with a diminished capacity to provide instructions discharges counsel, or counsel is required to withdraw, there may be merit in counsel's offering her services to the court as *amicus curiae*.[231]

9) No matter the difficulties or what action is required, a client with diminished capacity should always be treated with respect.[232] The goal is to honour the client's autonomy and dignity in making decisions, to the extent reasonably possible given the nature of the impairment.

3) Fitness to Stand Trial

The *Criminal Code* provides that an accused is unfit to stand trial if unable on account of mental disorder to conduct a defence or to instruct counsel to do so, and, in particular, unable on account of mental disorder to understand the nature or object of the proceedings, understand the possible consequences of the proceedings, or communicate with counsel.[233] Caselaw holds that the ability to instruct counsel, as defined in the *Criminal Code*, does not require that the accused be able to appreciate his own best interests in providing instructions, or even be prepared to co-operate with counsel.[234] While the accused must be able

---

229 This duty is described in the paragraph associated with notes 212–13, above in this chapter; ABA, Opinion 404, above note 207. The situation may be different on appeal, as seen in *R v Ta* (2002), 164 CCC (3d) 97 (Ont CA) [*Ta*], where counsel withdrew and was appointed *amicus curiae* after the client became unable to provide instructions. The appeal was heard even though the appellant was unfit, the court holding that the *Criminal Code* fitness provisions do not apply at the appellate level and that the client's interests could be protected through other means.

230 See ABA Model Rule 1.14, comment 6; Third Restatement § 24(2); as well as the Canadian rules cited at note 214, above in this chapter.

231 See the somewhat analogous case of *Ta*, discussed in note 229, above in this chapter.

232 See ABA Model Rule 1.14, comment 2.

233 *Criminal Code*, above note 205, s 2.

234 *Taylor*, above note 51 at 566–67 [paras 48–55]; *R v Whittle* (1994), 92 CCC (3d) 11 at 25–26 and 31 [paras 32, 48, and 51] (SCC); *R v LSC*, 2003 ABCA 105 at paras 10–14; *R v Morrissey*, 2007 ONCA 770 at paras 24–47, leave to appeal to

to communicate so as to provide instructions, including on matters such as how to plead and whether to testify, and to relate the facts necessary to permit counsel to present a defence, there is no requirement that the instructions be sensible when objectively measured against her best interests.[235]

In many cases where an accused's fitness is debatable, the problem will be readily apparent to the Crown or the court and so will be addressed regardless of any initiative on the part of the defence.[236] Yet defence counsel may, by virtue of his close contact with the client, be the only one with reason to believe that fitness is a live issue. If the client is unable to provide instructions to raise the issue, can counsel nonetheless disclose his concerns to the court? Can he do so even against the wishes of the client? These are hard questions that do not yield easy answers.

We can start by noting that counsel may wish to obtain the advice of a mental-health expert regarding the client's condition, despite the absence of instructions to do so.[237] The objection can be made that without the client's express consent, such action violates the lawyer's duty of confidentiality. Yet disclosure to the expert likely falls within counsel's implied authority to release confidential information to protect the interests of a client with diminished capacity.[238] Provided that counsel has a real concern on the issue of fitness and that no more confidential information is revealed than is necessary, consultation with

---

SCC refused, [2008] SCCA No 102; *R v Jobb*, 2008 SKCA 156 at paras 18–26 and 39; *R v Penny*, 2010 NBCA 49 at paras 33–41.

235 This low "limited cognitive capacity" threshold for a finding of fitness has been questioned or outright criticized because an accused may be found to be fit yet utterly lack the capacity to make rational decisions and so to properly instruct counsel on any reasonable view of the matter, with the result that trial fairness is undermined: see Melody Martin, "Defending the Mentally Ill Client in Criminal Matters: Ethics, Advocacy, and Responsibility" (1993) 52 UT Fac L Rev 73 at 113–17; House of Commons, Standing Committee on Justice and Human Rights, *Review of the Mental Disorder Provisions of the Criminal Code* (June 2002) at 7–9 (Chair: Honourable Andy Scott); Hy Bloom & Richard Schneider, *Mental Disorder and the Law: A Primer for Legal and Mental Health Professionals* (Toronto: Irwin Law, 2006) at 76–78; Joan M Barrett & Riun Shandler, *Mental Disorder in Canadian Criminal Law* (Toronto: Thomson Carswell, 2006) (loose-leaf 2012 supplement release 4) at § 3.2(c); Hugh Harradence, "Re-applying the Standard of Fitness to Stand Trial" (2013) 59 Crim LQ 511 at 554–56.

236 The defence, prosecution, and court all have the power to request a fitness hearing: see *Criminal Code*, above note 205, s 672.23(1).

237 See American Bar Association, Standing Committee on Ethics and Professional Responsibility, Informal Opinion 1530 (1989).

238 See the text and rules associated with notes 214–15, above in this chapter.

an expert is justified. In this regard, it is worth remembering that the expert will ordinarily be bound by the same duty of confidentiality that applies to the lawyer.[239] And consulting with an expert may carry the benefit of providing counsel with an opportunity to initiate measures that restore fitness without having to raise the issue with the court.[240]

Nonetheless, after obtaining expert advice, counsel may reasonably believe that it is necessary to raise the fitness issue with the court. Or counsel may come to the same conclusion based simply on her dealings with the client.[241] In either case, raising the fitness issue even absent express instructions is justified, and probably mandated, where counsel has a good-faith basis for doubting the client's fitness to stand trial.[242] After all, by undertaking the conduct of the case in court, the lawyer is implicitly representing that the accused is fit to stand trial. The lawyer is also proceeding on the assumption that the client is exercising some level of decision making authority within the bounds of a workable professional relationship. If the relationship is fractured because of real fitness issues, proceeding with the trial creates an unacceptable risk of undermining the client's autonomy and subverting the proper role of counsel.[243]

Should a lawyer with serious misgivings regarding a client's fitness nonetheless be permitted *not* to raise the fitness issue if she reasonably believes that doing so may cause the client undue harm? The example is given of a client charged with a relatively minor offence who faces an

---

239 See *Chrusz*, above note 222 at 353–55 [paras 111–17].
240 See Christopher Slobogin & Amy Mashburn, "Ethics in Criminal Advocacy, Symposium: The Criminal Defense Lawyer's Fiduciary Duty to Clients with Mental Disability" (2000) 68 Fordham L Rev 1581 at 1622–23.
241 See *Szostak*, above note 58 at para 70.
242 See *ibid* at paras 69–70; *Brigham*, above note 37 at 379"g"–80"b"; *R v Gibbons* (1946), 86 CCC 20 at 21–22 [para 3] (Ont CA). *Szostak*, above note 58 at para 71, expressly declines to decide whether counsel can raise the fitness issue contrary to the client's express instructions. However, counsel did so without adverse comment from the court in *R v Gero*, 2000 ABCA 227 [*Gero*]. This course of action finds support in the policy driving s 672.24 of the *Criminal Code*, above note 205, which requires the court to appoint counsel for an unrepresented accused — even if against his will — where there are reasonable grounds to believe he is unfit to stand trial: see *R v Waranuk*, 2010 YKCA 5 at para 40. Several American cases suggest that counsel can raise the fitness issue against the client's wishes: *State v Johnson*, 395 NW2d 176 (Wis 1986); *United States v Boigegrain*, 155 F3d 1181 (10th Cir 1998), certiorari denied, 525 US 1083 (1999); *In re Fleming*, 16 P3d 610 at 616–17 (Wash 2001). See also American Bar Association, *ABA Criminal Justice Mental Health Standards* (Washington, DC: American Bar Association, 1989) standard 7-4.2(c); Third Restatement § 24, comment "d."
243 See *Szostak*, above note 58 at para 69; Martin, above note 235 at 127.

insurmountable Crown case and has served as much time in pre-trial detention as he would if sentenced after a guilty plea. Some commentators have suggested that, on these facts, it is ethical for counsel to represent the client on a guilty plea and not raise the competency issue in court.[244]

However, improvements made over the last two decades in the protections afforded to individuals whose fitness is being scrutinized by the court,[245] as well as those who have been found to be unfit,[246] make it much less likely that raising the fitness issue will be to the client's decided detriment, for instance in terms of time spent in custody. This is especially so in jurisdictions employing mental health courts, which offer a therapeutic jurisprudence option focused on treatment, support, and diversion.[247] Even where a mental health court is unavailable, Crown counsel may agree to divert a less serious matter given a client's condition.[248] In short, defence counsel can usually raise the fitness issue without risking a worse outcome for the accused, and doing so will often have precisely the opposite effect.[249]

Before raising the issue of fitness with the court, counsel must do her best to discuss the matter fully with the client. Counsel must also recognize that there may be valid reasons why an accused does not want to pursue the fitness inquiry. For instance, the client may wish to avoid the stigma of the assessment or an adverse finding, the treatment that can attend on such a process, or any delay that might be associated with an assessment. On the other hand, an assessment may work powerfully to the client's immediate benefit. Specifically, the process may occur quickly and involve treatment that results in drastic improvement in the client's mental state, allowing for a fairer and smoother trial process.

---

244 Rodney Uphoff, "The Decision to Challenge the Competency of a Marginally Competent Client: Defense Counsel's Unavoidably Difficult Position" in Rodney Uphoff, ed, *Ethical Problems Facing the Criminal Defense Lawyer: Practical Answers to Tough Questions* (Chicago: American Bar Association, 1995) ch 3 at 35; John D King, "Candor, Zeal, and the Substitution of Judgment: Ethics and the Mentally Ill Criminal Defendant" (2008) 58 Am U L Rev 207 at 234–45 and 258–64. *Contra* Slobogin & Mashburn, above note 240 at 1621–27.

245 For example, s 672.16 of the *Criminal Code*, above note 205, creates a statutory presumption against in-custody assessments.

246 See Harradence, above note 235 at 548–53.

247 See Richard Schneider, Hy Bloom, & Mark Heerema, *Mental Health Courts: Decriminalizing the Mentally Ill* (Toronto: Irwin Law: 2007).

248 *R v Proulx*, 2011 SKPC 128 at para 89.

249 Slobogin & Mashburn, above note 240 at 1623–24.

Counsel who raises the fitness issue, whether against the client's wishes or not, should always do so in the client's presence, and not while the client is absent from the courtroom.[250] In bringing the issue to the court's attention, counsel should also strive to protect the client's best interests to the greatest extent possible, for example by ensuring that the client is not unnecessarily subjected to an in-custody assessment.

4) Raising the NCRMD Defence

The NCRMD defence applies where an accused commits an act while suffering from a mental disorder that renders her incapable of appreciating the nature and quality of the act or of knowing it was wrong.[251] The party seeking to establish NCRMD bears the onus of proving it on the balance of probabilities.[252]

The question of overriding a competent client's decision not to raise an NCRMD defence is distinct from the fitness issue. The major point of differentiation derives from the fact that the client is presumably fit to stand trial and thus generally competent to make decisions regarding the conduct of the defence.[253] As we have seen, Canadian constitutional law accords the client total freedom in deciding whether to plead guilty.[254] The reasoning behind this conclusion applies equally to the decision to put forward, or not, an NCRMD defence. Indeed, the Supreme Court of Canada's decision in *Swain* holds that an accused person has a constitutional right to control the conduct of the defence in various respects including the decision whether to rely on the NCRMD defence.[255]

It is true that *Swain* also recognizes that society has an interest in preventing the conviction of people who are not truly guilty of a criminal offence by reason of incompetence.[256] The Court went so far in this regard as to permit the Crown to raise the NCRMD issue of its own accord, and against the wishes of the accused, following a guilty verdict.[257] The Court stated that "[t]he accused is not the only person who

---

250 *Szostak*, above note 58 at para 72.
251 *Criminal Code*, above note 205, s 16(1).
252 *Criminal Code*, ibid, s 16(3).
253 See the paragraph associated with notes 233–35, above in this chapter.
254 See Section F, above in this chapter.
255 *Swain*, above note 47 at 505–6 [paras 35–36].
256 *Ibid* at 508–9 [paras 44–45].
257 *Ibid* at 512–18 [paras 54–75]. The Crown can also raise NCRMD at the conviction stage where the accused has put in issue his ability to form the intent necessary to prove the charged offence (*ibid* at 508 [para 41]).

has an interest in the outcome of the trial; society itself has an interest in ensuring that the system does not incorrectly label insane people as criminals."[258] Unlike defence counsel, however, the prosecutor does not owe the accused a duty of loyalty, and to the contrary is generally expected to conduct the case in a manner inimical to the accused's best interests. A distinction must therefore be drawn between the Crown's ability to raise NCRMD against the accused's wishes and the propriety of a defence lawyer doing so.

In line with this way of thinking, in R v Szostak the Ontario Court of Appeal held that defence counsel must obtain the client's instructions before pursuing an NCRMD defence and *a fortiori* cannot raise the defence over the client's objections.[259] The court recognized that an accused person who is fit for trial may act irresponsibly in deciding whether to advance the NCRMD defence, despite having received proper advice from counsel, but held that this is her right.[260] It is not for defence counsel, however well intentioned, to pursue the defence without proper instructions.[261]

The approach recommended in *Szostak* sits uneasily with defence counsel's conduct in the earlier Ontario case of *R v David*.[262] There, the client had taken the stand to deny having committed three homicides, after which his counsel called psychiatric evidence to support a finding of NCRMD. In closing submissions, defence counsel relied on NCRMD and explained its inconsistency with his client's testimony by suggesting the accused may have confabulated his denial rather than admit to lacking a memory of the homicides. Counsel also told the jury that the accused, "of course, himself, doesn't promote the same defence."[263] The Court of Appeal accepted the propriety of the Crown counsel's countering these comments by submitting to the jury that defence counsel must have had instructions to mount the NCRMD defence.[264] Another possibility, not raised by the Crown or the court, is that counsel called the expert witnesses and ran the NCRMD defence without obtaining his client's consent.[265]

---

258 *Ibid* at 512 [para 56].
259 *Szostak*, above note 58 at paras 77–78. The preponderance of American cases and commentators share this view, as noted by Johnson, above note 74 at 105–10, and Poulin, above note 42 at 1244–45.
260 *Szostak*, above note 58 at para 78.
261 *Ibid* at para 80.
262 (2002), 169 CCC (3d) 165 (Ont CA).
263 *Ibid* para 82.
264 *Ibid* at paras 79–83.
265 Contrast Guy Paul Morin's first trial, where Morin did not testify but steadfastly denied to his counsel committing the charged murder. Counsel recommended

Though bound to obtain and follow the client's instructions regarding whether to raise NCRMD, counsel has a duty to inform the client fully as to the advantages and disadvantages of doing so and should provide her considered opinion on the point.[266] When engaging in this consultation process, counsel should recognize that a client may have legitimate reasons for viewing an NCRMD defence with distaste. He may want to obtain total vindication with an acquittal and may reject any notion that the alleged offence involved incompetent behaviour. The client may also prefer a set and limited jail term to the more indeterminate confinement that can result from an NCRMD finding.[267] Furthermore, the stigma of an NCRMD finding and any treatment imposed as a result may be anathema to some clients. There can also be tactical reasons to avoid an NCRMD defence, including the hope that withholding the defence from the trier of fact will improve the chances of acquittal or focus more attention on a diminished responsibility defence. These are points worth discussing with the client in arriving at a final decision on the matter.

Perhaps the greatest ethical challenge in this area arises out of the fact that the fitness test employed by Canadian courts requires only that the accused be able to communicate with counsel, and not that she have the capacity to engage in rational decision making.[268] An accused may therefore be fit for trial yet because of a serious mental illness irrationally refuse to raise a promising NCRMD defence that would yield a much better result than an otherwise certain conviction. It has been suggested that in these very narrow and exceptional circumstances, counsel should be permitted to raise NCRMD without the client's instructions.[269] Alternatively, because the client's instructions amount to an insistence that the defence be conducted in an incompetent manner,[270] counsel has the option of withdrawing for "ethical reasons" and simultaneously asking to be appointed as *amicus curiae*, in which

---

that Morin run NCRMD as an alternative to the main defence of identity. Though highly reluctant, Morin agreed because counsel stated that otherwise he would withdraw. See Woolley, above note 35 at 52–54 and 58; *Report of the Kaufman Commission on Proceedings Involving Guy Paul Morin*, by The Honourable Fred Kaufman (Toronto: Ontario Ministry of the Attorney General, 1998) at 35–39, 1049–63, and 1069, online: www.attorneygeneral.jus.gov.on.ca/english/about/pubs/morin/.

266 See Section E, above in this chapter.

267 See *R v Kankis*, 2012 ONSC 378 at paras 20–22; *Szostak*, above note 58 at paras 64 and 74.

268 See the comments at note 235, above in this chapter.

269 Slobogin & Mashburn, above note 240 at 1631–37.

270 See Section K, above in this chapter.

guise he may be able to raise the NCRMD defence at either the conviction or the postconviction phase. The option of complying with the client's wholly irrational instructions, perhaps hoping that NCRMD can be raised for the first time on appeal, is hardly an ideal result.[271]

Of course, in many cases the imprudence of not raising NCRMD will not be so obvious, and reasonable people may see the pros and cons of running the defence differently. A client's refusal to employ the defence is therefore not necessarily tantamount to an insistence that the lawyer act incompetently, nor does it invariably justify the view that there has been an irreparable loss of confidence or breakdown in the relationship so as to allow, or mandate, withdrawal. Even where withdrawal is permissible because of the client's refusal to run NCRMD, counsel should not wait until the eleventh hour to raise the issue of the defence, at least not where the issue has been foreseeable for some time. Otherwise, the client may be faced with the Hobson's choice of losing counsel shortly before or during the trial or of adopting a strategy she finds highly objectionable.

O. THE REPRESENTATION OF YOUNG PEOPLE

To varying degrees, our society views children and adolescents as unable to make many fundamental decisions affecting their welfare and regards young people as dependent on the care and guidance of parents or legal guardians. The legal system has thus deemed that young people have limited capacity in many respects. A prime example is the inability of a minor to commence a civil action without a litigation guardian. In the realm of criminal law, no person can be convicted of an offence committed while under the age of twelve.[272]

Yet young people between the ages of twelve and seventeen who commit offences proscribed by the *Criminal Code* are subject to prosecution under the *Youth Criminal Justice Act*.[273] Importantly, the Act makes clear that a youth charged with a criminal offence has the right to "retain and instruct counsel without delay, *and to exercise that right personally*, at any stage of the proceedings."[274] The Act also stipulates

---

271 Although, as observed by Barrett & Shandler, above note 235 at § 4.4(a)(i), courts are fairly flexible in allowing NCRMD to be raised for the first time on appeal. See, for example, *R v IEM* (2003), 173 CCC (3d) 515 (Ont CA).

272 *Criminal Code*, above note 205, s 13.

273 SC 2002, c 1, ss 2(1) (definition of "young person") and 14(1).

274 *Ibid*, s 25(1) [emphasis added]. Parliament added the italicized words in response to *R v W(WW)* (1985), 20 CCC (3d) 214 (Man CA), which held that a

that young persons "have rights and freedoms in their own right, such as a right to be heard in the course of and to participate in the processes, other than the decision to prosecute, that lead to decisions that affect them."[275]

These statutory provisions strongly suggest that the relationship between a young person charged with a criminal offence and his lawyer is similar to any other client-lawyer relationship. Indeed, most Canadian ethical codes state that where a client's ability to make decisions is diminished because of "minority," the lawyer must, as far as reasonably possible, maintain a normal client-lawyer relationship.[276] Young persons who are able to comprehend the circumstances relevant to the charge and instruct counsel should therefore enjoy the same decision making authority vis-à-vis counsel as would an adult accused. This position is generally accepted in the United States[277] and is also advocated by commentators in Canada.[278]

In short, counsel who represents a young person must act as an advocate, zealously seeking to achieve the client's goals. Counsel must also keep the young person informed and follow her instructions, even if given against the advice of counsel and arguably not in the client's best interests. An *amicus curiae* model, where counsel attempts to aid the court in achieving a result that is fair for all participants and society as

---

youth charged criminally could only retain counsel by a guardian, next friend, or guardian *ad litem* and that the lawyer had to take instructions from the adult responsible for the retainer, as opposed to the youth.

275 Above note 273, s 3(1)(d)(i).

276 See the rules cited at note 207, above in this chapter. To similar effect, see ABA Model Rule 1.14(a).

277 See ABA Model Rule 1.2(a) and 1.14; Third Restatement § 24; National Juvenile Defender Center, *National Juvenile Defense Standards* (Washington, DC: National Juvenile Defender Center, 2012) § 1.2 [*NJD Standards*], online: www.njdc.info/pdf/NationalJuvenileDefenseStandards2013.pdf; Lee Teitelbaum, "Standards Relating to Counsel for Private Parties" in Robert E Shepherd, ed, *Juvenile Justice Standards Annotated: A Balanced Approach* (Chicago: American Bar Association, 1996) 69, parts III–V at 75–82, online: www.ncjrs.gov/pdffiles1/ojjdp/166773.pdf; *Standards for the Administration of Juvenile Justice: Report of the National Advisory Committee for Juvenile Justice and Delinquency* (Washington, DC: United States Department of Justice, 1980).

278 See Nicholas Bala & Sanjeev Anand, *Youth Criminal Justice Law*, 3d ed (Toronto: Irwin Law, 2012) at 415–20; Jeffery Wilson, *Wilson on Children and the Law* (Toronto: Butterworths, 1994) (loose-leaf 2013 supplement) at § 6.18; Larry Wilson, "The Role of Counsel in the *Youth Criminal Justice Act*" (2003) 40 Alta L Rev 1029 at 1032–34; Quebec Bar Committee on the Legal Representation of Children, "The Legal Representation of Children: A Consultation Paper," translated by Robin Ward (1996) 13 Can J Fam L 49 at 101–3.

a whole, is thus rejected, as is the "champion" or "guardianship model," whereby counsel's view of the client's best interests can override instructions to the contrary.

1) Making Sure That the Client-Lawyer Relationship Works

Defence counsel who represents a young person must take special care to ensure that the relationship operates properly. By dint of less extensive life experience and education, as well as developmental factors, young people may be at a cognitive and psychosocial disadvantage when it comes to making well-reasoned decisions.[279] They are also not as likely as adults to understand the workings of the criminal justice system. Studies suggest that young people often hold significant misconceptions about the system's nature and operation.[280] In many instances, the role of counsel therefore includes educating the young person as to how the system works, in language suitable to his stage of development.[281] This counselling function ensures that the young person is fully informed and thus able to make competent decisions pertaining to the legal representation. As in any client-lawyer relationship, the lawyer must be ready and willing to advise the client as to the pros and cons of various options and on occasion to be firm in recommending against a course of action the lawyer believes to be ill-advised.[282]

2) The Role of the Parent

Parental support and involvement can be of great value to a young person charged with a criminal offence. It is thus often appropriate for

---

279 See the caselaw, social science, and scientific studies cited in Abbe Smith, "'I Ain't Takin' No Plea': The Challenges in Counseling Young People Facing Serious Time" (2007) 60 Rutgers L Rev 11 at 18–21; Kristen Henning, "Loyalty, Paternalism, and Rights: Client Counseling Theory and the Role of Child's Counsel in Delinquency Cases" (2005) 81 Notre Dame L Rev 245 at 270–73. See also *Graham v Florida*, 130 S Ct 2011 at 2026 (2010); *NJD Standards*, above note 277 at § 2.6 (commentary).

280 M Peterson-Dadala, R Abramovitch, & J Duda, "Young Children's Legal Knowledge and Reasoning Ability" (1997) 39 Can J Crim 145; Michele Peterson-Dadala & Rona Abramovitch, "Children's Knowledge of the Legal System: Are They Competent to Instruct Legal Counsel?" (1992) 34 Can J Crim 139; *NJD Standards*, above note 277 at § 1.2 (commentary).

281 *NJD Standards*, ibid at § 2.6 & commentary.

282 We endorse the collaborative view of counselling described by Henning, above note 279 at 315–24.

counsel to meet with a youth's parents and keep them informed on the progress of the case. Parents may also be able to aid in the preparation of the case, for instance, by helping to put in place a rehabilitative program in anticipation of sentencing.[283]

Yet a young person and her parents may not see eye to eye regarding the proper conduct of the case. The parent may prefer a delay before seeking bail to teach the young person a lesson or insist on a guilty plea or view a custody disposition as preferable for the young person's future development. Conversely, where the parent risks liability arising out of the young person's acts, he may press for an acquittal at all costs even though such an approach is contrary to the youth's wishes and interests. Regardless of the parent's desires, counsel must leave the decision making authority with the client.

Ultimately, counsel's duties to the young person shape the degree and nature of counsel's interaction with the parents. Obligations of loyalty, competence, confidentiality, and disclosure are owed to the young person, not the parents, and dealings with the parents are permitted only where counsel holds a reasonable expectation that these obligations to the client will be bolstered as a result. The limited nature of the relationship between counsel and the young person's parents should be made clear to the young person and her parents at the beginning of the retainer.[284] As well, interaction with parents should take place only with the consent of the young person. Some young people may not want any parental involvement or may wish for only limited communication between lawyer and parents, in which case counsel must abide by these directions.

P. KEEPING A WRITTEN RECORD OF DISAGREEMENTS AND RESOLUTIONS

Prudent counsel will keep a written record of any substantial disagreement that occurs with a client during the retainer.[285] Matters that should be memorialized include the issue in dispute, the advice given, the client's reaction and instructions, and the course actually taken.

---

283 *NJD Standards*, above note 277 at § 2.5 (commentary).

284 *Ibid* at § 2.5 & commentary. See also Chapter 6, Section K(3), addressing conflict of interest concerns that can arise where a parent pays a child's legal fees.

285 See ABA Defense Standard 4-5.2(c). See also *R v GM*, 2012 NLCA 47 at para 123, rev'd on other grounds 2013 SCC 24, on the importance of obtaining written instructions where the client refuses to accept the lawyer's advice.

This record can help resolve factual disputes as to what happened and what was said if the lawyer's conduct is later attacked on appeal, in a civil suit, or in disciplinary proceedings.[286] Such a record can also on occasion aid the client, lending support to a version of events that is disputed by the Crown on appeal. Finally, the process of recording circumstances surrounding a dispute serves to remind lawyers of the importance of communicating fully with clients. The result may be a satisfactory resolution of the disagreement.

---

286 See, for example, *Archer*, above note 37 at paras 143–49; *R v Wells* (2001), 139 OAC 356 at para 61: signed instructions provided by the client at trial relied on by the appeal court to reject an ineffective assistance claim.

CHAPTER 4

CONFIDENTIALITY

A. INTRODUCTION

The lawyer's duty to keep confidential all information received as a result of representing a client is a core obligation of the professional relationship. The scope of this duty is exceptionally broad, demanding that counsel take great care in handling all information pertaining to or affecting a client. At the same time, there are exceptions to the duty of confidentiality that permit, and sometimes even demand, disclosure of such information by the lawyer. Determining the instances where exceptions should apply raises some of the most controversial and daunting ethical problems facing the criminal bar today.

This chapter examines the lawyer's duty of confidentiality to the client with an eye to some of the problems and concerns that can arise in a criminal practice. It also reviews instances where a lawyer owes a duty of confidentiality to *non*-clients, the most important of which concerns the proper handling of disclosure materials received from the Crown. Possible justifications for breaching confidentiality are discussed in other chapters, including Chapter 5 (confidentiality exceptions), Chapter 7 (client perjury), and Chapter 10 (physical evidence relevant to a crime).

B. RATIONALE

The standard justification for imposing a duty of confidentiality on lawyers is that the client who is assured of complete secrecy is more likely to reveal to his counsel all information pertaining to the case.[1] The lawyer who is in possession of all relevant information is better able to advise the client and hence provide competent service,[2] furthering both the client's legal rights and the truth-finding function of the adversarial system.[3] The obligation to maintain confidentiality also protects the client's privacy,[4] as well as promoting autonomy and dignity by facilitating her control over personal information and the conduct of the defence.[5] And the duty of confidentiality is closely connected to the overarching duty of loyalty owed by a lawyer to the client. The obligation to be loyal would be compromised if a lawyer could use information so as to adversely impact the client. A complete bar on the unauthorized use of confidential information by counsel, even where no adverse impact is possible, accordingly serves a prophylactic function that helps to ensure undivided loyalty.

What is more, solicitor-client privilege and thus by implication the ethical duty of confidentiality acquires "an added dimension" where

---

1   See *Smith v Jones* (1999), 132 CCC (3d) 225 at para 46 (SCC) [*Smith*]; *R v Mc-Clure*, 2001 SCC 14 at paras 31–33 [*McClure*]; *R v Brown*, 2002 SCC 32 at para 27 [*Brown*]; *Foster Wheeler Power Co v SIGED Inc*, 2004 SCC 18 at para 34 [*Foster Wheeler Power*]; *Pritchard v Ontario (Human Rights Commission)*, 2004 SCC 31 at para 14 [*Pritchard*]; *Canada (Privacy Commissioner) v Blood Tribe Department of Health*, 2008 SCC 44 at para 9 [*Blood Tribe*]; *R v Cunningham*, 2010 SCC 10 at paras 26–27 [*Cunningham*].

2   See Alta, Sask r 2.03(1) (commentary); BC, Man, Ont, NS, NL r 3.3-1, commentary 1; NB ch 5, commentary 1; CBA Code ch IV, commentary 1.

3   See *Maranda v Richer*, 2003 SCC 67 at para 37 [*Maranda*]; *R v Joanisse* (1995), 102 CCC (3d) 35 at 57 [para 64] (Ont CA) [*Joanisse*], leave to appeal to SCC refused (1996), 111 CCC (3d) vi (SCC). For a rights-based justification of solicitor-client privilege and so by extension confidentiality, see Adam Dodek, "Reconceiving Solicitor-Client Privilege" (2010) 35 Queen's LJ 493 at 519–20, 522, and 523–25.

4   See *Lavallee, Rackel & Heintz v Canada (AG)*, 2002 SCC 61 at paras 35 and 49 [*Lavallee*]; CBA Code ch IV, commentary 3.

5   The importance of autonomy and dignity in terms of controlling a criminal defence is recognized in *R v Swain* (1991), 63 CCC (3d) 481 at 505–6 [paras 35–36] (SCC). The autonomy-based rationale for protecting solicitor-client privilege is recognized in *General Accident Assurance Co v Chrusz* (1999), 180 DLR (4th) 241 at para 92 (Ont CA); *College of Physicians of British Columbia v British Columbia (Information and Privacy Commissioner)*, 2002 BCCA 665 at para 30. See also Alan Strudler, "Belief and Betrayal: Confidentiality in Criminal Defense Practice" (2000) 69 U Cin L Rev 245.

the client is the subject of a criminal investigation. The "promise of confidentiality" engaged by the privilege is particularly vital because the client is facing the state as a "singular antagonist."[6] More specifically, maintaining client confidences is especially important in the criminal context because doing so substantially furthers the client's ability to exercise constitutional rights against the state.[7]

In promoting effective legal advice, the duty of confidentiality not only benefits the individual client but also serves a broader societal interest. As already noted, a client who is able to rely on the assurance of confidentiality is more likely to receive sound legal counsel. As a result, he is more likely to obey the law and if charged with a crime is better able to mount a defence. It is in the public interest that these ends be encouraged, and the duty of confidentiality thus advances fundamental systemic goals.

C. THE RULES OF PROFESSIONAL CONDUCT

All Canadian rules of professional conduct strongly assert the lawyer's duty of confidentiality. The basic rule promulgated by most law societies states:

> The lawyer at all times must hold in strict confidence all information concerning the business and affairs of a client acquired in the course of the professional relationship and must not divulge any such information unless:
> (a) expressly or impliedly authorized by the client;
> (b) required by law or a court to do so;
> (c) required to deliver the information to the Society; or
> (d) otherwise permitted or required by this rule.[8]

The breadth of the duty of confidentiality imposed by the ethical rules is discussed in detail below. It is nonetheless worth stressing that the Canadian rules do not merely import a description of confidentiality that has independently been delineated elsewhere, for instance, by

---

6   *Lavallee*, above note 4 at para 23.
7   A largely rights-based justification of defence counsel's role is provided in Chapter 1, Section D. See also Section F, below in this chapter.
8   Alta, Sask r 2.03(1); BC, Man, NS, NL r 3-3.1. Ont r 3-3.1 uses almost the same wording. See also Que s 3.06; *Professional Code*, CQLR c C-26, s 60.4; *An act respecting the Barreau du Quebec*, CQLR c B-1, s 131; NB ch 5, rule; CBA Code ch IV, r 1.

statute or the common law. Rather, the rules provide lawyers with a freestanding, self-contained definition of confidentiality.

D. COMPARISON WITH SOLICITOR-CLIENT AND LITIGATION PRIVILEGES

The similarities and differences between the ethical rule of confidentiality and solicitor-client privilege are important, and are recognized in the rules of professional conduct.[9] Solicitor-client privilege is a class privilege that attaches to confidential communications passing between lawyer and client as part of the professional relationship.[10] The concept of confidentiality is accordingly central to the privilege.

Yet crucial distinctions exist between a lawyer's ethical duty of confidentiality and solicitor-client privilege.[11] First, the privilege encompasses only matters communicated in confidence by the client. The duty of confidentiality is broader, covering all information acquired by counsel whatever its source. Second, the privilege applies to the communication itself, does not bar the adduction of evidence pertaining to the facts communicated if gleaned from another source, and is often lost where other parties are present during the communication. In contrast, the ethical duty of confidentiality usually persists even where outside parties know the information in question or where the communication was made in the presence of others. Third, the application of an exception to solicitor-client privilege does not necessarily mean that information is exempt from the ethical duty of confidentiality. A comparable or some other exception to the ethical duty must apply before the lawyer can reveal the information.

It used to be accurate to say that the ethical duty of confidentiality was also different from solicitor-client privilege in that the latter was merely a rule of evidence preventing the use of privileged information in court whereas the former precluded release of the information for any purpose. This distinction is no longer valid. Since at least the 1982 decision in *Descôteaux v Mierzwinski*, courts have recognized that the

---

9   Alta, Sask r 2.03(1) (commentary); BC, Man, Ont, NS, NL r 3.3-1, commentary 2; CBA Code ch IV, commentary 2 & 3; NB ch 5, commentary 2.

10   See *Canada v Solosky* (1979), 50 CCC (2d) 495 at 507 and 509 (SCC) [*Solosky*]; *Descôteaux v Mierzwinski* (1982), 70 CCC (2d) 385 at 398 (SCC) [*Descôteaux*]; *R v Campbell* (1999), 133 CCC (3d) 257 at para 49 (SCC) [*Campbell*]; *McClure*, above note 1 at para 36; *Pritchard*, above note 1 at para 15; *R v Youvarajah*, 2013 SCC 41 at para 122 [*Youvarajah*], Wagner J, dissenting but not on this point.

11   See *R v Robillard* (2000), 151 CCC (3d) 296 at para 31 (Que CA) [*Robillard*].

privilege is also a "substantive rule" that protects against disclosure outside of the courtroom setting.[12] Thus, to provide a couple of examples, the privilege applies to prevent a journalist from obtaining client-lawyer communications through freedom of information legislation[13] and is also engaged when an inmate communicates with a lawyer from jail, whether by phone or letter.[14]

The subtle and complicated interplay between confidentiality and privilege is relevant to many ethical questions confronting criminal lawyers.[15] Unfortunately, discussion of the two concepts in the caselaw is occasionally muddled or, if taken out of context, confusing.[16] To provide but one example, courts will sometimes hold that a communication is not privileged, because it was not intended to be "confidential,"[17] yet this same communication may well be considered confidential within the meaning of the ethical rules. In other words, the term "confidential" can be used in different ways at different times. We will return to the distinction between the privilege and the ethical duty of confidentiality at various points in this chapter, as well as the following chapter on exceptions to the duty. For the moment, it may be helpful to provide a few examples.

Example 1: An accused is charged with robbery. Counsel has received disclosure detailing the results of police surveillance of her client during the day of the offence. The facts outlined in the disclosure are not privileged, and it is clear that the surveillance officers can testify at trial as to their observations. Nevertheless, the ethical rule of confidentiality prohibits the lawyer from revealing the facts set out in the disclosure to third parties.[18]

---

12   *Descôteaux*, above note 10 at 397–98 & 399–400. This point was made earlier in *Solosky*, above note 10 at 507–12, yet *Descôteaux* offers a fuller, clearer discussion. The substantive nature of the rule has since been affirmed in many cases, including *Smith*, above note 1 at paras 48–49; *McClure*, above note 1 at paras 17–24; *Lavallee*, above note 4 at para 49; *Maranda*, above note 3 at para 12; *Blank v Canada (Minister of Justice)*, 2006 SCC 39 at para 24 [*Blank*]; *Blood Tribe*, above note 1 at para 10.

13   See *Goodis v Ontario (Ministry of Correctional Services)*, 2006 SCC 31 [*Goodis*].

14   See *Solosky*, above note 10.

15   See, for example, David Layton, "The Public Safety Exception: Confusing Confidentiality, Privilege and Ethics" (2001) 6 Can Crim L Rev 217.

16   As recognized in *Foster Wheeler Power*, above note 1 at paras 28–29.

17   See, for example, *Ontario (Securities Commission) v Greymac Credit Corp* (1983), 41 OR (2d) 328 at 338 (Div Ct) [*Ontario (Securities Commission)*].

18   The disclosure may also be covered by an implied undertaking limiting the use to which it can be put: see Section R, below in this chapter.

Example 2: A client consults counsel with respect to the law concerning electronic surveillance. Counsel concludes that the client is seeking information to help avoid detection by police in connection with an upcoming drug deal. She tells him not to break the law and ends the interview. Counsel makes detailed notes of the meeting. Later, the police visit the lawyer asking her to reveal voluntarily the contents of the interview and provide them with any notes. The communications between counsel and client come within the crime-fraud exception to solicitor-client privilege and will probably not be protected if the lawyer is subpoenaed to testify or subjected to a search warrant. Yet the lawyer's ethical duty of confidentiality prevents her from revealing the communications or notes to police absent compulsion by legal process.[19]

Example 3: A client tells counsel he will be unable to pay her fees until after the trial, contrary to an express term of their written retainer. The half-day trial is still six months away. A client's failure to pay is usually not covered by solicitor-client privilege yet falls within the ethical duty of confidentiality because the information concerns the business and affairs of the client and was obtained in the course of the professional relationship.[20] The ethical duty thus precludes counsel from disclosing the client's failure to outside parties.

Litigation privilege is another privilege — one that is distinct from solicitor-client privilege yet similarly overlaps substantially with the ethical duty of confidentiality.[21] The privilege aims to create a zone of privacy regarding existing or anticipated litigation, so as to better facilitate each party's preparation for court.[22] Consistent with this rationale, litigation privilege applies to communications passing and materials created for the dominant purpose of litigation.[23]

Litigation privilege extends to cover interactions with third parties, whether conducted by a lawyer, an agent such as a private investigator,

---

19   The issues raised by this example are discussed in detail in Chapter 5, Section K.

20   *Cunningham*, above note 1 at paras 29–31. If the trial were closer in time so that the lawyer could not withdraw without jeopardizing the trial date, an exception to the duty of confidentiality would apply to allow the lawyer to disclose the failure to pay to the court (*ibid* at paras 47–48).

21   The contours of litigation privilege are extensively reviewed in Sidney Lederman, Alan Bryant, & Michelle Fuerst, *The Law of Evidence in Canada*, 4th ed (Markham, ON: LexisNexis, 2014) at § 14.194–234; S Casey Hill, David Tanovich, & Louis Strezos, *McWilliams' Canadian Criminal Evidence*, 5th ed (Toronto: Canada Law Book, 2013) (loose-leaf) at § 13.30; Adam Dodek, *Solicitor-Client Privilege* (Markham, ON: LexisNexis, 2014) at § 2.2.

22   *Blank*, above note 12 at paras 27–28 and 34.

23   *Ibid* at para 43.

or the client herself.[24] Unlike solicitor-client privilege, it therefore does not require that the communication be intended to be confidential as between a lawyer and client.[25] Litigation privilege further differs from solicitor-client privilege in typically ceasing to apply at the conclusion of the proceeding with respect to which it arose.[26]

All information covered by litigation privilege will necessarily be covered by the ethical duty of confidentiality. But the scope of the ethical duty is considerably broader. Most notably, the ethical duty neither depends on the existence of pending or anticipated litigation nor ends once the matter has concluded.

Example: Defence counsel retains a private investigator to collect statements from several witnesses for possible use at trial, but the witnesses end up not testifying. Litigation privilege covers the communications between the investigator and witnesses only until the criminal proceeding concludes. But the communications remain protected by the ethical duty of confidentiality even after the trial, because the duty survives the end of the retainer.

E. COMPARISON WITH CONFIDENTIALITY AT COMMON LAW AND EQUITY

Bodies of law external to the rules of professional conduct work to protect and enforce client-lawyer confidences. As we have just seen, the law of evidence gives effect to client-lawyer confidentiality by affording solicitor-client communications a class privilege. The law of agency also enforces client-lawyer confidences, the lawyer taking on many duties as agent, including the duty of confidentiality.[27] One also finds robust protection of a client's right to confidentiality in the law of fiduciaries more generally,[28] and in the willingness of equity to enjoin a breach of confidence.[29]

---

24 *Ibid* at para 27.
25 *Ibid* at para 32.
26 *Ibid* at paras 34–39.
27 See GHL Fridman, *Canadian Agency Law* (Markham, ON: Lexisnexis, 2012) at § 1.38 and §§ 4.30–35.
28 See Mark Vincent Ellis, *Fiduciary Duties in Canada* (Toronto: Carswell, 1988) (loose-leaf 2012 supplement) ch 9(6); *Strother v 3464920 Canada Inc*, 2007 SCC 24 at paras 34–35.
29 See *Slavutych v Baker* (1975), 55 DLR (3d) 224 at 229–30 (SCC).

These legal and equitable manifestations of confidentiality bear close resemblance to the ethical obligations imposed by codes of professional conduct. However, as the example of solicitor-client privilege shows, a lawyer's ethical obligations can differ from legal rules concerning confidences. The same can be said, though perhaps to a lesser degree, for the substantive duties of confidentiality imposed by the common law and equity. Though significant similarities exist, these legal and equitable duties are neither exactly coterminous with nor necessarily determined by the ethical obligations set out in the professional-conduct codes.[30]

F. CONSTITUTIONAL PRINCIPLES

The ability of an accused to make full answer and defence is often dependent on obtaining the help of a lawyer.[31] For this reason, the constitutional right to counsel has been recognized by many courts and in many contexts.[32] Yet the right to counsel requires more than simply a guarantee that counsel can act for an accused. Among other things, an accused must enjoy the benefit of confidentiality if the relationship with counsel is to operate effectively.[33] Courts have thus recognized a fundamental legal and civil right to maintain those confidences falling within the scope of solicitor-client privilege,[34] a right protected by

---

30 While often viewed as persuasive statements of public policy, the rules of professional conduct are not binding on courts: *MacDonald Estate v Martin*, [1990] 3 SCR 1235 at 1245–46 [paras 16–18] [*MacDonald Estate*]; *Galambos v Perez*, 2009 SCC 48 at para 29; *Cunningham*, above note 1 at para 38; *Canadian National Railway Co v McKercher LLP*, 2013 SCC 39 at para 16 [*McKercher*].

31 See Chapter 1, Section D.

32 Most obviously, s 10(b) of the *Canadian Charter of Rights and Freedoms*, Part I of the *Constitution Act, 1982*, being Schedule B to the *Canada Act 1982* (UK), 1982, c 11 [*Charter*], guarantees the right to counsel on arrest or detention. While the *Charter* does not expressly guarantee a free-standing right to representation by counsel at trial, appeal courts have located such a right in ss 7 and 11(d): *Smith*, above note 1 at para 5, Major J, dissenting but not on this point; *R v Bhandher*, 2012 BCCA 441 at para 50; *R v Rejzek*, 2009 ABCA 393 at para 15, leave to appeal to SCC refused, [2010] SCCA No 39; *R v Okafor*, 2009 ONCA 672 at para 12.

33 See, for example, the cases cited in note 1, above.

34 See *Solosky*, above note 10 at 510; *Descôteaux*, above note 10 at 409–13; *Geffen v Goodman Estate*, [1991] 2 SCR 353 at 383 [para 56] [*Geffen*]; *A(LL) v Beharriell* (1995), 103 CCC (3d) 92 at para 69 (SCC); *Smith*, above note 1 at paras 45–50; *McClure*, above note 1 at para 24; *Lavallee*, above note 4 at paras 34–36 and 49; *Maranda*, above note 3 at paras 12 and 23; *Foster Wheeler Power*, above note 1 at para 34; *Goodis*, above note 13 at paras 14–15; *Blood Tribe*, above note 1 at para 10; *Cunningham*, above note 1 at para 26.

sections 7 and 8 of the *Charter of Rights and Freedoms.*[35] What is more, constitutional protections such as the right to make full answer and defence and the principle against self-incrimination are necessarily furthered by solicitor-client confidentiality.[36] In short, as stated by the Supreme Court of Canada in *Maranda v Richer,* "the confidentiality of the solicitor-client relationship is essential to the functioning of the criminal justice system and to the protection of the constitutional rights of accused persons."[37]

G. REMEDIES

The lawyer who breaches the ethical duty of confidentiality is exposed to a panoply of possible legal proceedings brought at the client's behest. The client may make a complaint to the law society regarding violation of the rules of professional conduct.[38] He can also sue for breach of fiduciary duty, contract, or duty of care arising out of counsel's actions, seeking remedies as diverse as damages, an injunction enjoining misuse of the information, an accounting and disgorgement of profits, and delivery up or destruction of documents containing the confidential information.[39] Breach or threatened breach of a confidence may also lead to a claim of privilege in extant legal proceedings,[40] ground an application to have counsel removed from the record for conflict of interest,[41]

---

35 *Charter,* above note 32. See *McClure,* above note 1 at paras 2, 4, 17, and 41; *Lavallee,* above note 4 at paras 21, 24, and 34–36; *Goodis,* above note 13 at para 15; Mahmud Jamal & Brian Morgan, "The Constitutionalization of Solicitor-Client Privilege" (2003) 20 Sup Ct L Rev (2d) 213. Note, however, a recent *obiter* comment that solicitor-client privilege, though a fundamental rule of law that is supported by and impressed with the values underlying s 7 of the *Charter,* is generally *not* seen to be "constitutional": *R v National Post,* 2010 SCC 16 at para 39.

36 Regarding the latter, see *Smith,* above note 1 at paras 7 and 26–27, Major J, dissenting but not on this point; *Maranda,* above note 3 at para 12. Compare *Brown,* above note 1 at para 94.

37 *Maranda,* above note 3 at para 37.

38 See, for example, *Law Society of Upper Canada v Vujic,* [1995] LSDD No 7 [*Vujic*]; *Law Society of Upper Canada v Freedman,* [2005] LSDD No 20 [*Freedman*]; Iain Marlow, "Calgary Lawyer Resigns after Suspension for Leaking Client Info" *The Globe and Mail* (27 May 2014).

39 See, generally, F Bennett, "Confidentiality in a Solicitor and Client Relationship" (1989) 23 L Soc'y Gaz 257; Ellis, above note 28, ch 20; Fridman, above note 27 at §§ 4.36–40; *Wernikowski v Kirkland, Murphy & Ain* (2000), 141 CCC (3d) 403 at para 18 (Ont CA), leave to appeal to SCC refused, [2000] SCCA No 98.

40 See, for example, *Smith,* above note 1.

41 See, for example, *MacDonald Estate,* above note 30.

or fuel an appeal based on an allegation of ineffective counsel.[42] A serious breach of confidentiality may also contravene the *Criminal Code*.[43]

Caution: Lawyers sometimes face sanctions from governing bodies for breaching the duty of confidentiality as a result of reacting rashly and in anger during a dispute with the client.[44] No matter how badly the client may have behaved, the duty of confidentiality must be respected.[45] Even where it appears that an exception to the duty allows release of the information, it is prudent to obtain advice from the governing body or senior counsel before taking action that counsel may later regret.

H. SOME APPLICATIONS OF THE ETHICAL DUTY OF CONFIDENTIALITY

The duty of confidentiality owed a client by counsel has an expansive scope and comes to bear in countless situations. Indeed, a rebuttable presumption of fact extends the duty to all communications and information exchanged between a lawyer and client.[46] Some of the most important attributes of the duty, which serve to emphasize its great breadth, are set out below.

1) Information from All Sources Included

A key aspect of the duty of confidentiality, which is largely responsible for its tremendous reach, is that information from any and all sources is covered.[47] It matters not that the information comes from a third party rather than the client.[48] Nor does it necessarily matter that solicitor-

---

42   See, for example, *United States v Williams*, 698 F3d 374 (7th Cir 2012).
43   See, for example, *United States v ReBrook*, 837 F Supp 162 (SD W Va 1993): lawyer for a state lottery was charged with insider trading based on alleged misuse of confidential information.
44   See, for example, *Freedman*, above note 38.
45   Most codes state that a lawyer owes the client a duty of confidentiality "whether or not differences have arisen between them": Alta, Sask r 2.03(1) (commentary); BC, Man, Ont, NS, NL r 3.3-1, commentary 3; CBA Code ch IV, commentary 6.
46   *Foster Wheeler Power*, above note 1 at para 42.
47   Alta, Sask r 2.03(1) (commentary); BC, Man, Ont, NS, NL r 3.3-1, commentary 2; NB ch 5, commentary 2; CBA Code ch IV, commentary 2: the duty applies "without regard to the nature or source of the information or to the fact that others may share the knowledge."
48   *Wolfe v Wolfe*, 2003 SKQB 474 at para 20.

client privilege does not apply.[49] Confidentiality will even arise where information relating to the client comes unexpectedly or through unusual channels, for instance, where counsel happens to learn of the information from another client, through casual reading, or by overhearing gossip.[50]

2) All Forms of Information Are Covered

The duty of confidentiality applies to all forms of information relating to a client, including oral, documentary, electronic, photographic, and digital.[51]

3) Information Received by Employees and Agents

The ambit of confidentiality extends to information provided to agents for the lawyer. Information obtained by office staff or a private investigator must therefore be held in confidence and attracts the same ethical obligations as would information coming directly to the lawyer.[52]

4) Risk of Harm to Client and Lawyer's Altruistic Purpose Are Irrelevant

The prohibition against disclosing a client confidence does not dissipate simply because the client is not exposed to any risk of harm. The rules of professional conduct make no distinction between cases where disclosure or use will likely harm a client and those instances where the risk of adverse impact is non-existent.[53]

Comparison: The Third Restatement allows a lawyer to use or disclose confidential information where there is no reasonable prospect that doing so will adversely affect a client's material interest, provided the information is not used for the lawyer's gain and the client has not instructed the lawyer to the contrary.[54] We prefer the more cautious

---

49 See Section D, above in this chapter.
50 Alta, Sask r 2.03(1) (commentary); BC, Man, Ont, NS, NL r 3.3-1, commentary 8; NB ch 5, commentary 6; CBA Code ch IV, commentary 9.
51 Third Restatement § 59, comment "b."
52 See, for example, *Descôteaux*, above note 10 at 398; *Robillard*, above note 11 at para 6.
53 See the rules cited in note 8, above in this chapter.
54 § 60(1), comment "c(i)" & "c(ii)."

approach adopted by Canadian ethical codes, because it protects against unexpected harm or an erroneous assessment of risk by counsel.[55]

Similarly, the lawyer's duty to maintain confidentiality applies regardless of the purpose to which the information may be put. Use of confidential information for the benefit of a third party, be it another client of the lawyer or someone else, is clearly prohibited.[56] So is use for the lawyer's own benefit[57] or for a purpose that has a philanthropic, neutral, or undetermined effect.[58]

5) Both Disclosure and Use Prohibited

It is possible to make use of confidential information without disclosing it to a third party.[59] For example, counsel might learn from a client that a business opportunity exists and take advantage of the opportunity without revealing any information to a third party. Canadian rules of professional conduct typically prohibit use of confidential information for the benefit of the lawyer or a third party, or to the disadvantage of the client.[60]

Example: During the course of the representation, counsel learns that his client's marriage is in desperate straits and that the couple is experiencing sexual problems. Without discussing this matter with anyone else, counsel uses the information to embark on a sexual relationship with the client's wife. He has thereby breached the duty of confidentiality.[61]

---

55   Our view is shared by David Chavkin, "Why Doesn't Anyone Care about Confidentiality? (And, What Message Does That Send to New Lawyers?)" (2012) 25 Geo J Leg Ethics 239 at 258.
56   Alta, Sask r 2.03(2); BC, Man, NS, NL r 3.3-2; Ont r 3.3-1, commentary 11.1; Que s 3.06.01; CBA Code ch IV, commentary 14.
57   Alta, Sask r 2.03(2); BC, Man, NS, NL r 3.3-2; Ont r 3.3-1, commentary 11.1; Que s 3.06.01; CBA Code ch IV, commentary 14.
58   This is so because the basic rule of confidentiality does not contain an exception permitting use for such purposes: see the rules cited at note 8, above in this chapter.
59   Third Restatement § 60: prohibits both disclosure *and* use; Charles W Wolfram, *Modern Legal Ethics* (St Paul, MN: West, 1986) at 304–5: discusses how the duty of confidentiality can be breached absent overt disclosure.
60   See the rules cited at note 56, above in this chapter.
61   See *Szarfer v Chodos* (1986), 54 OR (2d) 663 (HCJ), aff'd (1988), 66 OR (2d) 350 (CA).

6) Information Can Be Confidential Even in the Absence of a Retainer

Most Canadian codes of professional conduct provide that information "acquired in the course of the professional relationship" is subject to the duty of confidentiality.[62] In *Descôteaux v Mierzwinski*, the Supreme Court of Canada made clear that solicitor-client privilege — and so too, by necessary implication, the duty of confidentiality — arises as soon as a potential client has her first dealing with a lawyer's office to obtain legal advice.[63] The wording used in the ethical rules is thus broad enough to cover pre-retainer discussions, and all information acquired at this point is confidential, even if the lawyer is retained only later or not at all.[64]

Caution: A lawyer who does not wish to be bound by a duty of confidentiality vis-à-vis a non-client, for instance because of a potential for conflict of interest, should exercise care in communicating with that person.[65] Simply refusing to accept a retainer may be inadequate to prevent the duty from arising.[66]

7) Duty Survives End of Retainer

The duty of confidentiality continues after the retainer has come to an end.[67] This persistence is justified given the basic rationale behind the obligation of confidentiality: if confidential information could be

---

62 See the rules cited in note 8, above in this chapter, except NB ch 5, rule.

63 *Descôteaux*, above note 10 at 401. See also *Pritchard*, above note 1 at para 16.

64 The commentary to most Canadian rules expressly states as much: Alta, Sask r 2.03(1) (commentary); BC, Man, Ont, NS, NL r 3.3-1, commentary 4; CBA Code ch IV, commentary 11. See also ABA Model Rule 1.18(b). However, where the individual never becomes a client, the lawyer arguably owes only a duty of confidentiality and not any broader duty of loyalty: CBA Code ch IV, commentary 11; CBA Task Force on Conflicts of Interest, *Conflicts of Interest: Final Report, Recommendations & Toolkit* (Ottawa: Canadian Bar Association, 2008) at 108–9.

65 This caution is made expressly in Alta, Sask r 2.03(1) (commentary); BC, Man, Ont, NS, NL 3.3-1, commentary 4. See also ABA Model Rule 1.18, comments 4 & 5.

66 Steps that can be taken to minimize risk in this regard are discussed in Chapter 6, Section J(2).

67 Alta, Sask r 2.03(1) (commentary); BC, Man, Ont, NS, NL r 3.3-1, commentary 3; NB ch 5, commentary 4; CBA Code ch IV, commentary 6. The same point is made in *Lavallee*, above note 4 at para 40, with respect to the lawyer's duty of loyalty, and thus by implication also the ethical duty of confidentiality.

revealed once the retainer ends, the client would be less likely to be completely candid with his lawyer while the relationship is ongoing.[68]

8) Duty Survives Death of Client

The duty of confidentiality is in a sense immortal, encompassing confidential information held by counsel even after the death of a client or former client,[69] and caselaw has endorsed a similarly strict application of solicitor-client privilege.[70]

9) Information Received After the Retainer Has Ended

None of the Canadian rules of professional conduct purport to extend the duty of confidentiality to information obtained by the lawyer *after* the professional relationship has ended. However, the rationale underlying these rules supports doing so where the lawyer comes by the information as a result of having formerly represented the client.

Example: Counsel A has been discharged by her client, who retains Counsel B. Shortly thereafter, Crown counsel calls Counsel A to discuss ongoing settlement negotiations and, despite learning that the retainer has ended, updates Counsel A as to the status of the case. Counsel B later phones Counsel A to obtain information regarding the early stages of the case and, in doing so, reveals recent non-public developments pertaining to the client's matter. The information acquired by Counsel A, whether from the Crown or Counsel B, should be kept confidential even though arguably not obtained "in the course of the professional relationship," which is the phrase used in most Canadian ethical rules to limit the reach of the duty of confidentiality.[71]

This limited extension of the obligation of confidentiality beyond the strict timeline of the professional relationship is warranted. If former counsel is free to publicize or exploit information acquired after but as a result of a prior professional relationship with the client, the

---

68   Some of the other justifications for the duty of confidentiality also arguably support continuation of the duty after the retainer ends: see Section B, above in this chapter.

69   The commentary to most Canadian rules states that the duty "continues indefinitely": see the rules cited at note 67, above in this chapter.

70   *Geffen*, above note 34 at 384; *Swidler & Berlin v United States*, 524 US 399 (1998). Although, as *Geffen* notes, the privilege is relaxed to permit a lawyer to give evidence in wills cases.

71   See the rules cited in note 8, above in this chapter.

client may delay discharging a lawyer in whom he no longer has confidence. Or the client may be less willing to provide complete disclosure to new counsel, at least initially, for fear that the information will be passed on to former counsel during discussions necessary for the transfer of the file. The client may also need to communicate with former counsel as part of the file-transfer process. The duty of confidentiality should thus ordinarily extend to cover any information "relating to the representation of the client,"[72] even when acquired after the retainer has concluded.

10) Literary Works

All Canadian rules of professional conduct refer to a lawyer's participation in literary works. Most expressly prohibit disclosure of confidential information in such works without the client's or former client's consent.[73] By contrast, the CBA Code merely states that the lawyer "should avoid" disclosure of confidential information in literary works,[74] although caselaw has interpreted this wording as confirming that the duty of confidentiality applies to literary works.[75] Canadian lawyers thus have no special licence to reveal confidential information in literary or artistic endeavours.[76]

11) Gossip and Shoptalk

A lawyer should never engage in indiscreet conversation or gossip that reveals confidential information, not even with close family or friends. This obvious proscription is set out in most Canadian rules of professional conduct.[77] These rules further provide that a lawyer who hears

---

72 This phrase is employed by the Third Restatement § 59 and ABA Model Rule 1.6(a) and is seen to cover post-retainer communications in *In re Investigating Grand Jury*, 887 A2d 257 at para 9 (PA Super 2005), appeal denied 902 A2d 1241 (2006).

73 Alta, Sask r 2.03(2) (commentary); Ont r 3.3-1, commentary 11.1; BC, Man, NS, NL r 3.3-2, commentary 1.

74 CBA Code ch IV, commentary 14.

75 See *Stewart v Canadian Broadcasting Corp* (1997), 150 DLR (4th) 24 at 112 (Ont Ct Gen Div) [*Stewart*], interpreting similar language used in a previous version of the Ontario code.

76 In the US, see *In re Smith*, 991 NE2d 106 (Ind 2013): lawyer disbarred for, among other things, revealing confidential information about client's criminal matters in a book published for personal gain.

77 Alta, Sask r 2.03(1) (commentary); BC, Man, Ont, NS, NL r 3.3-1, commentary 8; NB ch 5, commentary 6; CBA Code ch IV, commentary 9–10.

gossip concerning a client's affairs should keep such information confidential and not recount it to third parties.[78] The fact that information may reach a lawyer for reasons totally unconnected with the professional relationship, such as through scuttlebutt overheard in a restaurant, is irrelevant.

Social Media: The prohibition against gossip involving confidential client information encompasses a lawyer's social networking activity. An abject breach of this prohibition occurred in Florida when a lawyer received a bag of fresh clothes from her client's family, to be passed on to him to wear during a murder trial. She posted a photo of leopard-print underwear contained in the bag on Facebook, along with comments derogatory to her client. The posting came to the court's attention, and the lawyer was removed from the record and a mistrial declared. She was also fired by the public defender's office.[79]

"Shoptalk," used here to mean the discussion of legal matters between or among lawyers, ranging from an informal discussion at lunch to a question-and-answer session at a professional conference, raises more complicated issues. Lawyers routinely engage in shoptalk to aid in the conduct of a client's case, and shoptalk also serves the important function of continuing legal education. Starting with a non-contentious example, it makes sense to permit a lawyer to engage in such discussions with members of the same firm. Indeed, Canadian ethical rules provide that absent instructions to the contrary, the client's authority to do so is implied.[80] The other lawyers in the firm, as well as staff and agents, owe the client a duty of confidentiality regarding all information thereby received.

More complicated is shoptalk with non-firm lawyers, for they do not ordinarily owe the client a duty of confidentiality. A number of respected commentators nonetheless view "extra-firm" shoptalk as

---

78   Alta, Sask r 2.03(1) (commentary); BC, Man, Ont, NS, NL r 3.3-1, commentary 8; NB ch 5, commentary 6; CBA Code ch IV, commentary 9–10.

79   See "Lawyer's Facebook Photo Causes Mistrial in Miami-Dade Murder Case" *Miami Herald* (13 September 2012). On confidentiality issues arising from social media more generally, see Margaret DiBianca, "Ethical Risks Arising from Lawyers' Use of (and Refusal to Use) Social Media" (2011) 12 Delaware L Rev 179 at 187–90; Michael Lackey & Joseph Minta, "Lawyers and Social Media: The Legal Ethics of Tweeting" (2012) 28 Touro L Rev 149 at 155–58; Bob Tarantino & Omar Ha-Redeye, "Overview: The Rules of Professional Conduct and Their Application to the Legal Profession Online (and Off)" (2011–12) 12 Internet and E-Commerce Law in Canada 109 at 112.

80   Alta, Sask r 2.03(1) (commentary); BC, Man, Ont, NS, NL r 3.3-1, commentary 9; CBA Code ch IV, commentary 13; compare NB ch 5, commentary 7.

sometimes permissible.[81] We agree. If the discussion is discreet, creates no realistic risk of harm to the client, and the client's identity is not revealed unless necessary, one can view such shoptalk as impliedly authorized by the client.[82] After all, most clients would want counsel to canvas non-firm lawyers for ideas and strategies as a means of improving the quality of representation. Alternatively, communications with a non-firm lawyer can sometimes be purged of identifying characteristics to the point that no confidential information is disclosed.[83]

The Canadian rules of professional conduct are not completely clear regarding the propriety of shoptalk.[84] Words such as "gossip," "indiscreet," and "shoptalk" are not used in any precise way, and conversations with lawyers and non-lawyers are discussed without indicating what differences, if any, might exist. The rules are nonetheless reasonably open to the interpretation that discussion of a client's case with another lawyer is acceptable if carried out in the manner suggested in the previous paragraph.

The correlative question becomes, what duty, if any, is owed by the lawyer who *receives* information in this capacity? In our opinion, the recipient lawyer should maintain confidentiality provided it is reasonable in all the circumstances for him to expect that the information is intended to be kept secret.[85] Counsel who reveals confidential information to obtain the advice of a lawyer outside the firm should ensure that the recipient lawyer understands the need to preserve confidentiality. Sometimes the circumstances of the consultation make clear this need, but otherwise counsel should obtain the recipient lawyer's express agreement not to disclose or use information before proceeding with the discussion. Counsel should avoid seeking advice from a lawyer who might be in a conflict position vis-à-vis the matter or who is known to be a gossip.

---

81 Geoffrey Hazard & William Hodes, *The Law of Lawyering*, 3d ed (Gaithersburg, MD: Aspen, 2001) (loose-leaf 2013 supplement) § 9.15 at 9-67, 9-69, & 9-70; John Wesley Hall, *Professional Responsibility in Criminal Defense Practice* (St Paul, MN: Thomson/West, 2005) (loose-leaf 2012 supplement) at § 28:52; Third Restatement § 60, comment "h."

82 See also Chapter 5, Section G.

83 See ABA Model Rule 1.6, comment 4: use of a hypothetical to discuss issues relating to representation is acceptable provided there is no reasonable likelihood that a listener could ascertain the identity of the client or the situation involved.

84 See the rules cited at note 77, above in this chapter.

85 Dodek, above note 21 at § 6.56. See also Section Q, below in this chapter.

I. POSITIVE DUTY TO SAFEGUARD CONFIDENTIAL INFORMATION

The duty of confidentiality requires more of a lawyer than merely keeping quiet about client secrets. The ethical obligation also imposes a positive duty to safeguard client confidences by taking reasonable steps to secure all such information.[86] Consequently, the acquisition, storage, retrieval, and communication of confidential information must be subject to controls reasonably designed and managed to prevent unauthorized disclosure. Whether the steps taken are reasonable will depend on a number of factors, including the degree of risk that disclosure will occur, the foreseeability and seriousness of any resulting damage, the burden of taking steps to avoid the damage, and any relevant instructions provided by the client.

1) Safeguarding Confidential Information and Shared Office Space

The security of physical items, such as hard-copy documents, can be easily maintained by using locks, alarm systems, and adequate storage facilities. However, special care must be taken where two or more lawyers share office space but are not members of the same firm. A lawyer who shares space in this way must ensure that non-associated lawyers do not access her clients' confidential information, whether intentionally or by accident. In this vein, most Canadian rules state that lawyers who practise together in space-sharing arrangements "should be mindful of the risk of advertent or inadvertent disclosure of confidential information."[87] Measures that can be taken to protect against information leakage, plus a discussion of conflict-of-interest problems that can arise out of space sharing, are reviewed elsewhere.[88]

2) Phones and Electronic Devices

Security concerns can be difficult to address with respect to newer, constantly advancing technologies. Nevertheless, the obligation to be reasonably competent in the use of technology, and to use it responsibly

---

86   See *Lavallee*, above note 4 at para 35. See also Alta, Sask r 2.05(1) (commentary); BC, Man, Ont, NS, NL r 3.5-2, commentary 2: lawyer has a duty to safekeep and maintain confidentiality of client files.

87   Alta, Sask r 2.03(1) (commentary); BC, Man, Ont, NS, NL r 3.3-1, commentary 7.

88   See Chapter 6, Section N(1).

and ethically, extends to require the proper protection of confidential information located on or transmitted through phones and electronic devices.[89]

The nature of a defence lawyer's practice makes electronic surveillance a possibility in certain instances. Despite the protection afforded solicitor-client communications by Part VI of the *Criminal Code*,[90] some criminal lawyers avoid communicating on issues of substance by phone unless urgent circumstances offer no reasonable alternative.

There is a reasonable expectation of privacy in email, which should permit its general use without the need for the express consent of the client.[91] Yet there is merit in attaching a standard warning to all emails to the effect that the communication may be privileged and confidential and if received by mistake should be deleted and the sender notified immediately. Where information is particularly sensitive, it is safest to obtain the client's consent before using email or to utilize encryption.[92]

Counsel should be alert to any real risk that a third party can access solicitor-client emails. An example would include emails that can be accessed from a computer shared by others in the client's home or from a computer, smartphone, or tablet device owned by an employer.[93] The client should be warned about such risks, and alternative means of communicating should be used instead.

Finally, lawyers must ensure that adequate steps are taken to protect confidential information stored on electronic devices or third-party servers through measures such as firewalls, secure wireless networks, strong password protection, full-disk encryption, antivirus software, and proper backup. Sensitive metadata should be removed from electronic

---

89   The duty to be competent regarding advances in technology is recognized in CBA Code ch II, commentary 4; ABA Model Rule 1.1, comment 8.

90   See ss 186(2) & (3) of the wiretap provisions in the *Criminal Code*, RSC 1985, c C-46, the aim of which is to exclude *bona fide* communications between lawyer and client.

91   Encryption may nonetheless be necessary for very sensitive information: see CBA Ethics and Professional Responsibility Committee, *Practising Ethically with Technology* (Ottawa, Canadian Bar Association, 2014) at 4 [*Practising Ethically with Technology*].

92   Peter Joy & Kevin McMunigal, "The Ethical Risks of Technology" (2012) 27 Criminal Justice 57.

93   The risks associated with use of an employer's computer are discussed in American Bar Association, Standing Committee on Ethics and Professional Responsibility, Formal Opinion 11-459, "Duty to Protect the Confidentiality of E-mail Communications with One's Client" (4 August 2011).

files provided to opponents or third parties. And all confidential information must be irrevocably wiped from devices before recycling.[94]

3) Cloud Computing

"Cloud computing" can refer to a number of things, including the storage of electronic data on a third-party server, as opposed to on an individual's computer hard drive.[95] There are a number of benefits to storing data in this way, including the ability to access the information over the Internet from any device and the ease with which it can be shared with others simply by emailing them a link.

Storing and sharing data through cloud computing raises confidentiality concerns because the information is kept on a server by a third party who is not part of the client-lawyer relationship. Governing bodies in Canada and the United States that have examined the use of cloud computing have generally concluded that a lawyer may use such services provided adequate steps are taken to protect a client's confidential information, the service provider maintains acceptable security, and the lawyer has adequate access to the information being stored.[96] To put it another way, counsel should use cloud computing only where reasonably satisfied after exercising due diligence that doing so will not jeopardize his professional responsibilities.[97]

Determining whether adequate steps have been taken to protect client confidentiality when using cloud computing is heavily context dependent. A number of resources canvass specific factors that a lawyer should consider,[98] and this is an area where it may be prudent to obtain input from an information technology consultant.

---

94 For sample recommendations with respect to confidentiality and new technologies, see *Practising Ethically with Technology*, above note 91; Joy & McMunigal, above note 92.

95 For an expansive definition of the term, see Law Society of British Columbia, *Report of the Cloud Computing Working Group* (Vancouver: Law Society of British Columbia, 2012) appendix 2. See also Florida State Bar, Proposed Advisory Opinion 12-3 (25 January 2013) [Florida State Bar], where cloud computing is "Internet-based computing in which large groups of remote servers are networked so as to allow sharing of data-processing tasks, centralized data storage, and online access to computer services or resources."

96 See, for example, the review of various state ethics opinions provided in Florida State Bar, *ibid*.

97 See Law Society of British Columbia, above note 95 at 22; Gavin Hume, "Use of Cloud Computing by Lawyers Requires Due Diligence to Stay Onside Regulatory Requirements" (2012) 70 Advocate 51.

98 See, for example, Law Society of British Columbia, above note 95, appendix 1; Florida State Bar, above note 95.

4) Handling Confidential Information in a Public Place

A lawyer must exercise caution when handling confidential material in a public space. Leaving a confidential document in an office reception area or courtroom may result in the improper disclosure of information to others. The same goes for working or talking at close quarters, such as in an airplane or courthouse corridor.[99]

5) Supervising Employees and Agents

The lawyer's positive duty to guard against breaches of confidentiality extends to require proper training of lawyers and non-lawyers who work at the firm and to ensure that confidences are protected by agents who come into contact with confidential material, such as bank employees, private investigators, couriers, photocopy service employees, and experts. Most Canadian rules impose this aspect of the positive duty on lawyers as a *quid pro quo* for recognizing the implied authority to disclose confidential information to such people.[100]

6) Protecting against Disclosure to Other Clients

Lawyers must take reasonable measures to ensure that a client's confidential information is not disclosed to other clients.[101] Lawyers must also decline any retainer that, if accepted, might require disclosure of confidential information to the new client or vice versa. This latter duty is expressly recognized in most ethical codes[102] but is also subsumed within the broader obligation to avoid conflicts of interest.[103]

---

99 See, for example, *R v Hunter* (2001), 155 CCC (3d) 225 (Ont CA): conversation overheard by a third party in courthouse corridor is led by Crown at trial, albeit excluded on appeal.

100 Alta, Sask r 2.03(1) (commentary); BC, Man, Ont, NS, NL r 3.3-1, commentary 9; NB ch 5, commentary 7; CBA Code ch IV, commentary 13. See also Wolfram, above note 59 at 892–95; ABA Model Rule 5.3.

101 Alta, Sask r 2.03(1) (commentary); BC, Man, Ont, NS, NL r 3.3-1, commentary 6; NB ch 5, commentary 5; CBA Code ch IV, commentary 7–8. See also Alta r 2.03(2) (commentary). For an egregious example of criminal counsel's disclosing confidential information to another client, see *Law Society of Upper Canada v Kaminer*, [2012] LSDD No 210.

102 Alta, Sask r 2.03(1) (commentary); Alta r 2.03(2) (commentary); BC, Man, Ont, NS, NL r 3.3-1, commentary 6; Que s 3.06.02; NB ch 5, commentary 5; CBA Code ch IV, commentary 7–8.

103 *R v Neil*, 2002 SCC 70 at para 19(i); *McKercher*, above note 30 at para 24.

7) Keeping Confidential Information Secure After the Retainer Has Ended

The obligation to safekeep a client's information continues after the retainer has ended. The lawyer must therefore handle a closed file with care.[104] It should be returned to the client or stored in a secure location, whether in hard copy version, electronic, or both. Generally, the file should not be destroyed unless the client consents, in which case the destruction must be carried out so as to prevent any breach of confidentiality. Shredding will usually be required.

It may be okay to destroy a closed file without the client's permission, provided doing so creates no realistic chance of harm to the client. Given that appeals and retrials can extend the life of a case and that details regarding a closed file can be relevant to a subsequent civil or criminal proceeding, counsel should wait at least six years before destroying a file absent consent of a client. Even then, to be safe, counsel should consider taking reasonable steps to contact the client and determine her wishes. A lawyer must never destroy a client's file, no matter how much time has elapsed, where there are legitimate grounds to believe that the client's interests may be harmed as a result.[105]

Example: To avoid storage costs, trial counsel always returns her disclosure materials to the Crown and destroys all work product after rendering a final account to the client. This practice is unwise. It risks depriving the client of information that may be relevant to postconviction matters and may also impede counsel's ability to respond if ineffective assistance is raised as a ground of appeal or if she is later sued for negligence or reported to the law society by the client or a third party.[106]

J. DUTY TO ASSERT CONFIDENTIALITY

Closely related to the positive duty to safeguard information is the obligation of counsel to assert confidentiality over client information sought by a third party. This duty has been recognized at common law,[107] and

---

104 See the rules cited at note 86, above in this chapter.

105 Hall, above note 81 at § 28:54 and § 4:30, argues that a criminal file can never be destroyed absent a client's consent, or if there is a possibility that its contents may be of use to the client regarding a parole or probation matter.

106 See the facts and court's comments in *R v EG*, 2010 ONSC 3667 at para 15.

107 *Bell v Smith* (1968), 68 DLR (2d) 751 (SCC); *Lavallee*, above note 4 at paras 24–25; *Simcoff v Simcoff*, 2009 MBCA 80 at paras 16–17; *Cunningham*, above note 1 at paras 32–34.

particularly applies where counsel is served with a subpoena to testify or produce documents relating to a client or is subject to a search warrant pertaining to a client's file.[108] Counsel who is subject to the compulsion of court process must raise any non-frivolous claim of privilege in response and should be generally aware of the applicable common law, statutory provisions, and constitutional principles.[109]

1) Subpoenas

Counsel who is served with a subpoena usually has adequate time to consider her response. It is wise to begin by contacting another lawyer to obtain legal assistance. Another lawyer should also represent the client in any attempt to quash or otherwise challenge the subpoena, and in any event, the client must be informed of the subpoena so that he can decide whether to assert solicitor-client privilege. Depending on the circumstances, the subpoenaed counsel may want or require separate counsel, for instance, where a conflict of interest arises and where counsel's unique concerns warrant representation.

Counsel acting on behalf of the client and/or the subpoenaed lawyer in an attempt to resist a subpoena should determine the availability of an immediate appeal in case of an adverse ruling.[110] If an appeal route has any realistic potential, and the client so instructs, preparations should be made in advance of the ruling so that the necessary procedural steps, including an application for a stay pending appeal, can be undertaken immediately if the subpoena is upheld.

If the subpoena is valid and if the sought-after information is confidential but not privileged, counsel must answer all proper questions once sworn or affirmed as a witness.[111] If answering a question requires counsel to reveal information that may be privileged, she must assert the privilege unless there has been an effective waiver by the client.

---

108 *Lavallee*, above note 4 at paras 24 and 35.
109 Alta, Sask r 2.05(6) (commentary); Man r 3.5-2, commentary 2A; Ont, NS, NL r 3.5-7, commentary 1; NB ch 7, commentary 4; CBA Code ch VIII, commentary 6. See also BC r 3.3-2.1.
110 Where the client asserting the privilege is not an accused, it may be that an interlocutory appeal can be brought, with leave, directly to the Supreme Court of Canada: see Chapter 5, Section D.
111 See Chapter 5, Section D.

2) Search Warrants

Being the subject of a search warrant puts counsel in a difficult position, with little time to carefully consider all options before reacting. Lawyers and employees of the firm should know in advance how to react, just as the inhabitants of an office are generally aware of the required procedure for a fire drill. It may be helpful to provide lawyers and staff with a written checklist of steps to take when confronted with a search warrant.[112] Such steps may include the following:[113]

1) If notified in advance of the search warrant,[114] separate the materials sought by the police and place them in a secure place. Take careful notes to document this procedure so that continuity can be established if need be. Under no circumstances should any materials be destroyed or hidden.
2) Make copies of the materials for the client to aid him in making informed decisions regarding the search.[115] If time permits, it may be useful to compile an inventory.
3) Immediately notify the client of the impending search. It may be appropriate to suggest that he retain independent legal counsel, for instance, where the propriety of a lawyer's conduct may be in issue or where any other potential for conflict of interest arises.[116] Any instructions of import should be memorialized in writing.

---

112 A handy two-page list is provided at the beginning of the Law Society of Upper Canada's *Guidelines for Law Office Searches* (Toronto: Law Society of Upper Canada, 2012) [*Ont Guidelines for Law Office Searches*], online: www.lsuc.on.ca/ guidelines-for-law-office-searches/.

113 These recommendations are derived from (1) the first edition of this text, (2) the Federation of Law Societies of Canada's draft "Protocol on Law Office Searches" (Ottawa: Federation of Law Societies of Canada, 2004) [*FLSC Draft Protocol*], (3) the *Ont Guidelines for Law Office Searches*, above note 112, and (4) the Law Society of British Columbia's *Guidelines: Recommended Terms for Law Office Search Warrants* (Vancouver: Law Society of British Columbia, 2013) [*BC Recommended Terms for Law Office Search Warrants*], online: www.lawsociety. bc.ca/docs/lawyers/search-warrants.pdf.

114 *R v Tarrabain, O'Bryne & Company*, 2006 ABQB 14 at para 25 [*Tarrabain*]; *R v AB*, 2014 NLCA 8 at para 49 [*AB*]: lawyer should have advance notice so he can be present during the search, provided the lawyer is not a target of the investigation. See also *Lavallee*, above note 4 at para 49(5): every effort must be made to contact lawyer and client at the time of execution of the search.

115 This step avoids the need to bring an application to obtain copies, and was employed by the lawyer in *Tarrabain*, above note 114 at paras 40–41.

116 The risk of conflicting interests is noted in *Lavallee*, above note 4 at para 40.

4) If time permits, review the law governing law office searches. Section 488.1 of the *Criminal Code*,[117] which sets out a procedure for law office searches, has been struck down as unconstitutional by *Lavallee, Rackel & Heintz v Canada (AG)*.[118] As Parliament has not seen fit to pass a *Charter*-compliant replacement provision, the principles applicable to law office searches are set out in the jurisprudence.[119] Protocols or guidelines available from professional governing bodies can be very useful in this regard.[120]

5) Consider obtaining legal advice from another lawyer and also calling the governing body for input.[121] The governing body will assist in providing advice to the lawyer but usually will *not* get involved in overseeing the search or taking other direct action to ensure that solicitor-client privilege is protected.[122]

6) Call a meeting of lawyers and staff to review the procedure to be followed once police arrive.

7) When the police arrive, ask for and record the officers' names and badge numbers. Also ask to see the search warrant and supporting materials, and to make copies.[123]

8) Review the terms of the warrant to ensure facial validity, for instance, that the law office is named as a place to be searched, that the warrant is valid on the date in question, and that the warrant is signed by a judicial officer. Deficiencies should be brought to the attention of the police, with the suggestion that a new warrant be

---

117 Above note 90.

118 *Lavallee*, above note 4 at paras 48 and 50. The import of *Lavallee* is to strike down as well comparable provisions in other federal statutes (for example, s 232 of the *Income Tax Act*, RSC 1985, c 1 (5th Supp)) and provincial legislation (for example, s 160 of the Ontario *Provincial Offences Act*, RSO 1990, c P.33).

119 Most important are the principles reviewed in *Lavallee*, above note 4 at para 49; *Maranda*, above note 3 at paras 10 and 14–20.

120 See the resources mentioned in note 113, above in this chapter.

121 *Tarrabain*, above note 114 at paras 24 and 27. See also *BC Recommended Terms for Law Office Search Warrants*, above note 113 at para 2, which envisions the law society providing guidance regarding a lawyer's professional obligations.

122 Some, mostly earlier, cases arguably suggest that a law society representative may participate in collecting the sought-after materials: *Lavallee*, above note 4 at paras 20, 41, and 49(5); *Maranda*, above note 3 at para 20; *AB*, above note 114 at paras 48–50. But the current approach is either to have the lawyer whose office is being searched collect the materials or to have the court appoint an independent referee to do so, as explained at step 12, below.

123 Section 29 of the *Criminal Code*, above note 90, requires police to carry the warrant with them and produce it when requested. If no search warrant is proffered, counsel must refuse to provide police with any files: *Agnes Securities Ltd v British Columbia* (1976), 31 CCC (2d) 154 (BCSC).

obtained. However, counsel must not obstruct the police, and if they insist on proceeding despite facial deficiencies, counsel must be content with noting the objection.[124] Deficiencies in the warrant can be raised with the court at a later date.

9) If no warning has been given before the arrival of the police, ask for some time to carry out as many of steps 1–6, above, as possible. If this request is refused, try to play catch-up on a triage basis as the search progresses, with a particularly high priority placed on contacting the client.

10) Absent a clear, express, and fully informed waiver by the client, advise the police that all of the materials sought in whatever form are confidential and claim privilege on behalf of the client.[125]

11) A search warrant does not determine the application of privilege, and therefore the police should not be permitted to see the contents of any of the sought-after material.[126] If the police insist on doing so, note their conduct and the objection to it. Any impropriety on the part of the police can be raised with the court on review.

12) Sometimes the lawyer is a target of the police investigation or is otherwise in a conflict of interest with the client whose material is the subject of the warrant. Or the lawyer may be absent, and no other lawyer in the firm may be available to stand in her stead. In each of these instances, there is a real concern that solicitor-client privilege will not be properly safeguarded. The police, Crown, or court will often foresee the problem, leading to the appointment of a referee as a condition attached to the warrant.[127] A referee is a lawyer who is independent of the police, Crown, and conflicted counsel and who acts as the court's agent as mandated by the warrant to ensure that the search and postsearch procedures are carried out in accordance with the warrant and with proper solicitude for solicitor-client privilege.[128]

---

124 Scott Hutchison, "Search and Seizure Checklist Redux 2005: What to Do When the Police Arrive to Search a Law Office" (2005) 24 Advocates' Soc J 18 No 2 at 23(8).

125 Remember that in rare cases even the name of a client may be protected by privilege: see Section L, below in this chapter.

126 See *Lavallee*, above note 4 at para 49(4); *Robillard*, above note 11 at paras 37–38; *Re Law Society of Upper Canada*, 2006 ONCJ 470 at paras 54–55.

127 A referee should be appointed in such circumstances because the lawyer cannot be relied upon to fulfill the critical function of safeguarding solicitor-client privilege: *Tarrabain*, above note 114 at paras 25–26 and 29.

128 The referee's function is described in *Tarrabain*, *ibid* at paras 22–30; *R v Law Office of Simon Rosenfeld*, [2003] OJ No 834 at paras 12–15 (SCJ) [*Rosenfeld*]; *Ont Guidelines for Law Office Searches*, above note 112 at 8–9; *FLSC Draft Protocol*, above note 113

13) If a referee is required but has not been appointed under the warrant, the police should be alerted to the problem and urged to re-apply to the court so an appointment can be made. If the police refuse to do so, the lawyer must not obstruct the search but should note the objection and response, and can raise the matter with the court at a later point. The lawyer must do her best to safeguard the privilege in the meantime, despite the perceived need for a referee, and may want to contact the governing body to obtain input.

14) Counsel or the referee should ask to be allowed to locate and collect the sought-after materials, rather than having the police conduct the search of the law office themselves. This minimizes disruption in the office and, more importantly, guards against the possibility that the police will see privileged material while executing the warrant.

15) If the sought-after materials are located in files on a computer or other electronic device and are easily retrievable, the lawyer or referee should ask police to be allowed to obtain them from the device himself, either printing hard copies or copying the data onto media provided by police, to minimize the possibility that privileged information will be revealed.

16) The warrant may permit the search for and seizure of electronic devices or media. If so, the lawyer or referee should ask police to be allowed to locate these items. If the warrant authorizes a comprehensive search of the electronic devices or media after seizure, an application should be brought to appoint an independent forensic computer examiner for this purpose. This examiner is independent of the Crown and the police and works as agent of the court, often in conjunction with the referee or lawyer, to ensure that the search

---

at para 4; *BC Recommended Terms for Law Office Search Warrants*, above note 113 at para 1. Referees were also appointed in *R v Hanington*, 2006 ABQB 378 [*Hanington*], and *Ontario (Ministry of the AG) v Law Society of Upper Canada*, 2010 ONSC 2150 [*Ontario (AG)*], and their use is endorsed in *Directeur des poursuites criminelles et pénales et Shérif de la Chambre criminelle et pénale*, 2010 QCCS 2362 at paras 81–89, leave to appeal to CA refused, [2010] JQ No 10775 (CA). Contrast *Re Law Society of Upper Canada*, above note 126, where a request for appointment of a referee was rejected, the court instead requiring that the materials be located by "a person under the direction of the officer who conducts the search, but removed from the investigation, and bound by a term of secrecy in the warrant or assistance order" (*ibid* at paras 115 and 117(4)). In our view, appointing a referee is much preferable, for he will be independent of the police and, as a lawyer, familiar with solicitor-client issues. On a different point, the warrant may require that a conflicted lawyer assist the referee in certain limited respects, for instance, by providing the names and last known addresses of the clients whose materials are or may be involved in the seizure: *Rosenfeld*, above in this note at paras 17, 21(i), & (ii).

and postsearch procedures are carried out in accordance with court orders and with proper solicitude for solicitor-client privilege.[129]

17) Where the warrant permits the creation of a forensic image of an electronic device or media without removing the device or media from the law office, the lawyer or referee should ask police whether the process will result in the forensic images being stored on an electronic device or media belonging to police. If so, the lawyer or referee should ask the police to hold off conducting the imaging process until the process can be conducted without an image's being stored on a police electronic device or media. In any event, while the forensic image is being created, the lawyer or referee should attempt to ensure that neither any displays on the electronic device nor any data stored on the electronic device or media are visible to police.[130]

18) If the police wish to verify that the forensic image has been created, it will be necessary to use an independent forensic computer exa-miner for this purpose.[131] The warrant may already have provided for the examiner's appointment. If not, the lawyer or referee should urge the police to reapply to the court so that such an appointment can be made.

19) If the police refuse a request made in steps 17 or 18, above, the lawyer or referee must not obstruct the search but should note the objection and response, and can raise the matter with the court at a later point.

20) All of the materials collected by the lawyer or referee pursuant to the warrant, in whatever form, should be placed in packages and sealed by the lawyer or referee. The packages should be marked for identification and initialled by the police and the lawyer or referee.

21) The lawyer or referee should check with police to ensure they are going to deposit the seized materials with the court or an independ-ent third party as required by the terms of the warrant. If the war-rant does not so provide, an application should be brought for this purpose, seeking that the materials stay in the custody of the court or an independent third party until further direction of the court.

---

129 An independent forensic computer examiner was appointed in *Ontario (AG)*, above note 128. See also *Ont Guidelines for Law Office Searches*, above note 112 at 6 and 11–12; *BC Recommended Terms for Law Office Search Warrants*, above note 113 at para 5.

130 See *AB*, above note 114 at paras 29 and 42–43: risk of inadvertent disclosure will arise even if a police officer tries not to look at the screen or hard data while copying files.

131 See *Ontario (AG)*, above note 128 at para 19, as well as sections B and C of the order attached to the judgment.

22) A search warrant does not provide the bearer with a right to conduct interviews with lawyers or staff members. To protect against inadvertent slips and ensure a consistent approach, it is advisable that a single lawyer or the referee handle all interaction with the police executing the warrant. It may be impractical to limit contact in this manner for a larger-scale search, but a single lawyer or the referee should nonetheless play the primary role in communicating with police on substantive matters.

23) Counsel should make thorough notes regarding the entire process, recording the individuals present and relevant occurrences and times. If an issue arises as to how the search was conducted or any other matter, such notes may be invaluable. It may also be wise to have at least two lawyers present at all times so that corroboration will be available if a factual dispute arises, or, if the technology is available, to audio or video record events.

24) Once the search has been completed, discuss the events with the client, or independent counsel acting on behalf of the client, and seek further instructions from the client if necessary.[132] If independent counsel has not been retained, consider whether a conflict of interest might exist so as to necessitate new counsel for the client.

25) If instructed to continue acting for the client, the lawyer should act promptly to take any steps required or advisable to protect the privilege. These may include applying to a court for an order or directions regarding

- storage of the seized materials with the court or an independent third party;[133]
- issues regarding client notification;
- unsealing, accessing, and copying the seized materials or data contained therein;
- appointing a referee or independent forensic computer examiner;
- challenging the validity of the warrant or its execution; and
- ascertaining whether solicitor-client or any other privilege applies.[134]

---

132 An extensive list of matters for discussion with the client is provided in *Ont Guidelines for Law Office Searches*, above note 112 at 12. If a referee has been appointed, it will likely fall on her to notify and discuss these matters with the client: *Rosenfeld*, above note 128 at paras 15 and 21(i)–(iii); *Hanington*, above note 128; *FLSC Draft Protocol*, above note 113 at paras 4(h), (i), & (j).

133 See *Ontario (AG)*, above note 128.

134 The referee and Crown counsel may also wish to apply to the court for an order or directions following execution of the warrant: see *Ont Guidelines for Law Office Searches*, above note 112 at 12. Or the search warrant may already have

K. DUTY TO INFORM CLIENT REGARDING SCOPE OF CONFIDENTIALITY

Lawyers should inform clients regarding the scope of the confidentiality obligation at or near the beginning of the retainer, mentioning the general categories of exception.[135] Failure to do so could leave the client with a false sense of security and result in counsel's liability where information not covered by the confidentiality rule is later used or released.

On the other hand, unless the client has specific questions, a lawyer need not provide a detailed review of every possible exception to the duty of confidentiality. Such detail is required only where there is a realistic risk that an exception may be engaged. The case of two or more co-accused represented by the same lawyer provides a good example: the special application of the duty of confidentiality must always be fully discussed with all co-accused.[136] Other examples include the client who is about to be assessed by a defence psychiatrist (future-harm exception)[137] and the appellant who contemplates raising ineffective assistance of counsel as a ground of appeal (self-defence exception or waiver).[138]

Caveat: The duty to explain the scope of confidentiality must not be used as a veiled threat to dissuade a client from making a complaint against counsel. For instance, a trial lawyer should not cow a client with horror stories of widespread loss of confidentiality and privilege to head off a claim of ineffective assistance. If the circumstances present a possible conflict between counsel's desire to avoid a complaint or civil liability and the client's best interests, independent legal advice will probably be necessary.

---

included terms dealing with such matters: see *BC Recommended Terms for Law Office Search Warrants*, above note 113 at paras 9–17.

135 See ABA Defense Standard 4-3.1(a) & comments; Cecelia Klingele, "Confidentiality and Disclosure: What the New ABA Criminal Justice Standards (Don't) Say about the Duties of Defense Counsel" (2011) 38 Hastings Const LQ 983 at 986–93, discussing the difficulty in determining exactly what should be said to the client and when; Elisia Klinka & Russell Pearce, "Confidentiality Explained: The Dialogue Approach to Discussing Confidentiality with Clients" (2011) 48 San Diego L Rev 157, proposing an approach similar to that advocated for in the text above.

136 See Section O, below in this chapter.

137 See Chapter 5, Section I.

138 See Chapter 5, Section E.

L. CONFIDENTIALITY AND INFORMATION REVEALING THE IDENTITY OF A CLIENT

Information indicating the identity of a client, as well as the related fact that a retainer exists, is typically not the subject of solicitor-client privilege.[139] An exception to this general rule appears to exist where the fact of identity is closely connected to the nature of the retainer, where disclosure by the lawyer would represent the last link in connecting the client to a crime, or perhaps where identity is inextricably intertwined with other clearly privileged information.[140] Where solicitor-client privilege does apply, there is no doubt that a client's identity will be confidential within the meaning of the rules of professional conduct. The ethical rules in Canada go much further, however, by placing a general obligation on counsel not to reveal the identity of a client or the fact of being consulted or retained unless required by the nature of the retainer.[141] Whether privilege covers the information is irrelevant. Imposing this duty of confidentiality on counsel is warranted, for revelation of a client's name by criminal counsel may fuel gossip and cause embarrassment, ridicule, or financial harm.

Two Examples: Our first example sees a lawyer approached by a prospective client. The client tells the lawyer that he has been involved in a fatal car accident and wishes to determine whether he can come forward without risking a criminal charge. The lawyer accepts the retainer, the purpose of which is to attempt negotiations with the authorities so as to achieve the client's objective. Our second example sees the lawyer retained to act for a prominent businesswoman who has been charged with shoplifting. In only the first scenario will privilege operate to shield the lawyer from the operation of legal process that attempts to expose the client's identity.[142] However, leaving the possibility of legal compulsion aside, in *both* examples counsel is forbidden

---

139 *Ontario (Securities Commission)*, above note 17 at 338; *Lukas v Lawson* (1993), 13 OR (3d) 447 (Gen Div); *Rosenfeld*, above note 128 at paras 10–12.

140 *Thorson v Jones* (1973), 38 DLR (3d) 312 (BCSC) [*Thorson*]; *Lavallee*, above note 4 at para 28, aff'g (2000), 143 CCC (3d) 187 at paras 50–61 (Alta CA); *R v Sauvé*, [1965] CS 129. But see *R v Murtha*, 2009 NSSC 342 at paras 24–26: exception applied much more broadly.

141 Alta, Sask r 2.03(1) (commentary); BC, Man, Ont, NS, NL r 3.3-1, commentary 5; NB ch 5, commentary 3; CBA Code ch IV, commentary 4.

142 Privilege was found to exist on facts resembling those in this example in *Thorson*, above note 140.

188 ETHICS AND CRIMINAL LAW

from revealing the client's identity to any third party because of the ethical duty of confidentiality.[143]

Despite the general ethical prohibition against revealing a client's identity, it would be wrong to say that the fact of retainer and the identity of one's client can never be disclosed. Disclosure of this confidential information will often be permitted in accordance with the client's implied or express authorization.[144] In particular, counsel has the implied authority to reveal information pertaining to a client's identity where to do so is a necessary part of the retainer.[145] In the vast majority of cases, a defence lawyer cannot effectively represent a client without informing the court, Crown counsel, and others of this fact. On the other hand, this implied authority obviously does not permit disclosure for purposes unrelated to the proper representation of the client.[146]

M. WHEREABOUTS OF THE UNLOCATED OR FUGITIVE CLIENT

Somewhat related to the question of whether counsel can reveal a client's identity is the case of the unlocated or fugitive client. A client may seek advice from a lawyer regarding police attempts to conduct a suspect interview or execute an arrest warrant. A client may also contact counsel after absconding while on bail or escaping from prison. Yet another possibility is that a subpoenaed witness contacts counsel after failing to appear in court as required. In any of these circumstances, counsel may learn of the client's whereabouts or obtain information that could help to reveal the client's location. It is also possible that friends or relatives of the client provide counsel with similar information. How does the duty of confidentiality operate in these sorts of situations?

As was the case regarding a client's identity, it is helpful to consider both solicitor-client privilege and the duty of confidentiality. Looking first to the privilege, we find scant Canadian authority on point, but

---

143 It has been suggested that solicitor-client privilege usually does not cover the client's identity because such information is not confidential: see, for example, *Ontario (Securities Commission)*, above note 17 at 338. This comment is clearly made in the context of a privilege claim and should not be taken to mean that the ethical duty of confidentiality does not apply to a client's identity.

144 See the discussion of express and implied authority in Chapter 5, Section B.

145 Revelation of a client's identity is expressly permitted by many rules of professional conduct where "the nature of the matter requires such disclosure": see the rules cited at note 141, above in this chapter.

146 Compare *Hanington*, above note 128 at paras 13 and 22.

the law regarding identity appears to be applicable.[147] That is to say, the location of one's client is usually not protected by privilege, but the privilege will apply where the client's location is closely connected to the subject matter of the retainer. Of course, if the client seeks advice regarding how to evade capture, the crime-fraud exception to the privilege may apply.[148]

Turning to the related question of confidentiality, we find that where counsel is compelled by judicial process to reveal a client's location and where a court determines that the privilege is inoperative, the rules of professional conduct clearly mandate disclosure.[149] Nonetheless, before the application of court process, the better view is that counsel's broad obligation to keep information confidential precludes the revelation of an unlocated or fugitive client's whereabouts.[150] Certainly, no Canadian code of professional conduct contains an exception that unambiguously mandates disclosure of this sort of information. Yet, if in the circumstances it can be said that the client's continued status as a fugitive constitutes on ongoing criminal offence, three Canadian ethical codes contain a future-crime exception that permits — but does not mandate — disclosure.[151]

In other provinces, there is only a future-harm exception, which permits disclosure where necessary to prevent death or serious bodily harm.[152] In these jurisdictions, the strict prohibition against disclosure of a fugitive client's location will usually apply. This is so even where the client seeks counsel's help in avoiding capture. In such a case, counsel must advise the client against breaking the law and seek to convince her to surrender. But as long as Canadian law does not criminalize mere non-disclosure by counsel,[153] and absent the applicability

---

147 See, for example, Lederman, Bryant, & Fuerst, above note 21 at § 14.57, where a client's identity and whereabouts are impliedly treated in a similar way.

148 See Chapter 5, Section K(1).

149 See Chapter 5, Section D.

150 The American Bar Association, Standing Committee on Ethics and Professional Responsibility, in Formal Opinion 84-349, effectively adopts this position by withdrawing previous opinions that held to the contrary. However, the American position is subject to some debate, in part because of the legacy wrought by these various opinions.

151 Sask r 2.03(4)(d); Man r 2.03(5)(d); and NB ch 5, commentary 9(c). See also Chapter 5, Section I(5).

152 See Chapter 5, Section I(4).

153 See, for example, *Criminal Code*, above note 90, s 139 (obstructing justice), "the gist of which is *doing an act* which has a tendency to pervert or obstruct the course of justice and which is done for that purpose": *R v May* (1984), 13 CCC (3d) 257 at 260 (Ont CA) [emphasis added].

of the future-harm exception, counsel cannot violate the confidence by revealing the client's location to the authorities.

Warning: Counsel must never aid or abet a fugitive client's efforts to evade capture. Any action that helps the client in this regard is unethical[154] and also exposes counsel to criminal censure.[155]

N. INADVERTENT DISCLOSURE

At one time, solicitor-client privilege was considered lost by virtue of accidental interception or even theft of the underlying confidential information.[156] But Canadian courts no longer take such an unforgiving stance.[157] Rather, the privilege will likely be maintained despite inadvertent disclosure to a third party if in the circumstances it can be said that waiver has not occurred. Factors applicable in determining whether there has been waiver include how the materials were released, whether prompt attempts were made to recover them once disclosure was discovered, the timing of the application to retrieve the materials, the number and nature of the third parties who received the materials, whether or not unfairness would result if other parties were not allowed to use the materials, and the impact on the court process.[158] We can thus say that in cases where counsel takes reasonable precautions to protect a confidence, there is a strong argument that waiver does not occur, and hence privilege is not lost merely because information has been unintentionally disclosed.

---

154 See Chapter 2, Section B(1).

155 See *Criminal Code*, above note 90, ss 22 (counselling), 23 and 463 (accessory after the fact), and s 139 (obstructing justice).

156 *Calcraft v Guest*, [1898] 1 QB 759 (CA); *Descôteaux*, above note 10 at 396, n 3 and 400; *R v Dunbar* (1982), 68 CCC (2d) 13 at 42 [paras 73–74] (Ont CA) [*Dunbar*]. Limited respite from this strict rule was traditionally offered by equity, which would enjoin use of confidential documents that had been unlawfully or improperly obtained: *Ashburton (Lord) v Pape*, [1913] 2 Ch 469 (CA).

157 *Airst v Airst* (1998), 37 OR (3d) 654 at 657–60 (Gen Div) [*Airst*]; *Supercom of California Ltd v Sovereign General Insurance Co* (1998), 37 OR (3d) 597 at 606 (Gen Div); *Chapelstone Developments Inc v Canada*, 2004 NBCA 96 at paras 42–60; *R v Bruce Power Inc*, 2009 ONCA 573 [*Bruce Power*]; *R v Barros*, 2010 ABCA 116 at para 45, rev'd but not on this point 2011 SCC 51 [*Barros* SCC]; *Re Mahjoub*, 2012 FC 669 [*Mahjoub*]; *R v KB*, 2014 NSPC 23 at paras 63–80 [*KB*].

158 *Airst*, above note 157 at 659–60; *R v Serfaty*, [2004] OJ No 1952 at paras 61–62 (SCJ); *Brass v Canada*, 2011 FC 1102 at para 84 (Proth); *Canada (MNR) v Thorton*, 2012 FC 1313 at paras 58–74.

A lawyer's ethical duty of confidentiality is implicated in two ways by the accidental disclosure scenario. First, the positive duty to protect confidences from disclosure means that counsel must take steps to prevent accidental disclosure from occurring.[159] Second, if unintentional disclosure does occur, counsel has an obligation, pursuant to the same duty, to take prompt and reasonable steps to retrieve the information and prevent further dissemination.[160] This obligation exists even if the information is irrelevant to matters at issue in a court proceeding.

What happens where the tables are turned, so that a lawyer finds himself in receipt of confidential information that has been obtained by improper means or inadvertently disclosed? A number of Canadian ethical codes address this scenario, but they differ with respect to the type of materials covered and the nature of the obligations imposed on the recipient lawyer.

The rule in British Columbia is fairly expansive in both regards.[161] It applies whenever a lawyer obtains access to or comes into possession of materials that the lawyer has reasonable grounds to believe belong to or are intended for an opposing party and were not intended for the lawyer to see. The rule is *not* restricted to materials that are privileged. The recipient lawyer must return the materials unread and uncopied to the other side. If the lawyer has read part or all of the materials before realizing they were inadvertently sent, the other side must also be informed of the extent to which the lawyer is aware of the contents and what use she intends to make of them.

By contrast, the applicable rule in Alberta is only triggered where the materials inadvertently sent contain an opposing party's privileged information.[162] The Alberta code instructs recipient counsel to inform the opposing party and not make use of the materials. However, where there is a genuine dispute as to whether privilege continues to apply, recipient counsel is allowed to "secure the communication pending resolution of the dispute," during which time it is improper to use the

---

159 See Section I, above in this chapter. See also ABA Model Rule 1.6(c): lawyer must make reasonable efforts to prevent inadvertent disclosure of confidential information.

160 See, for example, *R v Widdifield*, 2014 BCCA 170 at paras 77 and 84: prosecutor has a duty to seek return of privileged materials inadvertently included in disclosure provided to defence.

161 BC r 7.2-10. NB ch 15, commentary 2(viii) is similar but applies to documents intended for or belonging to any person, and not only those intended for or belonging to the opposing party.

162 Alta r 6.02(12) & commentary.

materials or disclose their contents.[163] The obligations where recipient counsel has read part or all of the materials before realizing they may be privileged echo those set out in the British Columbia rule.

The comparable ethical rule in Saskatchewan, Manitoba, Ontario, Nova Scotia, and Newfoundland is similar to British Columbia's in that it covers any material that recipient counsel knows or reasonably should know has been inadvertently disclosed by the other side, whether privileged or not.[164] Yet the only obligation imposed on recipient counsel in these provinces is to promptly inform the sender that the material has been received. Whether additional steps need be taken, such as returning the document to the other side, is said to be beyond the scope of the rule, as is the issue of whether privilege is lost.[165] In all of these provinces except Ontario, a commentary adds that unless required by law, the decision whether to return the material is left to the recipient lawyer's professional judgment.[166]

A crucial gloss on the ethical rules in all Canadian jurisdictions is the caselaw governing counsel's obligations in the inadvertent-disclosure context. This jurisprudence holds that on receipt of privileged material inadvertently disclosed by the opposing party, a lawyer must promptly return the material and advise the adversary of the extent to which it has been reviewed, or if there is a reasonable basis to argue privilege has been lost should seal the material and immediately seek a ruling on the privilege issue.[167] Where despite the inadvertent disclosure, privilege is found to remain in place, recipient counsel cannot employ the material as part of his case and, pursuant to the Supreme Court of Canada's decision in *Celanese Canada Inc v Murray Demolition Corp*, may even be disqualified from acting further in the matter.[168]

---

163   *Ibid.* See also Third Restatement § 60, comment "m," and related Reporter's Note: counsel is under obligation to return materials only where circumstances of disclosure do not destroy privilege.

164   Sask r 6.02(10); Man, Ont, NS, NL r 7.2-10.

165   Sask r 6.02(10) (commentary); Man, Ont, NS, NL r 7.2-10, commentary 1. ABA Formal Opinion 05-437 favours a comparable approach.

166   Sask r 6.02(10) (commentary); Man, NS, NL r 7.2-10, commentary 2.

167   See *Celanese Canada Inc v Murray Demolition Corp*, 2006 SCC 36 at para 62 [*Celanese Canada*]; *KB*, above note 157 at paras 59–60; *White v 123627 Canada Inc (cob Algonquin Petro Canada)*, 2014 ONSC 2682 at para 16; *Chan v Dynasty Executive Suites Ltd*, [2006] OJ No 2877 at para 74 (SCJ) [*Chan*]; *2054476 Ontario Inc v 514052 Ontario Ltd*, [2006] OJ No 4383 at para 39 (SCJ).

168   *Celanese Canada*, above note 167 at paras 42–67. Where Crown counsel is the recipient of the material, another possibility is that the charges will be judicially stayed, as occurred in *Bruce Power*, above note 157.

The fact that recipient counsel obtained the material solely because of a slip-up by the opposing party does not preclude disqualification.[169] Rather, as *Celanese Canada* makes clear, counsel will be disqualified if there exists a real risk that the privileged information will be misused if she stays on the case.[170] Once the privilege holder establishes that opposing counsel received confidential material attributable to a solicitor-client relationship, the onus shifts to the recipient counsel to prove, with "clear and convincing evidence," the absence of any resulting prejudice.[171] *Celanese Canada* provides a detailed list of factors bearing on whether this onus will be met.[172] Yet it is probably safe to say that where recipient counsel can show she was blameless in receiving the material, and on realizing privilege might apply acted promptly to return the material unread, disqualification will be unlikely.[173]

Given the decision in *Celanese Canada*, counsel in jurisdictions where the ethics code does not mandate return or sealing of material that is inadvertently disclosed by the other side and may be *privileged* should nonetheless very seriously consider returning or sealing the material pending a judicial determination as to whether privilege has been waived. Doing so ensures a timely resolution of the privilege issue and minimizes the risk that recipient counsel will be disqualified.[174] Responding in this way also avoids breaching the rule that prohibits a lawyer from taking advantage of a mistake on the part of another lawyer where to do so would obtain for the former lawyer's client a benefit to which the client has no *bona fide* claim or entitlement.[175] Returning the material

---

169 See *Celanese Canada*, above note 167 at paras 34 and 57. But counsel's complicity in impropriety relating to the material's disclosure makes disqualification more likely: *Celanese Canada Inc v Murray Demolition Corp* (2004), 244 DLR (4th) 33 at para 35 (Ont CA), rev'd but not on this point, *Celanese Canada*, above note 167; *National Bank Financial Ltd v Potter*, 2005 NSSC 113 at para 78, aff'd 2006 NSCA 73; *Chan*, above note 167 at para 85.

170 *Celanese Canada*, above note 167 at paras 42–55: this test is derived from *MacDonald Estate*, above note 30, a leading case on conflict of interest.

171 *Celanese Canada*, above note 167 at paras 42–55: onus not met, and counsel removed from record; *Bruce Power*, above note 157 at para 55: onus not met, and judicial stay entered; *Mahjoub*, above note 157 at paras 70–73: onus met, but several counsel nonetheless removed based on abuse of process doctrine.

172 *Celanese Canada*, above note 167 at paras 59–65.

173 *Ibid* at para 57.

174 This point is made in the last paragraph of American Bar Association, Standing Committee on Ethics and Professional Responsibility, Formal Opinion 11-460, "Duty When Lawyer Receives Copies of a Third Party's E-mail Communications with Counsel" (4 August 2011).

175 Alta r 6.02(3); Sask r 6.02(2); BC, Man, Ont, NS, NL r 7.2-2; NB ch 15, commentary 4; CBA Code ch XVI, commentary 4.

has the further advantage of bolstering the credibility and integrity of the individual lawyer, not to mention the profession as a whole.

Example: In reviewing disclosure materials, counsel sees that the Crown has inadvertently neglected to redact information revealing the identity of a confidential informant. Counsel should immediately tell the Crown and return the materials without making copies. Counsel should also inform the Crown of the extent to which the privileged information has been viewed. If counsel takes the view that privilege has been lost, she should alert the Crown and seek a ruling on the point.[176]

Mining metadata: Controversy exists as to whether, and if so to what extent, counsel can review and use metadata contained in electronic documents disclosed by an opponent. Some argue that it is always improper to mine for metadata absent actual knowledge the information was intentionally sent. Others contend that metadata can generally be reviewed by a recipient lawyer, although this contention is sometimes accompanied by important caveats, for example, that the sending lawyer be notified if the metadata contains information of material significance or that the recipient lawyer stop mining for metadata, and perhaps even return or destroy the file, if advised the information was inadvertently disclosed.[177] The safest approach is to treat metadata like any other material received from the other side, and to apply to it the ethical and legal rules that govern in the particular jurisdiction.[178]

A lawyer who comes into possession of confidential material that may have been illegally obtained from a complainant or other third party must consider several additional factors. First, retention of the material may constitute the criminal offence of possession of property obtained by crime.[179] Second, while the ethical rules in British Columbia

---

176 Cases commenting on the Crown's mistakenly disclosing informer-privileged information to the defence include *R v Hirschboltz*, 2004 SKQB 17; *Barros* SCC, above note 157 at para 37; *R v Santos*, 2007 ONCJ 633; *R v Akleh*, [2008] OJ No 5577 (SCJ); *R v Lucas*, [2009] OJ No 2251 (SCJ) [*Lucas* ON]. See also *R v Gauthier*, 2004 NLSCTD 71: withdrawing defence counsel returns disclosure to Crown and accidentally includes confidential client material.

177 For a review of various American state bar opinions pro and con, see Pennsylvania Bar Association Committee on Legal Ethics and Professional Responsibility, Formal Opinion 2009–100, "Ethical Obligations on the Transmission and Receipt of Metadata"; Wisconsin State Bar Professional Ethics Committee, Formal Opinion EF-12-01, "Prevent Disclosure of Metadata" (15 June 2012). See also A Perlman, "The Legal Ethics of Metadata Mining" (2010) 43 Akron L Rev 785.

178 See Perlman, *ibid* at 798–99.

179 *Criminal Code*, above note 90, s 354. The ethical rules applicable to handling physical evidence of a crime may also be engaged, as discussed in Chapter 10.

and Alberta require notification of the other party no matter how the documents come into counsel's possession, the remaining Canadian ethical rules apply only to documents that have been "inadvertently sent." It could be argued that these latter rules do not require notification where the material has been stolen.[180] Yet this interpretation hardly seems to accord with the spirit of the rules. And the law may require notification in any event, especially where the material is or may be privileged.[181] On the other hand, notification may have significant adverse consequences for the lawyer's client, if he was complicit in obtaining the documents or data in question.

O. CO-CLIENTS

Where not prevented from doing so by conflict-of-interest problems, counsel may represent two or more co-accused in the same matter. In such an instance, counsel is not bound by the duty of confidentiality as between the clients. To the contrary, she has a positive obligation to disclose to each client any relevant information received from the other(s).[182] The duty of confidentiality owed to co-clients thus operates only as against the rest of the world.[183] Importantly, counsel must fully explain the workings of the duty of confidentiality to all affected clients before taking on a joint retainer.[184]

---

180 See New York State Bar Association, Committee on Professional Ethics, Opinion 945, "Disclosure of Client Wrongdoing" (7 November 2012) at para 3: inadvertent disclosure rules do not apply, but no opinion given regarding whether notification is nonetheless required by law. *Contra* State Bar of California Standing Committee on Professional Responsibility and Conduct, Formal Opinion No 2013-188, "Confidential Information and Unsolicited Email Correspondence" at 4–5: same ethical rules apply whether disclosure is inadvertent or intentional but unauthorized.

181 See the paragraphs associated with notes 167–73, above. See also *1784049 Ontario Ltd (cob Alpha Care Studio 45) v Toronto (City)*, 2010 ONSC 1204 at para 45: on receiving a potentially privileged document leaked by a councillor with the defendant city, the lawyer for the plaintiff should have promptly sought to have the court rule on any disputed claim of privilege.

182 See Alta r 2.03(1) (commentary) and 2.04(2) (commentary); Sask r 2.04(5)(b); Man r 2.04(7)(b); Ont r 2.04(6)(b); BC, NS, NL r 3.4-5(b). See also the discussion in Chapter 6, Section O(1)(b).

183 See *Dunbar*, above note 156 at 37 [para 57]; *Pritchard*, above note 1 at para 23; *R v B(BP)* (1992), 71 CCC (3d) 392 at 399 (BCSC); *Boreta v Primrose Drilling Ventures Ltd*, 2010 ABQB 383 at para 58.

184 See Sask r 2.04(5)(b); BC, Man, Ont, NS, NL r 3.4-5(b); Alta r 2.04(3)(c); CBA Code ch V, commentary 6. Counsel must also ensure that the retainer is not

Counsel who is jointly representing two clients faces a dilemma if one client tries to renege on the usual information-sharing arrangement. Suppose that despite having given informed consent to multiple representation, Client A provides information to counsel with the express instruction that it not be shared with Client B. This puts counsel in a position of divided loyalty: failure to disclose will betray the duty to keep Client B informed while disclosure will violate Client A's instructions. Counsel must therefore withdraw unless Client A can be persuaded to share the information.[185] Where counsel is forced to do so, the question remains, can she disclose the information to Client B? It has been suggested that there is a discretion to disclose if the adverse impact of non-disclosure on Client B exceeds the adverse impact that disclosure will have on Client A.[186] There may also be a discretion, whether in the alternative or not, to at least inform Client B that a matter seriously affecting his interests has arisen.[187]

P. DUTY OF CONFIDENTIALITY OWED TO ORGANIZATIONAL CLIENT

Where a lawyer acts for a corporation or other organization, the ethical duty of confidentiality is owed to the organization, and not to the individuals within it, be they employees, officers, or directors.[188] Information received from such individuals must not be kept secret from the person or persons who instruct the lawyer. This is reflected in provisions found in several Canadian ethical codes, which require a lawyer who has received information suggesting past or future illegality on the part of an organization, including from an inside source, to bring the information to the attention of the person who normally instructs the lawyer. If a satisfactory response is not forthcoming, the lawyer must engage in "up-the-ladder" reporting, to the board of directors if necessary, in an attempt to ensure that any ongoing or planned illegality ceases.[189]

---

precluded because of conflict of interest: see Chapter 6, Section H.

185 Alta r 2.04(2) (commentary); Sask r 2.04(8); BC, Man, Ont, NL r 3.4-8; NS r 3.4-8 & 8A; NB ch 6, commentary 3; CBA Code ch V, commentary 7.

186 See Third Restatement § 60, comment "l."

187 *Ibid.*

188 See Alta r 2.02(6); Sask r 2.02(3); BC, Man, Ont, NS, NL r 3.2-3; CBA Code ch IV, commentary 18; Third Restatement § 96, comment "b."

189 Alta r 2.02(11); Sask r 2.02(8); BC, Man, Ont, NS, NL r 3.2-8; CBA Code ch IV, commentary 18.

Q. DUTY OF CONFIDENTIALITY OWED TO NON-CLIENTS

Caselaw and ethical codes typically speak of duties of confidentiality owed to current and former clients. Yet on occasion a lawyer may owe a duty of confidentiality to a non-client. Examples already discussed include

1) where a lawyer receives confidential information from a potential client who ends up not retaining the lawyer,[190]
2) where a lawyer receives confidential information from a non-firm colleague who is seeking advice regarding how best to conduct some aspect of a case,[191] and
3) where a lawyer receives confidential material inadvertently disclosed by opposing counsel.[192]

More generally, a duty of confidentiality to a non-client may arise where the non-client provides a lawyer with confidential material with the reasonable expectation that it will remain confidential as against the rest of the world and where the lawyer knows or ought to know that the information is confidential.[193]

R. HANDLING CROWN DISCLOSURE MATERIALS

Disclosure materials received from the Crown in the course of a criminal matter are covered by the duty of confidentiality owed to the client.[194] Accordingly, neither the materials themselves nor their contents can be used or released without the client's express or implied consent absent the application of an exception to the duty. Of course, implied consent will almost always exist to allow counsel to use disclosure to prepare and advance the client's defence; after all, that is its purpose. But consent cannot be implied where counsel seeks to use the materials to advance other aims, especially where doing so risks harming the client.

---

190 See Section H(6), above in this chapter.
191 See Section H(11), above in this chapter.
192 See Section N, above in this chapter.
193 CBA Code ch IV, commentary 12; CBA Task Force on Conflicts of Interest, above note 64 at 118–21.
194 See Example 1 associated with note 18, above. See also *Law Society of Upper Canada v Anber*, 2014 ONLSTH 143 [*Anber*]: lawyer disciplined for breaching duty of confidentiality by posting client's disclosure on Internet.

For example, disseminating disclosure to third parties may cause significant damage to a client's reputation.

Altogether apart from the duty of confidentiality owed to a client, defence counsel is restricted in handling disclosure materials by ethical obligations owed to the administration of justice. By way of explanation, it is helpful to begin by examining the harm to the proper functioning of the criminal justice system that can flow from the improper use of disclosure.

1) Rationale for Handling Disclosure with Care

The 1991 decision in *R v Stinchcombe* radically changed the scope and extent of disclosure provided to defence counsel.[195] Nowadays, every prosecution generates disclosure materials. Cases involving thousands of pages of disclosure are not at all uncommon. Importantly, disclosure often contains information that engages third-party privacy interests, for instance, outlines of unproven allegations, complainant or witness statements that touch on highly personal matters, medical reports, financial information, intercepted communications, criminal records, and so on.[196] If relevant, such information must be disclosed to the accused so that he can make full answer and defence, and it is generally available for use at trial provided it is admissible. This curtailment of third-party privacy rights is necessary to ensure the fair and reliable operation of the criminal justice system.

Yet the accused does *not* have a *Charter* right to disseminate disclosure for purposes other than making full answer and defence in the extant criminal proceeding. Nor is disclosure the property of the accused to do with as he wishes.[197] Legitimate privacy interests must as a general rule give way so that the accused can make full answer and defence but otherwise are usually deserving of protection.[198] To put it another way, "individuals involved in a criminal investigation do not forfeit their privacy interests for all future purposes; they reasonably

---

195 (1991), 68 CCC (3d) 1 (SCC) [*Stinchcombe*]. See Chapter 12, Section G.

196 A list of the private information that can be found in disclosure materials is provided in *R v McNeil*, 2009 SCC 3 at para 19 [*McNeil*]; *R v Quesnelle*, 2014 SCC 46 at paras 32–33 [*Quesnelle*].

197 See *R v Kim*, 2004 ABQB 157 at paras 17–18.

198 See *R v Basi*, 2011 BCSC 314 at paras 15–18, 43, and 72 [*Basi*]; Ontario, *Report of the Attorney General's Advisory Committee on Charge Screening, Disclosure, and Resolution Discussions*, ed by G Arthur Martin (Toronto: Ontario Ministry of the Attorney General, 1993) at 181 [*Martin Report*]; *P(D) v Wagg* (2004), 184 CCC (3d) 321 at para 46 (Ont CA) [*Wagg*]. See also *McNeil*, above note 196 at paras 12, 19–20, 38, and 42; *Quesnelle*, above note 196 at paras 2 and 37.

expect that personal information in police reports will not be disclosed in unrelated matters."[199] Use of disclosure for purposes collateral to the criminal proceeding can severely undermine these privacy interests, and in egregious cases — for example, when the statement of a vulnerable witness is circulated within a criminal milieu — may create a real threat to personal safety.[200]

The use of disclosure for collateral purposes may also make people less willing to co-operate with police investigations, to the substantial detriment of the administration of justice.[201] As noted in the influential 1993 *Martin Report*:

> The administration of justice is highly dependent upon witnesses coming forward to provide information that will lead to the proper conviction and punishment of those who have committed crimes. For a witness, courtroom proceedings may be inconvenient, or even traumatic, in the best of circumstances. Therefore, even occasional misuse of disclosure materials can potentially persuade large numbers of already reluctant witnesses to refrain from co-operating for fear that they will suffer the consequences of similar misuse.[202]

Furthermore, disclosure materials may also include information over which the Crown could make a successful claim of public interest immunity or another privilege to prevent its dissemination or use for purposes other than making full answer and defence.[203] It is thus incorrect to assume that privileges otherwise applicable to portions of investigatory materials are necessarily lost for all purposes simply on the materials' being shared with the defence as part of the disclosure process.[204]

Defence counsel should keep two further considerations in mind if asked by a client to release disclosure for a purpose collateral to the subject matter of the case. First, counsel will almost always have been retained solely to assist the client in making full answer and defence. Absent exceptional circumstances, counsel has no obligation, ethical or otherwise, to assist the client in employing the disclosure for other purposes. Second, counsel must be alive to the possibility that the client or

199 *Quesnelle, ibid* at para 2. See also *ibid*, paras 29–44.
200 See *Martin Report*, above note 198 at 180.
201 See *Basi*, above note 198 at paras 18 and 43; *Martin Report*, above note 198 at 180.
202 Above note 198 at 180.
203 See *Basi*, above note 198 at paras 17 and 43; *Wagg*, above note 198 at para 46; *Jourdain v Ontario* (2008), 91 OR (3d) 506 at paras 50–58 (SCJ).
204 In addition to the cases cited in the preceding note, see Lederman, Bryant, & Fuerst, above note 21 at §§ 14.141–42.

a third party wishes to use disclosure for an illegal purpose, such as to harass a witness or obtain intelligence on behalf of a criminal organization.[205] Most Canadian ethical codes provide that a lawyer must not knowingly assist in any dishonesty or illegal conduct and should be on guard against becoming the tool of an unscrupulous client or others.[206] If the lawyer has suspicions or doubts in this regard, reasonable inquiries must be made to clarify whether the conduct in question is illegal or otherwise unethical.[207]

2) Duty to the Administration of Justice and the Implied Undertaking

These arguments for placing restrictions on defence counsel's handling of disclosure materials, *in addition* to the restrictions imposed by the duty of confidentiality owed to a client, are highly compelling. There can thus be no doubt that defence counsel has an ethical obligation to the administration of justice to act responsibly with respect to disclosure materials.[208] As stated in the *Martin Report*:

> Full disclosure invariably enhances counsel's ability to advise his or her client, and to prepare for the trial or the plea and sentencing. However, in the Committee's view, these broad disclosure rights cannot be misused by the defence. Disclosure is an accused's constitutional right because of its crucial role in making full answer and defence. However, it cannot be overlooked that, while the right to make full answer and defence is paramount in the realm of disclosure, there are other important, and competing, values at stake. These values include public safety, the privacy interests of victims or witnesses, and the need to maintain the integrity of the administration of criminal justice. These important values must be accommodated to the greatest extent possible.[209]

---

205 See, for example, *R v Mastop*, 2013 BCCA 494, leave to appeal to SCC refused, [2014] SCCA No 23 [*Mastop*]: lawyer convicted for assisting criminal organization by, among other things, providing it with disclosure materials.

206 See Chapter 2, Section B(1).

207 *Ibid.*

208 See *Stinchcombe*, above note 195 at 12 [para 23]; *Martin Report*, above note 198 at 179–80 (discussing comment in *Stinchcombe*); *R v Pickton*, 2005 BCSC 967 at para 3; *R v Floria*, [2008] OJ No 4418 at para 23 (SCJ) [*Floria*], appeal quashed 2009 ONCA 117.

209 *Martin Report*, above note 198 at 175.

The question becomes, what restrictions on defence counsel's handling of disclosure are justified? And more particularly, should an implied undertaking attach to disclosure materials, as it does to information exchanged between parties as part of the discovery process in civil proceedings?

The *Martin Report* does not expressly endorse an implied undertaking in the criminal disclosure context. But it plumps for even *stricter* restrictions, recommending that defence counsel keep disclosure materials in her custody or control to protect against improper dissemination, and not even provide copies to the client.[210] A number of courts have cited the *Martin Report*'s approach with apparent approval.[211] Some have recognized an implied undertaking,[212] the existence of which is especially entrenched in British Columbia.[213] Other courts, though demonstrating a marked attraction to arguments favouring an implied undertaking, have declined to decide the issue, the prime example being the well-reasoned decision of the Ontario Court of Appeal in *P(D) v Wagg*.[214] A few decisions have held that criminal disclosure materials are not subject to an implied undertaking, but these tend to be of older vintage, and none provides a reasoned basis for the conclusion.[215]

---

210 *Martin Report, ibid* at 179–84. The defence lawyers on the committee responsible for the report, dissenting on this point, took the less restrictive view that disclosure should be subject to an implied undertaking (*ibid* at 181).

211 *R v Smith* (1994), 146 Sask R 202 at paras 14–15 (QB); *R v Mohammed*, [2007] OJ No 5806 at paras 25–28 (SCJ) [*Mohammed*].

212 *Hedley v Air Canada* (1994), 23 CPC (3d) 352 paras 30–33 (Gen Div); *R v Lucas* (1996), 104 CCC (3d) 550 at paras 8–10 (Sask CA), aff'd without reference to this issue (1998), 123 CCC (3d) 97 (SCC) [*Lucas SK*]; *Fullowka v Royal Oak Mines*, [1998] NWTJ No 45 at para 7 (SC) [*Fullowka*]; *Bourgeois v Bolen*, 2004 ABQB 35 at para 47; *R v Little*, 2001 ABPC 13 at paras 36–38; *R v Wiebe*, 2007 ABPC 47 at paras 25–27; *Pelletier v Pelletier*, 2013 ABPC 141 at para 5; *D(P) v Wagg* (2002), 61 OR (3d) 746 at para 41 (Div Ct), issue expressly left undecided on further appeal, *Wagg*, above note 198 at para 47; *R v Hathway*, 2005 SKQB 504 at paras 9–18 [*Hathway*]; *Children's Aid Society of Algoma v DP*, 2006 ONCJ 170 at paras 16–18; *LeBlanc v Haché*, 2014 NBQB 99 at paras 42–46.

213 *Basi*, above note 198; *Mastop*, above note 205 at para 58; *R v Basi*, 2009 BCSC 755 at para 9; *Wong v Antunes*, 2008 BCSC 1739 at para 38 [*Wong*], var'd on other grounds 2009 BCCA 278; *Henry v British Columbia (AG)*, 2012 BCSC 1878 at para 42 [*Henry*].

214 Above note 198 at paras 29–47: "compelling reasons" to recognize implied undertaking rule. See also *R v Schertzer*, [2004] OJ No 5879 at para 4 (SCJ): "highly likely" that implied undertaking attaches; *Ontario (AG) v Holly Big Canoe* (2006), 80 OR (3d) 761 at para 36 (SCJ): "powerful case" for recognizing implied undertaking; *Lucas ON*, above note 176 at paras 18–20. Contrast *Jackson v DA*, 2005 ABQB 702 at paras 4–6 and 44–47, simply holding that the law is unsettled.

215 See, for example, *R v Masilamany*, [2004] OJ No 701 at para 32 (SCJ).

Ultimately, there are strong justifications for subjecting criminal disclosure materials to an implied undertaking, recognition of which is also supported by a clear preponderance of caselaw. Defence counsel should therefore treat disclosure as covered by an implied undertaking even if the law is not firmly settled in his jurisdiction.

The contours of the implied undertaking in the criminal context remain to be fully worked out. The most comprehensive discussion of the implied undertaking is presently found in the British Columbia decision of *R v Basi*.[216] Based on the approach taken there, as well as in the civil context, the following principles likely apply:

1) The implied undertaking prevents counsel from using disclosure for any purpose other than to make full answer and defence in the criminal proceedings in which the materials are provided.[217]

2) The implied undertaking restricts not only counsel's use of disclosure materials but the client's as well.[218] It is *not* an undertaking of the sort that one lawyer gives another but rather is an obligation owed to the court by both counsel and the client. To hold otherwise would undermine the rationale for recognizing the implied undertaking in the first place, for an unrepresented accused or client in possession of disclosure would be free to use the materials in any way.

3) The implied undertaking covers not only the material disclosed but also the information contained in the material.[219]

4) The implied undertaking continues even after the criminal matter has concluded.[220] Presumably, it would not prevent counsel from using the materials at a parole hearing in the matter in which they were disclosed or in relation to a postappeal application to re-open the case because of a possible miscarriage of justice, brought under section 696.1 of the *Criminal Code*.[221]

5) The implied undertaking is extinguished where the materials have been used at trial or with the consent of the Crown and/or police or leave of the court.[222]

6) The court will relieve a party from an implied undertaking, in whole or part, where the party can demonstrate "on a balance of prob-

---

216 Above note 198.
217 See *ibid* at paras 42 and 45.
218 See *ibid* at para 42, stating that the rule applies to "the accused."
219 See *ibid*.
220 See *ibid* at para 45. See also *Juman v Doucette*, 2008 SCC 8 at para 51 [*Juman*].
221 Above note 90.
222 See *Wong*, above note 213 at para 38; *Huang (litigation guardian of) v Sadler*, 2006 BCSC 559 at para 18 [*Huang*], leave to appeal to BCCA refused, 2006 BCCA 279; *Juman*, above note 220 at paras 25 and 51.

abilities the existence of a public interest of greater weight than the values the implied undertaking is designed to protect."[223] The use to which the party wishes to put the materials in question and any perceived prejudice to the party in whose favour the implied undertaking operates are key considerations.[224]

7) Counsel who receives disclosure in one case cannot use it in another proceeding, whether civil or criminal, without consent of the Crown and/or police or leave of the court.[225] Where the other proceeding is criminal, there should be no problem obtaining consent or leave if the material is relevant to that other proceeding within the meaning of *Stinchcombe*. Where the other proceeding is civil, consent or leave will likely be forthcoming if the litigation arises out of the same incident.[226]

8) Although using disclosure material at trial typically extinguishes the implied undertaking, counsel should be wary of assuming that *any* court use leads to this result. For instance, there is a good argument for concluding that filing disclosure materials at a pre-trial proceeding does not put an end to the implied undertaking, especially in jurisdictions where the public is not automatically granted access to all documents contained in criminal court files.[227]

9) A court can order that disclosure materials be returned to the Crown at the conclusion of a criminal matter where there is a real risk they will otherwise be used in violation of the implied undertaking.[228]

3) Express Undertakings

It is not uncommon for the Crown to require defence counsel to enter into an express undertaking to ensure the protection of privacy interests engaged by disclosure materials. Express undertakings are usually employed with respect to portions of disclosure that engage especially strong privacy interests or concerns about possible misuse. Examples include an express undertaking not to create copies of a video statement made by a sexual assault complainant or depicting the appearance of an undercover police officer,[229] or precluding counsel from plugging an

---

223 *Juman, ibid* at para 32.
224 See *ibid* at para 33.
225 See *Henry*, above note 213; *Hwang v Saskatoon*, 2003 SKQB 395 [*Hwang*].
226 See *Hwang, ibid*; *Henry*, above note 213.
227 See *Basi*, above note 198 at paras 47–64.
228 See *ibid* at paras 65–79.
229 See *Wagg*, above note 198 at para 79 (sexual assault example); *Hathway*, above note 212 (undercover officer example). See also *Floria*, above note 208 at para 21.

external drive containing disclosure into a computer that is connected to the Internet, to prevent access to sensitive material by hackers.[230] Express undertakings are also sometimes used where the defence seeks disclosure of material outside of the main investigative file, which is only potentially relevant and raises real confidentiality concerns.[231]

In some jurisdictions, British Columbia being a prime example, the Crown will occasionally seek an express undertaking preventing counsel from sharing a portion of the disclosure with the client absent consent or leave of the court.[232] Defence counsel should be careful about agreeing to such a request, given the ethical duty to keep the client reasonably informed and the fact that the client's input may be required to understand the relevance of a particular piece of information.[233] Accepting information on the condition that it not be shared with the client may also strain the professional relationship; a client may find it difficult to trust counsel who is sharing a secret with the lawyer for the opponent.[234] In extreme cases, where the information viewed pursuant to the express undertaking is clearly material to the defence but protected by an impenetrable privilege, counsel's inability to share the information with the client or use it in court may lead to an incurable conflict of interest.[235]

Nonetheless, express undertakings that prevent counsel from sharing information with a client may, in some circumstances, be extremely beneficial for the defence. They permit counsel access to information without the need to bring a disclosure application, which can be a time-consuming process and may end in failure. If, after reviewing the material, defence counsel determines that the information is relevant and that no privilege applies, the Crown may consent to remove the express undertaking. If not, counsel can bring a disclosure application, and in doing so will have the considerable advantage of knowing the

---

230 See *Mohammed*, above note 211 at paras 54–60.
231 See Patrick J LeSage & Michael Code, *Report of the Review of Large and Complex Criminal Case Procedures* (Toronto: Ontario Ministry of the Attorney General, 2008) at 53–54, online: www.attorneygeneral.jus.gov.on.ca/english/about/pubs/lesage_code/default.asp. The authors are referring to court-ordered express undertakings, but the same process can be implemented without the involvement of the court.
232 See also Ont r 3.2-2, commentary 1.2: in limited circumstances, it may be appropriate for a lawyer to receive information on a "for counsel's eyes only" basis.
233 See Chapter 3, Section E.
234 See *R v Basi*, 2009 SCC 52 at paras 45–47; *R v Ahmad*, 2011 SCC 6 at para 49.
235 See cases cited in preceding note.

precise nature of the sought-after information.[236] An express undertaking preventing counsel from sharing information with the client may therefore be justified in the right circumstances. Before agreeing to such an express undertaking, however, counsel must ensure the client fully understands and consents to its terms.

Honouring Undertakings: Undertakings given to another counsel or the court must be "strictly and scrupulously" fulfilled.[237] They constitute a lawyer's promise and reflect an acceptance of personal responsibility unless the contrary is clearly stated.[238] Counsel must therefore not give an undertaking she cannot carry out. Undertakings should also be written or confirmed in writing, and the terms should be absolutely unambiguous.[239] Counsel taking over a file may be bound by former counsel's undertakings and so should make inquiries as to whether any such undertakings exist before accepting the retainer.[240]

4) Providing Disclosure Materials to a Client or the Client's Associates

Providing copies of disclosure to the client can facilitate both the client's understanding of the case and the process by which counsel obtains instructions and relevant information from the client. Leaving copies with the client for such purposes thus often legitimately assists in preparing the defence and is not improper provided counsel takes reasonable steps to ensure that the copies are not improperly disseminated or otherwise misused.[241] In jurisdictions where the implied undertaking applies, the client should be told about its requirements. In jurisdictions, if any, where the implied undertaking does not apply, it is nonetheless prudent for counsel to inform the client that disclosure must not be

---

236 It is prudent to draft the express undertaking to allow defence counsel to file the material with the court on a disclosure application, to remain sealed but be accessible by the court in deciding the application.

237 See Alta r 4.01(7) and 6.02(13); Sask r 4.01(6) and 6.02(11); BC, Man, Ont, NS, NL r 5.1-6 and 7.2-11; CBA Code ch XVI, commentary 7. See also *Anber*, above note 194: lawyer disciplined for breaching express undertaking to Crown by posting disclosure materials on Internet.

238 See rules and commentary cited in preceding note.

239 Alta r 6.02(13) & commentary; Sask r 6.02(11) & commentary; BC, Man, Ont, NS, NL r 7.2-11 & commentary 1; CBA Code ch XVI, commentary 7.

240 Allan McDonell, "Undertakings in BC: Don't Get Buried" (2012) 70 The Advocate 375 at 380.

241 *Contra Martin Report*, above note 198 at 179, recommendation 35, and 182–84 (discussion of same).

used for any improper purpose. The client should be urged to contact counsel for advice before acting if unsure as to what is permitted.

Where counsel reasonably suspects that the client may misuse the disclosure materials if provided with copies, precautions should be taken to prevent this from happening.[242] This due diligence requirement may be satisfied simply by having a serious talk with the client regarding the importance of using the disclosure for proper purposes only and the consequences that may flow from a failure to do so. In other cases, counsel may be justified in refusing to hand over copies of the disclosure and instead utilizing alternative means to have the client review the materials, such as by providing access in counsel's office.

Recommendation: Matters that counsel should consider in determining whether there is a realistic risk a client will misuse disclosure materials if provided with copies include

1) whether the nature of the materials makes them susceptible to misuse;
2) whether the client has a discernible interest in misusing the materials;
3) the extent to which receiving copies of the materials, as opposed to reviewing them in counsel's office, will help the client to make full answer and defence;
4) whether the character of the client makes misuse more likely; and
5) the client's stated reason for wanting a copy of the materials, including whether his interest appears focused on the very parts of the materials that give counsel cause for concern based on factors (1) or (2).

Counsel must never provide disclosure materials to a client's associates in an attempt to convince them that the client is not co-operating with police or has not absconded with assets related to a criminal enterprise. Providing disclosure to a lawyer who acts on behalf of such associates is also improper. In the vast majority of instances, relaying information from disclosure materials to the client's associates does nothing to advance the client's defence, and for this reason alone cannot be said to fall within the ambit of counsel's professional retainer. More importantly, using the disclosure in this way may assist a criminal enterprise in its illegal activities and so violate the ethical prohibitions against aiding the client or anyone else in committing a crime or fraud.[243] Finally, and in any event, release of disclosure to a client's associates will almost always breach the terms of the implied undertaking in those provinces where the implied undertaking operates.

---

242 See the paragraph associated with notes 205–7, above in this chapter.
243 *Ibid.*

If the client refuses to accept limitations on his access to or use of disclosure that counsel reasonably believes are necessary to ensure that the materials are not used for an improper purpose, counsel must withdraw from the case. On withdrawing, the disclosure materials should be returned to the Crown, not given to the client. The Crown should not, however, be told the reason for counsel's withdrawal, because such information falls within counsel's duty of confidentiality.

CONFIDENTIALITY EXCEPTIONS

A. INTRODUCTION

The duty of confidentiality is central to the integrity of client-lawyer relationships, and the profession and administration of justice more generally. However, there are other societal values that in some cases trump the duty, permitting or even mandating disclosure of confidential information. For this reason, the rules of professional conduct contain various exceptions to the obligation of confidentiality, often grappling with the question of exactly when confidentiality can give way because of inconsistency with important countervailing values. Other exceptions are based on the client's authority to release information or on the recognition that widespread public awareness of information may render the lawyer's obligation otiose. While the exceptions most commonly suggested by Canadian ethical rules are dealt with in this chapter, their application in certain special circumstances is canvassed separately elsewhere in this book.[1]

As we shall see, in some instances an exception is only vaguely described or hinted at by the rules, which as a result may offer only minimal guidance for practising lawyers. In other cases, exceptions provide a discretion as to whether disclosure should be made, which may leave counsel with a difficult decision as to the proper course to take. Finally, the exceptions to the duty of confidentiality can be controversial,

---

1   See, for example, Chapters 7 and 10.

and probably as a result are sometimes framed differently in different provinces. It is therefore important that counsel consult the ethical rules applicable in his jurisdiction and not blithely assume complete consistency from province to province. With these forewarnings, we can now look at some of the instances where Canadian ethical rules may operate to relieve counsel from the usual obligation to keep client information confidential.

B. AUTHORIZED DISCLOSURE

The disclosure of otherwise confidential information is permitted where authorized by the client.[2] After all, the lawyer's duty of confidentiality is for the benefit of the client, and the rationale for maintaining confidentiality dissipates where the client can be said to permit disclosure. Authorized disclosure can be viewed either as an exception to the duty of confidentiality or as not coming within the scope of the duty to begin with. The Canadian rules of professional conduct tend to the former view,[3] which has the advantage of emphasizing the importance of protecting confidentiality in the ordinary course. Authorization comes in two forms, express or implied, each of which will be considered in turn.

1) Express Authority

Disclosure can be expressly authorized by the client.[4] If waiver of confidentiality is clear and unambiguous, consent can even permit use or disclosure that risks harm to the client.[5] In any case of express consent, however, counsel must make sure that the client fully understands the ramifications of disclosure, including all reasonably foreseeable advantages and disadvantages.[6] Counsel need competently advise the client

---

2   See Alta, Sask r 2.03(1)(a) & commentary; BC, Man, Ont, NS, NL r 3.3-1(a) and commentary 9; *An act respecting the Barreau du Quebec*, CQLR c B-1, s 131(2); NB ch 5, rule and commentary 9(a) and 13; CBA Code ch IV, rule and commentary 13.
3   See rules and commentary cited in preceding note.
4   *Ibid.*
5   See Third Restatement § 61, comment "b."
6   See *McClure v Thompson*, 323 F3d 1233 at paras 54–56 (9th Cir 2003), certiorari denied, 540 US 1051 (2003): client's consent to release the location of his murder victims was not informed, because counsel failed to make clear possible adverse consequences; *Commonwealth v Downey*, 65 Mass App Ct 547 at 552 (2006): consent to lawyers wearing concealed recording devices during trial at the request of film company was not informed, because clients were not alerted to risk that privileged communications would be broadcast in the media.

in this respect, and where the action being considered raises a possible conflict of interest, independent legal advice may be necessary.[7] It is possible that although fully-informed consent is obtained, conflict concerns cannot be alleviated.[8] It may be, for example, that a potential conflict of interest involving two clients is waived only by one or that despite a knowing waiver by both clients, the court is not prepared to treat the conflict problem as resolved.

In the United States, ABA Model Rule 1.6(a) and the Third Restatement § 61 require counsel to consult with the client before obtaining express consent. In contrast, most Canadian rules of professional conduct dealing with confidentiality do not make clear that express consent must be fully informed. However, this requirement is surely mandated as part of a lawyer's duty to be honest and candid when advising a client.[9]

Example: A client is in custody on serious charges and has prepared and provided to counsel a summary of his whereabouts on the day of the offence. The client wants his parents to have a complete understanding of the case, and to this end he asks counsel to send them a copy of the summary. Counsel should not take this step without first making the client aware of the possible loss of privilege and any attendant harm.[10]

2) Implied Authority

A lawyer is also permitted to reveal or use confidential information based on the implied authority of a client.[11] Authority can ordinarily be implied where disclosure or use is necessary to advance the client's interests regarding the subject matter of the retainer. Often included in the scope of implied authority is disclosure to other lawyers, secretaries, and paralegals working with or for the firm, as well as outside contractors such as lawyers, private investigators, and prospective expert witnesses. These sorts of people are frequently employed by counsel to

---

7   See Chapter 6, Section O(1)(d).
8   See Chapter 6, Section O(2).
9   See Chapter 3, Section E.
10 See *R v Kotapski* (1981), 66 CCC (2d) 78 (Que SC), aff'd (1984), 13 CCC (3d) 185 (Que CA): counsel sent such a document to a former client's wife and privilege was lost.
11 See the rules cited at note 2, above in this chapter.

aid a client's cause, and disclosure or use of confidential information is required for this purpose.[12]

Implied authority will also permit counsel to disclose or use confidential information as required in the ordinary course of running a law practice. Bookkeepers, accountants, bankers, governing body auditors, computer technicians, and others may thus come into contact with client information without breaching the duty of confidentiality.[13] The general wording used in most Canadian ethical codes easily accommodates such disclosure.[14]

Authority may also be implied to permit counsel to disclose or use confidential information when dealing with people who are not employed to work on behalf of the client or lawyer. For instance, in certain circumstances counsel may divulge confidential information to the police or Crown. Examples include information provided to the authorities in an effort to avoid charges being laid, to negotiate a plea resolution, and to press any other point on behalf of the client.[15] In disclosing confidential information to third parties who are adverse in interest, counsel must naturally exercise caution. While a lawyer has some discretion in this regard, authority should not be implied to permit disclosure that presents a real risk of harm to the client. Where the lawyer has any doubt on this score, the issue of disclosure should be fully canvassed with the client and express instructions obtained.[16]

Implied authority works to legitimize a myriad of disclosures and uses of client information that would otherwise be considered confidential. It must always be remembered, however, that implied authority is subject to countermand by the client. Where a client forbids a particular disclosure or use of confidential information, authority to do so can never be implied. The client's will is sovereign in this respect, and she can restrict dissemination of information to any number of people, including even a lawyer's own associates.[17] Implied authority to release

---

12 These people owe a duty of confidentiality to the client, and the lawyer is responsible for ensuring they honour the duty: see Chapter 4, Sections H(3) and I(5).

13 The point made in the preceding note applies equally here.

14 See the rules cited at note 2, above in this chapter.

15 See, for example, ABA Model Rule 1.6, comment 5, which extends implied authorization to include disclosure of confidential information to an opponent regarding "a fact that cannot properly be disputed."

16 See, for example, R v L(CK) (1987), 39 CCC (3d) 476 (Ont Dist Ct): counsel improperly undertook to disclose defence psychiatric assessment to Crown without informing client.

17 The commentary to the rules cited at note 2, above in this chapter, expressly recognizes that a client can rescind the implied authority to disclose confidential information to others in the lawyer's firm.

confidential information may also be precluded by screening measures taken to avoid a conflict-of-interest problem.[18]

Some ethical codes grant implied authority to disclose confidential information to permit the lawyer to take action on behalf of a client who lacks the capacity to provide instructions, to protect the client until a legal representative can be appointed.[19] This implied authority will exist if fairly viewed as necessary to protect the client's interests in all the circumstances, including factors suggesting the client lacks capacity, the risk of harm to the client if confidential information is not used, and any instructions the client may have provided with respect to the use of confidential information before becoming incapacitated.[20]

Example: A client discloses information to counsel regarding the events surrounding the charged offence. This information together with the client's general behaviour reasonably leads counsel to believe that the client may not be fit to stand trial. Counsel raises the fitness issue with the court at the start of trial and in doing so discloses confidential information regarding the client's version of events. Counsel did not obtain instructions from the client before doing so. On these facts, counsel has acted properly in raising the fitness issue with the court, which necessarily required the use and some very limited disclosure of the client's confidential information. But he should not have disclosed any more information than was necessary to obtain a fitness hearing, and in particular should not have revealed his client's version of events without first obtaining instructions.[21]

C. PUBLIC KNOWLEDGE

As already mentioned, the ethical duty of confidentiality applies to much information that would not attract solicitor-client privilege, because it has been shared with third parties.[22] For example, a lawyer may receive information regarding a client's case from many potential witnesses. These communications are clearly not solicitor-client privileged, but they are nonetheless confidential under the rules of professional conduct.

---

18 See Chapter 6, Section N(2).
19 Alta, Sask r 2.03(1) (commentary); BC, Man, Ont, NS, NL r 3.3-1, commentary 10. See also Chapter 3, Section N.
20 See commentary cited in preceding note.
21 See *R v Szostak*, 2012 ONCA 503 at paras 69–71, as well as Chapter 3, Section N(3).
22 See Chapter 4, Section D.

It matters not that others besides the lawyer have exactly the same information.[23]

The question arises as to whether the duty of confidentiality persists even where the information is commonly known in the public sphere. The Third Restatement answers this question no, defining confidential information so as *not* to encompass "information that is generally known."[24] Some Canadian caselaw holds that "notorious" information is not confidential,[25] but the jurisprudence also suggests that "widely known" information may still be covered by the ethical duty.[26]

The Canadian rules of professional conduct do not shed a lot of light on this issue. They obliquely suggest that information may be so well known or readily available as to release counsel from any obligation of confidentiality. Specifically, one of the commentaries states with respect to the rule of confidentiality, "Although the rule may not apply to facts that are public knowledge, the lawyer should guard against participating in or commenting upon speculation concerning the client's affairs or business."[27] The codes touch on the same issue in dealing with conflict problems that can arise when a lawyer transfers from one firm to another. In this context, confidential information is specially defined to mean "information that is not generally known to the public obtained from a client."[28] Does this mean that for all other purposes, information is treated as confidential even though it may be a matter of general public knowledge? Or is the special definition meant simply to reflect the approach that should apply universally, and not only in the context of conflict screening?

The public-knowledge exception hinted at in the professional-conduct rules must be approached with caution. At the very least, the knowledge must beyond all doubt be a matter of public record, to such an extent that it can be said to be "generally known." In this regard, it has been suggested that information accessible to members of the public will nonetheless remain confidential where acquisition requires

---

23   See *Stewart v Canadian Broadcasting Corp* (1997), 150 DLR (4th) 24 at 111 [para 209] (Ont Ct Gen Div) [*Stewart*]: "widely known information" may fall within the ethical duty of confidentiality.

24   Third Restatement § 59.

25   *Ott v Fleishman* (1983), 46 BCLR 321 at 322–23 [para 6] (SC); *Le Soleil Hospitality Inc v Louie*, 2010 BCSC 1954 at para 31.

26   *Stewart*, above note 23 at 111 [para 209].

27   Alta, Sask r 2.03(1) (commentary); BC, Man, NS, NL r 3.3-1, commentary 8; CBA Code ch IV, commentary 10. Ont r 3.3-1, commentary 8.1 is to the same effect.

28   Sask r 2.04(17); BC, Man, Ont, NS, NL r 3.4-17; CBA Code ch V, commentary 33. Alta r 2.04(8) (commentary) is similar in effect. Note, however, that this passage was deleted from the FLSC Code in October 2014.

special knowledge, unusual effort, or substantial expenditure.[29] A more demanding, and in our view preferable, approach is to ask whether the information is sufficiently public that its disclosure by the lawyer cannot reasonably be said to create a realistic risk of prejudice or embarrassment to the client.[30]

Public trials: It can be argued that information pertaining to most criminal trials, though available to members of the public who attend court or order transcripts, is not sufficiently notorious to fall outside the duty of confidentiality. On this view, the client whose case is not reported in the media does not lose protection of the duty of confidentiality with respect to all matters that take place in open court. Public knowledge arguably means more than simply knowledge revealed in a form accessible to the public.

Moreover, and crucially, other ethical obligations also come to bear where counsel is considering the use or disclosure of information that is potentially within the public's knowledge. Notably, the duty of loyalty prevents counsel from taking any action that can reasonably be said to cause harm to a client or former client, at least where the harm is caused in relation to the subject matter of the retainer or a related matter.[31] This prohibition applies regardless of whether the duty of confidentiality is engaged. The existence of a public-knowledge exception is thus irrelevant where the broader duty of loyalty nonetheless prohibits disclosure or use of information to the disadvantage of a client or former client.

One of the most detailed discussions of confidentiality, loyalty, and public knowledge in Canadian caselaw is found in *Stewart v Canadian Broadcasting Corp.*[32] In *Stewart*, defence counsel participated in a television broadcast that examined a former client's case. The information revealed by the broadcast was readily available in trial transcripts

---

29   See Third Restatement § 59, comment "d." David Chavkin critiques this definition as too broad in "Why Doesn't Anyone Care about Confidentiality? (And, What Message Does That Send to New Lawyers?)" (2012) 25 Geo J Leg Ethics 239 at 258–63.

30   Compare *Stewart*, above note 23 at 99 [para 181]: criminal defence counsel should take into account the risk of harm to the client even when the information in question is public knowledge.

31   See Chapter 6, Section B. See also *R v Neil*, 2002 SCC 70 at paras 17–19; *Canadian National Railway Co v McKercher LLP*, 2013 SCC 39 at para 25 (current clients); *Consulate Ventures Inc v Amico Contracting & Engineering (1992) Inc*, 2010 ONCA 788 at paras 22–34; *Brookville Carriers Flatbed GP Inc v Blackjack Transport Ltd*, 2008 NSCA 22 at paras 20–49 (CA) (former clients).

32   Above note 23.

and had been the subject of widespread media coverage roughly twelve years previous.[33] An important holding in *Stewart* is that defence counsel did not run afoul of Ontario's ethical rule of confidentiality by participating in the program. In the court's view, the information disclosed by the broadcast was "public" within the meaning of Ontario's then-extant version of the commentary quoted above. The information was therefore not confidential.[34]

The court in *Stewart* nonetheless held that the duty of loyalty owed a former client can operate to prevent a lawyer from employing widely known information — or indeed taking any steps — to the former client's disadvantage. Specifically, the court held that "careful, competent and responsible criminal defence counsel should and do take into account the risk of harm to a former client in deciding whether to discuss publicly a former client or the former client's case, [even] when all relevant information is in the public domain."[35] Counsel in *Stewart* was thus found to have acted inappropriately by participating in a broadcast that was harmful to the former client's interests.

In sum, counsel contemplating the use or disclosure of information that might be "public" within the meaning of applicable ethical rules must consider both the duty of confidentiality and the wider duty of loyalty. The safest course is to err liberally on the side of non-disclosure. Where possible, counsel should check with the client or former client to obtain express authorization rather than relying on this rather foggy limitation to the duty of confidentiality. If the client objects to the requested use or disclosure, then absent exceptional circumstances, counsel should comply.[36]

D. DISCLOSURE REQUIRED BY LAW

The rules of professional conduct make clear that the duty of confidentiality does not apply where the lawyer is required to divulge client

---

33   *Ibid* at 112–13 and 127–28 [paras 212 and 253–54].
34   *Ibid* at 110–13 [paras 206–13]. See also the rules cited at note 27, above in this chapter.
35   *Ibid* at 97 [para 178]. The court reached this result based on legal and equitable principles, but we believe the rules of professional conduct support the same conclusion regarding the duty of loyalty owed to a former client: see the sources cited at note 31, above in this chapter, plus Chapter 6, Section I(2).
36   Contrast *Stewart, ibid* at 100 [para 186], where counsel proceeded with the television broadcast over his client's express objection.

confidences by law or court order.[37] Some codes add that the lawyer must release no more information than is required,[38] a caution that surely applies in every jurisdiction, given the vital and broad nature of the duty of confidentiality.

The ethical rules in Manitoba, Ontario, and New Brunswick expressly state that a lawyer must disclose confidential information where required to do so by law or court order,[39] meaning that counsel has no discretion on the point. The other Canadian jurisdictions are not so clear in this regard. The distinction can be important. Some counsel might choose to risk contempt of court rather than disclose a confidence if given the choice under the rules of ethics. Yet the better view, in light of a lawyer's general duty to abide by the dictates of the law,[40] is that counsel must disclose information when compelled by statute or court order.[41]

When faced with a third party's attempt to use statutory or other legal process to obtain confidential information, counsel has a duty to raise any non-frivolous argument that might reasonably serve to thwart disclosure.[42] Most obviously, solicitor-client privilege can often be asserted, but other legal arguments may also be apposite. For instance, another exclusionary rule may apply, such as the prohibition against hearsay or bad character evidence. Similarly, rules of statutory interpretation can be brought to bear or constitutional arguments invoked. While any reasonably tenable objection to disclose must be raised, indisputably frivolous attempts to mount legal arguments against disclosure are improper.[43]

---

37   Alta, Sask r 2.03(1)(b); BC, Man, Ont, NS, NL r 3.3-1(b); *Professional Code*, CQLR c C-26, s 60(4); *An act respecting the Barreau du Quebec*, above note 2, s 131(2); NB ch 5, rule; CBA Code ch IV, r 2 and commentary 17.

38   Man r 3.3-2; NB ch 5, commentary 10; CBA Code ch IV, r 2 and commentary 17.

39   Man r 3.3-2; Ont r 3.3-1.1; NB ch 5, rule and commentary 8(a).

40   See Chapter 2, Section B(1); *Wood v Schaeffer*, 2013 SCC 71 at para 109, LeBel and Cromwell JJ, dissenting but not on this point. Note too that contempt of court can constitute a criminal offence: see *Criminal Code*, RSC 1985, c C-46, s 9; Alan Mewett & Peter Sankoff, *Witnesses* (Toronto: Carswell, 2012) at § 8.3.

41   A lawyer's duty to reveal non-privileged confidential information when compelled by court process is affirmed in *Lavallee, Rackel and Heintz v Canada (AG)*, 2000 ABCA 54 at para 63 [*Lavallee* Alta CA], aff'd 2002 SCC 61 [*Lavallee*]. See also Rebecca Aviel, "The Boundary Claim's Caveat: Lawyers and Confidentiality Exceptionalism" (2012) 86 Tul L Rev 1055: lawyers must disclose confidences when required to do so by law.

42   See Chapter 4, Section J, discussing counsel's obligations when served with a subpoena or subjected to a search warrant.

43   See Third Restatement § 63, comment "b." See also Chapter 3, Section L.

E. LAWYER SELF-DEFENCE

Most jurisdictions recognize that a lawyer has the right to use or disclose confidential information to the extent necessary to defend against an allegation of wrongdoing. The best rationale for this exception is that lawyers would otherwise be defenceless against groundless charges of impropriety and that where it is a client who makes the allegation, the duty of confidentiality has been waived. Yet where the information in question is solicitor-client privileged and where it cannot be said that waiver or any other exception to the privilege applies, it is difficult to justify allowing the lawyer to release the information. Such dispensation would provide lawyers with a benefit not available to anyone else, which hardly seems fair.[44]

The majority of Canadian ethical codes set out the self-defence exception in the following terms:

> If it is alleged that a lawyer or the lawyer's associates or employees:
> (a) have committed a criminal offence involving a client's affairs;
> (b) are civilly liable with respect to a matter involving a client's affairs;
> (c) have committed acts of professional negligence; or
> (d) have engaged in acts of professional misconduct or conduct unbecoming a lawyer,
> the lawyer may disclose confidential information in order to defend against the allegations, but must not disclose more information than is required.[45]

1) Basic Scope of the Self-Defence Exception

Instances where the exception might apply include where a client accuses counsel of a criminal act or brings a civil suit or disciplinary complaint against counsel. Or the exception might be engaged because a client casts aspersions on counsel's performance in seeking to strike a guilty plea or argues ineffective assistance of counsel on appeal.[46] As

---

44   See the arguments made in Adam Dodek, "Reconceiving Solicitor-Client Privilege" (2010) 35 Queen's LJ 493 at 536–37 [Dodek, "Reconceiving"]; Adam Dodek, *Solicitor-Client Privilege* (Markham, ON: LexisNexis, 2014) ch 8, s 9, "The Lawyer's Exceptions" [Dodek, *Solicitor-Client*]; Alice Woolley, *Understanding Lawyers' Ethics in Canada* (Markham, ON: LexisNexis, 2011) at 132–33.

45   Alta r 2.03(4); Sask r 2.03(5); BC, Man, Ont, NS, NL r 3.3-4. See also NB ch 5, commentary 9(b); CBA Code ch IV, r 4.

46   Regarding ineffective assistance, see *R v Archer* (2005), 202 CCC (3d) 60 at paras 158–60 (Ont CA); *R v Le*, 2011 MBCA 83 at para 175; *R v West*, 2009 NSCA

the ineffective-assistance example makes clear, it does not matter that the allegation has been made in a proceeding to which the lawyer is not a party.

The self-defence exception permits disclosure of confidential information not only to defend a lawyer from attack by a client but also to protect associated lawyers and non-lawyers who are subject to allegations of impropriety. The text of most Canadian rules expressly covers a lawyer's associates or employees.[47] Those rules that do not on their face extend so far should be interpreted the same way, provided the allegations can be seen to constitute waiver by the client. Indeed, the logic behind protecting associates or employees arguably justifies extending the exception to any agent who is subject to attack.[48]

2) Use of Confidential Information Only to the Extent Necessary

As with all exceptions to the duty of confidentiality, use or disclosure of the information is permitted only to the extent necessary to achieve the countervailing purpose, in this case to mount a defence. The lawyer must therefore assess the seriousness of the allegation and determine the minimum amount of confidential information required to counter effectively the charge of misconduct. Some allegations may be so far-fetched or ludicrous as to call for no response or perhaps simply a blanket refutation. Others may on their face appear to be valid and so justify an extensive revelation of client-lawyer communications.

The need to keep the disclosure or use of confidential information to a minimum also applies with respect to the people to whom confidences are revealed. For instance, dissemination to the media might be warranted if the client's allegations are made or reported in that forum[49] but otherwise would not normally be permitted. Similarly, an allegation of misconduct made solely to a governing body would probably not justify the revelation of confidences to any person or entity other than that body.

---

94 at paras 15–17; *R v Ballantyne*, 2012 BCCA 372 at paras 70–71 and 89, leave to appeal to SCC refused, [2012] SCCA No 482; *R v Li* (1993), 36 BCAC 181 at paras 48–73 [*Li*]; *R v Delisle* (1999), 133 CCC (3d) 541 at 548 [para 14] (Que CA).

47   See the rules cited at note 45, above in this chapter.

48   See Third Restatement § 64, comment "d."

49   See, for example, Edward Greenspan, "Edward Greenspan Rebuts Conrad Black" *Globe and Mail* (30 September 2011): opinion piece by defence counsel responding to allegations made by client in book about criminal trial.

Ineffective-Assistance Claim: The most common instance where a client asserts defence counsel's performance has been inadequate is where a claim of ineffective assistance of counsel is brought on appeal. Absent the former client's express consent, the better view is that counsel should respond by providing information to Crown appeal lawyers only as part of a judicially sanctioned process.[50] Otherwise, there is a realistic risk that more information than necessary will be revealed to rebut the claim[51] and that the duty of confidentiality will be unjustifiably breached. Once a judicially sanctioned process has been invoked, the extent to which the duty of confidentiality has been waived will be clear, and counsel can safely co-operate with appellate Crown counsel in providing information in response to the ineffective-assistance claim.[52]

Warning: A lawyer must never threaten to use the self-defence exception as a means of dissuading a client from making or proceeding with a disciplinary complaint or allegation of incompetence. In some instances,

---

50   See American Bar Association, Standing Committee on Ethics and Professional Responsibility, Formal Opinion 10-456, "Disclosure of Information to Prosecutor When Lawyer's Former Client Brings Ineffective Assistance of Counsel Claim" (14 July 2010): absent client consent, disclosure should only be made as part of a judicially supervised process. This opinion is discussed in David Siegel, "What (Can) (Should) (Must) Defense Counsel Withhold from the Prosecution in Ineffective Assistance of Counsel Proceedings?" (December 2011) 35 Champion 18; Peter Joy & Kevin McMunigal, "Confidentiality and Claims of Ineffective Assistance" (2011) 25 Criminal Justice 42; Cecelia Klingele, "Confidentiality and Disclosure: What the New ABA Criminal Justice Standards (Don't) Say about the Duties of Defense Counsel" (2011) 38 Hastings Const LQ 983 at 1002–4. For positions generally consistent with that expressed in the opinion, see *R v EG*, 2010 ONSC 3667 at para 12; Canadian Bar Association, Ethics and Professional Responsibility Committee, *Frequently Asked Questions about Solicitor-Client Privilege and Confidentiality* (Ottawa: Canadian Bar Association, 2010) at 26–27; Felicia Folk, "Two Exceptions to a Lawyer's Duty of Confidentiality: The Right to Reveal Confidential Information in Defence of Reputation and in Pursuit of Fees" (2000) 58 The Advocate 33 at 41–42. But see DC Bar, Ethics Opinion 364, "Confidentiality Obligations When Former Client Makes Ineffective Assistance of Counsel Claim" (January 2013).

51   See *R v West*, 2009 NSCA 63 at para 33; *Li*, above note 46 at 194 [paras 71–73].

52   Judicially supervised processes for addressing privilege disputes can be found in Ontario Court of Appeal, *Procedural Protocol Re Allegations of Incompetence of Trial Counsel in Criminal Cases* (1 May 2000) at paras 10–11 and 14–15, online: www.ontariocourts.ca/coa/en/notices/adminadv/protocol.htm; British Columbia Court of Appeal, *Practice Directive (Criminal): Ineffective Assistance of Trial Counsel* (12 November 2013) at paras 4, 8–10, and 11(f), online: www.courts.gov. bc.ca/court_of_appeal/practice_and_procedure/criminal_practice_directives_/ Criminal-Ineffective%20Assistance%20of%20Trial%20Counsel.htm.

the potential divergence of the client's interests from those of the lawyer will make necessary independent legal advice for the client.

3) Allegations by a Third Party

Sometimes a lawyer is subject to allegations of wrongdoing made not by the client but by a third party such as the police or Crown. Most Canadian self-defence rules are framed broadly enough to encompass such third-party claims.[53] By contrast, the New Brunswick rule applies only to an allegation made "in a dispute with the client."[54] Yet this distinction will frequently be of limited importance. Allegations made against a lawyer by the police or Crown often occur in circumstances where solicitor-client privilege is lost owing to the crime-fraud or innocence-at-stake exceptions,[55] in which case the lawyer can use confidential information in her defence regardless of whether the allegation comes from a third party as opposed to the client. Similarly, a complaint by a third party to the lawyer's governing body concerning non-criminal conduct will fall within special regulatory provisions that permit the lawyer to disclose relevant file materials and information.[56]

In rare cases, however, a third party's allegation will arise where there has been no waiver by the client and where no other exception to the duty of confidentiality or solicitor-client privilege applies. It is presumably for this reason that most ethical codes allow for a self-defence exception where a third party alleges impropriety. Yet justifying so broad an exception is difficult, especially where the information in question is both confidential *and* privileged.[57]

Before counsel uses or discloses information in response to a third-party allegation, it is especially important that he make efforts to discuss the matter with the client. Unlike the more usual case, where it is the client who makes the allegation, the client may be unaware of the dispute. Counsel should request that the client authorize use or revelation of confidential information to the extent necessary to counter

---

53   See the rules cited at note 45, above in this chapter; *Wilder v Ontario (Securities Commission)* (2001), 197 DLR (4th) 193 at para 33 (Ont CA) [*Wilder*]. See also Third Restatement § 54; ABA Model Rule 1.6(b)(5).

54   NB ch 5, commentary 9(b).

55   See, for example, *R v Murray*, [2000] OJ No 685 (SCJ) (crime-fraud exception); *R v Murray* (2000), 144 CCC (3d) 322 (Ont SCJ) (innocence-at-stake exception). The innocence-at-stake exception applied in the latter decision has since become much stricter: see Section M(1), below in this chapter.

56   See Section H, below in this chapter.

57   See note 44, above in this chapter, and the associated text.

the allegation.[58] Where notifying the client would jeopardize counsel's ability to mount an effective defence, it may be appropriate to dispense with this requirement.

The interests of counsel and client may diverge where the police or Crown alleges criminal conduct by counsel. Rendering advice to the client in these circumstances will be impossible because of conflict-of-interest concerns. In this regard, consider *R v Joubert*,[59] where police executed a search warrant at a lawyer's office regarding transactions carried out for a client. It seems clear the police had not ruled out the possibility that counsel was implicated in money-laundering activities. Counsel nonetheless continued to provide legal advice to the client — in our view improperly — following execution of the warrant.

Prohibition: Using or disclosing confidential information to defend oneself against allegations of misconduct by the police or Crown is permitted only where the allegation pertains to the client's representation. Counsel is not allowed to breach confidentiality as a means of obtaining leniency from the police or Crown with respect to conduct unrelated to the retainer.[60] Conversely, Crown counsel should never threaten or bring unfounded charges against a defence lawyer in an effort to force the revelation of otherwise confidential information that can then be used against the client.[61] Defence counsel who encounters such a tactic is placed in a terrible bind. If at all possible, she should hold off making disclosure, all the while protesting vigorously, but there may be no choice except to reveal some information if charges are in fact laid.

4) Anticipated Allegation

To the extent Canadian rules of professional conduct speak of the lawyer's defending against "allegations," the rules may be broad enough to cover the use or disclosure of confidential information where an allegation of misconduct, though made, has not yet led to a formal complaint or charge.[62] But do the rules permit counsel to mount a purely pre-emptive defence, where an assertion of misconduct has not yet been made?

---

58   See Third Restatement § 64, comment "e" (Reporter's Note).

59   (1992), 69 CCC (3d) 553 (BCCA), reconsideration refused (1992), 13 BCAC 116 (CA), leave to appeal to SCC refused, [1992] SCCA No 105.

60   See *In re Shwiller*, 612 SE2d 305 (2005): lawyer appears to have released client confidences to police after being arrested on a drug matter.

61   See *Wilder*, above note 53 at para 34.

62   See the rules cited at note 45, above in this chapter. This broad approach is expressly acknowledged in ABA 1.6(b)(5), comment 10.

The impetus for such action could occur when counsel discovers part way through a retainer that the client is using his services for a criminal purpose. Remaining silent may increase the risk of being charged, convicted, or held civilly liable. Where no other option can reasonably be seen to protect counsel, the argument for disclosure holds some weight.[63] For instance, in *Finers v Miro*,[64] a law firm managing assets for a client learned that the assets were potentially subject to a constructive trust in favour of a third party who alleged fraud by the client and that the firm also faced possible liability to the third party. In these circumstances, the court permitted the firm to make partial disclosure of otherwise confidential information.

On the other hand, most Canadian rules speak of permitting disclosure where "it is alleged" there has been misconduct by the lawyer or the lawyer's associates or employees. This wording suggests that an anticipated allegation is not enough.[65] Counsel who expects but has not yet received an accusation of misconduct should thus consider alternatives short of whistle-blowing, including immediate cessation of the retainer and action to preserve evidence that will aid in demonstrating innocence if and when the accusation crystallizes. It would also be wise to obtain and confirm in writing legal advice from a senior practitioner and/or the law society ethics adviser.[66]

F. FEE DISPUTES

Very closely related to the self-defence exception is the widespread recognition that lawyers can use confidential information to the extent necessary to establish or collect fees.[67] Though currently well-established, this exception has been criticized on the ground that lawyers are merely favouring their own financial interests, avoiding the much more stringent rules applicable when the interests of non-lawyers are

---

63   See Geoffrey Hazard & William Hodes, *The Law of Lawyering*, 3d ed (Gaithersburg, MD: Aspen, 2001) (loose-leaf 2013 supplement) at § 30: favours permitting pre-emptive disclosure where it is reasonably certain that a serious fraud is underway and that a plausible accusation of complicity could be made against the lawyer.

64   [1991] 1 All ER 182 (CA).

65   See ABA Model Rule 1.6(b)(5), comment 10: lawyer's right to respond is triggered by *an assertion* of wrongdoing.

66   A more extensive discussion of the "duped lawyer" problem can be found in Section L, below in this chapter.

67   See Alta r 2.03(5); Sask r 2.03(6); Man r 3.3-3B; BC, Ont, NS, NL r 3.3-5; NB ch 5, commentary 9(b); CBA Code ch IV, r 4.

put in jeopardy.[68] Certainly, it is difficult to justify except in instances where it can be said that the client has acted so as to waive the benefit of confidentiality and privilege. In any event, the restriction of this exception to circumstances where disclosure is *necessary* to protect the lawyer's interests demands special emphasis. The mere fact that a lawyer seeks to advance her position in a fee dispute does not justify widespread revelation of all confidences.[69]

A wrinkle arises where counsel has an agreement with a third party to pay the fee. It may be possible to infer the client's authority to reveal a confidence where a fee-related dispute occurs with the third party. However, relying on implied authority may be untenable where disclosure would harm the client. And absent express consent, or a reasonable basis to conclude the client has somehow waived confidentiality, there is a good argument that counsel should be barred from even a necessary use of confidential information in these circumstances.[70]

In this vein, the Manitoba and New Brunswick rules appear to envision the fee exception as applying only where the lawyer's dispute is with the client.[71] Yet most Canadian rules of professional conduct on their wording seem to permit the same scope for using confidential information even where a fee dispute concerns a third party.[72] Counsel can often avoid the entire controversy when arranging the terms of the retainer, for instance, by obtaining express authority from the client in advance or carefully crafting the terms of the contract with the third party.[73]

As a final point, the jurisprudence permits criminal defence counsel to disclose a client's failure to pay the agreed retainer in advance of trial when applying to the court to withdraw from the record for non-payment of fees.[74] This exception to the duty of confidentiality does not fall within the exception in the ethical codes permitting disclosure to

---

68 See David Layton, "*R v McClure*: The Privilege on the Pea" (2001) 40 CR (5th) 19 at 26–27. Dodek, "Reconceiving," above note 44 at 516–17 and 537, argues that the exception should be abolished.

69 See, for example, *Piercy v Piercy* (1990), 48 BCLR (2d) 145 at 152 (CA), implicitly criticizing counsel for releasing reams of privileged information during a taxation hearing.

70 See Third Restatement § 65, comment "e"; Charles W Wolfram, *Modern Legal Ethics* (St Paul, MN: West, 1986) at 310–11.

71 Man r 3.3-3B, commentary 1; NB ch 5, commentary 9(b). See also ABA Model Rule 1.6(b)(5).

72 See the rules cited at note 67, above in this chapter.

73 Such steps may raise conflict-of-interest concerns, but then again many third-party payment arrangements do so: see Chapter 6, Section K.

74 *R v Cunningham*, 2010 SCC 10 at paras 47–48.

establish or collect fees, but it is closely related and is designed to protect a lawyer from having to conduct a trial for free for a client who has
breached an agreement to provide funds in advance.

G. SECURING ADVICE REGARDING LEGAL AND ETHICAL MATTERS

Many Canadian ethical codes expressly permit counsel to disclose confidential information to a lawyer from outside the firm or an advisory
lawyer from the governing body to secure legal or ethical advice about
the lawyer's proposed conduct.[75] In some situations, the client could be
seen to impliedly consent to the lawyer's disclosing confidential information for this purpose.[76] But where the result of obtaining advice may
be to cause prejudice to the client, this assumption may not be justified.
In such circumstances, the "ethical advice" exception allows the lawyer
to disclose confidential information to reduce the prospect of future allegations of misconduct. But much more than this, the exception helps
to ensure that lawyers act legally and ethically and thus furthers the
proper functioning of the administration of justice.[77]

A lawyer who encounters an ethical issue while representing a
client may wish to post a request for help and input on a criminal defence counsel listserv to which he belongs. Such listservs are usually
governed by a confidentiality agreement precluding the release of information to non-members. But the number of lawyers to whom information circulates can create a real risk of disclosure to the outside
world, and in some cases other listserv members may represent clients
who have interests adverse to the client on whose behalf the question
arises.[78] Listserv postings should thus be restricted to queries that can

---

75   Alta r 2.03(6); Sask r 2.03(7); Man r 3.3-3B; BC, Ont, NS, NL r 3.3-6. See also
     ABA Model Rule 1.6(b)(4). If the consultation is with a lawyer in the same firm,
     these same rules apply, but see also BC, Man, Ont, NS, NL r 3.3-1, commentary 9;
     Alta, Sask r 2.03(1) (commentary); CBA Code ch IV, commentary 13.
76   See ABA Model Rule 1.6(b)(4), comment 9; Chapter 4, Section H(11).
77   See ABA Model Rule 1.6(b)(4), comment 9.
78   See Oregon State Bar, Formal Opinion No 2011-184, "Confidentiality, Conflicts
     of Interest: Consulting between Lawyers Not in the Same Firm" (March 2011)
     at 556–57, albeit written in the context of ethical rules that do not expressly
     permit disclosure of confidential information to other lawyers for the purpose
     of obtaining advice on ethical matters. See also Caroline Buddensick, "Risks
     Inherent in Online Peer Advice: Ethical Issues Posed by Requesting or Provid-
     ing Advice via Professional Electronic Mailing Lists" (2009) 22 Geo J Leg Ethics
     715 at 721–25.

be made without disclosing any confidential information that could serve to identify the client. Where the revelation of sensitive information is necessary to obtain advice on an ethical matter, counsel should forgo the listserv and consult directly with a senior practitioner or a law society ethics adviser.

Caution: Counsel who is asked to provide ethical advice to a lawyer from another firm should assume that all information concerning the consultation is privileged and confidential and approach the exchange as if she is in a solicitor-client relationship with the consulting lawyer. The consulting lawyer should nonetheless remind his colleague of the need to keep their communications confidential and should never seek advice from a colleague whose discretion in this regard is open to question.[79]

Counsel has a duty to disclose to the client any conclusions he reaches as a result of consultation with another lawyer on a legal or ethical matter where impacting in a material way on the course of the representation. Counsel must also disclose any related facts, including his own acts or omissions. These disclosures are simply part of the general duty to keep the client informed and advised.[80] Counsel probably need not disclose the contents of the consultation to the client, or even that he has engaged in such consultation.[81] Yet there is no prohibition against doing so, and revealing the fact and details of the consultation may assist greatly in explaining to the client the nature and import of the issue.[82]

H. INFORMATION REQUIRED BY THE LAW SOCIETY

A lawyer must disclose information when required to do so by her governing body.[83] This exception to the duty of confidentiality is justified by

---

79   See also Chapter 4, Sections H(6), H(11), and Q.
80   See Chapter 3, Section E.
81   See New York State Bar Association, Committee on Professional Ethics, Opinion #789, "Consultation with a Law Firm's In-house Counsel on Matters of Professional Ethics Involving One or More Clients of the Law Firm" (26 October 2005) at paras 17–20; American Bar Association, Formal Opinion 08-453 at 3 [ABA Formal Opinion 08-453]; Dodek, *Solicitor-Client*, above note 44 at § 6.60.
82   See ABA Formal Opinion 08-453, above note 81 at 3.
83   See Alta, Sask, BC, Man, Ont, NS, NL r 3.3-1(c). In other jurisdictions, this obligation falls within the "required by law" exception, given that the duty to

the need for law societies to regulate lawyers' conduct so as to help up-hold the integrity and proper operation of the legal system and protect the public interest.[84] It applies even where the confidential information is also privileged[85] and regardless of whether the client consents to the disclosure,[86] although clients usually do. Where a lawyer makes disclosure under this exception, the client loses the protection of con-fidentiality only as against the governing body, and not as against the rest of the world.[87]

I. FUTURE HARM OR PUBLIC SAFETY

The exception to the duty of confidentiality covering the prevention of future harm relaxes the lawyer's ordinary obligation to the client in an attempt to strike a balance with the need to protect members of the public from preventable harmful acts. Every Canadian ethical code contains at least one future-harm exception, and in a few cases more than one. Plus, in *Smith v Jones*, the Supreme Court of Canada recognized a comparable exception to both the common law duty of confidentiality and solicitor-client privilege.[88] As we shall see, ascer-taining the scope of, and relationship between, the ethical-code and judge-made exceptions is not always easy. We will begin by looking at the ethical rules and the Supreme Court's decision in *Smith v Jones* and then move on to examine some of the issues raised by these exceptions.

---

provide information to the law society is mandated by statute or regulation: see Section D, above in this chapter.

84   See *Law Society of Saskatchewan v Merchant*, 2008 SKCA 128 at paras 53–58 [*Merchant*], leave to appeal to SCC refused, [2008] SCCA No 538; *Stewart McK-elvey Stirling Scales v Nova Scotia Barristers' Society*, 2005 NSSC 258 at paras 18, 23, and 29 [*Stewart McKelvey*]; *Federation of Law Societies of Canada v Canada (AG)*, 2011 BCSC 1270 at paras 188–201, aff'd 2013 BCCA 147, leave to appeal to SCC granted, [2013] SCCA No 235 but appeal subsequently discontinued [*Federation of Law Societies*].

85   See *Skogstad v Law Society of British Columbia*, 2007 BCCA 310 at paras 18–20 [*Skogstad*]; *Merchant*, above note 84 at paras 53–58; *Federation of Law Societ-ies*, above note 84 at paras 193–201 (BCSC) and paras 144–46 (BCCA); *British Columbia (Auditor General) v British Columbia (Ministry of AG)*, 2013 BCSC 98 at paras 131–37.

86   The clients did not waive production in *Skogstad*, above note 85; *Merchant*, above note 84; *Stewart McKelvey*, above note 84.

87   See *Skogstad*, above note 85 at paras 16–20; *Stewart McKelvey*, above note 84 at para 16; *Federation of Law Societies*, above note 84 at para 195 (BCSC); *Merchant*, above note 84 at paras 60–69.

88   (1999), 132 CCC (3d) 225 (SCC).

As a prelude, however, note that we use the term "future harm" to refer to the exceptions found in all Canadian rules of professional conduct. On occasion, we refer to a "future-crime" exception, by which we mean a future-harm exception that is restricted to the prevention of crime. The term "public safety" is used to refer to the exception to the duty of confidentiality and solicitor-client privilege in *Smith v Jones*. Another term sometimes used when the prevention of harm is being discussed is the "crime-fraud" exception. As elaborated on in Section K, below in this chapter, we use "crime fraud" to refer to a particular exception to solicitor-client privilege and argue against the existence of a comparable exception to the ethical duty of confidentiality. There is no magic in the use of these various terms. For instance, in *R v Campbell*, the Supreme Court of Canada occasionally speaks of a "future-harm" exception in discussing what we choose to call the "crime-fraud" exception.[89] What *is* important, however, is to define one's terms carefully and be consistent in their use.

1) The Rules of Professional Conduct

The various rules of professional conduct reveal some disparity in delineating the future-harm exception. The most expansive approach is arguably employed in New Brunswick. There, disclosure of otherwise confidential information is permitted when the lawyer has reasonable grounds to believe that a crime is likely to be committed[90] and is required where necessary to prevent a crime involving violence.[91]

British Columbia, Alberta, Ontario, Quebec, Nova Scotia, and Newfoundland have adopted a future-harm exception aimed solely at preventing death or serious bodily harm, regardless of whether criminal conduct is anticipated, and that provides a lawyer with the discretion whether to make disclosure. The following rule is typical: "A lawyer may disclose confidential information, but must not disclose more information than is required, when the lawyer believes on reasonable grounds that there is an imminent risk of death or serious bodily harm, and disclosure is necessary to prevent the death or harm."[92]

The future-harm exceptions in Saskatchewan and Manitoba represent an amalgam of the above approaches. Lawyers are given a discretion to disclose confidential information if they reasonably believe that

---

89 (1999), 133 CCC (3d) 257 at paras 55–64 (SCC) [*Campbell*].

90 NB ch 5, commentary 9(c).

91 NB ch 5, commentary 8(b).

92 BC, Ont, NS, NL r 3.3-3. Alta r 2.03(3) is almost identical. Que s 3.06.01.01 is worded slightly differently, but the import is the same.

a crime is likely to be committed and that disclosure could prevent the crime.[93] But disclosure is mandatory if the lawyer reasonably believes that an identifiable person or group is in imminent danger of death or serious bodily harm and that disclosure is necessary to prevent such harm.[94] The requirement to disclose to prevent death or serious bodily harm is downgraded to a discretion where the lawyer reasonably believes that doing so will result in harm to the lawyer or his family or colleagues.[95]

The CBA Code contains a future-harm exception akin to the mandatory component of the Saskatchewan and Manitoba rules but without the operation of a discretion in circumstances where the lawyer is reasonably concerned about harm to self, family, or colleagues.[96] Moreover, the CBA Code does not provide lawyers with the general discretion to disclose confidential information to prevent likely crimes.

2) The Genesis of Most of the Current Ethical Rules: *Smith v Jones*

Before 1999, most Canadian ethical codes had fairly expansive, entirely crime-focused future-harm exceptions along the lines of the rules that currently operate in New Brunswick.[97] But that year, the Supreme Court of Canada for the first time recognized a public-safety exception to solicitor-client privilege in the still-leading decision of *Smith v Jones*.[98] This public-safety exception was found to apply where "the facts raise real concerns that an identifiable individual or group is in imminent danger of death or serious bodily harm."[99] The Court was of the view that the clarity, seriousness, and imminence of the danger are the three most important factors in assessing whether the exception is engaged, and discussed each of these factors in some detail.[100]

---

93 Sask r 2.03(4)(d); Man r 3.3-3B(d).

94 Sask r 2.03(3); Man r 3.3-3A.

95 Sask r 2.03(3) (commentary); Man r 3.3-3A, commentary 4.

96 CBA Code ch IV, r 2. The absence of such a discretion can put lawyers in a real bind: see Connecticut Bar Association, Committee on Professional Ethics, Informal Opinion 08-06, "Duty to Disclose Client's Threat" (17 September 2008) at 4: mandatory disclosure requirement must be honoured even if lawyer has reasonable concern that disclosure will jeopardize her own safety.

97 For a description of the rules as they then existed, see Michel Proulx & David Layton, *Ethics and Canadian Criminal Law*, 1st ed (Toronto: Irwin Law, 2001) at 231–32.

98 Above note 88.

99 *Ibid* at para 85.

100 *Ibid* at paras 19 and 77–85.

The public-safety exception to solicitor-client privilege recognized in *Smith v Jones* was broader than the Canadian ethical rules as they then stood because it was not restricted to preventing crime. Yet it was simultaneously narrower than most insofar as disclosure was permitted only to prevent the most serious types of bodily harm.[101] In the years following the decision, most Canadian law societies amended their future-harm exceptions to reflect the public-safety exception articulated by *Smith v Jones*, using language taken directly from the Supreme Court's judgment. But these amended future-harm exceptions are not identical. As noted in Section I(1), immediately above, some law societies have redrafted their rule to provide lawyers with a discretion to disclose where the standard set out in *Smith v Jones* has been met. Others make disclosure mandatory in such cases. And these latter law societies have at the same time retained the pre-existing — and generally much broader — future-harm exception that permits disclosure of confidential information to prevent any likely crime.

The disparity in the various ethical codes regarding the nature and scope of the future-harm exception is not in itself problematic; lawyers are often governed by different ethical rules depending on their jurisdiction of practice. Difficulty for lawyers may arise, however, to the extent that some of the ethical rules are broader than the public-safety exception to privilege adopted in *Smith v Jones*. This subject is discussed in Section I(13), below in this chapter.

3) New Brunswick Rule's Exclusive Focus on Crimes

One of the most striking features of the exception utilized in New Brunswick is that it is restricted to future *crimes*.[102] In this province, it would therefore not be out of place to refer to a "future-crime" exception. The distinction between the New Brunswick rule and the rules in the remaining Canadian jurisdictions, which have been modified to remove the crime requirement in response to *Smith v Jones*, can be illustrated using the following examples.

Example 1: X gets into a car accident with another driver, who is injured and sues X civilly. X's counsel retains a doctor to examine the plaintiff. The doctor's report reveals that the plaintiff has an aortic aneurysm probably caused by the accident, which will almost certainly

---

101 Only British Columbia's future-harm exception was limited to preventing death or serious bodily harm, but it was narrower than the *Smith v Jones* exception because disclosure was permitted only to prevent *crimes* causing such harm.

102 See the text associated with notes 90–91, above in this chapter.

kill him if left untreated. The matter settles soon after, and the plaintiff does not request production of X's expert report. X is adamant that his counsel not disclose the report to the other side and cannot be convinced otherwise. Under the New Brunswick ethical rules, counsel must comply with X's instructions. Lawyers in the rest of Canada will be permitted or required to disclose the information to prevent death or serious bodily harm to the plaintiff.[103]

Example 2: Counsel acts for a client who is severely depressed as a result of an outstanding child pornography charge. The client tells counsel that he is going to commit suicide by overdosing on sleeping pills at his home that evening. Counsel attempts to dissuade him but makes little headway. That night, counsel drives to the client's house. The lights and a flat screen TV are on, and the client's car is in the driveway, but no one answers the door. Repeated phone calls go unanswered. Because suicide is not a crime in Canada, the future-crime exception in New Brunswick will not allow counsel to call for help. Lawyers in the rest of Canada are not so restricted.

The failure of the future-harm exception in New Brunswick to cover cases where very serious harm may occur as a result of a non-criminal act is highly problematic. The fact that future harm flows from a crime perhaps imposes a greater moral obligation on a lawyer to make disclosure, given the lawyer's position as an officer of the court. Nevertheless, providing not even a *discretion* to reveal information where necessary to prevent serious but non-criminal future harm places confidentiality on too high a plane. The approach taken with respect to the public-safety exception to solicitor-client privilege in *Smith v Jones*, under which criminality is not a necessary precondition, is to be much preferred where the harm to be prevented involves death or serious physical injury.

4) Timing and Type of Harm: Imminent Danger of Death or Serious Bodily Harm

While *Smith v Jones* took an expansive approach by forgoing a "crime" requirement, the Supreme Court of Canada embraced a restrictive view of the type of harm sufficient to activate the public-safety exception, at least compared to most Canadian ethical rules then in force. The exception is engaged only in the face of serious bodily harm or death,

---

103 This example borrows heavily from *Spaulding v Zimmerman*, 116 NW2d 704 (Minn 1962).

the Court holding that anything less would be insufficient to justify overriding the privilege.[104] As noted, the governing bodies in British Columbia, Alberta, Ontario, Quebec, Nova Scotia, and Newfoundland have, over time, responded by modifying their future-harm exception to impose this same "death or serious bodily harm" limitation.[105]

We agree that the future-harm exception to the ethical duty of confidentiality should permit or mandate disclosure to prevent death or serious bodily harm. But the types of adverse impact sufficient to trigger a future-harm exception should arguably be broader. A multimillion dollar fraud may hold no risk of physical harm yet have a devastating impact on many individuals. In our view, lawyers should thus at least have a discretion to make disclosure where serious, criminal economic harm is threatened.[106] Another option would be to permit disclosure to prevent substantial economic harm but only where the client has used the lawyer's services to perpetrate a crime or fraud.[107]

Our criticism is somewhat tempered, however, by the definition of "serious bodily harm" proffered in Smith v Jones. Specifically, the majority notes that serious psychological harm may constitute serious bodily harm where the psychological harm "substantially interferes with the health or well-being of the complainant."[108] Most ethical rules that have adopted the Smith v Jones formulation of future harm include "serious psychological harm" within the definition or in the accompanying commentary.[109] The exact scope of this phrase remains to be determined, but there is a decent argument that catastrophic economic loss to one or more individuals could come within the definition.[110]

---

104 Smith v Jones, above note 88 at para 82.
105 See the paragraph associated with note 101, above in this chapter.
106 Our view is shared by Dodek, Solicitor-Client, above note 44 at § 8.16. The Law Society of Upper Canada considered including substantial financial injury in the post–Smith v Jones future-harm exception, but the proposal was defeated: see David Layton, "The Public Safety Exception: Confusing Confidentiality, Privilege and Ethics" (2001) 6 Can Crim L Rev 217 at 235.
107 See Section L(6), below in this chapter.
108 Smith v Jones, above note 88 at para 83. Compare the narrower definition in the Third Restatement § 66, comment "c": "Serious bodily harm . . . includes life-threatening illness and injuries and the consequences of events such as imprisonment for a substantial period and child sexual abuse. It also includes a client's threat of suicide."
109 The exceptions are Man r 3.3-3A and Que s 3.06.01.01.
110 For an expansive view of the Smith v Jones–influenced future-harm exceptions, see David Tanovich, "Law's Ambition and the Reconstruction of Role Morality in Canada" (2005) 28 Dal LJ 267 at 298–300, arguing that removal of the "crime" requirement in conjunction with recognition that bodily harm includes

The ethical rules adopting the *Smith v Jones* formulation require the existence of "imminent danger" of death or serious bodily harm before a lawyer is permitted to disclose.[111] Importantly, it is the danger of harm that must be imminent, not the harm itself. Suppose, for example, that a client company informs its lawyer of a chemical-plant spill. Absent immediate remediation, there will be serious adverse health effects beginning in five to ten years.[112] The *danger* of death or serious bodily harm is imminent, and so the imminence requirement as found in most Canadian ethical rules is met. It matters not that the harm itself will not occur until many years in the future.

5) The Need for *Future* Harm

The future-harm rules in the ethical codes apply to certain types of harm that may occur in the future and are preventable. The same can be said for the public-safety exception described by *Smith v Jones*. Both the ethical rules and the Supreme Court's exception are broad enough to encompass an ongoing or developing event that may in the future create or exacerbate harm.

Example: Client X has kidnapped and hidden a young child. Now under arrest, he refuses to co-operate with the police. However, X tells his counsel that the child is tied up in a locked storage shed on a deserted country lot and was alive when he last saw her two days previous. X refuses to provide this information to the police or allow the lawyer to do so because the girl can identify him. Under the future-harm rules, as well as the public-safety exception articulated in *Smith v Jones*, counsel is either permitted or mandated to release this information to save the child's life.[113]

---

psychological injury creates a much broader future-harm exception than existed before the decision in *Smith v Jones*.

111 See the rules referenced at notes 92 and 94, above in this chapter.

112 The future-harm exception in ABA Model Rule 1.6 as it stood when *Smith v Jones* was decided used the term "imminent" to qualify the harm, not the *danger* of harm. It has since been amended to remove the imminence requirement altogether, on the sensible view that disclosure should be permitted to prevent death or serious bodily harm that is reasonably certain to occur even if not imminent: see ABA Model Rule 1.6(b)(1), comment 6.

113 A more complicated version of this scenario occurred in *Henderson v State*, 962 SW2d 544 (Tex Crim App 1997), certiorari denied, (1998) 525 US 978 [*Henderson*]. See also *McClure v Thompson*, above note 6: lawyer released confidential information based on belief that abducted children were alive, and the majority and dissent disagreed as to whether this belief was reasonable.

In contrast, where the harm has already occurred, the exceptions do not apply, and counsel cannot reveal confidential information. Limiting the exceptions to instances where the harm is prospective is justified because a completed injury can no longer be prevented. Thus, in the famous Lake Pleasant Bodies Case, two lawyers were ethically prohibited from revealing the location of two murder victims after being given the information by their client, at least absent their client's consent.[114] Of course, if the client were acquitted and if the lawyers reasonably formed the opinion that he would kill others on being released, the future-harm and public-safety exceptions would apply to permit or mandate the disclosure of confidential information to prevent the anticipated future deaths.[115]

Finally, the Saskatchewan, Manitoba, and New Brunswick future-crime exceptions permit the release of confidential information to prevent a criminal offence.[116] Some crimes can continue over an extended period. A client who is unlawfully at large is committing an offence as long as she manages to avoid capture. A fraudulent investment scheme may be composed of many illegal acts that occur over the life of the scam. In these and similar cases, there is a prospective crime that comes within the meaning of the Saskatchewan, Manitoba, and New Brunswick rules.

6) Degree of Likelihood That Disclosure Will Prevent Harm

Canadian rules of professional conduct stipulate that disclosure can be made only where "necessary to prevent" the specified future-harm, at least in the case of death or serious bodily harm.[117] This precondition emphasizes the importance of maintaining confidentiality wherever possible, although one might legitimately ask whether "necessary to prevent *reasonably* certain" harm strikes a better balance between client confidentiality and the protection of third parties from such substantial injury.[118] In any event, where the harm can be prevented other than by revealing confidential information, the exception is not engaged.

---

114   For the facts and legal aftermath of the case, see *People v Belge*, 372 NYS2d 798 (Co Ct 1975), aff'd 376 NYS2d 771 (NY App Div 1975), aff'd 359 NE2d 377 (NY 1976). The lawyers tried to use the information to plea bargain, a tactic also seen in *Henderson*, above note 113; *McClure v Thompson*, above note 6.
115   See also *Smith v Jones*, above note 88 at para 84: referencing a scenario where an inmate promises to commit a murder once released from jail.
116   See the text associated with notes 90 and 93, above in this chapter.
117   See Section I(1), above in this chapter. See also the discussion in the paragraphs associated with notes 165 and 167–68, below in this chapter.
118   The quoted words are used in ABA Model Rules 1.6(b)(1) (covering death or substantial bodily harm) and 1.6(b)(2) & (3) (covering substantial injury to

Interestingly, the future-crime exceptions found in Saskatchewan and Manitoba set a lower standard for the release of confidential information, for it is enough that disclosure "could prevent" the crime.[119] Query whether a more demanding standard, on par with that employed in the context of death or serious bodily harm, would be preferable. On the other hand, lawyers in these provinces have a discretion whether to disclose under the future-crime exception, the exercise of which will undoubtedly be influenced by the odds that revelation will stop the offence from occurring. And both the Saskatchewan and Manitoba codes state that a decision to disclose under this exception should be made only in exceptional circumstances.[120]

7) Duty to Confer with the Client

A duty to confer with the client before making disclosure is not expressly mentioned in the Canadian future-harm rules or *Smith v Jones*.[121] Yet this duty surely exists for two reasons. First, counsel has a general obligation to keep the client informed regarding matters relevant to the representation.[122] Second, it will often be impossible to determine whether disclosure is necessary to prevent the feared harm without first speaking with the client. The ensuing discussion may assuage counsel's fears. Or where the client has the power to prevent the harm, counsel may be able to convince the client to do so, especially once the client learns that counsel is required or permitted, depending on the jurisdiction and the circumstances, to release confidential information to prevent future harm. In other cases, counsel may actually secure the client's consent to use or reveal a certain amount of confidential information.[123] Even if some information is eventually revealed over the objections of the client, a pre-revelation discussion may better equip counsel to make disclosure in the manner least damaging to the client. These examples illustrate why counsel should make all reasonable efforts to speak to the client before acting under the future-harm

---

financial interests or property caused by a client crime).

119 See the text associated with note 93, above in this chapter.

120 Sask r 2.03(4) (commentary); Man r 3.3-3B, commentary 3.

121 By contrast, a duty to confer is recognized in The State Bar of California, *California Rules of Professional Conduct* (San Francisco: State Bar of California, 2014) r 3-100(C); Third Restatement § 66(2).

122 See Chapter 3, Section E.

123 Consent must be informed: see Section B(1), above in this chapter.

exception. Failure to do so may result in disclosure of confidential information that was not necessary to prevent future harm.[124]

Granted, it may not always be possible or prudent to confer with one's client before disclosing information pursuant to the future-harm exception. Time constraints or the unavailability of the client may reasonably justify forgoing this step. Or speaking with the client may jeopardize efforts to prevent the harm or create a new risk of serious harm to the lawyer or a third party. And in very rare cases, it may be that discussing the issue with the client is so obviously futile as to not be worth pursuing. Counsel's default approach, however, should be to consult with the client in advance of releasing any information, absent good reason not to do so. If advance consultation is imprudent or impossible, counsel must nonetheless discuss the matter with the client after the fact[125] unless there is an overriding justification for not doing so, such as the protection of the lawyer or third persons from death or serious bodily harm.[126]

8) Duty to Undertake Reasonable Investigation If Feasible

Counsel should make inquiries or undertake other investigations where uncertain as to the degree of likelihood that the anticipated future harm will actually occur. Information thereby acquired will bear on the reasonableness of counsel's belief that the harm will or may crystallize if confidential information is not released.[127] An obvious source of information in this regard is the client, as discussed in Section I(7), immediately above in this chapter. However, time constraints may make it infeasible to carry out much in the way of investigation, especially if the threatened harm is extremely serious. The ability to make inquiries or otherwise investigate may also be limited by the need to maintain the client's confidentiality.

---

124 See *United States v Williams*, 698 F3d 374 (7th Cir 2012), in which a lawyer disclosed information to the prosecutor under a future-crime exception without attempting to dissuade the client from committing the planned offence. We agree with the dissent that the lawyer acted unethically in this regard.

125 See, for example, Sask r 2.03(4)(d) (commentary); Man r 3.3-3B, commentary 4: obligation to inform client of disclosure made under the future-crime exception.

126 See Chapter 3, Section E(3).

127 See *McClure v Thompson*, above note 6 at para 61.

9) Duty to Minimize Harm to the Client

Disclosure should be made to the extent necessary to prevent harm, but no more.[128] Only information sufficient to avoid the harm should be released and only to those persons who need to be notified to achieve this purpose. For example, to minimize the risk that police will trace the information back to the client through counsel, it may be advisable to retain another lawyer with instructions to make the necessary disclosure without revealing the client's or retaining counsel's name.[129]

The best way to protect a client from harm caused by disclosure under a future-harm exception is to preclude the state from using the disclosed information, as well as any information derived therefrom that was not otherwise discoverable, against the client in a criminal prosecution. This sort of "use and derivative use immunity" was not expressly considered by the majority in *Smith v Jones*.[130] Yet the information disclosed in *Smith v Jones* was later used against the accused at trial to his very significant detriment, something that would not have occurred had the immunity been recognized.[131]

After the decision in *Smith v Jones*, the Supreme Court of Canada recognized use and derivative use immunity in the somewhat comparable context of the innocence-at-stake exception to solicitor-client privilege.[132] And immunity has been employed in closely analogous circumstances to exclude from evidence at a criminal trial confidential information provided to a corrections ombudsman staff member, who released the information to counter a bomb threat made by an irate inmate.[133] Use and derivative use immunity has also been recognized in a number of American cases so as to maintain attorney-client privilege

---

128 See *Smith v Jones*, above note 88 at para 86; Que s 3.06.01.02; Sask r 2.03(4)(d) (commentary); Man r 3.3-3B, commentary 4.

129 In such a case, the identity of counsel who retains the disclosing lawyer will likely be privileged: see Chapter 4, Section L.

130 Nonetheless, the point of dispute between the majority and Major J in dissent involved a related issue, insofar as Major J would have precluded disclosure under the public-safety exception of any information that could be used as "conscriptive evidence against the accused" (*Smith v Jones*, above note 88 at paras 3 and 24–31).

131 See *R v Leopold*, 2001 BCCA 396, leave to appeal to SCC refused, [2001] SCCA No 551; David Layton, "*R v Leopold*: The Public Safety Exception and Defence Counsel as Confidential Informant" (2001) 43 CR (5th) 319.

132 *R v Brown*, 2002 SCC 32 at paras 90–104 [*Brown*]. See also Section M(1), below in this chapter.

133 *R v Paquin* (1999), 26 CR (5th) 356 (Ont SCJ) [*Paquin*], although the court was dealing with rather unique statutory provisions that do not exist in the context of solicitor-client privilege.

over information at a criminal trial despite its having been disclosed by a lawyer under an ethical-code future-harm exception.[134]

The policy arguments in favour of employing use and derivative use immunity in the future-harm context are compelling.[135] Immunity would reduce substantially the potential for harm to the client and thus the degree of incursion against the duty of confidentiality. And the likelihood that a lawyer would exercise the discretion to release information under the exception would probably rise.[136] Affording the client use and derivative use immunity makes further sense because the policy concern driving the exception is the avoidance of serious future harm, not the collection of evidence to use in the prosecution of the client.[137] Granted, in some cases the only way to protect the public might be to use the information against the client in a criminal prosecution.[138] But in all but the most exceptional cases, the threat of harm will have passed or can be alleviated in other ways,[139] and so using the information against the client in a criminal matter is not necessary to advance the policy goals that led to the disclosure.[140]

---

134 *In re Grand Jury Investigation*, 902 NE2d 929 (Mass 2009); *Purcell v District Attorney for the Suffolk District*, 676 NE2d 436 at 440–41 (Mass 1997); *Newman v State*, 863 A2d 321 at 331–33 (Md 2004); *Kleinfeld v State*, 568 So 2d 937 at 939–40 (Fla Dist Ct App 1990). See also Mitchell Simon, "Discreet Disclosures: Should Lawyers Who Disclose Confidential Information to Protect Third Parties Be Compelled to Testify against Their Clients?" (2007) 49 S Tex L Rev 307; Jean Powers, "Comparing Exceptions to Privilege and Confidentiality relating to Crime, Fraud, and Harm — Can Hard Cases Make Good Law?" (2010) 79 UMKC L Rev 61 at 74–79 and 86–93.

135 See Layton, above note 106 at 248–52; Richard Mahoney, "A Public Safety Exception to Solicitor-Client Privilege" (2005) 34 Comm L World Rev 295 at 312–15 (though arguing against derivative use immunity); Woolley, above note 44 at 156; Wayne Renke, "Case Comment: Secrets and Lives — The Public Safety Exception to Solicitor-Client Privilege: *Smith v Jones*" (1999) 37 Alberta L Rev 1045 at 1069; as well as the authorities and articles cited at note 134, above in this chapter.

136 This conclusion is supported by the empirical research recounted in Simon, above note 134 at 339–43.

137 See the comments to similar effect in the context of the innocence-at-stake exception in *Brown*, above note 132 at para 89.

138 See Layton, above note 131 at 320. *Smith v Jones*, above note 88, could be viewed as such a case, for the client was planning a series of torture-murders against vulnerable women.

139 See, for example, *Paquin*, above note 133 at paras 19 and 32.

140 As a safety valve intended to address such exceptional cases, Woolley, above note 44 at 156, suggests that use and derivative use immunity be denied where the Crown establishes that public safety cannot otherwise be protected.

The Supreme Court's post–*Smith v Jones* jurisprudence solidly establishes that solicitor-client privilege is a fundamental right protected by section 7 of the *Charter of Rights and Freedoms*,[141] which must remain as close to absolute as possible, especially in the criminal context, and can only be overridden in exceptional cases and in a manner that intrudes upon the privilege holder's rights as minimally as possible.[142] The points set out above provide a strong basis to argue that minimal impairment in the case of the public-safety exception should include use and derivative use immunity for the client whose privileged information is disclosed. Consequently, although recognition of immunity is not supported by the decision in *Smith v Jones*, there appears to be some room for the law to develop in this direction in the future.

10) Lawyer's Discretion in Jurisdictions That Permit Disclosure to Prevent Any Crime[143]

The governing bodies in Saskatchewan, Manitoba, and New Brunswick afford lawyers a discretion to release confidential information to prevent any crime.[144] In these jurisdictions, the question arises as to what factors a lawyer should consider in deciding whether to exercise the discretion. In our view, relevant considerations include the following:

1) *Probability that harm will occur*: These codes give the lawyer a discretion to disclose only where she believes the crime is likely to occur.[145] However, some "likely" harms are more probable than others. A lawyer may be more inclined to disclose a confidence where the commission of the crime is absolutely certain if the information is not revealed, as opposed to some high yet lesser degree of likelihood.

2) *Type (including extent) of harm*: The seriousness and permanence of any harm that will flow from the anticipated crime is a factor for

---

Affording immunity to the client in the future-harm context is also favoured by Dodek, *Solicitor-Client*, above note 44 at §§ 8.26 and 8.48.

141   Part I of the *Constitution Act, 1982*, being Schedule B to the *Canada Act 1982* (UK), 1982, c 11 [*Charter*]. See Chapter 4, Sections B and F.

142   *Lavallee*, above note 41 at para 36; *Brown*, above note 132 at paras 81 and 96; *Maranda v Richer*, 2003 SCC 67 at paras 12 and 33 [*Maranda*].

143   As discussed below, however, there is an argument that *Smith v Jones* operates to prevent a lawyer from disclosing privileged information under a future-crime exception unless it is necessary to prevent an imminent danger of death or serious bodily harm: see Section I(13), below in this chapter.

144   See the text associated with notes 90 and 93, above in this chapter.

145   Sask r 2.03(4)(d); Man r 3.3-3B (d); NB ch 6, commentary 9(c).

the lawyer to take into account in exercising the discretion.[146] The more serious and permanent the harm, the more likely disclosure will be made.

3) *Immediacy of harm*: Another consideration is the immediacy of the forecast crime.[147] The more imminent the danger, the more likely the lawyer will be to disclose.

4) *Likelihood that release of information will prevent crime*: The more likely it is that disclosure will prevent the anticipated crime, the stronger the case for exercising the discretion to release the information.[148]

5) *Role of the client*: Counsel may be more inclined to reveal a confidence where the client has used him as an unwitting dupe to carry out the intended crime.[149] A related consideration is whether the information in question falls within the crime-fraud exception to solicitor-client privilege.[150] However, counsel must be wary of too quickly judging a client's moral culpability. For this reason, the possibility that a client is implicated in creating the risk of harm should not be overemphasized.

6) *Role of the lawyer*: As just mentioned, the lawyer may have unwittingly played a role in exposing a third party to future harm, whether or not arising out of a client's improper manipulation of the professional relationship. The lawyer may harbour legitimate concerns regarding personal responsibility for causing the harm and take these into account in exercising the discretion.[151] A valid desire to circumvent subsequent attribution of blame by a party poised to suffer harm may also be a proper consideration.[152]

7) *Impact on the client*: In exercising discretion under a future-crime exception, counsel should consider whether revealing the information risks adverse impact on the client, and if so to what degree.[153] The discretion is more likely to be exercised in favour of disclosure if the risk of harm to the client is low. Conversely, serious repercussions for the client will make counsel less likely to disclose.

---

146 Sask r 2.03(4)(d) (commentary "b"); Man r 3.3-3B, commentary 3.

147 See, generally, the discussion of "imminence" in *Smith v Jones*, above note 88 at para 84, and in Section I(4), above in this chapter. See also the reference to "urgency" in Sask r 2.03(4)(d) (commentary "d"); Man r 3.3-3B, commentary 3.

148 Sask r 2.03(4)(d) (commentary "c"); Man r 3.3-3B, commentary 3.

149 Sask r 2.03(4)(d) (commentary "e"); Man r 3.3-3B, commentary 3.

150 Sask r 2.03(4)(d) (commentary "f"); Man r 3.3-3B, commentary 3.

151 Sask r 2.03(4)(d) (commentary "e"); Man r 3.3-3B, commentary 3.

152 See Section E, above in this chapter.

153 Sask r 2.03(4)(d) (commentary "h"); Man r 3.3-3B, commentary 3. The availability of use or derivative use immunity for the client is discussed in Section I(9), above in this chapter.

8) *Impact on the lawyer*: Counsel may fear that her professional practice will suffer harm because of being labelled a whistle-blower.[154] Existing or prospective clients may view disclosure as tantamount to working with the police or Crown and avoid retaining counsel in the future. A lawyer may also take into account a realistic risk that disclosure will lead to threats or other harm to her family or colleagues.[155]

9) *Reliance on the lawyer by the victim*: If the lawyer knows that the potential victim of the crime is placing some reliance on him with respect to the matter,[156] for example, an elderly and unsophisticated parent who is acting as surety, this factor can be taken into account.

10) *Impact on the legal system*: It is legitimate for counsel to consider the impact her decision will have on the administration of justice.[157] Counsel should not cower before the vagaries of public opinion but, on the other hand, may want to consider the view of the hypothetical reasonable person apprised of all the facts.[158]

11) *Lawyer's personal view*: Lawyers are human beings and can reasonably differ on the proper approach to certain ethical issues. Counsel's moral compass will play a role in the decision whether to disclose a confidence under a future-crime exception.[159] Some counsel may feel so strongly that confidences must be preserved, even while recognizing that not everyone takes this view, as to almost always decide in favour of non-disclosure.

These factors are not intended to be all-inclusive. Moreover, all relevant factors must be considered together, the ultimate question being whether in counsel's view the need to keep client information confidential is outweighed by the importance of preventing a likely future crime. It is our view that counsel should generally be given significant leeway in exercising the discretion.[160]

---

154 Sask r 2.03(4)(d) (commentary "i"); Man r 3.3-3B, commentary 3.
155 Sask r 2.03(4)(d) (commentary "j"); Man r 3.3-3B, commentary 3.
156 Sask r 2.03(4)(d) (commentary "g"); Man r 3.3-3B, commentary 3.
157 Sask r 2.03(4)(d) (commentary "k"); Man r 3.3-3B, commentary 3.
158 It is, after all, this same hypothetical person who helps to ascertain whether a disqualifying conflict of interest exists: see *MacDonald Estate v Martin*, [1990] 3 SCR 1235.
159 Sask r 2.03(4)(d) (commentary "l"); Man r 3.3-3B, commentary 3.
160 See Third Restatement §§ 66(3) and 67(4), granting counsel an absolute, unreviewable discretion. On a related point, *Smith v Jones*, above note 88 at para 59, expressly leaves unanswered the question whether a doctor — and hence, presumably, a lawyer too — can be held liable for deciding not to make a discretionary disclosure. Caselaw bearing on a doctor's civil liability for failing

11) Lawyer's Discretion in Jurisdictions That Permit Disclosure to Prevent Death or Serious Bodily Harm

Smith v Jones appears not to *require* that a lawyer disclose otherwise solicitor-client privileged information to prevent an imminent danger of death or serious bodily harm to an identifiable person or group. It is true that at certain points, the Court uses language to suggest that the exception *must* apply if the necessary preconditions are met.[161] But nowhere does the Court say that the lawyer *must disclose* where the exception applies. In fact, the Court affirms the decision of the court below, which modified the mandatory order made by the judge at first instance to rule that disclosure of the information in question was permitted.[162]

Nonetheless, the law societies in Saskatchewan, Manitoba, and New Brunswick all mandate disclosure to prevent violence or serious bodily harm or death (albeit in New Brunswick, only where the harm flows from a crime). Accordingly, once the necessary preconditions are met, lawyers in these jurisdictions have no discretion and must always disclose the confidential information.[163]

By contrast, and seemingly more in line with the judgment in *Smith v Jones*, the governing bodies in British Columbia, Alberta, Ontario, Quebec, Nova Scotia, and Newfoundland provide lawyers with a discretion in deciding whether to disclose to prevent a future harm.[164] In these jurisdictions, as well as in Saskatchewan and Manitoba, when the lawyer reasonably believes that disclosure will bring harm upon self, family, or colleagues,[165] counsel should consider most of the factors set out in Section I(10), above in this chapter, in deciding whether to exercise the discretion. But some additional comments are worth making in this regard, given the special context of these *Smith v Jones*–influenced rules.

---

to disclose confidential information where public safety is at stake is cited in Layton, above note 106 at 241, n 113.

161 Above note 88 at paras 74, 85, and 95. For an argument that the public-safety exception should be modified to make disclosure mandatory, see Dodek, "Reconceiving," above note 44 at 536. *Contra* Tanovich, above note 110 at 297–98.

162 Above note 88 at para 105. The lower-court decisions are *Smith v Jones*, [1997] BCJ No 3136 (SC) [*Smith* (BCSC)], var'd (1998), 62 BCLR (3d) 198 (CA) [*Smith* (BCCA)]. However, the Court of Appeal's modification was based not on a reasoned consideration of the public-safety exception but rather on the remedial limits of the court's rules concerning declaratory relief.

163 Leaving aside the discretion that exists in the former two provinces where disclosure would bring harm to the lawyer or his colleagues or family: see the text associated with note 95, above in this chapter.

164 See the rules cited at note 92, above in this chapter.

165 See the text associated with note 95, above in this chapter.

First, the ethical rules that follow the formulation in *Smith v Jones* state that the lawyer can only release information where she "believes disclosure is necessary to prevent the death of serious bodily harm." This precondition arguably requires that the lawyer be certain the harm will occur if disclosure is not made, for if there is no certainty, how can it be said that disclosure is necessary to prevent the harm? If this interpretation is correct, the lawyer's conclusion that she is permitted to release the information is tantamount to a determination that there is a high likelihood of death or serious bodily harm.[166]

Second, a determination that a *Smith v Jones*–influenced rule is engaged necessarily means the lawyer has concluded that the anticipated harm is very serious and the danger of it occurring is imminent. Nonetheless, some situations falling within the rule may involve a risk of greater harm and more urgency than do others.

Third, the harm to which the client may be exposed if confidential information is released under these rules will be significant if the result is to provide the authorities with information leading to his prosecution for a serious offence. But the consequences for the client will sometimes be worse if disclosure is not made. Assume, for example, that counsel receives a call from the client's brother. The brother says that the client has left the house with a gun, intent on killing a Crown witness. Calling the witness and/or the police might lead to a charge of attempted murder or possession of a loaded, prohibited firearm yet still be to the client's advantage because timely intervention potentially avoids the more serious charge of first-degree murder. This example also demonstrates how the disclosure of information received from a third party who is not himself bound by a duty of confidentiality (viz, the brother) may present less risk of adverse impact to the client than if the information comes directly from the client. Where the third party's information is likely discoverable by the police, even if only after the crime has been committed, revelation by the lawyer may have little additional adverse impact on the client.

Fourth, counsel should be exceedingly slow to rely on possible detriment to her own business interests, by virtue of being labelled as a whistle-blower, in deciding whether to disclose to prevent death or serious bodily harm. Favouring financial gain over the prevention of serious physical harm to a third party smacks of unseemly self-interest and tends to lower the public's level of respect for the legal profession and the administration of justice.

---

166 See also Section I(6), above in this chapter.

Finally, the commentary in some of the jurisdictions adopting a discretionary *Smith v Jones*–influenced ethical rule states that in assessing whether disclosure is justified, lawyers should consider a number of factors including seriousness, likelihood, and imminence of harm; the existence of alternatives short of disclosure for preventing harm; and circumstances under which the information in question was acquired.[167] These factors are obviously highly relevant to determining whether disclosure is permitted under the rule, but as noted above, they are also pertinent in assessing whether the discretion to disclose should be exercised once the rule is engaged.

Example: Counsel's client is convicted and sentenced for sexual interference after a single incident of oral sex on a twelve-year-old boy. Over a year later, the client tests positive for HIV and tells counsel. It is impossible to know whether the client was HIV positive when the offence occurred. Moreover, the risk of transmitting the virus through a single incident of oral sex appears low, although the medical evidence is not entirely clear.[168] And the frequency with which HIV tests are conducted in some jurisdictions makes it entirely possible that transmission, if it occurred, will be detected before long or, at the worst, will come to light once symptoms begin to show, at which point treatment can commence. Counsel must also consider the possibility that the complainant, if infected, will unknowingly pass on the virus to others. Finally, because the client was unaware of his HIV-positive status until tested and has already been sentenced, disclosure will probably cause him little if any prejudice. On these facts, is the future-harm exception engaged? If so, should counsel exercise the discretion to make disclosure? These questions will be elided if, after discussing the matter fully with counsel, the client consents to disclosure being made to the complainant through Crown counsel.[169]

12) Procedure for Disclosure

In *Smith v Jones*, a defence psychiatric expert believed that the release of confidential information was necessary to prevent future serial mur-

---

167 Alta r 2.03(3) (commentary); BC, Ont, NS, NL r 3.3-3, commentary 3.
168 See, for example, *R v JTC*, 2013 NSPC 88 at para 61 (YJC); *R v Boone*, 2012 ONCA 539 at para 45; *Canadian Blood Services v Freeman*, 2010 ONSC 4885 at paras 95 and 569 (SCJ); *R v Mumford*, 2010 ONSC 5624 at para 21.
169 This example is loosely based on *R v Butt*, 2012 ONSC 4326 at paras 1–5, where counsel disclosed the information to the Crown. It is unclear whether disclosure was made under the future-harm exception or based on the client's consent, but the fact counsel remained on the record for an appeal strongly suggests the latter.

ders by an offender who had pleaded guilty to a lesser offence and was awaiting sentencing. The psychiatrist brought an action in the Superior Court for a declaration permitting him to release the information and gave notice to the offender's counsel. The psychiatrist also sought and was granted leave to commence the action using pseudonyms for both parties and for an in camera hearing.[170] The court record was sealed and a publication ban was imposed, measures the Court of Appeal and Supreme Court of Canada continued pending a final determination of the matter.[171] Once the Supreme Court released its decision, the record was unsealed and the publication ban removed to the extent that solicitor-client privilege had been overridden.[172]

The decision of the majority in *Smith v Jones* generally approves of the procedure undertaken by the psychiatrist.[173] More detailed guidance is provided by several of the *Smith v Jones*–influenced future-harm exceptions. These rules encourage counsel to obtain ethical advice from the law society and suggest that a judicial order permitting disclosure can be sought where practicable.[174] A judicial determination that disclosure is permitted or mandated will presumably protect counsel from disciplinary or civil proceedings by the client, while an order forbidding disclosure may have the same effect in relation to a third party who suffers harm as a result of non-disclosure.

Obtaining a court ruling to resolve a problem involving the future-harm exception is ideal, but circumstances may not permit the luxury of a court proceeding. *Smith v Jones* recognizes as much, the majority suggesting that it may be necessary simply to notify the potential victim, the police, or a Crown prosecutor, depending on the specific circumstances.[175] The ethical rules modelled on *Smith v Jones* are consistent in this regard, recognizing that how and when disclosure should be made will depend on the circumstances.[176]

The rule in Quebec provides the most detail on this point. It stipulates that information disclosed to prevent death or serious bodily harm can only be provided to a person exposed to danger, that person's repre-

---

170 *Smith* (BCSC), above note 162 at para 38.
171 *Smith v Jones*, above note 88 at para 98. However, the Supreme Court refused to hear the appeal in camera: *ibid* at para 102.
172 *Ibid* at para 100.
173 *Ibid* at paras 96–97.
174 Alta r 2.03(3) (commentary); BC, Ont, NS, NL r 3.3-3, commentary 4. See also Que s 3.06.01.04: consultation with Barreau du Quebec permitted if time allows.
175 *Smith v Jones*, above note 88 at para 97. See also *ibid* at para 29, Major J, dissenting but not on this point.
176 Alta r 2.03(3) (commentary); BC, Ont, NS, NL r 3.3-3, commentary 4.

sentative, or those who can come to the person's aid.[177] The rule further requires that in making disclosure, the lawyer mention (1) her identity and membership in the bar, (2) that the information communicated is protected by confidentiality and is being disclosed to prevent imminent death or serious bodily harm under the future-harm exception, and (3) the nature and imminence of the anticipated harm and the identity of the person in danger.[178] A lawyer in Quebec is also permitted to communicate the identity and contact details of the person who prompted her to make the disclosure.[179]

Finally, several of the *Smith v Jones*–influenced rules require that a lawyer who makes disclosure prepare a written note as soon as possible containing the date and time of disclosure, the identity of the person to whom it was made, the content of the information provided, and the grounds supporting the decision to disclose.[180]

13) A Dilemma for Lawyers in Jurisdictions That Have a Future-Crime Exception

The public-safety exception to solicitor-client privilege is much narrower than the future-crime exceptions found in the ethical codes in Saskatchewan, Manitoba, and New Brunswick, because the latter allow lawyers to disclose confidential information — presumably including solicitor-client privileged information — to prevent *any* crime, and not only where necessary to avoid death or serious bodily harm. There is a decent argument that these future-crime exceptions impermissibly clash with the *Charter*-protected principle of fundamental justice that protects solicitor-client privilege,[181] insofar as they countenance the release of privileged information in instances not encompassed by the exception in *Smith v Jones*.[182] Given lawyers' strong duty to protect against the disclosure of information covered by the privilege,[183] practitioners in Saskatchewan, Manitoba, and New Brunswick may decide that the safest course is *never* to exercise the discretion to release solicitor-client privileged information unless necessary to prevent death or serious

---

177 Que s 3.06.01.01.

178 Que s 3.06.01.02.

179 Que s 3.06.01.03.

180 Alta r 2.03(3) (commentary); BC, Ont, NS, NL r 3.3-3, commentary 5; Que s 3.06.01.05.

181 See Chapter 4, Section F.

182 See Dodek, "Reconceiving," above note 44 at 529–30.

183 See Chapter 4, Section I.

bodily harm.[184] This approach, if adopted, will mean that lawyers in these provinces will use the future-crime exception only to release confidential information that is not also privileged.

J. COURT SECURITY

The Saskatchewan, Manitoba, and New Brunswick codes contain a confidentiality exception that, depending on the jurisdiction, permits or requires a lawyer who has reasonable grounds for believing a dangerous situation is likely to develop at a court facility to inform the persons having responsibility for security at the facility and give particulars.[185] The "likely development of a dangerous situation" seems to equate with the likelihood that a crime involving violence will be committed. On this reading, the court-security rule adds little to the future-harm exceptions as found in these codes.[186]

British Columbia, Ontario, Nova Scotia, and Newfoundland have similar court-security provisions but in the section of the code concerning "The Lawyer and the Administration of Justice."[187] The associated commentary states that where client information is involved, "the lawyer should be guided by" the provisions of the rule regarding confidentiality.[188] Disclosure of a client's confidential information will thus only be permitted where one of the exceptions to the duty of confidentiality is triggered. As each of these provinces has adopted a discretionary future-harm exception based on the standard endorsed in *Smith v Jones*, the disclosure of confidential information will only be permitted, and never required, where necessary to prevent imminent danger of death or serious bodily harm at a court facility.[189]

---

184 See Woolley, above note 44 at 139; Adam Dodek, "Doing Our Duty: The Case for a Duty of Disclosure to Prevent Death or Serious Harm" (2001) 50 UNBLJ 215 at 219–20.

185 Sask r 2.03(4)(e); Man r 3.3-3B(e); NB ch 5, commentary 11. See also CBA Code ch IV, r 3.

186 These future-harm exceptions are described in the text associated with notes 91 and 94, above in this chapter.

187 BC, Ont, NS, NL r 5.6-3.

188 *Ibid.*

189 The future-harm exceptions are described in the text associated with note 92, above in this chapter.

K. POSSIBLE CRIME-FRAUD EXCEPTION

A question that has garnered little attention in Canada is whether there exists a crime-fraud exception to the ethical duty of confidentiality. By "crime-fraud exception," we mean an exception that would permit disclosure by counsel *even in the absence of compulsion by court process* whenever circumstances exist sufficient to engage the crime-fraud exception to solicitor-client privilege. Answering the question requires that we examine the nature and parameters of this exception to the privilege.[190]

1) The Crime-Fraud Exception to Solicitor-Client Privilege

The crime-fraud exception to solicitor-client privilege applies to communications with a lawyer that are in themselves criminal or are knowingly made for the purpose of obtaining legal advice to facilitate a crime.[191] The justification for this exception is inextricably linked with the grounds necessary to establish the privilege in the first place. Communications between lawyer and client are protected by privilege if made within the usual and ordinary scope of professional employment.[192] The communications thus need to be for the purpose of seeking legal advice, as opposed to some other purpose.[193] Where the client seeks advice to help perpetrate a crime, there can be no privilege

---

190 Several leading authorities view crime-fraud communications as falling within an exception to the privilege: *Campbell*, above note 89 at para 55; *Smith v Jones*, above note 88 at para 55; *Maranda*, above note 142 at paras 35 and 52; *Juman v Doucette*, 2008 SCC 8 at para 47; *Canada (Privacy Commissioner) v Blood Tribe Department of Health*, 2008 SCC 44 at para 10 [*Blood Tribe*]. The better view is that the communications are not privileged in the first place, because they are made for an illegal purpose: Dodek, *Solicitor-Client*, above note 44 at § 3.74. See also *Ontario (Public Safety and Security) v Criminal Lawyers' Association*, 2010 SCC 23 at para 53: the only two exceptions to the privilege are for innocence-at-stake and public safety.

191 See *Campbell*, above note 89 at paras 55–64. The trend is to extend this exception to non-criminal conduct that nonetheless breaches a regulatory statute or constitutes a civil wrong: Dodek, *Solicitor-Client*, above note 44 at § 3.80; Sidney Lederman, Alan Bryant, & Michelle Fuerst, *The Law of Evidence in Canada*, 4th ed (Markham, ON: LexisNexis, 2014) at § 14.89.

192 See *Canada v Solosky* (1979), 50 CCC (2d) 495 at 507 (SCC) [*Solosky*]; *Descôteaux v Mierzwinski* (1982), 70 CCC (2d) 385 at 398 (SCC) [*Descôteaux*]; *Pritchard v Ontario (Human Rights Commission)*, 2004 SCC 31 at para 14 [*Pritchard*].

193 See *Solosky*, above note 192 at 507; *Descôteaux*, above note 192 at 398 and 413; *Campbell*, above note 89 at para 50.

because such advice is not within the usual and ordinary scope of a lawyer's professional employment.[194] At bottom, a policy decision is being made to the effect that these communications constitute an abuse of the client-lawyer relationship, do nothing to advance the rationale underlying solicitor-client privilege, and so should not be fostered through the protection afforded by a privilege.

Some comments in the caselaw might be read to suggest that the crime-fraud exception is engaged only where the client is trying to dupe the lawyer or where the lawyer has actually assisted in carrying out the client's improper purpose, whether knowingly or not.[195] On this view, a client who is unabashedly honest in asking the lawyer to assist in committing a crime enjoys the protection of solicitor-client privilege provided the lawyer does nothing to further the improper proposal.[196] Yet this reading of the crime-fraud exception clashes with leading statements of law and departs from the rationale that drives the exception.[197] Accordingly, solicitor-client privilege should not apply whenever a client knowingly seeks to use a lawyer's services to commit a crime, regardless of whether the client is upfront about the intended criminal purpose or whether the lawyer actually participates in furthering the client's aims.

2) Envisioning a Similar Exception to the Duty of Confidentiality

Is there a crime-fraud exception, not only to solicitor-client privilege, but also to *the ethical duty of confidentiality*? Such an exception would allow a lawyer to disclose information received from a client to a third party, for instance the police or Crown counsel, completely apart from

---

194 See *Solosky*, above note 192 at 507; *Descôteaux*, above note 192 at 398 and 413; *Campbell*, above note 89 at paras 55–58.

195 *Campbell, ibid* at para 63.

196 This is the view taken by Woolley, above note 44 at 113 and 170.

197 *R v Cox and Railton* (1884), 14 QBD 153 at 168: "If his criminal object is avowed, the client does not consult his adviser professionally, because it cannot be the solicitor's business to further any criminal object"; Lederman, Bryant, & Fuerst, above note 191 at § 14.88: "If a client seeks out a lawyer for the purpose of assisting him or her to perpetrate a crime or fraud, there can be no privilege"; *Smith v Jones*, above note 88 at para 55: "communications . . . intended to obtain legal advice to facilitate criminal activities are not privileged"; *R v McClure*, 2001 SCC 14 at para 37 [*McClure*]: "only communications made for the legitimate purpose of obtaining lawful professional advice or assistance are privileged"; *Blood Tribe*, above note 190 at para 10: "no privilege attaches to communications . . . intended to further criminal purposes."

any question of compulsion by court process. Suppose, for example, that a client asks a lawyer to assist in a money-laundering scheme but abandons the plan after receiving a stern lecture from the lawyer. No one else has reason to suspect that the client was considering this criminal plan. The lawyer will therefore not be subpoenaed or served with a search warrant regarding the communications, and the crime-fraud exception to privilege will never come into play. But if the crime-fraud exception also works to release the lawyer from the ethical duty of confidentiality, counsel is free to disclose at least some of the communications to the police. The result might be catastrophic for the client.

There are many less exotic instances where a crime-fraud exception to the duty of confidentiality might come to bear. Consider the client who suggests fabricating an alibi or offering perjured testimony, seeks advice regarding the best way to ensure that a Crown witness does not attend at trial, or provides counsel with an obviously forged employer's letter for use on sentencing. A crime-fraud exception to the duty of confidentiality would permit counsel to report the client to the authorities in these and many other cases, even where counsel has succeeded in dissuading the client from the proposed illegality. Such an incursion into the duty is potentially enormous, making it important to determine whether this sort of exception in fact exists.

3) Searching for Guidance in the Ethical Rules

No Canadian ethical code expressly addresses whether there exists a crime-fraud exception to the duty of confidentiality, and arguments can be marshalled either way. In support of the exception, one can point to judicial pronouncements to the effect that crime-fraud communications are not confidential.[198] The non-confidential nature of such communications would by definition relieve counsel of any obligation to keep the information secret. There is also a statement in *Smith v Jones* to the effect that, by necessary implication, an exception that applies to solicitor-client privilege also applies to all duties of confidentiality.[199] On this reasoning, communications falling within the crime-fraud exception to the privilege are also not protected by the ethical duty of confidentiality. Finally, from a policy perspective it can be argued that the client who attempts to utilize counsel's services to commit a crime has perverted the proper purpose of the professional

---

198 See, for example, *Descôteaux*, above note 192 at 398 and 413–14; *Campbell*, above note 89 at para 55.
199 *Smith v Jones*, above note 88 at para 44.

relationship. Communications that are themselves criminal or know-ingly made to obtain an illegal end are in no way necessary to promote a client's legal representation and fall outside the rationale that justifies the ethical duty of confidentiality.

These points in favour of a crime-fraud exception to the duty of confidentiality cannot be dismissed outright. But in our view the eth-ical rules as currently constituted do not permit such an exception. For one thing, the Canadian ethical codes arguably define the general duty of confidentiality broadly enough to cover communications knowingly made for the purpose of facilitating a crime or fraud. Remember that these ethical rules do not rely on common law or equitable definitions of confidentiality in delineating the scope of the duty,[200] a fact that weakens the relevance of judicial pronouncements regarding crime-fraud communications, solicitor-client privilege, and confidentiality.

In the same vein, the caselaw that at first glance appears to support an exception must be seen in context. Usually the courts are speaking of a loss of the confidentiality that is necessary to ground solicitor-client privilege, with the result that disclosure can be compelled by court process.[201] Permitting voluntary disclosure by a fiduciary, who has a duty of loyalty to the client, including a duty not to reveal infor-mation received regarding a client's affairs, is taking matters signifi-cantly further. That is to say, caselaw forcing compliance with court process does not necessarily equate with an ethical rule that condones voluntary disclosure by counsel. Confidentiality as defined by the rules of professional conduct can be, and in many cases is, wider than confi-dentiality at common law.[202]

What is more, several ethical codes include provisions dealing with client illegality that are framed so as to strongly suggest that there exists no crime-fraud exception to the duty of confidentiality. For instance, a commentary found in the Ontario rule on confidentiality, relating to the issue of crime-fraud and disclosure in the context of representing an organization, states:

> A lawyer employed or retained to act for an organization, including a corporation, confronts a difficult problem about confidentiality when he or she becomes aware that the organization may commit a dishon-est, fraudulent, criminal, or illegal act. This problem is sometimes described as the problem of whether the lawyer should "blow the whistle" on their employer or client. Although the rules make it clear

200 See Chapter 4, Section C.
201 See, for example, *Campbell*, above note 89 at para 55.
202 See the discussion in Chapter 4, Sections C–E.

that the lawyer shall not knowingly assist or encourage any dishonesty, fraud, crime, or illegal conduct (rule 3.2-7), and provide a rule for how a lawyer should respond to conduct by an organization that was, is or may be dishonest, fraudulent, criminal or illegal (rule 3.2-8), it does not follow that the lawyer should disclose to the appropriate authorities an employer's or client's proposed misconduct. *Rather, the general rule, as set out above, is that the lawyer shall hold the client's information in strict confidence, and this general rule is subject to only a few exceptions. Assuming the exceptions do not apply, there are, however, several steps that a lawyer should take when confronted with the difficult problem of proposed misconduct by an organization.* The lawyer should recognize that their duties are owed to the organization and not to the officers, employees, or agents of the organization (rule 3.2-3) and the lawyer should comply with rule 3.2-8, which sets out the steps the lawyer should take in response to proposed, past or continuing misconduct by the organization.[203]

Rules 3.2-7 and 3.2-8, referred to in this commentary, guide the lawyer in avoiding complicity in and responding to past, current, or anticipated client fraud or illegality. Neither suggests counsel can disclose otherwise confidential information to third parties, and the rule dealing with organizations (3.2-8) expressly states that counsel must comply with the rules governing confidentiality. Similar provisions are found in the codes in British Columbia, the Prairie provinces, Nova Scotia, and Newfoundland.[204] If these law societies meant to exempt lawyers from the duty of confidentiality by virtue of a crime-fraud exception, surely these rules would have said so. Instead, the clear implication is that the duty remains in place unless one of the listed exceptions applies.

Furthermore, in Saskatchewan and Manitoba, where the ethical codes include a future-crime exception giving lawyers the discretion to disclose confidential information to prevent an offence, the commentaries note that a factor to consider in applying this discretion is whether the information is in furtherance of a crime, in which case "no (evidentiary) privilege attaches to it as it cannot be said to be a legitimate communication for the purpose of obtaining legal advice."[205]

---

203 Ont r 3.3-3, commentary 5.1 [emphasis added].

204 Regarding organizational clients and up-the-ladder reporting, see Alta r 2.02(11); Sask r 2.02(8); BC, Man, NS, NL r 3.2-8; CBA Code ch IV, commentary 18. Regarding the avoidance of becoming involved in client fraud or illegality, see Alta r 2.02(10); Sask r 2.02(7); BC, Man, NS, NL r 3.2-7; CBA Code ch III, commentary 7.

205 Sask r 2.03(4) (commentary "f"); Man r 3.3-3B, commentary 3.

These commentaries mention as another factor bearing on the exercise of the discretion whether the lawyer is being duped into participating in a fraud or otherwise involved in a future crime.[206] If the crime-fraud exception to privilege also operated as an exception to the duty of confidentiality, surely the Saskatchewan and Manitoba codes would have included a stand-alone exception, rather than mentioning the crime-fraud scenario as a factor to take into account in deciding whether to disclose to prevent a future crime.

Finally, where carefully crafted future-harm or self-defence exceptions do not apply, there is little reason to permit disclosure by counsel simply because a crime-fraud communication has occurred. There will usually be no risk of harm to the public, no past harm to mitigate, and the lawyer's own interests will not be unfairly jeopardized. And disclosure will frequently provide the police with evidence to be used in prosecuting the client. In sum, even though crime-fraud communications are not protected by solicitor-client privilege, we believe that counsel cannot disclose such communications to outside parties unless required by law or permitted by another recognized exception to the duty of confidentiality.[207]

L. THE PROBLEM OF UNWITTING INVOLVEMENT BY COUNSEL IN CRIMINAL ACTS

Our discussions of the future-harm exception and the apparent absence of a crime-fraud exception to the ethical duty of confidentiality segue nicely into the examination of a potentially difficult problem: the case of the lawyer who learns that she has been unwittingly used by a dishonest client to further a crime. Looking at this problem illuminates the relationship among some of the exceptions to the lawyer's obligation to keep client confidences secret. The exercise also identifies possible weaknesses in ethical rules as they currently stand and points the way to remedial amendments.

---

206 Sask r 2.03(4) (commentary "e"); Man r 3.3-3B, commentary 3.
207 This is not to say, however, that the status quo is satisfactory: see Section L, below in this chapter.

1) The Crime-Fraud Exception to Solicitor-Client Privilege

By virtue of the crime-fraud exception, solicitor-client privilege will not cover client-lawyer communications where the client uses the lawyer's services to perpetrate a crime.[208] Yet there appears to be no analogous exception to the ethical duty of confidentiality.[209] Accordingly, the absence of privilege does not by itself license the lawyer to disclose the same information absent legal compulsion.[210] The crime-fraud exception to solicitor-client privilege thus does not help the duped lawyer who wishes to make voluntary disclosure, for instance to remedy harm already caused by the client's illegal activities.

2) The Future-Harm Exception

What about the future-harm exception? If the duped-lawyer scenario involves an entirely completed crime, the obligation of confidentiality is not abrogated by this exception, which applies only to prospective harms. The case where the crime is still ongoing raises different possibilities. In Saskatchewan, Manitoba, and New Brunswick the ethical rules provide counsel with a discretion to reveal confidential information to prevent any future crime,[211] including one that is ongoing.[212] And the fact that the client used counsel's services for an illegal purpose can be considered in deciding whether to exercise this discretion.[213] Yet in other provinces, this approach will probably be foreclosed because the future-harm exception applies only to death or serious bodily harm.[214] Unless their services have been used to create a risk of such harm, duped lawyers in these provinces cannot rely on the exception to reveal confidential information to prevent harm to potential victims.

3) The Self-Defence Exception

Lawyers have a discretion to reveal confidential information to defend against allegations of misconduct.[215] Whether this self-defence exception should apply in our duped-lawyer scenario depends on whether its scope extends to cover *anticipated* allegations. It is questionable

---

208 See Section K(1), above in this chapter.
209 See Section K(3), above in this chapter.
210 See Sections K(1)–(3), above in this chapter.
211 See the text associated with notes 90 and 93, above in this chapter.
212 See Section I(5), above in this chapter.
213 See Section I(10), above in this chapter.
214 See the text associated with note 92, above in this chapter.
215 See Section E, above in this chapter.

whether the exception can be read this broadly.[216] It may therefore be inapplicable to the duped-lawyer scenario before a point at which aspersions are cast against the lawyer.

4) The Possible Inapplicability of Any Exception

As the above discussion shows, a client may have duped a lawyer into assisting with an illegal scheme, yet no recognized exception to the ethical duty of confidentiality applies. In such a case, the lawyer should nonetheless try to persuade the client to take any action necessary to avoid future harm or to remedy past damage. If consultation with the client is impractical or proves fruitless, the lawyer should immediately end the retainer. The delicate question of how counsel should withdraw, and whether he can disaffirm or retract any opinion, document, or statement connected with the illegal act, is dealt with elsewhere.[217] At this juncture, suffice it to say that the distinction between a "noisy" withdrawal and the overt and unequivocal release of confidential information is sometimes difficult to discern. One should therefore guard against viewing the noisy withdrawal option as a simple way to avoid the problem concerning confidentiality.

5) The ABA Model Rules and Third Restatement Approach

The foggy interstices of the crime-fraud exception to solicitor-client privilege and the various exceptions to the ethical duty of confidentiality can be troubling when held up against the duped-lawyer scenario. Where the client has misused the professional relationship to plan or commit a crime and refuses to abandon the project or, if applicable, rectify or mitigate any damage done, there is a good policy argument in favour of permitting disclosure. A liberal interpretation of the self-defence exception could conceivably cover most such cases, but justifying increased disclosure in the name of lawyer self-interest does little to improve the reputation of the profession in the eyes of the public. If there is to be a change in the ethical rules on this point, protecting society from serious harm and discouraging individuals from abusing the client-lawyer relationship should be the guiding principles.

Adopting a wholesale crime-fraud exception constitutes too great an impingement on the duty of confidentiality. Yet there is much to

---

216 See Section E(4), above in this chapter.
217 See the paragraph associated with notes 222–24, below in this chapter, as well as Chapter 11, Sections F, G, and M(2).

recommend an attenuated, more focused exception that takes account of the policy factors just mentioned. For example, ABA Model Rule 1.6(b)(2) allows a lawyer to disclose confidential information to the extent necessary to prevent the client from committing a crime or fraud that is reasonably certain to result in substantial injury to the financial interests or property of another and in furtherance of which the client has used or is using the lawyer's services. The Third Restatement includes a similar exception,[218] and both sets of standards also permit disclosure of confidential information to the extent reasonably necessary to rectify or mitigate a substantial financial loss arising from a crime or fraud committed through the client's use of the lawyer's services.[219]

Disclosure under the ABA Model Rules and the Third Restatement is permitted only where the lawyer fails to persuade the client to take action necessary to prevent, rectify, or mitigate the loss. And in these attempts at persuasion, counsel should advise the client of the ability to disclose absent consent as a last resort. As the commentary to the Third Restatement recognizes, these exceptions may to some indeterminable degree dampen some clients' desire to consult freely with counsel, but the social benefits of allowing a lawyer to avoid, mitigate, or rectify substantial financial loss in the described circumstances warrant such a risk.[220]

6) Suggestion for Reform in Canada: Re-adopting the American Approach

Over the past decade the strong trend in Canada has been to restrict the ethical future-harm exceptions to instances involving death or serious bodily harm. The model for the new exceptions has been the public-safety exception to solicitor-client privilege formulated in *Smith v Jones*. The public-safety exception was in turn undoubtedly influenced by the future-harm exception set out in ABA Model Rule 1.6 as it read in the late 1990s.[221]

Even at that time, however, limiting the future-harm exception to death or serious bodily harm, as did rule 1.6, was rejected by most state

---

218 Third Restatement § 67(1).

219 ABA Model Rule 1.6(b)(3); Third Restatement § 67(2).

220 Third Restatement § 67, comment "b."

221 When the first edition of this book was published, in 2001, ABA Model Rule 1.6(b)(1) provided that "a lawyer may reveal [confidential] information to prevent the client from committing a criminal act that the lawyer believes is likely to result in imminent death or substantial bodily harm."

bar and regulatory rules governing American lawyers.[222] Moreover, the ABA Model Rules contained — and still contain — an exception to the duty of confidentiality to permit lawyers to disclose client confidences to avoid misleading the court.[223] They arguably also permitted a lawyer whose services had been used by a client to advance a future crime to announce her withdrawal to third parties and to disaffirm any tainted documents.[224] In short, in the late 1990s the American legal ethics landscape did not justify the blanket conclusion that lawyers in that country could disclose confidential information to prevent future harm only where it involved death or serious bodily injury.

What is more, since *Smith v Jones* was decided, the ABA has reacted to a number of high-profile corporate frauds by broadening its future-harm exception in two significant ways:[225] first, by adding the provisions encompassing substantial injury to property or financial interests caused by client crime involving a lawyer's services, described in Section L(5), above in this chapter;[226] and second, by permitting a lawyer to disclose an organizational client's confidential information to outside parties where necessary to prevent substantial injury to the client caused by an employee's or officer's ongoing or intended misconduct.[227]

---

222 See Ellen J Bennett, Elizabeth J Cohen, & Martin Whittaker, *Annotated Model Rules of Professional Conduct*, 7th ed (Chicago: Center for Professional Responsibility, American Bar Association, 2011) at 105.

223 ABA Model Rule 3.3.

224 This "noisy" withdrawal option was referred to in a comment to ABA Model Rule 1.6, but has been superseded by the 2003 inclusion of r 1.6(b)(2) & (3), dealing with client crimes involving the use of a lawyer's services.

225 A third amendment arguably broadening the ABA future-harm exception is removal of the requirement that death or serious bodily harm be "imminent": see note 112, above in this chapter.

226 Also part of the matrix of American future-harm exceptions are rules passed pursuant to s 307 of the federal *Sarbanes-Oxley Act of 2002*, 15 USCA § 7245 [*Sarbanes-Oxley Act*]. Specifically, 17 CFR § 205.3(d)(2) (2012) permits lawyers licensed before the Securities and Exchange Commission to release confidential information to the commission, without the client's consent, (1) to prevent the client from committing a material violation that is likely to cause substantial injury to financial interests or property, (2) to prevent the client from committing any act likely to perpetrate a fraud on the commission during a commission investigation or administrative proceeding, or (3) to rectify the consequences of a material violation by the client that has caused or may cause substantial injury to financial interests or property in furtherance of which the lawyer's services have been used.

227 ABA Model Rule 1.13(c)(2). The *Sarbanes-Oxley Act*, above note 226, contains a somewhat similar "up-the-ladder and out" reporting requirement: see 17 CFR § 205.3(b).

The arguments in favour of adopting a future-harm exception broader than that found in most Canadian jurisdictions are compelling, especially if the broadening resembles the just-mentioned modifications enacted by the ABA.[228] To begin with, all Canadian governing bodies had expansive future-crime exceptions for many years. There is no indication that client confidentiality was unduly harmed during that period. Moreover, the ABA exception described in Section L(5), above, is much narrower than the old Canadian exceptions, applying only where the threatened harm is serious and where the lawyer's services have been used to advance the client's crime or fraud. The incursion against client confidentiality is thus much reduced, covering only circumstances where the client is undeserving of protection and where the public interest in disclosure is high. It is also important to remember that the ABA client-fraud exceptions afford lawyers the discretion whether to disclose, so the revelation of client confidences is not compelled. Extending future-harm exceptions in this way has the additional benefit of giving lawyers an important lever to encourage client compliance with the law — the threat of disclosure to third parties — with attendant benefits for society, the integrity of the legal system, and sometimes even the client.

M. DISCLOSURE WHERE INNOCENCE IS AT STAKE

Another area where there is uncertainty as to whether Canadian ethical codes permit the disclosure of confidential client information concerns those rare circumstances where a lawyer has information suggesting that an innocent person will be, or has been, convicted of a crime. It is helpful, in laying out the problem, to begin with a review of the innocence-at-stake exception to solicitor-client privilege.

1) The Innocence-at-Stake Exception to Solicitor-Client Privilege

The innocence-at-stake exception operates to set aside solicitor-client privilege where necessary to enable an accused to make full answer

---

228 This view is shared by Paul Paton, "Corporate Counsel and Corporate Conscience: Ethics and Integrity in the Post-Enron Era" (2006) 84 Can Bar Rev 533 at 555–56.

and defence.[229] To activate the exception, the accused must meet two stringent preconditions: first, the sought-after information must be unavailable from any other admissible source;[230] and second, absent the information he must be unable to raise a reasonable doubt.[231]

If these threshold requirements are satisfied, the court proceeds to apply the two-stage innocence-at-stake test.[232] Stage one requires the accused to demonstrate "some evidentiary basis" to conclude that a privileged communication exists that *could* raise a reasonable doubt as to guilt. Mere speculation as to the contents of the privileged communication is insufficient.[233] However, given that the accused has not seen the material in question, a description of the possible communication may be all that is possible, and it would be unfair to require anything more precise.[234]

If stage one is met, the trial judge will examine the privileged materials and may also require that counsel in possession of the materials provide an affidavit, for the judge's eyes only, indicating that all relevant information is memorialized in the file or, if not, containing all other information necessary to complete the record.[235] The judge then determines whether the privileged materials are *likely* to raise a reasonable doubt as to the guilt of the accused.[236] If this burden is met, the judge will order disclosure of the communications that are likely to raise a reasonable doubt.

The application to set aside the privilege will usually not be brought until after completion of the Crown case, because by that point the trial judge will have a good idea as to whether the accused is in a position to raise a reasonable doubt without the sought-after material.[237] Where the application is successful, the exception is carefully crafted to provide several protections to the privilege holder. First, only information

---

229 The two leading cases are *McClure*, above note 197, and *Brown*, above note 132. The exception had been recognized in earlier decisions but without thorough analysis or the adoption of a comprehensive framework for its application: see, for example, *Smith v Jones*, above note 88 at para 54; *Campbell*, above note 89 at para 65.
230 See *McClure*, above note 197 at para 48; *Brown*, above note 132 at paras 30–35.
231 See *McClure*, above note 197 at paras 48–49; *Brown*, above note 132 at paras 46–48, 54, and 72.
232 The components of the test are succinctly itemized in *Brown*, *ibid* at para 4.
233 See *McClure*, above note 197 at paras 52–53.
234 See *ibid* at para 54.
235 See *Brown*, above note 132 at paras 60–65.
236 See *McClure*, above note 197 at para 57.
237 See *Brown*, above note 132 at paras 52–55.

necessary to raise a reasonable doubt will be released.[238] Second, the information will not be given to the Crown unless used by the defence at trial.[239] Third, even if used at trial, the judge can restrict the degree to which the information is disseminated to trial participants and members of the public.[240] Finally, the privilege holder will receive use and derivative use immunity under section 7 of the *Charter*, which means that the information, and any evidence that would not have been obtained but for its release, cannot be used against him in a later proceeding.[241]

2) The Ethical Duty of Confidentiality Where Innocence Is at Stake

The innocence-at-stake exception to solicitor-client privilege is very difficult to trigger.[242] The chances of its being invoked are reduced still further because Canadian ethical codes do not recognize a comparable exception to the duty of confidentiality.[243] The lawyer is often the only person aware of the exculpatory information, meaning that no other interested party has reason or basis to invoke the court process to defeat the privilege. If the client decides to keep the information secret and if the lawyer cannot make disclosure, because there is no exception to the ethical duty of confidentiality, there is no prospect of the information ever coming to light, not even where the innocence-at-stake exception to solicitor-client privilege clearly applies.

Fortunately, most Canadian future-harm exceptions permit or mandate disclosure where necessary to prevent serious bodily harm, and regardless of whether the harm flows from a criminal act.[244] And serious bodily harm is defined to include serious psychological harm

---

238 See *ibid* at paras 74–77.

239 See *ibid* at paras 78–86.

240 See *ibid* at para 87.

241 See *ibid* at paras 90–104; David Layton, "*R v Brown*: Protecting Legal-Professional Privilege" (2002) 50 CR (5th) 37.

242 Arguably too much so: see Layton, above note 68 at 25–27.

243 Two American ethical codes recognize an innocence-at-stake exception: Massachusetts Rules of Professional Conduct r 1.6(b)(1); Alaska Rules of Professional Conduct r 1.6(b)(1), both permitting disclosure where reasonably likely to prevent the wrongful execution or incarceration of another. Contrast Peter Joy & Kevin McMunigal, "Confidentiality and Wrongful Incarceration" (2008) 23 Criminal Justice 46, arguing for an exception limited to where the client whose confidential information is implicated is deceased.

244 See the text associated with notes 92 and 94–96, above in this chapter.

that substantially interferes with health and well-being.[245] These exceptions can surely be read to permit disclosure of otherwise confidential information to prevent or cut short the lengthy incarceration of an innocent individual.[246] They might even apply after a sentence has been served given the significant stigma, economic, and therefore psychological harm that can continue indefinitely following a conviction for a serious offence.

A lawyer who practises in a jurisdiction where the future-harm exception permits disclosure and who decides to exercise the discretion to release the information should seek to ensure that her client has the protection of the use and derivative use immunity that arises where the innocence-at-stake exception to solicitor-client privilege arises. This can be done by applying to the court for an order requiring disclosure.[247] Or counsel can release to the lawyer for the wrongfully incarcerated individual, or to an innocence project if there is no lawyer, just enough confidential information to prompt a successful innocence-at-stake application on behalf of the individual.[248] In either case, disclosure will be compelled by court order thus triggering use and derivative use immunity for the client's benefit.

---

245 See Section I(4), above in this chapter.

246 Our view is shared by Dodek, *Solicitor-Client*, above note 44 at § 8.50. Unlike in Canada, where most future-harm exceptions clearly apply to prevent serious psychological harm, there is significant debate in the United States as to whether future-harm exceptions permit disclosure to prevent wrongful incarceration. Arguing that the future-harm exception in ABA Model Rule 1.6(b)(1) should apply in such cases are James E Moliterno, "Rectifying Wrongful Convictions: May a Lawyer Reveal Her Client's Confidences to Rectify the Wrongful Conviction of Another?" (2011) 38 Hastings Const LQ 811; Colin Miller, "Ordeal by Innocence: Why There Should Be a Wrongful Incarceration/Execution Exception to Attorney-Client Confidentiality" (2008) 102 Nw UL Rev Colloquy 391. Arguing that r 1.6(b)(1) is unlikely to apply but that this lacuna should be remedied are Ken Strutin, "Preserving Attorney-Client Confidentiality at the Cost of Another's Innocence: A Systemic Approach" (2011) 17 Tex Wesleyan L Rev 499; Inbal Hasbani, "When the Law Preserves Injustice: Issues Raised by a Wrongful Incarceration Exception to Attorney-Client Confidentiality" (2010) 100 J Crim L & Criminology 277; Powers, above note 134 at 80–82. Arguing against permitting disclosure to prevent wrongful incarceration is J Vincent Aprile II, "Confidential Information and Wrongful Convictions" (2010) 25 Criminal Justice 50.

247 Many codes encourage a court application before disclosing under the future-harm exception, if time permits: see Section I(12), above in this chapter.

248 See *People v Vespucci*, 745 NYS2d 391 (Co Ct 2002): lawyer reveals to counsel for accused that he has information suggesting accused is innocent but cannot disclose anything further because of privilege owed to deceased client; counsel for accused applies to the court in an attempt to have privilege set aside.

N. DISCLOSURE OF INFORMATION PERTAINING TO JUROR ELIGIBILITY

Defence counsel has an obligation, recognized in the jurisprudence and most ethical codes, to disclose promptly to the Crown and court information in her possession regarding juror eligibility or impropriety, unless the Crown and court are already aware. Specifically, counsel must make disclosure where she has good reason to believe that a potential juror (1) has engaged in criminal conduct that makes him ineligible for jury duty under provincial law or is subject to being challenged for cause under section 638(1)(c) of the *Criminal Code*,[249] or (2) cannot serve in a particular case due to matters of obvious partiality.[250] Counsel must also make disclosure where she becomes aware of improper conduct by a jury panel member or a juror.[251]

This exception to the duty of confidentiality can be justified on the basis that selection of a jury and the proper conduct of jurors once empanelled are fundamental to the fair and accurate operation of the justice system, and ought not to be subject to the rules that typically govern defence counsel's obligation of confidentiality to the client in an adversarial, rights-based system.[252]

It is not totally clear whether this exception to the duty of confidentiality applies where the information in counsel's possession is covered by solicitor-client privilege. Importantly, the caselaw on privilege does not recognize such an exception. It is true that the Supreme Court of Canada has affirmed a lawyer's duty to disclose information to prevent the selection of ineligible or partial jurors, but in doing so the Court said nothing to suggest the creation of a new exception to solicitor-client privilege.[253] There is thus a very strong argument that privileged information regarding problems with a prospective juror or a jury member cannot be disclosed to the Crown or court absent the

---

249 *Criminal Code*, above note 40. See R v *Yumnu*, 2012 SCC 73 at paras 66 and 69 [*Yumnu*]; BC r 5.5-2(d). The British Columbia code rule refers to ineligibility generally, and makes no mention of s 638(1)(c), which provides that an individual cannot serve if he has been convicted of an offence resulting in a term of imprisonment exceeding twelve months.

250 See *Yumnu*, above note 249 at paras 67–68; Alta, Sask r 4.05(2); BC, Man, Ont, NS, NL r 5.5-2.

251 See Alta, Sask r 4.05(3); BC, Man, Ont, NS, NL r 5.5-3.

252 See *Yumnu*, above note 249 at para 71.

253 *Ibid* at paras 66–71.

client's consent or operation of a recognized exception to the privilege, such as for public safety or crime-fraud.[254]

---

254 The argument in this respect is analogous to that set out in Section I(13), above in this chapter.

CHAPTER 6

CONFLICT OF INTEREST

A. INTRODUCTION

A conflict of interest occurs whenever a lawyer is placed in a position where loyalty to a client is compromised. There are an inexhaustible number of situations in which a conflict problem can arise. The conflicting interests may involve current, former, or prospective clients, and sometimes even third parties with whom a client-lawyer relationship is never established or contemplated. A lawyer's loyalty may also be compromised by her own interest or the interest of an affiliated lawyer. Categorizing scenarios according to the type of conflict raised is a helpful way to address the ethical and legal obligations of criminal counsel in this area. A discussion of any particular scenario, however, is incomplete without examining the principles that make conflict avoidance so important, as well as the professional-conduct standards, common law rules, and constitutional guarantees that are derived from and reflect these principles.

B. BASIC PRINCIPLES

The client-lawyer relationship is based on the highest of trusts, where the lawyer's loyalty is unquestioned. The duty to be loyal, born of the fiduciary relationship between counsel and client, guides and informs every aspect of the lawyer's dealing with a client.[1] It underpins important related obligations such as the duty of confidentiality. As we shall see, the duty of confidentiality is particularly important in the realm of conflict of interest. Yet a threat to confidentiality is not a precondition to the existence of a conflict problem. The leitmotif of conflict of interest is the broader duty of loyalty.[2] Where the lawyer's duty of loyalty is compromised by a competing interest, a conflict of interest will exist even when there is no possibility that confidential information will be misused.

The importance of loyalty to the client-lawyer relationship is underlined by the adversarial nature of the criminal justice system. An adversarial system gives litigants the right and responsibility to present their own cases and to challenge the evidence and arguments of their opponents. As agents for the litigants, lawyers operate within this adversarial setting, making loyalty towards the client absolutely essential — a lawyer must act as zealous advocate for the client's cause.[3] Failure to provide loyal service may harm the client's ability to exercise important constitutional rights.[4] It can also undermine the reliability of a result and the public's confidence in the legal process.

The duties necessary for a healthy client-lawyer relationship are thus, by extension, fundamental to the entire administration of justice.[5] It follows that guarding against conflict of interest prevents harm to both the client and the criminal justice system.[6]

---

1   See *R v Neil*, 2002 SCC 70 at paras 12, 16, and 25–27 (SCC) [*Neil*]; *Strother v 3464920 Canada Inc*, 2007 SCC 24 at paras 34–35 [*Strother*]; *Amato v Welsh*, 2013 ONCA 258 at paras 58–59.

2   See *Strother*, above note 1 at para 35. See also Alta, Sask r 2.04(1) (commentary); Man r 3.4-2, commentary 2; BC, Ont, NS, NL r 3.4-1, commentary 5; NB ch 6, rule.

3   See *Canadian National Railway Co v McKercher LLP*, 2013 SCC 39 at para 25 [*McKercher*].

4   For example, the rights discussed in Chapter 1, Section D.

5   See *Neil*, above note 1 at para 12.

6   See Sask r 2.04(1) (commentary); BC, Ont, NS, NL r 3.4-1, commentary 5: public confidence in the justice system depends on lawyers' respecting the duty of loyalty. See also *MacDonald Estate v Martin*, [1990] 3 SCR 1235 at 1244 [paras 13, 15, and 18] [*MacDonald Estate*]; *Neil*, above note 1 at para 24; *Strother*, above note 1 at para 34; *McKercher*, above note 3 at para 13; *R v Robillard* (1986), 28 CCC (3d) 22 at 27 (Ont CA) [*Robillard*]; Richard Devlin & Victoria Rees, "Beyond Conflicts of Interest to the Duty of Loyalty: From *Martin v Gray* to *R v Neil*" (2005) 84 Can Bar Rev 433 at 443.

C. RELATED RULES OF PROFESSIONAL CONDUCT

Many rules of professional conduct emphasize the principles driving the proscription against conflict of interest. Most importantly, Canadian governing bodies have adopted comprehensive rules that specifically address conflict issues.[7] The content of these rules is discussed extensively throughout this chapter. For now, suffice it to say that they recognize that the client's interests and the administration of justice more broadly may be seriously impaired when a lawyer's judgment and ability to act on the client's behalf is not free from compromising influences.

Other rules of professional conduct further reflect the concerns raised when a lawyer confronts a possible conflict of interest, for instance

1) *Integrity*: Lawyers are required to discharge with integrity all duties owed to a client, the court, the public, and other members of the profession.[8] Integrity is the fundamental quality of a lawyer,[9] representing a key element of each rule of professional conduct, and from the perspective of the client finds expression in absolute trustworthiness.[10] Trustworthiness, or loyalty, is seen to be the essential element of the client-lawyer relationship.[11]

2) *Confidential information*: A lawyer has a duty to hold in strict confidence all information concerning the business and affairs of the client acquired in the course of the professional relationship.[12] The information cannot be used for the benefit of the lawyer or a third party, or to the detriment of the client,[13] and this duty persists even after the professional relationship ends.[14]

---

7   Alta, Sask r 2.04; BC, Man, Ont, NS, NL r 3.4; Que s 3.06; NB ch 6; CBA Code ch V & VI.

8   BC r 2.2-1; Alta, Sask r 1.01(1); Man, Ont, NS, NL r 2.1-1; Que s 2.00.01; NB ch 1, rule; CBA Code ch I, rule.

9   BC r 2.2-1, commentary 1; Alta, Sask r 1.01(1) (commentary); Man, Ont, NS, NL r 2.1-1, commentary 1; NB ch 1, commentary 1; CBA Code ch I, commentaries 1 & 2.

10   See rules and commentaries cited at preceding note.

11   CBA Code ch I, commentary 1.

12   Alta, Sask r 2.03(1); BC, Man, Ont, NS, NL r 3-3.1; Que s 3.06, *Professional Code*, CQLR c C-26, s 60.4, and *An act respecting the Barreau du Quebec*, CQLR c B-1, s 131; NB ch 5, rule; CBA Code ch IV, r 1.

13   Alta, Sask r 2.03(2); BC, Man, NS, NL r 3.3-2; Ont r 3.3-1, commentary 11.1; Que s 3.06.01; CBA Code ch IV, commentary 14.

14   Alta, Sask r 2.03(1) (commentary); BC, Man, Ont, NS, NL r 3.3-1, commentary 3; NB ch 5, commentary 4; CBA Code ch IV, commentary 6.

3) *The lawyer as advocate*: When acting as advocate, the lawyer must represent the client resolutely, honourably, and within the limits of the law.[15] The lawyer is duty bound to raise every issue, advance every argument, and ask every question, however distasteful, that he thinks will help the client's case and to endeavour to obtain for the client the benefit of every remedy or defence available at law.[16]

4) *The lawyer and the administration of justice*: The lawyer should encourage public respect for and try to improve the administration of justice.[17] Judicial institutions will not function effectively unless they command the respect of the public, and constant efforts must be made to improve the administration of justice and thereby maintain its respect in the eyes of the public.[18]

Each of these rules engages the lawyer's duty of loyalty to the client, as well as broader obligations to the justice system, and is potentially jeopardized when a conflict arises.

D. THE COURT'S JURISDICTION TO REMOVE COUNSEL FROM THE RECORD

Courts have the jurisdiction to remove conflicted counsel from the record, to protect clients and the administration of justice from prejudice.[19] The rules of professional conduct, while not binding on the courts, are afforded close attention in determining whether a lawyer should be disqualified due to a conflict of interest and are considered important expressions of public policy.[20]

---

15   Alta, Sask r 4.01(1); BC, Man, Ont, NS, NL r 5.1-1; NB ch 8, rule; CBA Code ch IX, rule.

16   Alta, Sask r 4.01(1) (commentary); BC, Man, Ont, NL r 5.1-1, commentary 1; NB ch 8, commentary 14(b) & (c); CBA Code ch IX, commentary 1.

17   Alta, Sask r 4.06(1); BC, Man, Ont, NL r 5.6-1; NB ch 20, rule; CBA Code ch XIII, rule.

18   Alta, Sask r 4.06(1) (commentary); BC, Man, Ont, NL r 5.6-1, commentary 2; NB ch 20, commentaries 2 & 3; CBA Code ch XIII, commentary 1.

19   See *MacDonald Estate*, above note 6 at 1245 [para 18]; *McKercher*, above note 3 at paras 13 and 61–63; *R v Brissett* (2005), 74 OR (3d) 248 at para 51 (SCJ) [*Brissett*].

20   See *MacDonald Estate*, above note 6 at 1244–46 [paras 16–18]; *McKercher*, above note 3 at para 16. The role of the court and law societies is also discussed in FLSC Code r 3.4-1, commentary 12, which was added in October 2014 and will likely be included in most law society codes in the next year or so.

E. CONSTITUTIONAL RIGHTS TO EFFECTIVE COUNSEL AND COUNSEL OF CHOICE

In criminal cases, the justification for prohibiting counsel from representing an accused while labouring under a conflict takes on constitutional dimensions. By definition, where counsel for the accused has an actual conflict of interest, the client suffers through representation by an advocate whose loyalty is suspect. If counsel's performance is impaired as a result, the accused has been denied the assistance of effective counsel in violation of the *Canadian Charter of Rights and Freedoms*.[21] We thus see the important interface between conflict of interest and the right to effective counsel. A lawyer can render effective assistance only when she gives the accused's cause the undivided loyalty that is a prerequisite to proper legal representation.[22] Failure to do so means that the adversarial system cannot function properly, the appearance of fairness suffers, and the reliability of the verdict is called into question.[23]

A conflict-of-interest problem may also implicate an accused's right to counsel of choice. This right has been recognized at common law as fundamental, is by implication entrenched in section 10(b) of the *Charter*, and most likely is among the principles of fundamental justice protected by section 7 of the *Charter*.[24] The rationale underlying the right to counsel of choice shares much with the principles that justify prohibiting a lawyer from acting while under a conflict of interest. The loyalty and confidentiality owed a client by counsel can flourish only in a setting where counsel enjoys the client's full trust. This trust relationship by its

---

21 Part I of the *Constitution Act, 1982*, being Schedule B to the *Canada Act 1982* (UK), 1982, c 11 [*Charter*]. See, for example, *R v Silvini* (1991), 68 CCC (3d) 251 at 257–61 [paras 10–22] (Ont CA) [*Silvini*]; *R v WW* (1995), 100 CCC (3d) 225 at 234–37 [paras 22–28] (Ont CA) [*WW*]; *R v Kim*, 2007 BCCA 25 at para 28 [*Kim*]; *R v Ross*, 2012 NSCA 56 at para 59; *Côté v Rancourt*, 2004 SCC 58 at para 11 [*Côté*].

22 See *WW*, above note 21 at 235 [para 23]; *R v MQ*, 2012 ONCA 224 at paras 26–27 [*MQ*].

23 See *WW*, above note 21 at 234 [para 22].

24 Many conflict cases recognize this right, for example, *R v Speid* (1983), 8 CCC (3d) 18 at 20 [para 5] (Ont CA) [*Speid*]; *Robillard*, above note 6 at 26; *WW*, above note 21 at 235, n 4 [para 24, n 6]; *R v McCallen* (1999), 131 CCC (3d) 518 at paras 32–39 and 80 (Ont CA) [*McCallen*]; *Neil*, above note 1 at paras 13–14; *R v Sandhu*, 2011 BCSC 1137 at paras 26–32 [*Sandhu*], appeal quashed, 2012 BCCA 73; *R v Cadorette*, 2011 ONSC 5772 at paras 28–33 [*Cadorette*]; *R v Parsons*, [2010] OJ No 6254 at para 6 (Ct J) [*Parsons* ONCJ]; *R v Downey*, 2013 ONSC 138 at paras 26–28 [*Downey*]. In the civil context, see *Strother*, above note 1 at para 62; *MacDonald Estate*, above note 6 at 1243 [para 13].

nature has a special personal quality and so will be most sedulously fostered where the client can choose her own lawyer.[25] Additionally, an accused has a constitutional right to present her own case to the trier of fact, a right derived from a desire to protect personal autonomy and dignity from unjustified state intrusion.[26] The choice of lawyer is an important part of an accused's presentation of her defence and thus falls within the scope of this *Charter* protection.

An appreciation of the interplay between the constitutional right to the effective assistance of counsel and the right to choice of counsel is necessary when approaching any conflict-of-interest problem. Sometimes these rights will combine to force the removal of a conflicted lawyer before or during trial. For example, an accused may decide that he wishes to retain new counsel — that is, to exercise the right to choose counsel — because a conflict of interest has arisen that if permitted to continue will fatally undermine the ability of existing counsel to provide loyal representation, thus infringing the right to be represented by effective counsel.

In other cases, the rights to choice of counsel and the effective assistance of counsel may diverge or even clash. For instance, the Crown may worry that a conflict-of-interest problem will lead to a postconviction appeal based on ineffective assistance and so bring an application to disqualify defence counsel, and the accused may oppose the application by relying on the right to counsel of choice. Or consider an application to remove defence counsel who formerly represented a Crown witness. The accused's right to effective counsel may be scarcely threatened by the spectre of conflict. Instead, the witness's claim to loyalty and confidentiality from former counsel comes up against the accused's right to counsel of choice.[27]

F. THE TEST FOR CONFLICT OF INTEREST BEFORE OR DURING TRIAL

In *R v Neil*, the Supreme Court of Canada endorsed the definition of conflict of interest set out in the Third Restatement,[28] defining a conflict as

---

25 See *McCallen*, above note 24 at paras 34–36.

26 See *R v Swain* (1991), 63 CCC (3d) 481 at 504–6 [paras 33–36] (SCC); *McCallen*, above note 24 at para 37.

27 Indeed, the witness may assert countervailing constitutional rights, such as the rights to privacy and the protection of solicitor-client privilege.

28 Third Restatement § 121.

"a substantial risk that the lawyer's representation of the client would be materially and adversely affected by the lawyer's own interests or by the lawyer's duties to another current client, a former client, or a third person."[29] This definition has been affirmed in several of the Court's subsequent decisions.[30] It has also been adopted in most rules of professional conduct, albeit usually with the addition of language expressly referencing the duty of loyalty. The definition found in the rules, with the salient added language italicized, reads as follows: "'conflict of interest' means the existence of a substantial risk that a lawyer's *loyalty to or* representation of a client would be materially and adversely affected by the lawyer's own interest or the lawyer's duties to another client, a former client, or a third person."[31]

It is helpful, in unpacking the meaning of this definition, to focus on four questions: (1) When will the representation of the client be "materially and adversely affected"? (2) When is the risk of such an effect "substantial"? (3) What is the role of confidential information in the analysis? and (4) How does the accused's right to choice of counsel factor in to the definition?

1) When Will the Representation of the Client Be Materially and Adversely Affected?

A good source of guidance in sussing out the meaning of the phrase "materially and adversely affected" is the Third Restatement, the highly respected American Law Institute publication from which the definition in *Neil* and the ethical codes is taken. The Third Restatement emphasizes that there is no conflict unless the effect is adverse and states that an adverse effect is measured against the quality of the representation and not necessarily the quality of the ultimate result.[32] It further suggests that determining whether the adverse effect is material requires an assessment of the obligations necessarily assumed by the lawyer or assumed by agreement with the client in the retainer

---

29   Above note 1 at para 28.
30   *Strother*, above note 1 at para 51; *Galambos v Perez*, 2009 SCC 48 at para 31; *McKercher*, above note 3 at para 8.
31   Alta, Sask definitions; BC, Ont, NS, NL r 1.1-1. The same definition but without the reference to loyalty is used in Man r 1.1-1; CBA Code ch V, commentary 1. Most codes repeat the definition in one of the commentaries to the rule dealing specifically with conflict of interest: see Alta, Sask r 2.04(1); Man r 3.4-2; BC, Ont, NS, NL r 3.4-1.
32   Third Restatement § 121, comment c(i).

or during the course of the representation.[33] The importance the client ascribes to a particular element of the representation is pertinent in assessing materiality.[34]

2) When Is the Risk of a Material and Adverse Effect Substantial?

When will the risk of a material and adverse effect be viewed as "substantial" within the meaning of the definition in *Neil* and the ethical codes? The codes themselves offer some guidance on this point. In Alberta and Manitoba, the rules provide that "a substantial risk is one that is significant, and while not certain or probable is more than a mere possibility."[35] Somewhat similarly, the codes in British Columbia, Saskatchewan, Nova Scotia, and Newfoundland say that "the risk must be more than a mere possibility; there must be a genuine, serious risk to the duty of loyalty or to client representation arising from the retainer."[36] Ontario's ethical rules contain both statements.[37]

The governing bodies' views as to what constitutes a substantial risk are clearly influenced by the Supreme Court of Canada's holding in *Strother v 3464920 Canada Inc* that "while it is sufficient to show a possibility (rather than a probability) of adverse impact, the possibility must be more than speculation."[38] The notion that a conflict will exist where the risk of harm is realistically possible, even if not probable, finds further support in the Court's earlier decision in *MacDonald Estate v Martin*.[39] These are civil decisions, but there is no reason why the standard should be any higher in the criminal context.

Not surprisingly, then, the criminal law jurisprudence establishes that a conflict of interest will exist at the trial stage where there is "any realistic risk" of an adverse effect, which connotes something less

---

33   *Ibid*, comment c(ii).

34   *Ibid*.

35   Alta r 2.04(1) (commentary); Man r 3.4-2, commentary 1. For the reasons set out below at note 36, there is a good possibility that the Manitoba law society will move these words to commentary 2 in the future.

36   Sask r 2.04(1) (commentary); BC, NS, NL r 3.4-1, commentary 1. In October 2014 FLSC Code r 3.4-1 was amended to move this statement to commentary 2. These law societies may follow suit in the months to come.

37   Ont r 3.4-1, commentary 1. The comment made in the preceding note regarding the October 2014 FLSC Code amendment applies here as well.

38   Above note 1 at para 61.

39   Above note 6 at paras 19 and 44–45.

than a probability but more than mere conjecture or speculation.[40] The leading discussion of the "any realistic risk" standard is found in the Ontario Court of Appeal decision of *R v WW*, a multiple representation case in which Doherty JA stated:

> Where the issue [of conflict of interest] is raised at trial, the court must be concerned with actual conflicts of interest and potential conflicts that may develop as the trial unfolds. In deciding whether counsel should be permitted to act for co-accused, trial judges must, to some degree, speculate as to the issues which may arise and the course the trial will take. The trial judges' task is particularly difficult since they cannot be privy to the confidential discussions which may have passed between the clients and counsel and which may reveal the source of potential conflicts. Given those circumstances, trial judges must proceed with caution and when there is any realistic risk of a conflict of interests they must direct that counsel not act for one or perhaps either accused.[41]

A key point here is that a conflict exists not only where counsel's duty of loyalty is *actually* divided, for example because she cannot advance one client's best interests without harming those of another client. A conflict will also exist where there is a *realistic risk* that an actual conflict will occur at a future point in the proceedings. A contingent threat of harm to the duty of loyalty owed a client can thus suffice to disqualify counsel from acting.

---

40 See *WW*, above note 21 at 238 [para 33]; *R v Brown*, [1998] OJ No 6270 at para 15 (Gen Div) [*Brown* 1998]; *R v Bogiatzis* (2002), 162 CCC (3d) 374 at paras 14 and 23 (Ont SCJ) [*Bogiatzis*]; *R v Billy*, [2009] OJ No 4737 at paras 20–21 (SCJ) [*Billy*]; *R v Whittington*, [2009] OJ No 3313 at para 23 (SCJ) [*Whittington*]; *R v Desmond*, 2010 ONSC 2945 at paras 56 and 69 [*Desmond*]; *R v LK*, 2010 ONSC 2964 at para 18 (SCJ) [*LK*]; *R v Ta*, 2011 ONSC 6525 at paras 31(2) and 37–38 [*Ta*]; *R v Toor*, 2010 ONSC 2903 at para 16 [*Toor*]; *Cadorette*, above note 24 at para 23; *Downey*, above note 24 at paras 37–44; *R v McCall*, 2013 ONSC 4157 at para 27 [*McCall*]; *R v Karmis*, 2008 ABQB 525 at para 35 [*Karmis*]; *R v Caines*, 2011 ABQB 82 at paras 338–39 [*Caines*]; *R v Lewis*, 2011 ABQB 227 at para 7 [*Lewis*]; *R v Aitken*, 2007 BCSC 2041 at para 48 [*Aitken*]; *Sandhu*, above note 24 at para 87; *R v Quiriconi*, 2011 BCSC 1737 at para 13 [*Quiriconi*]; *R v Cocks*, 2012 BCSC 1336 at paras 10(14) and 37–38 [*Cocks*]; *R v Clarke*, 2012 NSSC 406 at paras 50, 106, 121, 129, and 156 [*Clarke*]; *R v Edkins*, 2002 NWTSC 9 at para 20 (SC) [*Edkins*].

41 Above note 21 at 238 [para 33]. See also *MQ*, above note 22 at para 33; *Neil*, above note 1 at para 38: test less onerous at trial stage because the court must proactively prevent harm; *Consulate Ventures Inc v Amico Contracting & Engineering (1992) Inc*, 2010 ONCA 788 at para 14: conflict rules serve prophylactic purpose [*Consulate Ventures*].

What is more, the realistic risk test is less demanding than proof on the civil standard. It is "any realistic" risk that a material and adverse effect will occur — not a "likely or probable" risk. The adjective "realistic" nonetheless indicates the need for some evidentiary foundation from which risk can reasonably be said to flow; mere conjecture and bare possibility is insufficient to justify disqualifying counsel.[42] But on the whole, the standard suggested in WW is not terribly imposing, and it would seem that any conflict scenario that could reasonably occur during the course of the trial will suffice to require the removal of counsel.[43]

The "any realistic risk" test represents, to some extent at least, a preference for avoiding mistrials and overturned convictions over the competing interest of the accused's right to counsel of choice. If the court is being asked to decide a conflict issue, the client — or in a case of multiple representation, at least one client — must wish the allegedly conflicted counsel to continue. Let us assume that the client is not prepared to allow counsel to act in the face of an actual conflict but asserts a strong desire that counsel stay on the record unless and until such a conflict occurs. Removing counsel before trial, on a showing of any realistic risk of conflict as opposed to an actual material and adverse effect, or even some other standard in-between, is to cause immediate and certain prejudice to the ability to retain counsel of choice in order to avoid the possibility of future harm occasioned by the crystallization of a conflict.

It will be necessary for the trial judge in assessing whether the "realistic risk" test is met to obtain an appreciation of the nature and strength of the Crown case, to discern the course that the trial might take and hence assess the degree of likelihood that an actual conflict will occur. For example, a weak Crown case may make it less likely that two jointly represented co-accused will adopt antagonistic defences, and thus reduce the chances of a conflict arising. By contrast, a strong Crown case that encourages *mens rea* defences might force one accused to take the stand and adopt a defence detrimental to the co-accused. It is also possible that an accused whose counsel is the target of a removal application is able and willing to indicate probable defences, thus providing further valuable information to the trial judge.[44] The scenarios

---

42   See, for example, many of the cases cited in note 40, above in this chapter, plus
      McCallen, above note 24 at para 75; *R v Parsons* (1992), 72 CCC (3d) 137 at 142
      (NLCA) [*Parsons* NLCA].
43   See *R v Con-Drain Co* (1983), 2008 ONCJ 114 at para 39 [*Con-Drain*].
44   Tactical issues arise at this point, as does the applicability of the principle
      against self-incrimination. It has been suggested that the accused has an obliga-

may be varied and complex. A trial judge will often face a difficult challenge in divining whether there is a realistic risk that a proffered conflict scenario will come to pass if counsel stays on the case.

a) Addressing a Conflict Issue Raised Late in a Trial

Sometimes a conflict issue will arise only late in a trial, perhaps because the implicated lawyer has until then forgotten about the underlying facts or because an unexpected Crown witness is called. In such a case, the judge should keep three things in mind. First, it may be clear that the trial has proceeded to that point without any actual harm arising, and so there is no need to remedy existing prejudice.[45] Second, the trial may be sufficiently close to finishing that the risk of prejudice occurring through the crystallization of an actual conflict in the future is minimal.[46] Third, the main concern at the beginning of a trial lies in avoiding the harm that will arise if a conflict later crystallizes. But where a risk of conflict is detected late in a trial, the harm caused if counsel is disqualified — including the likelihood of a mistrial — may be greatly accentuated so as to shift the balance of convenience.[47]

A court asked to consider a conflict issue arising late in a trial must therefore take into account the advanced stage of the proceeding in applying the "realistic risk" test.[48] Given the factors just discussed, the court may decide to allow counsel to continue even though a different result might have been reached had the issue been addressed before trial. This is especially so where all affected parties consent to counsel continuing.[49]

3) What Is the Role of Confidential Information in Determining Whether a Conflict of Interest Exists?

The definition of conflict of interest adopted in *Neil* and the codes makes no express mention of a lawyer's duty to guard a client's confidences.

---

tion to reveal the nature of his defence, albeit *ex parte* and in camera: see David Littlefield, "*Silvini*: Divided Loyalty" (1992) 9 CR (4th) 250 at 257. *Contra R v Kalenderian*, [1999] OJ No 802 at paras 25–28 (Gen Div).

45 See *MQ*, above note 22 at para 41, noting no adverse impact on accused to that point in the trial.

46 See *ibid* at para 42, noting a smaller risk of harm occurring than might have existed at the start of trial.

47 See *ibid* at paras 43–44: trial judge can take into account that disqualifying counsel will cause a mistrial.

48 See *ibid* at paras 38–45; *R v Henderson*, 2012 MBCA 93 at para 104, leave to appeal to SCC refused, [2012] SCCA No 524 [*Henderson*].

49 See *MQ*, above note 22 at para 34.

This duty is nonetheless accommodated within the definition because the obligation to maintain client confidences is embraced by the broader duty of loyalty.[50] Indeed, a commentary to the conflict rules found in most ethical codes recognizes that a number of obligations arise from the duty of loyalty, one of which is the duty of confidentiality.[51]

A conflict can nonetheless arise even though there is no risk that confidential information might be misused.[52] This is so because the duty of loyalty is broader than the duty of confidentiality. A conflict occurs simply upon there being a realistic possibility that a lawyer's personal interests or obligations owed to another client or a third party will adversely affect the lawyer's duty of loyalty to the client. For example, conflict concerns regarding the joint representation of two co-accused often have nothing to do with a risk that confidential information might be misused, the problem rather arising because the lawyer may be unable to advance one client's defence without prejudicing the interests of the other.[53] Disloyalty divorced from any concern about confidential information can also justify disqualifying a lawyer from acting against a former client on the same or a related matter.[54]

4) How Does the Right to Counsel of Choice Impact the Conflict Determination?

While the prejudice caused by a conflict can be serious, disqualifying counsel from acting may prevent a client from being represented by counsel of choice.[55] The right to counsel of choice is thus taken into account in deciding whether counsel should be removed from the record. It is sometimes said that given this right, counsel should not be disqualified absent "compelling reasons."[56]

---

50 See *Neil*, above note 1 at para 1. The close connection between the duties of loyalty and confidentiality is discussed in Chapter 4, Section B.

51 Alta, Sask r 2.04(1) (commentary); Man r 3.4-1, commentary 2; BC, Ont, NS, NL r 3.4-1, commentary 5.

52 See, for example, *Neil*, above note 1 at paras 17–18; *McKercher*, above note 3 at para 23; *Brookville Carriers Flatbed GP Inc v Blackjack Transport Ltd*, 2008 NSCA 22 at paras 20–49 [*Brookville Carriers*]; *Consulate Ventures*, above note 41 at paras 22–34; *Speid*, above note 24 at 22 [para 15]; *Sandhu*, above note 24 at paras 35–39; *R v Stewart*, 2011 ONCJ 114 at paras 29–31 and 38 [*Stewart*].

53 See the paragraph associated with notes 64–65, below in this chapter.

54 See the paragraph associated with notes 97–98, below in this chapter.

55 See note 24, above in this chapter, and the accompanying text.

56 *Neil*, above note 1 at para 13; *R v Baltovich* (2003), 170 OAC 327 at para 11 (CA) [*Baltovich*]; *Speid*, above note 24 at 20–21 [para 6]; *MacDonald Estate*, above note 6 at 1243 [para 13]; *Brissett*, above note 19 at paras 49–50, 54, and 56; *Billy*,

Yet the right to counsel of choice does not include an entitlement to be represented by counsel who suffers from a disqualifying conflict.[57] The definition of conflict of interest in *Neil* and the codes does not cease to apply simply because an accused asserts this right. The interest in choice of counsel has already been taken into account in formulating the definition, and is not further balanced on a case-by-case basis as part of the application of the test.[58]

G. ACTING FOR CONCURRENT CLIENTS WITH DIRECTLY ADVERSE INTERESTS IN UNRELATED MATTERS: THE "BRIGHT-LINE" RULE

Although *Neil* is a criminal case, its greatest repercussion has perhaps come in the civil realm by virtue of the "bright-line" rule articulated by the Supreme Court of Canada. This rule operates when a lawyer concurrently represents two clients — that is, acts for them in separate matters, as opposed to jointly on the same brief. As expressed in *Neil* and affirmed in subsequent cases such as *Canadian National Railway Co v McKercher LLP*:

> The bright line is provided by the general rule that a lawyer may not represent one client whose interests are directly adverse to the immediate interests of another current client — *even if the two mandates are unrelated* — unless both clients consent after receiving full disclosure (and preferably independent legal advice), and the lawyer reasonably believes that he or she is able to represent each client without adversely affecting the other.[59]

In *McKercher*, now the leading case in this area, the Court clarified that the bright-line rule amounts to more than a particular application of the conflict-of-interest test discussed in Section F, above in this

above note 40 at para 19; *Sandhu*, above note 24 at paras 26–27; *Downey*, above note 24 at 27.

57   See most of the cases cited at notes 24 and 56, above in this chapter, plus *R v Lall*, 2013 ONSC 864 at para 67 [*Lall*]; *R v Colpaert*, [2013] OJ No 6126 at paras 5–6 (SCJ) [*Colpaert*]; *Billy*, above note 40 at para 37; *Brissett*, above note 19 at paras 50 and 57; *Aitken*, above note 40 at paras 30 and 44–46; *McCall*, above note 40 at paras 23–24; *Bogiatzis*, above note 40 at para 8.

58   *Strother*, above note 1 at para 51; *Sandhu*, above note 24 at para 52.

59   *Neil*, above note 1 at para 29 [emphasis in original]; *McKercher*, above note 3 at para 27; *Strother*, above note 1 at paras 51–55.

chapter: it constitutes a separate conflicts hurdle applicable in the context of concurrent representation. If this hurdle is cleared, it still remains to consider whether there is a substantial risk that the lawyer's representation of a client will be materially and adversely affected by her personal interests or duties to another client, a former client, or a third person.[60]

The bright-line rule applies when a lawyer concurrently acts for two clients whose immediate legal interests are directly adverse.[61] The prohibition against taking on such retainers where the matters are related is uncontentious and fully in accord with long-accepted conflicts principles.[62] What took many lawyers by surprise was *Neil*'s assertion that, absent consent, a lawyer cannot represent two current clients with adverse legal interests in respect of *unrelated* matters.[63] However, we can largely ignore the debate sparked by *Neil* and the subsequent development of the bright-line rule in *McKercher* because criminal defence counsel almost never act for concurrent clients whose immediate interests are directly adverse in unrelated matters, all litigation being conducted against the Crown. In those rare instances where the bright-line rule is engaged regarding unrelated matters, defence counsel must comply with the guidelines in *Neil* and *McKercher*.

---

60   See *McKercher*, above note 3 at paras 8, 38, and 41; FLSC Code r 3.4-1, commentaries 1 & 2 as amended in October 2014, which will likely be adopted by most law societies in the next year or so. Why there should be two separate rules is not explained, but presumably the rationale underlying both is the same: avoiding prejudice to clients and the administration of justice.

61   The concepts of "immediate legal interests" and "directly adverse" are fleshed out in *McKercher*, above note 3 at paras 31–35. See also Alta, Sask r 2.04(1) (commentary); Man r 3.4-3; BC, NS, NL r 3.4-1, commentaries 6 & 7; FLSC Code r 3.4-1, commentary 1. The FLSC Code shifted its description of the bright-line rule to commentary 1 in October 2014. Most of the law societies will probably follow suit in the future.

62   Such a conflict may occur where defence counsel concurrently represents clients charged on separate indictments involving related matters: see, for example, *Caines*, above note 40 at paras 311–33; *Ta*, above note 40; *R v Greene*, 2014 ABPC 77 [*Greene*].

63   For a discussion of the debate engendered by the bright-line rule following *Neil*, see Adam Dodek, "Conflicted Identities: The Battle over the Duty of Loyalty in Canada" (2011) 14 Leg Ethics 193.

H. MULTIPLE OR JOINT REPRESENTATION (REPRESENTING CO-ACCUSED)

The simultaneous representation of two or more jointly charged accused presents one of the most dangerous conflict-of-interest dilemmas for defence counsel. Counsel must be wary of representing multiple accused and should do so only after extremely careful consideration of the conflict issue. Moreover, Crown counsel confronted with a case of multiple representation should make it a practice to address conflict concerns promptly, at the least with defence counsel if not with the court. And trial judges would do well to make formal inquiries whenever co-accused share a single counsel.

1) Accentuated Danger of Conflict in the Joint Retainer Context

The danger arising from multiple representation has nothing to do with the risk that confidential information will be improperly shared between the clients, because the duty of confidentiality does not operate vis-à-vis clients who jointly retain the same lawyer in a single matter.[64] Rather, the risk of conflict exists because the advice or action necessary to best promote the interests of one client may operate to prejudice the other. This is not to say that the duty of confidentiality owed to the clients is never implicated; it may help one client to use confidential information but harm the other to do so. Ultimately, the conflict danger is a function of the increased likelihood of incompatible demands on counsel's loyalty in representing multiple clients in the same matter. The jurisprudence thus recognizes that the right to the effective assistance of counsel is especially susceptible to harm in cases of multiple representation.[65]

Some commentators view the dangers of multiple representation as sufficiently grave to warrant a blanket prohibition against the practice.[66] Yet there are valid arguments as to why, sometimes, two or more co-accused may in fact benefit from representation by a single counsel. They may value the expertise of a particular counsel, have a deep trust

---

64 See the discussion in Chapter 4, Section O.

65 *R v Moyse*, 2013 MBCA 71 at para 15 [*Moyse*]; *Silvini*, above note 21 at 257–58 [paras 11–12]; *WW*, above note 21 at 235–36 [para 24]; *R v Berrardo* (1994), 93 CCC (3d) 571 at 573 [para 8] (Que SC); *Côté*, above note 21 at para 11. See also note 72, below in this chapter, and the associated text.

66 See, for example, *Littlefield*, above note 44.

and confidence in counsel because of prior dealings, or wish to mini-mize costs by jointly retaining one lawyer.[67] It may also work to the advantage of jointly charged individuals to adopt a unified stance via a single lawyer, and so present a solid, seamless defence to the trier of fact.[68] And the risk of an actual conflict materializing at trial may in some circumstances be very low.

It is for these reasons that the courts have stopped short of impos-ing an absolute prohibition on multiple representation.[69] Yet the argu-ments favouring joint representation cannot be blithely accepted or overidealized. Costs and delay occasioned when a conflict crystallizes during trial can overwhelm any savings incurred by sharing a single counsel, and the risk of crystallization will often be very real. More-over, separate lawyers can work together to present a common defence to the jury where strategically advisable,[70] without courting the risk of a jury's assuming that all the accused are guilty because of associa-tion with a single counsel. If the common defence falls apart and the accused need to point fingers at one another, separate lawyers can do so with impunity because they owe no duty of loyalty to each other's clients.

Ultimately, the potential for conflict in taking on a joint retainer in a criminal case is "so grave that ordinarily a lawyer should decline to represent more than one codefendant."[71] And so Canadian courts have held that defence lawyers who act for multiple accused "assume the heavy burden of ensuring that they are not placed in a position of representing interests which are or may be in conflict."[72] Sensible coun-sel will thus ordinarily refuse to accept joint retainers and will agree to act only in those rare cases where the presumption of fatal conflict can be rebutted.

---

67   See Alta r 2.04(3) (commentary); Sask r 2.04(2) (commentary); Man r 3.4-2, com-mentary 6; BC, Ont, NS, NL r 3.4-2, commentary 3; CBA Code ch V, commentary 4.

68   See Man r 3.4-2, commentary 6; *WW*, above note 21 at 235, n 4 [para 24, n 6]; *R v Graff* (1993), 80 CCC (3d) 84 at 88–89 (Alta CA), leave to appeal to SCC refused (1993), 83 CCC (3d) vi (SCC) [*Graff*]; *Whitebear v Alberta*, 2012 ABQB 626 at para 116 [*Whitebear*]; *Glasser v United States*, 315 US 60 at 92 (1942).

69   See *WW*, above note 21 at 235 [para 24]; *R v Le*, 2013 BCCA 455 at para 36 [*Le*]; *Cocks*, above note 40 at para 10(2); *Whitebear*, above note 68 at para 113; *Caines*, above note 40 at para 334.

70   Separate counsel might refuse to cooperate, but if so, this suggests the clients have conflicting interests.

71   ABA Model Rule 1.7(b), comment 23. Basically the same language is found in ABA Defense Standard 4-3.5(c).

72   *WW*, above note 21 at 235–36 [para 24]; *Kim*, above note 21 at para 25; *Cocks*, above note 40 at para 10(4).

2) Ethical Code Provisions Addressing Joint Retainers

The professional-conduct rules impose special conditions that must be met before counsel can act for multiple clients in the same matter. To begin with, each client must be told that (1) the lawyer has been asked to act for all of them, (2) the duty of confidentiality does not operate as between them, and (3) if a conflict develops that cannot be resolved, counsel cannot continue to act for all of them and may have to withdraw completely.[73]

While the rules do not mandate that the lawyer advise the clients to obtain independent legal advice, they stipulate that in some cases a lawyer should do so to ensure that the clients' consent is informed, genuine, and uncoerced, especially where one of the clients is less sophisticated or more vulnerable than another.[74] Moreover, if the lawyer has had a continuing relationship with one of the clients, he must advise the others and recommend they receive independent legal advice about the joint retainer.[75]

Once these informational requirements have been met, the codes state that the lawyer must obtain each client's consent.[76] The consent must be in writing, or the lawyer must record it in a separate written communication provided to each client.[77] Even where everyone consents, the codes caution against acting on a joint retainer where it is likely that a contentious issue will arise between the clients or that their interests will diverge as the matter progresses.[78] If a contentious issue does arise, the lawyer cannot advise the clients with respect to it, and if the issue is not resolved, she must withdraw from the joint representation.[79]

---

73 Sask r 2.04(5); BC, Man, Ont, NS, NL r 3.4-5; Alta r 2.04(3); CBA Code ch V, commentary 6.
74 Sask r 2.04(5) (commentary); BC, Man, Ont, NS, NL r 3.4-5, commentary 1; Alta r 2.04(3) (commentary); CBA Code ch V, commentary 7.
75 Sask r 2.04(6); BC, Man, Ont, NS, NL r 3.4-6; Alta r 2.04(3) (commentary); CBA Code ch V, commentary 6.
76 Sask r 2.04(7); BC, Man, Ont, NS, NL r 3.4-7; Alta r 2.04(3) (commentary); CBA Code ch V, commentary 6.
77 Sask r 2.04(7) (commentary); BC, Man, Ont, NS, NL r 3.4-7, commentary 1. In other codes, written confirmation is advised but not mandated: Alta r 2.04(3) (commentary); CBA Code ch V, commentary 6.
78 Sask r 2.04(7) (commentary); BC, Man, Ont, NS, NL r 3.4-7, commentary 1; Alta r 2.04(3) (commentary); CBA Code ch V, commentary 6.
79 Sask r 2.04(8); BC, Man, Ont, NS, NL r 3.4-8; CBA Code ch V, commentary 8. There may, however, be instances where the lawyer can keep acting for one client even though the contentious issue is not resolved: Sask r 2.04(9); BC, Man, Ont, NS, NL r 3.4-9; Alta r 2.04(3) (commentary); CBA Code ch V, commentary 8.

The rules governing joint retainers reflect the indisputable fact that the risk of a conflict is generally heightened in this context. Most codes do not advert specifically to multiple representation in criminal cases,[80] but as explained in Section H(1), above in this chapter, these types of joint retainers create an especially grave risk of conflict and in our view should only very rarely be accepted.

3) Examples of Conflict Problems Arising in the Joint Retainer Context

In meeting the heavy burden of justifying a joint retainer, criminal defence counsel must ascertain whether there is a realistic risk that the clients' interests will clash at any point in the proceeding so as to preclude multiple representation. This requires careful examination of the potential course of the trial, in light of the anticipated Crown case and the possible defences available to the clients, and scrupulous assessment of any scenario where counsel's loyalty might be called into question. Examples of divided loyalties that can arise in the context of multiple representation are set out below.

a) Plea Discussions

The most obvious example of a conflict related to plea bargaining occurs when one client is offered immunity from prosecution or a light sentence in return for testimony against the other client or perhaps merely "off the record" information that would harm the other's interests. However, counsel must not assume that plea bargaining raises no other conflict-of-interest dangers. For instance, while not actively seeking co-operation, the Crown may decide to call the client who pleads guilty as a witness at the other client's trial.

Indeed, any aspect of plea negotiations that can help one client but harm the other presents a conflict problem.[81] Perhaps one client wishes to rely on the other, who is more articulate and has no record, to testify in support of a joint defence. An offer by the Crown that is attractive to the articulate client may thus be harmful to the other. Or take the case of an aggregate deal offered by the Crown, only available if accepted by all of the accused, that provides a more favourable result to one client than the other.[82] Remember that because the Crown has discretion in

---

80   An exception is Alta r 2.04(3) (commentary).
81   On the problem of conflicts and plea negotiations generally, see *Greene*, above note 62 at para 46.
82   ABA Defense Standard 4-6.2(e) aptly provides that counsel representing multiple co-accused should not participate in making an aggregate plea agreement unless each client provides informed consent.

fashioning a plea arrangement, multiple accused may be competing for the best deal possible. If even one client is interested in the possibility of a plea or is approached by the Crown regarding a plea, a conflict could arise.

Example: A lawyer represents three men charged with trafficking controlled substances. Accused X pays the lawyer's entire fee, including the fee for representing his two co-accused. The lawyer reaches a plea agreement with the prosecutor under which charges against Accused X will be dropped, and the other co-accused will plead guilty with a joint recommendation for penitentiary time. On these facts, the lawyer almost certainly has a fatal conflict of interest, for the plea arrangement substantially benefits Accused X but is probably to the detriment of the other two clients.[83]

It is not uncommon to see spouses jointly charged with offences in the wake of a police search that turns up drugs or stolen property at the family home. One accused, usually the man, may plead guilty in return for the Crown's agreeing to drop the charges against the other, usually the woman. Some lawyers see no difficulty in acting for both spouses in these circumstances. Certainly, there may be excellent reasons for the man to plead guilty, and retaining one counsel saves money. But it is difficult to see how a lawyer can properly advise both clients about the merits of the plea deal.[84] The man is taking complete responsibility for the wrongdoing and forgoing any chance of an acquittal after a contested trial. How can the lawyer give loyal counsel regarding this decision while simultaneously remaining true to the woman, who will emerge without a conviction if the plea arrangement is accepted? At the very least, the lawyer should not act absent the clients' informed consent following independent legal advice.[85]

b) Pre-trial Applications

Many pre-trial applications focus on the exclusion of Crown evidence. If evidence is harmful to one client but helpful to the other and if there exists a reasonable prospect of excluding it, a conflict arises. Non-evidentiary pre-trial applications can also present problems. It

---

83 This example is based on *R v Stork* (1975), 24 CCC (2d) 210 (BCCA) [*Stork*]. See also *Kim*, above note 21.

84 See David Layton, "*R. v Sundstrom*: At the Nexus of Informant Privilege and Conflict of Interest" (2013) 135 The Verdict 21 at 23–24.

85 See *Ta*, above note 40 at paras 19 and 36, not a case involving spouses but one in which conflict concerns regarding plea negotiations were answered by a waiver based on independent legal advice.

may, for example, be in the interest of one accused but not the other to obtain severance.[86]

c) Attacking the Crown Case

A Crown case can be attacked in many ways, including by challenging the evidence of witnesses in cross-examination. Such attacks may help one client but hurt the other, perhaps because the evidence is clearly favourable to one co-accused but unfavourable to the other.[87] Loyalty may be impossibly compromised in this way where, for example, one accused is able to shift blame to the other or where they have inconsistent defences. Mounting or refraining from an attack on the Crown case to bring out such distinctions will almost invariably breach the duty of loyalty owed to one of the clients.

d) Building an Affirmative Defence

Evidence called by the Crown can often be used to build an affirmative defence, and cross-examination of a Crown witness is sometimes undertaken with this purpose in mind. Where a defence can be furthered in this way by one client but will harm the other, a conflict exists.

A defence can also be put forward by calling evidence once the Crown case has closed. A conflict will arise in this respect whenever a witness helpful to one accused will harm the other. Classic examples of inconsistent affirmative defences include a case where one accused argues alibi while the other relies on a *mens rea* defence or where two or more accused put forward inconsistent alibis. Additionally, where all accused share a single, common defence, it may be that one accused is able to make use of an alternative defence. If this accused decides to present the alternative, the inability of the other accused to follow suit may be viewed adversely by the trier of fact.

e) Decision to Testify and Testimony of a Client

A key instance where an attempt to build a defence may lead to conflict occurs at the point where the clients must decide whether to testify.[88]

---

86   See *R v McCaw* (1971), 5 CCC (2d) 416 (Ont CA); *Silvini*, above note 21 at 260–61 [para 19]; *R v Chen* (2001), 53 OR (3d) 264 at para 63 (SCJ) [*Chen*].

87   See *Silvini*, above note 21 at 259 [para 16]; *R v Bullis* (1990), 57 CCC (3d) 438 at 443 (BCCA) [*Bullis*]; *Chen*, above note 86 at para 64; *Moyse*, above note 65 at paras 12–14; *Greene*, above note 62 at paras 43–44; *R v Thanigasalam*, 2007 ONCJ 672 at para 17 [*Thanigasalam*]; *R v Badali*, [2004] OJ No 1012 at para 4 (Ct J) [*Badali*].

88   See *Silvini*, above note 21 at 259 [para 16]; *Bullis*, above note 87 at 443; *Chen*, above note 86 at para 65; *Greene*, above note 62 at para 44; *Badali*, above note 87 at para 4.

The testimony of one client may harm the other, leading to divided loyalties when counsel is advising one or both clients whether to take the stand. Similarly, one client may not want or need to testify, yet the other, who is poorly spoken or has a bad record, may desire the former to give evidence to present a joint defence. Also, putting one client on the stand but not the other may unavoidably lead the jury to speculate about the silence of the non-testifying client. That is to say, the trier of fact may wonder whether the lawyer's decision to have one client testify but not the other reflects the lawyer's belief in the guilt of the non-testifying client.

Once one client takes the stand, an intractable problem arises if any element of the ensuing testimony is adverse to the other. Counsel cannot cross-examine on the point without attacking her own client and thus breaching the duty of loyalty. But a failure to cross-examine will be disloyal to the other client.

f) Closing Arguments

The availability of any argument in closing that would help one client but hurt the other creates a conflict. Suppose that one client testifies but that the other does not. Commenting on the non-testifying client's silence is disloyal to him, but saying nothing may be adverse to the testifying client's best interests.[89] The same insoluble conflict occurs where the evidence is stronger against one client than the other.[90] Pointing this out will hurt one client. Not doing so will hurt the other. Ultimately, the feasibility of presenting a closing argument for one client that in any way points to the other's guilt, perhaps in so subtle a way as by highlighting the absence of a corresponding argument for the latter, raises a possible conflict problem.

g) Sentencing

Taking account of the comparative roles played in the offence by jointly involved offenders is often important in arriving at a proportionate and just sentence. However, counsel who acts for two or more individuals convicted of an offence will have difficulty in accentuating or minimizing distinct roles without harming one or both clients.[91] The same problem arises if the clients have markedly different criminal records or substantially divergent prospects for rehabilitation, or exhibit any number of other differences that may have an impact on sentencing.

---

89   See *Thanigasalam*, above note 87 at para 18.
90   See *Silvini*, above note 21 at 259 [para 16]; *Bullis*, above note 87 at 443.
91   See *Greene*, above note 62 at para 45.

h) Bail Hearings

The limited function of a bail hearing makes conflict less likely, but the problem of divided loyalty can nonetheless arise. Comparisons available to counsel at a bail hearing may be helpful to one client but harmful to the other. By the same token, one client may want a separate bail hearing because her circumstances are much more favourable than those of the other, who is likely to be detained. Finally, even though a bail hearing will occur early on in proceedings, the possibility of plea discussions, with the associated conflict concerns, may exist at this point.

i) Preliminary Inquiries

As with a bail hearing, the limited function of a preliminary inquiry makes conflict somewhat less of a problem.[92] Yet even where committal is not in issue, a conflict can arise. For instance, the preliminary inquiry creates a record that can be used at trial, most often by cross-examining a witness on his earlier testimony but sometimes also for substantive purposes.[93] The preliminary inquiry is thus important in laying a groundwork for attacking the Crown case and building a defence at trial, and to the extent the clients' interests may clash in either regard, a conflict can arise.

It may also be in the interests of one client to waive the preliminary inquiry to avoid the possibility of committal on additional offences, while the other client would be better served by not waiving. Or one client may benefit from a trial in provincial court, where such an option is available, while the other is best advised to take the matter to a higher court. Finally, the possibility of plea negotiations, and the attendant conflict problems, may exist at the preliminary inquiry stage.

j) Conflicting Instructions

Even where the clients' interests seem totally congruent from an objective standpoint, an irreconcilable conflict may arise because they in fact disagree as to the proper course of action to take regarding an aspect of the case. For instance, bringing a pre-trial application or calling a certain defence witness may affect both clients in exactly the same

92   See *Stewart*, above note 52 at paras 27, 36, 39, and 44; *R v Brown*, 2011 ONCJ 189 at para 71 [*Brown* 2011]; *R v Piersanti* (2005), 192 CCC (3d) 449 at paras 5–6 (Ont CA) [*Piersanti*]; *Cadorette*, above note 24 at paras 21–22; *R v Zarelli*, 2004 BCPC 378 at paras 21–26 [*Zarelli*]; *R v Amundson*, 2011 SKPC 131 at para 19 [*Amundson*]; *R v Miller*, 2013 SKPC 87 at para 8 [*Miller*].

93   See *R v Alcantara*, 2012 ABQB 219: admissibility of witness's preliminary inquiry testimony for its truth opposed on ground that defence counsel was fatally conflicted when cross-examining the witness at the preliminary inquiry.

way, yet they take inconsistent positions as to the best course of action. The clients' personalities and subjective priorities come into play in this respect, and counsel should attempt to forecast important strategic and tactical decisions to determine whether inconsistent instructions might arise.[94]

k) Conclusion

The examples in sections H(3)(a) to (j), above, highlight a leading hall-mark of conflict-of-interest problems in the context of multiple representation: adversity of interest arises where clients have inconsistent defences or are implicated in the charged criminality to varying degrees, and with adversity of interest comes conflicting demands on counsel's loyalty. Ultimately, the danger in taking a multiple-representation retainer is significant, and while doing so is not absolutely prohibited, spurning such retainers goes a long way towards avoiding conflict problems.

I. SUCCESSIVE REPRESENTATION (FORMER CLIENTS)

Because there is a duty of loyalty, and hence confidentiality, owed to former clients, a conflict of interest can occur where counsel previously acted for an individual connected to a current criminal matter. The duties owed to a former client may lead to a conflict problem where counsel previously represented a co-accused or a Crown witness in the same or a related matter or in a matter that, while seemingly unrelated, saw counsel acquire confidential information relevant to the current representation. In such cases, the present and former clients may both be exposed to harm if the current retainer is allowed to continue. It is to this question of harm that we now turn.

1) Harm Potentially Caused by Successive Representation

The former client is perhaps most susceptible to harm given that the retainer has come to an end and counsel has now, in the former client's view, taken on a new allegiance. Often the former client's greatest fear is that confidential information relevant to the current matter will

---

94 See Alta r 2.04(3) (commentary): counsel considering multiple representation should assess the "probability that the conflict or potential conflict will ripen into a dispute due to the respective positions *or personalities of the parties*, the history of their relationship or other factors" [emphasis added].

be improperly used.[95] Misuse can occur in many ways. But the most common misuse scenario arises where the former client is a testifying co-accused or Crown witness. In cross-examining the former client, counsel may improperly disclose confidential information to further the current client's representation. Even if client-lawyer confidences are not disclosed in this way, the ex-client may be unduly prone to her former lawyer's suggestions on cross-examination because of fear of misuse or because of familiarity and trust arising from the erstwhile relationship.[96]

The above examples of harm involve the spectre of confidential information's being misused. Yet a former client has a claim to counsel's continuing loyalty regarding the subject matter of the completed retainer even where there is no possibility of such misuse occurring. This duty of loyalty may not be as broad as the fealty owed a current client. But it precludes a lawyer from acting so as to attack, undermine, or undo the work performed in the concluded matter, in other words, to change sides or become a "turncoat" on an issue central to the matter.[97] A reasonable member of the public would hold the integrity of the justice system in considerably less esteem if lawyers were permitted to act against former clients in this way.[98]

The current client may also suffer prejudice where his counsel is poised to take a position adverse to a former client in the same or a related matter or has obtained from the former client information relevant to the extant representation. For one thing, counsel arguably breaches the duty of candour owed the current client if she refuses to disclose relevant but confidential information received from the former client.[99]

---

95   See *Speid*, above note 24 at 22 [para 12]; *MQ*, above note 22 at paras 29–30; *Brissett*, above note 19 at para 39.

96   See *MacDonald Estate*, above note 6 at 1261 [para 47]; *Toor*, above note 40 at para 19; *Edkins*, above note 40 at paras 12 and 26; *Con-Drain*, above note 43 at para 39.

97   See *Consulate Ventures*, above note 41 at paras 22–34; *Brookville Carriers*, above note 52 at paras 20–49; *Speid*, above note 24 at 22; *McCall*, above note 40 at para 31; *Billy*, above note 40 at paras 23–30; *Lewis*, above note 40 at para 11; *Lall*, above note 57 at paras 47–48 and 57–58; *Con-Drain*, above note 43 at paras 40–52; *R v S & V Service Centers Ltd*, [2012] OJ No 3634 at paras 43–63 (Ct J) [*S & V*]; *Stewart v Canadian Broadcasting Corp* (1997), 150 DLR (4th) 24 at 161–63 [paras 318–19] (Ont Ct Gen Div); *R v B(BP)* (1992), 71 CCC (3d) 392 at 399–402 (BCSC) [*B(BP)*]; *Quiriconi*, above note 40 at para 12. "Turncoat" is the apt term used by Paul Perell in *Conflicts of Interest in the Legal Profession* (Toronto: Butterworths, 1995) at 38–42.

98   See *Consulate Ventures*, above note 41 at para 27; *Brookville Carriers*, above note 52 at paras 48 and 51; *B(BP)*, above note 97 at 400–2.

99   See *Quiriconi*, above note 40 at para 12; *Toor*, above note 40 at para 22.

There is also a risk of "soft-pedalling,"[100] meaning that counsel may dial down her zeal to the detriment of the current representation to avoid or mitigate harm to the former client. For instance, the obligations owed to a former client may cause counsel to go easier in cross-examining a witness she previously represented, whether a Crown witness or a testifying co-accused.[101] Or the current client may have concerns that counsel is reluctant to object to Crown evidence that is harmful to him but useful to a co-accused who is a former client.

Example: Counsel acts for a client charged with murder. The client will advance self-defence at trial based in part on the deceased's prior record for violence. Counsel represented the deceased regarding a number of violent offences. In doing so, she obtained no confidential information. She is nonetheless in a conflict. Advancing self-defence at trial will involve attacking the deceased's character using offences on which counsel earlier acted for the deceased and is thus disloyal to a former client regarding the subject matter of the retainers. Yet not using the offences in this way will be disloyal to the current client, who must rely on them to advance his defence.[102]

2) Rules of Professional Conduct regarding Conflict of Interest and Former Clients

Consonant with what has been said to this point, most Canadian ethical codes contain a rule providing that unless a former client consents, a lawyer must not "act against" that former client in (1) the same or any related matter, or (2) any other matter if the lawyer has relevant confidential information arising from the representation of the former client that may prejudice that client.[103] This rule thus stops a lawyer from acting against a former client where there may be a temptation to reveal confidential information obtained during the course of the concluded retainer. But it also precludes attacking the legal work done during the previous retainer or undermining the former client's position on a matter that was central to that retainer.[104] It is nonetheless permissible,

---

100 See *Neil*, above note 1 at para 19(2); *McKercher*, above note 3 at para 23.

101 See *Brissett*, above note 19 at paras 59 and 75(4); *Caines*, above note 40 at para 329; *Lewis*, above note 40 at para 9; *Con-Drain*, above note 43 at paras 45 and 52.

102 The facts and result are based on *Billy*, above note 40 at paras 31–35.

103 Alta r 2.04(4); Sask r 2.04(10); Ont, NS, NL r 3.4-10. To similar effect, see BC r 3.4-10; Man r 3.4-4A.

104 Alta r 2.04(4) (commentary); Sask r 2.04(10) (commentary); BC, Ont, NS, NL r 3.4-10, commentary 1; Man r 3.4-4A, commentary 1. The language in these commentaries is from *Brookville Carriers*, above note 52 at para 51. In October 2014

say the codes, for a lawyer to act against a former client in a fresh and independent matter wholly unrelated to any work the lawyer has done for that client provided that any previously obtained confidential information is irrelevant to the new matter.[105]

It could be argued that the phrase "act against" found in the rule dealing with former clients limits the prohibition to cases where the former client is a party in a proceeding involving the lawyer's current client. On this view, defence counsel who cross-examines a former client called as a Crown witness does not "act against" the former client, because a witness is not a party in a criminal case.[106] But this interpretation is unconvincing. The duty of loyalty owed to a former client is broad and should not be attenuated simply because the former client is not a named party in a proceeding.[107] The "turncoat" scenario can cause serious prejudice to the current and/or former clients and the administration of justice regardless.

3) *MacDonald Estate*: Determining Whether There Is a Realistic Risk That Confidential Information Will Be Misused

The improper disclosure of confidential information is often a key concern in cases of successive representation. When it comes to determining whether a conflict arises because of a threat to the duty of confidentiality, courts apply the analytical framework set out by the Supreme Court of Canada in *MacDonald Estate v Martin*.

MacDonald Estate holds that a conflict exists whenever there is a "possibility of real mischief" regarding the misuse of confidential information.[108] The case also sets out rules and presumptions for determining when a possibility of real mischief exists. Specifically, one must ask whether the public, as represented by a reasonably informed

---

the FLSC Code was amended to state expressly that the duty of loyalty includes the duty not to attack the legal work done during a retainer or to undermine the former client's position on a matter that was central to the retainer: see FLSC Code r 3.401, commentary 7. This new commentary will likely be added to most law society codes as well.

105 See the commentaries cited in the preceding note.

106 See *R v Dix*, 1998 ABQB 92 at para 37 [*Dix*]; *R v Woodcock*, 2010 ONSC 484 at para 11(1) [*Woodcock*].

107 See *Brissett*, above note 19 at para 40; *Sandhu*, above note 24 at paras 54–69; *Caines*, above note 40 at para 311; *Edkins*, above note 40 at para 11.

108 Above note 6. This standard is commensurate with the "any realistic risk" test: see Section F(2), above in this chapter.

person, would be satisfied that no use of confidential information will occur. Two questions must typically be answered in so satisfying this hypothetical person: (1) Did the lawyer receive confidential information attributable to a client-lawyer relationship relevant to the matter at hand? and (2) Is there a risk that any such information will be used to the prejudice of the former client?[109]

a) Did the Lawyer Receive Confidential Information Relevant to the Matter at Hand?

MacDonald Estate states that the starting point in answering the first question is to determine whether there existed a previous client-lawyer relationship that is sufficiently related to the retainer in the matter before the court. If so, a court should infer that confidential information has passed unless the lawyer satisfies the court that no information was imparted that could be relevant.[110] In attempting to discharge this burden — termed "heavy" by Sopinka J, writing for the majority — the lawyer must not reveal the specifics of any confidential communication.[111] Moreover, the degree of satisfaction necessary to justify a holding that no confidential information was communicated must be gauged from the perspective of the reasonably informed member of the public.[112]

b) Is There a Risk That Such Information Will Be Used to Prejudice the Former Client?

As for the second question, pertaining to risk of prejudice to the client, *MacDonald Estate* holds that a lawyer with confidential information from a professional relationship sufficiently related to the matter in question simply cannot act against a former client. The prohibition is strict, for in the words of Sopinka J:

> No assurances or undertakings not to use the information will avail. The lawyer cannot compartmentalize his or her mind so as to screen out what has been gleaned from the client and what was acquired legitimately because it might be perceived to have come from the client. This would prevent the lawyer from adequately representing the new client. Moreover, the former client would feel at a disadvantage.

---

109 See *MacDonald Estate*, above note 6 at 1259–60 [paras 44–46]; *McKercher*, above note 3 at para 24.

110 *MacDonald Estate*, above note 6 at 1260–61 [para 47]. In *Desmond*, above note 40 at paras 40–71, the transfer of relevant information was not inferred, because counsel had acted only at a consent-release bail hearing.

111 *MacDonald Estate*, above note 6 at 1260–61 [para 47].

112 *Ibid.*

Questions put in cross-examination about personal matters, for example, would create the uneasy feeling that they had their genesis in the previous relationship.[113]

Automatic disqualification is the mandated result, even where, as in *MacDonald Estate* itself, affidavits are sworn by the counsel concerned to the effect that confidential information will not be misused. This is so because a reasonably informed member of the public would look askance at continued representation based on the assurances of the lawyers in whose financial interest it is to keep the case. Nonetheless, *MacDonald Estate* recognizes that the use of screening devices to prevent the misuse of confidential information may work to alleviate conflict concerns, a topic discussed in sections I(5) and N(2), below in this chapter.

It is important to remember that *MacDonald Estate* concludes that a possibility of real mischief arises where counsel acts *against* a former client from whom she obtained information relevant to the current matter. In other words, it is only where adversity or the realistic prospect of such arises that a lawyer should be disqualified because of a conflict.[114] If there is no such prospect, there is insufficient basis to conclude the lawyer may breach the duty of confidentiality owed the former client, and the test for disqualification is not met.

4) Relevance of Confidential Information or Concluded Retainer to the Matter at Hand

MacDonald Estate notes that the confidential information needs be "relevant to the matter at hand" to create a conflict of interest.[115] Relevance to the matter at hand is thus a vital consideration in assessing whether a conflict exists; the greater the relevance, the more likely the information will be misused in the proceeding, provided the interests of the current and former clients are adverse. Even where the concern relates only to the "turncoat" lawyer scenario, it is important to assess the relevance of the former client's retainer to the matter at hand. This is so because acting against the former client is more likely to undermine or undo legal work performed for him in the past where the two matters are related.[116]

---

113 *Ibid.*
114 See *Cadorette*, above note 24 at paras 16–17 and 20.
115 Above note 6 at 1260.
116 The notion of "relevance" or "relatedness" is nonetheless somewhat different depending on whether one is concerned with a breach of the duty of confidenti-

It is worth emphasizing that the lawyer who seeks to fight off a removal application is severely constricted in arguing that the subject matter of any implicated confidential information is not relevant to the matter at hand. Counsel cannot put information before the court in an attempt to rebut an assertion of relevance if to do so would reveal the specifics of a client-lawyer communication.[117] It is therefore likely that the court will accept any reasonable assertion by the former client that relevant confidential information passed. Yet a former client may willingly reveal the contents of any confidential communications, thereby demonstrating that they are unrelated to the case at hand.[118] Taking this tack rebuts any suggestion that counsel possesses information that can be misused in the current representation. It also extinguishes the duty of confidentiality by revealing the contents of the communications for the world to see.

Many of the criminal cases in this area look at the subject matter of the former and current retainers in the context of potential conflict between the interests of the accused and a Crown witness formerly represented by counsel for the accused. Where the subject matters of the two retainers are the same or closely related, a finding of conflict is much more likely.[119] Yet even where the witness was represented on criminal charges totally unconnected to the case at hand, these charges may form an important part of defence counsel's cross-examination on the issue of credibility, or there may be reason to believe that personal information passed between counsel and the former client that can be used in cross-examination.[120] In either case, sufficient relevance is established, and counsel will be disqualified. In other instances, a court

---

ality or the "turncoat" lawyer scenario: see *Brookville Carriers*, above note 52 at paras 17 and 50–51.

117 See *MacDonald Estate*, above note 6 at 1260–61 [para 47].

118 This is what happened in *R v Cobb*, [1993] QJ No 881 (SC) [*Cobb*]. See also *R v Sterling* (1993), 108 Sask R 243 (QB). A former client may also submit an affidavit stating that no relevant confidential information was imparted: see, for example, *S & V*, above note 97 at paras 20 and 42; *R v Rowley*, 2008 ONCJ 394 at paras 13–18 and 26 [*Rowley*].

119 See *Caines*, above note 40 at paras 296–309; *Lall*, above note 57 at paras 59–66; *R v DePatie* (1970), 2 CCC (2d) 339 (Ont CA); *Speid*, above note 24; *Robillard*, above note 6; *R v K(P)*, 2007 MBPC 52; *LK*, above note 40; *B(BP)*, above note 97; *R v Munro*, [1990] OJ No 2485 (Prov Ct); *R v AS* (1996), 28 OR (3d) 663 at 668–69 (Gen Div) [*AS*]; *Badali*, above note 87 at paras 5–6; *R v DD*, [2006] OJ No 4913 at paras 202–91 (Ct J) [*DD*]; *R v Cote*, 2011 BCPC 501.

120 See *Toor*, above note 40 at paras 20 and 26; *Brissett*, above note 19 at paras 41–45; *Edkins*, above note 40 at para 21; *R v Lewis*, [2001] OJ No 6343 at para 12 (SCJ) [*Lewis* Ont SCJ]; *R v Leask* (1996), 1 CR (5th) 132 at paras 29–31 (Man Prov Ct) [*Leask*].

may perceive the former retainer between counsel and the witness as unproblematic for a variety of reasons, including that it occurred in the distant past,[121] was very limited or unrelated to any disputed issue that could arise during trial,[122] or involved matters already known to the public.[123]

5) The Use of Independent (Screened) Counsel

It is sometimes suggested that a conflict arising out of successive representation can be avoided by using independent counsel at those points during the trial when the former and current clients' interests are adverse.[124] Using independent counsel in this way is most easily envisaged where the former client is a Crown witness and where the site of adversity is easily delineated, for instance, the cross-examination of the former client. Because the duty of loyalty owed to a former client requires counsel not just to refrain from taking an adverse position in the same or a related matter but also to protect all confidential information, the use of an independent counsel typically requires the employment of screening devices. The possibility that a screen might satisfactorily address a conflict problem involving former clients is rec-

---

121 See *R v Marr*, [1992] BCJ No 1782 (SC Chambers); *R v GK*, [1994] SJ No 612 (QB Chambers) [*GK*]; *R v Johnson*, [1995] BCJ No 2754 (SC) [*Johnson*]; *R v Bouchard*, [2005] OJ No 4133 at para 28 (SCJ) [*Bouchard*]; *Woodcock*, above note 106 at para 11(2).

122 See *R v Joyal* (1990), 55 CCC (3d) 233 at 239 (Que CA) [*Joyal*]; *Parsons* NLCA, above note 42; *R v Dafoe*, [1995] OJ No 5128 (Gen Div); *R v Judge* (1997), 201 AR 186 (Prov Ct) [*Judge*]; *GK*, above note 121; *R v Cousins* (1998), 176 Nfld & PEIR 1 (NLSCTD) (counsel however disqualified on other grounds); *R v Spence*, [1996] OJ No 3134 (Gen Div) [*Spence*]; *Bouchard*, above note 121 at paras 28 and 31; *Woodcock*, above note 106 at para 11(2); *Bogiatzis*, above note 40; *Rowley*, above note 118.

123 *Spence*, above note 122.

124 See *Dix*, above note 106 at 33–34 [paras 57–58]; *R v Stephenson* (1999), 138 CCC (3d) 562 at paras 16–17 (Ont SCJ) [*Stephenson*]; *R v Baptiste*, [1999] OJ No 5343 at para 44 (SCJ); *Baltovich*, above note 56 at para 11; *R v Zeneli* (2003), 176 Man R (2d) 15 at paras 22–29 (Prov Ct); *Woodcock*, above note 106 at paras 11(7) and 12; *R v Turner*, [2000] NJ No 385 at paras 38–40 and 46 (SCTD); *Parsons v Newfoundland (Minister of Justice)* (1999), 142 CCC (3d) 347 at para 13 (NLCA); *Lewis* Ont SCJ, above note 120 at para 14; *R v Pangman*, [1999] MJ No 418 (QB); *R v Trieu*, 2002 ABPC 34 at para 15.

ognized in many ethical codes[125] and has also been acknowledged by the judiciary.[126]

A number of steps are advisable in constructing a screen for maximum effect. We can illustrate using the example of counsel in a murder case who receives new disclosure regarding an important Crown witness. Counsel realizes that he and members of his firm have represented the witness on many criminal matters in the past. The firm should immediately seal all of its files regarding the witness. Counsel should retain an outside lawyer to cross-examine the witness. All firm members, including support staff, should undertake in writing not to discuss confidential information received from the witness with one another or anyone else, including outside counsel. All firm members should agree in writing that breach of the undertaking must be reported immediately to the Crown and is grounds for dismissal from the firm. For her part, outside counsel should undertake in writing that she will not receive any confidential information from counsel for the accused or his firm regarding the witness and will receive all disclosure relevant to the witness directly from the Crown. Finally, the accused should obtain independent legal advice from yet another lawyer and if satisfied with the screening steps should execute a waiver to this effect.[127]

Even if screening devices can be employed, some courts have with good reason been reluctant to permit the use of independent counsel as a means of side-stepping a conflict issue.[128] There may be a lingering concern that confidential information can be misused in ways other than the cross-examination of the former client. It may also be that while confidential information can be insulated from misuse, employing independent counsel fails to answer adequately the concern that a lawyer should not take a position adverse to a former client regarding the same or a related subject matter. There are a myriad of

---

125 Alta r 2.04(5); Sask r 2.04(11); Man r 3.4-4B; BC, Ont, NS, NL r 3.4-11; CBA Code ch V, commentary 14. These rules deal with screening within a firm, but they can surely apply, with necessary modification, to independent counsel retained to cross-examine a Crown witness. Also analogous are the screening rules applicable where a lawyer transfers to a new firm: see Section N(2), below in this chapter.

126 See the cases cited at note 124, above in this chapter.

127 These measures approximate those taken in *Dix*, above note 106.

128 *Leask*, above note 120 at para 45; *R v Werkman* (1997), 6 CR (5th) 221 at paras 4 and 15–20 (Alta QB) [*Werkman*]; *R v EJA* (2000), 198 Nfld & PEIR 103 at para 15 (NLSCTD); *Brissett*, above note 19 at paras 67–69 and 78; *Lewis*, above note 40 at paras 11–21; *Colpaert*, above note 57 at para 9; *Parsons* ONCJ, above note 24 at paras 14–15; *Con-Drain*, above note 43 at paras 70 and 73–75; *DD*, above note 119 at paras 237–88.

points during the conduct of the defence when counsel can arguably be disloyal in exactly this manner, for example, by criticizing the former client during a defence opening, eliciting testimony from Crown witnesses that helps to attack the former client's credibility, calling witnesses who contradict the former client, or disparaging the former client in the closing to the trier of fact. Indeed, when we leave specific examples aside, the general function of helping an accused who takes a position materially adverse to the former client on a related matter can be seen as highly problematic in light of counsel's persisting duty of loyalty to ex-clients.

J. CLIENTS AND PROSPECTIVE CLIENTS

Conflict problems almost always arise regarding those whom a lawyer has represented or is representing as clients. It can therefore be important to determine whether a client-lawyer relationship was ever established. But a lawyer may also owe a duty of confidentiality to a person never taken on as a client that results in disqualification from acting in a matter. The most common example involves a prospective client who ends up not following through with a retainer.[129]

1) Determining Whether a Client-Lawyer Relationship Is Formed

Where counsel for an accused has had previous contact with a Crown witness or a co-accused but was never formally retained, there may be a preliminary issue as to whether the communications occurred in the context of a client-lawyer relationship. Not every contact with a lawyer results in such a relationship.[130] And if there was no client-lawyer relationship, no fiduciary duty exists, and the attendant obligations of loyalty and confidentiality generally do not arise.[131]

The assessment as to whether a client-lawyer relationship ever existed is based on the perspective of a reasonable member of the public fully informed of the circumstances. In this vein, many Canadian

---

129 Other examples are discussed in Chapter 4, Section Q.

130 See *R v McCulloch* (1992), 73 CCC (3d) 451 at 453–54 (Ont Ct Gen Div): mere contact with a witness does not create a client-lawyer relationship; *R v Doucet* (1994), 89 CCC (3d) 474 at 476–77 [paras 11–12] (Man CA), aff'd (1995), 95 CCC (3d) 287 (SCC) (same principle enunciated).

131 Subject to scenarios where a duty of confidentiality is owed to a non-client: see, for example, Section J(2), below in this chapter, and Chapter 4, Section Q.

ethical codes define "client" to include a person who has consulted a lawyer and reasonably concludes that the lawyer has agreed to render legal services on her behalf.[132] The subjective belief of the person consulting the lawyer is therefore not governing on the point. Yet courts will not rely on technical and esoteric analyses to avoid finding that a client-lawyer relationship was formed.[133] The relationship can be established without formality and in the absence of an express retainer or remuneration.[134] It is telling that the codes impose a duty of care on each lawyer to ensure that unrepresented persons do not proceed under the impression that the lawyer will protect their interests.[135]

Example 1: A lawyer's firm acts for Client A, who is charged with fraud. The lawyer expects that B will soon be charged as a co-accused. Wanting to act for B in the matter, he obtains information from Client A that can be used to help B in a cutthroat defence. B is later charged with the fraud. Even though the firm was not formally retained by B when the confidential information was obtained from Client A, the lawyer will be viewed as acting for B at that time and thus to have harboured divided loyalties regarding A and B.[136]

Example 2: A Crown witness approaches defence counsel seeking legal advice regarding her involvement in the matter. Counsel immediately says he cannot represent her because he acts for the accused. Counsel nevertheless requests an interview with the express stipulation that the communications are not taking place in the context of a client-lawyer relationship and attract no duty of confidentiality. The witness agrees, and an interview takes place. No client-lawyer relationship can reasonably be seen to exist, and any understanding to the contrary by the witness is irrelevant.[137]

---

132 Sask definitions; BC, Man, Ont, NS, NL r 1.1-1; CBA Code "Interpretation." To similar effect, see Alta definitions.

133 See *Lall*, above note 57 at paras 41–42.

134 See Man, Ont r 1.1-1, "client," commentary 1; *R v Stewart*, [1997] OJ No 1084 at para 41 (Gen Div). See also Stephen Grant, Linda Rothstein, & Sean Campbell, *Lawyers' Professional Liability*, 3d ed (Markham, ON: LexisNexis, 2013) at § 1.9–§ 1.10.

135 See Chapter 8, Section C."

136 The facts and result are based on *Neil*, above note 1 at paras 8(i) and 32.

137 This example is based on *R v Bennett*, [1991] OJ No 2503 (Prov Ct). See also *R v Bilotta* (1999), 139 CCC (3d) 183 (Ont SCJ), and, to somewhat similar effect, *McCall*, above note 40 at paras 34–61.

2) Prospective Clients and the Duty of Confidentiality

Even where a client-lawyer relationship is never formed, a duty of confidentiality attaches to information obtained by a lawyer from an individual inquiring about the possibility of entering into a retainer.[138] This duty may conflict with an obligation the lawyer owes to a client so as to create conflict problems. A lawyer should therefore exercise caution in meeting with a prospective client whose interests may clash with those of an existing client or a client whom the lawyer wishes to represent in the future.[139]

Steps that may minimize conflict concerns involving potential clients include avoiding contact with any individual whose interests appear incompatible with those of a current client, restricting the initial discussion to matters required for a conflict check and then making the check before going any further, asking the prospective client to waive confidentiality regarding the preliminary discussions, and if a conflict is perceived in a firm context, immediately screening the lawyer who met with the potential client.[140]

It is important to keep an accurate record of contacts with prospective clients, including the nature of any information received, in case an issue later arises as to what occurred. Accurate records also ensure that future conflict checks identify potential problems in a timely way.

K. THIRD-PARTY PAYMENT OF FEES

An arrangement whereby a third party pays a client's fees and disbursements often raises the spectre of an impermissible conflict of interest. The obvious danger created by a third-party payment, no matter the size or proportion of the total fee paid, is that the lawyer will favour the interests of the third party over those of the client. Any potential for adversity of interest between the client and a third-party payor should thus trigger alarm bells for counsel.

---

138 See *MQ*, above note 22 at para 29; *Lall*, above note 57 at paras 39–40. See also Chapter 4, sections H(6) and Q.

139 This caution is set out in a general way in Alta, Sask r 2.03(1) (commentary); BC, Man, Ont, NS, NL r 3.3-1, commentary 4. See also the specific conflicts-related recommendations in Alta r 2.04(4) (commentary).

140 For guidance in this latter respect, see Section N(3), below in this chapter.

1) Rules of Professional Conduct

Canadian rules of professional conduct say little about third-party payment of fees and the risk of conflict of interest. Most codes state only that a lawyer must disclose to the client that a fee is being paid by another person and obtain the client's consent before proceeding with the arrangement.[141] The Alberta code goes further, however, providing that the lawyer must be satisfied that the payor understands the significance of not being the client, including that she will have no right to receive confidential information regarding the matter.[142]

By contrast, the ABA Model Rules expressly recognize that payment of a client's fees by a non-client can lead to conflict problems. They seek to counter this risk by precluding a lawyer from accepting compensation from a third party unless (1) the client gives informed consent, (2) there is no interference with the lawyer's independence of professional judgment or the client-lawyer relationship, and (3) the client's information is protected as required by the duty of confidentiality.[143] The ABA Defense Standards list these same requirements and add an introductory caution to the effect that counsel must remember that his loyalty is due entirely to the accused and must ensure that accepting third-party payment will not lead to a conflict of loyalty.[144]

2) Ensuring That Third-Party Payment Does Not Create Conflict Problems

Although payment by a third party may cause conflict issues, the arrangement can afford the client the immense benefit of having the cost of legal representation footed by another. It is therefore proper to accept a third-party payment provided the lawyer's duties of loyalty and zealous advocacy to the client remain unaffected by the third party's interests. Also, counsel's instructions must come from the client, not the third party. And the duty of confidentiality owed to the client must remain strong, meaning that confidential information cannot be shared with the third party absent the client's consent. Finally, relevant information emanating from the third party must be shared with the client, for the lawyer owes the third party no duty of confidentiality.

---

141 Alta, Sask r 2.06(1) (commentary); BC, Man, Ont, NS, NL r 3.6-1, commentary 2; CBA Code ch XI, commentary 7.

142 Alta r 2.02(5) (commentary).

143 ABA Model Rule 1.8(f). See also Third Restatement § 134(1).

144 ABA Defense Standard 4-3.5(e).

Recommendation: It is always wise to discuss the terms of the retainer and the risk of conflict with the third party, in addition to the client.[145] Although the third party is owed no duty of loyalty, failure to alert her to the preconditions upon which the retainer is accepted risks discord down the road. A third party could stop payment or seek the return of funds on becoming disenchanted with the limits imposed by counsel's duties to the client.

A very different route for avoiding conflict is to have the third party lend or give the client money sufficient to cover legal fees. However, a third party may be unwilling to cede control over the financial aspects of the retainer, in which case the conflict problem cannot be circumvented in this manner.

This leads us to the related issue of whether the third-party payor should ever be permitted to direct the course of the representation. He may naturally wish some control over how, or at least how much, money is spent. Or a third party with responsibility for the accused, such as a parent or caregiver, may desire involvement in decisions that an accused, if more sophisticated or mature, would ordinarily make alone. If a third party is to play this latter role, the client's fully informed consent is a mandatory precondition. And the involvement permitted by a third party must be "reasonable in scope and character."[146] Directions that are clearly to the disadvantage of the client can never be countenanced, and the client must always receive full disclosure as to what is happening and why. In the event of disagreement between the third party and the client, the latter's wishes must prevail.

3) Young Person's Fees Paid by a Parent

The funding of a young person's defence by his parents provides especially rich potential for conflict of interest.[147] The parents may have a particular idea as to how the matter should be handled, one that clashes with the young person's wishes or best interests. The parents may, for instance, insist that their son plead guilty regardless of a strong *Charter* argument. Or they may demand that all information received by counsel be relayed to them, in violation of the duty of confidentiality counsel owes to the young person. Perhaps because of these sorts of concerns, the *Youth Criminal Justice Act* obliges a court to ensure that a

---

145 This point garners some support from the Alberta rule discussed in the text associated with note 142, above in this chapter.

146 Third Restatement § 134(2).

147 See also Chapter 3, Section O(2).

young person is represented by counsel independent of a parent where it appears that the best interests of the young person and the parent are in conflict.[148] In any event, it is important for counsel to remember that his professional obligations are owed to the young person, not the parents, even though the parents are paying for counsel's services. Providing financial aid does not give the parents the right to assume the position of instructing client, nor to exercise greater influence over counsel.

4) Fees Paid by a Third Party Allegedly Involved with the Client in Crime

Conflict klaxons should be screaming where the client's legal expenses are to be paid in whole or part by a co-accused, an unindicted co-conspirator, or someone counsel suspects is head of a criminal organization.[149] This sort of third party may fear that the accused will co-operate with the prosecution or adopt a defence that blames the third party, and so may pressure counsel to prevent such outcomes. Or the third party may wish the matter to go to trial, despite the availability of a favourable plea bargain for the accused, to resolve a legal issue important to the third party.[150] Conversely, it may be in the third party's interests for the non-paying accused to plead guilty as part of a plea deal that sees the Crown stay the charges against the third party.[151] Counsel's loyalty to the client may also be put at risk where the lawyer is benefiting, or hopes to benefit, from an ongoing arrangement under which the third party will pay legal fees for other clients in the future. This is so because running the defence in a way that threatens harm to the third party's interests not only jeopardizes the lawyer's remuneration in the particular case but also risks cutting off a stream of revenue in the future.

Where fees are being paid by someone alleged to be involved with the client in crime, a lawyer will almost never be able to comply with the guidelines discussed in Section K(2), above in this chapter, so as to avoid a fatal conflict. But, more than this, two other restrictions may prevent counsel from proceeding with the proposed payment arrangement.

---

148 SC 2002, c 1, s 25(8).

149 See *Wood v Georgia*, 450 US 261 at 268–69 (1981) [*Wood*], recognizing that an inherent danger arises where an accused is represented by a lawyer paid by a third party who allegedly operates a criminal enterprise.

150 See *Wood, ibid* at 267–70.

151 This is what happened in *Stork*, above note 83, and probably also *Kim*, above note 21.

First, a lawyer is ethically prohibited from accepting funds she knows or ought to know are proceeds of crime. This is because knowingly handling proceeds of crime is an offence under the *Criminal Code*,[152] and the lawyer's ethical duty to the administration of justice precludes any conduct the lawyer knows or ought to know is criminal.[153] Counsel must therefore exercise extreme caution where he suspects that the funds may be the fruits of crime.

Second, the same ethical duty to the administration of justice prevents a lawyer from accepting a retainer he knows or ought to know will operate to assist anyone in committing crimes. The lawyer cannot therefore accept payments made in furtherance of a criminal conspiracy, for instance when a criminal organization has agreed in advance to compensate lower-level members for their criminal conduct in part by paying for legal representation if arrested.[154] Nor can the lawyer accept a third-party payment meant to reward the client for running a defence that avoids placing blame on the third party or others involved in a criminal enterprise, because to do so would further a criminal attempt to obstruct justice.

L. LAWYER AS WITNESS OR ALLEGEDLY INVOLVED WITH MATERIAL FACTS

A lawyer appearing as a witness in a matter in which she also acts as counsel may harm the client's interests and also unfairly prejudice the opposing party. Most notably, counsel's personal interest in being found a credible witness may clash with the duty of loyalty owed to the client. Moreover, the lawyer who takes the stand may find that her credibility with the trier of fact as an advocate is compromised. Conversely, unacceptable harm may be visited on the opponent because the trier may be more inclined to believe the closing submissions of a lawyer who is personally aware of material facts.

---

152 See, for example, *Criminal Code*, RSC 1985, c C-46, ss 354 (offence to possess the "proceeds of crime," defined to include any property obtained by or derived directly or indirectly from an indictable offence) and 462.31 (offence to deal with proceeds of crime with an intent to convert or conceal).

153 See Chapter 2, Section B(1).

154 See Chapter 2, Section B(2), and in particular see the example associated with note 16.

1) Lawyer as Witness: Ethical Rule and Jurisprudence

It is for the above reasons that the ethical codes state that a lawyer who appears as an advocate must not testify or submit his own affidavit before the court unless the matter is purely formal or uncontroverted or unless he is permitted to do so by law or the rules of the court.[155] A commentary adds that the lawyer must also refrain from asserting as fact that which is properly subject to legal proof, cross-examination, or challenge, because to do so is to put oneself forward as an unsworn witness and place one's own credibility in issue.[156] Where the lawyer is a necessary witness, says the commentary, she should testify and entrust the conduct of the case to another lawyer.[157] Finally, the codes provide that where a lawyer does become a witness in a case, she cannot appear as counsel on appeal unless the matter with respect to which she testified is purely formal or uncontroverted.[158]

Commensurate with the policy behind these rules, the caselaw provides that counsel will be removed from the record where there is a realistic risk he will become a witness at trial.[159] The biggest concern occurs where the lawyer's evidence may be contested, meaning that it will be challenged by the opposing party either through cross-examination or by eliciting contradictory evidence from another source.[160] In some cases, courts have disqualified counsel on this basis,[161] but in others they have refused to do so because the risk of counsel's being

---

155 Alta, Sask r 4.02(1); Man, Ont, NS, NL r 5.2-1; NB ch 8, commentary 6(a) & (b); CBA Code ch IX, commentary 5. See also BC r 5.2-1, which is to the same effect but also allows a lawyer to give evidence where such "is necessary in the interests of justice."

156 Alta, Sask r 4.02(1) (commentary); BC, Man, Ont, NS, NL r 5.2-1; CBA Code ch IX, commentary 5.

157 See the commentaries cited in the preceding note.

158 Alta, Sask r 4.02(2); BC, Man, Ont, NS, NL r 5.2-2. See also NB ch 8, commentary 6(c); CBA Code ch IX, commentary 5. Similarly, a lawyer should generally not act on an appeal in which his conduct as trial counsel is in issue: see *R v Bhatti*, 2006 BCCA 16 at para 30.

159 *Bogiatzis*, above note 40 at paras 22–23; *R v Charles*, 2012 ONSC 2001 at paras 18–24 [*Charles*]. The same principle applies where the witness is a partner or associate of a lawyer acting for the accused: see *R v Pyszniak*, 2000 ABPC 199 at paras 74 and 80(b) [*Pyszniak*]; *R v Marshall*, 2002 SKQB 107 at para 9 [*Marshall*]; *Whittington*, above note 40 at para 20.

160 See *Pyszniak*, above note 159 at paras 73 and 80(d).

161 *Downey*, above note 24; *R v Bevan*, 2009 ONCJ 487 [*Bevan*]; *R v Buhr*, 2009 MBPC 22 [*Buhr*]; *Zarelli*, above note 92; *R v McCarroll*, [2005] OJ No 961 (SCJ); *Marshall*, above note 159.

302 ETHICS AND CRIMINAL LAW

called was not sufficiently high.[162] If counsel is to be a witness on a *voir dire* only, it may be possible for her to hand carriage of that part of the case only over to another counsel, and otherwise to remain on the record.[163]

The jurisprudence further mirrors the ethical rules in forbidding a lawyer from seeking to avoid becoming a witness by relating facts based on personal involvement from counsel table.[164] If it is necessary to put the facts before the court, counsel should either find someone else who can testify to the events or give up the brief and take the stand as a witness.[165] Failure to heed this advice raises the same sort of conflict problems that occur when a lawyer testifies on a disputed point while remaining on the record.[166] It is also unfair to the opponent, who is unable to test the asserted facts through cross-examination.[167]

In determining whether counsel must be disqualified because he may be a witness, it is worth remembering that a party cannot call opposing counsel as a witness merely because he has material evidence to give. Counsel can only be called where an evidentiary foundation establishes he has evidence that is both relevant *and necessary*.[168]

2) Conflict May Occur Even Where Advocate-Witness Rule Not Directly Engaged

Counsel's alleged involvement in facts relevant to the retainer can raise conflict concerns even where she is unlikely to become a witness and whether the allegations are accurate or not. The lawyer's self-interest in protecting her reputation may influence the retainer in a myriad of ways, including the cross-examination of Crown witnesses, decisions on whether and how to call a defence, and the substance of submissions to the judge or jury.

---

162 *Bogiatzis*, above note 40; *Karmis*, above note 40; *Whittington*, above note 40; *R v Robinson*, [2012] OJ No 6616 (Ct J) [*Robinson*]. See also *Pyszniak*, above note 159: defence counsel's partner was to be Crown witness at preliminary inquiry; court ordered that independent counsel be retained to conduct the cross-examination.

163 See *Charles*, above note 159 at paras 26–37; *R v Liard*, 2013 ONSC 5457 at paras 407–13 [*Liard*].

164 *R v Leduc* (2003), 176 CCC (3d) 321 at paras 132–34 (Ont CA) [*Leduc*].

165 See *ibid* at para 132.

166 See *ibid* at paras 132–34.

167 See *ibid* at para 132.

168 See *R v 1504413 Ontario Ltd*, 2008 ONCA 253 at paras 13–14; *R v Elliott* (2003), 181 CCC (3d) 118 at paras 114–15 (Ont CA); *Liard*, above note 163 at paras 403–6; Marcus Pratt, "Defending the Right to Choose Counsel in Times of Conflict" (2001) 6 Can Crim L Rev 261 at 278–79.

For example, counsel may have evidence helpful to a client but wish to avoid testifying, perhaps to side-step damage to reputation, an attack on credibility, or, most obviously, loss of a retainer fee. A decision not to testify avoids contravening the advocate-witness rule yet raises a real concern regarding conflict of interest. Somewhat similarly, counsel may resist eliciting helpful facts from a Crown witness because doing so will mean revealing his own role in a less than flattering light. Another possibility is that counsel's involvement becomes known to the jury through other witnesses, in a way that improperly bolsters or undermines his credibility as an advocate with the trier of fact.[169]

M. LAWYER'S FINANCIAL AND OTHER PERSONAL INTERESTS

There are many instances where counsel's financial or other interests come into conflict with the duty of loyalty to a client. Some have already been discussed.[170] The general approach must be to look out for and avoid any situation where a decision must be made or action taken on behalf of the client that simultaneously affects the lawyer's personal interests. As the Alberta ethical code states, "a lawyer must not act when there is a conflict of interest between a lawyer and client, unless the client consents and it is in the client's best interests that the lawyer act."[171] A few instances where a conflict may arise from the lawyer's personal interests are discussed below.

1) Acting as a Surety

Acting as a surety creates a substantial risk of conflict of interest, for the lawyer's duty of loyalty can easily clash with the obligations owed to the court as a surety, as well as the desire to avoid the monetary loss

---

169 These sorts of concerns are discussed in *R v Henry* (1990), 61 CCC (3d) 455 at 467–69 (Que CA) [*Henry*]; *Bogiatzis*, above note 40 at paras 24–25; *Downey*, above note 24 at paras 78–84; *Aitken*, above note 40 at paras 50–55; *Bevan*, above note 161 at paras 14–20; Pratt, above note 168 at 276–78.

170 See sections K & L, above in this chapter.

171 Alta r 2.04(1). See also BC, Ont, NS, NL r 3.4-1, commentary 3: conflicts rule applies where a lawyer is tempted to prefer the lawyer's own interests over the interests of the client. The definition of conflict of interest adopted in the caselaw and codes also references the lawyer's own interests: see Section F, above in this chapter.

that may result if the client breaches his recognizance.[172] It is for this reason that many ethical codes state that a lawyer must not act as surety, deposit money or other valuable security, or act in a supervisory capacity for an accused client.[173]

The rules nonetheless allow a lawyer to so act for an accused with whom the lawyer is in a family relationship where the accused is represented by the lawyer's partner or associate.[174] This exception is no doubt motivated by compassion for lawyers unfortunate enough to find themselves with family members charged criminally. Yet the mechanism of having the accused represented by the lawyer's partner or associate does not ensure that potential conflicts are alleviated. There may remain a real risk of a clash between the lawyer's duty to the court as a surety, security-giver, or supervisor, as well as her personal interests, and the partner's or associate's duty to loyally serve the client. The safer course is to have outside counsel handle the file.

2) Taking an Assignment of a Bail Deposit or Seized Funds

A lawyer who takes an assignment of a bail deposit to cover payment of fees and disbursements runs into a problem similar to that faced by counsel who acts as a surety. Acquiring a property interest in deposited funds gives the lawyer a strong interest in seeing that the funds are not depleted because of the client's breaching bail or absconding. The lawyer in this position may be less inclined to fight strenuously against a Crown application to revoke bail following conviction or may be tempted to encourage subtly a nervous surety to pull the bail.

In a similar vein, counsel who takes an assignment of funds that have been seized under proceeds of crime provisions has an interest in protecting his property interest. The client's best interests may dictate that the funds be relinquished to the Crown as part of a plea agreement or that the client willingly concede forfeiture at a sentencing hearing to avoid a fine or in exchange for reduced jail time. Yet counsel who has an interest in the funds will obtain the greatest benefit from exactly the

---

172 See Gary T Trotter, *The Law of Bail in Canada*, 3d ed (Toronto: Carswell, 2010) (loose-leaf 2013 supplement) at § 7.3(a): lawyer ought not to stand as client's surety due to very real potential for serious conflict.

173 Sask r 2.04(40); BC, Man, Ont, NS, NL r 3.4-40; NB ch 23, commentary 3; CBA Code ch XIX, commentary 9.

174 Sask r 2.04(41); BC, Man, Ont, NS, NL r 3.4-41; NB ch 23, commentary 3; CBA Code ch XIX, commentary 9.

opposite result, and for this reason an assignment of such funds creates a dangerous conflict problem.[175]

3) Business Relations with a Client

The opportunity for a lawyer to have business dealings with a client is more likely to occur in non-criminal settings. Nonetheless, criminal lawyers should be wary of conflict-of-interest problems if such an opportunity arises. There are certainly circumstances particular to criminal proceedings that can leave counsel with an interest potentially adverse to the client who is also a business associate. For instance, it may be in counsel's interest to have the client plead guilty to minimize the possibility of jail and thus increase the ability to pay back a loan or continue with a joint business enterprise.

Recommendation: An appearance of impropriety can arise by virtue of business dealings with a client who is under investigation or charge. Such dealings may attract police attention. In these circumstances, the lawyer may have an interest in self-protection that is adverse to the best interests of the client. It has thus been said that prudent criminal defence counsel should not engage in any kind of business dealings, however minor, with a client.[176]

4) Sexual Relationship with a Client

The ethical codes recognize that conflict concerns can arise out of a sexual relationship with a client.[177] Such a relationship is fraught with danger. The lawyer may act to prolong or shorten proceedings depending on whether he wishes to continue the relationship. A sexual relationship that ends in acrimony may lead the lawyer to act out of spite and revenge to harm the client's case. Or the relationship may operate to skew the client's view of the matter and adversely impact her instructions. There is also a more fundamental concern that in initiating

---

175 See *R v Pawlyk* (1991), 65 CCC (3d) 63 (Man CA); *R v Wilson* (1993), 86 CCC (3d) 464 (Ont CA).

176 See *R v White* (1997), 114 CCC (3d) 225 at 264 [para 128] (Ont CA), leave to appeal to SCC refused, [1997] SCCA No 248.

177 Sask r 2.04(1) (commentary); Man r 3.4-2, commentary 8; BC, Ont, NS, NL r 3.4-1, commentary 8(e). The FLSC Code moved this topic to r 3.4-1, commentary 11(d) in October 2014. It is anticipated that most law society codes will eventually follow suit.

or acceding to a sexual relationship, the lawyer may be exploiting the client's vulnerability.[178]

N. AFFILIATED LAWYERS AND TRANSFERS TO OTHER FIRMS

Lawyers in a firm usually discuss cases and often work on them together. They also have contractual, business, and personal ties. A fee received by one lawyer may benefit everyone in the firm. There is thus a strong presumption that firm members share confidential information,[179] and a conflict affecting one lawyer is normally imputed to all lawyers in the firm.[180] As stated in *Neil*, "it is the firm not just the individual lawyer, that owes a fiduciary duty to its clients."[181] It is therefore unsurprising that some codes define "client" to include a client of a firm in which a lawyer is a partner or associate whether or not the lawyer handles the client's work.[182] This definition reflects the view that the conflict rules generally extend to capture lawyers who practise together.

The question arises as to when, if ever, a similar imputation should apply to space-sharing arrangements even though the lawyers neither practise in the same firm nor hold themselves out as doing so. Another topic deserving attention is the extent to which screens can be used to alleviate the conflict problems that arise when a lawyer for a client transfers to a firm that represents the client's opponent in litigation.

---

178 See *Adams v Law Society of Alberta*, 2000 ABCA 240: defence counsel had initiated a sexual relationship with a young client and was convicted of sexual exploitation and disbarred.

179 See *MacDonald Estate*, above note 6 at 1262 [para 49]. Indeed, lawyers have implied consent to share a client's confidential information within the firm: see Chapter 5, Section B(2).

180 See *MacDonald Estate*, ibid; *Speid*, above note 24 at 21 [paras 8–10]; *Werkman*, above note 128 at paras 2 and 11; *Stephenson*, above note 124 at 565 [paras 4 and 11]; *Chen*, above note 86 at 278 [paras 44–47]; *Brissett*, above note 19 at paras 46 and 72; *Cocks*, above note 40 at paras 48–49; *Aitken*, above note 40 at paras 32–34; *Lewis*, above note 40 at paras 2 and 10.

181 Above note 1 at para 29. See also *McKercher*, above note 3 at para 19.

182 See Alta definitions, "client"; Ont r 1.1-1. In October 2014 the definition of "client" in FLSC Code r 1.1-1 was amended to the same effect. It is likely that most of the other law society codes will adopt this expanded definition too.

1) Office-Sharing Arrangements: Avoiding Conflicts

Criminal defence lawyers often work alone but share office space with other independent practitioners in an effort to reduce costs. Given their close physical proximity and common area of practice, these lawyers may discuss files with one another and in doing so share client confidences, whether inadvertently or otherwise. Depending on the space-sharing arrangement, a client may thus have a reasonable concern that his confidences will be revealed to other lawyers.

Most Canadian governing bodies recognize that a danger of conflict can arise where lawyers share office space, even though their practices are separate. Several codes allude to the possibility of leaked confidences, and attendant conflict concerns, in the following commentary to the rule on confidentiality:

> Sole practitioners who practise in association with other lawyers in cost-sharing, space- sharing or other arrangements should be mindful of the risk of advertent or inadvertent disclosure of confidential information, even if the lawyers institute systems and procedures that are designed to insulate their respective practices. The issue may be heightened if a lawyer in the association represents a client on the other side of a dispute with the client of another lawyer in the association. Apart from conflict of interest issues such a situation may raise, the risk of such disclosure may depend on the extent to which the lawyers' practices are integrated, physically and administratively, in the association.[183]

These codes revisit the space-sharing issue in the rule dealing with conflicts, usually while illustrating circumstances that may give rise to conflict problems. Typical is the Nova Scotia code, which describes the potential for conflict arising where "[s]ole practitioners who practise with other lawyers in cost-sharing or other arrangements, represent clients on opposite sides of a dispute. The fact or the appearance of such a conflict may depend on the extent to which the lawyers' practices are integrated, physically and administratively, in the association."[184]

These ethical code provisions send a clear message to criminal lawyers who practise as independents but work in common office areas:

---

183 Sask r 2.03(1); BC, Man, Ont, NS, NL r 3.3-1, commentary 7. To somewhat similar effect, see Alta r 2.03(1) (commentary).

184 NS r 3.4-1, commentary 8(g). See also Man r 3.4-2, commentary 9; Ont r 3.4-1, commentary 8(f); BC, NL r 3.4-1, commentary 8(g). The FLSC Code moved this topic to r 3.4-1, commentary 11(f) in October 2014. Most law society codes will likely do the same.

space sharing may lead to a fatal conflict of interest. The jurisprudence suggests the same.[185] Consequently, a lawyer may be disqualified where a reasonable person would conclude that given the particularities of the office arrangement, the representation of clients adverse in interest by the space-sharing lawyers creates a realistic risk that confidential information will be misused.

Policies that will assist in avoiding space-sharing conflict problems include

1) not sharing a firm name, website, letterhead, or business cards;
2) not integrating work spaces or file storage areas, and perhaps even locking individual office doors after hours;
3) not leaving client files unattended in common spaces and taking care when conversing in such areas;
4) not sharing staff, bookkeepers, or accountants and implementing policies to prevent confidences' being leaked through interactions with a common receptionist;
5) not having one lawyer's mail opened by an employee who works for a lawyer not in the same firm;
6) using separate computer systems;
7) having lawyers and staff sign a formal agreement stating that no client confidences will be shared; and
8) implementing special screening mechanisms for clients known to be adverse in interest.

In addition to the ethical code provisions set out earlier in this section, the British Columbia code contains special conflict rules forbidding space-sharing lawyers from acting for clients adverse in interest unless the lawyers agree to disclose in writing to all of their clients (1) the identity of the lawyers who make up the firm acting for the client, (2) that the space-sharing arrangement exists, and (3) that the lawyers sharing space with the firm are free to act for individuals adverse in interest to the client.[186] If space-sharing lawyers choose not to represent clients adverse in interest, they must run conflict checks to promote compliance.[187] In either case, the British Columbia conflict rules stipu-

---

185 *Neil*, above note 1 at paras 5, 8(i), & 9; *Stewart*, above note 52 at paras 22–27; *R v Luk*, 2008 BCPC 377 at paras 41–42 and 52. In the civil context, see *Baumgartner v Baumgartner* (1995), 122 DLR (4th) 542 (BCCA); *Bezzeg v Bezzeg* (1994), 153 NBR (2d) 212 (QB).
186 BC r 3.4-42 & 3.4-43.
187 BC r 3.4-43, commentary 1.

late that space-sharing lawyers must take reasonable steps to ensure that each client's confidential information is protected.[188]

The Alberta code takes a more stringent position still. Lawyers who practise from the same premises are treated as a firm even where they hold themselves out as independent.[189] They are required to carry out conflict checks, as would any firm,[190] and unlike in British Columbia, and presumably other provinces, do not have the option of taking measures to avoid being treated as a firm for conflicts purposes.

2) Transfers and Screening

In *MacDonald Estate*, the majority was prepared to impute a conflict of interest to all lawyers working in the same firm yet appeared willing to allow for continued representation where the firm to which a "tainted" lawyer transferred had implemented formal screens approved by the legal profession to prevent the problematic confidential information from passing to other lawyers in the firm.[191] The Federation of Law Societies of Canada later adopted a rule applicable when a lawyer moves to a new firm,[192] from which derived the transfer and screening rules currently employed by most Canadian governing bodies.[193] The imputation of a conflict to all members of a firm is therefore now subject to rebuttal provided appropriate, code-based steps have been taken to screen the lawyer who possesses confidential information.

Screens are commonly used where a lawyer with confidential information regarding a former client moves to a firm representing the client's opponent. The screening measures may be physical in that materials related to the new firm's client are kept away from the tainted lawyer, who does not work on or discuss the case with anyone at the firm. Measures may also be non-physical in that the new firm adopts and circulates a written policy outlining the screening steps taken, requires that firm members provide affidavits or undertakings setting out their adherence to the policy, and informs all affected clients of the

---

188 BC r 4.4-43, commentary 2.

189 Alta definitions, "law firm."

190 Alta r 2.03(1) (commentary) & 2.04(1) (commentary)

191 *MacDonald Estate* above note 6 at 1261–63 [paras 48–49].

192 The rule was based on a report by the Canadian Bar Association Task Force on Conflicts of Interest, *Conflict of Interest Disqualification: Martin v Gray and Screening Methods* (Ottawa: CBA, 1993).

193 Alta r 2.04(6)–2.04(9); Sask r 2.04(17)–2.04(26); BC, Man, Ont, NS, NL r 3.4-17–3.4-26; NB ch 6, commentary 7; CBA Code ch V, commentaries 20–40. In October 2014 the FLSC Code was amended to address this topic in r 3.4-17–3.4-23. Most law society codes will likely be amended to follow suit over the next year or so.

conflict problem and the steps taken. It is important that the measures be implemented in a timely way. Ultimately, the ability of screens to alleviate a conflict problem depends on whether a reasonable person fully informed of the facts would be satisfied that no misuse of confidential information would occur.[194]

Transfers and space sharing: The ethical codes in British Columbia and Alberta apply the rules governing a lawyer's transfer between law firms to space-sharing arrangements.[195] Lawyers in these jurisdictions who move into a space-sharing arrangement must therefore comply with these transfer rules.

Can screening be effective when applied to the small firms in which defence lawyers almost always practise? The viability of a screen can be questioned because sharing a small physical space and interacting frequently with the same close colleagues makes meaningful implementation a real challenge. For this reason, and given the weighty public and constitutional interests at stake in criminal matters, it has been argued that screening can never cure a firm conflict problem in a criminal case.[196] Certainly, Canadian courts have at times been slow to accept that criminal-firm screens can completely dispel reasonable concerns that confidential information may be misused.[197] While an absolute bar for small firms may be going too far,[198] courts should not condone

---

194 See *MacDonald Estate*, above note 6 at 1262 [para 49]; *Ford Motor Company of Canada Ltd v Osler, Hoskin & Harcourt* (1996), 131 DLR (4th) 419 at 440–43 [paras 62–70] (Ont Ct Gen Div); *Canada Southern Petroleum v Amoco Canada Petroleum Co* (1997), 144 DLR (4th) 30 at 41–42 [paras 38–39] (Alta CA), leave to appeal to SCC refused, [1997] SCCA No 162; *Davies, Ward & Beck v Baker and McKenzie* (1998), 40 OR (3d) 257 at 261 (CA); *Bank of Montreal v Dresler*, 2002 NBCA 69 at para 2 [*Dresler*]; *Robertson v Slater Vecchio*, 2008 BCCA 306 at para 1 [*Robertson*]. The viability of screens is also discussed in *DD*, above note 119 at paras 202–24, albeit not in relation to a lawyer-transfer scenario.

195 BC r 3.4-17, commentary 2. In Alberta, the transfer rules apply by virtue of the definition of "law firm," which includes space-sharing lawyers: Alta definitions and r 2.04(1) (commentary).

196 See John Wesley Hall Jr, *Professional Responsibility in Criminal Defense Practice* (St Paul, MN: Thomson West, 2005) (loose-leaf 2012 supplement) at § 13.5.

197 *Chen*, above note 86 at para 57; *Brissett*, above note 19 at para 46; *R v Borbely*, 2012 ONSC 5639 at para 20 [*Borbely*].

198 See *Borbely*, *ibid* at paras 20–27, recognizing the difficulty in setting up screens but finding such is possible on the facts of the case. In the civil context, see the useful discussions in *Dresler*, above note 194 at paras 80–83; *Robertson*, above note 194 at para 27; Canadian Bar Association Task Force on Conflicts of Interest, *Conflicts of Interest: Final Report, Recommendations & Toolkit* (Ottawa: CBA, 2008) at 81–83.

screening mechanisms in criminal cases absent real satisfaction as to their effectiveness.

The effectiveness of screens may be less difficult to establish where Crown counsel or public defenders are concerned. These lawyers often work in larger offices, where screening measures are easier to implement. Moreover, their offices usually have multiple locations, which goes some way to creating a natural screening mechanism. It has thus been recognized that a Crown or public defender office "may be able to demonstrate that, because of its institutional structure, reporting relationships, function, nature of work, and geography, relatively fewer 'measures' are necessary to ensure the non-disclosure of client confidences."[199] Still, where acceptable screening measures cannot be implemented, the Crown or public defender will have to refer the matter to outside counsel.[200]

3) Other Screening Contexts

Screening can be employed to address conflict issues in contexts other than the transfer of lawyers. As discussed in Section I(5), above in this chapter, some courts have allowed a screened lawyer from another firm, retained expressly for the purpose, to cross-examine a Crown witness formerly represented by counsel for the accused. It may also be possible to screen a lawyer who has received confidential information from a prospective client never taken on by a firm so as to enable other firm members to act against that individual in the same matter.[201]

O. WAIVER (CONSENT)

Canadian professional-conduct rules suggest that at least in some circumstances, a conflict of interest can be waived. In particular, the basic prohibition against counsel's acting where there is a conflict is typically

---

199 Sask r 2.04(19) (commentary) and 2.04(26) (commentary); BC, Man, Ont, NS, NL r 3.4-19, commentary 4 and 3.4-26, commentary 15; CBA Code ch V, commentaries 32(D) and 37. See also Alta r 2.04(8) (commentary). In October 2014 the FLSC Code was amended to address this topic in r 3.4-20, commentary 2. Most law society codes will probably make the same change.

200 This result is implicitly recognized by the commentaries mentioned in the preceding note.

201 See Alta r 2.04(4) (commentary). This possibility is supported by analogy to the rules governing former clients and firm screening: Alta r 2.04(5); Sask r 2.04(11); Man r 3.4-4B; BC, Ont, NS, NL r 3.4-11; CBA Code ch V, commentary 14.

said to apply "except as permitted under this Code,"[202] and a subsequent rule states that a lawyer must not represent a client where there is a conflict unless there is express or implied consent from all affected clients and unless the lawyer reasonably believes she can still properly represent the clients.[203]

Allowing a conflict to be "cured" by a waiver reflects the belief that a client should be permitted to accept a risk of material impairment of representation or loyalty.[204] After all, the client may reasonably conclude that the benefits from retaining the lawyer justify running such a risk.[205] Perhaps the best way of rationalizing waiver in the criminal context, however, is to say that a client's informed consent deserves some weight in assessing whether there is a realistic risk that a conflict will actually crystallize during the proceeding.

1) Effective Waiver: The Need for Informed Consent

A client who considers waiving a conflict concern in a criminal case usually has a constitutional right at stake. The accused whose current lawyer faces a potential conflict risks harm to his right to effective counsel.[206] The accused whose former lawyer is acting for a co-accused may face a possible breach of the *Charter* rights to a fair trial and to have solicitor-client communications remain confidential.[207] Even a witness who is not an accused will likely be able to assert a *Charter* right in the face of cross-examination by a current or former lawyer who acts for an accused.[208] In sum, whether the conflict problem concerns an accused or a witness, or a current as opposed to a former client, constitutional rights are potentially engaged.

---

202 Alta, Sask r 2.04(1); BC, NS, NL r 3.4-1; Ont r 3.4-1 (slightly different wording but to the same effect). See also Man r 3.4-2; NB ch 6, commentary 1; CBA Code ch V, r 1.

203 Sask r 2.04(2); BC, Man, Ont, NS, NL r 3.4-2. Similar are Alta r 2.04(1) (commentary); Man r 3.4-2; NB ch 6, commentary 1; CBA Code ch V, r 1.

204 See Ont r 3.4-2, commentary 0.1, nonetheless noting that actual material impairment cannot be waived.

205 See Sask r 2.04(2) (commentary); Man r 3.4-2, commentary 6; BC, Ont, NS, NL r 3.4-2, commentary 3. See also Alta r 2.04(3) (commentary).

206 See Section E, above in this chapter.

207 The latter right is discussed in Chapter 4, Section F.

208 Discussions as to how the *Charter* might apply in the third-party production context are of interest regarding this point: see, for example, *R v O'Connor* (1995), 103 CCC (3d) 1 at paras 17 and 110–19 (SCC); *R v Mills* (1999), 139 CCC (3d) 321 at paras 69–89 (SCC); *R v McClure*, 2001 SCC 14 at paras 2 and 17–25; *AM v Ryan* (1997), 143 DLR (4th) 1 at paras 19–23 and 30 (SCC).

There is no general prohibition against waiving a *Charter* guarantee,[209] and the possibility of a valid waiver regarding conflict of interest has been recognized.[210] As with the relinquishment of any important right, the standard for waiver in the conflict context is high, especially where one of the affected clients is an accused whose liberty is in jeopardy. In *R v Silvini*, the Ontario Court of Appeal thus emphasized the need for clear and unequivocal evidence "that the person is waiving the implicated right and is doing so with full knowledge of the purpose of the right and the effect of a waiver."[211] Canadian rules of professional conduct similarly stress the need for fully informed disclosure as a basis for waiver and typically state that consent to a conflict must be either express or implied.[212]

a) Express Consent: General Principles Set Out in the Codes

Most codes state that express consent must be fully informed and voluntary after disclosure.[213] They further provide that it must be either (1) in writing, signed by each person consenting, or (2) oral, provided that each person consenting receives a written communication recording the consent as soon as practicable.[214]

Many governing bodies define "disclosure" to mean full and fair disclosure of all information relevant to the person's decision in sufficient time for the person to make a genuine and independent decision, and the taking of reasonable steps to ensure understanding of the matters disclosed.[215] This definition applies in the conflicts context and

---

209 See *R v Turpin* (1989), 48 CCC (3d) 8 at 22–23 [paras 21–22] (SCC) [*Turpin*].

210 See *Silvini*, above note 21 at 261 [paras 20–21]; *Henry*, above note 169 at 471–74; *AS*, above note 119 at 669; *McCallen*, above note 24 at para 72; *Booth v Huxter* (1994), 16 OR (3d) 528 at 538–39 (Div Ct) [*Booth*]; *R v Brown*, [1996] OJ No 5320 at para 9 (Gen Div); *Amundson*, above note 92 at para 21; *Cadorette*, above note 24 at para 27. See also the rules cited at note 203, above in this chapter.

211 Above note 21 at 261 [para 21]. *Silvini* adopts the standard applied whenever an accused seeks to waive a procedural safeguard, including one that is constitutionally protected: see *Korponey v Canada (AG)* (1982), 65 CCC (2d) 65 at 74 (SCC). See also *Neil*, above note 1 at para 19(iii): lawyer has a duty to inform the client regarding matters relevant to conflict issues; *Strother*, above note 1 at para 1: consent to lawyer acting despite conflict problem must be based on disclosure.

212 Sask r 2.04(2); BC, Man, Ont, NS, NL r 3.4-2.

213 Alta definitions; Sask definitions and r 2.04(2); Man r 1.1-1; BC, Ont, NS, NL r 1.1-1 and 3.4-2.

214 Alta definitions; Sask definitions; BC, Man, Ont, NS, NL r 1.1-1.

215 Alta definitions; Sask definitions; BC, Man, NS, NL r 1.1-1. In October 2014 the FLSC Code was amended to move the definition of "disclosure" to r 3.4-2, commentary 2. Most law society codes will likely do the same in the months to come.

jibes with the approach taken in *Silvini*.[216] The fundamental importance of timely disclosure to the client is also supported by counsel's general duties of loyalty and candour to the client.

The ethical codes elaborate on the nature and importance of disclosure in the rules addressing conflict of interest. First, these rules stress that disclosure is an essential requirement to obtaining a client's consent.[217] Second, they state that where it is impossible to make adequate disclosure to a client because of a duty of confidentiality owed to another client, consent cannot be obtained, and the lawyer must decline to act.[218] Third, most governing bodies require that the lawyer inform the client of the relevant circumstances and the reasonably foreseeable ways the conflict could adversely affect the client's interests, including because of the lawyer's relations to the parties and any interest in or connection with the matter.[219] Finally, many codes contain special provisions relating to consent and disclosure in the context of multiple representation, which have already been reviewed above.[220]

b) Criminal Defence Counsel's Consultation with a Current Client

The information to be disclosed to the client will vary with the circumstances. But defence counsel must appreciate that, as a general rule, no client can make an informed decision regarding a conflict issue without a full and accurate explanation of the material risks of continued representation.[221] Matters that should be discussed with the client, where relevant, include the following:

1) *Importance of avoiding a conflict*: Counsel should define the notion of a conflict of interest for the client and explain why, in light of a lawyer's duties of loyalty and confidentiality, a conflict could have a negative impact on the quality of representation. The client should also understand that she has a constitutional right to a lawyer who has no conflict.

---

216 See the text associated with note 211, above in this chapter.
217 Alta r 2.04(1) (commentary); Sask r 2.04(2) (commentary); BC, Ont, NS, NL r 3.4-2, commentary 1. Also pertinent is FLSC Code r 3.4-1, commentary 9, added in October 2014, which states that the duty of candour requires a lawyer to advise an existing client of all matters relevant to the retainer. Most law societies will probably add this commentary to their codes as well.
218 Alta r 2.04(1) (commentary); Sask r 2.04(2) (commentary); BC, Ont, NS, NL r 3.4-2, commentary 1. See also *McKercher*, above note 3 at para 47.
219 Sask r 2.04(2) (commentary); Man r 3.4-1, commentary 5; BC, Ont, NS, NL r 3.4-2, commentary 2. Similar is Alta r 2.04(1) (commentary).
220 Section H(2), above in this chapter.
221 See *Brissett*, above note 19 at para 60.

2) *Manner in which a conflict may arise*: The discussion should be wide-ranging, covering tactics and strategies at all stages of the retainer and how the conflict may affect or even foreclose certain options. Counsel should raise any conflict scenario that realistically may arise on the facts of the case and provide concrete examples to help the client's understanding. Counsel must also take care to inform himself as to the client's circumstances to ensure an accurate and realistic review of the possible conflict scenarios.

3) *Impact on confidentiality and privilege*: Counsel must take special care to explain how the ethical duty of confidentiality and the substantive rule of privilege might operate. For example, two co-accused represented by a single counsel must be told clearly that no confidentiality can exist as between them but that confidentiality and privilege generally exist in full force against the outside world.[222]

4) *Office sharing*: If a conflict problem involves an office-sharing arrangement, all pertinent facts concerning the office set up must be disclosed.[223]

5) *Conflict could hurt client in ways unrelated to quality of representation*: A client should be told of the financial cost, delay, and any other harm that may occur if a conflict, though presently contingent, crystallizes later in proceedings.

6) *Possibility that currently resolvable conflict will later become fatal*: The risk of a material and adverse effect on the client's representation though presently "non-fatal" because of the client's informed consent may in the future crystallize so as to make the representation impossible on any terms, and the client should be advised of this possibility.

7) *Conflict involving another client*: If the conflict involves another client, it is important to canvass the nature of the relationship with that other client, including the length, number, and type of retainers.[224] Further, a client should be told of any possibility that, in the future, the conflict may develop so that counsel continues to act only for the other client.[225]

8) *Advantages of continuing with retainer*: The client must be told of any potential advantages that come with keeping present counsel. The

---

222 See the rules and text associated with note 73, above in this chapter.
223 See Section N(1), above in this chapter.
224 See the rules and text associated with note 75, above in this chapter, regarding joint retainers.
225 See, for example, the rules and text associated with note 73, above in this chapter, regarding joint retainers.

closeness and comfort of an existing relationship, counsel's familiarity with the client's case or circumstances, financial savings, special expertise held by the lawyer or the lawyer's firm, avoiding any delay, and where co-accused are involved presenting a unified front to the trier of fact may all be implicated.[226] In this regard, the client should be told of her constitutional right to counsel of choice.

9) *Independent legal advice*: Counsel should explain the role and importance of independent legal advice, even where the client appears uninterested in obtaining an opinion from an independent lawyer. The importance of independent legal advice in avoiding conflict problems is discussed in Section O(1)(d), below in this chapter.

Where after receiving full disclosure the client decides to continue the retainer, consent must be obtained from or promptly confirmed with the client in writing.[227] Prudent counsel will use a consent specific to the client, detailing the nature of the disclosure and advice given. If independent legal advice has been provided, counsel should obtain a copy of the client's written consent from the lawyer who did so.

c) Criminal Defence Counsel's Consultation with a Former Client

Where the conflict affects a former client, counsel may wish to approach him to obtain consent to act for the current client. If the former client has counsel in the matter, contact should be made through that lawyer.[228] The former client should be informed of the implications of the current representation, the fact that the lawyer possesses confidential information regarding the former client, any measures that have been or will be taken to guard against misuse of such information, and the former client's right to refuse consent.

In dealing with a conflict involving a former client, counsel must be careful not to disclose confidential information while informing the current and former clients of the problem. The affected clients may consent to a limited relaxation of the duty of confidentiality for the purpose of explaining the conflict issue. In other cases, it may be possible to make adequate disclosure absent a partial waiver of confidentiality. However, a lack of consent could conceivably make any disclosure of confidential information impossible, thus foreclosing the possibility of obtaining consent to continued representation.[229]

---

226 See also the paragraphs associated with notes 66–70, above in this chapter.
227 See the rules cited at note 214, above in this chapter.
228 See Chapter 8, Section C(1).
229 See the rules and text associated with note 218, above in this chapter.

d) Independent Legal Advice

The value of independent legal advice lies in the fact that the client obtains an opinion from a lawyer whose loyalties are not at all suspect and who has no interest in whether the retainer continues. Independent legal advice is not necessarily required to validate a client's waiver of a conflict issue.[230] But it certainly helps to ensure that the client understands the issue and comes to an informed view as to her position. Unless conflict concerns can fairly be described as trifling, prudent counsel will thus encourage a client to obtain independent legal advice and in some circumstances will absolutely insist.[231] This is especially so given that most criminal clients are in a vulnerable position.

There is nothing improper in counsel recommending a particular lawyer to the client for the purpose of obtaining independent legal advice.[232] But the lawyer who is recommended cannot suffer from the same conflict, as would a partner or associate in the same firm.[233] Nor should counsel attempt to streamline matters by personally obtaining independent legal advice, to be passed on to the client. Acting as a conduit could render the advice useless, given that the opinion would be filtered through the lawyer who may have a conflict. Finally, the current or former clients whose legal interests are potentially impacted should not be referred to the same lawyer for independent legal advice. To do so risks replicating the conflict problem and fatally undermining the advice, for the individuals may have adverse interests as to how the conflict should be handled.

Counsel who provides independent legal advice must take the retainer seriously and not perfunctorily discharge the duty. This is a client-lawyer relationship with all the attendant responsibilities, including

---

230 See, for example, the rules pertaining to joint retainers and independent legal advice, discussed in the text associated with note 74, above in this chapter. See also Alta r 2.04(1) (commentary). In October 2014 the FLSC Code's conflict rule regarding consent was amended to add commentary 2A. This new commentary states that in some cases, independent legal advice should be recommended to ensure the client's consent is informed, genuine, and uncoerced, especially if the client is vulnerable or disadvantaged. Most law socieities will probably amend their codes to add this commentary as well.

231 See *Neil*, above note 1 at para 29, which expresses a preference for independent legal advice where a client is being asked to consent to a conflict. A lack of independent legal advice may militate against allowing counsel to remain on the record: see, for example, *Buhr*, above note 161 at para 8; *Brissett*, above note 19 at para 77; *Robillard*, above note 6 at 27–28.

232 See *MQ*, above note 22 at para 49.

233 Compare *Buhr*, above note 161 at para 8: counsel not independent, because acting for both the client and the firm subject to application to disqualify.

strong duties of loyalty and competence. The provision of independent legal advice "is an undertaking to be taken seriously and not lightly assumed or perfunctorily discharged."[234] Sometimes the client's trial counsel, often the one who has referred him for independent legal advice, believes the purpose of independent legal advice is to facilitate a waiver. This view is manifestly wrong.

It follows that counsel providing independent legal advice on a conflict issue must become fully informed of all relevant facts and provide carefully considered advice to the client. A two-minute conversation with trial counsel for the affected client for the purpose of getting background information will rarely if ever be sufficient. Reviewing the synopsis or report prepared for the Crown by police is usually a minimum requirement, but it may be necessary to read other parts of the disclosure materials as well.[235] Absent exceptional circumstances, counsel should personally meet with the client, without original counsel or the other affected individuals being present, and render or confirm the opinion in writing.

e) Implied Consent

The ethical codes recognize that a client's consent to a conflict may be implied or inferred.[236] So do the courts.[237] The concept of implied consent will be unfamiliar to many criminal lawyers. It appears intended to soften the impact of *Neil*'s bright-line rule against a lawyer concurrently acting for clients whose immediate legal interests are directly adverse in unrelated matters.[238] In any event, consent will be inferred only in exceptional circumstances.[239] The professional-conduct rules thus limit implied consent to situations where

1) the client is a government, financial institution, publicly traded or similarly substantial entity, or an entity with in-house counsel;
2) the matters are unrelated;
3) the lawyer has no relevant confidential information from one client that might reasonably affect the other; and

---

234 CBA Code ch III, commentary 12; Man r 3.2-2A, commentary 4.
235 Counsel providing independent legal advice appeared to receive inadequate disclosure in *Con-Drain*, above note 43 at paras 57–62; *Stewart*, above note 52 at paras 17–19.
236 See note 212, above in this chapter, and the associated text.
237 See *Neil*, above note 1 at para 28. See also *Strother*, above note 1 at para 37.
238 This explanation is provided in Alta r 2.04(1) (commentary).
239 See *Neil*, above note 1 at para 28.

4) the client has commonly consented to lawyers' acting for and against it in unrelated matters.[240]

These conditions will almost never be satisfied in a case involving criminal clients. In the vast majority of criminal matters, consent to act in the face of a conflict issue must therefore be express and memorialized in writing.

Example: Private counsel whose practice is largely devoted to defence work is retained by the attorney general to prosecute a case. Counsel represents many clients on unrelated matters who are currently being prosecuted by the Crown. The attorney general's consent to counsel's prosecuting this file despite the bright-line rule can be implied because the preconditions set out in the ethical codes and caselaw are met.[241]

2) Instances Where Waiver Cannot Overcome the Conflict Problem

A fully informed waiver by all affected parties will not always provide a complete answer to a conflict problem.

a) Counsel Reasonably Believes Representation Will Be Adversely Affected

If counsel is reasonably of the view that acting in the case will have a material adverse impact on the representation or duty of loyalty owed to all affected clients, the retainer cannot be accepted or if already accepted must be terminated.[242] A lawyer who legitimately feels unable to adhere to the duties owed to a client can never act, not even where the client has provided fully informed consent, because to do so would breach ethical obligations fundamental to the client-lawyer relationship.[243]

---

240 Sask r 2.04(2)(b); Man r 3.4-3, commentary 1; BC, Ont, NS, NL r 3.4-2(b). To similar effect, see Alta r 2.04(1) (commentary).

241 This example is given in *Neil*, above note 1 at para 28.

242 See *Neil*, *ibid* at para 29; Sask r 2.04(2); Man r 3.4-3, commentary 1; BC, Ont, NS, NL r 3.4-2. See also Alta r 2.04(3)(b) and commentary (in the context of multiple retainers); Man r 3.4-3, commentary 1 (in the context of acting for current clients whose interests are directly adverse).

243 See Chapter 3, Section J.

b) Society's Interest in a Conflict-Free Proceeding Overrides the Waiver

Society has an interest, altogether apart from that of an accused, or anyone else, in promoting the administration of justice by avoiding conflict of interest. Canadian rules of professional conduct thus make clear that consent will not solve every conflict-of-interest problem.[244] This is especially so where the reliability of a criminal verdict may be threatened.[245] The informed consent of all affected clients to a lawyer's continuing with a case will therefore not necessarily satisfy the societal interest in avoiding conflicts. To put it another way, an accused does not have a right to a trial that will be unfair by virtue of her counsel's fatal conflict of interest.[246]

Society's interest may override an informed consent even when the conflict has not crystallized to the point where there is actual adversity between the competing interests. The risk of adversity occurring during the trial, with all the attendant harm to the justice system, may simply be too high to countenance. Accordingly, even where all interested individuals have provided informed waivers, a lawyer will be disqualified from acting in a criminal matter where necessary to prevent an unacceptable risk of harm to the justice system as a whole.[247]

3) Possible Revocation of the Waiver

An accused may be willing to waive conflict concerns based on expected and explained contingencies but not where an unexpected conflict scenario develops. A cautious accused may thus phrase a waiver to allow for revocation in certain circumstances. Similarly, a court may be loath to interpret a waiver as extending to an unanticipated crystallization of a conflict.[248]

---

244 For instance, counsel cannot act on a joint retainer where a conflict develops that cannot be resolved: Alta r 2.04(3)(d); Sask r 2.04(5)(c); BC, Man, Ont, NS, NL r 3.4-5(c).

245 See *Côté*, above note 21 at para 11; *Robillard*, above note 6 at 26.

246 See also Section F(4), above in this chapter.

247 See *Robillard*, above note 6 at 27–28; *McCallen*, above note 24 at para 72; *Booth*, above note 210 at 538–39; *MQ*, above note 22 at paras 33 and 37; *LK*, above note 40 at paras 20–21; *Quiriconi*, above note 40 at paras 21–26; *Sandhu*, above note 24 at paras 111–14; *Cocks*, above note 40 at para 10(17); *Aitken*, above note 40 at paras 46–47; *Whitebear*, above note 68 at para 113; *Caines*, above note 40 at paras 340–43; *Lall*, above note 57 at paras 50–54 and 66; *Ta*, above note 40 at para 31(6); *Con-Drain*, above note 43 at paras 65–69; *Brown 1998*, above note 40 at para 25; *R v Martin* (1989), 86 Nfld & PEIR 246 at paras 6–8 (Nfld SCTD).

248 See *Chiefs of Ontario v Ontario* (2003), 63 OR (3d) 335 at paras 47–97 (SCJ).

Even where a waiver purports to be irrevocable, it is hard to envisage a court's rejecting a revocation attempt by an accused who subsequently faces a serious crystallized conflict.[249] To do so would be to force a reluctant accused to proceed with ineffective counsel, with potentially catastrophic consequences for the integrity of the administration of justice. The accused's revocation should therefore be accepted in such a case. However, a court may be more inclined to reject a revocation attempt made by a Crown witness, given that he does not risk conviction as a result of the conflict.[250]

P. CONFLICT OF INTEREST INVOLVING CROWN COUNSEL

The great majority of conflict cases involve defence counsel. But conflict problems can bedevil prosecutors too.[251] For example, a defence lawyer will sometimes move to a Crown law office, leading to a conflict problem when she then acts against a former client.[252] The same issue may arise where a private sector lawyer is retained *ad hoc* to prosecute a particular matter. It is also possible, albeit rarer, for a conflict to arise because of a lawyer's moving to the defence bar after practising as a prosecutor or in-house counsel for a police service.[253]

The basic principles that apply to defence counsel, or any other lawyer for that matter, should also govern whether a prosecutor need be disqualified for reasons of conflict of interest. We do not support the notion that because Crown prosecutors have a duty to act fairly in

---

249 See *Cocks*, above note 40 at paras 34 and 39–43; *Lewis*, above note 40 at para 16; *Miller*, above note 92 at para 6; *Lall*, above note 57 at paras 53–56 and 66; *Brown* 1998, above note 40 at paras 15 and 25.

250 See *Bouchard*, above note 121 at para 32: court gives weight to waiver by Crown witness despite subsequent attempt at revocation. See also the comments in *Parsons* NLCA, above note 42 at 143, regarding the witness's waiver.

251 See Deborah MacNair, *Conflicts of Interest: Principles for the Legal Profession* (Aurora, ON: Canada Law Book, 2005) (loose-leaf 2013 supplement) at § 5:40; Deborah MacNair, "Crown Prosecutors and Conflict of Interest" (2002) 7 Can Crim L Rev 257.

252 See *Joyal*, above note 122; *R v Dobrotic* (1995), 162 NBR (2d) 379 (CA); *R v Covington*, [1999] OJ No 217 (CA); *R v Foster* (1997), 90 BCAC 243 (CA) [*Foster*]; *Johnson*, above note 121; *R v Stokes*, [1999] NSJ No 170 (SC) [*Stokes*]; *R v Zwicker* (1995), 169 NBR (2d) 350 (CA); *R v Lindskog* (1997), 117 CCC (3d) 551 (Sask QB) [*Lindskog*]; *Henderson*, above note 48 at paras 84–106; *R v Standingwater*, 2007 SKQB 484 [*Standingwater*].

253 See *Sandhu*, above note 24.

the public interest, they are somehow better able to resist the pull of conflicting interests or should otherwise be subject to a less rigorous conflicts test.[254]

Some of the cases involving a lawyer's transfer to or from a Crown law office focus on whether the conflict problem should be imputed to the transferring lawyer's new office colleagues. Whether imputation is justified will depend on the adequacy of screening measures.[255] A somewhat analogous imputation issue arises where an accused has allegedly threatened a Crown counsel, and evidence of the threat is to be led at a trial conducted by a lawyer from the same prosecution service.[256]

The potential for conflict can also arise where a prosecutor works on a case in which the accused is a police officer, judge, defence counsel, or government employee or representative.[257] Where a police officer is the accused, a risk of divided loyalties may flow from the close working relationship between Crown and police in the criminal justice system, a relationship that can exist at both the personal and the institutional levels.[258] The issue will be whether this ongoing relationship creates an unacceptable risk that Crown counsel handling the matter will show favouritism towards the accused officer, whether intentionally or not. The risk will be unacceptable if it would cause a reasonable and informed person to lose confidence in the criminal justice system. But a mere possibility of harm is not enough to justify intervention — there must be a realistic risk that injury will occur.

---

254 We agree with the view taken in *Stokes*, above note 252 at paras 6–8.

255 See the discussion in Section N(2), above in this chapter. See also *Henderson*, above note 48 at paras 97–106; *Standingwater*, above note 252 at paras 1(b), 1(c), and 37; *R v Le*, 2001 ABQB 195 at paras 2 and 50–53; *R v DPF* (2000), 193 Nfld & PEIR 68 (SCTD); *Joyal*, above note 122; *Stokes*, above note 252.

256 See *R v Hundert*, 2010 ONSC 6759 at paras 8 and 25–32; *R v Atatise*, 2011 MBQB 82 at paras 40–46.

257 See Bruce MacFarlane, "Sunlight and Disinfectants: Prosecutorial Accountability and Independence through Public Transparency" (2001) 45 Crim LQ 272 at 273; *R v Figueroa* (2003), 176 CCC (3d) 63 at para 18 (Ont CA). See also *Public Prosecution Service of Canada Deskbook* (Ottawa: PPSC, 2014) ch 2.2, section 3: prohibition against participating in prosecution involving anyone in respect of whom there is an objectively reasonable perception of conflict.

258 See the comments in *R v Thiessen*, 2002 MBQB 149 at para 25, aff'd 2003 MBCA 121, leave to appeal to SCC refused, [2003] SCCA No 460.

Q. DUTY TO ADDRESS A CONFLICT ISSUE IN A TIMELY WAY

A conflict of interest can cause substantial harm to one or more affected clients. Defence counsel who permits a conflict to develop unchecked may also suffer. He may be removed from the record, forced to return fees paid or forgo compensation for work already done, exposed to disciplinary proceedings, or faced with a civil lawsuit by a disaffected client. Tardiness in addressing a conflict issue can also redound to the significant detriment of the administration of justice. The case may be delayed in getting to trial, or if the trial has already commenced, a mistrial may be required. Another possibility is that a conviction is overturned on appeal, and a new trial ordered.

It is therefore no surprise that the caselaw and ethical codes recognize that lawyers have a duty to avoid conflicts of interest.[259] The jurisprudence further holds that defence and Crown counsel alike have a duty to address conflict issues *in a timely way*.[260] And these obligations are ongoing, meaning that counsel must look out for conflict problems and take timely remedial steps where necessary, throughout the proceeding, as new information is received and as the complexion of the case changes.[261]

Because of the serious impact that a conflict of interest can have on legal representation and given the lawyer's obligations to protect and foster public respect for the administration of justice, any counsel who has a client involved in a matter is completely justified in drawing the attention of the presiding judge to a non-frivolous conflict problem.

---

259 *Neil*, above note 1 at para 19(i); *McKercher*, above note 3 at para 19; Alta, Sask r 2.04(1) (commentary); Man r 3.4-2, commentary 4; BC, Ont, NS, NL r 3.4-1, commentary 2. In October 2014 the FLSC Code was amended to make this point in r 3.4-1, commentaries 1, 5, and 10. It is probable that most law societies will adopt these same amendments.

260 *Neil*, above note 1 at para 38; *Brissett*, above note 19 at para 23; *Whitebear*, above note 68 at paras 107 and 120–23; *Caines*, above note 40 at paras 348–60; *Lewis*, above note 40 at para 6; *R v Fleetham*, 2009 BCCA 379 at para 63; *R v Poole*, 2008 BCSC 543 at para 28; *Con-Drain*, above note 43 at para 22; *R v Kajak*, 2004 ONCJ 311 at paras 15–21.

261 See *Whitebear*, above note 68 at para 122. See also the rules cited at note 259, above in this chapter.

1) Defence Counsel

Defence counsel must take proactive steps to deal with a conflict issue and should not leave the matter for the court or Crown counsel to raise.[262] This is especially so because she is usually in the best position to know whether a real potential for conflict exists. Indeed, defence counsel is sometimes the only one who is aware of the issue.[263] Counsel with a potential conflict problem thus has a duty to address the issue promptly, most definitely with all affected clients, and frequently also with Crown counsel or the court. Responsible counsel who wants to be sure that a potential conflict is not of a disqualifying nature may, for example, wish to inform the court of the circumstances and any steps taken to resolve concerns.[264]

It may be preferable for defence counsel not to argue an application opposing his removal and instead for the client to retain separate counsel for the purpose. Bringing in an outside lawyer avoids the difficulties that can arise if counsel is required to defend his own actions or submit an affidavit in support of the client's position and also ensures that the client obtains independent legal advice.[265]

2) Crown Counsel

Crown counsel who becomes aware of a conflict problem should raise the matter with the defence counsel who is so affected.[266] A prosecutor faced with the multiple or successive representation of co-accused should always do so, even if the potential for fatal conflict is not readily apparent. Given that confidential information or defence strategies to which Crown counsel is not privy almost certainly bear on the likelihood of serious conflict, insisting on a clear and unequivocal waiver from all affected accused is the safest course.[267] In some cases, for example those involving prosecution witnesses with long criminal records, Crown counsel may wish to have inquiries made of the witness

---

262 See the authorities cited at notes 258–59, above in this chapter, plus the extensive and trenchant criticism of a firm's systemic failure to properly handle conflict issues in *Brown* 2011, above note 92 at paras 59–66 and 78–81.

263 See *Whitebear*, above note 68 at para 139.

264 See *Werkman*, above note 128 at para 6: defence appears to have raised issue with court and then argued against disqualification.

265 See *Chen*, above note 86 at para 69.

266 Implicit support for this point is derived from the authorities cited at notes 259–60, above in this chapter. For a particularly persistent approach in this regard, see *Brown* 2011, above note 92 at paras 10 and 62.

267 See, for example, *Aitken*, above note 40 at paras 21–24.

whether a client-lawyer relationship exists or existed with counsel for the accused.

Where defence counsel fails or is unable to address a conflict concern adequately, the prosecutor should apply to the court for directions or to remove counsel from the record.[268] Responsible Crown counsel may wish to raise the matter with the court regardless to ensure that any waivers are put on the record and to provide the court with the opportunity to make any inquiries thought necessary in the circumstances.

If the Crown concludes that defence counsel should be disqualified, the objection should be made and any application brought at "the earliest practicable stage."[269] But Crown counsel must never use a conflict application as a tactical tool to harry the defence. To do so would be unprofessional, constitute an illegitimate attack on the accused's right to choice of counsel, and undermine public confidence in the justice system.[270]

3) Ability of Judge to Raise the Conflict-of-Interest Issue

A trial judge can raise a conflict-of-interest issue of her own accord, based on the court's inherent jurisdiction to prevent harm to the administration of justice.[271] In some instances, the judge may have a positive obligation to inquire into the possibility of a conflict, for instance where a single counsel appears for two or more jointly charged accused.[272] Given the risks associated with joint representation and the ease with which an inquiry can be made, placing this duty on the judge does not seem onerous.

The court also has an obligation to inquire sufficiently into the propriety of counsel's continuing to act once a conflict issue has been

---

268 See *Edkins*, above note 40 at para 7.
269 See the authorities cited at note 260, above in this chapter, plus *Chen*, above note 86 at paras 22–23; *R v Bilmez* (1995), 101 CCC (3d) 123 at 124 [para 5] (Ont CA) [*Bilmez*]; *Edkins*, above note 40 at para 7; *Ta*, above note 40 at paras 31(1) and 35; *Bogiatzis*, above note 40 at paras 28–29; *Cocks*, above note 40 at para 10(5).
270 See *Neil*, above note 1 at para 14; *Strother*, above note 1 at para 36; *Whitebear*, above note 68 at para 124; *Aitken*, above note 40 at para 31.
271 See the cases cited at note 19, above in this chapter, plus *Caines*, above note 40 at para 294.
272 See *WW*, above note 21 at 236, n 5 [para 27, n 7]; *Robillard*, above note 6 at 26; *Henry*, above note 169 at 473; *Caines*, above note 40 at paras 344–45 and 360; *Badali*, above note 87 at para 8. See also *Leduc*, above note 164 at para 135: trial judge should raise advocate-witness rule with a lawyer who is asserting contested facts from the counsel table.

raised. Simply accepting the assurance of counsel that no conflict exists does not necessarily satisfy this obligation.[273]

4) Conflict Issue Can Be Raised with the Court at Any Time

A conflict problem can be raised with the court at any point during the life of a criminal matter. This includes during[274] and even before[275] the preliminary inquiry. The conflict issue need not, and usually should not, be reserved for consideration by the trial judge, as opposed to any judge of the court then having jurisdiction over the matter, because the propriety of counsel's continuing to act should be resolved propitiously so as to avoid delay and wasted resources.[276]

R. THE TEST FOR CONFLICT OF INTEREST FOLLOWING CONVICTION

The issue of conflict is sometimes raised for the first time at a postconviction appeal,[277] usually as part of a claim that the appellant's right to effective counsel was infringed at trial. In such a case, the appellant will presumably argue that he could not be expected to have raised the issue at trial, given the nature of the allegation that counsel was ineffective because of an alleged conflict.[278] However, where the alleged conflict does not involve the appellant's trial counsel — for instance, where the complaint concerns counsel for the Crown or a co-accused, who formerly represented the appellant — failure to raise the matter at trial, while not fatal, may be detrimental to the argument.[279]

---

273 See *Bilmez*, above note 269 at 123–24 [para 4]; *Chen*, above note 86 at para 25; *Desmond*, above note 40 at para 4; *McCall*, above note 40 at para 28; *Aitken*, above note 40 at para 29; *Robinson*, above note 162 at para 8.

274 See *Robillard*, above note 6 at 26; *R v Greenwood*, [1995] OJ No 387 at para 6 (Gen Div); *Pyszniak*, above note 159 at paras 12–28; *R v Anderson*, 2003 MBQB 92 at para 20; *Zarelli*, above note 92 at para 10; *Amundson*, above note 92 at para 11.

275 See, for example, *Aitken*, above note 40; *Sandhu*, above note 24.

276 See *R v Kerzner* (1991), 3 OR (3d) 272 at 273 [para 3] (CA).

277 Regarding the ability to challenge an order disqualifying counsel before the conclusion of trial, see David Layton, "The Pre-trial Removal of Counsel for Conflict of Interest: Appealability and Remedies on Appeal" (1999) 4 Can Crim L Rev 25.

278 See *Silvini*, above note 21 at 261 [para 20].

279 See, for example, *Joyal*, above note 122 at 239–40; *Foster*, above note 252 at paras 4–7. See also the comments made in *Lindskog*, above note 252 at 561 [para 21].

When an appellant seeks to overturn a conviction on the ground of an alleged conflict at trial, the standard applied by the appeal court differs from that utilized by a trial judge. In *R v WW*, Doherty JA noted that, in contrast to the trial judge,

> [t]he appellate court looks backward at the completed trial. The court has the full trial record and may have further material detailing the circumstances surrounding the joint representation and the effects of that representation on counsel's ability to defend the appellant. Unlike the trial court, the appellate court is not concerned with pro-phylactic measures intended to avoid the potential injustice which may flow from compromised representation. Instead, the appellate court must determine whether counsel's representation was in fact compromised in such a way as to result in a miscarriage of justice. The concern on appeal must be with what happened and not with what might have happened. It makes no more sense to find ineffect-ive representation based on the possibility of a conflict-of-interest, than it does to find ineffective representation based on the mere pos-sibility of incompetent representation.[280]

Given the discrete perspectives and roles of trial judge and appeal court, Doherty JA concluded that the appellant alleging denial of effect-ive counsel because of a conflict at trial must demonstrate (1) an actual conflict of interest between the respective interests represented by trial counsel and (2) as a result of a conflict, some impairment of counsel's ability to represent effectively the interests of the appellant.[281] This test has been adopted in many other cases.[282]

An actual conflict of interest exists where a course of conduct fa-vouring a lawyer's personal interests or dictated by duties owed another client or a third person would, if followed, be inconsistent with the best interests of the accused.[283] It is thus necessary that the appellant point

---

280 Above note 21 at 239 [para 34]. To similar effect, see *Neil*, above note 1 at para 38; *MQ*, above note 22 at para 34.

281 *WW*, above note 21 at 237 and 239 [paras 27 and 36].

282 *Graff*, above note 68 at 90; *R v Phalen* (1997), 160 NSR (2d) 371 at paras 21–23 (CA); *R v Barbeau* (1996), 110 CCC (3d) 69 at 80 [paras 35–36] (Que CA); *R v Dean* (1997), 95 BCAC 278 at para 76 (CA); *R v Samra* (1998), 129 CCC (3d) 144 at para 36 (Ont CA); *Neil*, above note 1 at paras 38–39; *MQ*, above note 22 at para 52; *Piersanti*, above note 92 at para 5; *Kim*, above note 21 at para 26; *R v Sherif*, 2012 ABCA 35 at paras 13–17; *R v Walsh*, 2014 BCCA 326 at para 45.

283 See *WW*, above note 21 at 239 [para 37] (speaking in the context of joint repre-sentation).

to a specific instance at trial where her interests diverged from those said to be in conflict, requiring counsel to choose between interests.[284]

As for the second precondition — some impairment of counsel's ability to represent effectively the appellant's interests — it is enough that the appellant point to a single instance where when faced with an actual conflict of interest, counsel chose the course of action detrimental to the interest of the appellant.[285] There is no need to show prejudice in terms of adverse impact on the verdict, because impaired performance flowing from an actual conflict is a miscarriage of justice and so cannot be cured by the proviso in section 686(1)(b)(iii) of the *Criminal Code*.[286]

---

284 See *ibid* at 240 [para 38].
285 See *ibid* at 240–41 [paras 41–42].
286 See *ibid* at 237 and 240–41 [paras 28 and 41–42]; *Neil*, above note 1 at para 39. Section 686(1)(b)(iii) of the *Criminal Code*, above note 152, allows an appeal court to dismiss an appeal notwithstanding an error of law where it is of the opinion that no substantial wrong or miscarriage of justice has occurred.

CHAPTER 7

CLIENT PERJURY

A. INTRODUCTION

What should a defence lawyer do on learning that a client intends to give false testimony or has already lied on the stand? The proper response to anticipated or completed client perjury is a hotly debated issue in criminal law ethics. Almost every commentator who addresses the ethical aspects of criminal law practice devotes special attention to the thorny problem of client perjury. The topic has become a paradigmatic scenario for examining defence counsel's sometimes conflicting duties, on the one hand of loyalty to the client and on the other to maintain the integrity of the truth-seeking function of the criminal justice system. The impact of the perjury issue on broader questions of ethics has been substantial, as have been the repercussions for those who take challenging positions. In the United States, a provocative conference address on the topic by Professor Monroe Freedman in 1966 led several appellate court judges, including soon-to-be-Chief-Justice-of-the-Supreme-Court Warren Burger, to seek Freedman's disbarment and academic dismissal.[1] Freedman's controversial writings on client perjury constituted an important impetus for the American Bar Association

---

1   The judges' attempt was fortunately unsuccessful: see Monroe Freedman, "Getting Honest about Client Perjury" (2008) 21 Geo J Leg Ethics 133 at 133–34 and 136–39.

to launch a reconsideration of its model code and eventually, in 1983, to adopt the replacement model rules.[2]

The client-perjury problem can often be seen as a particular instance of defence counsel's difficulty in representing the client who is irresistibly known to be guilty.[3] This is because the perjury issue will frequently arise where the client admits guilt but nonetheless insists on testifying falsely at trial in the hope of securing an acquittal. Yet the spectre of client perjury can loom even where counsel is in no position to conclude that the client is guilty. The client may contend that false testimony is crucial to bolster an otherwise valid defence.[4] The issue of client perjury is also discrete because it implicates the accused's constitutional right to testify on his own behalf. Ultimately, the unique and labyrinthine range of possible responses to anticipated or completed client perjury warrants an in-depth examination of the topic.

B. COMPETING PRINCIPLES

The principles bearing on the resolution of any client-perjury problem are by now largely familiar. Defence counsel owes the client a duty of loyalty, which includes obligations to keep secret all confidential information and to act as a competent and resolute advocate for the client's cause. A lawyer faced with anticipated or completed client perjury quickly recognizes the pull of the duty of loyalty. A response that explicitly or implicitly reveals the planned or already executed falsehood by definition serves to expose client secrets and, in many instances, to undermine the client's defence. Loyalty militates against rushing into action that will harm the client.

There are also closely associated constitutional principles that prevent counsel from improperly interfering with the client's defence. If defence counsel acts unreasonably to cause unfairness at the trial or compromise the reliability of the verdict, the right to the effective assistance of counsel is infringed.[5] The unjustified release of information

---

2   See John M Burkoff, *Criminal Defense Ethics 2d: Law and Liability*, 2008–9 ed (St Paul, MN: Thomson Reuters/West, 2008) at § 5:16 [199–200].

3   See Chapter 1.

4   See, for example, *Nix v Whiteside*, 475 US 157 (1986) [Nix], in which the accused told counsel that he believed the victim had been carrying a gun and insisted that he had killed in self-defence. The accused wanted to help along this defence by falsely testifying that he had seen a flash of metal in the victim's hand.

5   See Chapter 3, Section K(1). For instance, inadequate advice regarding the right to testify may lead to this result: *R v Ross*, 2012 NSCA 56 at paras 40–57; *R v*

received from the client by counsel may also violate the client's constitutional right to the protection of solicitor-client privilege, and perhaps too the principle against self-incrimination.[6] Furthermore, counsel must be cognizant of the client's constitutional rights to control the conduct of the defence,[7] to call evidence in defending against the charge,[8] and in particular to testify in his own defence.[9] In sum, interventions that keep the client from the stand or otherwise impede his free choice to testify risk undermining fundamental principles of justice to the client's severe detriment and attracting censure from the courts.

The power of these constitutional principles is undeniable, shaping every client-lawyer relationship and counsel's attendant ethical obligations. Yet a lawyer's allegiance to the client's cause is not without limits, and the same can be said for an accused's constitutional rights. A central objective of the adversarial criminal justice system is the search for truth. Granted, the principle against self-incrimination serves to temper the system's truth-finding function. But this principle operates to require only that the Crown prove its case without any compulsion of the accused and does not encompass the right to fabricate evidence in a criminal proceeding. It is also questionable whether the right of an accused to testify includes a licence to knowingly present false testimony.[10]

This is not to say that a court would refuse to allow an accused to testify on the basis that her proposed testimony was false. It is the lawyer's knowing involvement in assisting the client to commit perjury that is unacceptable. Doing so almost certainly makes counsel a party to the criminal offences of perjury and attempting to obstruct justice,[11] and represents unacceptable complicity in an attempt to subvert the truth-finding process. The prohibition against counsel knowingly misleading the court represents a justifiable limit on the duty of loyalty to the client[12] and concomitantly imposes restrictions on those constitutional rights that relate to the client's legal representation, such as the

---

Qiu, 2010 ONCA 736 at para 9 [Qiu]; R v Moore, 2002 SKCA 30 at paras 48–55 (Sask CA) [Moore].

6   See Chapter 4, Section F.

7   See R v Swain (1991), 63 CCC (3d) 481 at 505–7 [paras 33–36] (SCC) [Swain].

8   See R v Seaboyer (1991), 66 CCC (3d) 321 at 389 [para 34] (SCC); R v Murphy, 2012 ONCA 573 at paras 16–25; R v Bishop, 2013 NUCA 3 at para 51.

9   See R v Brigham (1992), 79 CCC (3d) 365 at 380–83 and 390–91 (Que CA) [Brigham]; R v Smith (1997), 120 CCC (3d) 500 at paras 14–15 and 26 (Ont CA); R v Dunbar, 2003 BCCA 667 at para 126, leave to appeal to SCC refused, [2004] SCCA No 30; Qiu, above note 5 at para 15.

10   See Section F(4)(b), below in this chapter.

11   Criminal Code, RSC 1985, c C-46, ss 131 and 139 respectively.

12   See Chapter 1, Section E.

rights to counsel, to counsel of choice, and to the effective assistance of counsel.[13]

The question becomes, how can the profession's ethical standards best accommodate the competing principles of loyalty to the client and solicitude to the truth-finding function of the criminal justice system? If there are instances where the principles clash, which, as we shall see, is certainly the case when it comes to client perjury, which interest must give way, and how? The answers to these questions are far from easy, but the rules of professional conduct provide a decent starting point for any lawyer seeking to resolve a client-perjury problem.

C. RELATED RULES OF PROFESSIONAL CONDUCT

The ethical standards promulgated by Canadian governing bodies do not include provisions that address the issue of client perjury in all its complexity. Yet the general guidelines relating to "The Lawyer as Advocate" found in most ethical codes are highly relevant because they include direction and prohibitions concerning misleading the court. We have discussed some of these guidelines already, in the context of the defence of the client known to be guilty.[14] The main interdictions against misleading the court bear repeating at this juncture, as do the commentaries pertaining to remedial measures and withdrawal:

Advocacy
- When acting as an advocate, a lawyer must represent the client resolutely and honourably within the limits of the law, while treating the tribunal with candour, fairness, courtesy, and respect.[15]
- Notwithstanding the lawyer's private opinion on credibility or the merits, a lawyer may properly rely on any evidence or defences including so-called technicalities not known to be false or fraudulent.[16]
- If the accused clearly admits to the lawyer the factual and mental elements necessary to constitute the offence, the lawyer must not

---

13 These and other constitutional rights relating to counsel's role in the adversary system are discussed in Chapter 1, Section D.
14 See Chapter 1, Section B.
15 Alta, Sask r 4.01(1); BC, Man, Ont, NS, NL r 5.1-1. See also the introductory rules in NB ch 8, and CBA Code ch IX is almost identical.
16 Alta, Sask r 4.01(commentary); BC, Man, Ont, NS, NL r 5.1-1, commentary 9; NB ch 8, commentaries 14(b) & (c); CBA Code ch IX, commentary 10.

call any evidence that because of the admissions, the lawyer believes to be false.[17]

- When acting as an advocate, a lawyer must not knowingly assist or permit a client to do anything that the lawyer considers to be dishonest or dishonourable.[18]
- When acting as an advocate, a lawyer must not knowingly attempt to deceive a tribunal or influence the course of justice by offering false evidence, misstating facts or law, presenting or relying upon a false or deceptive affidavit, suppressing what ought to be disclosed, or otherwise assisting in any fraud, crime, or illegal conduct.[19]

Disclosure of Error or Omission

- A lawyer who has unknowingly done or failed to do something that if done or omitted knowingly would have been in breach of this rule and who discovers it must, subject to the rules governing confidential information, disclose the error or omission and do all that can reasonably be done in the circumstances to rectify it.[20]
- If a client desires that a course be taken that would involve a breach of this rule, the lawyer must refuse and do everything reasonably possible to prevent it. If that cannot be done, the lawyer should, subject to the rules governing withdrawal, withdraw or seek leave to do so.[21]

Two Canadian ethical codes contain provisions that directly address the problem of how a lawyer should respond to a completed client perjury. The Alberta code contains a rule and commentary very similar to the "disclosure of error or omission" provisions set out above[22] but also states regarding the duty to correct a falsehood that "it may be a

---

17 Alta, Sask r 4.01(commentary); BC, Man, Ont, NS, NL r 5.1-1, commentary 10; CBA Code ch IX, commentary 11.

18 NL, NS, BC, Ont r 5.1-2(b); Alta r 4.01(2)(d); Sask, Man, Ont r 4.01(2)(b); NB ch 8, commentary 10(ii); CBA Code ch IX, commentary 2(b).

19 Alta r 4.01(2)(g); Sask r 4.01(2)(e); BC, Man, Ont, NS, NL r 5.1-2(e); NB ch 8, commentary 10(v); CBA Code ch IX, commentary 2(e). See also Alta r 4.01(2)(m), which prohibits a lawyer from counselling a witness to give untruthful or misleading evidence, and r 4.01(5), which prohibits a lawyer from assisting a client or witness in misleading a tribunal. Que s 3.02(1)(c) prohibits a lawyer from "leading or attempting to lead the court into error or, by illegal means, creating doubt in favour of the client."

20 Sask r 4.01(4); BC, Man, Ont, NS, NL r 5.1-4; NB ch 8, commentary 11; CBA Code ch IX, commentary 3. Alta r 4.01(5)(b) is comparable.

21 Alta r 4.01(5) (commentary); Sask r 4.01(4) (commentary); BC, Man, Ont, NS, NL r 5.1-4, commentary 1; NB ch 8, commentary 12(b); CBA Code ch IX, commentary 4.

22 Alta r 4.01(5)(b) & first para of commentary, which resemble the rule and commentary set out in the text associated with notes 20 & 21, above in this chapter.

sufficient discharge of this duty to merely advise the tribunal not to rely on the impugned information."[23]

The New Brunswick code includes the usual error and omission provisions[24] but in addition contains a commentary that provides counsel with three alternatives when it comes to rectifying completed witness perjury on a material point: (1) make immediate disclosure to the court and to other counsel, (2) continue without making reference to the false testimony and in argument without explanation advise the court that it should not be relied on, or (3) seek leave of the court to withdraw from the matter.[25]

Finally, and altogether apart from the prohibition against misleading the court, most ethical codes forbid lawyers from knowingly assisting a client or anyone else in dishonesty, crime, fraud, or illegality.[26] A client who testifies to facts knowing them to be false is acting dishonestly and committing the crimes of perjury and attempting to obstruct justice. The prohibition against assisting in dishonesty or crime is thus engaged where a lawyer knows that the client intends to give perjured evidence on being called to testify.

D. MONROE FREEDMAN AND THE LAWYER'S TRILEMMA

We have already alluded to Professor Monroe Freedman's controversial contribution to the legal profession's discussion of client perjury. Freedman's influence on the debate is hard to overstate. It is thus worth reviewing his position in more detail.[27]

The centrepiece of Freedman's position lies in the so-called trilemma presented whenever a lawyer is confronted with client perjury. This trilemma derives from three competing ethical obligations. First, the lawyer is expected to acquire full knowledge of the case, a vital prerequisite to the competent representation of the client. Second, counsel

---

23   Alta r 4.01(5), fourth para of commentary.
24   NB ch 8, commentaries 11 and 12(b).
25   NB ch 8, commentary 12(a).
26   Alta r 2.02(10); Sask r 2.02(7); BC, Man, Ont, NS, NL r 3.2-7; CBA Code ch III, commentary 8. See also Chapter 2, Section B(1).
27   Freedman's extensive writings on the subject include the pioneering "Professional Responsibility of the Criminal Defence Lawyer: The Three Hardest Questions" (1966) 64 Mich L Rev 1469, and the latest edition of his book, co-authored with Professor Abbe Smith, *Understanding Lawyers' Ethics*, 4th ed (New Providence, NJ: LexisNexis, 2010) ch 6.

must maintain all client confidences, an essential means of encouraging full disclosure by the client. Third, the lawyer has a duty to be candid with the court, and thus not to undermine the judicial process by knowingly perpetrating falsehoods.

In Freedman's opinion, any proposed resolution to the client-perjury problem puts at least one of these three obligations at risk. For instance, counsel can attempt to circumvent the problem by striving never to acquire knowledge of the true facts from the client, but at significant cost to the duty of competence. If, instead, the lawyer discloses the client's intended or completed perjury, confidentiality suffers and clients will learn not to be open with counsel. On the other hand, keeping the confidence secure and proceeding with a defence that utilizes the perjured testimony means that the lawyer is consciously playing a role in misleading the court.

Freedman concedes that the trilemma yields to no simple solution and professes that he has never been entirely comfortable with any response.[28] But his preferred approach, based on the great importance that he ascribes to client-lawyer confidentiality within an adversarial criminal justice system, is to adopt the following course. The lawyer must start by attempting to dissuade the client from committing perjury. If the client is unswayed, the lawyer can withdraw from the case provided the client suffers no attendant prejudice. However, where prejudice cannot be avoided, for instance because the trial is in progress when counsel learns of the anticipated perjury, withdrawal will not be an option. The lawyer must therefore conduct the defence as though nothing is amiss, calling the client to the stand, bringing out the perjured testimony through examination-in-chief and re-examination, and relying on the false evidence in closing argument.

The notion that a lawyer can sometimes knowingly lead and rely on perjured evidence remains shocking to many lawyers, judges, academics, and members of the public. Few other commentators go so far as Freedman in protecting client-lawyer confidentiality.[29] And as just seen, the rules of professional conduct clearly prohibit counsel from

---

28   Freedman & Smith, *ibid* at 163.
29   In 1988, Norman Lefstein, "Client Perjury in Criminal Cases: Still in Search of an Answer" (1988) 1 Geo J Leg Ethics 521 at 523–24, noted irony in the fact that such a hotly debated position has never really been endorsed by any court or other commentator. Since then, however, Freedman's position has been supported in two well-argued academic articles: Jay Silver, "Truth, Justice, and the American Way: The Case *Against* the Client Perjury Rules" (1994) 47 Vand L Rev 339; Nathan Crystal, "Limitations on Zealous Representation in an Adversarial System" (1997) 32 Wake Forest L Rev 671.

knowingly eliciting perjured evidence.[30] Freedman's position is thus definitely not a viable option for Canadian lawyers.[31] Yet the force of his illuminating work persists, a valuable touchstone in assessing the suitability of any suggested response to client perjury. We will therefore periodically return to Freedman's ideas as this chapter progresses.

E. OVERVIEW OF THE ISSUES AND ANALYTICAL FRAMEWORK

Many issues flow from the client-perjury problem, most of which can be examined by looking at the various options available to defence counsel in response. Remonstrating with the client, withdrawal, calling the client as a witness, eliciting testimony, arguing before the trier of fact, and making disclosure to the court or Crown: when, if ever, is each of these options permitted, mandated, or forbidden? Another important aspect of the problem concerns the initial determination as to whether perjury is truly planned or has in fact already occurred. For ease of reference, we will discuss these issues by considering anticipated and completed client perjury separately.

F. ANTICIPATED CLIENT PERJURY

Often a lawyer will suspect or believe that a client intends to commit perjury. Sometimes there will be plenty of time to consider and address the possibility. But the issue may arise immediately before the client is scheduled to testify,[32] in which case an already difficult problem is compounded by the pressures and time constraints of the trial process. Regardless, the lawyer must begin by considering the nature of her suspicion or belief.

1) Acquiring Knowledge That the Client Intends to Commit Perjury

We have already discussed in detail the crucial role a lawyer's knowledge plays in triggering the ethical limitations applicable in defending

---

30   See Section C, above in this chapter.
31   As explained in Section F(4)(d), below in this chapter.
32   This appears to have occurred in *Sankar v State of Trinidad and Tobago*, [1995] 1 All ER 236 (PC).

a client who is known to be guilty.[33] Assessing the nature of the lawyer's knowledge is equally important when it comes to client perjury. In either instance, counsel must determine whether he has the state of mind necessary to trigger the interdiction against misleading the court.

The requisite state of mind has two discrete but closely related elements. First, the lawyer must know that a certain version of facts is false and if recounted by the client would constitute perjury. Second, the lawyer must know that the client steadfastly plans to testify to the false version of facts, the intention being to mislead the court. If either element is missing — the version of facts is not false, or the client does not plan to recount the false facts in her testimony — the client-perjury problem does not arise. The question becomes, what level of awareness is necessary to fix counsel with knowledge that the client is going to testify falsely?

We can start by emphasizing that counsel should not jump to rash conclusions about a story's falsity or the client's nefarious intention.[34] The role of counsel in the adversarial system is to act as the accused's advocate, not to assume the part of judge. The conduct of the defence must not be limited simply because defence counsel suspects that perjury will occur. Imposing such restrictions too quickly may impinge on the client's constitutional rights and when counsel's assumption that perjury will occur is erroneous may also contribute to an unreliable verdict.

Example: Counsel's client is charged with sexual assault and asserts his innocence. But the client fails a defence-administered polygraph test. Counsel tells the client that this failure precludes him from testifying at trial. Counsel does not mention that other lawyers would not necessarily view the defence as being restricted in this way. The client does not take the stand and is convicted based on the complainant's evidence. Given that polygraph results are far from infallible, counsel too quickly concluded that the client was guilty, thereby undermining his right to testify in his own defence.[35]

Having reiterated the basic presumption against judging the client, we can move on to focus on counsel's knowledge in relation to the possible falsity of a version of facts proffered by the client. Assume, for example, that the client tells counsel she intends to testify that she was

---

33   See Chapter 1, Section F.
34   See Chapter 1, Section F(1).
35   This example is based on the facts and result in *Moore*, above note 5. While *Moore* does not expressly state that counsel believed his client to be guilty, the implication that he had come to this conclusion is strong.

at home sleeping at the time of the crime. When can counsel be said to "know" that this alibi is false? The possible thresholds and their justifications have been reviewed in Chapter 1.[36] Here, suffice it to say that counsel can be said to know that a version of events is untrue where he reasonably draws an *irresistible conclusion* of falsity from available information, by which we mean a conclusion that not even a zealous but honest partisan could deny.[37] Yet two caveats are necessary. First, the lawyer's determination must be based on a careful investigation of all relevant facts.[38] Second, it is improper to use avoidance techniques as a means of cultivating ignorance so as to evade the ethical strictures associated with client perjury.[39]

A common instance where counsel may turn her mind to the possibility of client perjury occurs where the client has provided inconsistent statements.[40] Yet inconsistency on its own does not warrant a conclusion that the client plans to lie on the stand. A client may quite legitimately have remembered additional facts or realized that an earlier version of events was incorrect. Counsel must therefore refrain from equating inconsistency with planned perjury. Rather, counsel should explore the inconsistency with the client at the first available opportunity. Only if the lawyer thereby acquires irresistible knowledge that the client intends to offer false testimony, do the restrictions pertaining to client perjury apply.[41]

Consultation with the client: Counsel should discuss with the client any reasonable suspicion that perjury is being planned. Such a discussion is a necessary part of determining whether a proffered story is perjurious, and is equally important in ascertaining whether the story will hold up under cross-examination. Even where counsel cannot be said to possess irresistible knowledge that the client's version of events is false, the discussion may serve to dissuade the client from perjuring himself.

36   See Chapter 1, Section F(2).

37   This test is endorsed in *R v Youvarajah*, 2013 SCC 41, citing the first edition of our text, and has found favour with Michael Code, "Ethics and Criminal Law Practice" in Alice Woolley et al, *Lawyers' Ethics and Professional Regulation*, 2d ed (Markham, ON: LexisNexis, 2012) ch 8, 435 at 463; Alice Woolley, *Understanding Lawyers' Ethics in Canada* (Markham, ON: LexisNexis, 2011) at 167 and 303–4 [Woolley, *Understanding Lawyers' Ethics*]; G Lafontaine, "Client Perjury and the Criminal Defence Lawyer as Lie Detector" (2006) 27:1 For the Defence 6.

38   Counsel's duties in this regard are described in Chapter 1, Sections F(2) & F(3).

39   See Chapter 1, Section F(4).

40   An example where an eleventh-hour change in the client's story caused counsel concern is described in *Brigham*, above note 9 at 373"a"–"d."

41   Dealing with a client's inconsistent statements is addressed in more detail in Chapter 1, Section F(3).

However, counsel must approach the issue with great sensitivity. Hasty, angry, or otherwise impolitic recriminations may strain or rupture the professional relationship and do more harm than good.

2) Admonishing the Client to Tell the Truth

Where counsel comes to an irresistible conclusion that a client intends to commit perjury, the immediate reaction should be to attempt to dissuade him from pursuing such a course. Admonishing against perjury serves two purposes. First, counsel acts in the best interests of the client by providing advice concerning the possible harmful repercussions of advancing a perjurious defence. Even if the client is not particularly interested in the ethical niceties of the perjury problem, he will surely want to hear about the strategic considerations that typically make perjury a bad idea. Second, the administration of justice benefits whenever counsel is successful in convincing the client not to testify falsely. The court is not presented with false evidence, counsel remains free of complicity in any deception, and the attendant harm to the truth-finding process is avoided.

For these reasons, it is widely accepted that defence counsel has a duty to remonstrate with the client against providing false evidence.[42] Even Monroe Freedman, who in certain circumstances condones counsel's participation in presenting false testimony from the client, recognizes that a lawyer must always try to dissuade the client from lying on the stand.[43]

Depending on the circumstances of the case, counsel's admonition should cover a number of points. Typically, the client must be told the following:

1) Perjury is a crime.
2) The prosecution will likely attack the perjured testimony, using cross-examination, reply evidence, or argument to the trier of fact (concrete examples should be provided if at all possible).
3) The perjury may well be discovered by the trier of fact, leading or contributing to the client's conviction.

---

42   See the rules cited at note 21, above in this chapter. Clearer still in requiring remonstration are ABA Model Rule 3.3, comment 6, and Third Restatement § 120, comment "g."
43   Freedman & Smith, above note 27 at 162.

4) Once revealed, the bogus defence may cause the court to impose a harsher sentence than would otherwise be the case.[44]
5) The client's falsehood may lead the authorities to lay a separate charge of perjury, with the attendant risk of an additional conviction and punishment.
6) Defence counsel has an ethical duty not to mislead the court, which may permit or mandate significant remedial measures if the client does not change her mind.

This last point, concerning possible remedial measures, deserves elaboration. The client must be advised as to exactly how an impending or completed perjury may limit the conduct of the defence. Counsel must be precise in outlining the possible responses if the client remains impervious to the admonition. The responses available, and hence the contents of this portion of the admonition, remain to be discussed below. At this juncture, we can nonetheless say that a client should never be threatened with a response that counsel knows to be improper or has no intention of carrying out.[45] Such an admonition would be duplicitous and might even operate to deny the client the effective assistance of counsel. Counsel must also tread carefully in admonishing the client. Employing too heavy a hand may destroy the client's sense of trust in counsel, causing the relationship to break down completely.

The close connection between admonishing the client and permissible remedial measures is demonstrated by the well-known decision of the United States Supreme Court in *Nix v Whiteside*.[46] Whiteside was charged with stabbing a drug dealer to death. He told defence counsel that the killing was precipitated by his belief the victim was about to shoot him with a gun. This belief was not based on Whiteside's having actually seen a gun, but the claim of self-defence was nonetheless

---

44   Trial judges are only permitted to take account of perjurious testimony on sentencing for the limited purpose of negating or discounting any suggestion that the offender is remorseful: see *R v Bradley*, 2008 ONCA 179 at paras 15–17; *R v Kozy* (1990), 58 CCC (3d) 500 at 506–7 [paras 14–16] (Ont CA); *R v Vickers* (1998), 105 BCAC 42 at para 15 (CA) [*Vickers*]; *R v Von Holtum*, 2013 BCCA 384 at para 31; Clayton Ruby, Gerald Chan, & Nader Hasan, *Sentencing*, 8th ed (Markham, ON: LexisNexis Canada, 2012) at §§ 6.1–12. The client may nonetheless harbour a concern that a trial judge will unconsciously react to perjury by increasing the sentence.

45   See *DB v British Columbia (Director of Child, Family and Community Service)*, 2002 BCCA 55 at paras 17–18, 29, 41, and 64 [*DB*]: though not a perjury case, counsel improperly discouraged the client from testifying by saying he would disclose his opposition to her doing so to the court if she insisted on taking the stand, a disclosure the court held he was not in fact permitted to make.

46   Above note 4.

feasible given the victim's reputation and comments and movements made just before the killing. Shortly before trial, however, Whiteside changed his story. He told his lawyer that the self-defence claim could not succeed unless he testified to having seen something metallic in the victim's hand: "If I don't say I saw a gun," said Whiteside, "I'm dead."[47]

Whiteside's counsel reacted to this last-minute revelation by trying to convince his client not to present false evidence.[48] The remonstration consisted of counsel's telling Whiteside that the proposed testimony would be perjurious and that the false assertion was not needed to establish a valid defence. Indeed, adding the bogus reference to seeing a metallic object could hurt the defence given that the victim was not found in possession of a gun.[49] Counsel told his client that he would move to withdraw from the case if Whiteside insisted on going ahead with the lie. He also indicated that in such an event, he would inform the court that the testimony was perjurious and probably would be allowed to attempt to impeach the testimony.

Whiteside responded to counsel's remonstration by agreeing not to testify falsely. The defence lawyer accepted this change of heart and took no further steps to prevent the previously anticipated perjury. This confidence in the client's sincerity was justified, for Whiteside took the stand and testified in chief without mentioning a metallic object. He even went so far as to admit in cross-examination that he did not see the victim holding a gun. The jury nevertheless found Whiteside guilty as charged, and he appealed on the ground that counsel's admonition had denied him a fair trial and the constitutional right to the effective assistance of counsel. In other words, Whiteside argued that he should have been allowed to present a perjurious defence.[50]

The opinion of the Court dismissing Whiteside's appeal was written by Freedman's old nemesis Burger CJ,[51] who recognized that counsel's first duty when confronted with proposed perjury is to try to dissuade the client from the unlawful course of conduct.[52] This assertion is not contentious.[53] Much more controversial was the Chief Justice's holding

---

47   The Court proceeded on the basis that this comment showed that Whiteside intended to commit perjury: *ibid* at 162–63, 180, and 190. For a critique of this view, see Lefstein, above note 29 at 531–33.

48   The content of the admonition is found in *Nix*, above note 4 at 161 and 179.

49   See Geoffrey Hazard & William Hodes, *The Law of Lawyering*, 3d ed (Gaithersburg, MD: Aspen, 2001) (loose-leaf 2013 supplement) at § 29.19.

50   *Nix*, above note 4 at 162.

51   See the text associated with note 1, above in this chapter.

52   *Nix*, above note 4 at 169.

53   But see the argument made by Silver, above note 29.

that defence counsel did not act improperly in threatening to with-draw and disclose the perjury to the court.[54] The Chief Justice also saw no problem in counsel's making reference to impeaching the client's testimony.[55] In affirming the content of counsel's admonition, most es-pecially regarding disclosure, the decision in *Nix v Whiteside* has at-tracted considerable attention. Many writers have criticized the Court's opinion[56] and have sought to limit the impact of the case by pointing out that Burger CJ's remarks are mere *dicta*.[57] We will examine the solu-tions condoned by *Nix* further below.[58] For the moment, we merely use the case to illustrate how the propriety of counsel's admonition depends on the legitimacy of the remedial responses proposed.

3) Client's Response to Admonition by Counsel

Defence counsel must carefully assess the client's response to an ad-monition against committing perjury. Only if the client is recalcitrant, will counsel be justified in taking further remedial measures. Always keeping in mind the basic presumption against judging the client, counsel must not assume that the client will persist in the desire to testify falsely. It has thus been suggested that a lawyer can ordinarily take for granted that the client will heed the advice to avoid perjury and that following an admonition the usual course is for counsel to proceed on this basis.[59] This assumption is especially justified where the client is clearly worried by the prospect of the lawyer's taking re-medial measures in response to a completed perjury, for instance by immediately seeking leave to withdraw.

Example: Counsel represents J on a charge of aggravated assault. The case against J is strong, and J candidly tells his lawyer that he commit-

---

54   *Nix*, above note 4 at 174.
55   *Ibid* at 172–73.
56   See, for example, Lefstein, above note 29.
57   See, for example, Donald Liskov, "Criminal Defendant Perjury: A Lawyer's Choice between Ethics, the Constitution and the Truth" (1994) 28 New Eng L Rev 881. While many writers take this view, the Third Restatement § 120, comment "i," notes that from the perspective of state and federal courts, *Nix* has settled most of the questions concerning client perjury.
58   See Sections F(4)(a) and F(4)(f), below in this chapter.
59   See Terence McCarthy & Carol Brook, "Anticipated Client Perjury: Truth or Dare Comes to Court" in Rodney Uphoff, ed, *Ethical Problems Facing the Criminal Lawyer: Practical Answers to Tough Questions* (Chicago: American Bar Association, 1995) ch 11 at 157; American Bar Association Committee on Ethics and Profes-sional Responsibility, Formal Opinion 87-353, "Lawyer's Responsibility with relation to Client Perjury" (20 April 1987) at 8 [ABA Formal Opinion 87-353].

ted the offence. J nonetheless wants to take the stand and put forth a mendacious alibi. Counsel admonishes J to abandon the scheme, following which he applies to be removed from the record. Without more, this immediate attempt to withdraw is imprudent. Counsel is justified in taking remedial measures beyond admonition, whatever those measures may be, only where the admonition clearly fails and where counsel can safely conclude that the client is recalcitrant.[60]

4) Remedial Measures Where the Client Cannot Be Dissuaded

In those instances where the client refuses to jettison the perjury plan, the lawyer's task becomes much more difficult. What steps can be taken to avoid complicity in misleading the court without fatally undermining the duty of loyalty to the client? Possible options include withdrawal, refusing to call the client as a witness, adopting a passive role in eliciting the client's testimony, refusing to use perjured testimony in closing submissions, and disclosing the planned falsehood to the court or other third party. We will look at the possible merits and demerits of each of these options in turn.

a) Withdrawal

Most Canadian ethical codes are unequivocal in providing that a lawyer should withdraw or seek the leave of the court to do so where the client insists on a course of conduct that involves dishonesty or deception upon the court.[61] Severing all connections with the client and the case certainly allows counsel to avoid having to make difficult choices concerning the best response to the perjury, both as it occurs and afterwards. But withdrawal is not an easy panacea to the perjury problem, and there exist valid criticisms of this option. Several American commentators take the position that withdrawal is rarely the ideal response to anticipated client perjury.[62] However, the arguments for and against withdrawal in Canada must be examined in light of our Supreme Court's decision in *R v Cunningham*,[63] which provides substantial guidance

---

60 This example is loosely based on the facts and decision in *State v Jones*, 923 P2d 560 (Mont 1996).

61 See the rules and commentaries cited at notes 15–21, above in this chapter.

62 See, for example, John Wesley Hall, Jr, *Professional Responsibility in Criminal Defense Practice* (St Paul, MN: Thomson/West, 2005) (loose-leaf 2012 supplement) at § 26.14; Lefstein, above note 29 at 525–27 and 533; Freedman & Smith, above note 27 at 157–59; Silver, above note 29 at 413–15.

63 2010 SCC 10 [*Cunningham*].

regarding counsel's ability to get off the record and strongly emphasizes the importance of counsel's protecting client confidentiality in
attempting to do so.

Before the decision in *Cunningham*, there was a legitimate concern
that counsel facing a certain prospect of client perjury might be denied
leave of the court to withdraw.[64] This concern is no longer justified provided counsel and the court comply with the following principles extracted from *Cunningham*. To begin with, where the trial is far enough
away that there is no realistic prospect that it will need to be resched-
uled, the court has no power to refuse counsel's request to withdraw.[65]
Even when withdrawal would require an adjournment, the court cannot refuse leave where counsel indicates that the application is based on
"ethical reasons."[66] "Ethical reasons" is a term of art used to describe any
situation in which an issue has arisen in the client-lawyer relationship
that makes it "impossible for counsel to continue in good conscience to
represent the accused."[67] The term includes instances where the client
insists that counsel conduct the defence in an unethical manner,[68] and
so covers the case in which a client is intent on taking the stand to
give false evidence. Importantly, the court must not inquire as to the
specifics of counsel's "ethical reasons": this generic explanation must
be accepted at face value, and the application to withdraw granted.[69]

Example: The accused has testified in chief at his murder trial and
is being cross-examined by the prosecutor when the court adjourns
for the day. On resuming the next morning, defence counsel tells the
court that a matter has arisen requiring a further adjournment. Counsel eventually applies to withdraw. Counsel explains to the court that
his basis for doing so is that he received information from the client
part way through cross-examination the nature of which means he
will mislead the court if forced to present further any defence evidence,

---

64 See Michael Proulx & David Layton, *Ethics and Canadian Criminal Law*, 1st ed
    (Toronto: Irwin Law, 2001) at 377 and 381–82. For some American commenta-
    tors, this concern continues to represent a significant ground, though not the
    only one, for rejection of the withdrawal option: see, for example, Freedman
    & Smith, above note 27 at 157–58; Susan Thrower, "Neither Reasonable nor
    Remedial: The Hopeless Contradictions of the Legal Ethics Measures to Prevent
    Perjury" (2010) 58 Clev St L Rev 781 at 804–9.
65 *Cunningham*, above note 63 at paras 47 and 59.
66 *Ibid* at paras 49 and 59.
67 *Ibid* at para 48.
68 *Ibid*.
69 *Ibid* at paras 32–34, 48–49, and 59. For a more comprehensive discussion of
    withdrawal for ethical reasons, see Chapter 11, Section L(4)(a).

cross-examine any reply witnesses, or present a closing address except to advance the most basic of principles. In making these disclosures, counsel has improperly released confidential information that strongly supports the inference that client perjury has occurred. Counsel should have applied to withdraw based on "ethical reasons" and said nothing more about the underlying problem.[70]

Having set out the basic parameters of the withdrawal process where counsel is faced with anticipated client perjury, we can turn to examine some of the criticisms levelled at this option. One obvious weakness is that the perjury problem will merely be transferred to another lawyer. In theory, this raises the spectre of an endless series of applications to withdraw, the result being that the client can avoid ever having to face a trial by insisting on committing perjury with each successive counsel. Such a prospect is unrealistic, however, because an accused whose lawyers repeatedly apply to get off the record for ethical reasons will soon be taken to have waived the right to be represented by counsel and be forced on to trial without a lawyer.[71]

More likely is that the client will have learned to be circumspect about discussing the planned perjury and so pass off the false version of events as true to new counsel. New counsel will then elicit the perjurious evidence in court. This result is surely a lesser evil, for no lawyer is *knowingly* participating in the presentation of false evidence.[72] Yet the fact remains that in such a case the justice system's truth-finding goal may be undermined. This problem could be avoided by allowing withdrawing counsel to disclose the planned perjury to the new lawyer, even over the objections of the client. For this to be possible, an exception to the ethical duty of confidentiality would have to apply.[73] The obvious candidate is the future-harm exception, which in most provinces is modelled on the public-safety exception to solicitor-client privilege

---

70   This example is based on the pre-*Cunningham* case of R v *Jenkins* (2001), 152 CCC (3d) 426 (Ont SCJ), appeal dismissed, [2005] OJ No 282 (CA) [*Jenkins*]. For a discussion of *Jenkins* based on the then-applicable law and ethical code provisions, see David Layton, "R. v *Jenkins*: Client Perjury and Disclosure by Defence Counsel" (2001) 44 CR (5th) 259.

71   See, for example, R v *Downey*, [2002] OJ No 1524 at paras 103–10 (SCJ): accused's history of changing lawyers led to adjournment application's being denied; *Cunningham*, above note 63 at para 50 (last bullet point).

72   See Michael Franck, "Letter to the Editor: Response to Lefstein" (1988) 2 Geo J Leg Ethics 585 at 587. This position is ridiculed as self-centred and anti-accused in Silver, above note 29 at 414.

73   The client's instructions not to disclose confidential information to successor counsel are binding, absent the application of an exception to the duty of confidentiality: see Chapter 11, Section M(3).

set out in *Smith v Jones*.[74] However, a future-harm exception based on *Smith v Jones* is highly unlikely to permit disclosure to successor counsel for the purpose of averting perjury by a former client because it operates only where disclosure is necessary to prevent serious bodily harm or death.[75]

The situation may be different in Saskatchewan, Manitoba, and New Brunswick because the ethical codes in these provinces contain an additional exception to the duty of confidentiality permitting lawyers to make disclosure to prevent any crime.[76] These future-crime exceptions would appear, at least on their face, to permit withdrawing counsel to inform successor counsel of the anticipated perjury, which would probably serve to fix successor counsel with knowledge of the client's plan. The risk of harm to the truth-finding function of the justice system would thus be reduced. And the prejudice to the former client would be kept to a minimum because disclosure would only be made to successor counsel, who owes the client a duty of confidentiality, and not to the world at large.[77]

Criminal defence lawyers in Saskatchewan, Manitoba, and New Brunswick may nonetheless choose *never* to exercise their discretion to disclose the planned perjury to successor counsel under the future-crime exception. This may be so in whole or part because they view disclosure as clashing with the former client's constitutional right to the protection of solicitor-client privilege, a right that arguably trumps the applicability of the future-crime exception where the information does not fit within the narrow exception to the privilege recognized in *Smith v Jones*.[78] A viable counter-argument, however, is that the information in question, though confidential, falls within the crime-fraud exception to solicitor-client privilege,[79] at least where it has been conveyed in a knowing attempt to enlist the lawyer's aid in committing a perjury.[80] On this view, lawyers in New Brunswick, Manitoba and Saskatchewan

---

74   (1999), 132 CCC (3d) 225 (SCC). These future-harm exceptions are discussed in Chapter 5, Section I(1).

75   See Chapter 5, Section I(4).

76   These future-crime exceptions are discussed in Chapter 5, Section I(1).

77   Ordinarily, a lawyer should not disclose client confidences to a successor lawyer without the client's consent: see Chapter 11, Section M(3).

78   This argument is explained in Chapter 5, Section I(13).

79   In our view, there is no stand-alone crime-fraud exception to the ethical duty of confidentiality: see Chapter 5, Section K.

80   Woolley, *Understanding Lawyers' Ethics*, above note 37 at 170, argues that the crime-fraud exception to privilege does not apply in the typical perjury scenario because the client is being "up front" about the plan and the lawyer has not assisted in any way. In our view, however, the exception applies because the

are free to make disclosure, if they so wish, because the information was never privileged to begin with and fits within the future-crime exception to the duty of confidentiality operating in these provinces.[81]

Example 1: A client charged in Manitoba insists on counsel's calling her to the stand to testify falsely, even though she knows perjury is a crime. She says that if he withdraws, she will retain new counsel and give the perjurious evidence without that counsel knowing. On these facts, the crime-fraud exception to solicitor-client privilege applies because the client has knowingly attempted to obtain counsel's aid in committing perjury. The ethical duty of confidentiality still attaches to the communications, but Manitoba's future-crime exception permits counsel to disclose the client's planned perjury to successor counsel to prevent the false evidence from being led.

Example 2: If the facts are varied so that the trial occurs in Quebec, counsel cannot make disclosure to successor counsel even though solicitor-client privilege does not apply. This is so because in Quebec the ethical duty of confidentiality is not subject to a broad future-crime exception but only to a future-harm exception limited to the prevention of death and serious bodily harm.[82]

Example 3: A client charged in Saskatchewan wishes to testify. He has given several inconsistent statements to counsel. Under questioning from counsel about the inconsistencies, the client breaks down and admits that he is guilty. Counsel informs the client that if he insists on testifying, she will withdraw. The client advises her to do so and says he will try to retain new counsel. On these facts, the information that the proposed testimony is false does not fit comfortably within the crime-fraud exception to solicitor-client privilege, because the client's admission of guilt was not made in an effort to obtain assistance in committing a crime. If solicitor-client privilege applies, there is a good argument that it prevents counsel from relying on Saskatchewan's future-crime exception to the duty of confidentiality.

A different criticism of the withdrawal option is that getting off the record will usually cause harm to the client, in particular where it occurs shortly before or during the trial. Significant extra cost may be incurred in hiring new counsel, or the accused may have difficulty in finding counsel on short notice. Where a mistrial or lengthy adjournment

---

client has knowingly sought to use the lawyer's services to commit a crime: see Chapter 5, Section K(1).

81   *Contra* Woolley, *Understanding Lawyers' Ethics, ibid* at 171.
82   Que s 3.06.01.01.

is granted as a result of withdrawal, the resulting delay will prejudice the accused who is detained pending trial but ultimately acquitted. A mistrial or adjournment may also cause systemic harm in the form of wasted resources and delayed justice. On the other hand, where the court refuses to declare a mistrial or adjournment, the accused will probably be forced to finish the case unrepresented.[83]

It can also be argued that prejudice to the client will arise if counsel withdraws during the trial insofar as the judge or jury may thereby be alerted to the possibility of planned client perjury. Granted, in applying to withdraw, counsel will merely say that she seeks to get off the record for "ethical reasons" and will mention nothing about perjury or any improper course of action insisted on by the client.[84] Yet the timing and context of the application may implicitly raise a suspicion of perjury.[85] For instance, an application to get off the record for "ethical reasons" brought immediately before the accused is scheduled to testify may suggest to the trial judge at least the possibility of a dispute between counsel and client regarding planned perjury.

The concern that withdrawal will inferentially suggest that the client intends to commit perjury is greatest where the trial is by judge alone. Yet the danger of prejudice to the client should not be overstated. "Ethical reasons" can encompass legitimate bases for withdrawing apart from planned perjury, such as a profound disagreement between client and counsel as to the strategic advisability of the client taking the stand or covering certain subjects in direct examination. In a system where judges routinely act as triers of fact despite having excluded incriminating evidence such as an involuntary confession, a hearsay admission of guilt to a civilian, evidence of other crimes committed by the accused, or real evidence obtained by virtue of a breach of section 8

---

83   For a rare case where a new lawyer was able to take over the case right away, see *Jenkins*, above note 70.

84   There used to be a real concern about lawyers' alluding to planned misconduct by the client in seeking leave to withdraw, as in *Jenkins*, *ibid*, and *R v Pomeroy* (1984), 15 CCC (3d) 193 (Alta CA). See also Proulx & Layton, above note 64 at 379–81. But this danger has been dramatically reduced given changes in the law regarding withdrawal, as discussed in the paragraph associated with notes 64–69, above in this chapter.

85   Some American courts have even held that withdrawing counsel's statement "I cannot state the reason" represented in the circumstances an assertion that the client was planning perjury: *Lowery v Cardwell*, 575 F2d 727 at 729–31 (9th Cir 1978); *United States v Henkel*, 799 F2d 369 at 370 (7th Cir 1986), cert denied 479 US 1101 (1987) [*Henkel*].

of the *Charter of Rights and Freedoms*,[86] the risk of harm arising from a speculative possibility of client perjury seems acceptable in the absence of other clearly superior options for avoiding a lawyer's knowing complicity in eliciting perjured testimony.[87] Nonetheless, a prudent judge might consider expressly stating in the reasons for judgment that the withdrawal had no bearing whatsoever on his decision making process.

The risk that an inference of perjury will arise where counsel withdraws during the proceeding is even less of a concern in a jury trial because the jury will not have been privy to the withdrawal application and will have no idea why counsel has gone. Jurors may be puzzled by counsel's sudden disappearance, but it seems a leap to assume that as a result they will be predisposed to conclude that the client's testimony is perjured. This is especially so where the trial judge instructs them that counsel's withdrawal is completely irrelevant in deciding the case. In *R v Jenkins*, for example, the Ontario Court of Appeal rejected as speculative the argument that defence counsel's withdrawal during an adjournment in the appellant's cross-examination would have suggested to the jury that counsel did not believe the appellant's testimony. The court added that the trial judge's instructions to the jury — presumably to ignore the fact of withdrawal in deciding the case — in any event sufficiently answered any such concern.[88]

In Canada, a significant preponderance of commentators,[89] as well as existing judicial authority,[90] accept that withdrawal is the required or preferable response for counsel facing a client's planned perjury. This conclusion is especially compelling given the minimal risk of confidential information being disclosed on a withdrawal application

---

86   Part I of the *Constitution Act, 1982*, being Schedule B to the *Canada Act 1982* (UK), 1982, c 11.

87   Compare *R v Bolianatz*, 2012 ABCA 238 at paras 13–23, leave to appeal to SCC refused, [2013] SCCA No 82: rejects the argument that trial counsel's comments disparaging the clients' honesty when withdrawing created a reasonable apprehension of bias in a judge-alone trial.

88   *Jenkins*, above note 70 at para 2 (Ont CA).

89   A rare skeptic as to the propriety of withdrawal is B Finlay, "The Conduct of Lawyers in the Litigious Process: Some Thoughts" in Eric Gertner, *Studies in Civil Procedure* (Toronto: Butterworths, 1979) 15 at 27–28 (writing in the civil context). Finlay would have the lawyer remain on the case but expressly advise the court not to rely on the evidence (*ibid* at 30).

90   *Cunningham*, above note 63 at paras 48–49: not dealing with client perjury but implicitly suggesting that counsel must withdraw rather than continue with a case in breach of an ethical code rule; *Jenkins*, above note 70: pre-*Cunningham* case granting leave to withdraw in what was certainly a case of completed client perjury; *R v Legato* (2002), 172 CCC (3d) 415 at paras 83–88 (Que CA) [*Legato*]: *obiter* comments regarding proper response by counsel to client perjury.

under the process endorsed in *Cunningham*. It also jibes with Canadian codes of professional conduct, which *mandate* that counsel withdraw where the client insists that the defence be conducted so as to breach the ethical rules, including the rule against knowingly misleading the court.[91] We therefore conclude that withdrawal is the best answer to anticipated perjury. This is indisputably so when the application to get off the record can be brought well before trial. As the trial approaches, the dangers associated with withdrawal loom larger. Yet withdrawal remains the superior option, provided counsel strives, to the extent possible, to minimize even an inference that the client is intending to commit perjury.

Advice: In withdrawing from the case, counsel should document carefully and fully all relevant circumstances, including discussions with the client. Ideally, counsel will obtain written confirmation from the client as to the nature of the problem, the advice provided, and the client's refusal to change her course of action. Counsel is also well advised to obtain input from one or more senior criminal defence practitioners and/or a governing body ethics advisory service.

b)   Continuing with the Trial but Refusing to Call the Client as a Witness

Continuing with the trial but refusing to call the client as a witness in response to anticipated client perjury carries some superficial attraction.[92] Canadian ethical codes prohibit counsel from knowingly assisting or permitting the client to do anything dishonest and from knowingly participating in deceiving the court.[93] Facilitating the client's ruse by calling him to the stand and playing a role in eliciting false testimony obviously runs afoul of this prohibition. Staying on the case but refusing to call the client as a witness undeniably works to prevent the perjury from occurring and so avoids breaching the duty of candour owed by counsel to the court. The truth-finding function of the criminal justice system is also furthered. Moreover, the option

---

91   See the rules and commentaries cited at notes 15–21, above.

92   A rare commentator who endorses counsel's responding to anticipated client perjury in this way is David Pannick, *Advocates* (Oxford: Oxford University Press, 1992) at 160–61. A few American cases condone this option: *Stephenson v State*, 424 SE2d 816 (Ga Ct App 1992); *United States v Curtis*, 742 F2d 1070 at 1075–76 (7th Cir 1984); *United States v Rantz*, 862 F2d 808 at 811 (10th Cir 1988). But the great preponderance of American jurisprudence does not: see, for example, *People v Johnson*, 62 Cal App 4th 608 at 626 and 629 (1998), cert denied, 525 US 914 (1998) [*Johnson*].

93   See the rules and commentaries cited at notes 15–19 and 26, above in this chapter.

of overriding the client's instructions to testify arguably finds implicit support in the code commentaries providing that where the client wishes to adopt a course that would involve counsel's breaching the rule prohibiting knowingly misleading the court, counsel "must refuse and do everything reasonably possible to prevent it."[94]

Yet preventing a client from testifying in the face of instructions to the contrary runs up against insurmountable problems. For one thing, the code commentaries just mentioned, after stating that the lawyer must refuse to carry out instructions that would involve breaching the prohibition against knowingly misleading the court, provide that counsel must withdraw where the client cannot be persuaded to change the instructions.[95] In other words, the codes require that counsel refuse and withdraw, not refuse and override. This approach makes sense. Conducting litigation in express defiance of a client's instructions is a cardinal breach of counsel's role as loyal advocate and marks the solicitor-client relationship as irreparably broken. Withdrawal is always to be preferred over running the case counter to the client's express direction regarding a material point.[96]

Furthermore, while the dominant view in Canada is that defence counsel, and not the client, has the final say regarding most of the decisions pertaining to the conduct of the case, one of the few exceptions is the decision whether to testify.[97] This decision is seen to be of superordinate importance in mounting a defence, leading virtually all courts and commentators to accept that it belongs to the client.[98] Counsel can strongly advise a client not to testify, but she cannot ignore and override a client's decision to the contrary. As observed by Fish J in *R v Brigham*, citing many sources including an influential 1970 article on ethics by the esteemed G Arthur Martin, where an irreconcilable conflict arises between counsel and client as to whether the latter should take the stand, counsel must withdraw rather than disregard the client's instructions.[99]

---

94 See the commentaries cited at note 21, above in this chapter.

95 *Ibid.* Further support for this position is found in the code provisions that address withdrawal more generally, which mandate getting off the record where the client persists in instructing the lawyer to act unethically: see Chapter 11, Section F.

96 See Chapter 3, Section J.

97 See Chapter 3, Section F.

98 *Ibid.* See, for example, *Swain*, above note 7 at 506 [para 36]; *R v Strauss* (1995), 100 CCC (3d) 303 at para 48 (BCCA).

99 *Brigham*, above note 9 at 380"h"–383"g." See also *DB*, above note 45 at para 17, commenting that counsel who disagrees with client's desire to testify should either accede to the client's wishes or withdraw. In the context of anticipated

The view that the client and not counsel makes the decision whether to testify is supported by the accused's constitutional right to take the stand as part of the defence.[100] Granted, *Nix v Whiteside* opines that the accused has no constitutional right to give perjured testimony,[101] and caselaw in Canada leans in the same direction.[102] But it is difficult to envisage a trial judge refusing to allow an accused to take the stand on the basis that the evidence would be false.[103] Cases where a judge has refused to allow an accused to testify are almost unicorn rare and appear confined to instances where a contumacious self-represented accused has acted incredibly disruptively while on the stand.[104] Indeed, one could feasibly argue that absent waiver, an accused has a constitutional right to testify *regardless* of whether the testimony is true or false. What he does *not* have is a constitutional right to avoid the *consequences* of testifying falsely, which can include being found guilty at trial and prosecuted for perjury.

In any event, cases suggesting there is no constitutional right to testify falsely must be seen in their context, which in the American jurisprudence usually involves an appellant's attacking the effectiveness of trial counsel's representation on the basis that counsel convinced her not to testify falsely or threatened to withdraw or make disclosure if she insisted on lying on the stand. Such arguments have failed because an accused intent on perjury does not have a constitutional right to the knowing assistance of counsel in carrying out a planned perjury. But this is not the same as saying that counsel who ignores the client's instructions and completes the case without calling him to the stand has acted ethically. Very few American cases[105] and no Canadian ones suggest that counsel faced with the prospect of client perjury is ethically permitted to respond in such a manner.

---

perjury, however, acceding to the client's wishes is not a viable option: see Section F(4)(d), below in this chapter.

100 See the cases cited at note 9, above in this chapter.

101 *Nix*, above note 4 at 173–74. See also *United States v Midgett*, 342 F3d 321 at 325 (4th Cir 2003); *People v DePallo*, 96 NY2d 437 at 441 (2001) [*DePallo*].

102 *Vickers*, above note 44 at para 12; *R v Ford* (1993), 78 CCC (3d) 481 at 498 [paras 63–64] (BCCA) [*Ford*]; *Legato*, above note 90 at para 88.

103 How would the judge make such a determination, absent an evidentiary hearing that would likely mirror the accused's testimony at trial in any event? Denial of the accused's right to testify, even if justified, would never be permitted without a full inquiry by the court.

104 See *R v Fabrikant* (1995), 97 CCC (3d) 544 at 572–74 [paras 79–88] (Que CA), leave to appeal to SCC refused, [1995] SCCA No 211.

105 See note 92, above in this chapter.

There may be considerable merit in refusing to overturn a conviction simply because trial counsel has ignored instructions to testify and continued with the trial in the face of an accused's insistence on testifying falsely. But this is not because counsel has acted competently, which is to say ethically. Rather, the result is justified because a claim of ineffective assistance of counsel cannot be made out unless the lawyer's incompetence has resulted in prejudice.[106] Overriding the client's instructions regarding the decision whether to testify probably *does* amount to incompetence. But where the appeal court concludes, based on fresh evidence put before it, that the proposed testimony was obviously false, the incompetence has not resulted in the sort of prejudice necessary to breach the right to effective assistance of counsel, namely, a real possibility that the result would have been different or a denial of procedural fairness.[107]

Two final, more practical objections can be made to the contention that a lawyer should be permitted to override a perjurious client's instructions and complete the trial without calling him to the stand. First, such action may prevent the client from presenting other *non-perjurious* testimony to the fact-finder and thereby deprive him of a valid defence. Second, it is difficult to envision how counsel would go about overriding the client's instructions when faced with a determined client. Such a client might simply inform the court that he wishes to testify. At this point, the lawyer cannot physically intervene to stop the client. Making submissions to the court in an effort to obtain a ruling that the client cannot testify would only be possible if disclosure is acceptable as a last alternative, but it is not.[108] Airing the disagreement publicly would simply accentuate that a fundamental breakdown in the professional relationship has occurred, underlining the need for counsel to withdraw rather than continue to act for the accused.

c)   Eliciting Testimony with Free or Open Narrative

"Free or open narrative" refers to a special mode of eliciting the client's testimony. Counsel identifies the accused as the next witness and conducts the examination-in-chief in the normal manner where the anticipated answers are not known to contain falsehoods. However, when it comes to eliciting testimony counsel knows to be untrue, the conventional

---

106 See *R v GDB*, 2000 SCC 22 at paras 28–29.

107 See Dale Ives, "The Role of Counsel and the Courts in Safeguarding the Accused's Opportunity to Decide Whether to Testify" (2006) 51 Crim LQ 508 at 522, n 61, apparently accepting that trial fairness will not be undermined where counsel has ignored a client's instructions to testify falsely.

108 See Section F(4)(f), below in this chapter.

examination-in-chief is abandoned. Instead, the lawyer is confined to asking the client whether she wishes to make any additional statement concerning the case to the fact-finder. Counsel provides no guidance in the form of follow-up questions. Counsel can make objections during cross-examination or elicit evidence in reply but only regarding matters that do not relate to the perjurious testimony.[109] And counsel is not permitted to rely on the perjurious evidence in closing submissions.[110]

The strength of the narrative approach, according to proponents, is the ability to accommodate the competing principles at stake. The lawyer does not fatally undermine the duty of loyalty to the client, and the client's ability to testify is preserved. At the same time, counsel is distanced from participation in the perjury and to this extent is not complicit in attempting to mislead the court.

A leading source of support for the narrative approach is the first edition of the ABA Defense Standards, approved in 1971.[111] Granted, the ABA House of Delegates rejected this option when considering the proposed second edition, and the current standards contain no reference to the narrative approach.[112] However, a growing number of courts in the United States have accepted the narrative approach as a valid response to anticipated client perjury, including in large jurisdictions such as California, New York, Massachusetts, Illinois, Pennsylvania, and Florida.[113] Several academic commentators have followed

---

109   See *Brown v Commonwealth*, 226 SW3d 74 at 84–85 (Ky 2007) [*Brown*]; *State v Chambers*, 994 A2d 1248 at 1264 (Conn 2010) [*Chambers*]. *Chambers* also proscribes objections on matters going to the accused's credibility.

110   Nonetheless, in *Chambers*, above note 109, the accused was offered an opportunity to make representations directly to the jury in closing regarding his testimony. *Contra Commonwealth v Mitchell*, 438 Mass 535 at 550 (2003) [*Mitchell*]: accused should not be afforded such an opportunity.

111   First edition ABA defense standard 4-7.7(c), reproduced in *State v Lowery*, 523 P2d 54 (Ariz 1974) [*Lowery*].

112   See the discussion in the Third Restatement § 120, reporter's note to comment "i." The narrative approach endorsed by the first edition was altered slightly in the proposed second edition: see Lefstein, above note 29 at 542.

113   *Johnson*, above note 92; *People v Bolton*, 166 Cal App 4th 343 (2008); *DePallo*, above note 101; *People v Andrades*, 4 NY3d 355 (2005) [*Andrades*]; *Mitchell*, above note 110; *People v Bartee*, 566 NE2d 855 at 857 (Ill App 1991) [*Bartee*]; *Commonwealth v Mascitti*, 534 A2d 524 (Pa Super 1987) [*Mascitti*]; *Commonwealth v Jermyn*, 620 A2d 1128 (Pa 1993), cert denied, 510 US 1049 (1994); *Sanborn v State*, 474 So 2d 309 (Fla 3rd DCA 1985); *Rubin v State*, 490 So 2d 1001 (Fla Dist Ct App 1986), review denied, 501 So 2d 1283 (Fla), cert denied, 483 US 1005 (1987); *Shockley v State*, 565 A2d 1373 at 1377 (Del Super Ct 1989); *Chambers*, above note 109; *State v McDowell*, 681 NW2d 500 (Wis 2004), cert denied, 543 US 938 (2004) [*McDowell*]; *Brown*, above note 109; *Scott v State*,

suit,[114] as have the ethical codes in Massachusetts and the District of Columbia.[115]

Yet compromise positions sometimes end up doing unacceptable harm to all of the interests at stake, and this appears to be so with the narrative approach. The lawyer, though admittedly adopting a more passive role, is still knowingly facilitating the presentation of false evidence. At the same time, counsel's unusual approach will likely signal to the judge and prosecution that the client is lying.[116] A moderately astute jury will probably arrive at the same conclusion on perceiving that the lawyer's closing submissions make no reference to key testimony by the accused. Confidentiality thus suffers in a way that may significantly harm the client when it comes to the final determination as to guilt and the imposition of a sentence. This real risk of harm will be readily apparent to the client, and so adopting the narrative approach may cause almost as much damage to the client-lawyer relationship as would outright disclosure.

A further problem arises from the prosecutor's possible objection to defence counsel's use of the narrative approach. On observing that counsel is not eliciting testimony in the normal manner, the prosecutor might demur on the ground that there is no opportunity to object to inadmissible evidence prior to its being heard by the trier of

---

8 So 3d 855 (Miss SC 2008) [*Scott*]; *State v Layton*, 432 SE2d 740 at 754–55 (W Va 1993).

114 Lefstein, above note 29; Wayne Brazil, "Unanticipated Client Perjury and the Collision of Rules, Evidence, and Constitutional Law" (1979) 44 Mo L Rev 601. The narrative approach also finds some favour in Michael Asimow & Richard Weisberg, "When the Lawyer Knows the Client Is Guilty: Client Confessions in Legal Ethics, Popular Culture, and Literature" (2009) 18 S Cal Interdisciplinary LJ 229 at 242–43; L Timothy Perrin, "The Perplexing Problem of Client Perjury" (2007) 76 Fordham L Rev 1707 at 1737–42; Peter Henning, "Lawyers, Truth, and Honesty in Representing Clients" (2006) 20 Notre Dame JL Ethics & Pub Pol'y 209 at 264–66.

115 Massachusetts Rules of Professional Conduct, r 3.3(e) and comments 9–10; District of Columbia Rules of Professional Conduct, r 3.3(b).

116 Indeed, the narrative approach as used in many jurisdictions involves defence counsel before calling the client to the stand disclosing to the trial judge or another judge of the same court, whether expressly or by strong implication, that she believes the client will give perjured testimony: see *Mitchell*, above note 110 at 542–43 and 549 (disclosure to the trial judge); *McDowell*, above note 113 at 526 (disclosure to the trial judge); *Andrades*, above note 113 at 365–66 (disclosure to the trial judge); *Chambers*, above note 109 (disclosure to another judge); *Brown*, above note 109 at 80–81, 84, and 87 (disclosure to the trial judge *ex parte*, sealed record); *Scott*, above note 113 at 859–61 (disclosure to the trial judge *ex parte*, sealed record).

fact.[117] The defence lawyer would then be in the awkward position of trying to explain the basis for proceeding by way of narrative without breaching confidentiality. On the other hand, asking an open-ended question arguably does not breach the rules usually applicable to the proper conduct of an examination-in-chief. Plus, given that the narrative approach will usually result in the client's version of events being presented in a less than organized and coherent manner, few prosecutors may bother objecting in the first place.[118] However, if an objection is made and upheld, defence counsel is in a terribly difficult position, forbidden to continue using the narrative method but ethically barred from facilitating perjury by eliciting testimony in the normal manner.[119]

Ultimately, as Professor Wolfram observes, the narrative approach tries to have it both ways, in his view incoherently so, and ends up causing substantial harm to all of the principles at stake.[120] Wolfram's view appears to find support in *Nix v Whiteside*.[121] The ABA Model Rules also appear to reject the narrative approach,[122] albeit with the important caveat that a lawyer acts ethically in employing the approach if

---

117 However, in jurisdictions where defence counsel obtains permission to proceed by way of narrative after bringing an *inter partes* application — see all but the final two cases cited in the preceding note — the prosecutor will have no basis to object.

118 See Freedman & Smith, above note 27 at 159. Note that prosecutors virtually never object both for this reason and because they know that the narrative approach severely weakens the accused's case insofar as defence counsel does not rely on the evidence thereby elicited in final submissions.

119 The proposed but rejected client-perjury provision in the second edition of the ABA Defense Standards attempted to resolve this problem by allowing counsel to engage in something closer to a normal examination-in-chief following a sustained prosecution objection to the narrative form: see Lefstein, above note 29 at 542.

120 Charles W Wolfram, *Modern Legal Ethics* (St Paul, MN: West, 1986) at 661. To similar effect, see Stephen Gillers, "Monroe Freedman's Solution to the Criminal Defense Lawyer's Trilemma Is Wrong As a Matter of Policy and Constitutional Law" (2006) 34 Hofstra L Rev 821 at 829–31; Thrower, above note 64 at 790–97; Raymond McKoski, "Prospective Perjury by a Criminal Defendant: It's All about the Lawyer" (2012) 44 Ariz St LJ 1575 at 1625–26.

121 In *Nix*, above note 4 at 170–71, Burger CJ describes the narrative approach in note 6 without providing any sign of approval.

122 ABA Model Rule 3.3. Nathan Crystal, "False Testimony by Criminal Defendants: Still Unanswered Ethical and Constitutional Questions" [2003] U Ill L Rev 1529 at 1548, argues that comment 6 implicitly endorses the narrative approach, but we do not believe this to be a convincing interpretation of this comment, which states that "a lawyer may not elicit *or otherwise permit* a witness to present testimony the lawyer knows is false" [emphasis added].

required to do so by the jurisprudence in her jurisdiction.[123] Tellingly, no Canadian case or commentator supports the open-narrative option.

As a final point, it is worth observing that while counsel who employs the narrative approach is not allowed to rely on the perjurious testimony in making closing arguments, the trial judge is not in the same position. Rather, a judge is under a positive obligation to present the accused's version of events to the jury as part of the charge provided the testimony if believed would support a valid defence.[124] In *R v Colpitts*,[125] counsel in closing conspicuously neglected to make mention of a key element in his client's testimony. We do not know for certain that this tack was prompted by knowledge that the testimony was false. But the hallmarks of client perjury were present. The trial judge followed counsel's suit, making no reference to the accused's potentially perjurious testimony in his charge. The Supreme Court of Canada ruled that the judge thereby erred, and ordered a new trial.[126]

d) Eliciting Testimony in the Normal Manner

As we have seen, Professor Freedman is the leading exponent of the view that counsel should elicit and use perjurious testimony in the normal manner.[127] Freedman's view is also adopted in an opinion promulgated by the National Association of Criminal Defense Lawyers,[128] which he helped to draft. This same view has been strongly endorsed by Professor Silver in a comprehensive article addressing many aspects of the client-perjury problem,[129] while Professors Asimow and Weisberg argue that criminal lawyers should at least have a discretion to follow Freedman's approach if they so choose.[130]

Proceeding in this manner has the advantage of bolstering the client's right to testify and preventing any breach of counsel's duty of loyalty. Counsel is arguably not wilfully procuring perjured evidence,

---

123 ABA Model Rule 3.3, comment 7.

124 See *R v Gauthier*, 2013 SCC 32 at para 24; *R v Caron* (1998), 126 CCC (3d) 84 at 91 [paras 16–17] (Que CA); *R v Cerra*, 2002 BCCA 515 at para 11.

125 [1966] 1 CCC 146 (SCC).

126 Query whether the prosecutor who closes last can ask the jury to draw an adverse inference from a failure in the defence closing to rely on the client's testimony: see *State v Long*, 714 P2d 465 at 467 (Ariz Ct App 1986), holding that a prosecutor's request that the jury draw this inference is improper.

127 See Section D, above in this chapter.

128 "The Ethics Advisory Committee of NACDL, Formal Opinion 92-2" *The Champion* (March 1993) 23, online: www.nacdl.org/WorkArea/DownloadAsset. aspx?id=22098&libID=22068, set out in Hall, Jr, above note 62 at § 26.6.

129 Silver, above note 29.

130 Asimow & Weisberg, above note 114 at 243–44.

for she must have made good-faith efforts to dissuade the client from leading false testimony.[131] Silver goes so far as to propose that this approach best serves the goal of promoting truth in criminal proceedings on the grounds that perjury is almost always detected by the trier of fact and that counsel is particularly ill-equipped to determine on his own whether proposed testimony is false.[132]

Yet most ethical codes in the United States firmly reject Freedman's approach,[133] as do a large majority of academic commentators in that country. In Canada, learned writers are even less likely to endorse Freedman's recommended response to anticipated client perjury.[134] More importantly still, the Canadian rules of professional conduct expressly prohibit counsel from knowingly offering false evidence,[135] as does the jurisprudence.[136] The ethical codes also contain a more general interdiction against counsel knowingly assisting a client in any dishonesty or illegality.[137]

It is thus clear that Canadian lawyers cannot adopt Freedman's arguments and proceed in the normal manner when confronted by a client who wishes to testify falsely. At bottom, allowing counsel to knowingly lead and use false evidence is too great an impingement on the truth-finding function of the adversarial criminal justice system. The duty of loyalty simply does not extend to embrace such conduct, nor do the client's constitutional protections include obtaining counsel's knowing assistance in presenting false evidence.[138] Indeed, counsel

---

131 See Freedman & Smith, above note 27 at 165–66. Contrast Silver, above note 29 at 418–19: counsel should make no effort to dissuade the client apart from pointing out any tactical disadvantages of lying on the stand.

132 Silver, *ibid* at 423.

133 See, for example, ABA Model Rule 3.3(a)(3), comments 5–7; Third Restatement § 120.

134 See, for example, Randal Graham, *Legal Ethics*, 2d ed (Toronto: Emond Montgomery, 2011) at 411–12 & 413–14. Professor Woolley, in Woolley, *Understanding Lawyers' Ethics*, above note 37 at 180–83, stands alone in arguing that Freedman's proposal is the best solution to the perjury trilemma but acknowledges that it is precluded by Canadian ethical codes (*ibid* at 169).

135 See the provisions cited at notes 15–21 and 26, above in this chapter.

136 This is the implicit holding in the leading cases on client perjury: *Jenkins*, above note 70 at 432–37 [paras 18–36]; *Legato*, above note 90 at paras 83–88. See also *R v Li* (1993), 36 BCAC 181 at para 59 (CA), leave to appeal to SCC refused, [1994] SCCA No 209: *obiter* observation that lawyer who knows of client's guilt cannot call client to testify otherwise. The general prohibition against counsel knowingly misleading the court is affirmed in the jurisprudence discussed in Chapter 1, Section E.

137 See the rules cited at note 26, above in this chapter.

138 See the discussions in Sections B and F(4)(b), above in this chapter.

who knowingly leads false evidence is likely guilty of a criminal offence.[139] Proceeding in the normal manner is therefore not at all recommended for the lawyer who faces a client-perjury problem.

e) Permitting the Client to Offer Only Non-perjurious Testimony

Still another approach is to call the client as a witness but only for the
purpose of testifying to facts that counsel does not know to be false.
This option, less commonly presented as a viable response to anticipated client perjury, seeks to alleviate some of the criticisms directed at
refusing to call the client as a witness, and it garners support from both
the ABA Standing Committee on Ethics and Professional Responsibility and the Third Restatement.[140] For instance, the Third Restatement
states, "If the client nonetheless insists on the right to take the stand,
defense counsel must accede to the demand of the accused to testify.
*Thereafter defense counsel may not ask the accused any question if counsel
knows that the response would be false.*"[141]

Yet restricting the client's testimony presents its own serious problems. It is quite probable that, once on the stand, the client will testify to those facts that he wishes, regardless of counsel's attempts to
guide the examination in a particular direction. Even if the client can
be restricted to providing non-perjurious testimony, the result will frequently be that no testimony whatsoever is offered regarding crucial
aspects of the case. Such a failure will leave the fact-finder highly unimpressed and may alert other trial participants to the client-perjury
problem. Finally, there is no guarantee that the Crown will not delve
into the problematic area during cross-examination. Presumably, the
client will respond by providing the false evidence, undermining the
entire point of the exercise.

f) Disclosure of the Intended Perjury

The suggestion that a lawyer may be required or permitted to disclose a
client's intended perjury is highly controversial. Those who advocate disclosure of an intended perjury rely primarily on the point that counsel
must not allow false evidence to skew the truth-finding function of the

---

139 See note 11, above in this chapter. Canadian courts would be highly unlikely to
     accept the argument made by Freedman & Smith, above note 27 at 165–66, that
     counsel who undertakes such action has a defence to a criminal prosecution
     because she does so only as a last resort "under the compulsion of her role in
     our constitutionalized adversary system."
140 ABA Formal Opinion 87-353, above note 59 at 8; Third Restatement § 120, com-
     ment "i." See also *Lowery*, above note 111.
141 Third Restatement § 120, comment "i" [emphasis added].

criminal justice system.[142] On this view, where revelation is necessary to prevent such an occurrence, all other attempts at prevention having failed, counsel must or may take this final remedial step. A somewhat different argument in favour of disclosure focuses on the benefits to be derived from involving a neutral arbiter in the process. Depending on the nature of the procedure governing the act of disclosure, a judge may be able to examine and assess the disagreement between counsel and client. Judicial intervention at this stage might conceivably serve to fashion a resolution to the problem or even to discover that counsel's fears are unjustified.

The arguments against disclosure are familiar and powerful. Disclosure represents a huge incursion against the duties of loyalty and confidentiality normally owed to the client. Indeed, disclosing the intended perjury may require the revelation of a whole raft of confidential information, especially if the client disputes counsel's allegations and if an evidentiary hearing is held. Obvious harms to the client may arise from counsel's disclosure, including conviction at trial, a harsher sentence, and the laying of new criminal charges.[143] Clients may decide to avoid the risk of such injury by becoming less candid in their dealings with lawyers, with the result that the overall quality of representation suffers. Ironically, less candid dealing may actually cause the incidence of completed perjury to *rise*. Clients who fear disclosure are more likely to hide planned perjury from their counsel, with a resulting decrease in the prospect that counsel will discover such plans and be able to dissuade clients from carrying them out.

The ethical guidelines promulgated by Canadian governing bodies shed substantial light on the propriety of counsel's disclosing otherwise confidential information in an effort to prevent anticipated client perjury. The starting point is the commentary, found in most codes, stipulating that the lawyer whose client insists on conduct that if carried out would breach the rule prohibiting the knowing presentation of false evidence "must refuse and do everything reasonably possible to prevent it."[144] One could perhaps argue that the reference to "doing everything reasonably possible to prevent the perjury," to paraphrase given our context, should be read to include the option of making disclosure.

---

142 See, for example, Franck, above note 72; ABA Formal Opinion 87-353, above note 59 at 6 and 8.

143 These harms become more or less likely depending on the procedure under which disclosure is made, as well as the reaction by Crown counsel and the court.

144 See the rules cited at note 21, above in this chapter.

But this interpretation is unconvincing because the commentary immediately goes on to provide that where the client continues to insist that counsel act unethically, counsel must withdraw or seek leave to do so.[145] Withdrawal, not disclosure, is thus the response of last resort mandated by the codes.[146] What is more, the commentary further provides that counsel must comply with the ethical rule dealing with withdrawal in seeking to get off the record. In many Canadian codes, the withdrawal rule expressly states that counsel must strive to protect the client's confidences and cannot reveal the reason for withdrawing when terminating the retainer, a position that is also supported in the caselaw.[147] This prohibition makes sense only if there has been no prior disclosure of the problem.

Interpreting the commentary's requirement that the lawyer do everything reasonably possible to prevent a client's perjury so as to permit or mandate disclosure runs up against a further objection. As will be seen, most Canadian codes seem fairly clear in rejecting disclosure as an option in the case of *completed* perjury.[148] The fact that disclosure of a completed perjury is prohibited militates strongly against interpreting the commentary under discussion to countenance disclosure of an anticipated falsehood, absent a clear expression of intent otherwise.

What about the future-harm exception to the duty of confidentiality? Might it apply to permit disclosure of an anticipated perjury? The notion that counsel can ethically make disclosure of a client confidence to prevent future harm is certainly well-established in Canada, and is discussed at length in Chapter 5.[149] Yet in most provinces the future-harm exception only permits disclosure to prevent death or serious bodily harm[150] and so is unlikely ever to be engaged by the prospect of client perjury.[151]

---

145 *Ibid.*
146 The cases cited at note 90, above in this chapter, also seem to reject disclosure as a response to anticipated client perjury, insofar as they endorse counsel's withdrawing where the client insists on giving false testimony.
147 See Chapter 4, Section H(7), and Chapter 11, Section M.
148 See Section G(3)(b), below in this chapter.
149 See Chapter 5, Section I.
150 The provinces in question are British Columbia, Alberta, Ontario, Quebec, Nova Scotia, and Newfoundland and Labrador. The CBA Code is to the same effect. See Chapter 5, Section I(1).
151 Exceedingly improbable hypotheticals might nonetheless trigger the exception in these provinces. Consider, for instance, a case in which counsel represents a client who intends to testify falsely to the detriment of a co-accused where both are charged with first-degree murder. If believed by the jury, the perjury might

Yet the situation may be different in Saskatchewan, Manitoba, and New Brunswick. As noted above, each of these provinces has a confidentiality exception that affords lawyers a discretion to disclose confidential information where reasonably necessary to prevent any crime.[152] Lawyers in these jurisdictions thus appear to have the option of making disclosure where necessary to prevent a client's intended perjury. However, as explained already, lawyers may be justifiably reluctant to exercise this discretion for fear of undermining the client's constitutional right to the protection of solicitor-client privilege.[153] Lawyers who have no such fear should nonetheless not make disclosure without first weighing very carefully the advantages and disadvantages of doing so.[154]

Given our view that counsel in Saskatchewan, Manitoba, and New Brunswick may have the option of disclosing *after* the perjury has occurred[155] and the difficulty in ascertaining whether the client will really act to implement the perjurious plan, we believe that the discretion to disclose to prevent anticipated client perjury should rarely if ever be exercised.[156] The one limited circumstance where disclosure of anticipated perjury by lawyers in these three provinces *may* be permissible, though not required, involves revelation to new counsel for the client following withdrawal. Doing so may fix successor counsel with knowledge sufficient to prevent him from acting unless the client agrees not to testify falsely.[157]

If counsel feels justified in making disclosure of a client's intended perjury to anyone other than successor counsel, settling on the mechanics of the revelation raises many problems. In a trial by jury, counsel could make disclosure to the judge and prosecutor, in the absence

---

lead to the co-accused's wrongful conviction and thus cause him serious bodily harm, which includes serious psychological harm: see Chapter 5, Section M(2).

152 See the paragraph associated with notes 76–77, above in this chapter.

153 See the paragraph associated with notes 78–81, above in this chapter.

154 For a discussion of factors that might impact on counsel's exercise of the discretion, see Chapter 5, Section I(10).

155 See Section G(3)(b), below in this chapter.

156 Woolley, *Understanding Lawyers' Ethics*, above note 37 at 169–70, argues that counsel should never disclose an intended client perjury. Although she does not discuss the future-crime exceptions in Saskatchewan, Manitoba, and New Brunswick, elsewhere in her book she contends they should only be used to disclose client confidences where the test in *Smith v Jones*, above note 74, has been met (Woolley, *Understanding Lawyers' Ethics*, above note 37 at 139), based on an argument similar to that mentioned in the text associated with note 78, above.

157 This argument is explained in the paragraphs associated with notes 76–81, above in this chapter.

of the trier of fact.[158] It has also been suggested that disclosure could be made to the judge alone, without notifying the Crown attorney or perhaps even the client.[159] However, keeping the client in the dark is of dubious ethical validity, given counsel's duty to keep the client informed.[160] Moreover, counsel must remonstrate with the client before making disclosure, during which the client must be warned that disclosure is a possible remedial measure. It seems nonsensical to provide such a warning only to hide the fact of disclosure from the client. Going behind the client's back in this way would probably also violate the accused's right to be present during the trial.[161]

A variation is for counsel to bring the disclosure application before a judge other than the trial judge, without notice to the prosecutor.[162] Yet once the trial has started, obtaining an adjournment for such a purpose without alerting the trial judge to the reason may be difficult.

Once a judge has been informed of the anticipated problem, the client may indicate an intention not to offer the testimony in question. At this point, the possibility of perjury will be remote and counsel can proceed to call the client to the stand, if the professional relationship has not been destroyed by the disclosure. But the client may deny that he intends to offer false testimony. A judge may therefore be forced to hold an evidentiary hearing on the issue, obviously in the continued absence of the jury.[163] However, if this route is taken, the defence lawyer may

---

158 See *United States v Long*, 857 F2d 436 (8th Cir 1988) [*Long*]. In the United States, this often occurs in the closely related context of counsel's obtaining prior judicial authorization to employ the narrative method of questioning: see *Mitchell*, above note 110 at 542–43 and 549; *McDowell*, above note 113 at 526; *Andrades*, above note 113 at 365–66.

159 See *United States v Litchfield*, 959 F2d 1514 (10th Cir 1992).

160 See Chapter 3, Section E.

161 See *Mitchell*, above note 110 at 547–48; *contra Andrades*, above note 113 at 362. In Canada, s 650(1) of the *Criminal Code*, above note 11, gives an accused the right to be present during "the whole of his or her trial." Recent cases where the s 650(1) right has been breached by counsel and the judge meeting in the absence of the accused to discuss witness credibility issues include *R v James*, 2009 ONCA 366; *R v Schofield*, 2012 ONCA 120.

162 This possibility is discussed in *Long*, above note 158; Carol Reiger, "Client Perjury: A Proposed Resolution of the Constitutional and Ethical Issues" (1985) 70 Minn L Rev 121 at 151. It is occasionally used by counsel seeking advance permission to elicit evidence by narrative method: see *Brown*, above note 109 at 80–81, 84, and 87; *Scott*, above note 113 at 859–61.

163 See, for example, *Long*, above note 158; *Butler v United States*, 414 A2d 844 (DC 1980); *Thornton v United States*, 357 A2d 429 at 432 (DC 1976); *Witherspoon v United States*, 557 A2d 587 (DC 1989). However, courts receiving disclosure from counsel seeking permission to use the narrative method tend to reject the

be removed from the record for conflict of interest, given his fundamental disagreement with the accused and probable role as a witness,[164] leaving the accused unrepresented at the hearing. A further conundrum arises if new counsel is appointed and if that counsel concludes that the accused is going to commit perjury at the evidentiary hearing.[165]

If the trial judge is unable to determine that the client is intent on committing perjury, the client should be permitted to testify. But where the judge concludes that perjury will occur if the accused takes the stand, the next step is far from obvious. The judge will in effect face many of the options that initially bedevilled defence counsel. She may try to dissuade the accused from carrying out the perjury and if unsuccessful may rule that counsel can withdraw from the case. Or the judge might allow counsel to remain and have the accused testify in narrative form[166] or adopt Freedman's view and encourage counsel to proceed in calling the client as though nothing were amiss. Yet this latter result means that the client's confidence has been violated without achieving much in return, apart from the court's permission to elicit and rely on false evidence. A very different approach would be to hold that the disclosed information is neither confidential nor privileged and permit the Crown counsel to lead evidence of the accused's plan and/or cross-examine the accused on the matter if he takes the stand. It is even conceivable that a judge once convinced the proposed testimony is perjurious might conclude that there is no constitutional right to present false evidence and so rule that the accused cannot testify.[167]

Another possible judicial response is to declare a mistrial, perhaps on the ground that counsel has withdrawn or been discharged. An objection to the mistrial option is that an accused could derail proceedings and delay a feared conviction by repeatedly asserting a firm intention to lie on the stand. This problem can be partially alleviated by making the record from the first trial available if the perjury issue

---

idea that a hearing is necessary: see, for example, *Bartee*, above note 113 at 857; *Mitchell*, above note 110 at 547–48 and 552; *Johnson*, above note 92 at 630.

164 See Chapter 6, Section L.

165 See Liskov, above note 57 at 903.

166 In the United States, this is the usual judicial response to a disclosure of anticipated perjury by counsel: see, for example, *Henkel*, above note 85; *Long*, above note 158 at 44; *Mascitti*, above note 113 at 528; McKoski, above note 120 at 1631–34. Indeed, disclosure by counsel is typically made in jurisdictions where the narrative method is condoned.

167 Yet this result is unlikely: see the discussion in Section F(4)(b), above in this chapter. We are aware of no case in Canada or the United States in which a trial judge has responded to counsel's disclosure of anticipated client perjury in this fashion.

arises during the second proceeding and ruling that the accused's actions represent waiver of the right to counsel. Yet any mistrial that comes late in the proceedings has a cost in terms of wasted resources and may cause harm to the client who is awaiting trial in custody, not to mention the course of justice where witnesses become unavailable or memories fade.

Until now, we have assumed that the perjury problem is disclosed during a jury trial. But the same issue can arise when the accused is being tried by a judge alone. In such a case, the revelation is made to the trier of fact, which increases the risk of subsequent prejudice to the accused.[168] For this reason, a mistrial may be the only valid course of action for the trial judge once the accused's planned perjury is revealed. Others have suggested that disclosure to the court, while permissible in a jury trial, can never be countenanced in a trial by judge alone.[169] Yet another option is to make disclosure to a judge other than the trial judge. Of course, if one takes the view that the disclosed information is not confidential or privileged and on the particular facts can reasonably be viewed as consciousness of guilt, no problem arises because the Crown can properly lead it in seeking a conviction at trial.

Unfortunately, on most of these disclosure scenarios the perjury problem is merely foisted on the trial judge. Granted, the duties that make counsel's handling of the problem so difficult are not replicated exactly in the judicial context. In particular, the judge does not owe the accused a duty of loyalty or confidentiality. But any solution implemented by the court will have to take account of counsel's duties, and there are also difficult constitutional and procedural issues to consider.[170] Indeed, because the court may be in no better position to solve the problem than is defence counsel, it has been very sensibly argued that disclosure of anticipated perjury should be avoided.[171]

---

168 The risk is much greater than where counsel withdraws for "ethical reasons," which does not involve disclosure of counsel's belief that the client will commit perjury: see the paragraphs associated with notes 84–87, above in this chapter.

169 See Third Restatement § 120, comment "i," suggesting disclosure be made to the prosecutor, who is not permitted to inform the judge of the matter.

170 The implicated constitutional rights are canvassed in Sections B and F(4)(b), above in this chapter.

171 See Lefstein, above note 29 at 538–41; Asimow & Weisberg, above note 114 at 240–41.

G. COMPLETED CLIENT PERJURY

Several of the issues canvassed above in relation to anticipated perjury arise in much the same fashion with respect to perjury that has already occurred. Yet the difference in timing does lead to distinctions. For instance, dealing with completed client perjury focuses more closely on remedial steps. Sometimes, however, the line between anticipated and completed perjury blurs. Consider defence counsel who while conducting an examination-in-chief of her client is stunned to hear testimony that she irresistibly knows to be false. As the client waits on the stand for the next question, obviously preparing to tell a series of associated lies, counsel anticipates further perjury. The worst sort of problem has arisen: perjury is both completed and anticipated, and counsel is under pressure to continue with the client's examination at a crucial point in the trial.[172]

1) Acquiring Knowledge That the Client Has Committed Perjury

Irresistible knowledge that perjury has occurred is a vital prerequisite to counsel's taking any remedial action. We have discussed the importance and nature of counsel's knowledge in relation to anticipated perjury.[173] The principles remain the same when counsel is confronted with client perjury that has already taken place. It is worth emphasizing that counsel should not jump to any conclusions without discussing the matter with the client. Where the problematic testimony has taken counsel by surprise, it is especially important that counsel confront the client confidentially, if necessary obtaining an adjournment for the purpose.

2) Admonishing the Client to Correct the Perjury

Once defence counsel knows that a perjury has occurred, she must seek to convince the client to correct the falsehood.[174] In doing so, counsel should ensure that the client understands the consequences of disclosing, or not, the lie to the court. If the client is steadfast in

---

172 A combination of completed and anticipated client perjury probably occurred in *Jenkins*, above note 70, although counsel seems to have first learned of the lies during his client's cross-examination by Crown counsel.

173 See Section F(1), above in this chapter.

174 See the code provisions set out at notes 20–21, above in this chapter.

refusing to retract the perjury, counsel must take appropriate remedial measures. The admonition to correct a perjury is thus analogous to the requirement that counsel attempt to dissuade a client from committing an anticipated perjury.[175]

Comparison: Most Canadian rules urge counsel to rectify a known falsehood by making disclosure to the court. The client must therefore be counselled to accept this remedial route. But the Alberta and New Brunswick codes condone an additional remedial option, namely, informing the court that the evidence in question should not be relied on.[176] In these two provinces, a lawyer should thus present this option to the client as an alternative to making disclosure outright.

It has been suggested that in some circumstances it may be appropriate for counsel to attempt to correct the perjury by asking further questions of the accused.[177] Such an approach does not constitute a knowing attempt to mislead the court, for the lawyer's purpose is to retract the falsehood. However, this tack is not generally recommended. Because counsel cannot be sure of the client's answers or reaction, the exercise will be difficult to control. Any harmful result, such as an angry verbal attack directed at counsel or the revelation of confidential information, will take place in front of the fact-finder. The better approach is to consult with the client in private. If the client is amenable to correcting the perjury, further questions can be asked with counsel fairly secure in anticipating the client's responses.

A related point arises as to how, exactly, counsel can engineer a confidential meeting with the client without alerting Crown counsel, the judge, or the jury that something has gone terribly wrong. It may be that the perjury is discrete, and counsel has no fear that further lies will be told. If so, counsel can perhaps continue with the examination in the normal fashion and talk to the client at the next break in proceedings. Where the examination is almost over, however, counsel may have no choice but to request an adjournment.[178] The adjournment should be suggested without fanfare, as casually as possible. If counsel anticipates problems, it is prudent to make the request in the absence of the jury. It is also a good idea, if possible, to continue with at least a few innocuous questions before asking for a break. This delay lessens

---

175   With respect to which, see Section F(2), above in this chapter.

176   See the paragraphs associated with notes 23–25, above in this chapter.

177   See Beverley Smith, *Professional Conduct for Lawyers and Judges*, 4th ed (Fredericton, NB: Maritime Law Book, 2011) ch 7 at para 48.

178   See *Law Society of Saskatchewan v Segal*, [1999] LSDD No 9 [*Segal*]: in the context of perjury committed during examination in discovery.

368 ETHICS AND CRIMINAL LAW

the chances that the requested adjournment will trigger suspicion that the accused has lied.

The difficulties in obtaining an adjournment are immeasurably increased where the lawyer predicts that further perjury is sure to occur. One option is to ask for an immediate adjournment. Another is to shift the questions to an unproblematic area and then to make the request. A more daring avenue is to continue as though nothing is wrong, in effect embracing, at least for a time, the Freedman approach.[179] Or counsel could decide to complete the examination on the areas of concern by utilizing the narrative method.[180] Given the problems associated with both Freedman's approach and the narrative method, we believe that counsel is best advised to cut short the examination as soon as possible, or in any event without eliciting further perjurious responses. Successful remonstration, it is to be hoped, can address the problem before it gets worse.

3) Remedial Measures Where the Client Refuses to Correct the Perjury

There are three main options available to the lawyer who, coming to know of a completed perjury, and despite admonition, is faced with a recalcitrant client. First, counsel can attempt to withdraw from the case. Second, counsel can disclose the falsehood to the court or Crown counsel. Third, counsel can continue to act on the case as though nothing is amiss.

a) Withdrawal
We have already discussed many of the issues surrounding withdrawal as a response to client perjury, though in the context of perjury that has yet to occur.[181] In the case of completed perjury, counsel by definition finds himself in the midst of the trial. At this stage in the proceedings, counsel cannot withdraw as of right but rather must seek leave.[182] In doing so, counsel can inform the court only that he is applying to get off the record for "ethical reasons."[183] The court has no power to

---

179   See Section F(4)(d), above in this chapter.
180   See Section F(4)(c), above in this chapter.
181   See Section F(4)(a), above in this chapter.
182   See the discussion in the paragraph associated with notes 64–69, above in this chapter.
183   *Ibid.*

demand further information regarding the reason for counsel's request
and is required to grant leave.[184]

Despite the paucity of information revealed by counsel in withdrawing, given the context the judge and prosecutor will probably be
alerted to at least the potential of a client perjury problem. Yet, as explained in the context of anticipated client perjury, the risk of the judge
or Crown being so alerted is not so serious as to disqualify withdrawal
as a viable response to client perjury.[185]

In any event, Canadian caselaw addressing the issue of completed
client perjury views withdrawal as a proper remedial action.[186] Withdrawal also appears to be mandated by most Canadian codes of professional conduct. Specifically, the ethical rules concerning advocacy
found in the majority of codes state that counsel who has unknowingly
done something that if done knowingly would have been in breach of
the duty not to mislead the court must, on obtaining the knowledge in
question, and subject to the rule concerning confidentiality, disclose
the error and do all that can reasonably be done to rectify it.[187] Importantly, these rules go on to provide that where the client insists that
counsel act unethically — which is the case here because she refuses to
allow counsel to rectify the perjury — counsel should withdraw.[188] The
need to get off the record is further supported by the code provisions
governing withdrawal more generally, which provide that counsel must
terminate a retainer where the client has instructed counsel to act contrary to professional ethics.[189]

It is also worth mentioning the unique provisions found in the
codes in two provinces. The code in New Brunswick states that counsel who becomes aware of a material perjury by a client or witness has
three options: withdraw, make immediate disclosure to the court and
other counsel, or continue in the proceedings without referencing the
false evidence except to advise the court that the evidence should not
be relied upon.[190] In Alberta, the rules contain language to the effect that
on becoming aware a client has given false evidence, a lawyer has a
duty to immediately correct the misapprehension,[191] but the commentary

---

184 *Ibid.*
185 See the paragraphs associated with notes 84–87, above in this chapter.
186 See the cases cited at note 90, above in this chapter.
187 See the rules cited at note 20, above in this chapter.
188 See the commentaries cited at note 21, above in this chapter.
189 See Chapter 11, Section F.
190 NB ch 8, commentary 12(a).
191 Alta r 4.01(5)(b) & first and fourth paras of associated commentary.

adds that "it may be sufficient discharge of this duty to merely advise the tribunal not to rely on the impugned information."[192]

The provisions in Alberta and New Brunswick can perhaps be read to provide a lawyer whose client refuses to correct a perjury with options other than mandatory withdrawal. A more compelling interpretation, however, is that these other options are available only where the client is in agreement. If the client refuses to countenance their use, the lawyer's only recourse is to apply to withdraw. We prefer this view because in both codes the provisions setting out counsel's various options appear to be subject to the overriding rule that a lawyer must withdraw where the client insists that a lawyer act so as to breach the duty of candour to the court.

b) Disclosure

Most of the arguments for and against disclosure have been covered in the discussion concerning anticipated client perjury.[193] While the reasons for not revealing a perjury that is merely planned are quite strong, once the client has perpetrated the falsehood, the balance shifts somewhat in favour of disclosure. The possibility that counsel is over-reacting to a feared course of action dissipates. Moreover, the client will have knowingly used the lawyer's services to commit the crimes of perjury and attempting to obstruct justice, the latter of which will be ongoing at least until the verdict is rendered. There is good reason to deny a client the benefits of the duties of loyalty and confidentiality where he has abused the solicitor-client relationship in an effort to pervert the course of justice.[194] In our opinion, disclosure is therefore justified *from a policy point of view* where perjury has occurred and where the client refuses to correct the falsehood.[195] This is the position taken in the ABA Model Rules and the Third Restatement, both of which expressly require counsel to make disclosure of a client's completed perjury on a material matter.[196]

---

192 Alta r 4.01(5)(b) & fourth para of associated commentary.
193 See Section F(4)(f), above in this chapter.
194 See Chapter 5, Section L.
195 To the same effect, see Graham, above note 134 at 414. *Contra* Woolley, *Understanding Lawyers' Ethics*, above note 37 at 169–71.
196 ABA Model Rules 3.3(a)(3) & 3.3(b), plus comments 10–11; Third Restatement § 120(2). Freedman argues that lawyers tend to disclose under Model Rule 3.3 only when representing indigent or minority clients and that the rule therefore operates in an unconstitutionally discriminatory fashion: Freedman & Smith, above note 27 at 184; Freedman, above note 1 at 148–52. See also Gillers, above note 120 at 843.

Yet the majority of Canadian ethical codes appear to preclude counsel from disclosing a completed client perjury to the court. Formidable support for this conclusion is found in the rule requiring counsel who realizes she has unknowingly done something that if done knowingly would have breached the duty not to mislead the court to disclose the error or omission *subject to the rules governing confidentiality*.[197] Crucially, the confidentiality rules adopted by most governing bodies contain no exception that would allow disclosure for the purpose of remedying a client's perjury. In particular, these rules permit disclosure to prevent future harm but only where the harm involves death or serious bodily injury, a precondition that will almost never be met in the client-perjury scenario.[198] It is therefore unsurprising that in the Ontario case of *R v Jenkins*, the court implicitly accepted that counsel could not disclose a completed perjury by the client.[199]

The situation may be different in Saskatchewan, Manitoba, and New Brunswick, for the codes in these provinces permit disclosure of otherwise confidential information to prevent any crime, whether or not it involves death or serious bodily harm.[200] The difficult issue remains, however, as to whether lawyers in these provinces will treat this future-crime discretion as largely inoperative because of the narrower public-safety exception to solicitor-client privilege set out in *Smith v Jones*.[201]

Finally, the code in New Brunswick is unique in Canada in expressly allowing counsel to make immediate disclosure to the court and Crown on learning that a client or other defence witness has committed perjury.[202] Yet the better view, as explained above, is that this provision can only be relied on with the client's consent.[203] Regardless, the provision is arguably unavailable because it impermissibly clashes with the narrower *Smith v Jones* exception to solicitor-client privilege.[204]

---

197 See the rules cited at note 20, above in this chapter.

198 See the paragraph associated with notes 149–51, above in this chapter, making the same point regarding anticipated client perjury.

199 *Jenkins*, above note 70, although it is hard to agree with the court's conclusion that withdrawing counsel maintained the client's confidences: see Layton, above note 70 at 262–63 and 270–74.

200 See the paragraphs associated with notes 152–57, above in this chapter, making the same point regarding anticipated client perjury.

201 See the paragraph associated with notes 152–54, above in this chapter.

202 See the text associated with note 190, above in this chapter.

203 This point is made in an analogous context in the last paragraph of Section G(3)(a), above in this chapter.

204 See the paragraph associated with notes 152–54, above in this chapter.

c) Other Options

Some other options have been advanced that fall short of full disclosure of the completed perjury. In particular, it has been suggested that counsel can continue to conduct the case in the normal manner but make no reference to the false testimony in closing.[205] If counsel discovers the falsehood during direct examination and if further perjury is anticipated, this option could also entail shifting to the narrative method for the remainder of the client's testimony. A variation, which while still not the equivalent of full disclosure comes very close, would have counsel expressly inform the court that the evidence should not be relied upon.[206]

These options are problematic for several reasons. First, if one accepts that disclosure against the client's wishes is precluded by the codes in most Canadian jurisdictions, it is difficult to nonetheless justify conduct that implicitly but nonetheless strongly signals that the evidence in question is false. Second, it may be difficult if not impossible to make effective closing submissions in favour of acquittal without relying on the perjured evidence. In such a case, making no mention of the false evidence or telling the trier of fact to disregard it reduces the defence to a tiny rump, consisting of little more than counsel exhorting the trier of fact to abide by the requirement that the Crown prove guilt on the criminal standard. Third, and most importantly, we believe that counsel should not conduct the defence in a manner contrary to the client's express instructions regarding a material point. Rather than override the client's wishes in a manner that effectively sabotages the defence, counsel whose client resists exhortations to remedy a completed perjury should withdraw for ethical reasons.

H. PREVENTATIVE MEASURES: EARLY ADVICE TO THE CLIENT

The risk of the perjury problem arising can be reduced if at the outset of the relationship counsel makes clear to the client a lawyer's role and

---

205 See Richard Peck, "Ethical Problems in Defending a Criminal Case: The Serbo-nian Bog" (Paper delivered at Federation of Law Societies, National Criminal Law Program, Saskatoon, SK, July 1992) at 11–12. This option is similar to that proposed by the Crown in *Jenkins*, above note 70 at 436 [para 34].

206 As noted in Section G(3)(a), above in this chapter, this approach is countenanced in Alberta and New Brunswick as an alternative to making remedial disclosure to the court, but in our view neither jurisdiction permits counsel to adopt it against the client's wishes.

responsibilities. Of course, it would be inappropriate, and likely fatal to the relationship, to accuse the client of perjurious plans without any basis in fact. But counsel should diplomatically explain not only the nature and operation of client-lawyer confidentiality and privilege but also possible limits on the lawyer's duties connected with the prohibition against assisting in the presentation of false evidence.[207] This approach has been criticized by those who view such counselling as an invitation to not inform the lawyer of planned perjury or who fear that the client will in any event develop a distrust of the lawyer.[208] Yet surely openness in the client-lawyer relationship runs both ways. As long as counsel approaches the matter in a sensitive, non-accusatory fashion, it makes sense to give the client accurate information as to what a defence lawyer can and cannot do in representing an accused.[209]

---

207 See Chapter 4, Section K.
208 See Silver, above note 29 at 394–95. To be clear, we do not favour counselling directed at avoiding knowledge of planned or executed perjury: see Chapter 1, Section F(4).
209 See Allan Hutchinson, *Legal Ethics and Professional Responsibility*, 2d ed (Toronto: Irwin Law, 2006) at 174: "lawyers would save themselves and their clients a lot of trouble and disappointment if they covered such matters in an initial interview"; *Canadian National Railway Co v McKercher LLP*, 2013 SCC 39 at paras 45 and 58: a lawyer has a duty to disclose to the client any factors relevant to the lawyer's ability to provide effective representation.

CHAPTER 8

WITNESSES

A. INTRODUCTION

The outcome of a criminal case usually depends on the testimony of witnesses. A central role for counsel thus lies in determining whether witnesses are available to assist the client's case, in preparing witnesses to testify and eliciting their evidence in court, and in deciding whether and how to challenge the reliability of witnesses called by the opposing party. Ethical principles guide counsel at all stages of these interactions with witnesses. We have already examined the interplay of these principles in a number of areas, such as the problem of client perjury and the cross-examination of a witness known by the lawyer to be truthful.[1] In this chapter, the discussion continues with the focus predominantly, though not entirely, on counsel's out-of-court interactions with witnesses and potential witnesses. In each area reviewed, counsel's obligation to advance resolutely the client's best interests plays a substantial role in conceptualizing what constitutes ethical conduct. Yet the obligation to promote the client's best interests is often limited by a concomitant duty to avoid conduct that creates an unacceptable risk of misleading the court or treating a witness unfairly.

---

1   See Chapter 7 and Chapter 1, Section K(1).

B. THE DUTY TO LOCATE AND INTERVIEW WITNESSES

Canadian ethical codes describe a competent lawyer as one who applies relevant knowledge, skills, and attributes in a manner appropriate to each matter including, among other things, investigating the facts.[2] They also state that "unless the client instructs otherwise, the lawyer should investigate the matter in sufficient detail to be able to express an opinion rather than mere comments with many qualifications."[3] In the same vein, the ABA Defense Standards oblige defence counsel to "conduct a prompt investigation of the circumstances of the case and explore all avenues leading to facts relevant to the merits."[4]

Defence counsel's duty of competence thus includes the obligation to take reasonable steps to investigate whether an individual has information that might assist in advancing the client's case at trial. Timely action will often be necessary to ensure that the best possible information can be obtained, for example by interviewing a witness promptly about an ordinary occurrence that might otherwise soon be forgotten or imperfectly remembered.[5] An unreasonable failure to interview a witness soon enough, or at all, may amount to incompetence. Where the result is real prejudice to the client at trial, counsel's oversight will constitute ineffective assistance so as to require that a conviction be overturned and a new trial ordered.[6]

Yet counsel need not interview everyone who might conceivably have information relevant to the case. He must exercise sound professional judgment, based on all of the circumstances, to determine whether there is a reasonable possibility the information will assist the

---

2   Alta, Sask r 2.01(1)(b); BC, Man, Ont, NS, NL r 3.1-1(b). See also Chapter 3, Section K(1).

3   Alta, Sask r 2.01(2) (commentary); BC, Man, Ont, NS, NL r 3.1-2, commentary 8.

4   ABA Defense Standard 4-4.1(a).

5   See G Arthur Martin, "Preparation for Trial" in Law Society of Upper Canada, *Defending a Criminal Case* (Toronto: Richard De Boo Ltd, 1969) 221 at 230–32.

6   See, for example, *R v Delisle* (1999), 133 CCC (3d) 541 at 555–58 [paras 47–55 and 60] (Que CA) [*Delisle*], *R v McKellar* (1994), 34 CR (4th) 28 (Ont CA); *R v Michelin*, [1999] OJ No 848 at paras 35–38 and 42 (Gen Div); *R v Jim*, 2003 BCCA 411 at paras 8–9 and 13; *R v Giroux*, [2004] OJ No 2054 at paras 1–2 (CA) [*Giroux*]; *R v McKoy*, 2011 ONCA 41 at paras 4–5; *R v Fraser*, 2011 NSCA 70 at paras 86–93 and 97–104 [*Fraser*]. See also Dale Ives, "Failure to Interview a Potential Defence Witness as the Basis for an Ineffective Assistance of Counsel Claim" (2008) 53 Crim LQ 490.

client's defence.[7] Factors to consider in deciding whether to seek out and interview a potential witness include the degree of likelihood that the witness exists and can be located, whether the witness's information relates to a viable defence, the extent to which the information advances that defence and is reliable, whether the witness is likely to be co-operative, and any instructions received from the client.[8]

Recommendation: Counsel should generally ascertain whether the client knows of anyone who might have information that could be relevant to the case. It is usually advisable to interview those individuals who have personally witnessed material events,[9] although the need to do so will vary depending on the extent to which their evidence may assist the defence and the contents of any interview materials produced by police and included in the disclosure.

Defence lawyers have finite resources with which to conduct investigations, especially where the client is of modest means or relies on legal aid, and a paucity of resources can present serious challenges.[10] Counsel's ethical duties cannot be dictated simply by reference to the amount of funding available.[11] Yet she cannot be expected personally to finance expensive investigations into whether a witness exists and has information helpful to the defence.[12]

C. STRICTURES ON CONTACTING A WITNESS BEFORE TRIAL

A lawyer is free to contact any potential witness in an attempt to obtain information material to the client's case, regardless of whether the witness

---

7   In the context of ineffective assistance of counsel claims, the view that only *reasonable* steps to investigate a potential witness need be taken is endorsed in *Strickland v Washington*, 466 US 668 at 691 (1984); *R v White* (1997), 114 CCC (3d) 225 at 254 [para 94] (Ont CA) [*White*]; *Giroux*, above note 6 at para 1.

8   Similar factors are mentioned in *White*, above note 7 at 254 [para 94]; *R v RW* (2006), 207 CCC (3d) 137 at paras 55–58 and 76 (Ont CA), leave to appeal to SCC refused, [2007] SCCA No 337. The issue of whether counsel *must* follow a client's instructions, including those relating to interviewing and calling witnesses, is canvassed in Chapter 3, Section C.

9   See *R v Strauss* (1995), 100 CCC (3d) 303 at paras 48 and 56 (BCCA); *White*, above note 7 at 254 [para 93].

10   See ABA Model Rule 4-4.1(a), comment "The Importance of Prompt Investigation."

11   See, for example, *R v LCB* (1996), 104 CCC (3d) 353 at 370–71 and 374 [paras 64–67 and 77] (Ont CA) [*LCB*]: low legal aid rates no excuse for failing to meet client until day of trial.

12   *Fraser*, above note 6 at 80; *R v Aulakh*, 2012 BCCA 340 at para 89.

is or will be under subpoena by the other side.[13] In other words, there is no property in a witness.[14] The search for truth that is central to the adversarial criminal justice system would be unduly hampered were it otherwise.[15] The accused's right to make full answer and defence would also be jeopardized. Of course, a potential witness is free to refuse to speak to counsel for a party barring a statutory or common law obligation to the contrary. But the starting proposition is that counsel should be permitted to seek the witness's assistance, whether or not it is likely to be forthcoming.

While counsel has a general right to contact potential witnesses for the purpose of preparing a client's case, this right is sometimes curtailed. The ethical rules also restrict the manner of counsel's interaction with a witness. The aim of these limitations is to ensure that counsel's actions in pursuit of the client's best interests do not override the witness's legitimate rights or cause damage to the truth-seeking goal of the justice system.

1) Persons Represented by a Lawyer in the Matter: The No-Contact Rule

The ethical codes prohibit counsel from approaching, communicating with, or dealing with a person who is represented by a lawyer "in respect of the matter" except through or with the consent of the person's lawyer.[16] This no-contact rule applies whenever counsel knows or should know that the witness is so represented.[17] However, the interdiction does not operate where the person is represented by a lawyer only on an unrelated matter.[18] Nor does it prevent parties from communicating with each other directly.[19]

---

13   See Alta, Sask r 4.03; Ont r 5.3-1; BC, Man, NS, NL r 5.3.

14   See Alta r 4.01(3) (commentary); *R v Johnson*, 2007 ONCA 419 at paras 14–18 [*Johnson*]; *R v Downey*, 2013 ONSC 138 at para 54 [*Downey*].

15   See *R v Blais*, 2008 BCCA 389 at para 31.

16   Alta r 4.03 and 6.02(8); Sask r 4.03 and 6.02(6); BC, Man, Ont, NS, NL r 5.3-1 and 7.2-6.

17   Alta r 6.02(8) (commentary); Sask r 6.02(6) (commentary); BC, Man, Ont, NS, NL r 7.2-6, commentary 2.

18   Alta r 6.02(8) (commentary); Sask r 6.02(6) (commentary); BC, Man, Ont, NS, NL r 7.2-6, commentary 1. See also *Everingham v Ontario* (1992), 88 DLR (4th) 755 at 760 (Ont Div Ct): rule does not cover casual or unavoidable contact during which counsel and the person do not discuss the matter in question.

19   See rules and caselaw cited in preceding note.

a) Rationale for the No-Contact Rule

Several justifications have been offered for the no-contact rule. First, the rule guards against a lawyer taking undue and unfair advantage of the represented person.[20] Second, it minimizes the risk that a lawyer will obtain confidential information from the person.[21] Third, the no-contact rule prevents a lawyer from interfering with the solicitor-client relationship that the person enjoys with his own counsel.[22] Finally, the rule ensures that a person who has gone so far as to obtain representation has a chance to obtain legal advice before deciding whether to proceed with the requested communications.

There are countervailing arguments against imposing so broad a no-contact rule for represented individuals. A main concern is that the party whose lawyer wishes to communicate with the witness will be denied important information relevant to the matter, which may lead to an unreliable verdict and could be seen as unfair to the party as well. The no-contact rule can also cause mischief where the represented person's lawyer is acting unethically to shield the person from information highly relevant to the retainer. It also favours individuals who have the means and sophistication to retain counsel.

b) No-Contact Rule Applies to Witnesses, Not Just Parties

Does the no-contact rule apply to *any* person who is represented by counsel in respect of a matter, including witnesses? Or does it apply only to parties? The discrete ethical rule setting out the general right to communicate with a witness in most Canadian codes states that it is "subject to the rules on communication with a represented *party*," then cross-references the no-contact rule outlined above.[23] It could be argued that the intention is thus to limit the prohibition to parties only.

Yet the cross-referenced no-contact rules say nothing to suggest they are limited to parties.[24] To the contrary, the associated commentary states that they apply to communications "*with any person, whether or not a party to a formal adjudicative proceeding* . . . who is represented by

---

20   See ABA Model Rule 4.2, comment 1; Third Restatement § 99, comment "b."

21   See the comments cited in the preceding note.

22   *Ibid*. See also *US v Lopez*, 4 F3d 1455 at 1459 (9th Cir 1993) [*Lopez*], noting that the person's lawyer might view the contact as a betrayal by her client and withdraw.

23   Alta, Sask r 4.03; BC, Man, Ont, NS, NL r 5.3-1 [emphasis added]. The no-contact rules are set out at note 16, above in this chapter.

24   Alta r 6.02(8); Sask r 6.02(6); BC, Man, Ont, NS, NL r 7.2-6. Contrast CBA Code ch IX, commentary 6, which expressly confines the no-contact rule to an opposite *party* who is represented by counsel.

a lawyer concerning the matter to which the communication relates."[25] There is thus a very strong argument for interpreting the no-contact rule to apply to any represented person, including a witness.[26] This conclusion makes sense given that the justifications for the rule apply equally to represented witnesses.

Of course, Crown counsel does not represent a witness in a criminal matter,[27] not even a complainant. And very few witnesses have their own lawyer. Consequently, the no-contact rule will usually not be triggered with respect to witnesses in a criminal proceeding.

c) Contact with a Separately Represented Co-accused

The no-contact rule typically applies to prevent counsel from communicating directly with the client's represented co-accused in a case.[28] Such contact may be countenanced, however, by a joint defence agreement pursuant to which participating defence teams share information and resources in mounting the defence. Yet joint defence agreements are often informal and not in writing. If there exists any reasonable doubt as to whether the agreement permits direct communication between a lawyer and his client's co-accused, the lawyer should assume that the no-contact rule applies.

d) Contact by Lawyer's Agent

Canadian no-contact rules do not expressly prohibit a lawyer from engaging a private investigator or office staff member to communicate with a represented witness. Still, doing so is surely forbidden absent consent of the witness's lawyer. If a lawyer could avoid the import of ethical rules simply by employing an agent to engage in prohibited conduct, the rules would lose all effectiveness, and public confidence in the integrity of the profession would collapse. In the United States, ethical

---

25 See the commentaries cited at note 18, above in this chapter [emphasis added].

26 Sources supporting this view include the Third Restatement § 99, comment "c"; American Bar Association, Standing Committee on Ethics and Professional Responsibility, Formal Opinion 95-396, "Communications with Represented Persons" (28 July 1995) Part II, especially at text associated with note 21 [ABA Formal Opinion 95-396]; Geoffrey C Hazard & W William Hodes, *The Law of Lawyering*, 3d ed (Gaithersburg, MD: Aspen Law & Business, 2001) (loose-leaf 2013 supplement) at § 38.10; *US v Smallwood*, 365 F Supp 2d 689 at 695 (ED Va 2005) [*Smallwood*].

27 See *R v WRD* (1994), 89 CCC (3d) 474 at para 12 (Man CA), aff'd [1995] 1 SCR 785; *R v GPJ*, 2001 MBCA 18 at para 55; *R v Evic*, 2005 NUCJ 25 at paras 16–19; *R v Légaré*, 2010 ONSC 4662 at paras 38–42.

28 See ABA Formal Opinion 95-396, above note 26, Part I, especially at text associated with note 11.

codes make clear that a lawyer must not engage an agent to violate the no-contact rule on her behalf.[29] The same interdiction should operate in Canada.[30]

e) Contact Initiated by the Represented Person

The no-contact rule applies even if it is the represented witness who approaches the lawyer and not vice versa,[31] the reason being that the contact is made without the benefit of legal advice and so cannot be seen to flow from an informed waiver.

This aspect of the rule is open to challenge as overpaternalistic because the lawyer and not the represented person is being given the power to consent.[32] We accept that individuals can waive their right to consult with counsel, and the protection of ethical code provisions, in other instances — why not here as well? On the other hand, the witness's lawyer has an obligation to advise his client competently regarding the advisability of entering into requested communications and must abide by any instructions from the client to do so.[33] It would be wrong to assume that the lawyer will unethically obstruct the litigant's ability to communicate with the witness.

f) Subpoenas and Courtroom Contact

An obvious implied exception to the no-contact rule permits counsel to examine or cross-examine a represented witness in a court proceeding. Counsel and her agent can also serve a represented witness with a subpoena because such is permitted by court process[34] and because it is doubtful whether service on the witness's lawyer would be viewed as effective if the witness failed to attend in response.

---

29   ABA Model Rule 4.2, comments 4, 5.3, and 8.4(a), plus comment 1; Third Restatement § 99, comment "b"; ABA Formal Opinion 95-396, above note 26, Part IX; *Smallwood*, above note 26 at 396–97.

30   See *Cowles v Balac* (2006), 83 OR (3d) 660 at paras 195–97 (CA), Borins JA, writing for the entire court on this narrow point, leave to appeal to SCC refused, [2006] SCCA No 496.

31   See *Nelson v Murphy* (1957), 9 DLR (2d) 195 at 203–4 and 212–13 (Man CA); ABA Model Rule 4.3, comment 3; ABA Formal Opinion 95-396, above note 26, Part VII; *Smallwood*, above note 26 at 695; *Lopez*, above note 22; *In re Howes*, 940 P2d 159 at 165–66 (NM 1997).

32   See Third Restatement § 99, comment "b."

33   See Third Restatement § 99, comment "j."

34   See *In re Seizure of $143,265.78 from Comerica Checking Account No 185513495446*, 616 F Supp 2d 699 at 706 (ED Mich 2009).

g) Contact in an Emergency

Although no such exception exists in the Canadian codes, there is good reason to permit a lawyer to make direct contact with a represented witness where reasonably necessary to prevent death or serious bodily harm, and perhaps other significant harm as well.[35] Such communication is justified by the need to protect the witness and will rarely if ever risk undermining the policies that drive the no-contact rule.

h) Second Opinions

Although not strictly speaking relevant to the topic of witnesses, an important exception to the no-contact rule permits a lawyer who is not otherwise interested in the matter to give a second opinion to a represented person.[36] In such a case, it is not necessary to obtain the consent of or inform the person's existing counsel. Nonetheless, the lawyer must obtain sufficient information to allow for a competent second opinion, which in some instances will only be possible by consulting incumbent counsel.[37]

i) Limited Scope Retainers

A final exception to the no-contact rule applies in the context of limited scope retainers. These are retainers pursuant to which counsel is to provide legal services for a part, but not all, of the client's legal matter.[38] The no-contact rule allows another lawyer to communicate with a represented person regarding matters that are not included within the limited scope retainer.[39]

This limited retainer exception comes into play where an accused contacts another lawyer or Crown counsel directly with a request to explore the possibility of a plea resolution under which he will become a prosecution witness.[40]

---

35   See Third Restatement § 99(d), plus comment "i"; Geoffrey Hazard & Dana Irwin, "Toward a Revised 4.2 No-Contact Rule" (2009) 60 Hastings LJ 797 at 828–30.

36   Alta r 6.02(9); Sask r 6.02(7); BC, Man, Ont, NS, NL r 7.2-7.

37   Alta r 6.02(9) (commentary); Sask r 6.02(7) (commentary); BC, Man, NS, NL r 7.2-7, commentary 3; Ont r 7.2-7, commentary 4.

38   For a definition of "limited scope retainer," see Alta, Sask definitions; BC, Man, NS, NL r 1.1-1.

39   See Alta r 6.02(8.1); Sask r 6.02(6.1); Man, Ont, NS r 7.2-6A; BC, NL r 7.2-6.1.

40   See Chapter 9, Section I(1); Chapter 12, Section I(9).

2) Provisions Governing the Manner of Contact[41]

The ethical codes contain rules governing the manner in which lawyers, and their agents,[42] deal with prospective witnesses. These provisions justifiably temper counsel's ability to pursue a client's best interests based on a need to prevent unfairness to witnesses and harm to the proper operation of the justice system.

a) General Rules Pertaining to Communications with a Witness

Most codes provide that in seeking information from a potential witness "the lawyer must disclose the lawyer's interest."[43] This disclosure obligation should usually include explaining the nature of the matter in question, the fact that the lawyer is representing a particular client, and the client's part in the dispute. The obligation probably does not require that the person be told that he might be asked or subpoenaed to testify at trial. But it may be tactically advisable to do so at some point during the encounter.

In our view, counsel need not caution the prospective witness that he can choose whether to talk or may wish to speak to a lawyer before doing so[44] or that providing information may harm his interests. Assuming that nothing is said to misrepresent the witness's legal rights or interests, the lawyer's duty of loyalty to the client overrides concern about the potential for harm to the witness. Once again, however, there may be tactical reasons for mentioning such matters to the witness during an interview. And there is nothing wrong with counsel's telling the witness that protections may be afforded regarding the subsequent use of any testimony compelled at trial,[45] as long as the witness understands that the lawyer is not representing his interests and cannot provide legal advice on this or any other issue.[46]

The ethical codes further stipulate that the lawyer "must take care not to subvert or suppress any evidence or procure the witness to stay out of the way."[47] This prohibition applies not only to acts intended to obstruct justice but also probably to sloppy interviewing that undermines the evidentiary integrity of a witness's evidence. So, for example,

---

41   This topic overlaps with Section G, below in this chapter.
42   This is so for the reasons set out in Section C(1)(d), above in this chapter.
43   Alta, Sask r 4.03; Ont r 5.3-1; BC, Man, NS, NL r 5.3.
44   See ABA Defense Function 4-4.3(c).
45   These protections arise from s 5(2) of the *Canada Evidence Act*, RSC 1985, c C-5, and s 13 of the *Canadian Charter of Rights and Freedoms*, Part I of the *Constitution Act, 1982*, being Schedule B to the *Canada Act 1982* (UK), 1982, c 11 [*Charter*].
46   See Section C(2)(b), below in this chapter.
47   Alta, Sask r 4.03; Ont r 5.3-1; BC, Man, NS, NL r 5.1-2(j) and 5.3.

counsel should interview witnesses separately to avoid tainting their recollections of relevant events.[48]

b)   Rules Governing Contact with Unrepresented Persons
In addition to the provisions directly addressing contact with prospective witnesses, many law societies have a rule governing a lawyer's dealings with unrepresented persons. This rule typically states that the lawyer shall

1) urge the unrepresented person to obtain legal representation,
2) take care to see that the person is not proceeding under the impression his interests will be protected by the lawyer, and
3) make it clear to the person that the lawyer is acting exclusively in the interests of the client.[49]

These requirements appear to apply to any unrepresented person, including a witness, and not simply to other parties to the litigation. They overlap considerably with the obligations imposed by the rule that focuses more directly on communicating with witnesses.[50] Yet several aspects of the unrepresented persons rule are distinctive and so warrant further comment.

First, the rule imposes an ongoing obligation on the lawyer to ensure that the unrepresented person is not operating under the misapprehension that the lawyer is looking out for her interests. Accordingly, when the lawyer knows or reasonably should know that the person is mistaken as to the lawyer's role in the case, the lawyer must take reasonable steps to correct the mistake.[51] What steps need be taken will depend on the circumstances, including the witness's level of sophistication, relationship to the lawyer's client, and the nature of the matter.[52]

Second, it is difficult to understand why the rule adopted by several governing bodies requires that a lawyer urge an unrepresented person to obtain independent legal representation. True, there may be situations where a lawyer should do so, for example where Crown counsel encounters an accused who is self-represented by choice in a serious matter and likely to suffer significant harm to his legal interests absent representation at trial. But for a run-of-the-mill unrepresented witness,

---

48   See also Section G(3)(c), below in this chapter.
49   Alta r 6.02(11); Sask r 6.02(9); BC, Man, NS, NL r 7.2-9.
50   See Section C(2)(a), above in this chapter.
51   See ABA Model Rule 4.3. To similar effect, see Third Restatement § 103. See also *In re Millett*, 241 P3d 35 (Kan 2010): defence counsel failed to disabuse witness of belief that counsel was acting in witness's interests.
52   See Alta r 6.02(11) (commentary).

who is not vulnerable and whose legal interests are not put at significant risk by speaking to counsel, a requirement that the lawyer urge the witness to seek independent legal representation is unnecessary and potentially even confusing. We therefore prefer the approach taken in Ontario, where the rule governing dealings with an unrepresented person does not require counsel to urge the person to obtain legal representation.[53]

Third, the import of the rule governing contact with an unrepresented person is that a lawyer must not give the person legal advice. After all, the lawyer must make clear that she is acting "exclusively" in the interests of the client and is not protecting the person's interests. But this should not mean that the lawyer is prohibited from making an accurate statement of the law to an unrepresented witness provided the lawyer reasonably ensures that the witness does not view the statement as constituting legal advice.

There may be occasions where the lawyer can take on the unrepresented person as a client, in which case giving legal advice is permissible. Yet acting for the person is not permissible if in breach of the rules governing conflict of interest, particularly those pertaining to joint retainers.[54] In our view, conflict problems will always or almost always preclude defence counsel from acting for the accused and a witness in the same matter, even where the witness's testimony is highly favourable to the defence.[55]

c) Prohibition against Dealing with a Witness Abusively or in Bad Faith

The codes prohibit a lawyer from dealing with any person in bad faith.[56] They also warn lawyers against communicating with any person "in a manner that is abusive, offensive, or otherwise inconsistent with the proper tone of a professional communication from a lawyer."[57] These general proscriptions apply to counsel's dealings and communications

---

53   Ont r 7.2-9. Nor is such a requirement included in ABA Model Rule 4.3 or Third Restatement § 103.
54   Alta r 6.02(11) (commentary); Sask r 6.02(9) (commentary); BC, Man, Ont, NS, NL r 7.2-9, commentary 1.
55   See, generally, Chapter 6.
56   Alta, Sask r 6.02(1); BC, Man, Ont, NS, NL r 7.2-1.
57   Alta r 4.01(2)(o) and 6.02(6); Sask r 4.01(2)(j) and 6.02(4); BC, Man, Ont, NS, NL r 7.2-4. Somewhat similar is ABA Defense Standard 4-4.3(a). See also *Florida Bar v Buckle*, 771 So 2d 1131 (Fla 2000): counsel disciplined for sending abusive letter to complainant.

with a witness.[58] More specifically, the codes also state that when acting as an advocate a lawyer must not needlessly abuse, hector, or harass a witness.[59] Contravening these rules unjustifiably harms the witness, discredits the justice system, sullies the lawyer's reputation, and may inure to the client's detriment in the extant proceeding.

d) Keeping Sufficient Record of the Contact and the Propriety of Surreptitious Recording

If possible, counsel should have an agent such as a private investigator interview the witness or do so in the presence of a third person.[60] Otherwise, it may be difficult to use a statement from the interview to impeach the witness at trial without counsel taking the stand himself to testify. If forced to testify, counsel will have to withdraw from the case.[61]

It is also important to create an accurate interview record. The best and easiest way to do this is by recording with an electronic device. A good quality recording serves several purposes. It can assist in refreshing the witness's memory before testifying, be instrumental in impeaching a witness whose testimony changes at trial, or help to rebut allegations of interview impropriety directed at counsel by the witness or others.

Being candid about making a recording will usually help to gain the witness's trust and give her some comfort that an accurate record will be available if there is future disagreement as to what was said. Sometimes, however, a lawyer will prefer a surreptitious recording based on a reasonable concern that the witness will be less open if aware the statement is being memorialized. Making such a recording is not contrary to the *Criminal Code*, because at least one party to the conversation is consenting to the recording.[62] And most Canadian ethical codes prohibit only the surreptitious recording of a client or another

---

58 Directly on point is "Principles of Civility for Advocates" in The Advocates' Society, Institute for Civility & Professionalism, *Principles of Professionalism for Advocates / Principles of Civility for Advocates* (Toronto: The Advocates' Society, 2009) at 14, r 35, online: www.advocates.ca/assets/files/pdf/publications/principles-of-civility.pdf ["Principles of Civility"]: advocates must always be courteous and civil in their communications with witnesses.

59 Alta r 4.01(2)(s); Sask r 4.01(2)(m); BC, Man, Ont, NS, NL r 5.1-2(m). These rules appear directed at in-court behaviour, but we see no reason why they should not also apply to out-of-court contact.

60 See, for example, *R v Bevan*, 2009 ONCJ 487 at para 17 [*Bevan*], stating that prudent counsel will not interview an opposing witness alone; *Downey*, above note 14 at paras 57–58: prudent counsel will not interview a contentious witness alone. See also *R v Charles*, 2012 ONSC 2001 at paras 18–37.

61 See Chapter 6, Section L.

62 *Criminal Code*, RSC 1985, c C-46, ss 184(1) & (2)(a).

lawyer,[63] which strongly implies that counsel is free to secretly record a conversation with a non-lawyer witness.[64]

For these reasons, counsel should be permitted to surreptitiously record a witness interview, especially where there is reason to believe that evidence of the same quality will not otherwise be obtained.[65] In such a case, counsel's duty of loyalty to the client overrides any scruples about hiding the act of recording from the witness. Indeed, being recorded should come as no surprise to many witnesses given the proliferation and easy deployment of unobtrusive recording devices. But a lawyer must not combine secret recording with conduct that is deceitful, such as actively misleading the witness into thinking that no recording is being made.[66] Lying to a witness contravenes the ban against counsel's engaging in dishonest or bad faith behaviour.[67]

3) Covert or Sting Operations

The police are sometimes unable to obtain evidence by using a direct and honest approach, in particular when dealing with a person they suspect has committed the crime under investigation. The law thus accords the police some leeway to employ deceptive means in attempting to acquire evidence.[68] Examples include making modest misrepresentations regarding the nature of evidence during a formal interview,[69] employing an undercover cell plant,[70] and running a "Mr Big" operation.[71]

---

63 Alta r 6.02(4); Sask r 6.02(3); BC, Man, Ont, NS, NL r 7.2-3.
64 Contrast CBA Code ch XVI, commentary 5: prohibits a lawyer from surreptitiously recording a conversation with *anyone*.
65 This precondition, though not employed in Canadian codes, is adopted in the Third Restatement § 106, comment "b."
66 See American Bar Association, Standing Committee on Ethics and Professional Responsibility, Formal Opinion 01-422, "Electronic Recordings by Lawyers without the Knowledge of All Participants" (24 June 2001); *In re PRB Docket No 2007-046*, 989 A2d 523 (Vt 2009). The trend in the United States is to permit surreptitious recording provided it is not carried out in a way that violates the ethical rules: see Hazard & Hodes, above note 26 at § 40.5; John Wesley Hall, Jr, *Professional Responsibility in Criminal Defense Practice* (St Paul, MN:Thomson/West, 2005) (loose-leaf September 2012 supplement) at § 3.18.
67 See Alta r 2.02(10) (commentary) and 4.01(2)(d); Sask r 2.02(7) and 4.01(2)(b); BC, Man, Ont, NS, NL r 3.2-7 and 5.1-2(b) (prohibiting dishonest activity). See also Section C(2)(c), above in this chapter.
68 See *R v Oickle*, 2000 SCC 38 at para 66 [*Oickle*]: police must be able to use deceit in investigating crime provided doing so would not "shock the community."
69 *Ibid* at para 44.
70 *R v Liew* (1999), 137 CCC (3d) 353 (SCC).
71 *R v Hart*, 2014 SCC 52.

Can defence counsel also use deceptive investigative measures, for instance where doing so holds the best prospect of uncovering information to undermine a key Crown witness or support an alternative-suspect defence? Several of the ethical-code rules canvassed earlier in this chapter suggest that the answer to this question is a resounding "no," in particular,

- a lawyer must not knowingly assist in or encourage dishonesty,[72]
- a lawyer must act in good faith towards those with whom he deals in practising law, and[73]
- in seeking information from a potential witness a lawyer must disclose his interest in the matter.[74]

Textual arguments to the contrary are not totally without attraction. For example, one could argue that the prohibition against engaging in dishonesty should be restricted to misrepresentations that undermine the integrity of the administration of justice.[75] Yet governing bodies may be reluctant to read into these rules an exemption for defence counsel whose aim in encouraging dishonesty is to advance the cause of justice.[76] Unless and until the codes are amended to include such an exemption, the safest course for counsel is to neither advise on nor help to carry out covert investigations.

Example: Counsel's client is charged with sexual assault against a college classmate. The defence is consent. The client learns from a reliable source that the complainant and her friends have been discussing the incident on Facebook, but he has no access to these conversations. Counsel should not pose as someone else in an attempt to "friend" the complainant and view the conversations. Doing so, or using an agent to carry out the task, probably violates the ethical rules mentioned above, and may also constitute a crime.[77] There is nothing wrong, however,

---

72 See the rules and commentary cited at note 67, above in this chapter.

73 See Section C(2)(c), above in this chapter.

74 See sections C(2)(a) & (b), above in this chapter.

75 See William Fortune, "Lawyers, Covert Activity, and Choice of Evils" (2008) 32 J Leg Prof 99 at 100–3. See also the exception read into comparable rules against deceit in Utah State Bar Ethics Advisory Opinion Committee, Opinion No 02-05 (18 March 2002) [Utah Opinion No 02-05] (dealing with government lawyers); New York County Lawyers' Association, Committee on Professional Ethics, Formal Opinion No 737, "Non-government Lawyer Use of Investigator Who Employs Dissemblance" (23 May 2007) (in civil context).

76 See, for example, In re Gatti, 8 P3d 966 at 974–76 (Or 2000), refusing to interpret the rule prohibiting deceit to permit a lawyer to conduct covert investigation.

77 Posing as another person may constitute fraudulent personation under s 403 of the Criminal Code, above note 62.

with viewing the portions of the complainant's profile that are available to any member of the public.

Preventing dishonesty by lawyers is important to the integrity of the profession and the administration of justice. Yet misrepresentation is sometimes necessary to uncover wrongdoing and injustice. After all, we countenance the police engaging in such conduct. And it seems to be generally accepted that prosecutors do not act unethically in providing police with legal advice regarding covert investigations.[78] Permitting defence counsel to supervise covert operations ensures they will be carried out lawfully, in the same way that prosecutorial advice undeniably helps prevent impropriety with respect to investigative subterfuge employed by police.

Granted, a police officer does not act as the prosecutor's agent in carrying out such subterfuge but rather as a constitutionally independent investigator.[79] Moreover, there is no principle of perfect parity regarding state and defence investigations,[80] as exemplified by the special tools available only to the police such as Part VI authorizations and search warrants. Yet these special tools tend to derive from express statutory authority. The ability to run a covert operation is arguably different because only the rules of ethics appear to bar similar defence conduct, rules with respect to which prosecutors appear to enjoy *de facto* immunity.

In the United States, concern about unfairness and injustice caused by an absolute ban on lawyers engaging in covert operations has led some states to amend their ethics codes to permit subterfuge in narrowly defined circumstances.[81] The best known of the new rules, from Oregon, permits a lawyer to supervise or provide advice about lawful covert activity — i.e. that which relies on misrepresentation or other subterfuge — in the investigation of violations of civil or criminal law or constitutional rights provided the lawyer otherwise complies with the ethical rules and has a good faith belief in the reasonable pos-

---

78   See Chapter 12, Section H(8)(a).

79   *Ibid.*

80   See *R v Quesnelle*, 2014 SCC 46 at para 64: the principles of fundamental justice and trial fairness do not guarantee defence counsel the right to precisely the same privileges and procedures as the Crown and police.

81   See Kevin C McMunigal, "Investigative Deceit" (2011) 62 Hastings LJ 1377 at 1387–91. By contrast, some state rules permit only prosecutors to advise on or supervise covert operations: see, for example, Florida, *Rules of Professional Conduct*, r 4-8.4(c); Alabama, *Rules of Professional Conduct*, r 3.8(2); Missouri, *Rules of Professional Conduct*, r 4-8.4(c); Tennessee, *Rules of Professional Conduct*, 8.4(c), comment 5; Utah Opinion No 02-05, above note 75.

sibility that the targeted violative activity has occurred or will occur in the foreseeable future.[82] In our view, Canadian law societies would be justified in adopting a similar rule applicable to lawyers practising in their jurisdictions.[83]

4) Ascertaining the Identity of a Confidential Informant

The privilege protecting a confidential informant's identity from disclosure is fundamental to the proper working of the criminal justice system.[84] It protects those who provide confidential information to police from retribution and encourages co-operation by future informers,[85] and it will only be set aside where the accused successfully engages the demanding innocence-at-stake exception.[86]

The question arises as to whether defence counsel is legally and ethically permitted to conduct an independent investigation to ascertain the identity of a confidential informant for the purpose of assisting the client in advancing a legitimate defence. The policy argument against allowing counsel to do so is that the result may be to place informants in physical danger and make individuals less willing to provide confidential information to police in the future, with concomitant negative effects on the investigation and prosecution of crime.[87]

However, in *R v Barros* the Supreme Court of Canada rejected this argument, holding instead that defence counsel is entitled to take lawful steps to ascertain a confidential informer's identity for the proper

---

82 Oregon, *Rules of Professional Conduct*, r 8.4(b). See also Alaska, *Rules of Professional Conduct*, r 8.4, comment 4; Ohio, *Rules of Professional Conduct*, r 8.4, comment 2A; Iowa, *Rules of Professional Conduct*, 32:8.4, comment 6; Wisconsin, *Rules of Professional Conduct*, r 20:4.1(b). A different approach is to prohibit only deceit that would reflect adversely on the lawyer's fitness to practise law: see Virginia, *Rules of Professional Conduct*, r 8.4(c); Michigan, *Rules of Professional Conduct*, r 8.4(b).

83 For more on this issue, see McMunigal, above note 81; Tory Lucas, "To Catch a Criminal, to Cleanse a Profession: Exposing Deceptive Practices by Attorneys to the Sunlight of Public Debate and Creating an Express Investigation Deception Exception to the ABA *Model Rules of Professional Conduct*" (2010) 89 Neb L Rev 219; Hazard & Irwin, above note 35 at 823–25.

84 See *R v Leipert* (1997), 112 CCC (3d) 385 at para 10 (SCC) [*Leipert*].

85 See *ibid* at paras 9–10; *R v Barros*, 2011 SCC 51 at para 30 [*Barros* SCC]; *Named Person v Vancouver Sun*, 2007 SCC 43 at para 2 [*Named Person*]; *R v Scott* (1990), 61 CCC (3d) 300 at 313 [para 31] (SCC).

86 See *Leipert*, above note 84 at para 15; *Named Person*, above note 85 at para 17; *R v Basi*, 2009 SCC 52 at para 22 [*Basi*].

87 See *R v Barros*, 2010 ABCA 116 at para 46, rev'd *Barros* SCC, above note 85.

purpose of putting forward the client's case at trial.[88] This is so, said the Court, even though the police and Crown are duty bound to prevent the release of any information that might reveal a confidential informer's identity. Informer privilege thus justifies the Crown withholding information from the accused but does not prevent defence counsel from attempting to discover the very same information so that full answer and defence can be made for the client.[89]

R v Barros nonetheless stresses that defence counsel can neither use unlawful means to obtain an informer's identity nor seek out such information for an illegal purpose.[90] Accordingly, an investigation must be carried out, and any resulting information handled, in a legal and ethical manner. Employing threats to discover the informant's identity is thus impermissible. So would be threatening to release an informer's identity, once discovered, in the criminal milieu unless a stay of proceedings is entered.

Defence counsel whose investigation reveals an informant's identity must think carefully before conveying the information to the client. Counsel has a basic obligation to share all relevant information with the client.[91] Yet disclosing the identity to the client may create a real risk of serious physical danger to the informant. Arguably, counsel is thus permitted to withhold the information from the client, especially where it turns out to be of no real assistance to the defence.[92] The client must nonetheless be told that counsel has the information. Moreover, the act of withholding may so undermine the professional relationship that the lawyer is forced to withdraw or is discharged by the client.[93] A different option is to convey the information to the client but at the same time to utilize the future-harm exception to the duty of confidentiality if reasonably thought necessary to prevent ensuing death or serious bodily harm to the informant.[94]

---

88 *Barros* SCC, above note 85.
89 *Ibid* at paras 1–2 and 37–43.
90 *Ibid* at paras 40–43.
91 See Chapter 3, Section E.
92 See Chapter 3, Section E(3).
93 See *Basi*, above note 86 at paras 44–47; *R v Ahmad*, 2011 SCC 6 at para 49.
94 See Chapter 5, Section I.

D. DUTY NOT TO INTERFERE WITH OPPONENT'S ABILITY TO CONTACT WITNESSES

It is generally improper for a lawyer to discourage a witness from speaking to counsel for an opponent. Doing so may unfairly deny the opponent the opportunity to marshal a case at trial and undermine the system's truth-seeking goal. This prohibition against impeding an opponent's access to evidence represents a justifiable limit on the lawyer's duty of loyalty to the client, made necessary to protect superordinate systemic interests.

Most Canadian ethical codes comment on communications between criminal defence counsel and a complainant, stipulating that counsel "must never influence a complainant or potential complainant not to communicate or cooperate with the Crown."[95] There is no reason why this prohibition should not extend to all witnesses. The rules of professional conduct arguably do so by stating more generally that a lawyer "must take care not to subvert or suppress any evidence or procure the witness to stay out of the way"[96] and "must not improperly dissuade a witness from giving evidence or advise a witness to be absent."[97]

But Alberta's code is clearest on this point, providing expressly that a lawyer must not improperly dissuade a witness from communicating with other parties.[98] Similarly, the ABA Model Rules prohibit a lawyer from requesting "a person . . . to refrain from voluntarily giving relevant information to another party."[99] And a basic rule applicable to criminal defence counsel is nicely formulated in the ABA Defense Standards: "Defense counsel should not discourage or obstruct communication between prospective witnesses and the prosecutor. It is unprofessional conduct to advise any person other than a client, or cause such person to be advised, to decline to give to the prosecutor or defense counsel for codefendants information which such person has a right to give."[100] The ABA Prosecution Standards include an analogous rule for prosecutors.[101]

---

95 Alta r 2.02(9) (commentary); Sask r 2.02(6) (commentary); BC, Man, NS, NL r 3.2-6, commentary 2.

96 Alta, Sask r 4.03; Ont r 5.3-1; BC, Man, NS, NL r 5.3.

97 Alta r 4.01(2)(o); Sask r 4.01(2)(j); BC, Man, Ont, NS, NL r 5.1(2)(j).

98 Alta r 4.01(2)(o). The Alberta code repeats the same point in r 4.01(3).

99 ABA Model Rule 3.4(f). See also Third Restatement § 116(4).

100 ABA Defense Standard 4-4.3(d).

101 ABA Prosecution Standard 3-3.1(d).

Of course, in sharp contrast to the prosecution,[102] an accused has no obligation to disclose her case in advance of trial. Accordingly, defence counsel is not required to reveal the existence or location of witnesses to the prosecution unless and until those witnesses are called.[103] What is more, a witness usually has a right to choose whether to speak to the police or counsel's opponent. There is nothing wrong with counsel's informing a witness of this right,[104] especially if asked.[105] But in doing so, counsel must neither leave the impression he is acting as the witness's lawyer nor encourage the witness to exercise the right to silence if approached by opposing counsel or police.[106] It is also improper for a lawyer to threaten counsel for an opponent with criminal or disciplinary proceedings in an attempt to foreclose legitimate attempts to interview a witness.[107]

In talking to a witness about communications with the other side, counsel must be careful to say nothing that can be construed as suggesting that untruths be told or that material information be withheld.[108] There is nothing wrong, however, with counsel's asking the witness to inform him of the content of any communications that might occur.

1) Exceptions to Prohibition against Advising Witnesses Not to Speak to Opponent

The general prohibition against discouraging a witness from speaking to the opponent or police has a number of exceptions. Most importantly, it does not apply to counsel's client.[109] The client has a legal right not

---

102 The prosecution's expansive duty to disclose is discussed in Chapter 12, Section G.

103 See Chapter 10, Section D, which also discusses some limited exceptions involving alibi and expert witnesses.

104 See Third Restatement § 116, comment "e"; "Principles of Civility," above note 58, r 34.

105 See Alta r 4.03 (commentary); ABA Defense Standard 4-4.3(d) (comment, "Obstructing Communications between Witnesses and the Prosecution"); ABA Prosecution Standard 3-3.1(d) (comment, "Obstructing Communications between Witnesses and the Defense").

106 See, for example, *In re Stanford*, 48 So 3d 224 at 229–30 & 231–32 (La 2010): defence counsel violated ethical rules by having a complainant sign a confidentiality agreement covering everything said at a meeting between her, counsel, and the defendant.

107 See *Johnson*, above note 14: court criticizes prosecutor for such conduct.

108 See the rules cited at note 96, above. See also *R v Mattson*, 2012 ONSC 2381 [*Mattson*]: lawyer charged with attempt to obstruct justice for directing a witness on what not to say to the Crown, although committal was quashed on review.

109 See Alta r 4.01(3) (commentary (a)); ABA Model Rule 3.4(f); Third Restatement § 116(4)(a).

to speak to the police or anyone else and is entitled to guidance regarding how the right should be exercised. There is thus nothing wrong with defence counsel advising the accused not to make a statement to police. Nor is there anything wrong with a lawyer for a prosecution witness advising the client to not speak to defence counsel or to impose preconditions for an interview such as a requirement that the lawyer be present.[110]

Somewhat similarly, the ban on advising a witness not to talk to an opponent or police does not apply to decision makers and certain others within a corporate client.[111] These people are viewed as the equivalent of the client for the purposes of the ethical rule in this area. Yet counsel can only advise such a person not to speak to the opponent or police where the advice can reasonably be said to not be adverse to the person's own best interests.[112] Moreover, the person must understand that counsel is acting for the corporation and not as her own lawyer.[113]

It has also been suggested that the rule against discouraging a witness from speaking to an opponent or police does not extend to close relatives of a client provided once again that the advice can reasonably be said to not be adverse to the relative's own best interests.[114] As stated in the Alberta code, the basis for this exception is that a close relative may be so closely connected with the client that it would be contrary to that person's legitimate interests to discuss the case with opposing parties.[115]

However, we believe that the safest course in criminal matters is for defence counsel *never* to advise a client's close relative or a decision maker within a corporate client not to speak to the police. Counsel should simply inform such individuals that they can choose for themselves whether to accede to an interview request but may want to obtain independent legal advice before making a decision. We say this for two reasons. First, in criminal matters there will often be a real risk that the person's legal interests are adverse to those of the client, in which case advising the person not to communicate with police is never justified. Second, there is a danger that advising an individual not to speak

---

110 See *US v Medina*, 992 F2d 573 at 579 (6th Cir 1993).

111 See Alta r 4.03 (commentary (b)). This conclusion applies in other jurisdictions by implication from the no-contact rule that covers certain individuals within a corporate client: see Sask 6.02(8); BC, Man, Ont, NS, NL 7.2-8.

112 See ABA Model Rule 3.4(f)(2); Third Restatement § 116(4)(b)(ii).

113 The rule governing contact with an unrepresented person should apply: see Section C(2)(b), above in this chapter.

114 See ABA Model Rule 3.4(f); Third Restatement § 116(4)(b).

115 See Alta r 4.03 (commentary (c)).

to police will lead to allegations that defence counsel has obstructed justice. Even if unfounded, the allegations may sabotage counsel's ability to remain on the case as an effective advocate for his client.

A final exception to the rule against defence counsel advising a person not to speak to the prosecution or police arises where that person owes a duty of confidentiality to the accused.[116] Examples include an accountant or doctor in relation to the client's financial or medical information, a former lawyer regarding client confidences, a private investigator who has worked on the client's case, a translator who has assisted during solicitor-client meetings, an expert witness retained to offer an opinion in the case, and so on.[117] Provided there is a reasonable basis for concluding that a duty of confidentiality operates to preclude the person from releasing the information to the Crown or police absent proper legal process, counsel can convey this position to the person.

2) Advising a Witness regarding a Subpoena

Defence counsel must never advise a prosecution witness to avoid service of a subpoena.[118] Counsel must also take care when a witness seeks advice regarding the legal import of a subpoena, such as by asking what will happen if she does not appear as required. A reply that implicitly encourages non-attendance is highly improper.[119] By contrast, defence counsel will be on firm ethical ground in telling a witness that she is legally compelled to attend court in response to a subpoena.

Indeed, it will usually be difficult to say much more without risking an allegation that counsel has unethically encouraged the witness to stay away from court. Telling a witness in a minor case, truthfully, that the Crown may simply stay the charge if she does not attend, and not seek a material witness warrant, can be seen as subtle encouragement to ignore the subpoena. Informing a witness that she may have a proper legal basis to resist a subpoena is unproblematic, however, for counsel is not suggesting that the witness disobey court process.[120]

---

116 See Third Restatement § 116, comment "e."

117 The exception for expert witnesses is acknowledged in Alta r 4.03 (commentary (d)).

118 See Third Restatement § 116(3); "Principles of Civility," above note 58, r 34.

119 *Ibid.* See also *In re Geisler*, 614 NE2d 939 at 943 (Ind 1993): lawyer disciplined for giving witness caselaw intimating that prior statements are inadmissible if witness does not show for trial; *R v Gillis*, 2013 NBPC 3: lawyer had urged manager of organizational victim in fraud case to make sure organization's employees did not show for trial and was convicted of attempt to obstruct justice.

120 See Third Restatement § 116, comment "d."

Ultimately, defence counsel should avoid giving advice in this area, not only because doing so risks allegations of attempting to obstruct justice, but also because the witness's interests and those of counsel's client will usually be in conflict. When counsel is approached by a prosecution witness regarding subpoena-related issues, the sensible course is to encourage the witness to obtain independent legal advice, and to do nothing that might lead the witness to believe counsel is looking after her interests.[121]

E. DEFENCE COUNSEL'S DEALINGS WITH A COMPLAINANT

The ethical rules that govern defence counsel regarding contact with witnesses apply to contact with complainants in a criminal matter. However, special considerations often arise regarding counsel's dealings with a complainant.

1) Prohibition against Inducing Complainant to Attempt to Exercise Influence over Prosecution

The ethical codes prohibit a lawyer from offering valuable consideration to another person in exchange for that person's influencing the Crown's conduct of a criminal charge or complaint unless the lawyer obtains the consent of the Crown to do so.[122] More generally, the codes also state that a lawyer must not "wrongfully influence" any person to prevent the Crown from proceeding with a charge or complaint or to cause the Crown to withdraw the complaint or stay the charge.[123] Finally, the codes provide that defence counsel must never influence a complainant or potential complainant to not communicate or co-operate with the Crown.[124]

These rules do not prevent counsel for an accused or potential accused from contacting a complainant or potential complainant for the purpose of conducting a defence in a civil matter, including discussing

---

121 See also Section C(2)(b), above in this chapter.
122 Alta r 2.02(9)(a); Sask r 2.02(6)(a); BC, Man, NS, NL r 3.2-6(a). The rationale for this prohibition is discussed in the text associated with note 140, below.
123 Alta r 2.02(9)(c); Sask r 2.02(6)(c); BC, Man, NS, NL r 3.2-6(c).
124 Alta r 2.02(9) (commentary); Sask r 2.02(6) (commentary); BC, Man, NS, NL r 3.2-6, commentary 2.

a civil settlement or making other restitution or an apology.[125] However, where counsel's overtures envision a benefit being provided in return for the complainant's influencing the criminal matter to the accused's advantage, the rules are engaged, and the Crown's consent must first be obtained.[126] Counsel engaging in settlement discussions should thus make clear that there is no expectation the complainant will attempt to exercise influence over the criminal matter. The prudent course is to document this understanding in writing at the beginning of discussions and in any settlement agreement that is reached.

2) Interviewing a Complainant

Most Canadian rules of professional conduct contain a commentary that expressly addresses a lawyer's duties in approaching a complainant on behalf of a client who is or may become an accused in a criminal matter:

> A lawyer representing an accused or potential accused may communicate with a complainant or potential complainant, for example, to obtain factual information, to arrange for restitution or an apology from the accused, or to defend or settle any civil claims between the accused and the complainant. However, when the complainant or potential complainant is vulnerable, the lawyer must take care not to take unfair or improper advantage of the circumstances. If the complainant or potential complainant is unrepresented, the lawyer should be governed by the rules about unrepresented persons and make it clear that the lawyer is acting exclusively in the interests of the accused or potential accused. When communicating with an unrepresented complainant or potential complainant, it is prudent to have a witness present.[127]

The ethical rules do not suggest that counsel has an obligation to notify the Crown or seek the Crown's consent before making contact with a complainant. In this regard, it is vital to remember that a prosecutor does not represent his witnesses, not even the complainant.[128]

---

125 See commentaries cited in preceding note. To the same effect, see Ont r 3.2-4, commentary 1.1, and r 5.1-2, commentary 2.

126 See the rules cited at note 122, above.

127 BC, Man, Ont, NS, NL r 5.1-2, commentary 2. Almost all of this wording is repeated in the rule governing inducements offered for a withdrawal of criminal proceedings: Alta r 2.02(9) (commentary); Sask r 2.02(6) (commentary); BC, Man, NS, NL r 3.2-6, commentaries 2 and 4.

128 See the cases cited at note 27, above in this chapter.

Nonetheless, some defence counsel may choose to notify the Crown in advance of contacting a complainant where doing so will reduce the risk of allegations of improper dealings with the witness and will not put the client in a materially worse position in terms of advancing a proper defence.

The rules discussed earlier in this chapter regarding contact with witnesses apply to counsel's dealings with an unrepresented complainant,[129] if anything with special emphasis given the centrality of the complainant to the prosecution case. Accordingly, counsel

- must clearly identify his interest as lawyer for the accused and not do anything to subvert the complainant's evidence or procure the complainant to stay out of the way;[130]
- must ensure that the complainant is under no illusion that her interests are being looked after by defence counsel;[131]
- must keep at the top of his mind the express prohibition against taking unfair or improper advantage of a complainant, though arguably applicable to any witness;[132] and
- must take steps to accurately memorialize the encounter and protect against becoming a witness if a dispute later arises as to what occurred during the interview.[133]

Some defence lawyers generally avoid interviewing complainants as a matter of tactics. This is especially so in domestic assault prosecutions, where there may be little benefit to be obtained for the client. Either the complainant is sticking to her story, in which case an interview will gain nothing and may give away the advantage of surprise in cross-examination, or the complainant wants to recant or seek an outcome other than the accused's conviction, in which case the safest course is to have her obtain independent legal advice. In any event, the risk of accusations of impropriety where counsel or counsel's agent interviews the complainant is very real because domestic cases are often highly volatile, emotional, and acrimonious. Reducing this risk is important, not only to preserve counsel's reputation, but also because the allegations may harm counsel's ability to properly defend

---

129 In the rare case where the complainant is represented by her own lawyer, the no-contact rule will apply: see Section C(1), above in this chapter.

130 See Sections C(2)(a) & (b), above in this chapter.

131 *Ibid.* See also District of Columbia Bar, Ethics Opinion 321, "Communications between Domestic Violence Petitioner and Counsel for Respondent in a Privately Litigated Proceeding for Criminal Contempt (July 2003).

132 See the text and rules associated with note 127, above in this chapter.

133 See Section C(2)(d), above in this chapter.

the accused. They may obscure or undermine points that are helpful to the defence at trial. They may also require that counsel withdraw, whether because he has become a potential witness or because the aspersions cast on his character threaten to bias the fact-finder against the accused.[134]

Not infrequently, a complainant will ask defence counsel to recommend a lawyer to provide independent legal advice. There is nothing wrong with counsel doing so, but the lawyer who is recommended must truly be independent. A lawyer who works in counsel's firm is not independent,[135] nor is a lawyer who shares office space with counsel absent compliance with the ethical-code rules on space-sharing arrangements and conflict of interest.[136]

F. COUNSEL WHO ACTS FOR A COMPLAINANT

The vast majority of witnesses go through the criminal process unrepresented. But issues relating to the proper representation of witnesses do arise on occasion, mostly regarding complainants who have retained their own counsel. For example, the question is sometimes raised as to when, if ever, a complainant can negotiate with an accused to obtain a benefit for harm allegedly caused by a criminal act. Ethical issues can also arise where counsel is asked to provide independent legal advice to a complainant who desires to have the criminal charges against the accused dropped.

1) Prohibition against Using Criminal Process to Obtain Personal Benefits

The rules of professional conduct prohibit counsel who acts for a complainant or potential complainant — or any other person for that matter — from attempting to gain a benefit for the client by threatening to initiate or proceed with a criminal charge or advising a client to make such a threat.[137] This restriction applies regardless of whether the client has a valid claim to receive a personal benefit because of

---

134 See Chapter 6, Section L. See also *Bevan*, above note 60 at paras 14–25: counsel fails to take precautions in interviewing a recanting domestic assault complainant, leading to his being removed from the record.

135 See Chapter 6, Section N, in particular the first paragraph.

136 See Chapter 6, Section N(1).

137 Alta r 2.02(8) and 4.01(2)(t); Sask r 2.02(5) (commentary) and 4.01(2)(n); BC, Man, Ont, NS, NL r 3.2-5 and 5.1-2(n).

another party's civil wrong[138] and regardless of whether the criminal complaint has merit. The ethical codes similarly proscribe a lawyer from accepting or offering to accept, or advising a client to accept or offer to accept, any valuable consideration in exchange for influencing the Crown's conduct of a criminal charge, unless the lawyer obtains the consent of the Crown to enter into such discussions.[139]

These prohibitions are driven by the belief that it is an abuse of judicial process to attempt or threaten to exercise influence over the state's criminal law machinery, which is directed at punishing and remedying public wrongs, for personal gain.[140] It would be nonsensical, however, to deny a complainant access to civil remedies merely because her personal loss is caused by conduct that also amounts to a criminal offence. Counsel for a complainant is thus free to launch civil proceedings before, during, or after the client has made a criminal complaint, as long as no attempt is made to use the criminal process for personal advantage.[141]

2) Providing Independent Legal Advice to a Complainant

It is not uncommon in domestic assault cases for defence counsel to hear from a complainant who expresses a wish to have the charges against her spouse dropped. Defence counsel will often refer the complainant to another lawyer for independent legal advice.

The lawyer providing the independent legal advice cannot be labouring under a conflict of interest.[142] Moreover, he must never forget that the complainant is a client who, like any other, is owed strong duties of loyalty and competence.[143] The purpose of independent legal advice is manifestly *not* to facilitate the best possible result for the accused or to make life easier for the lawyer who has made the referral.

Accordingly, counsel providing independent legal advice must obtain sufficient information regarding the matter to properly assist the

---

138 Alta r 2.02(8); Sask r 2.02(5) (commentary); BC, Man, Ont, NS, NL r 3.2-5, commentary 1.

139 Alta r 2.02(9)(b); Sask r 2.02(6)(b); BC, Man, NS, NL r 3.2-6(b).

140 See Alta r 2.02(8) (commentary) and 4.01(2) (commentary); Sask r 2.02(5) (commentary) and 4.01(2) (commentary); BC, Man, Ont, NS, NL r 3.2-5, commentary 1 and r 5.1-2, commentary 3. See also *R v Babos*, 2014 SCC 16 at para 37 [*Babos*]: using criminal court to collect civil debt is an abuse of process.

141 See Alta r 2.02(8); Sask r 2.02(5) (commentary); BC, Man, Ont, NS, NL r 3.2-5, commentary 2.

142 See the text associated with notes 135–36, above in this chapter.

143 The importance of treating the provision of independent legal advice seriously is discussed in more detail in Chapter 6, Section O(1)(d).

complainant. Counsel must then review with the complainant the advantages and disadvantages of taking steps to have the dispute removed from the criminal justice process. Is the complainant or her family at risk of harm in the future? How might not continuing with the prosecution affect any family law proceedings or future criminal proceedings in which her credibility may be in issue? If the complainant faces legitimate housing, financial, and emotional difficulties, might it be useful to consider options other than bringing the spouse back into the family dynamic? If the complainant wants to recant, she must understand the importance of telling the truth, and the serious repercussions of not doing so, whether with respect to her initial complaint or the proposed recantation.

The lawyer providing independent legal advice should also be cognizant of the possibility that a third party, in particular the accused, is improperly pressuring the complainant. If the lawyer reasonably suspects that the complainant's visit is part of an attempt to obstruct justice, for example because a proposed recantation is false, due diligence is required to avoid assisting in the illegal scheme.[144]

The result of independent legal advice may be, not recantation, but rather instructions from the complainant for counsel to explore with the Crown options other than proceeding with a criminal prosecution. As part of this exploration and if so instructed, the lawyer can indicate that the complainant will not meet with a prosecutor for the purpose of preparing for trial.[145] But counsel must never advise the client, whether expressly or implicitly, not to attend court in response to a subpoena, for such action constitutes a breach of a legal duty and may amount to contempt of court.[146]

Recommendation: Counsel providing independent legal advice to a complainant should make a complete record of the scope and nature of the retainer, the matters discussed, the advice given, the instructions received from the client, and any action taken as a result. It is prudent to set out at least some of this information in a reporting letter to the client.

---

144 See Chapter 2, Section B(1).

145 Counsel can do so because the complainant is his client: see Section D, above in this chapter.

146 See, for example, ss 700(2) (duty to attend court) and 708 (failure to attend without lawful excuse is contempt) of the *Criminal Code*, above note 62.

G. PREPARING A WITNESS TO TESTIFY[147]

Counsel who prepares a witness to testify not only furthers the client's best interests but also assists the criminal justice system in achieving a fair and accurate result. At the same time, a lawyer working in an adversarial system has no duty to assist the opponent by eliciting evidence that harms her client's case.[148] The task is thus to prepare the witness in a manner that will advance the client's position by bringing out helpful evidence in a credible and understandable way. Yet in preparing the witness, counsel cannot do anything to mislead the trier of fact and "must respect the important ethical distinction between discussing testimony and seeking to improperly influence it."[149] As stated long ago by the Chancellor of Ontario Sir John Boyd, "This interviewing of witnesses is to be done of course with quasi-judicial fairness and fidelity to truth, not so conducted as to shape their recollections or to harmonize their disagreements or to suggest what it is desirable to prove."[150]

Following this dictate is sometimes easier said than done. There can be a fine line between proper preparation and conduct that shapes a witness's evidence so as to materially change its import on a disputed matter. The ethical codes contain many rules directed at preventing a lawyer from misleading the court, including rules relating to the treatment of witnesses. But they often provide little guidance when it comes to discerning whether particular preparation practices are right or wrong. As in many areas of ethics, the lawyer must apply broad principles to the specific circumstances of his case and exercise discretion in deciding what is or is not appropriate. The goal is to prepare each witness in a way that permits partisan case development while minimizing the risk of impaired fact finding.[151]

---

147 Conducting an initial witness interview is treated separately in Section C(2), above in this chapter. In truth, it overlaps considerably with issues relating to witness preparation; the guidelines set out below thus apply *mutatis mutandis* to any encounter with a witness.

148 See Alta, Sask r 4.01(1); BC, Man, Ont, NS, NL r 5.1-1, commentary 3.

149 *United States v Geders*, 425 US 80 at 90, n 3 (1976).

150 J Boyd, "Legal Ethics" (1905) 4 Can Law Rev 85 at 90.

151 See Richard Wydick, "The Ethics of Witness Coaching" (1995) 17 Cardozo L Rev 1 at 39, steps 3 & 4.

1) Importance of Witness Preparation

Counsel's duty of competence generally includes the obligation to prepare a witness before calling her to the stand.[152] Witness preparation serves a number of valid goals in relation to the client's litigation interests. It aids in refreshing the witness's memory of relevant events. It gives counsel the chance to explain the process of testifying to witnesses for whom the experience is new. Preparation can also improve counsel's understanding of the case. Finally, good preparation allows counsel to structure a witness's testimony to emphasize relevant matters presented in a manner that is understandable to the trier of fact.

Good witness preparation also assists the adversarial criminal justice system in reaching a fair and accurate result. The client's position is coherently presented to the trier of fact during the witness's direct examination. The opponent then has a chance to test the witness's reliability or bring out additional facts through cross-examination. The process is focused, and time is not wasted. As long as the adversarial process remains a fundamental part of the justice system, witness preparation thus serves both the client's best interests and important systemic goals.[153]

2) Prohibition against Preparation That Misleads the Court

Witness preparation must not result in evidence that misleads the court, not even where doing so is to the client's advantage. The lawyer's duty not to mislead the court always trumps the duty of loyalty to the client.[154] There are many rules of professional conduct that bear on the duty not to mislead the court in the context of preparing a witness to testify, for example, a lawyer

- must not knowingly encourage or assist in activity that is dishonest, fraudulent, criminal, or illegal;[155]

---

152 Alan W Mewett & Peter J Sankoff, *Witnesses* (Scarborough, ON: Carswell, 1991) (loose-leaf 2013–14 supplement) at § 6.1 & 6.2; Earl Cherniak, "The Ethics of Advocacy" in Franklin R Moskoff, ed, *Advocacy in Court: A Tribute to Arthur Maloney, Q.C.* (Toronto: Canada Law Book, 1986) 101 at 103. Examples of courts criticizing counsel for failing to adequately prepare a witness to testify include *LCB*, above note 11 at 372 [para 72]; *R v Smith*, 2007 SKCA 71 at para 22; *Fraser*, above note 6 at paras 105–6; *R v Liard*, 2013 ONSC 5457 at para 424 [*Liard*].

153 See Bryan Finlay, Thomas A Cromwell, & Nikiforos Iatrou, *Witness Preparation: A Practical Guide*, 3d ed (Aurora, ON: Canada Law Book, 2010) at 34–35.

154 See Chapter 1, Section E.

155 Alta r 2.02(10) (commentary); Sask r 2.02(7); BC, Man, Ont, NS, NL r 3.2-7.

- has a duty to treat the tribunal with candour, fairness, courtesy, and respect;[156]
- cannot knowingly assist or permit a client to do anything that the lawyer considers to be dishonest or dishonourable;[157]
- cannot knowingly attempt to deceive a tribunal by offering false evidence;[158]
- cannot knowingly permit a witness to be presented in a false or misleading way or to impersonate another;[159]
- must act in good faith to the tribunal;[160] and
- must take care not to subvert or suppress any evidence.[161]

Misleading the court not only undermines the integrity of the justice system. It can lead to disciplinary or criminal sanctions for the lawyer[162] and cause irreparable harm to his reputation in the legal community. Improper witness preparation exposed in cross-examination will also usually harm the client's case.[163] And a witness who feels unduly pressured during preparation may grow to dislike counsel, resulting in less helpful testimony for the client at trial.

3) Preparation Guidelines

It is impossible to provide guidelines for every contingency that may arise while preparing a witness. The overriding principle for counsel, however, is to fulfill the duties of loyalty and competence owed to the client, which means preparation that assists in eliciting helpful evidence in a credible and coherent way, without creating an undue risk that the witness's narrative will change so as to mislead the trier of fact. This balancing act is harder to achieve in some circumstances than in

---

156 Alta, Sask r 4.01(1); BC, Man, Ont, NS, NL r 5.1-1.
157 Alta r 4.01(2)(d); Sask r 4.01(2)(b); BC, Man, Ont, NS, NL r 5.1-2-(b). See also Alta r 4.01(2)(m).
158 Alta r 4.01(2)(g); Sask r 4.01(2)(e); BC, Man, Ont, NS, NL r 5.1-2(e). See also Alta r 4.01(5)(a).
159 Alta r 4.01(2)(p); Sask r 4.01(2)(k); BC, Man, Ont, NS, NL r 5.1-2(k).
160 Alta r 4.01(6); Sask r 4.01(5); BC, Man, Ont, NS, NL r 5.1-5.
161 Alta, Sask r 4.03; Ont r 5.3-1; BC, Man, NS, NL r 5.3.
162 See *R v Sweezey* (1987), 39 CCC (3d) 182 (NLCA): lawyer who had advised a witness to be forgetful and evasive was convicted of attempting to obstruct justice; *Mattson*, above note 108: lawyer was charged with attempting to obstruct justice for directing a witness regarding the content of his testimony, although the committal was quashed on review.
163 Improper contact with a witness can justify the trier of fact's drawing an adverse inference regarding the witness's credibility: see the text and caselaw associated with note 228, below in this chapter.

others. What follows are some suggestions as to what constitutes ethical practice.

Recommendation: Counsel should prepare a witness on the assumption that everything said and done during the process will come out in cross-examination. A presumption of transparency encourages a perspective well-suited to avoid dubious preparation practices.

a) Stressing Paramount Importance of Truth-Telling

Counsel should tell a witness to speak the truth no matter what and not to worry about the impact that truthful testimony might have on the litigation's outcome. The witness should also be encouraged to correct testimony already given while still on the stand if she realizes that it is inaccurate or requires material qualification.[164]

b) Avoiding Speculation and Opinion

Counsel can and sometimes should tell a witness not to guess or speculate in providing answers and if a question is not understood to ask that it be repeated or clarified. The witness can also be told not to offer an opinion unless specifically asked and otherwise to recount only facts personally observed.

c) Avoiding Tainting

To avoid tainting, a lawyer should never prepare witnesses together.[165] It may also be worthwhile to caution a witness against conduct that may taint his independence or cause other harm. For instance, counsel may advise the witness not to discuss the subject matter of his testimony with others before testifying, most especially those who may be witnesses or have a palpable interest in the matter.[166]

d) Direction Not to Mention Particular Topics Unless Asked

Telling a witness that she should not broach a particular subject to prevent unfairness is entirely justifiable, and perhaps even required. Thus, counsel may want to caution the witness against mentioning an out-of-court statement that is inadmissible hearsay or past conduct by

---

164 See Finlay, Cromwell, & Iatrou, above note 153 at 51.

165 See Ontario, *Report of the Commission on Proceedings Involving Guy Paul Morin* (Toronto: Ministry of the Attorney General, 1998) (Chair: Fred Kaufman) at 1220, point (a) [*Morin Inquiry Report*]; *Gemmell v Reddicopp*, 2005 BCCA 62 at para 47. The concerns that can arise where witnesses discuss their evidence in each other's company are set out in *R v MB*, 2011 ONCA 76 at para 19.

166 Subject, of course, to the considerations mentioned in Section D, above in this chapter.

the accused that is caught by the exclusionary rule applicable to bad character evidence. Or counsel may tell an expert witness not to exceed the scope of her expertise in answering questions.

It is also proper to tell the witness, as a general proposition, not to volunteer information unless asked. More than this, counsel can ethically advise the witness not to bring up of her own accord particular pieces of information that might assist the opponent's case.[167] Doing so may come closer to crossing the line where the advice comes from Crown counsel.[168] But it must be remembered that all relevant information will have been disclosed to the defence before trial, including any information that Crown counsel suggests the witness not volunteer.[169]

In advising a witness not to mention a particular point unless asked, counsel must be exceedingly careful to say nothing to encourage the witness to cover up or modify his testimony regarding the topic or to leave out information so as to directly or implicitly contradict the rest of the witness's testimony. The witness must also understand that the information has to be revealed in response to a question asked by a lawyer or the court.

e) Courtroom Procedure and Etiquette

A lawyer should educate neophyte witnesses regarding courtroom procedure and etiquette. Doing so reduces nervousness and stress and thus assists the calling party in presenting the witness's evidence. Topics to canvas include how to address the judge and lawyers in court, the importance of speaking at a reasonable pace and volume, the need to answer questions verbally instead of simply nodding, and so on.

A witness should also be advised to stop talking and wait for a ruling if counsel for any party rises to object to a question posed. But the witness must understand that unless counsel or the judge intervenes, it is her job to answer the questions put, not to protest or complain about their relevance or propriety.

f) Courtroom Dress and Demeanour

Recommending that the witness take steps to present well in court, for instance by dressing in a presentable fashion and not wearing clothing that might distract the judge or jury, is unobjectionable. It is also permissible to advise the witness regarding demeanour, for example not to lose his temper if challenged in cross-examination or to avoid speech

---

167 See Mark M Orkin, *Legal Ethics*, 2d ed (Toronto: Canada Law Book, 2011) at 55.

168 See, for example, the clearly unethical conduct discussed in Bennett Gershman, "Witness Coaching by Prosecutors" (2002) 23 Cardozo L Rev 829 at 836–37.

169 See Chapter 12, Section G.

habits that might distract or grate on the trier of fact. But suggesting that demeanour be artificially shaped to bolster the reliability of the witness's testimony is improper. For example, a witness cannot be told to exaggerate her degree of confidence in recalling what happened. It is also wrong to tell a witness to dissemble regarding emotions expressed on the stand, such as by bursting into tears or feigning surprise when a particular matter is raised.

g) Advising as to Topics That Might Be Covered during the Witness's Testimony

Counsel should give the witness a good idea of the areas, and preferably even the specific questions, that will be covered in chief. Simulating a direct examination is perfectly acceptable. There is also nothing wrong with canvassing matters that might be of interest to the cross-examiner so that the witness is prepared to respond. Counsel may even conduct a mock cross-examination to give the witness a flavour of the areas and nature of challenge he may face when questioned by the opposing lawyer.

h) Refreshing Memory and Reviewing the Witness's Narrative of Events

A witness should be strongly encouraged to read carefully any prior statements and testimony transcripts to help refresh her memory. Counsel should also review with the witness documents or other physical items that will be introduced into evidence through her testimony.

How should counsel review the witness's narrative of events during the preparation process? Contemporary science tells us that memory is not like a video recording, always available to be discovered and played back, but rather is a constructive or additive process that can be prone to error.[170] And confabulation can be caused by questions that, whether intentionally or not, hint at the desired answer, or even arise from nothing more than an unconscious desire to compensate for a lack of actual memory.[171]

Consequently, a witness should not be pushed to conform his version of events to better accommodate counsel's theory of the case.

---

170 See *R v Trochym*, 2007 SCC 6 at para 41.

171 See *ibid* at para 42; *R v SGT*, 2011 SKCA 4 at para 63 [*SGT*]; Manitoba, *The Inquiry regarding Thomas Sophonow: The Investigation, Prosecution and Consideration of Entitlement to Compensation* (Winnipeg: Attorney General, 2001) (Commissioner: Peter Cory) at 28 ("The Experts' Position regarding Eyewitness Testimony"); Alice Woolley, *Understanding Lawyers' Ethics in Canada* (Markham, ON: LexisNexis, 2011) at 195–96.

Using leading questions during preparation may increase the danger of altering the witness's narrative to create unreliable testimony. Even subtle suggestions can be problematic, for example the repeated use of a descriptive word by counsel that is eventually adopted by the witness or causes the witness to adjust aspects of her narrative with the result that the import of her evidence has materially changed.

These dangers do not exist equally for every witness or for every matter with respect to which a witness might testify. Counsel must apply common sense in determining when leading questions are or are not appropriate. Concerns are much reduced regarding matters not in dispute between the parties. Conversely, some types of evidence may be more susceptible to confabulation, such as eyewitness testimony or the testimony of a co-operating accomplice or a child. Similarly, witnesses with an interest in the matter may be more likely to modify their testimony to favour a particular outcome if nudged in that direction by leading questions.

For all types of witnesses it will be necessary to ask questions to determine precisely what relevant information they possess regarding the issues in dispute. The witness will often be unaware of what exactly is relevant or may be taciturn or inarticulate and thus prone to leaving out relevant facts. So questions must be asked during preparation, sometimes a great many of them, on matters both general and precise. As a basic rule, however, the safest approach is to stick to non-leading questions when discussing disputed areas.[172] Counsel should also try to employ the witness's own language in discussing such areas, avoiding loaded descriptors that risk altering the evidence so as to mislead the trier of fact.

If a witness does not mention a relevant matter during preparation, it is permissible to draw his attention to the area and ask questions — preferably non-leading — in an effort to obtain information. It is also proper to ask the witness to explain apparent contradictions between information provided during preparation and prior statements or testimony.[173]

Example: Defence counsel applies to exclude wiretap evidence based on a constitutional attack on the Part VI authorization and is granted leave to cross-examine the officer whose affidavit was used in support. Counsel asks the court to make an order prohibiting Crown counsel from discussing the contents of the defence application materials with

---

172   See Peter A Joy & Kevin C McMunigal, *Do No Wrong: Ethics for Prosecutors and Defenders* (Chicago: American Bar Association, 2009) at 173.

173   See *Liard*, above note 152 at para 426.

the affiant. The order should be refused because it is proper and necessary for Crown counsel to canvass with the affiant the areas on which he is expected to testify in court. Crown counsel can be relied on to act ethically in preparing the affiant and not coach or lead him with respect to matters that may be in dispute.[174]

i) Suggesting That the Witness Use Particular Wording

It is usually best that a witness be encouraged to speak in her own words. Doing so makes it easier for the witness to communicate relevant information to the trier of fact in an understandable and credible way. But suggesting that a witness use particular wording to better convey his true meaning, as opposed to changing it, is permissible.[175] Discouraging a witness from an idiosyncratic use of language that would mislead the trier of fact as to what actually happened or from using unduly technical language or jargon is also acceptable. In other words, counsel can use the witness preparation process "to ensure clarity of testimony."[176] As stated in the Alberta code:

> While a lawyer may legitimately suggest alternative ways of presenting evidence so that it is better understood, it is improper to direct or encourage a witness to misstate or misrepresent the facts. An advocate's role is not to change or distort the evidence, but to assist the witness in bringing forth the evidence in a manner that ensures fair and accurate comprehension by the court and opposing parties.[177]

j) Confronting a Witness with Contradictory Evidence

It is usually permissible for counsel to confront a witness with evidence anticipated to come from other sources that the witness has not mentioned or perhaps even contradicted and to ask the witness whether this new information assists in refreshing her memory or to explain an apparent contradiction between the information and her recollection.[178] Only by doing so can counsel definitely ascertain what

---

174 The facts and conclusion are based on *R v Poloni*, 2006 BCPC 166.
175 See Joseph D Piorkowski, "Professional Conduct and the Preparation of Witnesses for Trial: Defining Acceptable Limitations of 'Coaching'" (1987) 1 Geo J Legal Ethics 389 at 399–402.
176 See Alta r 4.04(2) (commentary); Sask r 4.04(2) (commentary); BC, Man, NS, NL r 5.4-2, commentary 3.
177 Alta r 4.04(2) (commentary).
178 See Wydick, above note 151 at 14–15; *Morin Inquiry Report*, above note 165 at 1219–20; Woolley, above note 171 at 198 and 200–1; Gavin MacKenzie, *Lawyers & Ethics: Professional Responsibility and Discipline* (Scarborough, ON: Carswell, 1993) (loose-leaf revision 2013-3) at §§ 4.12 and 4-26.4; Earl J Levy, *Examination*

knowledge, if any, the witness purports to have regarding the matter. The witness's response on being confronted could lead to any number of results, from counsel's deciding the witness is not credible and so should not be called, to further investigation that leads to reliable evidence supporting the witness's version of events.

The danger, of course, is that mentioning other facts will provoke the witness to provide unreliable information, whether consciously or not, and thus risk misleading the trier of fact. Counsel should thus attempt to present the other facts in a way that presents the least risk of creating false evidence.[179] Where the witness is "patently impressionable or highly suggestible," the risk may be so high that counsel is best advised not to present the witness with the conflicting evidence.[180] On the other hand, in deciding what to do counsel can take into account the likelihood that a material change in the witness's evidence occasioned by the preparation process will be revealed in cross-examination. This will almost certainly be so where counsel acts for the prosecution because the Crown has a duty to disclose to the defence any new information that arises during a witness interview.[181]

k) Privileged Information

Counsel must not coax a witness to disclose privileged information during the preparation process, at least absent an informed waiver by the privilege holder. For example, an accused in a joint trial may decide to plead guilty and become a Crown witness. In interviewing this witness, Crown counsel should not dig for information that is privileged by virtue of having been shared by the remaining accused or their lawyers under a joint-defence arrangement.[182] To be safe, the witness should be initially briefed not to reveal any such information.

---

of *Witnesses in Criminal Cases*, 6th ed (Toronto: Carswell, 2011) at 31; Gershman, above note 168 at 858. See also Section G(6), below in this chapter.

179   See Wydick, above note 151 at 39–41. Especially helpful in this regard is the detailed interview process proposed for Crown counsel in the *Morin Inquiry Report*, above note 165 at 1219–20, later endorsed in *R v Spence*, 2011 ONSC 2406 at para 26, and by Levy, above note 178 at 49–50.

180   *Morin Inquiry Report*, above note 165 at 1220, point (j).

181   See Chapter 12, Section G(4).

182   This sort of "common interest privilege" is recognized in cases such as *Pritchard v Ontario (Human Rights Commission)*, 2004 SCC 31 at paras 23–24; *R v Dunbar* (1982), 68 CCC (2d) 13 at 36 [paras 54–56] (Ont CA); *General Accident Assurance Co v Chrusz* (1999), 45 OR (3d) 321 at paras 42–46 (CA); *Detlor v Brantford (City)*, 2013 ONCA 560 at paras 50–51.

4) Treating Witnesses Courteously and Respectfully

We have already discussed counsel's obligation to be civil and act in good faith in communicating with witnesses outside of court.[183] Most codes of professional conduct further state that a lawyer must not needlessly inconvenience a witness.[184] A person whom counsel intends to call as a witness should thus receive sufficient notice regarding trial scheduling, and counsel should strive to accommodate the person's work and personal commitments where possible.

5) Preparing the Client to Testify

A number of factors distinguish defence counsel's preparation of the client to testify from the process that occurs with other witnesses. To begin with, the client has a constitutional right to know the case against him, including everything the Crown witnesses will say. Counsel cannot sequester the client from relevant information that might, whether consciously or unconsciously, cause the client to modify his version of events. To the contrary, throughout the retainer counsel must keep the client apprised of relevant matters, including the nature and strength of the Crown case, the contents of the disclosure materials, and information obtained through defence investigation.[185]

And while there may be debate about whether an ordinary witness should ever be told of the law bearing on the case,[186] defence counsel must inform the accused of the legal parameters of any potentially applicable defences. True, the accused may use this information to concoct a false defence just as he may do after reviewing the disclosure provided by the Crown. Yet it would be ethically wrong for counsel as zealous advocate to presume that the client will use the information in this way. Not educating the client on the law may result in truthful factual points being withheld from counsel, to the client's substantial detriment at trial. Ultimately, the risk of fabrication is outweighed by

---

183   See Section C(2)(c), above in this chapter.

184   Alta r 4.01(2)(u); Sask r 4.01(2)(o); BC, Man, Ont, NS, NL 5.1-2(o).

185   See Chapter 3, Section E.

186   See, for example, Third Restatement § 116, comment "b": proper witness preparation may include discussing the applicability of law to the events in issue. We see little reason why an ordinary witness should be told about the applicable law but recognize that counsel's questions during preparation will be driven by the law governing any available defences and so may alert the witness as to what facts are legally relevant.

the client's right to know the strength of the Crown case based on the applicable law, including any viable defences.[187]

What is more, a lawyer's duty to advise the client includes the obligation to weigh in on the likelihood that the judge or jury will entertain a reasonable doubt regarding a pro-defence version of facts. Is the witness whose evidence assists in this regard credible? Or are credibility concerns so serious the witness should not be called? Is relying on other witnesses or other defences or perhaps even seeking a negotiated plea the better route? Counsel must provide this sort of advice to the client regarding ordinary witnesses. The same goes for the client's own account of what happened. It matters not that imparting such information to any other witness might be improper. The accused as witness is different because he is also a client and in that guise has a right to counsel's feedback on all aspects of the case.[188]

Another factor unique to the accused when it comes to witness preparation is that his communications with counsel are covered by solicitor-client privilege.[189] Although the privilege exists for very good reason where the client is a witness, it prevents the trier of fact from knowing anything about the preparation process. One could argue that this shield of privilege may tempt counsel to engage in improper conduct in readying the client to testify. We prefer the view that defence lawyers are aware of the sacrosanct duty never knowingly to encourage or assist in misleading the court and so will conduct themselves ethically regardless.

In sum, the accused's special position in the criminal justice system provides advantages that make easier the fabrication of evidence, whether knowingly or subconsciously. This is the unavoidable but necessary side effect of the various constitutional rights enjoyed by every accused. The accused's special position does not, however, give defence counsel licence to help the client fashion false evidence. Counsel can never knowingly participate in misleading the court, for example by

---

187 A strong proponent of this view is Monroe Freedman, who first articulated it in his famous article "Professional Responsibility of the Criminal Defense Lawyer: The Three Hardest Questions" (1966) 64 Mich L Rev 1469 at 1478–82. More recently, see Monroe H Freedman & Abbe Smith, *Understanding Lawyers' Ethics*, 4th ed (New Providence, NJ: LexisNexis, 2010) at 202–6. Professor Freedman's view appears to be adopted in *SGT*, above note 171 at paras 60–65. See also W William Hodes, "The Professional Duty to Horseshed Witnesses — Zealously, within the Bounds of the Law" (1999) 30 Tex Tech L Rev 1343 at 1354–56.

188 This view appears to be accepted, and certainly is not rejected, in *SGT*, above note 171 at para 61.

189 See Chapter 4, Section D.

412 ETHICS AND CRIMINAL LAW

telling the accused what to say in the stand.[190] And so the integrity of the justice system is not exposed to rampant abuse whenever defence counsel prepares the client to testify. To the contrary, solid protection exists in the form of ethical dictates that prohibit lawyers from knowingly assisting in any dishonesty.

6) Appellate Crown Counsel Interviewing Trial Defence Counsel regarding an Ineffective Assistance Claim

Where an appellant asserts that his counsel rendered ineffective assistance at trial, the Crown has a responsibility to investigate and respond to the allegation.[191] This will usually require that Crown counsel speak to the appellant's trial counsel and review with her in detail the allegations made by the appellant.[192] Doing so is a necessary part of preparing the Crown's response and does not amount to encouraging trial counsel to breach the duties of loyalty and confidentiality owed the former client.[193] Indeed, it has been suggested that trial counsel has an affirmative duty to provide information responsive to the appellant's allegations to ensure that the appeal court is not misled as to the facts.[194]

It is also acceptable for Crown counsel to draft an affidavit for trial counsel to be submitted to the court on appeal, based on the information received from trial counsel, this being a proper way to ensure that relevant matters are covered and inadmissible or extraneous information is excluded.[195] Of course, trial counsel remains responsible for the truth of the affidavit and cannot look to Crown counsel for legal advice in its preparation, and she will be subject to cross-examination on the affidavit if the appellant so desires.[196]

---

190 See *SGT*, above note 171 at para 60. See also Chapter 1, Section F(4); ABA Defense Standard 4-3.2(a): "defense counsel should probe [the accused] for all legally relevant information without seeking to influence the direction of the client's responses."

191 See *R v Archer* (2005), 202 CCC (3d) 60 at para 155 (Ont CA).

192 See *ibid* at paras 155 and 165–66.

193 See *ibid* at paras 158–59. Regarding the extent to which trial counsel is permitted to release information to the Crown or court in response to an ineffective assistance claim, see Chapter 5, Section E(2).

194 See *Archer, ibid* at paras 159 and 164–65.

195 See *ibid* at paras 155–56. But contrast this approach taken in British Columbia by virtue of the practice directive discussed in Chapter 5, note 52.

196 See *ibid* at paras 156–57 and 160–62.

H. QUESTIONING A WITNESS IN COURT

The ethical elicitation of testimony from witnesses in court is largely a matter of competent preparation and execution, and fidelity to the rules of evidence. But difficult issues can arise, many of which are addressed elsewhere in this text. For instance, the prohibition against eliciting false evidence is reviewed in Chapter 1,[197] as are the limits on cross-examining a witness counsel knows to be telling the truth.[198] The challenges that arise where a lawyer knows or suspects that a client intends to commit perjury are canvassed in Chapter 7. Many restrictions on cross-examination, some applicable only to prosecutors but many governing defence lawyers too, are discussed in Chapter 12. In this section of the text, we briefly review some further ethical issues that can arise when counsel questions a witness in court.

1) Presenting a Witness in a Misleading Way

Counsel's duty not to mislead the court means that he cannot knowingly permit a witness, or a party for that matter,[199] to be presented in a false or misleading way.[200]

2) Prohibition against Eliciting Inadmissible Evidence

Defence and Crown lawyers alike are prohibited from introducing evidence they know to be inadmissible.[201] The rules of evidence aim to promote justice by ensuring that information put before the trier of fact is relevant and not unduly prejudicial. Knowingly ignoring a rule of admissibility risks subverting trial fairness and causing an unreliable result.

---

197 See Chapter 1, Sections E and K.

198 See Chapter 1, Section K(1).

199 See the third example given in Chapter 2, Section B(1).

200 See Alta r 4.01(2)(p); Sask r 4.01(2)(k); BC, Man, Ont, NS, NL r 5.1-2(k). For a leading discussion on the impropriety of misleading the court as to a witness's circumstances, see *Meek v Fleming*, [1961] 3 All ER 148 at 154 and 156 (CA).

201 See Alta r 4.01(2)(j); "Principles of Civility," above note 58, r 55 and 57; *R v Tshiamala*, 2011 QCCA 439 at paras 118–21, leave to appeal to SCC refused, [2011] SCCA No 220 [*Tshiamala*]; *R v Lyttle*, 2004 SCC 5 at paras 55–61 [*Lyttle*]; *R v Felderhof* (2003), 180 CCC (3d) 498 at paras 73–75 (Ont CA); *R v Khan*, 2008 BCCA 63 at para 19. Compare *R v Youvarajah*, 2013 SCC 41 at para 129, Wagner J, dissenting but not on this point. See also ABA Prosecution Standard 3-5.6(b) and ABA Defense Standard 4-7.5(b). Regarding prosecutors, see also Chapter 12, Section H(7)(b).

It is thus unethical to ask a witness a question, whether in direct, cross-examination, or reply, that a lawyer knows will elicit inadmissible testimony. It is no answer to say that it is opposing counsel's job to object if the question is improper. Opposing counsel may not see the testimony coming or fail to appreciate that the evidence is inadmissible. Even where opposing counsel objects before the problematic testimony emerges, serious harm may arise because the trier has heard the facts suggested by the question.[202] For similar reasons, it is improper to refer to inadmissible facts in asking a question despite knowing that the witness will reject those facts in answering.[203]

If counsel reasonably believes that the opposing party or the court may object to the admissibility of evidence, the opponent and judge should be alerted to the intention to elicit the evidence so that a ruling on admissibility can be obtained if necessary.[204]

Example: In a murder case, the trial judge excludes several arguably irrational statements made by the accused shortly after the alleged offence on the basis that they constitute inadmissible hearsay. The defence calls an expert to testify on drug-induced psychosis as part of a *mens rea* defence. In questioning the expert, defence counsel refers to "other things that we haven't been able to present to you" and then asks a series of questions to elicit the expert's opinion that irrational statements made by the accused at the time in question would be indicative of cocaine psychosis. This questioning effectively circumvents the trial judge's ruling excluding the statements and is thus improper.[205]

3) Making Only Proper Objections and in a Timely Way

Cross-examination is a crucial forensic tool. Ill-considered attempts to interfere with a proper cross-examination are unethical, for even if rebuffed they can unfairly derail the opponent's ability to test a witness's evidence. The rules of professional conduct thus prohibit counsel for a calling party from obstructing a cross-examination "by unreasonable interruptions, repeated objection to proper questions, attempts to have the witness change or tailor evidence, or other similar conduct while the examination is ongoing."[206] The codes also contain another

---

202 See *R v RSW* (1990), 55 CCC (3d) 149 at 158–59 (Man CA).

203 See *R v Gaultois* (1989), 73 Nfld & PEIR 337 at paras 22–27 (Nfld CA).

204 See "Principles of Civility," above note 58, r 57; *Tshiamala*, above note 201 at paras 118–21; *R v Jacobson* (2004), 196 CCC (3d) 65 at para 16 (Ont SCJ).

205 See *R v Edgar* (2000), 142 CCC (3d) 401 at paras 26–29 (Ont CA).

206 Alta, Sask r 4.04(2) (commentary); BC, Man, NS, NL r 5.4-2, commentary 3.

broader rule that prohibits a lawyer from obstructive conduct during examination-in-chief and cross-examination.[207]

Where counsel has a legitimate objection to make and knows it, the objection must be made in a timely way.[208] Waiting to object until the end of the trial for tactical reasons can cause serious harm to the administration of justice. Prejudice arising from a jury's having heard inadmissible evidence may be more difficult to cure. And the course of the trial may have been dramatically different had a timely objection been made.

4) Prohibition against Harassing a Witness in Cross-examination

Counsel's brief sometimes mandates an aggressive attack on the credibility of a witness. The result may be to upset, embarrass, and humiliate. The justice system accepts this outcome as the cost of obtaining an accurate result via a fair adversarial process. Counsel is thus not only justified in conducting such a cross-examination but is ethically required to do so. As the rules of professional conduct state, "In adversarial proceedings, the lawyer has a duty to the client to raise fearlessly every issue, advance every argument and *ask every question, however distasteful*, that the lawyer thinks will help the client's case and endeavour to obtain for the client the benefit of every remedy and defence authorized by law."[209]

Yet lawyers also have a duty not to conduct a cross-examination that *needlessly* intimidates or humiliates the witness. The rules of professional conduct make this point,[210] and so does the jurisprudence.[211] It is proper to expose frailties in the witness's testimony on points relevant to the issue of guilt, including concerns relating to the witness's character. But the client who insists that the witness be degraded or demeaned purely out of spite must be told that such conduct is

---

207 Alta, Sask r 4.04(1); BC, Man, NS, NL r 5.4-1.

208 See *R v Dexter*, 2013 ONCA 744 at paras 30–41; *R v Graham*, 2013 BCCA 75 at para 34.

209 Alta, Sask r 4.01(1) (commentary); BC, Man, Ont, NS, NL r 5.1-1, commentary 1 [emphasis added]. See *Rondel v Worsley*, [1969] 1 AC 191 at 227–28 (HL); *Lyttle*, above note 201 at para 66.

210 Alta r 4.01(2)(s); Sask r 4.01(2)(m); BC, Man, Ont, NS, NL 5.1-2(m). See also ABA Prosecution Standard 3-5.7(a) and ABA Defense Standard 4-7.6(a).

211 *Lyttle*, above note 201 at para 44. Many cases on point deal with prosecutors, who probably face greater limits in this regard given their role as ministers of justice: see Chapter 12, Section H(7)(a).

impermissible.[212] Respect for the privacy and dignity of the witness, as well as the administration of justice, is pre-eminent where there can be no countervailing forensic benefit for the client.

5) Misstating a Witness's Evidence in Cross-examination

It is improper to ask a question in cross-examination that misstates the evidence of the witness or any other evidence.[213] Such questioning is unfair to the witness and risks misleading the court.

I. WITNESS EXCLUSION AND NO-COMMUNICATION ORDERS

Trial judges often make an order at the commencement of trial excluding witnesses from the courtroom until after they have testified and precluding them from speaking to any witness who has already given evidence. An order may also be made prohibiting a testifying witness from discussing her evidence with anyone during an adjournment. The aim of these exclusion and no-communication orders is to prevent the tainting of a witness's evidence.[214]

A lawyer often has a legitimate need to speak to witnesses before they are called, most importantly to prepare them to testify but also to make logistical arrangements. Absent good justification, an exclusion order should not be worded to prevent counsel from carrying out these important tasks.[215] But where an order uses language broad enough to interfere with counsel's legitimate trial preparation,[216] or there is any

---

212 See Chapter 3, Section J. See also *R v Beauchamp*, 2005 QCCA 580 at para 90: client's instructions can never justify an unethical cross-examination.

213 See Alta 4.01(2)(h); Sask r 4.01(2)(f); BC, Man, Ont, NS, NL r 5.1-2(f).

214 See *R v O'Callaghan* (1982), 65 CCC (2d) 459 at 464 [para 13] (Ont HCJ) [*O'Callaghan*]; *R v Collette* (1983), 6 CCC (3d) 300 at 306 (Ont HCJ), aff'd (1983), 7 CCC (3d) 574 (Ont CA), leave to appeal to SCC refused, [1984] SCCA No 334; *R v Murphy* (1994), 114 Nfld & PEIR 148 at para 54 (Nfld CA); *R v Dobberthien* (1973), 13 CCC (2d) 513 at 515 (Alta SCAD), aff'd (1974), 18 CCC (2d) 449 (SCC); *R v Dulle*, 2008 SKPC 56 at para 3(3); *R v Latimer*, [2003] OJ No 3841 at para 27 (SCJ).

215 See *O'Callaghan*, above note 214 at 465–68 [paras 13–21]. *O'Callaghan* and *R v Arsenault* (1956), 115 CCC 400 at 403 (NB SCAD), convincingly suggest that unless worded otherwise an exclusion order does not prevent counsel from communicating with excluded witnesses.

216 See, for example, *O'Callaghan*, above note 214.

doubt on the score, counsel should obtain dispensation from the trial judge before communicating with the witness.

As just noted, exclusion orders are rarely framed to prevent a lawyer from preparing a witness to give evidence at trial. Counsel should nonetheless think twice before relaying to a witness the content of testimony already presented in court. Doing so likely subverts the purpose of the court's order, namely, to sequester the witness from knowledge about what other witnesses have said in their testimony.[217] Alberta's code thus expressly forbids a lawyer from discussing the testimony of a witness with a person excluded from court during such testimony,[218] an interdiction that should be heeded by all Canadian lawyers.[219]

Counsel is not, however, barred from discussing facts with an excluded witness simply because they have been the subject of in-court evidence. Were it otherwise, out-of-court witness preparation would be unduly curtailed. The prohibition only precludes a lawyer's suggesting to an excluded person that particular facts have been recounted in another witness's testimony.[220] A problem may nonetheless arise where counsel plans to call an expert whose opinion is to be based on the testimony of previous witnesses. Counsel must obtain permission from the judge before relaying this testimony to the expert.

What should defence counsel do on learning that a client has defied a witness exclusion or no-communication order? In *R v Wiebe*,[221] the accused was in the midst of testifying when the court adjourned for the day. That evening, he exchanged emails with an excluded defence witness regarding a disputed issue that had arisen during testimony in chief. The accused must have told his lawyer about the emails, because when proceedings resumed, defence counsel disclosed their existence to the court. In rejecting the argument that the trial judge erroneously allowed the Crown to use the emails in cross-examination, the Ontario Court of Appeal observed that defence counsel had been under an ethical duty to advise the court of the emails.[222]

---

217 The precise wording of the order may not, on its face, bar a third party such as a lawyer from conveying such information to the excluded witness. Yet in many if not all jurisdictions, exclusion orders are viewed as impliedly having this effect: see *R v Robinson*, [1983] OJ No 2314 at para 1 (HCJ); Cherniak, above note 152 at 106–7.

218 Alta r 4.01(2)(q).

219 See Cherniak, above note 152 at 106–7; Finlay, Cromwell, & Iatrou, above note 153 at 113–14.

220 See Cherniak, above note 152 at 107; Finlay, Cromwell, & Iatrou, above note 153 at 114.

221 (2006), 205 CCC (3d) 326 (Ont CA) [*Wiebe*].

222 *Ibid* at para 8.

We agree that remaining silent and continuing with the examination-in-chief was not an option for defence counsel in *Wiebe*. Doing so would have meant knowingly assisting the client in testifying with the benefit of information obtained in breach of the exclusion order. Yet disclosing the breach absent the client's consent would have violated counsel's duty of confidentiality to the client. Counsel's only option was to urge his client to make disclosure to the court. This is no doubt what counsel did in *Wiebe*. Had the client refused to make disclosure, counsel would have had to apply to withdraw from the case for ethical reasons, remaining silent as to the precise reason why.[223]

Caution: No-communication orders directed at a testifying witness are sometimes of sufficient breadth to prohibit discussion with the lawyers involved in the case.[224] If counsel has a legitimate reason for speaking to a witness who is subject to such an order during a break in the testimony, she must first seek the court's leave.[225]

J. COMMUNICATING WITH A TESTIFYING WITNESS

We have just seen that a no-communication order may restrict a lawyer's ability to communicate out of court with a testifying witness. Far more likely to limit the scope for such communication, however, are provisions found in most Canadian ethical codes. These provisions seek to minimize the risk of improper tainting, which is seen to rise considerably once a witness begins to testify, and in particular once the opponent's strategy has been revealed through cross-examination. Of course, communication between counsel and a testifying witness that complies with the rules in this area must also adhere to the ethical principles prohibiting witness coaching.[226] Permission to communicate is not a licence to engage in improper coaching.[227]

---

223 The application would no doubt be granted: see Chapter 11, Section L.
224 See *R v Carson* (1994), 143 NBR (2d) 6 at para 4 (CA); *R v Willingham* (2004), 185 Man R (2d) 201 at para 14 (Prov Ct) [*Willingham*]; *R v Leung*, [1999] OJ No 5859 (Gen Div).
225 See *Willingham*, above note 224 at paras 26–35; Cherniak, above note 152 at 106.
226 See Section G, above in this chapter.
227 See Alta r 4.04(2) (commentary).

1) Relationship between Ethical Rules, Court Practice, and Agreements between the Parties

This is an area, like conflict of interest, where the law societies' ethical rules operate alongside jurisprudence developed by the courts. Breaching the law society rules may lead to disciplinary proceedings. Breaching the judicial rules may prejudice counsel's client by permitting the trier of fact to draw an adverse inference regarding the witness's credibility.[228]

The rules of professional conduct in this area, as in others, carry persuasive influence with the courts but are not binding.[229] Indeed, the rules typically state that they apply "subject to the direction of the tribunal,"[230] "unless the tribunal directs otherwise,"[231] or absent leave of the court for counsel to act otherwise.[232] The commentary to most rules further provides that their application "may be determined by the practice and procedures of the tribunal and may be modified by agreement of counsel."[233]

If counsel has any real concern as to whether a desired communication may clash with the court's expectations regarding what is permissible, he should seek direction from the judge.

2) Communication with Own Witness during Direct Examination

Nova Scotia has the most restrictive ethical rule governing counsel's ability to communicate with her witness during direct examination. It imposes a blanket prohibition on doing so absent leave of the court or consent of opposing counsel.[234] By contrast, the Ontario rule states

---

228 See *R v Peruta* (1992), 78 CCC (3d) 350 at 362 and 375 (Que CA), leave to appeal to SCC refused (1993), 81 CCC (3d) vi [*Peruta*]; Sidney Lederman, Alan Bryant, & Michelle Fuerst, *The Law of Evidence in Canada*, 4th ed (Markham, ON: LexisNexis, 2014) at § 16.148. A breach is not, however, likely to cause a court to exclude the witness's evidence: see, for example, *Polish Alliance of Canada v Polish Assn of Toronto Ltd*, 2011 ONSC 1851 at para 42 (Div Ct) [*Polish Alliance of Canada*].

229 See *MacDonald Estate v Martin*, [1990] 3 SCR 1235 at para 18; *R v Cunningham*, 2010 SCC 10 at para 18; *Canadian National Railway Co v McKercher LLP*, 2013 SCC 39 at paras 13–17; *Iroquois Falls Power Corp v Jacobs Canada Inc* (2006), 83 OR (3d) 438 at paras 31–39 (SCJ) [*Iroquois Falls Power*].

230 BC, Man, NL r 5.4-2; Sask r 4.04(2).

231 Alta r 4.04(2)(c). To similar effect, see Alta r 4.04(2)(b).

232 NS r 5.4-2; BC r 5.4-2(c).

233 Alta, Sask r 4.04(2) (commentary); BC, Man, NL r 5.4-2, commentary 1. See also Ont r 5.4-2, commentary 0.1.

234 NS r 5.4-2 & commentary 1.

that subject to the direction of the tribunal, "during examination-in-chief, the examining lawyer may discuss with the witness any matter that has not been covered in the examination up to that point."[235] This latter approach makes sense, for there is surely a reduced risk of harm in counsel's discussing matters yet to be covered during a break in the witness's evidence. Doing so is arguably no different from engaging in witness preparation before trial.

Yet distinguishing between evidence already given and that not yet elicited is not always easy. Where a witness's direct examination is lengthy, it may be difficult to discuss the evidence to come without mentioning that already given.[236] Such difficulties are rendered moot in British Columbia, Alberta, Saskatchewan, Manitoba, and Newfoundland, where the codes impose no prohibition at all on counsel communicating with her witness during direct examination. These codes state that subject to the direction of the tribunal, "during examination-in-chief, the examining lawyer may discuss with the witness any matter."[237]

We thus see a diversity of approaches across the country in terms of counsel's ability to communicate with the witness during examination-in-chief.[238] No matter where they practise, however, lawyers may wish to keep out-of-court communication with their testifying witness to a minimum during direct examination, to avoid allegations of improper coaching.

3) Communication with Own Witness between Direct Examination and Cross-examination

The rules in Ontario and Nova Scotia prohibit lawyers from communicating with their own witnesses during the interval between the end of direct examination and the beginning of cross-examination, absent leave of the court.[239] However, the codes in British Columbia, Alberta, Saskatchewan, Manitoba, and Newfoundland do not restrict communication with one's own witness until the commencement of

---

235 Ont r 5.4-2(a).
236 See John Sopinka, Donald B Houston, and Melanie Sopinka, *The Trial of an Action*, 2d ed (Toronto: Butterworths, 1998) at 128.
237 Sask r 4.04(2)(a); BC, Man, NL 5.4-2(a). Alta r 4.04(2)(a) is the same except for excluding the words "subject to the direction of the tribunal."
238 Diversity in this area may even exist *within* certain provinces: see Alta r 4.04(2) (commentary).
239 Ont r 5.4-2(b); NS r 5.4-2.

cross-examination.[240] Lawyers in these provinces are therefore not prohibited from speaking to the witness in the gap between direct and cross-examination.

4) Communication with Own Witness during Cross-examination

A lawyer is forbidden from speaking to his witness about the latter's evidence during cross-examination, absent leave of the court. The caselaw is uniform in this regard,[241] and so are the ethical rules.[242] The concern is that counsel's comments may expressly or implicitly suggest an answer that the witness can rely on when cross-examination resumes. Such a result unfairly interferes with the opposing party's ability to conduct an effective cross-examination and may lead to unreliable evidence that skews the trial result.[243]

There is, however, some differentiation between the rules in the various provinces. In Nova Scotia, the ban extends to any discussion about "the matter."[244] In Ontario, counsel is prevented from communicating "about the witness's evidence or any issue in the proceeding."[245] In British Columbia, Alberta, Saskatchewan, Manitoba, and Newfoundland, the interdiction is less expansive, applying only to "the evidence given in chief or relating to any matter introduced or touched on during the examination-in-chief."[246] Counsel in these latter provinces appear able to discuss with the witness matters not referenced in direct examination that it is anticipated might be canvassed in cross-examination.

The ethical code prohibitions do not encompass communication about administrative matters, for instance regarding the length of an

---

240 See the rules cited at note 237, above in this chapter, in conjunction with Alta, Sask r 4.04(2)(b); BC, Man, NL r 5.4-2(b).

241 *Polish Alliance of Canada*, above note 228 at para 23; *R v Cook*, 2012 ONSC 985 at paras 424–26; *R v Lawlor* (1999), 135 CCC (3d) 249 at para 13 (Nfld SCTD) [*Lawlor*]; *Iroquois Falls Power*, above note 229 at paras 12–14; *413528 Ontario Ltd v 951 Wilson Avenue Inc* (1989), 71 OR (2d) 40 at 42–44 and 46–47 (HCJ), appeal to Div Ct quashed [*413528 Ontario*]; *Seshia v Manitoba (Health Sciences Centre)* (2000), 48 CPC (4th) 33 at paras 7–11 (Man QB) [*Seshia*]; *R v Mayer*, 2011 BCPC 422 at para 35. See also *R v Savoy* (1977), 18 NBR (2d) 489 at para 21 (SCAD): improper for witness to speak to his own counsel during cross-examination.

242 Alta, Sask r 4.04(2)(b); BC, Man, NL r 5.4-2(b); NS r 5.4-2.

243 See *Lawlor*, above note 241 at para 13; *Polish Alliance of Canada*, above note 228 at paras 25–27.

244 NS r 5.4-2.

245 Ont r 5.4-2(b).

246 Alta, Sask r 4.04(2)(b); BC, Man, NL r 5.4-2(b).

adjournment or conversation entirely unrelated to the case.[247] It is nonetheless wise to minimize even innocuous discussion to avoid providing fodder for an allegation of impropriety.

5) Communication with Own Witness before Re-examination

The British Columbia, Ontario, and Nova Scotia codes do not allow communication between a lawyer and her witness about the evidence between the end of cross-examination and the start of re-examination, absent leave of the court.[248] These rules are driven by a concern that counsel may consciously or unconsciously suggest a re-examination answer that undermines headway made by the opponent in cross-examination.[249]

In stark contrast, the rules in Alberta, Saskatchewan, Manitoba, and Newfoundland allow counsel to speak to the witness once cross-examination is over — there is no bar on doing so either before or during re-examination, unless the court directs otherwise.[250] The governing bodies in these provinces have presumably concluded that counsel may have a legitimate reason to discuss evidentiary points with the witness before conducting re-examination. Specifically, counsel may not know all the facts regarding a topic covered in cross-examination and so be unaware as to whether the witness has relevant evidence that should be elicited in response. If barred from first speaking with the witness, counsel may decide to leave the area alone in re-examination, resulting in unfairness to the client and denying the trier of fact material information on a disputed issue.

It is for this reason that in British Columbia, where the rules require leave before speaking to one's own witness prior to re-examination, judges will only deny permission to do so in exceptional circum-

---

247 See *413528 Ontario*, above note 241 at 46–47; *Seshia*, above note 241 at paras 10–11. However, NS r 5.4-2 could be read to prohibit even discussions that are wholly administrative. Counsel in Nova Scotia should make sure that local practice permits a discussion on such topics before doing so, or seek leave of the court in advance.

248 BC r 5.4-2(c) (prohibition covers "any matter"); Ont r 5.4-2(c1) (prohibition covers evidence that will be dealt with on re-examination); NS r 5.4-2 (prohibition covers "the matter"). To similar effect, see *Peruta*, above note 228 at 362 and 372–73.

249 See *Peruta, ibid* at 362 and 372.

250 Alta, Sask r 4.04(2)(c); Man, NL r 5.4-2(c).

stances.[251] Courts in other jurisdictions may be more Scrooge-like in this regard.[252] Regardless, counsel whose law society rules require that leave be obtained before communicating with a witness prior to re-examination should be prepared to indicate the areas on which dialogue is desired.[253] Otherwise, it may be difficult for the court to ascertain whether leave is justified, and if so, regarding what matters.

Example: X is charged with murder in Quebec, where leave is required before counsel can speak to his own witness prior to re-examination. An expert testifies for the Crown, but after cross-examination his opinion decidedly helps the accused. Crown counsel obtains an adjournment before re-examination but says nothing about speaking to the expert. When the trial resumes, the expert is re-examined and changes his opinion to favour the Crown. In re-cross-examination, the expert admits that during the adjournment Crown counsel and the police expressed disappointment in his responses in cross-examination and spent time reviewing his testimony. Crown counsel has acted improperly in not seeking leave before discussing these matters with the expert, and also appears to have engaged in improper coaching.[254]

6) Applicability of Restrictions to the Testifying Accused

The restrictions discussed above should not apply holus-bolus to a testifying accused, at least not all of them. Unlike an ordinary witness, the accused is a party to the proceedings. More particularly, he faces the possibility of a criminal conviction and has a constitutional right to be represented by and consult with counsel during the trial.[255] It is for this reason that some cases support permitting communication between an accused and his counsel at any time before or after cross-examination, in contrast to imposing the leave requirement traditionally applicable

---

251 See *R v Montgomery* (1998), 126 CCC (3d) 251 at paras 11–13 (BCSC) [*Montgomery*]; *R v Hernandez*, 2008 BCSC 1467 at paras 1–2 [*Hernandez*]; *R v Violette*, 2009 BCSC 75 at paras 6–7 and 13. The British Columbia approach is cited with apparent approval in *MacLean v MacLean*, 2009 NSSC 126 at para 7 (FD).

252 See, for example, *Scavuzzo v Canada*, 2004 TCC 806 at para 15: the rule precluding communication with own witness between cross- and re-examination should be observed in the "vast majority of cases."

253 But see *Hernandez*, above note 251 at paras 3–4: counsel is not required to do so as a precondition for obtaining leave.

254 The facts and analysis are based on *Peruta*, above note 228.

255 See *Lawlor*, above note 241 at paras 10 and 13; *Montgomery*, above note 251 at para 14.

to a non-accused witness.[256] We believe that this same approach should apply everywhere in Canada, even where not permitted by the wording of the applicable ethical codes: the rules of professional conduct should never be allowed to override an accused's constitutional rights.[257]

And yet after the just-mentioned cases were decided, four law societies changed their rules to permit out-of-court communication between a lawyer and *any* witness she has called at any time before and after cross-examination.[258] In these provinces at least, allowing a testifying accused to speak to counsel at any time except during cross-examination hardly constitutes special treatment. In light of this trend in the law society rules, the more salient question may be whether the accused should have a general right to speak to counsel during cross-examination as well.[259]

In considering this question, one can start by recognizing that concerns about counsel improperly assisting her client are tempered because, unlike with an ordinary witness, the accused will have been present for the whole trial and had access to the entirety of the disclosure materials. The accused is thus less likely to be unaware of tactics that the prosecutor might employ to attack his credibility. We already accord the accused special treatment in the context of witness preparation by virtue of his role as a client to whom counsel owes duties of loyalty, candour, and advice.[260] For the same reason, why not accept differential treatment in this context too? Plus, the client and counsel may have a legitimate need to discuss trial matters unrelated to his testimony or matters concerning his testimony that are unrelated to the cross-examination to come. Finally, in communicating with the client, defence counsel will be prohibited from engaging in improper coaching and must be trusted to act ethically. Permitting communication during cross-examination does not mean condoning attempts to obstruct justice.

This is admittedly a difficult issue.[261] But in our view, during cross-examination an accused should *at least* be permitted to speak to his

---

256 *Lawlor*, above note 241 at para 13. The same view finds favour in *Montgomery*, above note 251 at para 14, albeit in *obiter*.

257 See Mewett & Sankoff, above note 152 at § 6.3(a), 6-14.

258 See the rules cited at note 250, above in this chapter.

259 See *Lawlor*, above note 241 at para 13, which seems to assume that an accused cannot communicate with counsel during breaks in cross-examination, although the comments on this point are *obiter*.

260 See Section G(5), above in this chapter.

261 See, for example, the controversy surrounding the issue in the United States, exemplified by the decisions in *Geders v United States*, 425 US 80 (1976), and especially *Perry v Leeke*, 488 US 272 (1989). There is ongoing debate in the United

lawyer without leave about matters other than his testimony to that point. The prohibitions in Nova Scotia, against discussing anything regarding "the matter,"[262] and in Ontario, against discussing not only the witness's evidence but also "any issue in the proceeding,"[263] are thus too broad. So too are the proscriptions in other provinces against discussing not only the witness's evidence in chief but also "any matter introduced or touched on" in chief.[264] These restrictions may preclude time-sensitive discussions about matters that legitimately require the client's input and instructions and yet have nothing to do with how the accused might best protect his credibility once cross-examination resumes. True, counsel can always ask for leave to be permitted to engage in such discussions, but doing so may reveal privileged and confidential matters to the detriment of the accused's trial strategy.

7) Sympathetic and Unsympathetic Witnesses: Ontario's Special Rules

Most law societies impose no restrictions on a lawyer's communicating with a testifying witness called by another party. The risk of tainting is usually minimal because there is generally no reason to assume the witness will favour an opposing counsel's client and so improperly adjust her evidence as a result of the communication.

Yet this reasoning does not apply in every case. The Crown may call a witness who unexpectedly gives testimony that exculpates rather than incriminates the accused. An accused bringing a *Charter* application may have to call police witnesses who are adverse to his claim for relief. Or one accused may call a witness who is sympathetic to all of the accused at a joint trial. In these and analogous cases, in contrast to the usual situation, there may be no risk of harm from out-of-court contact between calling counsel and the witness but a real possibility of mischief arising from communications with other counsel on the case.

The Ontario code seeks to address these atypical situations through special rules that impose or remove restrictions depending on whether

---

States as to whether a defendant has a right to speak to his counsel during an overnight or other significant adjournment about any matter, *including his testimony*: see *Serrano v Fischer*, 412 F3d 292 at 300 (2d Cir 2005); *Martin v United States*, 991 A2d 791 at 794–95 (DC 2010); *People v Hernandez*, 53 Cal 4th 1095 at 1110 (2012); *Beckham v Commonwealth*, 248 SW3d 547 at 553–59 (Ky 2008).

262 NS r 5.4-2.

263 Ont r 5.4-2(b).

264 Alta, Sask r 4.04(2); BC, Man, NL r 5-4.2(b).

the witness is sympathetic or unsympathetic to a particular lawyer's cause. These rules provide that, subject to the direction of the tribunal,

- during examination-in-chief by another legal practitioner of a witness who is unsympathetic to the lawyer's cause, the lawyer not conducting the examination-in-chief may discuss the evidence with the witness;[265]
- during cross-examination by the lawyer of a witness unsympathetic to the cross-examiner's cause, the lawyer may discuss the witness's evidence with the witness;[266]
- during cross-examination by the lawyer of a witness who is sympathetic to that lawyer's cause, any conversations ought to be restricted in the same way as communications during examination-in-chief of one's own witness;[267] and
- during re-examination of a witness called by an opposing legal practitioner if the witness is sympathetic to the lawyer's cause, the lawyer ought not to discuss the evidence to be given by that witness during re-examination. The lawyer may, however, properly discuss the evidence with a witness who is adverse in interest.[268]

These provisions represent a more nuanced approach to limiting a lawyer's communications with a testifying witness. Whether a witness is sympathetic or unsympathetic may be open to debate in a particular case. But imposing restrictions based on this criterion is principled, focusing on the factor that best predicts whether communications will present a real risk of harm. Ontario's special rules thus make sense and arguably merit export to other Canadian jurisdictions.

---

265 Ont r 5.4-2(a.1).
266 Ont r 5.4-2(c.2).
267 Ont r 5.4-2(c.3).
268 Ont r 5.4-2(c.4).

PLEA DISCUSSIONS

A. INTRODUCTION

Aside from instances where the prosecution stays or withdraws all charges, every accused person shares a common experience: entering a plea of guilty or not guilty in court. The large preponderance of these individuals plead guilty.[1] For them, the plea has an immediate and dramatic impact on the proceedings. A conviction is recorded, there is no trial on the issue of culpability, and the matter proceeds to sentencing. Deciding how to plead in response to a charge is thus the key decision for many, many accused, and not surprisingly the law accords them total freedom of choice in this regard.

Defence counsel almost always plays a central role in advising the accused with respect to the plea. A common and crucial aspect of counsel's role in this regard is participation in resolution discussions with the Crown, also sometimes known as plea discussions or plea bargaining. The vast majority of criminal cases are resolved through resolution discussions.[2] It is not going too far to say that "[i]n today's criminal justice system . . . the negotiation of a plea bargain, rather

---

1   See Ontario, *Report of the Criminal Justice Review Committee*, by Hugh Locke, John D Evans, & Murray D Segal (Toronto: Attorney General of Ontario, 1999) at 55–56 [*Criminal Justice Review Report*].
2   See *R v Nixon*, 2011 SCC 34 at para 47 [*Nixon*].

than the unfolding of a trial, is almost always the critical point for a defendant."[3]

In conducting plea discussions, defence counsel must respect the client's freedom of choice in entering a plea yet also fulfill the professional obligation to provide the client with competent advice. The very essence of the client-lawyer relationship is caught up in this mix and permeates any analysis of counsel's ethical duties when engaging in plea discussions. Counsel walks a fine line in undertaking plea discussions and advising the client. She must not dominate the client and impose a course of action without regard for the client's wishes. Nor should counsel act as a "dump truck," enabling rote and rushed justice by facilitating a guilty plea that is contrary to the client's best interests. Rather, the lawyer's duty is to support the client's freedom of choice through the provision of quality legal advice.

B. TERMINOLOGY AND SCOPE OF INQUIRY

A potentially confusing feature of the literature on plea discussions is the failure to articulate exactly what process is being studied. Moreover, certain phrases tend to raise the public's hackles, especially those employing the term "bargaining," and have thus taken on a distasteful meaning in some quarters. We will follow the lead of the Martin committee and use the term "resolution discussions" to refer to "any discussions between counsel aimed at resolving issues that a criminal prosecution raises."[4] The scope of resolution discussions is very wide, encompassing not only negotiations concerning a possible plea of guilty but almost any other aspect of the criminal proceeding, including an agreement to admit evidence, the adoption of an informal discovery process, or the scheduling of the trial itself. The primary focus of this chapter is plea discussions, or plea negotiations, by which we mean discussions directed towards a plea of guilty by the accused in return for the prosecutor agreeing to take or refrain from taking a particular course of action.[5] We are therefore confining ourselves to a particular aspect of resolution discussions.

---

3   *Missouri v Frye*, 132 S Ct 1399 at 1407 (2012) [*Missouri*].

4   Ontario, *Report of the Attorney General's Advisory Committee on Charge Screening, Disclosure, and Resolution Discussions* (Toronto: Attorney General of Ontario, 1993) (Chair: G Arthur Martin) at 282 [Martin Committee Report].

5   This definition is adapted from the Law Reform Commission of Canada, *Plea Discussions and Agreements* (Working Paper 60) (Ottawa: The Commission, 1989) at 40, recommendations 1 & 2 [*Plea Discussions and Agreements*].

While our focus is often on instances where negotiations occur between lawyers for the defence and the Crown, many of the obligations discussed in this chapter apply whenever an accused is considering whether to plead guilty. That is to say, the bulk of the duties discussed apply any time an accused person pleads guilty or considers doing so, whether or not plea discussions have occurred between the defence and the Crown.

C. LEGAL FACETS OF A GUILTY PLEA

An accused who pleads guilty is formally and publicly admitting to the crime.[6] There will be no trial on the general issue of culpability, the Crown will not be required to make its case on a standard of proof beyond a reasonable doubt, and the accused will relinquish many procedural rights, including some that are constitutionally enshrined.[7] The accused no longer asserts the right to make full answer and defence, abandons the rights to silence and non-compellability as a witness, and forgoes the presumption of innocence.[8] A guilty plea thus operates to waive many of the most sacrosanct rights afforded an accused.[9]

Flowing naturally from these observations is the proposition that the accused has complete control and freedom of choice over the decision whether to enter a guilty plea. This proposition is well-established by Canadian caselaw.[10] It also has constitutional dimensions, derived from the fundamental principle of justice that accords an accused the

---

6   See *R v Gardiner* (1982), 68 CCC (2d) 477 at 514 (SCC) [*Gardiner*]; *R v Parris*, 2013 ONCA 515 at para 121; *R v Eizenga*, 2011 ONCA 113 at para 43 [*Eizenga*]; *R v Le*, 2013 BCCA 455 at para 18; *R v Duong*, 2006 BCCA 325 at paras 9–10 [*Duong*].

7   See *R v RP*, 2013 ONCA 53 at para 39, leave to appeal to SCC refused, [2013] SCCA No 133 [*RP*]; *R v DMG*, 2011 ONCA 343 at para 41 [*DMG*]; *Eizenga*, above note 6 at paras 43 and 70; *R v RT* (1992), 17 CR (4th) 247 at para 13 (Ont CA) [*RT*]; *Duong*, above note 6 at para 12; *R v Hoang*, 2003 ABCA 251 at para 17 [*Hoang*]; *R v Messervey*, 2010 NSCA 55 at para 56 [*Messervey*]; *R v Brown*, 2006 PESCAD 17 at para 37 [*Brown*].

8   See *DMG*, above note 7 at para 41; *Brown*, above note 7 at para 37; *R v Adgey* (1973), 13 CCC (2d) 177 at 182–83 and 190 (SCC) [*Adgey*].

9   See *RP*, above note 7 at para 39; *Eizenga*, above note 6 at para 43; *RT*, above note 7 at para 13.

10 *R v GDB*, 2000 SCC 22 at para 34 [*GDB*]; *R v Murray*, 2000 NBCA 2 at para 10; *R v Laperrière* (1996), 109 CCC (3d) 347 (SCC) [*Laperrière*], aff'g the dissent of Bisson JA in (1995), 101 CCC (3d) 462 at 470–71 [para 69] (Que CA); *R v Lamoureux* (1984), 13 CCC (3d) 101 at 105 [para 24] (Que CA) [*Lamoureux*]; *DMG*, above note 7 at para 109; *RT*, above note 7 at para 16.

right to control the conduct of his defence.[11] Counsel who improperly pressures the accused to plead guilty or not guilty, so as to negate this liberty of choice, has thus undermined an important constitutional right.

It is worth mentioning several further attributes of a guilty plea that are perhaps not so immediately obvious. A guilty plea may also be used in subsequent civil or criminal proceedings to the disadvantage of the offender,[12] for instance in civil litigation commenced by a victim or in criminal litigation to help prove guilt as similar fact evidence or to attack her credibility as a prosecution witness. Moreover, the accused who pleads guilty will likely be prevented from challenging on appeal any adverse rulings that occurred before the plea.[13]

Perhaps most importantly, the ability to appeal the conviction following a guilty plea is greatly curtailed. A change of heart or dissatisfaction with the sentence meted out is not, on its own, sufficient.[14] The appellant bears the onus of convincing the appeal court to set aside the plea,[15] and the test for doing so is fairly demanding. A guilty plea will usually be overturned only where the appellant can establish that it was not voluntary and unequivocal or was uninformed,[16] although success on appeal will also occur where the facts accepted by the accused do not constitute the offence to which the plea is entered or where a constitutional guarantee such as the right to disclosure has been infringed.[17] It has also been suggested that the appellant stands a better

---

11   See *R v Swain* (1991), 63 CCC (3d) 481 at 504–6 [paras 33–36] (SCC) [*Swain*].

12   See, for example, *R v WBC* (2000), 142 CCC (3d) 490 at paras 59–60 (Ont CA) [*WBC*], aff'd 2001 SCC 17; *R v Ford* (2000), 145 CCC (3d) 336 at paras 34–36 (Ont CA); *Shah v Becamon*, 2009 ONCA 113 at paras 18–19.

13   See *R v Fegan* (1993), 80 CCC (3d) 356 at 358–59 [paras 3–6] (Ont CA) [*Fegan*]; *R v Davidson* (1992), 110 NSR (2d) 307 at paras 2–6 (SCAD); *Hoang*, above note 7 at paras 14–41; *R v Claveau*, 2003 NBCA 52 at paras 2–8; *Duong*, above note 6 at para 8.

14   See *R v Lyons* (1987), 37 CCC (3d) 1 at 53 [para 107] (SCC) [*Lyons*]; *R v Raymond*, 2009 QCCA 808 at paras 114–15 [*Raymond*]; *R v Kim*, 2011 SKCA 74 at para 35 [*Kim*], leave to appeal to SCC refused, [2011] SCCA No 406.

15   See *Adgey*, above note 8 at 189; *RT*, above note 7 at para 12; *R v Short*, 2012 SKCA 85 at para 3 [*Short*]; *R v Wiebe*, 2012 BCCA 519 at para 25; *R v Giles*, 2010 NLCA 28 at para 7; *R v Nevin*, 2006 NSCA 72 at para 7 [*Nevin*].

16   The leading decision on point is *RT*, above note 7 at paras 12–39, which has been affirmed by many subsequent decisions including *R v Taillefer; R v Duguay*, 2003 SCC 70 at para 85 [*Taillefer*].

17   See *R v Voorwinde* (1975), 29 CCC (2d) 413 (BCCA) (insufficient facts); *R v Fones*, 2012 MBCA 110 at paras 38–51 (insufficient facts); *Taillefer*, above note 16 at paras 86–90 (violation of right to disclosure).

chance of success if he can point to a valid defence at trial.[18] Ultimately, there is no finite set of grounds upon which a guilty plea can be overturned, and an appeal court will intervene whenever necessary to ensure justice.[19]

A guilty plea resulting from poor legal representation may be set aside on appeal. Most often, this will be because an error made by trial counsel operated to render the plea involuntary or uniformed, which as noted provides the most common basis on which a plea will be overturned.[20] An appellant can also assert that trial counsel's error has violated his *Canadian Charter of Rights and Freedoms*[21] right to the effective assistance of counsel, and the inclusion of ineffective assistance as a distinct ground is becoming more common.[22] However, this constitutional right has not been relied on in the context of guilty pleas nearly so often in Canada as in the United States. The difference may be that Canadian courts have long recognized special rules relating to the validity of pleas, while ineffective-assistance arguments are a more recent development. Moreover, appeal courts apply a demanding test in determining whether a new trial is warranted because of defence counsel's incompetence: there is a strong presumption of competence that works in favour of letting the conviction stand, and even where this presumption is overcome, the appeal will be allowed only where the appellant can establish resulting prejudice.[23]

18 See *R v Read* (1994), 47 BCAC 28 at para 43; *R v Morris* (1994), 53 BCAC 296 at para 18; *R v Lewis*, 2012 SKCA 81 at paras 23–27 [*Lewis*]; *R v Hunt*, 2004 ABCA 88 at paras 14–16; *R v Riley*, 2011 NSCA 52 at paras 39–40 and 44 [*Riley*]; *Messervey*, above note 7 at paras 73–75. But see *Nevin*, above note 15 at para 18, suggesting the contrary.

19 See *R v Hanemaayer*, 2008 ONCA 580 at paras 19–20 [*Hanemaayer*]; *R v Kumar*, 2011 ONCA 120 at para 34 [*Kumar*]; *R v Kim*, 2007 BCCA 25 at para 5; *Kim*, above note 14 at para 33; *Brown*, above note 7 at paras 43–45.

20 See, for example, *R v Henry*, 2011 ONCA 289 at paras 28–37, as well as the cases discussed in *Eizenga*, above note 6 at para 58, and at note 93, below in this chapter.

21 Part I of the *Constitution Act, 1982*, being Schedule B to the *Canada Act 1982* (UK), 1982, c 11.

22 See, for example, *RP*, above note 7; *R v Newman* (1993), 79 CCC (3d) 394 at 400–1 [para 15] (Ont CA) [*Newman*]; *Short*, above note 15; *Kim*, above note 14; *R v Ogden*, 2013 NSCA 25; *Riley*, above note 18 at para 18; *Messervey*, above note 7; *R v Laffin*, 2009 NSCA 19 [*Laffin*].

23 See *GDB*, above note 10 at paras 26–28. See also Chapter 3, Section K(1).

D. IMPORTANT BACKGROUND CONSIDERATIONS

There are several considerations that, while not strictly speaking concerned with lawyers' ethics, deserve mention as constituting an important part of the contextual background for any examination of plea discussions and guilty pleas.

1) Plea Discussions Are Privileged

Communications between defence counsel and prosecutor during plea discussions are covered by a class privilege, which is held jointly by both parties and applies whether or not an agreement is reached.[24] This privilege is justified by the need to encourage full and candid discussions between the parties and thus the prospect of a plea resolution, and ordinarily operates so that the contents of such discussions are inadmissible in court.

Plea-discussion privilege will be set aside, however, where the public interest in doing so outweighs the importance of encouraging plea resolutions.[25] This may occur where the communications contain threats or other illegal statements or demonstrate prosecutorial misconduct[26] or where adducing their contents is necessary or helpful in proving that a resolution was reached,[27] allowing an accused to make full answer and defence,[28] enabling the Crown to rebut allegations of improper conduct during the negotiations,[29] or facilitating a challenge to perjured testimony.[30]

---

24   See *Sable Offshore Energy Inc v Ameron International Corp*, 2013 SCC 37 at paras 11–17 [*Sable Offshore Energy*]; *Ahmadoun v Ontario (AG)*, 2012 ONSC 955 at para 18; *R v Delchev*, 2012 ONSC 2094 at paras 19–29 [*Delchev*]; *R v Legato* (2002), 172 CCC (3d) 415 at paras 78–80 (Que CA) [*Legato*]; *R v Griffin*, 2009 ABQB 696 at paras 49–65, rev'd on other grounds 2011 ABCA 197; *R v Delorme*, 2005 NWTSC 34 at paras 13–24 [*Delorme*]; *R v DSB*, 2006 MBQB 137 at paras 8–12 and 37–61 [*DSB*]; *R v Cater*, 2011 NSPC 75 at paras 15–17 [*Cater*].

25   See *Sable Offshore Energy*, above note 24 at para 19.

26   See *Delchev*, above note 24 at paras 31 and 34–46; *Delorme*, above note 24 at para 13; *Cater*, above note 24 at para 22; *Singh v Montreal (City of)*, 2014 QCCA 307 at paras 14–15 and 20, leave to appeal to SCC refused, [2014] SCCA No 166.

27   See *Delorme*, above note 24 at para 13.

28   See *Delchev*, above note 24 at paras 31–32; *Delorme*, above note 24 at paras 25–48; *R v CLS*, 2009 MBQB 224 at paras 12–14; *R v Bernardo*, [1994] OJ No 1718 at paras 16–18 (Gen Div).

29   See *R v Zarinchang*, 2010 ONCA 286 at para 28.

30   See *Legato*, above note 24 at paras 80–92.

Example: Before testifying at the accused's first-degree murder trial, the key Crown witness pleaded guilty to a lesser charge based on an agreed statement of facts negotiated by his lawyer and the prosecutor. The plea negotiations must be disclosed, as an exception to plea-discussion privilege, to allow the accused to make full answer and defence at trial. However, confidential communications between the witness and his lawyer about the negotiations remain covered by solicitor-client privilege[31] and so cannot be disclosed barring waiver by the witness or the application of the very demanding innocence-at-stake exception.[32]

2) Preconditions for Judge to Accept a Guilty Plea

The jurisprudence has long accepted that a guilty plea is only valid if voluntary, unequivocal, and informed, this last requirement meaning that the accused understands the nature of the allegations and the effect and consequences of the plea.[33] A 2002 amendment to the *Criminal Code* echoes and expands on these preconditions, providing that a court may accept a plea of guilty only if satisfied that the accused is making the plea voluntarily and understands (1) that the plea is an admission of the essential elements of the offence, (2) the nature and consequences of the plea, and (3) that the court is not bound by any agreement made between the accused and the prosecutor.[34] In accordance with this amendment, trial judges should generally make inquiries to satisfy themselves that a guilty plea is voluntary, unequivocal, and informed.[35]

3) Judges Are Not Obligated to Conduct a Plea Inquiry

Although a court should usually conduct an inquiry to ensure that the requirements for accepting a guilty plea are satisfied, the 2002 amendment to the *Criminal Code* expressly provides that a judge's failure to "fully inquire" into whether the preconditions are met does not affect

---

31 See *R v Youvarajah*, 2013 SCC 41 at paras 48–54 [*Youvarajah*].

32 See Chapter 5, Section M(1).

33 See note 16, above in this chapter.

34 *Criminal Code*, RSC 1985, c C-46, s 606(1.1).

35 See *DMG*, above note 7 at paras 54 and 60; *R v Gates*, 2010 BCCA 378 at paras 20–21 [*Gates*].

434 ETHICS AND CRIMINAL LAW

the validity of the plea,[36] a position that generally accords with the pre-amendment caselaw.[37]

Nevertheless, where the circumstances suggest that the plea may be equivocal, involuntary, or uninformed, the adequacy of the judge's plea inquiry, or the failure to hold one at all, will be considered in determining whether the plea should be struck on appeal.[38] Conversely, a thorough judicial inquiry that yields considerable information suggesting that the elements necessary to constitute a valid plea are present will make it more difficult for the accused to have the plea struck on appeal.[39]

4) Plea Agreement Is Not Binding on the Court

While a judge should give serious consideration to a joint submission from counsel, she has a discretion to depart from the recommended sentence in the interests of justice. We favour the view of the Martin Committee Report that a judge should reject counsels' recommendation only where the proposed sentence "would bring the administration of justice into disrepute, or is otherwise not in the public interest."[40]

Advice: Counsel should ensure that the factors justifying a joint submission — as opposed to the plea discussions, which are privileged

---

36 *Criminal Code*, above note 34, s 606(1.1); *DMG*, above note 7 at para 42; *R v Walsh* (2006), 206 CCC (3d) 543 at paras 27–28 (Ont CA); *Gates*, above note 35 at paras 21–22; *Laffin*, above note 22 at para 47; *Messervey*, above note 7 at para 58; *Raymond*, above note 14 at para 117.

37 *R v Brosseau*, [1969] 3 CCC 129 at 138–39 (SCC) [*Brosseau*]; *Adgey*, above note 8 at 188; *Lamoureux*, above note 10 at 104 [para 17].

38 See *Brosseau*, above note 37 at 137–38; *Lamoureux*, above note 10 at 104 [para 17]; *Lewis*, above note 18 at paras 18–19; *R v Jack*, 2012 BCSC 1991 at paras 62–64; *Hoang*, above note 7 at paras 21–23; *R v IBB*, 2009 SKPC 76 at para 81 [*IBB*].

39 See *R v Pelletier*, 2006 MBCA 126 at para 5; *R v Carty*, 2010 ONCA 237 at para 32 [*Carty*]; *R v McIntosh*, 2004 NSCA 19 at paras 2 and 6–7; *R v Miller*, 2011 NBCA 52 at paras 3 and 8.

40 Martin Committee Report, above note 4 at 327–30. This test, or one similar to it, is used in most provinces: see, for example, *R v DeSousa*, 2012 ONCA 254 at paras 15–25 [*DeSousa*]; *R v RWE* (2007), 2007 ONCA 461 at paras 22–31; *R v Douglas* (2002), 162 CCC (3d) 37 at paras 42–52 (Que CA); *R v Steeves*, 2010 NBCA 57 at paras 30–32; *R v Marriott*, 2014 NSCA 28 at paras 99–102 [*Marriott*]; *R v AN*, 2011 NSCA 21 at paras 19–21; *R v Oxford*, 2010 NLCA 45 at paras 61–62 [*Oxford*]; *R v Sinclair*, 2004 MBCA 48 at paras 8–17; *R v Omoth*, 2011 SKCA 42 at paras 15–19 and 50–51; *R v Bullock*, 2013 ABCA 44 at paras 14–17; *R v Roadhouse*, 2012 BCCA 495 at paras 42–53.

— are placed before the court on sentencing.[41] Doing so makes it much less likely that the trial judge will reject the joint submission as unfit, unreasonable, or otherwise contrary to the public interest and the proper administration of justice.

E. PLEA DISCUSSIONS AND AGREEMENTS: AN INTEGRAL PART OF THE CRIMINAL JUSTICE SYSTEM

In the not too distant past, there was considerable controversy in Canada as to whether plea agreements should be employed in the ordinary course of the criminal justice process. Some commentators argued against plea agreements,[42] and the Law Reform Commission of Canada took this view in an early working paper.[43] The respective advantages and disadvantages of plea discussions continue to spark debate today. But it is now widely accepted by the judiciary and practising criminal lawyers that discussion and agreement between defence counsel and the Crown on the matter of the accused's plea constitutes an important part of our justice system.[44] Support for plea discussions is also reflected in the rules of professional conduct.[45] Because of this widespread acceptance, our discussion will focus on defence counsel's ethical responsibilities in the plea-negotiation process and will not delve more deeply to consider whether the process should occur in the first place.

It is nonetheless helpful to review briefly some of the reasons why an accused might wish to make a plea agreement with the Crown.[46]

---

41   See *R v Tkachuk*, 2001 ABCA 243 at paras 33–34; *R v Knockwood*, 2009 NSCA 98 at para 17; *R v Sharpe*, 2009 MBCA 50 at para 61 [*Sharpe*].

42   G Ferguson & D Roberts, "Plea Bargaining: Directions for Canadian Reform" (1974) 52 Can Bar Rev 497.

43   Law Reform Commission of Canada, *Criminal Procedure: Control of the Process* (Working Paper 15) (Ottawa: The Commission, 1976) at 45. However, the commission later changed its view to approve of plea negotiations: see *Plea Discussions and Agreements*, above note 5.

44   See, for example, *Nixon*, above note 2 at paras 46–47; *R v Burlingham* (1995), 97 CCC (3d) 385 at para 23 (SCC); *Oxford*, above note 40 at paras 56–57; *Sharpe*, above note 41 at para 55; *DeSousa*, above note 40 at para 15; *DSB*, above note 24 at paras 40–58. See also Martin Committee Report, above note 4 at 281; *Criminal Justice Review Report*, above note 1, ch 6.

45   See Section F, below in this chapter.

46   The advantages of resolution discussions from the perspectives of the Crown and the system more generally are canvassed in the Martin Committee Report, above note 4 at 281–91.

Only by appreciating the possible benefits for the accused can we understand the importance of counsel's role in the process and formulate appropriate ethical guidelines.

Most obviously, the accused can obtain concrete concessions from the Crown in exchange for a guilty plea, including a promise to recommend a particular sentence, the withdrawal of a charge, or an acceptable stipulation as to the facts on which the plea will be based. Other benefits, sometimes less concrete, can also flow from a plea agreement. The agreement will often lead to a much faster resolution of the case, minimizing the uncertainty and stress that accompany pending charges. Avoiding a trial may spare an accused substantial legal costs where he has retained a lawyer privately. An accused may also desire to admit guilt quickly and publicly as a genuine expression of remorse and to make amends with a victim. The result may be a faster and more successful path towards rehabilitation. Finally, plea discussions arguably allow the accused, through counsel, to play an active role in the process and actually influence the outcome, to an extent not always matched at trial.

The benefits that can arise from plea discussions may be undermined or illusory, however, where defence counsel fails to provide the client with diligent and skilled representation. Counsel may see the plea agreement as an opportunity to avoid the effort of preparing for a trial and fail to discover or pursue a valid defence. Or the retainer may provide for a block-fee payment, regardless of the outcome, and hence give the lawyer an incentive to have the client plead guilty quickly. Other lawyers may seek to maintain a good relationship with prosecutors and judges and so shy away from running trials or taking truly adversarial positions during plea discussions. These sorts of problems cripple counsel's duty of loyalty to the client, often to the client's significant detriment, and may constitute incompetent representation.[47] The result can be excessive pressure or poor advice that leads the accused to plead guilty against her wishes or best interests. Constitutional rights may be too quickly waived, and valid defences forgone.

Ethical guidelines for defence counsel concerning plea discussions should strive to maximize the potential benefits to an accused while avoiding the disadvantages that can flow from ineffective or otherwise sloppy representation. Loyalty and competence must be the hallmarks of the lawyer's function. With these beacon principles in mind, we can now turn to look at the relevant rules of professional conduct.

---

47   See the paragraph associated with notes 20–23, above in this chapter.

F. RELATED RULES OF PROFESSIONAL CONDUCT

Given that plea agreements are extremely common and widely accepted in the criminal justice system and that they can afford substantial benefits to an accused, it is not surprising that most Canadian ethical codes address the topic of plea discussions. These codes typically state the following:

Agreement on Guilty Plea

5.1-7 Before a charge is laid or at any time after a charge is laid, a lawyer for an accused or potential accused may discuss with the prosecutor the possible disposition of the case, unless the client instructs otherwise.[48]

5.1-8 A lawyer for an accused or potential accused may enter into an agreement with the prosecutor about a guilty plea if, following investigation,

(a) the lawyer advises his or her client about the prospects for an acquittal or finding of guilt;

(b) the lawyer advises the client of the implications and possible consequences of a guilty plea and particularly of the sentencing authority and discretion of the court, including the fact that the court is not bound by any agreement about a guilty plea;

(c) the client voluntarily is prepared to admit the necessary factual and mental elements of the offence charged; and

(d) the client voluntarily instructs the lawyer to enter into an agreement as to a guilty plea.[49]

Commentary

[1] The public interest in the proper administration of justice should not be sacrificed in the interest of expediency.[50]

---

48   BC, Man, Ont, NS, NL r 5.1-7. Sask r 4.01(7) is identical. This rule is not included in the Alberta, New Brunswick, and CBA codes.

49   BC, Man, Ont, NS, NL r 5.1-8. Alta, Sask r 4.01(8) are identical. NB ch 8, commentary 15, and CBA Code ch IX, commentary 13, are also quite similar, though there are some distinctions, as discussed below.

50   BC, Man, Ont, NS, NL r 5.1-8, commentary 1. Alta, Sask r 4.01(8) (commentary) are identical. NB ch 8, commentary 15(b), and the last sentence of CBA Code ch IX, commentary 13, are somewhat similar.

In England and Wales, the new *Bar Standards Board Handbook* does not include guidelines regarding guilty pleas.[51] But the board's old *Code of Conduct*, superseded at the end of 2013, contains several provisions on the topic, and these appear still to represent good practice in England and Wales. For instance, the old code directs barristers to follow certain basic standards derived from the early leading decision of *R v Turner*.[52] These standards provide that a barrister should advise the client generally about the plea, if necessary expressing the advice in strong terms, but must make clear to the client that he has complete freedom of choice and is ultimately responsible for the plea.

Much more daring, at least from a Canadian perspective, is the approach taken in the old code with respect to the client who wishes to plead guilty despite protestations of innocence made to counsel:

> 11.5.1 Where a defendant tells his counsel that he did not commit the offence with which he is charged but nevertheless insists on pleading guilty to it for reasons of his own, counsel should:
>
> (a) advise the defendant that, if he is not guilty, he should plead not guilty but that the decision is one for the defendant; counsel must continue to represent him but only after he has advised what the consequences will be and that what can be submitted in mitigation can only be on the basis that the client is guilty.
>
> (b) explore with the defendant why he wishes to plead guilty to a charge which he says he did not commit and whether any steps could be taken which would enable him to enter a plea of not guilty in accordance with his profession of innocence.
>
> 11.5.2 If the client maintains his wish to plead guilty, he should be further advised:
>
> (a) what the consequences will be, in particular in gaining or adding to a criminal record and that it is unlikely that a conviction based on such a plea would be overturned on appeal;

---

51   Bar Standards Board, *Handbook* (London: Bar Standards Board, 2014).

52   Bar Standards Board, "Written Standards for the Conduct of Professional Work" in *Code of Conduct*, 8th ed (London: BSB, 2012) at § 11.3 [Superseded Written Standards], (superseded by Bar Standards Board, *Handbook*, above note 51, 1 January 2014). *R v Turner*, [1970] 2 All ER 281 at 285 [*Turner*]. To similar effect, see "Practice Direction (Criminal Proceedings: Substituted and Additional Provisions)," [2009] 1 WLR 1396 at 1398, § 45.1. Since *Turner* was decided, the prevalence of plea bargaining in England and Wales has increased, and the associated substantive and procedural rules have changed considerably: see Lee Bridges, "The Ethics of Representation on Guilty Pleas" (2006) 9 Leg Ethics 80 at 81–85.

(b) that what can be submitted on his behalf in mitigation can only be on the basis that he is guilty and will otherwise be strictly limited so that, for instance, counsel will not be able to assert that the defendant has shown remorse through his guilty plea.

11.5.3 If, following all of the above advice, the defendant persists in his decision to plead guilty

(a) counsel may continue to represent him if he is satisfied that it is proper to do so;
(b) before a plea of guilty is entered counsel or a representative of his professional client who is present should record in writing the reasons for the plea;
(c) the defendant should be invited to endorse a declaration that he has given unequivocal instructions of his own free will that he intends to plead guilty even though he maintains that he did not commit the offence(s) and that he understands the advice given by counsel and in particular the restrictions placed on counsel in mitigating and the consequences to himself; the defendant should also be advised that he is under no obligation to sign; and
(d) if no such declaration is signed, counsel should make a contemporaneous note of his advice.[53]

In the United States, the ABA Model Rules and the Third Restatement have little to say regarding the discrete topic of plea discussions. But the ABA Defense Standards provide a fairly comprehensive examination of the topic:

Standard 4-5.1 Advising the Accused

(a) After informing himself or herself fully on the facts and the law, defense counsel should advise the accused with complete candor concerning all aspects of the case, including a candid estimate of the probable outcome.
(b) Defense counsel should not intentionally understate or overstate the risks, hazards, or prospects of the case to exert undue influence on the accused's decision as to his or her plea.

Standard 4-5.2 Control and Direction of the Case

(a) Certain decisions relating to the conduct of the case are ultimately for the accused and others are ultimately for defense counsel. The decisions which are to be made by the accused after full consultation with counsel include:

---

53   Superseded Written Standards, above note 52 at § 11.5.

    (i)   what pleas to enter;

    (ii)   whether to accept a plea agreement; . . . .

Standard 4-6.1 Duty to Explore Disposition Without Trial

(a)   Whenever the law, nature, and circumstances of the case permit, defense counsel should explore the possibility of an early diversion of the case from the criminal process through the use of other community agencies.

(b)   Defense counsel may engage in plea discussions with the prosecutor. Under no circumstances should defense counsel recommend to a defendant acceptance of a plea unless appropriate investigation and study of the case has been completed, including an analysis of controlling law and the evidence likely to be introduced at trial.

Standard 4-6.2 Plea Discussions

(a)   Defense counsel should keep the accused advised of developments arising out of plea discussions conducted with the prosecutor.

(b)   Defense counsel should promptly communicate and explain to the accused all significant plea proposals made by the prosecutor.

(c)   Defense counsel should not knowingly make false statements concerning the evidence in the course of plea discussions with the prosecutor.

(d)   Defense counsel should not seek concessions favorable to one client by any agreement which is detrimental to the legitimate interests of a client in another case.

(e)   Defense counsel representing two or more clients in the same or related cases should not participate in making an aggregated agreement as to guilty or nolo contendere pleas, unless each client consents after consultation, including disclosure of the existence and nature of all the claims or pleas involved.

The ABA's Criminal Justice Section has also adopted a separate package of standards that solely concern guilty pleas. Regarding defence counsel's ethical obligations, these "Pleas of Guilty" standards generally reflect the ABA Defense Standard provisions just quoted.[54]

---

54   American Bar Association, Criminal Justice Standards Committee, Criminal Justice Section, *ABA Standards for Criminal Justice: Pleas of Guilty*, 3d ed (Washington, DC: ABA, 1999) standard 14-3.2 [ABA Pleas of Guilty Standards].

G. EXPLORING THE POSSIBILITY OF A RESOLUTION WITHOUT A PLEA

Sometimes a lawyer will be retained before any charges have been brought against the client. In such circumstances, a resolution of the case without a charge being laid is the best result that can be achieved. Prompt and effective negotiation with the authorities is crucial if such a resolution is to be reached. Accordingly, resolution discussions may be undertaken, and indeed mandated, even before a charge has been laid.[55] Counsel taking part in these discussions should be guided by the ethical duties and considerations reviewed in this chapter with necessary modifications as dictated by the circumstances.

The same approach should be taken where, although charges have been laid, circumstances make diversion from the criminal justice system a real possibility. Depending on the jurisdiction in question, the Crown may be open to diverting less serious criminal charges such as minor property offences. Both the ABA Defense Standards and Pleas of Guilty Standards provide that counsel should explore the possibility of an early diversion whenever the law, nature, and circumstances of the case permit.[56] In Canada, the broad duties of competence and loyalty to the client surely fix defence counsel with the same duty to explore a diversion resolution for the case.

H. DUTY TO NEGOTIATE

Canadian rules of professional conduct impose no express obligation on defence counsel to canvas the possibility of a plea agreement with the Crown. However, as just noted, counsel owes the client basic duties of loyalty and competence. Given that a plea agreement may be in the best interests of the client, counsel has a duty to negotiate where there is a reasonable prospect that the client will thereby receive a benefit,[57]

---

55   See the rules cited at notes 48–49, above in this chapter: resolution discussions can occur before a charge is laid and be carried out on behalf of a "potential accused."

56   ABA Defense Standard 4-6.1(a); ABA Pleas of Guilty Standards, above note 54, 14-3.2(e).

57   See *Criminal Justice Review Report*, above note 1, recommendation 6.9 and the associated discussion; Martin Committee Report, above note 4 at 335–44; Jenny M Roberts "Effective Plea Bargaining Counsel" (2013) 122 Yale LJ 2650 at 2664–65.

provided the client has not instructed otherwise.[58] Doing so has the added advantage of promoting the proper and efficient functioning of the criminal justice system.[59]

I. ACTING FOR AN ACCUSED WHO MAY WISH TO BECOME A CO-OPERATING WITNESS

Some defence lawyers refuse to act for clients who seek a plea agreement in exchange for informing on or testifying against another individual.[60] These lawyers may be uncomfortable with assisting such clients for one or more of several reasons.[61] They may believe that co-operating witnesses are especially prone to lie, and thus may be unwilling to assist in a possible miscarriage of justice, or they may view the rewards afforded such witnesses as anathema to fundamental principles of sentencing such as parity and specific deterrence.[62] Some lawyers may also think it immoral to turn on a former friend or associate. Many fear that helping a co-operating witness will scare away future clients from the criminal milieu, where the injunction against becoming a "rat" or "snitch" is strong. A reputation for acting for such clients may also make it hard to work on multi-accused trials because counsel for a co-accused may worry that information shared pursuant to a joint defence strategy could make its way to the Crown through a co-operation arrangement.

The argument against a defence lawyer's refusing to act for an accused who seeks to become a co-operating witness rests on the straightforward proposition that once a retainer is accepted, counsel has a duty to act loyally and zealously in the client's best interests. It is hard to see why this duty should stop simply because the client wants counsel

---

58   See *R v WW* (1995), 100 CCC (3d) 225 at 244 [para 52] (Ont CA).

59   See Martin Committee Report, above note 4 at 335–44.

60   See, for example, *United States v Lopez*, 765 F Supp 1433 at 1438–39 (ND Cal 1991), vacated 989 F2d 1032 (9th Cir 1993), amended and superseded 4 F3d 1455 (9th Cir 1993) [*Lopez*]; *Brown v Doe*, 2 F3d 1236 at 1240 (2d Cir 1993), cert denied 510 US 1125 (1994).

61   See Daniel C Richman, "Cooperating Clients" (1995) 56 Ohio St LJ 69 at 116–26; B Tarlow, "The Moral Conundrum of Representing the Rat" (1995) 29 The Champion 15, reproduced in John Wesley Hall, Jr, *Professional Responsibility in Criminal Defense Practice* (St Paul, MN: Thomson/West, 2005) (loose-leaf September 2012 supplement) § 15.12 at 642–58.

62   See Richard Lippke, "Rewarding Cooperation: The Moral Complexities of Procuring Accomplice Testimony" (2010) 13 New Criminal Law Review 90.

to attain a result that is in her best interests and is neither illegal nor contrary to the codes of professional conduct.[63] Indeed, counsel who refuses to assist an existing client to become a co-operating witness arguably risks allowing a criminal underworld ethos to subvert his professional ethical duties.

There being no cab-rank rule in Canada, it seems clear that defence counsel can decline a retainer from a prospective client who is interested in becoming a co-operating witness.[64] The much more difficult question is whether counsel can refuse to assist an existing client who expresses a desire to negotiate a co-operation agreement or may benefit from such an arrangement.

As a starting point, a lawyer who views acting for a co-operating witness as repugnant must make this position clear to a potential client for whom co-operation is a viable possibility.[65] The lawyer should also make sure the prospective client knows how counsel's position might impact the representation and what will happen if at some point after retaining counsel the client wants to explore the possibility of co-operating with the prosecutor. Where the availability of a plea agreement involving co-operation is very real, the prospective client should probably obtain independent legal advice before hiring counsel.

Ethical codes: The ethical rules in most provinces contain special provisions applicable to limited scope retainers, which presumably apply to retainers that excuse counsel from having to assist in negotiating a co-operation agreement. These provisions require that counsel candidly and honestly explain the nature, extent, and scope of the limitation on the retainer[66] and confirm the nature of the retainer with the client in writing,[67] or if the client is in custody, at the very least keep a written record of the discussions and agreement on file.[68]

Addressing counsel's unwillingness to assist in a co-operation agreement upfront will not always foreclose the risk of a future conflict between counsel's views and the duty of loyalty owed to the client. A client may start off quite happy with the lawyer's perspective and dead

---

63   Naturally, counsel cannot act if he knows that the client's proffered information is false, given the injunction against being a party to dishonest or illegal conduct: see Chapter 2, Section B(1).

64   See Chapter 2, Section H(2).

65   This is what occurred in *Lopez*, above note 60 at 1438–39.

66   Alta, Sask r 2.02(1.1); BC, NL r 3.2-1.1; Man, Ont, NS r 3.2-1A.

67   Alta, Sask r 2.02(1.1) & commentary; BC, NL r 3.2-1.1; Man, NS r 3.2-1A & commentary 1; Ont r 3.2-1A.1, commentary 1.

68   Ont r 3.2-1A.1, commentary 1.1.

set against co-operating only to have second thoughts as the matter progresses. Or the prosecutor may come to counsel with a resolution proposal that involves co-operation. It may also be that, as the matter progresses, unforeseen developments make the prospect of co-operation much more enticing than was initially the case.

In none of these circumstances can defence counsel simply rely on the pre-retainer discussion and ignore the co-operation option. Rather, counsel must remain loyal to the client and respond competently and directly to any new or increased possibility of co-operation that arises during the currency of the retainer:

1) Where the Crown raises the possibility of co-operation, the matter must be brought to the client's attention. The same applies when a change of circumstances opens up the possibility where one did not previously exist or makes a previous possibility more attractive.[69]

2) Counsel must discuss the new development fully with the client and provide information and advice.[70] It is a good idea to obtain independent legal advice for the client so as to ensure that his decision is fully informed and not the result of undue pressure from counsel. After all, counsel whose standing policy is not to act for co-operating witnesses is arguably compromised when it comes to providing sound advice as to the merits of co-operating.[71]

3) If the client wants no part of co-operation, especially after receiving independent legal advice based on full disclosure, the ethical dilemma has been satisfactorily avoided, and counsel can continue with the defence.

4) If the client wishes to enter into discussions with the Crown, then given the limited scope of the retainer, it may be acceptable for counsel to withdraw after helping the client obtain new counsel to conduct the negotiations. Another option is to retain new counsel to carry out the negotiations while original counsel continues to conduct all other aspects of the case. On this latter scenario, original counsel will fully cede the retainer to new counsel only if a co-operation agreement is reached.

5) A client's desire to explore the possibility of a co-operation agreement will sometimes be extremely difficult to accommodate.[72] The

---

69 See the general duties discussed in Chapter 3, Section E.

70 *Ibid.*

71 See *Matter of Maternowski*, 674 NE2d 1287 at 1290–92 (Ind 1996).

72 See M Etienne, "The Ethics of Cause Lawyering: An Empirical Examination of Criminal Defense Lawyers as Cause Lawyers" (2005) 95 J Crim L & Criminology 1195 at 1257–58, suggesting that lawyers should therefore never refuse to continue to act for clients who wish to explore the possibility of co-operating;

opportunity for co-operation may be time-sensitive, requiring fast action that precludes retaining new counsel. Or the client may have spent considerable funds on the first lawyer and lack the money to bring new counsel up to speed. These problems are most serious where counsel insists on withdrawing if the client embarks on co-operation negotiations, and refuses to stay on the case while another lawyer assists in trying to work out a plea resolution. In such circumstances, unless the lawyer's objection to negotiating is truly so strong as to impede her ability to act competently, there may be no choice but to continue as counsel.

1) Request from an Already Represented Accused for Assistance in Negotiating a Co-operation Agreement

An accused may wish to explore the possibility of a co-operation agreement but legitimately fear serious reprisals if his intentions become known to a co-accused or in the criminal milieu more generally. This fear may be so great that the accused is loath to involve current counsel in the negotiations, in particular where counsel for multiple accused in a joint trial have been working closely together in preparing the defence. The accused may therefore approach a new lawyer with a request to conduct negotiations without revealing the retainer to anyone else, including his current counsel.

The main bar against a lawyer's taking on such a retainer is the no-contact rule found in most Canadian codes. This rule provides that if a person is represented by a lawyer in respect of a matter, another lawyer must not approach, communicate, or deal with the person regarding that matter except through or with the consent of the person's lawyer.[73] This prohibition appears to preclude a lawyer from taking on the kind of retainer we are discussing. It matters not that the accused has contacted counsel, and not vice versa, and is desperate for counsel to accept the brief.[74] Query, however, whether counsel could bring a without notice application seeking a court order permitting her to act for the accused despite the no-contact rule.[75]

Richman, above note 61 at 126–38 and 151, expressing "nagging suspicion" that lawyers inclined not to assist in negotiating co-operation agreements may be harming the interests of clients for whom co-operation is a viable option.

73   See Chapter 8, Section C(1).

74   See Chapter 8, Section C(1)(e).

75   See American Bar Association, Standing Committee on Ethics and Professional Responsibility, Formal Opinion 95-396, "Communications with Represented Persons" (28 July 1995), part VIII, especially at the text associated with notes 51

In any event, the no-contact rule will likely not apply where existing counsel has accepted the retainer on condition that he not participate in any plea discussions that contemplate co-operation with the police or Crown.[76] In such a case, the representation is proceeding under a limited scope retainer. That is, the retainer does not include representation by the lawyer regarding plea discussions directed at the possibility of co-operation. The no-contact rule found in most Canadian jurisdictions contains an exception that allows a lawyer to communicate with a represented person on matters excluded from a limited scope retainer.[77] In these jurisdictions, we see nothing wrong with the new lawyer undertaking the plea negotiations and adhering to the client's instructions to keep them secret from existing counsel.

J. CONDITIONAL OR PRELIMINARY PLEA DISCUSSIONS

Canadian ethical codes are worded broadly enough to permit defence counsel to engage in plea discussions with the prosecution before providing complete advice and obtaining instructions and admissions from the client.[78] This position accords with the realities of criminal litigation. As the comment to ABA Defense Standard 4-6.2 observes:

> In many cases, it will be appropriate to make an early contact with the prosecutor to secure information concerning the charge. In the course of this contact, the possibility of reducing the charge or making a plea may arise and counsel may have an opportunity to advance the client's interest without making any disclosures concerning the defence. The client's consent ordinarily need not be sought and obtained before any approaches are made, as there will be occasions when some discussion, perhaps only of a tentative and preliminary nature, will occur before an opportunity arises to obtain the client's consent.[79]

This approach does not, however, give the lawyer carte blanche in conducting conditional or preliminary plea discussions. For one thing,

---

& 52. The possibility of obtaining such an order is also discussed in Chapter 12, Section I(9).

76 See the paragraphs associated with notes 65–68, above in this chapter.

77 See Chapter 8, Section C(1)(i).

78 See the rules cited at note 48, above in this chapter. Contra CBA Code ch IX, commentary 12.

79 See ABA Defense Standard 4-6.2 & comment.

absent proper preparation, advice, and instructions, counsel can only canvas the possibility of a plea and is not permitted to reach a final agreement. Making an agreement without authority is highly improper and, among other things, may create an impetus for defence counsel to pressure the client to accept the arrangement against the latter's will. Moreover, even tentative discussions are improper where forbidden by the client, as expressly noted by most Canadian rules.[80] Where counsel has good reason to believe that the client would disapprove of plea discussions taking place, the proper course is to avoid even tentative discussions absent reviewing the matter with the client. Finally, it is prudent for counsel to inform the Crown that the discussions are only tentative, making clear that any proposal is subject to the client's consideration and agreement. Frankness in this regard avoids misunderstandings and minimizes the possibility that defence counsel will be criticized if a resolution is not reached.

K. DUTY TO INVESTIGATE

Effective negotiations with the Crown and competent advice for the client require more than mere experience, instinct, or wisdom. The rules of professional responsibility impose on counsel a general duty to understand adequately the factual and legal elements of a case before providing advice to the client.[81] Moreover, in the specific area of plea agreements, most Canadian governing bodies implicitly recognize an obligation to investigate a matter adequately insofar as they countenance plea agreements "following investigation" by the lawyer.[82] In the words of G Arthur Martin, "before urging a defendant to plead guilty [counsel] should have conducted the same type of intensive investigation which a lawyer preparing for trial should undertake."[83] Absent such investigation, counsel is unable to provide the best possible advice to the client regarding the advantages and disadvantages of a proposed plea agreement. Failure to master the details of the case may also weaken defence counsel's negotiating position with the Crown, leading

---

80   See the rules cited at note 48, above in this chapter.

81   Alta, Sask r 2.01(a) & (b); BC, Man, Ont, NS, NL r 3.1-1(a) & (b): competence requires knowledge of facts and law. Alta, Sask r 2.01(2) (commentary); BC, Man, Ont, NS, NL r 3.1-2, commentary 8: sufficient investigation required to ground an opinion.

82   See the rules cited at note 49, above in this chapter.

83   G Arthur Martin, "The Role and Responsibility of the Defence Advocate" (1970) 12 Crim LQ 376 at 387.

to a mediocre result for the client. For these reasons, counsel has an obligation to investigate thoroughly the circumstances of the case before entering into a plea agreement.

The amount of investigation required will vary from case to case but should reflect the degree of preparation normally expected of competent counsel. In ascertaining the type and extent of investigation required, one must take into account the number and complexity of factual and legal issues, the strength and nature of the Crown case, the strategy favoured by counsel, and any information provided by the accused.

Some clients, in particular those with extensive criminal records who are charged with relatively minor offences, may wish to plead guilty very soon after their arrest, for instance immediately on bail being denied. At this stage of the proceedings, counsel will usually have minimal information regarding the Crown case, limited perhaps to a summary of the allegations prepared by a police officer. It may therefore be impossible to provide the client with comprehensive advice as to the likelihood of conviction. Provided that counsel makes the client aware of this limitation and that the client wishes to proceed with a guilty plea nonetheless, we see no problem in counsel's acting on the plea. Yet counsel must make sure the client's decision to plead guilty absent complete knowledge of the Crown case is informed, express, and voluntary. Counsel should make contemporaneous notes setting out the client's position, or better yet obtain written instructions.

A lawyer must be extremely wary of acting on a guilty plea for a client who is charged with a serious offence without first having had an opportunity to review the prosecution disclosure and provide the client with comprehensive advice. The client who wishes to plead guilty in such circumstances should ordinarily be counselled to hold off making a decision until substantial disclosure has been received. If the client persists in her instructions, the lawyer is justified in terminating the retainer on the basis that the client has refused advice on a matter important to the representation.[84]

L. DUTY TO INFORM AND ADVISE THE CLIENT

Inextricably entwined with counsel's preparation is the duty to provide information and advice to the client. After all, a main reason why counsel must become familiar with the facts and law surrounding the case, undertaking independent investigation if appropriate, is to ensure that

---

84 See Section S, below in this chapter.

the client receives fully informed and competent advice. In many if not most cases, an accused relies heavily on counsel's advice in choosing how to plead. The quality of advice therefore has a direct bearing on the proper exercise of the client's constitutional right to decide how to plead in response to criminal charges.

1) Canadian Rules of Professional Conduct

Canadian ethical codes usually contain several provisions that ground counsel's duty to provide advice with respect to a plea decision.[85] First, there is the duty to deliver competent service to the client, which includes advising the client regarding appropriate courses of action so that he can make informed decisions regarding the conduct of the case.[86] Second, ethical code rules pertaining to quality of service provide that a lawyer has a duty to communicate effectively with the client[87] and to keep the client reasonably informed.[88] These quality-of-service rules also state that a lawyer must inform the client of any "proposal of settlement" — a term that surely includes a plea resolution offer from the Crown — and explain the proposal properly.[89] Third, most ethical codes contain a separate duty to be honest and candid when providing advice and, in describing that duty, typically refer to the obligation to inform the client of all information known to the lawyer that may affect the client's interests in the matter.[90] As the commentary to the relevant rule states, a lawyer's duty to the client who seeks legal advice is "to give the client a competent opinion based on a sufficient knowledge of the relevant facts, an adequate consideration of the applicable law, and the lawyer's own experience and expertise."[91] Finally, the provisions dealing directly with plea discussions and agreements contain express reference to the need to provide an accused with advice. Specifically, they accept the ethical propriety of entering into a plea agreement on behalf

---

85 On the topic of providing advice more generally, see Chapter 3, Section E.

86 Alta, Sask r 2.01(b); BC, Man, Ont, NS, NL r 3.1-1(b).

87 Alta, Sask r 2.02(1) (commentary); BC, NS, NL r 3.2-1, commentary 3. To similar effect, see Alta, Sask r 2.01(d); BC, Man, Ont, NS, NL r 3.1-1(d); NB ch 2, commentary 5(d) and ch 3, commentary 2.

88 Alta, Sask r 2.02(1) (commentary); BC, Man, NS, NL r 3.2-1, commentary 5(a); NB ch 3, commentary 4(a); CBA Code ch II, commentary 7(a).

89 Alta, Sask r 2.02(1) (commentary); BC, Man, NS, NL r 3.2-1, commentary 5(j); Que s 3.02.10; NB ch 3, commentary 4(j); CBA Code ch II, commentary 7(j).

90 Alta, Sask r 2.02(2); BC, Man, NS, NL r 3.2-2; Ont r 3.2-2, commentary 1.1; NB ch 4, rule; CBA Code ch III, rule.

91 Alta, Sask r 2.02 (commentary); BC, Man, Ont, NS, NL r 3.2-2, commentary 2.

of a client where "following investigation . . . the lawyer advises the client of the implications and possible consequences of a guilty plea."[92]

2) Factors to Cover with the Client

What advice should the lawyer give once she is fully informed regarding the factual and legal issues at stake? While the proper guidance in each case is largely driven by the particular circumstances at hand, a number of factors must be considered by defence counsel and discussed with the client, including

1) the merits of the case, including the strengths and weaknesses of any available defences;[93]
2) the likelihood of a conviction following trial;[94]
3) the consequences to the client if he loses after a disputed trial, including the maximum sentence, the probable range of sentences, and any relevant impact on his personal life, for example regarding work, family, driving, firearms use, international travel, or immigration status;
4) any adverse impact associated with the trial process where guilt is disputed, including publicity and the stress and unpleasantness that may flow from a decision to testify;
5) the impact that a guilty plea has on the trial process, including the waiver of many fundamental constitutional rights;[95]
6) the factual basis for a guilty plea and the sentencing process in instances where disputed aggravating or mitigating facts are to be litigated by the parties;
7) the benefits that might accompany a guilty plea, including not only concessions made by the Crown under a proposed plea agreement but also those pertaining to speedier resolution, stress reduction, and minimized cost to the client;
8) the plea of guilty as a beneficial factor on sentencing, including the heightened mitigation that often accompanies an early plea;[96]

---

92 See the rules cited at note 49, above in this chapter.
93 See *Lamoureux*, above note 10 at 105 [para 24]. Cases where faulty advice on available defences led the client to make a bad decision regarding how to plead include *Lafler v Cooper*, 132 S Ct 1399 (2012); *R v Ahmad*, 2012 BCCA 479.
94 See *Lamoureux*, above note 10 at 105 [para 24].
95 See *Riley*, above note 18 at para 32.
96 Regarding the mitigation inherent in a guilty plea, see Clayton Ruby, Gerald Chan, & Nader Hasan, *Sentencing*, 8th ed (Markham, ON: LexisNexis, 2012) at §§ 5.211–5.225.

9) the possible methods of indicating remorse and commencing the process of rehabilitation, as well as any associated disadvantages, responsibilities, or benefits;

10) the impact of the accused's prior criminal record and any other personal circumstances on the sentencing outcome;

11) the nature and range of penalties attendant on a guilty plea, including any mandatory minimum penalty and the maximum possible penalty;[97]

12) if the circumstances warrant, parole and probation possibilities, long-term and dangerous offender designations, property forfeitures, restitution orders, firearms prohibitions, sex offender designations, and DNA orders;[98]

13) any reasonably anticipated collateral consequences of a guilty plea, such as its impact on personal life, civil litigation, criminal charges in a foreign jurisdiction, and deportation proceedings, and whether a plea can be structured so as to minimize or avoid such consequences;[99]

14) the judge's power to ignore a joint submission in some circumstances;[100]

15) if the identity of the judge hearing the case is known, the judge's sentencing predilections;

16) the precise process involved in entering a plea, including that the judge may embark on a plea inquiry and what this might entail; and

17) the client's complete freedom of choice regarding the plea decision.

3) Respect for the Client's Freedom of Choice

Diligent counsel will usually encounter no great difficulty in covering many of the topics set out in Section L(2), above, with the client. The

---

97 See *R v Al-Diasty* (2003), 174 CCC (3d) 574 (Ont CA): counsel provided the client with an unduly optimistic opinion as to the likelihood of a jail sentence if he pleaded guilty.

98 See *Riley*, above note 18 at para 32: duty to review penalties and orders that a court may impose at sentencing.

99 See ABA Pleas of Guilty Standards, above note 54, 14-3.2(f); Margaret Love, "Evolving Standards of Reasonableness: The ABA Standards and the Right to Counsel in Plea Negotiations" (2011) 39 Fordham Urb Law J 147 at 163–66. Compare *Padilla v Kentucky*, 559 US 356 (2010), which held that where the deportation consequence is clear, failure to advise the client that a plea carries the risk of deportation constitutes deficient advice, with *R v Tyler*, 2007 BCCA 142, where counsel did not advise that a guilty plea would result in deportation, but the plea was nonetheless voluntary because the accused knew that the conviction would put his immigration status in serious jeopardy.

100 See subparagraph (b) of the rules cited at note 49, above in this chapter.

real challenge often comes in providing a final opinion as to whether the client should plead guilty. While the pros and cons of pleading guilty usually involve considerations personal to the accused, defence counsel who studiously avoids giving an opinion on the matter is not doing the client any service. Lawyers should offer such advice where possible[101] and have licence to provide the opinion in "strong terms."[102] Counsel must not shy away from providing a firm recommendation on the advisability of a particular plea, even where doing so means challenging the client's perspective and results in an animated discussion.[103]

Yet it is improper to bully the client into accepting counsel's preferred option. Valid defences may be forgone, perhaps even leading to the conviction of an innocent person, and in any event it is inappropriate to interfere with the client's freedom of choice regarding the plea. Counsel should also keep in mind the ethical prohibition against usurping the role of the court by acting as judge of the client's culpability.[104] For all of these reasons, the lawyer should not "exert undue influence on the accused's decision as to his or her plea."[105] At the end of the day, counsel must strive to provide competent advice while fully respecting the client's freedom of choice.

Where a client is particularly vulnerable, whether because of emotional fragility or especially trying circumstances, special care should be taken to ensure that her free will is not subjugated. Counsel should also work hard to avoid placing a client in a position where the pressure to plead guilty is needlessly increased. Pressure of this type is created when a defence lawyer unjustifiably waits until the last minute to provide complete and candid advice on the issue of the plea. Even where circumstances beyond the control of counsel or the accused result in sudden pressure to plead guilty, counsel may be able to alleviate the problem by requesting an adjournment.

Example: Accused Y is charged with domestic assault. He protests his innocence and provides counsel with useful ammunition to cross-examine the complainant. However, advice provided by counsel leaves

---

101 See Alta, Sask r 2.02(2) (commentary); BC, Man, Ont, NS, NL r 3.2-2, commentary 2; NB ch 4, commentary 1; CBA Code ch III, commentary 1: lawyer's advice must be open, undisguised, and honest.

102 See *Turner*, above note 52 at 285; *R v Goodyear*, [2005] EWCA Crim 888 at para 34; *Carty*, above note 39 at para 42.

103 See Alta, Sask r 2.02(2) (commentary); BC, Man, NS, NL r 3.2-2, commentary 3.

104 See Chapter 1, sections B and D.

105 ABA Defense Standard 4-5.1(b). See also *Lamoureux*, above note 10 at 105 [para 24]; Meredith Blake & Andrew Ashworth, "Ethics and the Criminal Defence Lawyer" (2004) 7 Leg Ethics 167 at 179–82.

Y with the impression that a fair trial can never be expected on a domestic assault charge. Y strongly considers a guilty plea but makes no final decision before the trial. Y's lawyer arrives for the trial unprepared, in the expectation Y will likely plead guilty. In trying to convince Y to enter a guilty plea, counsel admits he is not ready for trial. Fearing that a conviction is certain in any event, Y agrees to plead guilty. In failing to prepare for the case, counsel has effectively denied Y the option of going to trial and hence subjected Y to undue pressure to plead guilty.[106]

4) The "Uncertain or Unlikely" Prospect of Acquittal

The Canadian Bar Association (CBA) and New Brunswick rules of professional conduct permit defence counsel to commence plea discussions and enter into a plea agreement only where she has concluded and advised the client that an acquittal of the offence charged is "uncertain or unlikely."[107] In rare cases, this precondition will not be met, because the lawyer in good faith concludes that acquittal is certain. Should the lawyer as a result be prohibited from negotiating a plea agreement, as the CBA and New Brunswick codes would have it?

We can begin by stating an obvious point: counsel who believes an acquittal is certain should ordinarily attempt to convince the Crown to withdraw or stay the charge. Indeed, barring unequivocal instructions to the contrary, a lawyer who reasonably entertains this belief should not participate in discussions with the Crown that are directed towards entering a guilty plea. To do so would not be in the client's best interests and would be at odds with the duties of loyalty and competence. It may be, however, that despite receiving complete and competent advice regarding the certainty of acquittal, the client instructs counsel that he is guilty and wishes to enter a plea to this effect. This possibility is not as outlandish as might be thought. The accused may feel genuine remorse for having done wrong and wish to acknowledge guilt publicly as part of the process of rehabilitation and to make amends to the victim and society.

Where the client so instructs counsel, there should be no bar to counsel's taking part in plea discussions, making a plea agreement, or representing the client on a guilty plea, even though the Crown

---

106 See *R v Ceballo* (1997), 14 CR (5th) 15 (Ont Ct Prov Div) [*Ceballo*]. For other cases where counsel placed significant last-minute pressure on the accused or failed to make reasonable efforts to alleviate such pressure, see *Laperrière*, above note 10; *R v Toussaint* (1984), 16 CCC (3d) 544 (Que CA); *DMG*, above note 7 at paras 114–17; *IBB*, above note 38 at paras 20, 26, and 65–73.

107 CBA Code ch IX, commentary 13(a); NB ch 8, r 15(a)(i).

would otherwise be unable to prove its case in court.[108] The objections that arise where an innocent client wishes to plead guilty are not applicable,[109] for the court will not be misled, and the truthfully admitted facts will be sufficient to support a conviction. Furthermore, the accused's constitutional right to choose whether or not to plead guilty means that counsel must comply with such instructions. We therefore take the view, contrary to the wording found in the CBA and New Brunswick codes, that counsel should not be prohibited from entering into or concluding plea resolution discussions simply because she has not concluded that acquittal is uncertain or unlikely.

5) Communicating a Crown Resolution Offer or a Client's Acceptance

Defence counsel must pass on all plea proposals to the client.[110] It matters not that an offer appears clearly to fall short of the client's expectations or is probably not in the client's best interests. It matters not that counsel is eager to proceed to trial and that the client has a strong defence. The final decision as to the plea is the client's, and failure to provide all information relevant to this decision risks subverting the client's freedom of choice. Indeed, given the general duty to keep the client informed,[111] counsel must communicate to the client not only firm plea offers and tentative proposals but also any other information reasonably bearing on the decision how to plead.

Counsel's duty to act as a conduit for relevant information runs in both directions. Where the client instructs counsel to take a particular position regarding the Crown's plea proposal, counsel must do so promptly and accurately. Failure to convey acceptance of a plea proposal to the Crown violates counsel's ethical obligations[112] and may also constitute denial of the right to the effective assistance of counsel.[113]

---

108 See Martin Committee Report, above note 4 at 299–300.

109 See Section M(6), below in this chapter.

110 See the text associated with note 89, above in this chapter. See also *Missouri*, above note 3 at 1408: failure to inform the client of a plea offer will generally meet the performance prong of the test for ineffective assistance of counsel.

111 See the text associated with note 88, above in this chapter.

112 See Alta, Sask r 2.02(1), commentary (e); BC, Man, NS, NL 3.2-1, commentary 5(e); NB ch 3, commentary 4(e); CBA Code ch II, commentary 7(e): counsel must take appropriate steps to do something promised to a client or inform or explain to the client where the promise cannot be fulfilled.

113 See, for example, *Aldrich v State*, 296 SW3d 225 at 243 (Tex App 2009).

M. THE CLIENT WHO MAINTAINS INNOCENCE

The client who maintains innocence yet wishes to plead guilty presents a complex and difficult problem for defence counsel. Few other hot topics in the field of ethics and criminal law generate such diverse responses from the various Anglo-American nations. In examining this issue, we will thus look at the differing approaches taken in Canada, the United States, and England and Wales, as well as the pertinent policy arguments. Along the way, we will review some of the various scenarios that may confront counsel. Crucial to a proper resolution of any scenario are the likelihood that the client's protestations of innocence are accurate and the precise manner in which he wishes to concede guilt.

1) The Client Who Maintains Innocence but Later Abandons the Claim

Most defence counsel have encountered clients who want to plead guilty all the while maintaining innocence. The large majority of these clients are guilty but simply have trouble admitting culpability, even in a confidential setting with counsel. Perhaps, given the nature of the crime, the client cannot confess guilt without confronting a terrible personal weakness or alienating family and friends. Other clients exhibit an initial braggadocio in talking to counsel, especially early on when Crown disclosure is not yet available and when the professional relationship is just beginning. They may feel counsel will work harder if under the belief that the charge is unfounded. Still others, after months of trying, may actually convince themselves of facts that, while supporting innocence, never actually happened. Whatever the reason, the client who maintains innocence despite being guilty often changes his tune as the process unfolds.

For such a client, it may be permissible to participate in plea discussions with the Crown even while guilt is being denied. However, counsel should first obtain express instructions from the client. While instructions are not always needed before undertaking plea discussions,[114] protestations of innocence represent a warning sign that the client may not be amenable. The better course is thus to obtain the client's consent in advance. Indeed, consent may be an initial step for the client on the road towards a legitimate acknowledgement of guilt.

---

114 See Section J, above in this chapter.

Once the client has genuinely abandoned the claim of innocence, the finalization of a plea agreement and representation on a guilty plea are no longer problematic.

2) The Client Who Maintains Innocence and Never Abandons the Claim

Rarer, but immensely more contentious, is the scenario where a client protests innocence and never abandons the claim yet desires to plead guilty. Any one of several possibilities may underlie the client's position. The client might be guilty but simply persist in denying culpability for some or all of the reasons mentioned above. Or there may be a valid question whether the client is guilty, even though he admits facts from which a jury could conceivably convict. A good example is the accused who asserts self-defence or a *mens rea* defence. Most troubling is the client who may indeed be innocent but nonetheless decide to accept responsibility for a crime he did not commit.

There may be understandable reasons for a true innocent to contemplate a guilty plea. He may wish to protect a third party who is the real culprit, for instance, a spouse or child. Maybe the publicity, stress, or cost of a trial is so daunting that the accused is willing to admit guilt falsely as an avoidance measure. A guilty plea may also prove attractive to the accused who desires a fast and relatively certain conclusion to proceedings. Still other accused individuals, lacking in self-confidence, may buckle to pressure from the police, Crown, or defence counsel who mistakenly believes her to be guilty.

Probably the greatest impetus for pleading guilty despite being innocent, however, is the discount in sentence that usually accompanies a guilty plea.[115] This discount can be extremely attractive where the Crown case appears strong and where possible defences suffer from inherent weaknesses — witnesses may be uncooperative or unavailable, the accused may make a terrible witness, and so on. This is precisely what happened in the wrongful convictions of Anthony Hanemaayer and Dinesh Kumar, both of whom were innocent of the very serious charges they faced but pleaded guilty to obtain a significant sentence discount.[116] Yet the incentive for an innocent person to plead guilty is likely strongest in minor cases where an accused with a lengthy record

---

115 See, for example, the comments in *Hanemaayer*, above note 19 at paras 11 and 18.

116 See *Hanemaayer, ibid; Kumar*, above note 19. One strongly suspects that the same accounts for Gerald Barton's guilty plea to a statutory rape offence he did not commit: see *Barton v Nova Scotia (AG)*, 2014 NSSC 192 at para 84 [*Barton*].

has no chance of obtaining bail and recognizes that the delay before trial will easily exceed the sentence handed out on an early plea.

The client who maintains innocence and adamantly refuses to admit guilt in court yet simultaneously wants to plead guilty presents counsel with no real problem. Canadian courts have consistently ruled that an accused who pleads guilty must admit facts sufficient to ground a conviction, and in particular have tended to view a guilty plea as exactly commensurate with an admission of culpability.[117] Where the accused equivocates or refuses to admit the facts or attempts to put forth facts that would constitute a valid defence, the plea will be rejected or struck. Simply put, a court will not allow an accused to plead guilty without admitting the essential elements of the offence in open court. And most ethical codes effectively prevent counsel from acting on such a plea by stating that before finalizing a plea resolution, counsel must ensure that the client is prepared to admit the elements of the offence.[118]

The tougher predicament for counsel occurs where the client is quite willing to plead guilty and admit to blameworthy facts in court but all the while asserts innocence in the confidential setting of the client-lawyer relationship. This is what happened in the Supreme Court of Canada case of *R v Taillefer; R v Duguay*.[119] Duguay had been convicted of first-degree murder but succeeded in having his conviction overturned on appeal. Faced with a new trial, he instructed his lawyer to negotiate a plea resolution with the Crown and ended up pleading guilty to manslaughter and admitting the facts necessary to ground the conviction in court. Years later, it emerged that the Crown had failed to disclose important information to the defence before the plea. Duguay appealed his conviction on the basis of this non-disclosure. Affidavits from Duguay and his trial lawyers filed on the appeal asserted that he had always maintained his innocence and had decided to plead guilty only to avoid what he viewed as a strong risk of being convicted of murder.[120] The Court overturned the guilty plea on the basis of non-disclosure[121] but did not comment on the propriety of trial counsel's

---

117 See the cases cited at note 6, above in this chapter, as well as *R v SK* (1995), 99 CCC (3d) 376 at 382 [paras 13–15] (Ont CA) [*SK*]; *R v Johnson*, [1976] OJ No 1189 at para 9 (CA) [*Johnson*]; *Adgey*, above note 8 at 189; *R v Lucas* (1983), 9 CCC (3d) 71 at 76 [para 17] (Ont CA), leave to appeal to SCC refused, [1984] SCCA No 389; *Newman*, above note 22 at 400–1 [para 15]; *R v GOM* (1989), 51 CCC (3d) 171 at 174 (Sask CA); *R v Yarlasky* (1999), 140 CCC (3d) 281 at paras 3–4 (Ont CA). See also Ruby, Chan, & Hasan, above note 96 at § 3.17.

118 See subparagraph (c) of the rules cited at note 49, above in this chapter.

119 Above note 16.

120 *Ibid* at paras 109–10.

121 *Ibid* at paras 111–13.

having negotiated and acted on the plea for a client who all the while privately maintained his innocence.[122]

There is little doubt that Canadian lawyers sometimes act as did defence counsel in *Taillefer*.[123] The question is whether doing so is ethical.

3) The Somewhat Uncertain Position in Canada

Canadian rules of professional conduct are not entirely clear as to whether counsel can act on a guilty plea for a client who maintains innocence. The usual text of these rules provides that counsel can only conclude a plea agreement where "the client voluntarily is prepared to admit the necessary factual and mental elements of the offence charged."[124] This wording could be interpreted to mean that counsel cannot represent an accused on a guilty plea where the client privately maintains innocence.[125]

Yet this interpretation is not necessarily compelled by the language of the rules. For one thing, the rules by their own terms apply only to plea agreements. It is thus arguably open to counsel to proceed with the guilty plea of a client who maintains innocence in the absence of any such agreement. Perhaps more importantly, the rules are worded to require only that the accused be "prepared to admit" the necessary factual and mental elements of the offence. This phrase can be taken to mandate that the accused be willing to make a public admission of culpability during the plea and sentencing proceedings but not that she make the same admission to counsel in confidence. On this interpretation, counsel does not violate the rules in allowing the privately defiant accused to plead guilty, and the plea will be accepted because the client will make the necessary admissions in court.

Even if one accepts this view of the rules of professional conduct, there is no doubt that counsel is forbidden from representing the ac-

---

122 See Davud Tanovich, "*Taillefer*: Disclosure, Guilty Pleas and Ethics" (2004) 17 CR (6th) 149 at 152–55.

123 Other cases where an accused who appears to have privately maintained innocence has pleaded guilty after which the plea has been struck include *Hanemaayer*, above note 19 at para 11; *R v Johnson*, 2014 ONSC 2093 [*Johnson* SCJ]; *R v Brant*, 2011 ONCA 362; *R v Abotossaway* (2004), 189 OAC 322 (CA); *R v NC* (2001), 151 OAC 249 (CA); *Johnson*, above note 117; *R v Sutton*, 2012 NLCA 35; *R v JPB*, 2007 BCPC 270; *R v Sterling*, 2007 SKPC 66 at paras 6–7. See also *R v Hector* (2000), 146 CCC (3d) 81 at para 11 (Ont CA) [*Hector*]: trial counsel's affidavit suggests he often acts on guilty pleas for clients who privately maintain innocence.

124 Alta, Sask r 4.01(8)(c); BC, Man, Ont, NS, NL r 5.1-7(c). To similar effect, see NB ch 8, commentary 15(a)(iii); CBA Code ch IX, commentary 13(b).

125 This appears to be the import of *SK*, above note 117 at 382 [para 13].

cused who maintains innocence on a guilty plea *where the result will be to mislead the court*. This conclusion is supported by the general prohibition in all ethical codes against a lawyer knowingly attempting to deceive the court.[126] This prohibition precludes a lawyer from representing to the court that a client is guilty where he knows that the representation is false and that the client is in fact innocent.

Yet the prohibition against knowingly misleading the court is arguably not engaged where the lawyer does not believe the client's private protestations of innocence or is unsure whether they are true. Consider, for example, the client who maintains innocence but on counsel's reasonable assessment of the evidence is probably guilty. Because counsel does not believe the accused is innocent, permitting her to enter a guilty plea and admit to facts that establish culpability does not constitute an intentional deception on the court. If anything, it is counsel who is likely being told falsehoods by the client and the court that is receiving the true admission of guilt.

On the other hand, it can be argued that the court will always be misled where an accused pleads guilty while privately denying responsibility to counsel, even where counsel is satisfied the accused is probably guilty, because a guilty plea must be a sincere acceptance of moral blame. The impermissible deception in counsel's acting on the plea comes, not from any inaccuracy in portraying the facts surrounding the offence, but rather from helping the client present a disingenuous expression of remorse. Perhaps, then, a good deal of the concern regarding the client who wishes to plead guilty while privately maintaining innocence flows from a belief that the guilty plea must constitute an *authentic and unfeigned* acceptance of culpability.

We see strong indications of this belief in the leading case of *R v SK*,[127] where the accused young person had been charged with many sexual offences. Following the close of the prosecution case, defence counsel worked out a resolution with the Crown under which the accused would plead guilty to several minor counts in exchange for the more serious counts being dropped. The accused had always maintained his innocence, and he continued to do so in discussions with his lawyer pertaining to the plea agreement. Counsel responded by advising the accused that "criminal courts do not necessarily deal in

126 Alta r 4.01(2)(d) and (g); Sask r 4.01(2)(b) and (e); NL, Man, Ont, NS, BC r 5.1-2(b) and (e); NB ch 8, commentary 10(ii) and (v); CBA Code ch IX, commentary 2(b) and (e). See also Chapter 1, Section E.

127 Above note 117.

truth, but they deal in evidence."[128] The accused pleaded guilty, and counsel admitted to an agreed statement of facts on behalf of the client.

At a meeting with a probation officer in preparation for a pre-disposition report, the accused's protestations of innocence continued and thereafter became known to the judge. The judge proceeded with the sentencing regardless, and there was no attempt by the accused to withdraw the pleas. An appeal was later launched. In holding that the guilty pleas should be set aside, the court observed:

> This case presents a graphic example of why it is essential to the plea bargaining process that the accused person is prepared to admit to the facts that support the conviction. The court should not be in the position of convicting and sentencing individuals, who fall short of admitting the facts to support the conviction unless that guilt is proved beyond a reasonable doubt. *Nor should sentencing proceed on the false assumption of contrition.* That did not happen here, but worse, the sentence became impossible to perform. Plea bargaining is an accepted and integral part of our criminal justice system but must be conducted with sensitivity to its vulnerabilities. *A court that is misled, or allows itself to be misled, cannot serve the interests of justice.*[129]

In other words, false contrition is in itself misleading and unacceptable. This view certainly provides some support for the conclusion that counsel cannot ethically act on a guilty plea where the client, though fully prepared to admit culpability in court, denies guilt within the confidential context of the client-lawyer relationship. It is a conclusion that finds some support in a number of statements in the caselaw and commentary,[130] in addition to the comments from *SK* set out above.

Nonetheless, the substantial increase in plea negotiating over the past several decades, taken together with the reality of significant and

---

128 *Ibid* at 379 [para 5].
129 *Ibid* at 382 [para 15] [emphasis added].
130 *Johnson* SCJ, above note 123 at paras 25–32; *R v Moser* (2002), 163 CCC (3d) 286 at paras 39 and 52 (Ont SCJ); *R v Benoist*, 2011 ONCJ 362 at para 45; *R v CS*, 2010 ONCJ 497 at para 83; *R v Tzeng*, [2007] OJ No 878 at para 5 (SCJ); *R v Lockhard*, 2004 NBPC 13 at paras 24 and 33–35; *Youvarajah*, above note 31 at para 145, Wagner J, dissenting but not on this point; Martin Committee Report, above note 4 at 295; Ontario, *Inquiry into Pediatric Forensic Pathology in Ontario: Report* (Toronto: Attorney General of Ontario, 2008) at 460; *Plea Discussions and Agreements*, above note 5 at 48; Earl J Levy, *Examination of Witnesses in Criminal Cases*, 6th ed (Toronto: Carswell, 2011) at 36–37. See also Alice Woolley, *Understanding Lawyers' Ethics in Canada* (Markham, ON: LexisNexis, 2011) at 308–9 & 310–11, albeit advocating a position more like that taken in Section M(7), below in this chapter.

early disclosure in most cases and the obvious benefits to be obtained by the accused who pleads guilty rather than having a contested trial, undercuts the traditional view that a guilty plea necessarily reflects an expression of remorse. This is not to say that remorse is unimportant as a mitigating factor at sentencing — only that the presumption that the accused who pleads guilty thereby expresses remorse, absent any statement to this effect by the defence, is open to serious question.[131] So too, then, is the contention that it is unethical for counsel to act on a guilty plea for an accused who privately maintains innocence because the court is being misled regarding remorse.

As explained below in Section M(7), we therefore prefer the view that counsel should have some leeway to act on a guilty plea even where the client in confidence insists he is guiltless. But regardless of where one stands on this issue, it is important for lawyers not to jump too quickly to the conclusion that a client is protesting his innocence in a way that potentially limits the ability to act on a guilty plea.

Consider, for example, the hypothetical where a client is charged with sexual assault and tells counsel that because of excessive alcohol and drug use he cannot recall anything about the night in question. The prosecution case is nonetheless solid. Moreover, the client tells counsel that, despite his memory loss, based on the disclosure he is sure he committed the crime and wishes to plead guilty. Even if one accepts that counsel is ethically prohibited from acting on a guilty plea for a client who privately claims innocence, this injunction is not engaged, because the client has admitted guilt to counsel and is not claiming innocence.[132] Of course, on these facts counsel has a duty to explore thoroughly and advise the accused regarding any possible defences.[133]

---

131 See Joseph Di Luca, "Expedient McJustice or Principled Alternative Dispute Resolution? A Review of Plea Bargaining in Canada" (2005) 50 Crim LQ 14 at 60–62; Gregory Lafontaine & Vincenzo Rondinelli, "Plea Bargaining and the Modern Criminal Defence Lawyer: Negotiating Guilt and the Economics of 21st Century Criminal Justice" (2005) 50 Crim LQ 108 at 125–26. In England and Wales, the administrative rationale for rewarding a guilty plea with a sentence discount has clearly overtaken the traditional remorse-based justification: see Bridges, above note 52 at 84.

132 For a case in which counsel acted in such circumstances without adverse comment from the court, see Brown, above note 7. See also Christopher Sherrin, "Guilty Pleas from the Innocent" (2011) 30 Windsor Rev Legal Soc Issues 1 at 32.

133 In R v Jawbone (1998), 126 Man R (2d) 295 (CA), the accused, who professed to have no memory of the incident due to excessive drinking, pleaded guilty to a very serious offence within days of being charged. Very soon after, evidence emerged pointing to another person as the true culprit, and the plea was overturned on appeal.

And if a guilty plea is entered, counsel should put the client's position regarding the memory loss on the record at the sentencing proceedings.

A different hypothetical sees a client charged with common assault. The client admits to counsel that he grabbed the complainant hard by the arm, without her consent, and shouted at her loudly. Counsel explains that such actions constitute an assault. The client rejects this conclusion. In his view, an "assault" requires substantial injury, and thus he has committed no crime. But the client is wrong. Counsel can therefore act on a plea of guilty provided that the facts to be admitted in court jibe with the client's version of events because the client genuinely accepts these facts and because they provide no defence in law.[134]

A final scenario involves counsel's acting for a client charged with first-degree murder. The client sometimes asserts innocence in speaking to counsel, but the Crown case is extremely strong, and the client refuses to provide counsel with any explanation for the incriminating evidence and forbids counsel to retain an investigator to explore possible defences. The client receives a plea offer from the Crown and is provided with comprehensive advice by counsel regarding its merits. The client reviews the Crown's proposed statement of facts and agrees to admit to these facts in court. He also provides counsel with written instructions accepting the Crown's offer. However, the client never expressly tells counsel that he is in fact guilty. The plea proceeding goes ahead, and the client is convicted.

The jurisprudence suggests that this guilty plea is valid and also seems to accept that counsel has not breached the ethical rules simply by acting on the plea absent a private admission of guilt.[135] This latter conclusion makes sense because a client's failure to admit guilt directly to counsel does not always equate with an affirmation of innocence. Rather, it may be clear in the circumstances that the client is implicitly acknowledging culpability by agreeing to plead guilty and accept the allegations of fact proposed by the Crown.[136] Still, a client's failure to expressly admit guilt in private may be a warning sign,[137] in response

---

134   See *R v Conflitti* (1999), 27 CR (5th) 63 (Ont Ct Prov Div) [*Conflitti*], which provides the basis for this hypothetical.

135   *Hector*, above note 123 at paras 6–17; *RP*, above note 7 at para 49; *R v Khaja*, 2010 ONCA 246 at paras 11–12; *R v Pivonka*, 2007 ONCA 572 at para 16 [*Pivonka*]; *R v Leonard*, 2007 SKCA 128 at para 23.

136   See *Pivonka*, above note 135 at para 16. Yet we question whether this conclusion is justified in *Hector*, above note 123, given the client's private assertion of innocence to counsel during the plea proceeding: see Michel Proulx & David Layton, *Ethics and Canadian Criminal Law* (Toronto: Irwin Law, 2001) at 454–56.

137   See *Pivonka*, above note 135; *Hector*, above note 123 at para 8.

to which prudent counsel will make further inquiries to ensure that the client is not privately asserting innocence.

4) The Position in England and Wales

We have already noted that barristers in England and Wales are permitted to proceed with a guilty plea despite the client's private assertions of innocence.[138] To recap, representing such a client is acceptable provided the barrister

1) advises the client that he should not plead guilty unless truly guilty but that the decision is ultimately the client's to make,[139]
2) asks the client why he wishes to plead guilty despite denying the charge and ascertains whether any steps can be taken to enable the client to enter a plea of not guilty,[140]
3) advises the client as to the consequences of pleading guilty and that the resulting conviction is unlikely to be overturned on appeal,[141]
4) informs the client that counsel's submissions on the plea will be on the basis that the client is guilty and that counsel will be precluded from suggesting the plea represents an expression of remorse,[142] and
5) records in writing the client's reasons for the plea and asks the client to sign a declaration outlining counsel's advice.[143]

The leading case on point in England and Wales is *R v Herbert*.[144] Herbert had been jointly charged with two others, including his wife, of narcotics offences. After the trial had started, counsel for Mrs Herbert worked out a conditional plea agreement with the Crown. Under the agreement, the Crown would drop the charges against Mrs Herbert in exchange for a guilty plea by her husband. This proposal was communicated to Herbert, who agreed to change his plea though continued to maintain his innocence to counsel. Herbert's lawyer basically followed the guidelines set out above, advising Herbert that if he was truly not guilty, the best course was to continue contesting the case. Counsel also told Herbert that a jail term was likely on a plea of guilty. Herbert

---

138 See the text accompanying notes 51–53, above in this chapter.
139 Superseded Written Standards, above note 52 at § 11.5.1(a).
140 *Ibid* at § 11.5.1(a).
141 *Ibid* at § 11.5.2(a).
142 *Ibid* at § 11.5.2(b).
143 *Ibid* at § 11.5.2(c). If the client refuses to sign the declaration, counsel should nonetheless make a contemporaneous note of the advice: *ibid* at § 11.5.2(d).
144 (1992), 94 Cr App R 230 [*Herbert*]. See also *R v Najera*, [2001] EWCA Crim 2621 at paras 46 and 73.

nevertheless changed his plea. The Crown offered no further evidence against the wife, and the judge sentenced Herbert to five and a half years imprisonment. In dismissing Herbert's conviction appeal, the Court of Appeal referred to the applicable provision of the bar's code of conduct[145] and held that defence counsel had behaved properly. In the court's opinion, Herbert had received complete and conscientious advice and had exercised his own free will in entering the plea.[146]

The practice and jurisprudence in England and Wales embrace a position that permits counsel to act on a guilty plea despite the client's assertions of innocence outside the courtroom.[147] But can a barrister go so far as to act on a guilty plea knowing that the accused is a true innocent? To do so would necessitate lying to the judge by asserting that the facts underlying the plea are accurate. Yet barristers in England and Wales are subject to a general prohibition against misleading the court.[148] The judiciary in England and Wales would thus be unlikely to apply the *Herbert* approach to the case of the true innocent. Indeed, in *Herbert* the prosecution evidence seemed strong, and the accused's exculpatory explanations largely unconvincing.[149] It is highly probable that the appeal court had no real doubt that Herbert was truly guilty. It is one thing to condone counsel's acting on a guilty plea where the accused faces a strong Crown case and where protestations of innocence are likely disingenuous. It is quite another to permit counsel to act where a true innocent insists on pleading guilty and where the lawyer is being asked to advance facts she knows are false.[150] In short, the English and Welsh position is almost certainly not so extreme as it might appear at first blush.

---

145 *Herbert*, above note 144 at 232. This provision is set out in Proulx & Layton, above note 136 at 423. It was later replaced with the more detailed provision replicated in the text associated with note 53, above in this chapter. However, as explained at note 51, above in this chapter, this issue is not addressed at all in the ethical rules that came into force in 2014.

146 *Herbert*, above note 144 at 233–34.

147 The *Herbert* approach has drawn some criticism: see, for example, Mike McConville, "Plea Bargaining: Ethics and Politics" (1998) 25 JL & Soc'y 562 at 566–72. Yet the contrary view is that the true innocent will only rarely plead guilty, the more common situation being the guilty client who falsely protests innocence: see United Kingdom, *Royal Commission on Criminal Justice: Report* (London: HMSO, 1993) at 110–11.

148 Bar Standards Board, *Handbook*, above note 51, r C3(1).

149 *Herbert*, above note 144 at 231–32.

150 Accordingly, Bridges, above note 52 at 95–97, makes sensible suggestions as to when lawyers in England and Wales can or must refuse to act for a client who wants to plead guilty despite privately maintaining innocence.

5) The Position in the United States

In the United States, the leading case regarding the client who wishes to plead guilty but maintains innocence is *North Carolina v Alford*.[151] The defendant, Alford, had been charged with first-degree murder arising out of a shooting death and faced the possibility of execution if convicted after a trial. Under the law as it then stood, however, the maximum penalty was life imprisonment if the accused pleaded guilty. The prosecution case was strong, and the defendant pleaded guilty to second-degree murder, with the prosecutor's consent. The prosecutor called several witnesses on the plea hearing, all of whom provided evidence in support of Alford's guilt. Yet, when given an opportunity to speak before the court, Alford protested his innocence, stating that the plea was entered only to ensure that he did not receive the death penalty.

On appeal, the Supreme Court held that the plea was valid given that it represented a voluntary and intelligent choice among the alternative courses of action open to the defendant.[152] The Court went on to observe as follows:

> Here the State had a strong case of first-degree murder against Alford. Whether he realized or disbelieved his guilt, he insisted on his plea because in his view he had absolutely nothing to gain by a trial and much to gain by pleading. Because of the overwhelming evidence against him, a trial was precisely what neither Alford nor his attorney desired. Confronted with the choice between a trial for first-degree murder, on the one hand, and a plea of guilty to second-degree murder, on the other, Alford quite reasonably chose the latter and thereby limited the maximum penalty to a 30-year term. When his plea is viewed in light of the evidence against him, which substantially negated his claim of innocence and which further provided a means by which the judge could test whether the plea was intelligently entered, see *McCarthy v. United States, supra*, at 466–467 (1969), its validity cannot seriously be questioned. In view of the strong factual basis for the plea demonstrated by the State and Alford's clearly expressed desire to enter it despite his professed belief in his innocence, we hold that the trial judge did not commit constitutional error in accepting it.[153]

There are several points to be gleaned from *Alford*. Foremost is the Court's holding that a trial judge can enter a conviction after a guilty

---

151 400 US 25 (1970) [*Alford*].
152 *Ibid* at 31.
153 *Ibid* at 37–38.

plea despite an accused's open refusal to admit guilt provided there exists a strong factual basis in support of a conviction. The Court emphasized that the "strong factual basis" requirement serves to protect the innocent and ensure that guilty pleas are a product of a free and intelligent choice.[154] Yet the Court did not hold that an accused has a constitutional right to plead guilty while protesting innocence. To the contrary, it ruled that the federal government and any of the states can quite properly, by statute or otherwise, prohibit a conviction absent an admission of guilt by the accused.[155] In other words, a defendant does not have an affirmative right to have a plea accepted in the face of a refusal to admit culpability. Finally, the Court in *Alford* nowhere stated that counsel can properly represent an accused who wishes to base a guilty plea upon facts known by counsel to be untrue. There is thus a good argument that the ambit of an *Alford* guilty plea does not extend to permit a knowing deception of the court through the presentation of inaccurate facts.[156]

In the United States, use is also made of the *nolo contendere* plea. This plea, which is not available in Canada,[157] allows the court to enter a conviction based on the accused's assertion that she is not contesting the prosecution case. *Nolo contendere* is thus an implied admission of guilt for the limited purpose of the particular proceeding at hand. The plea is used in federal and a majority of state courts but may not be available in all circumstances.[158] The United States Supreme Court observed in *Alford* that implicit in the *nolo contendere* cases is a recognition that the Constitution does not bar imposition of a prison sentence for an accused who is unwilling to admit his guilt but who, faced with

---

154 *Ibid* at 38, n 10. Whether this requirement is met can be a matter of dispute, as exemplified by the West Memphis Three, who proclaimed their innocence for almost twenty years before entering *Alford* pleas in 2011: see John H Blume & Rebecca K Helm, "The Unexonerated: Factually Innocent Defendants Who Plead Guilty" (2014) Cornell Law Faculty Working Papers 113, online: http://scholarship.law.cornell.edu/clsops_papers/113, expressing discomfort with the use of the *Alford* plea because the defendants were likely innocent; Kaytee Vota, "The Truth behind *Echols v State*: How an Alford Guilty Plea Saved the West Memphis Three" (2012) 45 Loy LA L Rev 1003, arguing that the "strong factual basis" precondition for an *Alford* plea was not met.

155 Above note 151 at 38, n 11. Most state and federal courts permit *Alford* pleas in at least some circumstances: see Stephanos Bibas, "Harmonizing Substantive Criminal Law Values and Criminal Procedure: The Case of *Alford* and *Nolo Contendere* Pleas" (2003) 88 Corn L Rev 1361 at 1372, n 52 and 1375–76.

156 See Charles W Wolfram, *Modern Legal Ethics* (St Paul, MN: West, 1986) at 591.

157 See *RP*, above note 7 at para 38; *DMG*, above note 7 at para 43.

158 See Bibas, above note 155 at 1370–71.

"grim alternatives," is prepared to waive a trial and accept sentence.[159] The Court noted the similarities between the *nolo contendere* plea and the method of plea used in Alford's case and reasoned that given the acceptability of a conviction where the client does not admit guilt and merely chooses not to contest the prosecution case, the same should follow for a protestation of innocence.[160]

6) The True Innocent

Having stirred up the pot by canvassing various approaches to the problem of the accused who protests innocence yet wishes to plead guilty, we will now focus more specifically on the case of the accused who is, to counsel's knowledge, innocent.

Several justifications can be marshalled in favour of permitting counsel to act on a guilty plea for a true innocent,[161] assuming always that the decision to plead is freely made and that counsel has otherwise performed in a competent manner. To begin with, pleading guilty may undeniably further the client's best interests, in particular where the Crown case is solid and where contesting the charge will likely result in a longer time in jail. Allowing counsel to act on such a plea finds further support in the ethical obligation to carry out a client's instructions. True, counsel is assisting the client in misleading the court, but this action furthers the accused's constitutional right to choose freely whether or not to plead guilty. Plus, counsel will have done her best to convince the accused not to plead guilty and hence cannot be viewed as encouraging a misleading plea. Along similar lines, some lawyers may feel justified in taking part in the plea as long as the client, and not counsel, admits to the false facts, whereupon counsel will make no submissions that rely directly on the inaccuracies and will not submit that the accused has demonstrated remorse by virtue of the plea. Finally, it can be argued that forbidding a guilty plea by a true innocent will merely encourage clients to lie to counsel as the only means of securing the system's permission to plead guilty with the assistance of legal representation.

Yet there are strong reasons for prohibiting counsel from representing an innocent client on a guilty plea. First, a central purpose of the criminal justice system is to identify and denounce the offender. Permitting the true innocent to plead guilty subverts this purpose;

---

159 *Alford*, above note 151 at 36.
160 *Ibid* at 37.
161 See Josh Bowers, "Punishing the Innocent" (2008) 156 U Penn Law Rev 1117 at 1170–79.

makes a mockery of the associated objectives of rehabilitation, deterrence, and punishment; and undermines public confidence in the system. Second, a fundamental goal of the system is to ascertain the truth. This truth-seeking process is damaged whenever a court is persuaded to accept a guilty plea based on facts that are inaccurate. Third, the rules of professional conduct and caselaw clearly prohibit counsel from knowingly misleading the court and do not appear to allow for any exceptions. Fourth, although the accused has a right to decide how to conduct his defence, including complete freedom of choice regarding the plea to be entered, this right does not entitle the accused to counsel's assistance in knowingly misleading the court.[162] Fifth, there are other situations where the law limits the accused's freedom of choice to waive important constitutional protections, for instance, the right to be represented by counsel who is not labouring under a serious conflict of interest.[163] The accused does not have an absolute right to eschew the protections of a trial, nor does he have untrammelled licence to subvert the truth-finding function of the process. Rather, there are important societal interests that justify limiting the accused's freedoms.

Finally, our criminal justice system has expended a great deal of energy on, and suffered considerable anxiety over, the prospect of the wrongfully convicted, as illustrated by cases such as those involving Donald Marshall, Guy Paul Morin, David Milgaard, Thomas Sophonow, Greg Parsons, and the victims of Dr Charles Smith's unreliable expert testimony. Importantly, the ranks of the wrongfully convicted in Canada include those who have pleaded guilty.[164] Mislabelling an individual as guilty, when he is truly innocent, runs counter to the basic principles that drive the system and can be viewed as a miscarriage of justice that rewards hypocrisy and fosters cynicism. Our justice system includes the "well-established principle that it can never be in a defend-

---

162 The analogous argument has already been made regarding anticipated client perjury: see Chapter 7, Section F(4)(d).

163 See Chapter 6, Section O(2)(b).

164 See *Hanemaayer*, above note 19; *Kumar*, above note 19; *Barton*, above note 116; *R v Marshall*, 2005 QCCA 852; Sherrin, above note 132 at 3–7. In the American context, see Lucian Dervan, "Bargained Justice: Plea-Bargaining's Innocence Problem and the Brady Safety-Valve" [2012] Utah L Rev 51 at 82–86; Blume & Helm, above note 154. Sherrin and Blume & Helm, both *ibid*, concede the number of innocents who plead guilty is difficult to determine but nonetheless view the problem as serious. Contrast Oren Gazal-Ayal & Avishalom Tor, "The Innocence Effect" (2012) 62 Duke LJ 339, arguing that innocent individuals are much less likely than culpable ones to plead guilty because they are more optimistic about trial outcome and view a guilty plea as an unjust result.

ant's interest to be wrongly convicted."[165] Condoning the conviction of the innocent is a defeatist approach that excuses a less than dedicated effort from counsel to prevent a wrongful conviction and more generally undermines systemic reforms aimed at avoiding the unjust conviction of the innocent.[166]

7) A Proposed Solution

We endorse a practical, and admittedly contentious, resolution to the problem of the accused who maintains innocence yet wishes to plead guilty. For the reasons just given, we reject the argument that counsel can knowingly participate in a guilty plea involving a true innocent. To do so misleads the court and stretches the truth-finding function of the criminal justice system beyond the breaking point. But we take a different view where the accused maintains innocence in the face of a strong Crown case and where nothing about the plea involves counsel deliberately misleading the court. Such an accused may carefully and reasonably ponder the pros and the cons of a trial and in the end voluntarily and unequivocally decide to plead guilty. The risk of an unsuccessful trial falls on the client, not counsel, and the client should be permitted some latitude to enter a guilty plea.

Counsel should therefore be permitted to act on a guilty plea despite the client's protestations of innocence where the following preconditions are met:

1) Counsel must provide complete advice regarding all aspects of the plea based on a thorough review of the disclosure and any other appropriate preparation or investigation.
2) The client must understand that he should not plead guilty unless truly guilty but that the decision is for him to make, not counsel.
3) Counsel must ascertain why the client wishes to plead guilty despite denying the charge and determine whether any steps can be taken to enable the client to enter a plea of not guilty.
4) The client needs to be prepared to admit in court the facts sufficient to ground a conviction, for the purposes of the plea proceeding, even though he refuses to concede to counsel in private that the facts are true.
5) Counsel must be satisfied that there is a strong factual basis for the guilty plea, meaning that a reasonable jury would likely convict

---

165 See *R v Pietrangelo*, 2008 ONCA 449 at para 6, leave to appeal to SCC refused, [2008] SCCA 309.
166 See Sherrin, above note 132 at 15–16.

after considering the evidence led by the Crown and defence at a contested trial. To put it another way, counsel must be satisfied that acting on the plea would not create a substantial risk of a miscarriage of justice.[167]

6) The client must understand and accept that counsel's submissions on sentencing will be based on the facts admitted in court and that the conviction is unlikely to be overturned on appeal. The client must also be advised that counsel cannot suggest to the court that the guilty plea demonstrates remorse.[168]

7) The client's instructions must be informed, voluntary, and unequivocal.

8) Given that counsel is entering an ethical grey area, the instructions should be detailed, in writing, and signed by the client.

Even where these preconditions are met, counsel should not be forced to represent the client on such a plea but rather should be afforded a discretion whether to do so. The lawyer who decides not to act on the plea may as a result be discharged by the client but otherwise should seek leave of the court to withdraw from the case for ethical reasons.[169]

8) An Alternative: The *Nolo Contendere*–Like Plea Described in *R v RP*[170]

In *R v RP*,[171] the accused had pleaded not guilty in a multiple-complainant sexual assault case. After the first complainant finished testifying, the accused recognized that the Crown case was strong and while continuing to profess his innocence to counsel, believed that health prob-

---

167 This latter formulation is suggested by Bridges, above note 52 at 97 and 99–100. Compare *R v Popal*, [2007] OJ No 1755 at para 27 (SCJ): unethical to act on a guilty plea where the lawyer has objective proof demonstrating the client's innocence; Christopher Sherrin, "Defending a Pediatric Death Case: Problems and Solutions," Research Paper for the Inquiry into Pediatric Forensic Pathology in Ontario (Toronto: Government of Ontario, 2007) at 62–63, online: www.attorneygeneral.jus.gov.on.ca/inquiries/goudge/policy_research/pdf/Sherrin_Defending-a-Ped-Death-Case.pdf: counsel should not act on a guilty plea for an accused who "plausibly maintains factual innocence."

168 It is nonetheless permissible to mention other mitigating factors, including cost or time savings and sparing witnesses the inconvenience or even trauma of testifying: see *R v Randhawa*, 2007 BCCA 598 at para 7.

169 See Section S, below in this chapter.

170 The procedure described in this section is called "*nolo contendere*–like" in *RP*, above note 7 at para 89.

171 *Ibid.*

lems would prevent him from performing well in cross-examination if he took the stand to deny guilt. The accused did not want to continue with a contested trial and was very concerned about the prospect of a jail sentence. The following procedure was therefore adopted, at the instance of the defence but with the full agreement of the Crown:

1) The jury was dismissed, a mistrial declared, and the accused re-elected trial by judge alone. He pleaded not guilty to the charges.

2) The Crown filed a statement of facts that reflected the allegations made by the complainants who did not testify before the jury, based on their evidence at the preliminary inquiry.

3) Crown and defence counsel both invited the trial judge to make findings of guilt on all counts based on the testimony of the complainant who had testified and the statement of facts filed by the Crown. Defence counsel did not state that any of these facts were admitted by the accused or acknowledge their accuracy but rather indicated that they were not contested.

4) The court convicted the accused on all charges, and the matter was adjourned so that a pre-sentence report could be prepared.[172]

When the matter resumed six months later, the pre-sentence report indicated that the accused was denying guilt. The judge raised the possible effect of the accused's denials, but neither counsel suggested that the validity of the convictions was undermined as a result.[173]

The accused appealed, apparently because he was dissatisfied with his sentence,[174] and argued that his convictions must be overturned because the procedure employed amounted to a *nolo contendere* plea, which is not permitted under Canadian law. The Ontario Court of Appeal disagreed. Trial counsel was an experienced lawyer who had obtained detailed written instructions from the accused outlining exactly what was to happen and why. Counsel had enlisted another lawyer to review these instructions with the accused and to witness the accused's signature. Appended to the instructions had been the statement of facts to be put before the court by the Crown. Each page had been reviewed and initialled by the accused. He had also signed the last page of the document. Before the plea was entered, the proposed procedure had been reviewed with the court in the accused's presence. In these circumstances, the accused's participation in the procedure was

---

172 *Ibid* at paras 10–22. Regarding the propriety of an accused's permitting the Crown to prove portions of the prosecution case through a statement of facts, albeit in a different context, see also *R v Korski*. 2009 MBCA 37 at para 124.

173 *RP*, above note 7 at paras 23–25.

174 *Ibid* at paras 64 and 93.

unequivocal, informed, and voluntary. The procedure, though not expressly provided for in the *Criminal Code*, was not prohibited at law and neither caused unfairness nor created any concern about the reliability of the verdict. Accordingly, the appeal was dismissed, and the convictions upheld.[175]

It is worth comparing *RP* with the judgment of the Ontario Court of Appeal in *R v DMG*,[176] decided the year previous. In *DMG*, a very similar procedure had been employed to permit a conviction to be entered based on allegations read into the record by the Crown. As in *RP*, the Court of Appeal accepted that the procedure was not prohibited at law.[177] Yet its flawed execution led to the conviction being overturned. For one thing, and unlike in *RP*, defence counsel had made no submissions at all regarding the facts read into the record by the Crown. In particular, counsel had not stipulated that the court could rely on these facts or submitted that the court should use them to convict.[178] Moreover, and again in contrast to *RP*, there was nothing on the record to suggest that the accused had understood and approved of the process being adopted. Given that the not guilty plea had been structured to operate like a guilty plea, the court should have made inquiries to ensure that the accused appreciated the nature and effect of the procedure and was participating voluntarily.[179] Finally, whereas in *RP* the accused had been extensively counselled by his lawyer and independent counsel regarding the procedure to be employed and had signed detailed instructions, there was no indication trial counsel in *DMG* had properly explained the procedure to his client in advance of the hearing.[180] To the contrary, there was a serious concern that counsel in *DMG* had at the last minute pushed for the procedure to be adopted to accommodate his failure to properly prepare for a contested trial.[181]

Clearly, the decision in *DMG* does not foreclose the approach taken in *RP*. The *nolo contendere*–like mechanism used in both cases is thus properly available provided that the Crown is amenable and that the accused understands and accepts the nature and consequences of the

---

175 *Ibid* at paras 51–66.

176 *DMG*, above note 7.

177 *RP*, above note 7 at para 89; *DMG*, above note 7 at para 51. See also *R v Evans*, 2012 ONSC 5801 at para 33.

178 *DMG*, above note 7 at para 56; *RP*, above note 7 at paras 46, 55, and 63.

179 *DMG*, above note 7 at para 60; *RP*, above note 7 at paras 47, 55, 59–61, and 64. To similar effect, albeit on somewhat different facts, see *R v Loi*, 2013 ONSC 1202 at para 84.

180 *DMG*, above note 7 at paras 63–66 and 117; *RP*, above note 7 at paras 47, 55–58, and 62.

181 *DMG*, above note 7 at paras 80–82 and 112–19.

procedure.[182] *RP* provides an excellent template for how counsel can structure such a plea, while *DMG* provides a cautionary tale as to the pitfalls that can arise where a lawyer fails to take sufficient steps to ensure that the client truly wishes to proceed in such a manner.

Advice: It has been suggested that counsel who engages in the *nolo contendere*–like procedure should ensure that the client receives protections equivalent to those imposed by Canadian ethical codes in the context of plea resolution agreements.[183] Defence counsel in *RP* afforded his client such protections, and then some. His counterpart in *DMG* did not.

N. AGREED STATEMENTS OF FACT

Sometimes a client is fully willing to plead guilty and admit culpability yet insists on denying certain aggravating facts alleged by the Crown. In such cases, two ethical issues may arise. First, is counsel ethically limited in negotiating a plea agreement that accommodates the client's concerns? And second, can counsel proceed with the plea where the client persists in the denials and where the Crown refuses to soften its position?

Canadian ethical codes and law prohibit lawyers from knowingly attempting to deceive the tribunal by offering false evidence or misstating the facts.[184] Accordingly, in effecting a plea resolution before the court, both defence and Crown counsel are forbidden from participating knowingly in deceiving or otherwise misleading the tribunal. In particular, as stated in the Martin Committee Report, "it is inappropriate for counsel, in private discussions, to tailor the facts of an event for the purposes of achieving a plea or sentence that appears to counsel to be desirable. This is treating the Court with less than the full candour which counsel's professional obligations require, and may even be said

---

182 Reference to a similar procedure being employed can be found in *R v Sherret-Robinson*, 2009 ONCA 886 at para 3; *R v Ohenhen*, 2008 ONCA 838 at para 2. The same option was proposed in the first edition of this book: Proulx & Layton, above note 136 at 457–58.

183 This point is made in the disciplinary decision examining the conduct of trial counsel in *DMG*, above note 7: *Law Society of Upper Canada v Besant*, [2013] LSDD No 69 at para 134 [*Besant*]. However, *Besant* seems to view the *nolo contendere*–like procedure as always improper, no matter how executed, a conclusion contrary to the holding in the later-released *RP*, above note 7, and so arguably incorrect in law.

184 See the text and sources associated with note 126, above in this chapter.

to bear some considerable resemblance to manipulating the Court."[185] More recently, in *R v Nixon* the Supreme Court of Canada recognized that defence and Crown counsel both have an ethical obligation at guilty plea or sentencing proceedings not to mislead the court with respect to the circumstances surrounding the offence and the offender.[186]

Naturally, defence counsel must *know* that the facts are false before this prohibition can apply, yet the standard of knowledge cannot be set too low given counsel's special role as resolute advocate for the accused. Counsel should be fixed with knowledge that a particular fact is untrue only where she draws an irresistible conclusion of falsity from the available information, by which we mean a conclusion that not even a zealous but honest partisan could deny.[187]

Defence counsel will therefore usually be entitled to put forth an agreed statement of facts based on the client's assertions, even if at odds with the information contained in the Crown disclosure. We also see nothing wrong with counsel's convincing the Crown to exclude contentious aggravating facts as long as the language in the agreed statement is carefully crafted. For instance, the wording, as well as counsel's submissions, may speak of facts that the Crown is in a position to prove and that the parties have agreed will form the basis of the sentencing.[188] As recognized in *Nixon*, the sentencing judge is typically provided only the product of plea negotiations, not the complete array of circumstances and considerations underlying the final agreement.[189]

What if counsel is unable to convince the Crown to tone down the statement of facts to make it more agreeable to the client? In *R v Newman*,[190] a 1993 decision of the Ontario Court of Appeal, counsel represented a client on serious drug charges. After discussions with the Crown, a tentative plea agreement was reached. The Crown proposed a statement of facts to be used as the factual basis for the plea in court. While prepared to admit facts sufficient to found a conviction, the accused balked at several aggravating aspects of the Crown's proposal. Defence counsel's efforts to amend the agreed statement were in vain, but

---

185 Martin Committee Report, above note 4 at 325.
186 *Nixon*, above note 2 at para 53. See also *R v Beswick*, [1996] 1 Cr App R 427 at 430 (CA): court criticizes lawyers for agreeing to put inaccurate version of the facts before the sentencing judge.
187 See *Youvarajah*, above note 31 at para 61, citing the first edition of this text. This standard is elaborated on in Chapter 1, Section F(2), and also discussed in Chapter 7, Section F(1).
188 See Martin Committee Report, above note 4 at 323–27.
189 *Nixon*, above note 2 at para 53.
190 *Newman*, above note 22.

he ultimately concluded that the plea agreement was a good one for the accused and went ahead with the sentencing. He apparently did not tell the client what the consequences of going ahead might be, nor did he make any attempt to contest the facts by way of a *Gardiner* hearing.[191]

At the sentencing hearing, the agreed statement of facts was presented to the court, signed by counsel on behalf of his client "subject to comment." Defence counsel's subsequent submissions to the court took issue with some of the facts. The Crown interjected that the agreed statement contained facts that both sides admitted could be proven beyond a reasonable doubt under the test articulated in *R v Gardiner*. Defence counsel agreed with this submission and also accepted that the facts could be used by the court as the basis for a sentence.[192] The court accordingly sentenced the accused based on these facts, and an appeal was launched alleging denial of the right to the effective assistance of counsel.

The court in *Newman* dismissed the appeal, holding that defence counsel was competent and had provided sound judgment as to the overall benefits of pleading guilty in the circumstances. Regarding counsel's acceptance of the agreed statement of facts, the court noted that there was nothing to indicate that the appellant had not been fully aware of the contents of the statement and his counsel's lack of success in modifying it. Furthermore, the appellant had provided no fresh evidence to suggest that the disputed facts were untrue. The court concluded that "the appellant was simply trying to improve on his situation" when he had told his trial counsel that he would not agree to the disputed facts, and was employing the same strategy by challenging these facts on appeal.[193]

The court thus did not find a denial of the right to the effective assistance of counsel and did not question counsel's approach to the plea. From an ethical perspective, however, we are not so sanguine regarding counsel's actions. If a client is steadfastly unprepared to admit to facts insisted upon by the Crown as part of a proposed plea agreement, there are three options. First, the client can reject the agreement and go to trial if necessary. Second, the client can require that the Crown prove the contested facts on a *Gardiner* hearing, whether or not as part of a

---

191 See *Gardiner*, above note 6, holding that disputed aggravating facts must be proven by the Crown based on evidence and on a standard of proof beyond a reasonable doubt. This principle has since been included in ss 724(3)(a) and (e) of the *Criminal Code*, above note 34.

192 *Newman*, above note 22 at 399–400 [paras 9–12].

193 *Ibid* at 404 [para 26]. The analysis and result in *Newman* are discussed with approval in the somewhat similar case of *Eizenga*, above note 6 at paras 55–57.

plea agreement. Third, while stopping short of accepting the contested facts as true, the client can admit in court that the Crown is able to prove them on the criminal standard, and accept their use by the judge on sentencing.[194]

This third option is essentially the same as that adopted by defence counsel in *Newman*, but the client appears not to have been told about or to have agreed to its adoption. Counsel's conduct may not have caused the client any prejudice, but neither was he entirely forthcoming with the client. Indeed, counsel left the client with the incorrect perception that the aggravating facts would *not* be conceded during the plea. The ethical propriety of such a course of conduct is definitely open to question.

O. DUTY NOT TO MISLEAD THE CROWN DURING PLEA NEGOTIATIONS

Defence counsel's overriding obligation is to further the best interests of the client. Yet this obligation does not permit counsel to mislead the prosecutor during plea negotiations.[195] Most Canadian ethical codes state that counsel has an ethical obligation to act in good faith with all persons with whom she has dealings in the course of representing the client[196] and must not knowingly attempt to influence the course of justice by misstating the facts or law.[197] Lawyers are further prohibited from assisting or permitting the client to do anything counsel considers dishonest or dishonourable.[198] Several codes also provide that a lawyer must not knowingly misrepresent the client's position in litigation.[199]

The clearest articulation of the prohibition against lying to opposing counsel is found in an Alberta rule, which provides that "a lawyer

---

194 This approach is analogous to that described in Section M(8), above in this chapter.

195 Regarding the arguments for and against prohibiting lawyers from lying during settlement negotiations, see Stephen Pitel, "Counselling and Negotiation," in Alice Woolley et al, *Lawyers' Ethics and Professional Regulation*, 2d ed (Markham, ON: LexisNexis, 2012) 411 at 421–30.

196 Alta, Sask r 6.02(1); BC, Man, Ont, NS, NL r 7.2-1; NB ch 15, rule; CBA Code ch XVI, rule.

197 Alta r 4.01(2)(g); Sask r 4.01(2)(e); BC, Man, Ont, NS, NL r 5.1-2(e); NB ch 8, commentary 10(v); CBA Code ch IX, commentary 2(e).

198 Alta r 4.01(2)(d); Sask r 4.01(2)(b); BC, Man, Ont, NS, NL r 5.1-2(b); NB ch 8, commentary 10(ii); CBA Code ch IX, commentary 2(b).

199 Alta r 4.01(2)(r); Sask r 4.01(2)(l); BC, Man, Ont, NS, NL r 5.1-2(l).

must not lie to or mislead another lawyer."[200] The commentary to this rule elaborates:

> This rule expresses an obvious aspect of integrity and a fundamental principle. In no situation, including negotiation, is a lawyer entitled to deliberately mislead a colleague. When a lawyer (in response to a question, for example) is prevented by rules of confidentiality from actively disclosing the truth, a falsehood is not justified. The lawyer has other alternatives, such as declining to answer. If this approach would in itself be misleading, the lawyer must seek the client's consent to such disclosure of confidential information as is necessary to prevent the other lawyer from being misled. The concept of "misleading" includes creating a misconception through oral or written statements, other communications, actions or conduct, failure to act, or silence . . . .[201]

The Alberta provisions are somewhat similar to the prohibition in the ABA Defense Standards against defence counsel knowingly making false statements concerning the evidence in the course of plea discussions with the prosecutor[202] and reflect the tenor of the more general rules found in other Canadian ethical codes.[203] In our view defence counsel must therefore resist the temptation to play fast and loose with the truth in negotiating with the Crown, most especially regarding the facts surrounding the charged offence, those surrounding the client's circumstances, and the state of the law.[204] Misleading information, if discovered, may provide a legitimate basis for the Crown to renounce a plea agreement[205] or to take a position less favourable to the client where an agreement has yet to be reached. Dishonest dealing may also

---

200 Alta r 6.02(2).

201 Alta r 6.02(2) (commentary) [cross-reference omitted]. See also "Principles of Civility for Advocates" in The Advocates' Society, Institute for Civility & Professionalism, *Principles of Professionalism for Advocates/Principles of Civility for Advocates* (Toronto: The Advocates' Society, 2009) at 13, r 3, online: www.advocates.ca/assets/files/pdf/publications/principles-of-civility.pdf: "Counsel shall always be honest and truthful with opposing counsel."

202 ABA Defense Standard 4-6.2(c).

203 See the rules cited at notes 196–99, above in this chapter.

204 See ABA Model Rule 4.1 and Third Restatement § 98(1), both prohibiting counsel from knowingly making a false statement of material fact or law to a third party in the course of representing a client.

205 See *R v Obadia* (1998), 20 CR (5th) 162 at para 37 (Que CA); *R v MacDonald* (1990), 54 CCC (3d) 97 at 105 (Ont CA), leave to appeal to SCC refused, [1990] SCCA No 436.

expose counsel to disciplinary action[206] or, in a particularly serious case, lead to a criminal charge of attempting to obstruct justice. In any event, defence counsel suspected of taking unfair advantage of prosecutors will soon garner a bad reputation, to the detriment of all future clients.

While defence counsel is not permitted to mislead the Crown during plea discussions, this duty is subject to a number of caveats. First, in many instances counsel's bargaining strategy involves attempting to convince the prosecutor that the Crown will be unable to prove the offence or aggravating factors relevant to sentence. This strategy can be pursued even though counsel knows the facts in question are true. Second, counsel remains under a strict duty to maintain a client's confidences absent the client's consent to the contrary. This duty may preclude counsel from revealing relevant information to the Crown, although it can never justify lying.[207] Third, counsel is ethically barred from positing a particular fact as true only where he *knows* that particular fact to be false.[208] Fourth, bluffing about matters such as the client's "bottom line" in terms of accepting a plea deal or counsel's opinion as to the client's likelihood of success on factual or legal issues is arguably unproblematic because in the context of plea negotiating Crown counsel does not expect absolute truth regarding these topics.[209] Defence counsel who makes a habit of posturing regarding such matters or who takes positions that strain credulity in doing so will nonetheless soon find that prosecutors are quick to call her bluff.

P. WRITTEN INSTRUCTIONS

A few Canadian codes of professional conduct suggest or mandate that counsel obtain instructions in writing before commencing plea discussions or securing a plea agreement.[210] Most codes do not address

---

206 See *Law Society of Newfoundland and Labrador v Regular*, 2005 NLCA 71: counsel disciplined for misleading opposing counsel regarding a fact highly material to a shareholder dispute.

207 See Alta r 6.02(2) (commentary).

208 The standard of knowledge to be applied is discussed in the text associated with note 187, above in this chapter.

209 See, for example, ABA Model Rule 4.1, comment 2; American Bar Association, Standing Committee on Ethics and Professional Responsibility, Formal Opinion 06-439 "Lawyer's Obligation of Truthfulness When Representing a Client in Negotiation: Application to Caucused Mediation" (12 April 2006) at 6; Third Restatement § 98, comment "c," at 59–60; *Westcom TV Group Ltd v CanWest Global Broadcasting Inc* (1996), 26 BCLR (3d) 311 at para 18 (SC).

210 NB ch 8, r 15(a)(v) (mandated); CBA Code ch IX, commentary 13(d) (suggested).

this issue as part of the rule on plea discussions but elsewhere contain a general provision suggesting that counsel are expected to obtain or confirm all instructions in writing.[211] Some judges have also offered the opinion that prudent counsel will obtain written instructions regarding the plea.[212]

If time and other circumstances permit, there is certainly no downside to obtaining written instructions. The process will serve to remind both counsel and the accused of the gravity of the decision and provide counsel with a contemporaneous record of events in case the client later challenges the plea. If counsel prefers not to obtain written instructions, the next best thing is to promptly make a written record setting out the advice given and the client's instructions and to keep this record in the file. Counsel should also consider confirming the instructions in a letter to the client.

Where there is a disagreement between counsel and the accused regarding the plea or where the accused is experiencing significant difficulty in reaching a decision, the lawyer should always protect himself by making a written record of the advice given, the instructions received, and any other pertinent factors.[213]

Q. HONOURING PLEA AGREEMENTS

Absent exceptional circumstances, defence counsel is ethically bound to honour a resolution agreement made with the Crown. As observed by the Martin committee:

> [T]he duty of counsel to honour resolution agreements [is] simply a particular example of the duties of integrity and responsibility discussed in some detail at the outset of this Report. As such, honouring resolution agreements lies at the heart of counsel's professional obligations. Implicit support for the requirement that resolution agreements be honoured can be found in the decisions of the Ontario Court of Appeal in *R. v. Brown* (1972), 8 C.C.C. (2d) 227 and *R. v. Agozzino* (1970), 1 C.C.C. 380. Agreements reached following resolution agreements are also, in the Committee's view, in the nature of

---

211 Alta, Sask r 2.02(1) (commentary (e)); Man r 3.2-1, commentary 5(f); BC, NS, NL r 3.2-1, commentary 5(e).

212 See *IBB*, above note 38 at paras 38–39; *R v Valencia*, [2008] OJ No 3692 at para 27 (SCJ); *Conflitti*, above note 134; *R v Snow*, [2000] OJ No 2462 at para 16 (Ct J); *R v Alessandro*, [1997] OJ No 4859 at paras 64–66 and 90 (Ct J Prov Div).

213 See ABA Defense Standard 4-5.2(c).

undertakings. The Law Society of Upper Canada's Rules of Professional Conduct, Rule 10, Commentary 8, states that undertakings given in the course of litigation, "must be strictly and scrupulously carried out."[214]

In *Nixon*, the Supreme Court of Canada rejected the contention that a plea agreement can be enforced against the Crown as a contractual or lawyer's undertaking.[215] The Court nonetheless quoted the Martin Committee Report with approval to the effect that plea agreements can usefully be seen as analogous to or in the nature of undertakings and that honouring them is not only an "ethical imperative" but also a "practical necessity" given that such agreements are used to settle most contentious issues that come before the criminal courts.[216] The Court further observed that "the *binding effect* of plea agreements is a matter of utmost importance to the administration of justice."[217]

Importantly, the comments in *Nixon* and the Martin Committee Report were made as part of discussions focusing on the obligations of the Crown and so require qualification before being applied in the defence context.[218] In particular, although defence lawyers are ethically required to abide by plea agreements, this obligation is subject to the crucial proviso that where the client changes her mind before sentencing, there may be no choice but to abandon the agreement. To hold otherwise would effectively treat the plea agreement as an irrevocable waiver of the accused's constitutional right to plead not guilty, a proposition for which no caselaw exists in support.

Example 1: After obtaining clear instructions from her client, defence counsel finalizes a plea agreement with Crown counsel. On the morning the guilty plea is to be entered, the client informs counsel that he no longer wishes to abide by the agreement. Counsel may well be justified in advising the client to adhere to the agreement and in pointing out the pitfalls of not doing so. If, however, the client remains firm in his desire to renege on the agreement, counsel has no choice but to inform the Crown and cannot push ahead with the agreement against her client's wishes. Counsel may also be justified in applying to withdraw from the case whether because the client has rejected counsel's advice on an important matter or because counsel believes that her efficacy in

---

214 Martin Committee Report, above note 4 at 312–13.
215 *Nixon*, above note 2 at paras 44–49.
216 *Ibid* at para 46.
217 *Ibid* at para 47 [emphasis in original].
218 The circumstances under which Crown counsel can ethically repudiate a plea resolution agreement are discussed in Chapter 12, Section I(8).

arguing for a different sentence will be compromised as a result of having earlier agreed to the joint submission.[219]

Example 2: Counsel in British Columbia makes a plea agreement for a joint submission with a Saskatchewan prosecutor as a condition for having her client's drug charges waived to Vancouver for a guilty plea. At the sentencing, defence counsel advises the judge of the joint submission. But she submits that the sentence agreed on with the Crown, though well within the acceptable range in Saskatchewan, is at the high end of the range by British Columbia standards and that a lower sentence would be more appropriate in the circumstances. In making these submissions, counsel has improperly breached the agreement with the Crown.

Example 3: Appellant counsel is approached by a client who wishes to appeal the trial judge's acceptance of a joint submission. Caselaw holds that the client is permitted to resile from a joint submission on appeal,[220] and so we see nothing wrong with counsel's taking on the retainer. Yet counsel should probably not act on the appeal if he was counsel at trial. To do so would involve disputing a result counsel supported in the court below and so compromise his credibility as an advocate on appeal. It can also be argued that trial counsel must not agree to and support a joint submission at trial all the while intending to attack the sentencing result on appeal, because doing so amounts to misleading the Crown and court on a material point.[221]

R. DUTY TO THE PUBLIC INTEREST

Most Canadian ethical rules addressing defence counsel's role in negotiating and concluding plea agreements include a commentary stating that "the public interest in the proper administration of justice should not be sacrificed in the interest of expediency."[222] Defence counsel obviously has obligations in relation to the public interest in this context, as we have seen in discussing the problems that can arise where an accused

---

219 See *R v CNH* (2002), 170 CCC (3d) 253 at paras 8–10 (Ont CA) [*CNH*], where counsel applied to withdraw after the client changed his instructions during the sentencing hearing.

220 *CNH, ibid* at para 19. But see *R v Bui*, 2013 BCCA 168 at para 23. Query also whether, although an appeal is not foreclosed, the standard of review is more demanding: see *Marriott*, above note 40 at paras 47–55.

221 See Section O, above in this chapter.

222 See the commentaries cited at note 50, above in this chapter.

who is truly innocent wishes to plead guilty and the prohibition against counsel's misleading the Crown during plea negotiations.

Yet concerns about the public interest should not be taken to go much further in limiting defence counsel's conduct in this area. In particular, it is not part of defence counsel's duty to determine whether a proposed agreement is too lenient and for this reason to defer to the public interest by seeking a resolution less favourable to the accused. This sort of consideration is within the Crown's bailiwick,[223] and the judge's too once a plea agreement is presented to the court.[224]

S. WITHDRAWAL BECAUSE OF DISAGREEMENT WITH THE CLIENT

Where counsel and a client fundamentally disagree as to the proper plea to enter, we believe that counsel can withdraw from the case, in particular where no undue harm is caused to the client.[225] However, because the client has a constitutional right to choose how to plead, the lawyer should avoid withdrawing in all but the most serious cases of disagreement. And counsel must not blithely threaten withdrawal to bully the client into entering a particular plea. Such pressure unduly interferes with the client's freedom of choice and may lead to later re-criminations against the lawyer.

---

223 See, for example, Martin Committee Report, above note 4 at 300–5.
224 See Section D(4), above in this chapter.
225 See Chapter 3, Section C(4).

PHYSICAL EVIDENCE RELEVANT TO A CRIME

A. SETTING UP THE PROBLEM: *R v COFFIN* AND *R v MURRAY*

A classic ethics problem posed to law students and practitioners alike is the dilemma of the "smoking gun" or "bloody shirt."[1] What is the proper response when a client brings a gun to his lawyer, confesses to using the weapon to commit a murder, and asks for help in handling this piece of damning physical evidence? This problem sets up a potential clash between some of counsel's most sacrosanct responsibilities. On the one hand, counsel owes duties of loyalty and confidentiality to the client that militate against taking any action that might harm the client. Yet, at the same time, counsel bears an obligation to the administration of justice that prohibits actively interfering with the availability of physical evidence relevant to a crime and forbids any action that would serve to compromise its evidentiary value.

We can gain a greater appreciation of the interests at stake by looking at the concrete example of *R v Coffin*,[2] a case from Quebec that garnered much attention in the 1950s and 1960s. While not typically known as a "smoking gun" case, *Coffin* illustrates a lawyer's unfortunate involvement in concealing physical evidence of a crime. In 1954

---

1   For the story of the "bloody shirt," see Austin M Cooper, "Shirtless in Toronto" (2010) 29:3 Adv J 23.

2   (1956), 114 CCC 1 (SCC) [*Coffin*].

Coffin was convicted of murdering one of three American tourists who were shot to death while visiting the Gaspé for a hunting trip. Two years later, he became the last person to be hanged in the province of Quebec. Movies, television programs, and popular writings made the case a *cause célèbre*, and many people doubted Coffin's guilt.[3] Because of these doubts, a royal commission was established in 1963 to examine the investigation and prosecution of the case.

New evidence heard by the Coffin commission cleared up a mystery that had previously surrounded the disappearance of the suspected murder weapon and in so doing revealed actions by defence counsel that by today's standards were almost certainly unethical and illegal. At trial, the Crown contended that a man named Eagle had loaned a rifle to Coffin before the crime, and led evidence that this rifle could well have been used to kill one of the victims. The Crown also led evidence suggesting that Coffin had made arrangements to dispose of the rifle before the police search of his camp.[4] A police officer testified at trial that acting on "precise information," the nature of which he did not disclose and was not asked to reveal, he had searched unsuccessfully for the rifle in the vicinity of Coffin's camp.

The fate of the rifle was undoubtedly relevant to the issue of guilt. Yet the failure of the trial record to provide a satisfactory answer to this factual question, as well as the police officer's strange reference to "precise information" connecting Coffin to the rifle, helped to fuel arguments in favour of Coffin's possible innocence. The Coffin commission heard new evidence concerning the rifle. This evidence revealed that after his arrest Coffin had instructed a lawyer to get rid of the weapon. The lawyer, in the company of others, had located and disposed of the rifle according to his client's direction.[5] Needless to say, this startling new evidence, coming years after the trial and execution, shed light on Coffin's involvement and his counsel's conduct. Clearing up the mystery of the rifle helped alleviate concerns Coffin may have been innocent. The new evidence also explained why in cross-examining the police officer at trial defence counsel had neither pressed for disclosure of the source of the "precise information" nor attacked the officer's credibility on the point: counsel had known that the information provided to the

---

3   See, for example, Jacques Hébert, *I Accuse the Assassins of Coffin* (Montreal: Les Éditions du Jour, 1964); John Edward Belliveau, *The Coffin Murder Case* (Toronto: Kingswood House, 1956).

4   *Coffin*, above note 2 at 29–30.

5   See Quebec, *Rapport de la Commission d'enquête Brossard sur l'affaire Coffin*, vol 2 (Montreal: La Commission, 1964) at 300–8 [*Rapport sur l'affaire Coffin*].

officer was true.[6] However, the commission made no comment as to the propriety of counsel's actions in helping to move the rifle.

More recently, the sorts of ethical issues raised by *Coffin* were publicly aired in the notorious Ontario case of *R v Murray*.[7] The accused, Ken Murray, was a defence lawyer who in February 1993 was retained to defend Paul Bernardo against many serious sexual assault counts, as well as a charge of assault against Bernardo's estranged wife, Karla Homolka. Bernardo was also the prime police suspect in the murder of two teenage girls. The police conducted a seventy-one-day search of the home Bernardo had shared with Homolka. The search concluded on 4 April, after which Bernardo, who was in custody, directed Murray in writing to remove some items from the house that "alone may first appear to be irrelevant and thus overlooked but together can be very important" to the defence.[8] On 6 May Murray retrieved the items — six videotapes — from their hiding spot above a ceiling pot light. Bernardo instructed Murray not to view them for the time being. Murray complied and locked the tapes in his office safe without screening their contents.

On 14 May Homolka finalized an agreement with the Crown to plead guilty to two counts of manslaughter in the deaths of the teenage girls. There was to be a joint submission for a twelve-year sentence, and Homolka agreed to assist the Crown in prosecuting Bernardo for the homicides — her testimony would be crucial to obtaining convictions. On 18 May Bernardo was charged with two counts of first-degree murder in the girls' deaths. Murray was retained to conduct the defence and obtained Bernardo's instructions to view the videotapes. On doing so, Murray learned that the tapes depicted Bernardo and Homolka engaged in the gross sexual abuse of four female victims, including the two murdered girls. There can be no doubt that the Crown would not have made the plea agreement with Homolka had the tapes then been available as evidence.[9]

Murray retained the tapes for another sixteen months without disclosing their existence to the Crown. His ostensible purpose was to use the tapes to help negotiate a plea agreement or, alternatively, to spring them on Homolka, who claimed to be a forced participant as opposed to a willing abuser of the girls during cross-examination at trial.

---

6   *Ibid* at 362. The limits on cross-examining a witness who is known to be truthful are discussed in Chapter 1, Section K(1).

7   (2000), 144 CCC (3d) 289 (Ont SCJ) [*Murray*].

8   *Ibid* at para 7.

9   See *Report to the Attorney General of Ontario on Certain Matters relating to Karla Homolka*, by Hon Patrick T Galligan (Toronto: Attorney General of Ontario, 1996) at 216–17.

In July 1994 Bernardo instructed Murray not to use the tapes and instead to run a defence that denied any connection to the murder victims. A few days later, new Crown disclosure indicated that a DNA profile matching one of the victims had been found in a closet where Homolka asserted the girl had vomited during her ordeal. Murray felt that he had to withdraw from the case. Another lawyer, John Rosen, agreed to take over the defence provided the court granted an adjournment to permit him time to get up to speed on the file. Murray did not tell Rosen about the tapes and obtained written instructions from Bernardo forbidding their transfer to Rosen even if the latter ended up as counsel. Murray's main explanation to Rosen for having to give up the file was that he was ill-prepared and lacked the skill set needed to handle such a complex case.

On 1 September the trial judge refused to allow Murray to withdraw without bringing a formal application supported by an affidavit. Murray retained his own lawyer, Austin Cooper, and informed Cooper about the videotapes' existence. The next day, Cooper sought the law society's advice as to what Murray should do with the tapes. On 8 September an ad hoc three-bencher committee advised that Murray should deliver the tapes in a sealed packet to the court. Murray did so. The court provided the tapes to Rosen, who after conducting extensive research determined that they had to be delivered to the authorities. Rosen delivered the tapes to the police on 21 September. Bernardo eventually went to trial with Rosen as his counsel. The Crown led the tapes as part of its case and called Homolka as its star witness. Rosen relied on the tapes in cross-examining Homolka to attack her credibility, but Bernardo was convicted of both murder counts on 1 September 1995.

Following Bernardo's conviction, Murray was charged with attempting to obstruct justice for concealing the tapes. Although he was acquitted, Murray's conduct was subject to criticism by the trial judge, Gravely J. The judgment in *Murray*, which is discussed in detail in Section E(2), below in this chapter, amply demonstrates that a lawyer who is provided with an opportunity to handle physical evidence relevant to a crime frequently faces an ethical minefield.

Certainly, the proper response where defence counsel is confronted by physical evidence is not always obvious. One potentially difficult issue is whether counsel should accept possession in the first place. Another is whether once in counsel's possession the item can be retained for use at trial or, if unhelpful to the defence, returned to the original source, as opposed to promptly delivered to the authorities. There is also some disagreement as to the kinds of physical evidence to which special ethical obligations should attach, in particular whether they should extend to cover *all* relevant physical evidence as opposed only to so-called "fruits or instrumentalities" of a crime or non-documentary evidence. The first step in examining these and other questions is to ascertain what guidance is provided in the rules of professional conduct.

B. RELATED RULES OF PROFESSIONAL CONDUCT

Broadly speaking, the various Canadian codes of professional conduct take one of two approaches to the physical-evidence problem. The first, more traditional approach, is to provide little or no express guidance to lawyers. Emblematic in this regard is the CBA Code, which offers almost nothing in the way of useful advice. The closest this code comes to commenting directly on the issue is in the following portion of the chapter dealing with "The Lawyer as Advocate": "The lawyer must not, for example: . . . knowingly attempt to deceive or participate in the deception of a tribunal or influence the course of justice by . . . *suppressing what ought to be disclosed or otherwise assisting in any fraud, crime or illegal conduct*."[10] In *Murray*, Gravely J aptly commented that this rule "provides no guidance as to the nature of evidence that 'ought to be disclosed'. It is of small help either to counsel or to clients who may believe that both their secrets and their evidence are safe with their lawyers."[11] The provincial governing bodies in British Columbia, Ontario, and Quebec continue to follow the CBA Code's cryptic lead, at least for the moment, with identical or similar rules that leave practising lawyers in these provinces largely in the dark as to how best to respond when confronted with physical evidence.[12]

The second, more contemporary approach to the physical-evidence problem, is to adopt a rule of professional conduct that attempts to address the issue head-on. At the time of Ken Murray's trial, only the

---

10   CBA Code, ch IX, commentary 2(e) [emphasis added].

11   *Murray*, above note 7 at para 148, referring to former Ont r 10, commentary 2(e), which replicated the CBA Code rule and is retained in the current Ontario code as r 5.1-2 (e). For similar sentiments on the unsatisfactory nature of this provision, see David Layton, "Incriminating Physical Evidence, Ethical Codes and Source Return" [2002] The Professional Lawyer (Symposium Issue) 59 at 79 and 81–82; Angus MacDonald & Joel Pink, "Murder, Silence and Physical Evidence: The Dilemma of Client Confidentiality" (1997) 2 Can Crim L Rev 111 at 113; Kent Roach, "Ethics and Criminal Justice" (2003) 47 Crim LQ 121 at 122.

12   BC, Ont r 5.1-2(e); Que s 3.02.01(e).

Alberta ethical code could be said to take this approach. The current Alberta rule, the commentary to which was recently modified, states as follows:

> 4.01(9) A lawyer must not counsel or participate in: . . .
> (c) the destruction of property having potential evidentiary value or the alteration of property so as to affect its evidentiary value; or
> (d) the concealment of property having potential evidentiary value in a criminal proceeding.
>
> Commentary
>
> Lawyers must uphold the law and refrain from conduct that might weaken respect for the law or interfere with its fair administration. A lawyer must therefore seek to maintain the integrity of evidence and its availability through appropriate procedures to opposing parties.
>
> The word "property" in paragraphs (c) and (d) includes electronic information. . . .
>
> Paragraph (c) is not intended to interfere with the testing of evidence as contemplated by the Rules of Court.
>
> Paragraph (d) applies to criminal matters due to the danger of obstruction of justice if evidence in a criminal matter is withheld. While a lawyer has no obligation to disclose the mere existence of such evidence, it would be unethical to accept possession of it and then conceal or destroy it. The lawyer must therefore advise someone wishing to deliver potential evidence that, if possession is accepted by the lawyer, it will be necessary to turn the inculpatory evidence over to appropriate authorities (unless it consists of communications or documents that are privileged). When surrendering criminal evidence, however, a lawyer must protect confidentiality attaching to the circumstances in which the material was acquired, which may require that the lawyer act anonymously or through a third party.

The post-*Murray* modification of the Alberta rule's commentary occurred in 2011, the main import of which was to restrict the obligation to deliver physical evidence to the authorities to instances where the evidence is *inculpatory*.[13] The previous iteration of the commentary imposed this delivery obligation for all property having potential evidentiary value, whether inculpatory of the client or not.

---

13 Another material change was to define the term "property" to include electronic information.

In late 2000, in the aftermath of the *Murray* decision, the law society in Ontario struck a special committee of experienced defence lawyers and prosecutors and a retired judge to study the issue of handling physical evidence of a crime and to prepare a rule and commentary for inclusion in the ethical code. Seven members of the committee supported a rule under which lawyers would have leeway to retain physical evidence relevant to a crime in certain narrow circumstances and sometimes to return the evidence to its source.[14] A minority, composed of the two Crown counsel on the committee, preferred a rule modelled closely on the Alberta provision, as it then stood, requiring lawyers to deliver the property to the authorities in every instance, whether it incriminated the client or not.[15] Faced with this disagreement, and some public controversy over the proper approach,[16] in the spring of 2002 the benchers postponed addressing the issue so that the legality of the majority's proposal could be reviewed by outside counsel.[17] Over a decade has since passed, and the Ontario rule remains as it was when criticized by Gravely J in *Murray*.[18]

While Ontario awaits progress on this issue, since 2011 the law societies in Saskatchewan, Manitoba, Nova Scotia, and Newfoundland have adopted, beginning with Manitoba in 2011, the following physical-evidence commentaries from the pre-October 2014 version of the Federation of Law Societies of Canada (FLSC) *Model Code of Professional Conduct*:[19]

---

14 See *Special Committee on Lawyers' Duties with respect to Property Relevant to a Crime or Offence: Report to Convocation* (Toronto: Law Society of Upper Canada, 2002) appendix C [*Special Committee Report*]. The text of the recommended rule minus the commentary is set out in Layton, above note 11 at 86–87.

15 *Special Committee Report*, above note 14, appendix A.

16 Most notably, the Attorney General asserted in a letter to the law society that the majority's rule would condone the obstruction of justice and so was "nothing short of scandalous" and "intolerable and would only serve to bring the administration of justice into disrepute": see *Special Committee Report*, ibid, appendix B.

17 An overview of the history of the draft rule is provided in David Layton, "The Criminal Defence Lawyer's Role" (2004) 27 Dal LJ 379 at 387–89.

18 A similar attempt to draft a physical-evidence rule foundered soon after in Nova Scotia: see K MacDonald & C Robinson, "Physical Evidence of a Crime: Rule, Law or No Man's Land" *The Society Record* (February 2004) at 6, setting out the proposed rule and the arguments pro and con; Richard Devlin & Porter Heffernan, "The End(s) of Self-Regulation?" (2008) 45 Alta L Rev 169 at 172–73, chronicling its demise. Around the same time, the Canadian Bar Association decided against attempting to draft a physical-evidence rule for inclusion in a revised code: see "Controversial Criminal Law Rule Left Out of Amended CBA Ethics Code" *National* (May 2004) 57.

19 Federation of Law Societies of Canada, *Model Code of Professional Conduct* (Ottawa: FLSC, 2012) r 3.5-7 and commentaries 2–4 as they stood prior to 10 October 2014.

[2] A lawyer is never required to take or keep possession of property relevant to a crime or offence. If a lawyer comes into possession of property relevant to a crime, either from a client or another person, the lawyer must act in keeping with the lawyer's duty of loyalty and confidentiality to the client and the lawyer's duty to the administration of justice, which requires, at a minimum, that the lawyer not violate the law, improperly impede a police investigation, or otherwise obstruct the course of justice. Generally, a lawyer in such circumstances should, as soon as reasonably possible:

(a) turn over the property to the prosecution, either directly or anonymously;

(b) deposit the property with the trial judge in the relevant proceeding;

(c) deposit the property with the court to facilitate access by the prosecution or defence for testing or examination; or

(d) disclose the existence of the property to the prosecution and, if necessary, prepare to argue the issue of retaining the property.

[3] When a lawyer discloses or delivers to the Crown or law enforcement authorities property relevant to a crime or offence, the lawyer has a duty to protect the client's confidences, including the client's identity, and to preserve solicitor and client privilege. This may be accomplished by the lawyer retaining independent counsel, who is not informed of the identity of the client and who is instructed not to disclose the identity of the instructing lawyer, to disclose or deliver the property.

[4] If a lawyer delivers the property to the court under paragraph (c), he or she should do so in accordance with the protocol established for such purposes, which permits the lawyer to deliver the property to the court without formal application or investigation, ensures that the property is available to both the Crown and defence counsel for testing and examination upon motion to the court, and ensures that the fact that property was received from the defence counsel will not be the subject of comment or argument at trial.[20]

However, on 10 October 2014, the FLSC replaced these three commentaries with the following stand-alone physical-evidence rule and extensive commentaries:

---

20 Sask r 2.05(6) (commentary); NS, Man, NL r 3.5-7, commentaries 2–4.

5.1-2A A lawyer must not counsel or participate in the concealment, destruction or alteration of incriminating physical evidence or otherwise act so as to obstruct or attempt to obstruct the course of justice.

Commentary

[1] In this rule, "evidence" does not depend upon admissibility before a tribunal or upon the existence of criminal charges. It includes documents, electronic information, objects or substances relevant to a crime, criminal investigation or a criminal prosecution. It does not include documents or communications that are solicitor-client privileged or that the lawyer reasonably believes are otherwise available to the authorities.

[2] This rule does not apply where a lawyer is in possession of evidence tending to establish the innocence of a client, such as evidence relevant to an alibi. However, a lawyer must exercise prudent judgment in determining whether such evidence is wholly exculpatory, and therefore falls outside of the application of this rule. For example, if the evidence is both incriminating and exculpatory, improperly dealing with it may result in a breach of the rule and also expose a lawyer to criminal charges.

[3] A lawyer is never required to take or keep possession of incriminating physical evidence or to disclose its mere existence. Possession of illegal things could constitute an offense. A lawyer in possession of incriminating physical evidence should carefully consider his or her options. These options include, as soon as reasonably possible:

(a) delivering the evidence to law enforcement authorities or the prosecution, either directly or anonymously;

(b) delivering the evidence to the tribunal in the relevant proceeding, which may also include seeking the direction of the tribunal to facilitate access by the prosecution or defence for testing or examination; or

(c) disclosing the existence of the evidence to the prosecution and, if necessary, preparing to argue before a tribunal the appropriate uses, disposition or admissibility of it.

[4] A lawyer should balance the duty of loyalty and confidentiality owed to the client with the duties owed to the administration of justice. When a lawyer discloses or delivers incriminating physical evidence to law enforcement authorities or the prosecution, the lawyer has a duty to protect client confidentiality, including the client's identity, and to preserve solicitor-client privilege. This may be accomplished by the lawyer retaining independent counsel, who is not

informed of the identity of the client and who is instructed not to disclose the identity of the instructing lawyer, to disclose or deliver the evidence.

[5] A lawyer has no obligation to assist the authorities in gathering physical evidence of crime but cannot act or advise anyone to hinder an investigation or a prosecution. A lawyer who becomes aware of the existence of incriminating physical evidence or declines to take possession of it must not counsel or participate in its concealment, destruction or alteration.

[6] A lawyer may determine that non-destructive testing, examination or copying of documentary or electronic information is needed. A lawyer should ensure that there is no concealment, destruction or any alteration of the evidence and should exercise caution in this area. For example, opening or copying an electronic document may alter it. A lawyer who has decided to copy, test or examine evidence before delivery or disclosure should do so without delay.[21]

The law societies that adopted the former FLSC physical-evidence commentaries — Saskatchewan, Manitoba, Nova Scotia, and Newfoundland — will probably incorporate these replacement provisions into their codes over the next year or so. Less easy to predict is whether the law societies in British Columbia, Ontario, and Quebec will also adopt the new FLSC provisions, with or without modification, and whether the Law Society of Alberta will decide to swap its long-standing physical-evidence rule and commentaries for the now more comprehensive FLSC versions. Regardless, the FLSC's recent amendments continue the welcome trend of providing Canadian lawyers with better and more comprehensive guidance regarding the proper approach to take when confronted with physical evidence relevant to a crime.

Other examples of ethical rules that address whether or how to handle physical evidence can be seen in the United States. ABA Model Rule 3.4(a) is slightly reminiscent of the CBA Code provision set out above, stating "A lawyer shall not: (a) unlawfully obstruct another party's access to evidence or unlawfully alter, destroy or conceal a document or other material having potential evidentiary value. A lawyer shall not counsel or assist another person to do any such act." The comment to this rule, added in 2002, observes that the law applicable in the jurisdiction may allow counsel to temporarily take possession of physical evidence of client crimes to conduct a limited examination that will not alter or destroy material characteristics of the evidence, but notes

---

21 FLSC Code r 5.1-2A and commentaries 1–6.

that depending on the circumstances the law may also require that the lawyer thereafter turn the evidence over to the authorities.[22]

The American Law Institute's Third Restatement has adopted a slightly less cautious guideline, insofar as counsel is granted express licence to take possession of physical evidence of a client crime for the purpose of examination or testing. The relevant provision states the following:

> With respect to physical evidence of a client crime, a lawyer:
>
> (1) may, when reasonably necessary for purposes of the representation, take possession of the evidence and retain it for the time reasonably necessary to examine it and subject it to tests that do not alter or destroy material characteristics of the evidence; but
>
> (2) following possession under Subsection (1), the lawyer must notify prosecuting authorities of the lawyer's possession of the evidence or turn the evidence over to them.[23]

Notably, the Third Restatement mandates delivery to or notification of the authorities once examination or testing is complete. Simply retaining the evidence for use at trial is forbidden. Nor can the lawyer return the evidence to the site from which it was originally taken.[24]

Much more adventurous is ABA Defense Standard 4-4.6, which provides as follows:

(a) Defense counsel who receives a physical item under circumstances implicating a client in criminal conduct should disclose the location of or should deliver that item to law enforcement authorities only: (1) if required by law or court order, or (2) as provided in paragraph (d).

(b) Unless required to disclose, defense counsel should return the item to the source from whom defense counsel received it, except as provided in paragraph (c) and (d). In returning the item to the source, defense counsel should advise the source of the legal consequences pertaining to possession or destruction of the item. Defense counsel should also prepare a written record of these events for his or her file, but should not give the source a copy of such record.

---

22   ABA Rule 3.4(a), comment 2.
23   Third Restatement § 119.
24   *Ibid*, comment "c."

494 ETHICS AND CRIMINAL LAW

(c) Defense counsel may receive the item for a reasonable period of time during which defense counsel: (1) intends to return it to the owner; (2) reasonably fears that return of the item to the source will result in destruction of the item; (3) reasonably fears that return of the item to the source will result in physical harm to anyone; (4) intends to test, examine, inspect, or use the item in any way as part of defense counsel's representation of the client; or (5) cannot return it to the source. If defense counsel tests or examines the item, he or she should thereafter return it to the source unless there is reason to believe that the evidence might be altered or destroyed or used to harm another or return is otherwise impossible. If defense counsel retains the item, he or she should retain it in his or her law office in a manner that does not impede the lawful ability of law enforcement authorities to obtain the item.

(d) If the item received is contraband, i.e., an item possession of which is in and of itself a crime such as narcotics, defense counsel may suggest that the client destroy it where there is no pending case or investigation relating to this evidence and where such destruction is clearly not in violation of any criminal statute. If such destruction is not permitted by law or if in defense counsel's judgment he or she cannot retain the item, whether or not it is contraband, in a way that does not pose an unreasonable risk of physical harm to anyone, defense counsel should disclose the location of or should deliver the item to law enforcement authorities.

(e) If defense counsel discloses the location of or delivers the item to law enforcement authorities under paragraphs (a) or (d), or to a third party under paragraph (c)(1), he or she should do so in the way best designed to protect the client's interests.[25]

It is of particular interest that ABA Defense Standard 4-4.6 permits counsel to return the item to the originating source, keep it for examination, testing, or use at trial, or retain possession indefinitely where return to source is impossible or may result in destruction of the item or cause physical harm to a person. But, as noted in standard 4-4.6(a)(1), counsel must always disclose the item or its location to the authorities where required to do so by law.

---

25 Recently proposed revisions to this rule are assessed by Rodney J Uphoff, "The Physical Evidence Dilemma: Does ABA Standard 4-4.6 Offer Appropriate Guidance?" (2011) 62 Hastings LJ 1177 at 1217–26.

C. BASIC ETHICAL OBLIGATIONS: LOYALTY/CONFIDENTIALITY AND THE ADMINISTRATION OF JUSTICE

Determining the proper response to the physical-evidence problem requires an appreciation of several fundamental ethical obligations owed by lawyers to the client and the court. These obligations aid in navigating the complicated common law, statutory, and constitutional rules and principles that bear on the problem.

1) Loyalty and Confidentiality

The lawyer faced with the option of taking possession of physical evidence relevant to a crime owes certain duties to the client. Notably, the client is owed a duty of loyalty and the closely associated duty of confidentiality.[26] These obligations are fundamental to counsel's role in the criminal justice system, their purpose being, among other things, to encourage individuals to seek legal advice and to be candid with lawyers, which arguably results in the best possible legal representation and the most robust protection of a criminal client's constitutional rights. For this reason, the client's right to confidentiality has been afforded constitutional status in the context of solicitor-client privilege.[27] Taking any action that is against the client's interests with respect to the subject matter of the retainer or that serves to reveal confidential information against the client's wishes is *prima facie* unethical. Counsel who is faced with handling physical evidence relevant to a crime must therefore determine whether and how the obligations of loyalty and confidentiality are engaged.

2) Administration of Justice

While the lawyer's duties of loyalty and confidentiality are integral to providing a client with the best possible defence, they are not absolute and inviolable. As we have seen, the duties are sometimes tempered by

---

26   For a fuller discussion of confidentiality and loyalty, see Chapter 4. That these duties are engaged by the physical-evidence problem is expressly recognized by the six Canadian codes that directly address the issue: Alta r 4.01(9) (commentary); Sask r 2.05(6) (commentary); NS, Man, NL r 3.5-7, commentary 2; FLSC Code r 5.1-2A, commentary 4.

27   See Chapter 4, sections D and F.

important competing systemic or societal interests.[28] Thus, confidential information may be released to the authorities where necessary to prevent anticipated serious bodily harm, the justification being that the value of avoiding such harm outweighs the need for confidentiality.[29] Another policy concern that can operate to limit the duties of loyalty and confidentiality is the need to prevent subversion of the administration of justice. For example, counsel cannot act in a manner that violates the law.[30] And such a violation may occur if a lawyer impedes a police investigation.[31] The destruction or concealment of physical evidence thus engages the prohibition against breaking the law or otherwise undermining the proper administration of justice.[32] The question becomes, where is the line to be drawn between counsel's duty to the administration of justice and her duties to the client?

D. LACK OF A DEFENCE DISCLOSURE OBLIGATION AND THE PRINCIPLE AGAINST SELF-INCRIMINATION

An accused has no duty to disclose the nature of his defence, including the evidence to be relied on at trial, to the police or Crown.[33] As stated in *R v MBP*, "With respect to disclosure, the defence in Canada is under no legal obligation to co-operate with or to assist the Crown by announcing any special defence, such as an alibi, *or by producing documentary or physical evidence.*"[34] These words must always be kept in mind in ascertaining the proper resolution of any physical-evidence problem.

Granted, there exist some modest limits to the general rule against a defence disclosure obligation. Failure to make timely disclosure of an

---

28   See, for example, Chapter 5.

29   See Chapter 5, Section I.

30   See Chapter 2, Section B(1).

31   See Section E, below in this chapter.

32   This point is expressly recognized in those Canadian codes that address the physical-evidence issue: Alta 4.01(9) (commentary); Sask r 2.05(6) (commentary); NS, Man, NL r 3.5-7, commentary 2; FLSC Code r 5.1-2A and commentary 4.

33   See *R v Stinchcombe* (1991), 68 CCC (3d) 1 at 7 [para 13] (SCC) [*Stinchcombe*]; *R v MBP* (1994), 89 CCC (3d) 289 at 304–5 [para 38] (SCC) [*MBP*]; *R v RJS* (1995), 96 CCC (3d) 1 at para 88 (SCC) [*RJS*]; *R v Brown*, 2002 SCC 32 at para 82; *R v Peruta* (1992), 78 CCC (3d) 350 at 356 (Que CA), leave to appeal to SCC refused (1993), 81 CCC (3d) vi (SCC); *Murray*, above note 7 at para 102.

34   *MBP*, above note 33 at 304 [para 38] [emphasis added].

alibi may justify an adverse inference against the accused at trial,[35] as may an accused's refusal to be examined by a prosecution expert after raising a state of mind or mental disorder defence.[36] The revelation of some defence information may also be required by statute, for instance in relation to a notice of intention to adduce records or to lead expert evidence.[37] Yet these limited, ad hoc exceptions relate only to evidence called by the defence at trial. And they do not necessarily mandate disclosure, as opposed to affording trial remedies for the Crown if disclosure is not made.[38] Consequently, these exceptions do not detract in any significant way from the basic principle against defence disclosure.

The reasons often advanced for rejecting a defence disclosure obligation include the disparate resources of the Crown/police and the accused as well as the more purely adversarial role accorded the defence by our criminal justice system.[39] Related constitutional principles also support the absence of a defence disclosure obligation. The right to silence and presumption of innocence, both examples of the overarching principle against self-incrimination, are important *Charter of Rights and Freedoms* guarantees that allow an accused to choose not to reveal information to the police or Crown.[40] Indeed, the absence of a defence disclosure obligation has been identified as an example of the principle against self-incrimination in action.[41] In many instances, defence counsel who keeps a client's confidences secret and refuses to provide information to the police or prosecutor is therefore acting in furtherance of the client's constitutional rights.

E. RELEVANT *CRIMINAL CODE* PROVISIONS

One or more *Criminal Code* provisions may be contravened if counsel makes a wrong move in handling physical evidence of a crime. The

---

35   See *R v Cleghorn* (1995), 100 CCC (3d) 393 (SCC).

36   See *R v Stevenson* (1990), 58 CCC (3d) 464 (Ont CA); *R v Charlebois*, 2000 SCC 53.

37   See *Canada Evidence Act*, RSC 1985, c C-5, ss 26, 29, & 30 (public, banking, and business records); *Criminal Code*, RSC 1985, c C-46, s 657.3(1) (expert evidence).

38   See Michael Code, "Ethics and Criminal Law Practice" in Alice Woolley et al, *Lawyers' Ethics and Professional Regulation*, 2d ed (Markham, ON: LexisNexis, 2012) 435 at 470.

39   See *Stinchcombe*, above note 33 at 7 [para 11]; *MBP*, above note 33 at 304–5 [para 38].

40   *Canadian Charter of Rights and Freedoms*, Part I of the *Constitution Act, 1982*, being Schedule B to the *Canada Act 1982* (UK), 1982, c 11. Broadly speaking, the principle against self-incrimination prohibits forcing an individual to furnish evidence against herself in a proceeding in which the state and individual are adversaries: see *R v Jones* (1994), 89 CCC (3d) 353 at 366–68 [paras 25–32] (SCC).

41   See *RJS*, above note 33 at para 88.

overriding guiding principle must therefore be never to contravene the *Criminal Code*. Not surprisingly, in effect the Canadian ethical codes that currently address this area caution that in handling physical evidence relevant to a crime the lawyer must obey the law, and not act so as to obstruct justice.[42] If the criminal law is genuinely unsettled in a particular area, counsel should be circumspect and seek if at all possible to resolve the dilemma without putting himself at risk of prosecution.

Certainly, the *Criminal Code* provisions do not always provide clear-cut answers to the issues thrown up by the physical-evidence problem. For one thing, these provisions typically make no special mention of the role of defence counsel. Yet a lawyer who acts in the *legitimate* furtherance of a client's constitutional rights presumably cannot be prosecuted for breaking the criminal law. Thus, the lawyer who advises her client not to provide a statement to investigating officers or who destroys a privileged document has not obstructed justice. To a certain extent, courts must take account of ethical principles and practices as well as the accused's constitutional protections in interpreting *Criminal Code* provisions.[43] But, as made clear in the discussion below, conduct that is otherwise criminal is not excused merely because defence counsel was handling the physical evidence in the course of representing a client.

Finally, counsel must avoid becoming a dupe of the client who seeks to use counsel to facilitate the concealment of incriminating physical evidence. If a lawyer suspects that this is the client's real aim, correspondingly strong due diligence is required to ensure that all salient facts are as the client claims and that any contemplated course of conduct is legal.[44]

1) Possession and Trafficking of Property Obtained by Crime and Laundering the Proceeds of Crime

The *Criminal Code* prohibits the possession of property known to have been obtained by or derived directly or indirectly from the commission of an indictable offence.[45] It is also a criminal offence to traffic in such property, which means to sell, give, transfer, send, deliver, or deal

---

42   Sask r 2.05(6) (commentary); NS, Man, NL r 3.5-7, commentary 2; FLSC Code r 5.1-2A and commentaries 2 & 3; Alta r 4.01(9) (commentary).

43   Compare *Murray*, above note 7 at para 87: ethical duties may integrate with the issue of *mens rea* but do not translate into legal obligations.

44   See Chapter 2, Section B(1).

45   *Criminal Code*, above note 37, s 354.

with it in any way.[46] As for the offence of laundering proceeds, it occurs where a person deals with property with the intent to conceal or convert that property when it is known or believed that the property was obtained by or derived directly or indirectly from the commission of certain specified crimes.[47] The possession of property obtained by crime and laundering the proceeds of crime are not criminal, however, where a peace officer or a person acting under his direction takes steps for the purposes of an investigation or otherwise in the execution of the officer's duties.[48]

The offences of possession or trafficking of property obtained by crime and laundering proceeds contain no exception for lawyers who are acting in the course of representing a client.[49] Consequently, counsel is almost never justified in handling such property, the main exception being where it is accepted for the purpose of prompt turnover to the police.[50]

Unauthorized use of computers: The unauthorized use of a computer or electronic data may constitute an indictable criminal offence.[51] The possession of electronic files or hard copies obtained through the commission of such a crime thus constitutes the offence of possession of property obtained by crime. Lawyers must therefore never knowingly accept such items from a client, or anyone else for that matter.[52]

2) Obstructing Justice

It is a crime wilfully to attempt in any manner to obstruct, pervert, or defeat the course of justice.[53] The phrase "course of justice" includes, but is not restricted to, the investigatory phase of a matter, and no prosecution need yet have been commenced.[54] The offence encompasses an

---

46 *Ibid*, s 355.2.
47 *Ibid*, ss 462.3 and 462.31.
48 *Ibid*, ss 354(4) and 462.31(3).
49 Relevant to this point is *Federation of Law Societies of Canada v Canada (AG)*, 2013 BCCA 147 at para 151, leave to appeal to SCC granted, [2013] SCCA No 235 [*Federation of Law Societies of Canada*]: the criminal provisions dealing with money laundering do not distinguish between lawyers and other members of society in their application.
50 See Section E(4), below in this chapter.
51 *Criminal Code*, above note 37, s 342.1.
52 Subject, that is, to the exception mentioned in the text associated with note 50, above in this chapter.
53 *Criminal Code*, above note 37, ss 139(1) & (2).
54 See *R v Wijesinha* (1995), 100 CCC (3d) 410 at paras 27–34 (SCC), also holding that the offence can extend to disciplinary investigations carried out by a governing body.

attempted improper interference with the functioning of any part of the justice system.[55]

In *R v Murray*, the facts of which are set out above,[56] Gravely J held that Ken Murray's actions in concealing the videotapes *prima facie* tended to obstruct justice in several ways:

1) The tapes were secreted by Murray, putting them beyond the reach of the police, who had failed to locate them, hence tending to obstruct the police in their duty to investigate the murders.[57]

2) The Crown's ability to conduct its case was hampered throughout by the absence of the tapes, given that the tapes formed an integral part of the crime and were exceptionally detrimental to the defence. Examples of this negative impact on the prosecution included the Crown's resolution offer to Bernardo and the deal struck with Homolka.[58]

3) Concealing the tapes also influenced the way new defence counsel approached the conduct of the case.[59]

4) Finally, hiding the tapes had the potential to deprive the jury of admissible evidence.[60]

Justice Gravely concluded that the "[c]oncealment of the tapes had the potential to infect all aspects of the criminal justice system."[61] Plus, since the tapes were overwhelmingly incriminating, Murray had no legal justification for retaining them in his possession. Continuing to do so therefore satisfied the *actus reus* of tending to obstruct the course of justice.[62]

Murray was nonetheless acquitted because the Crown failed to prove beyond a reasonable doubt the specific intent necessary to ground a conviction, namely, that he had intended to obstruct justice.[63] In particular, Gravely J was unable to accept the Crown's submission

---

55   See *Murray*, above note 7 at para 105; *R v Beaudry*, 2007 SCC 5 at para 52 [*Beaudry*]; *R v May* (1984), 13 CCC (3d) 257 (Ont CA), leave to appeal to SCC refused, [1984] SCCA No 197; *R v Spezzano* (1977), 34 CCC (2d) 87 (Ont CA). *May*, above in this note at 260, speaks of "an act which has a tendency to pervert or obstruct the course of justice, and which is done for that purpose."

56   Section A, above in this chapter.

57   *Murray*, above note 7 at para 107.

58   *Ibid* at paras 108–9.

59   *Ibid* at para 110.

60   *Ibid.*

61   *Ibid* at para 111.

62   *Ibid* at paras 112–25.

63   *Ibid* at paras 100 and 126. See also *Beaudry*, above note 55 at para 52: obstructing justice is a specific intent offence.

that Murray had intended to suppress the tapes permanently.[64] Rather, Gravely J entertained a reasonable doubt that Murray had believed the tapes would support Bernardo's defence and intended to use them at trial and that Murray also had believed there was no legal duty to disclose them beforehand.[65] This reasonable doubt was bolstered in part by Gravely J's conclusion that at the time Murray had dealt with the tapes there was general uncertainty in the profession surrounding the legality of temporarily concealing evidence.[66]

Much of this uncertainty has dissipated by reason of the decision in *Murray* and the adoption of physical-evidence provisions by numerous law societies and the FLSC. There can be no doubt that counsel who suppresses or conceals incriminating physical evidence so as improperly to interfere with the functioning of the justice system commits an offence. Along the same lines, it is an offence even temporarily to remove evidence of a crime for the purpose of preventing seizure by the police.[67] So too is the act of destroying such evidence for this purpose.[68] But the legality of other types of conduct is less clear. In particular, can counsel properly examine or test physical evidence relevant to a crime to ascertain whether it might assist in making full answer and defence, or retain possession of wholly or predominantly exculpatory physical evidence until it can be used at trial? These challenging issues are discussed in sections I(9) and (10), below in this chapter.

3) Being an Accessory After the Fact

The crime of accessory after the fact is committed where an accused knows that a person was party to an offence and provides assistance for the purpose of enabling that person to escape justice.[69] Counsel

---

64   *Murray*, above note 7 at para 132.

65   *Ibid* at paras 139–55. See also *Beaudry*, above note 55 at para 52, suggesting that a good faith but misguided attempt to fulfill a legal duty does not meet the *mens rea* requirement for obstruction of justice.

66   *Murray*, above note 7 at paras 144–51.

67   See *R v Akrofi* (1997), 113 CCC (3d) 201 (Ont CA): pawnbroker obstructed justice by disposing of stolen property after being told not to do so by the police; *R v Lajoie* (1989), 47 CCC (3d) 380 (Que CA): hiding a gun from police obstructs justice; *R v Tschetter*, 2009 ABPC 125 at paras 121–27: hiding a vodka bottle after a car accident obstructs justice; *R v Nordman*, 2004 BCSC 1151: disposing of a knife used in a homicide obstructs justice.

68   See *R v Zeck* (1980), 53 CCC (2d) 551 (Ont CA): removing parking tickets from parked cars obstructs justice.

69   *Criminal Code*, above note 37, s 23. See also *ibid*, s 463. For authority that the word "escape" as found in the former provision should be read as "escape justice,"

therefore cannot deal with physical evidence in a manner intended to provide such assistance to the client. Conduct by non-lawyers that has been held to constitute the crime of accessory after the fact includes[70] cleaning up blood and hiding a weapon,[71] disposing of clothing worn or a vehicle used during a crime,[72] assisting in concealing a body,[73] and wiping blood from a murder weapon.[74]

Example: A client tells counsel that the gun used in an armed robbery and the proceeds are hidden in his safety deposit box. To avoid discovery of the items by police, the client asks counsel to take possession of the weapon and cash. Counsel must refuse. Helping the client for the purpose of avoiding detection would constitute the criminal offences of possession of property obtained by crime, trafficking property obtained by crime, laundering the proceeds of crime, obstruction of justice, and accessory after the fact.[75]

4) Illegal Items: Advice regarding Destruction and Possession for Purpose of Delivery to Police

Counsel should in almost all instances scrupulously avoid taking possession of contraband, that is, an item the mere possession of which is illegal, such as property obtained by crime, a controlled drug, a prohibited weapon, or child pornography. Counsel's possession of an illegal item is not any less criminal because she is a lawyer. It is for this reason that the FLSC Code warns lawyers that "[p]ossession of illegal things could constitute an offense."[76]

---

see *R v Vinette* (1974), 19 CCC (2d) 1 at 7 (SCC) [*Vinette*].

70   The following list of examples is partly taken from Casey Hill, "Accessory after the Fact" (Paper delivered at the Federation of Law Societies of Canada, National Criminal Law Program: Substantive Criminal Law, July 1993) at 7–8.
71   See *R v Knuff* (1980), 52 CCC (2d) 523 (Alta CA).
72   See *R v McVay* (1982), 66 CCC (2d) 512 (Ont CA); *R v Waterfield* (1974), 18 CCC (2d) 140 (Ont CA); *R v Jayawardena*, [2008] OJ No 3406 (SCJ).
73   *R v Steadman*, 2010 BCCA 382; *R v REW* (2006), 205 CCC (3d) 183 (Ont CA); *Vinette*, above note 69; *R v George* (1934), 63 CCC 225 (BCCA).
74   *R v Gratton* (1971), 5 CCC (2d) 150 (NB SCAD).
75   See *In re Ryder*, 381 F2d 713 (4th Cir 1967) [*Ryder*]: counsel was disciplined for moving stolen money and a gun from the client's safety deposit box to his own. See also *State ex rel Oklahoma Bar Ass'n v Harlton*, 669 P2d 774 (Okla 1983): counsel became an accessory by concealing a weapon with the aim of foiling an investigation of the client.
76   FLSC Code r 5.1-2A, commentary 3. The adverb "could" is no doubt employed in recognition of the "innocent-possession" defence discussed in the next paragraph of the main text.

There is, however, a well-developed line of appellate authority that precludes criminal liability where an individual, whether a lawyer or not, handles contraband for the sole purpose of immediately destroying it or otherwise permanently removing it from his control.[77] This "innocent-possession" defence will operate to permit a lawyer to take possession of contraband in order to pass it on promptly to the police.[78] The jurisprudence does not, however, suggest that a lawyer can avoid criminal liability simply because he takes possession of contraband for the purpose of making full answer and defence for a client at trial.

The innocent-possession defence appears to allow an individual to take possession for the purpose of promptly destroying the contraband.[79] Somewhat similarly, ABA Defense Standard 4-4.6(d) permits counsel to advise a client to destroy an illegal item provided there is no pending case or investigation relating to the evidence. Yet such action can be very risky — the mere fact that the client has come to the lawyer with the item suggests a real possibility that the police are investigating related matters.[80] At the very least, counsel must exercise due diligence to alleviate any suspicion that the police might be looking for the contraband before suggesting that a client destroy it.[81]

The safer and much-preferred course, however, is for counsel never to advise a client to destroy contraband and never to do it himself.[82] Rather, the client should be told that the continued possession of the item is a criminal offence, as will be its destruction if there is a related ongoing police investigation, in which case the only available legal option may be to deliver the item to the police, whether via counsel or otherwise.[83] The client can then decide what action to take.

---

77   See *PHS Community Services Society v Canada (AG)*, 2011 SCC 44 at para 96 [*PHS Community Services Society*]; *R v Chaulk*, 2007 ONCA 815 at paras 23–25 [*Chaulk*]; *R v York*, 2005 BCCA 74 at paras 13–20 [*York*].

78   The application of the defence where contraband is remitted to police is mentioned in *PHS Community Services Society*, above note 77 at para 96; *Chaulk*, above note 77 at para 24; *York*, above note 77 at para 13.

79   See the cases at note 77, above in this chapter, especially *Chaulk* at paras 23 and 25.

80   The Third Restatement § 119, reporter's note (comment "c"), thus looks askance at *ever* advising a client to destroy contraband. See also *United States v Russell*, 639 F Supp 2d 226 (D Conn 2007), discussed in detail in Gregory Sisk, "The Legal Ethics of Real Evidence: Of Child Pornography on the Choirmaster's Computer and Bloody Knives under the Stairs" (2014) 89 Wash L Rev 819, Part III: lawyer who acted for church was convicted for destroying a church employee's laptop containing child pornography.

81   See Chapter 2, Section B(1).

82   A rare instance where the destruction of contraband by counsel appears justified is discussed at the end of Section J(2), below in this chapter.

83   The method of delivery is discussed in Section K, below in this chapter.

5) Improper Advice Constituting a Criminal Offence

The wrong advice to a client can lead to criminal charges being laid against a defence lawyer, even where the lawyer never takes possession or control of the physical evidence.[84] Encouraging a client or third party to conceal or destroy incriminating items could make counsel a principal or party to an offence.[85]

F. SOLICITOR-CLIENT AND LITIGATION PRIVILEGES

Closely connected with the ethical duty of confidentiality is the substantive and evidentiary rule of solicitor-client privilege, which attaches to confidential communications passing between client and lawyer as part of the professional relationship.[86] Solicitor-client privilege has been accorded constitutional status by Canadian courts and is also integral to several discrete constitutional rights enjoyed by criminal clients, including the right to counsel, the principle against self-incrimination, and the right to make full answer and defence.[87] The criminal law and ethical rules that restrict a lawyer's handling of physical evidence therefore do not apply to items that are themselves solicitor-client privileged, such as an email sent from client to counsel for the purpose of obtaining legal advice.[88]

Given that the concept of confidentiality is central to solicitor-client privilege, the physical-evidence scenario usually requires that counsel assess whether the privilege applies. In making such an assessment, counsel must remember that the ethical duty of confidentiality is not coterminous with the rule of privilege.[89] The ethical obligation

---

84   See the *Criminal Code*, above note 37, ss 21 (aiding and abetting), 22 (counselling), 464 (counselling an offence that is not committed), and 465(1)(c) (conspiracy).
85   Such conduct is prohibited by FLSC Code r 5.1-2A and commentary 5. See also *Clark v State*, 261 SW2d 339 at 347 (Tex Crim App 1953) [*Clark*]: lawyer became an accessory by advising the client on how to dispose of a murder weapon; *R v Martin*, 2013 NBQB 322: lawyer was convicted of obstructing justice for advising the client's wife to hide incriminating items.
86   See Chapter 4, Section D.
87   See Chapter 4, Section F.
88   This point is expressly recognized in FLSC Code r 5.1-2A, commentary 1, and implicitly accepted in *Murray*, above note 7 at para 115. See also Section F(3), below in this chapter.
89   See Chapter 4, Section D.

is broader, applying to a great deal of information that would not be subject to privilege, such as disclosure materials provided by the prosecution to defence counsel.

1) Client-Lawyer Communications versus Pre-existing Physical Evidence

Solicitor-client privilege extends only to the protection of communications exchanged as part of the professional relationship, and not to pre-existing items that are passed on to counsel.[90] If it were otherwise, clients could employ counsel as a clearinghouse for pre-existing incriminating evidence, thereby insulating the evidence from use by the prosecution and providing a blanket justification for counsel's keeping the evidence. In *Murray*, Gravely J thus had no trouble concluding that the videotapes created by Paul Bernardo as part of his crimes did not attract the protection of privilege on entering lawyer Ken Murray's possession.[91]

Example: A religious community elder provides counselling services to the accused and two complainants regarding sexual assault allegations. On learning that the police are preparing a subpoena to obtain his counselling records, the elder consults an out-of-province lawyer. He then sends the records to the lawyer. The records are not subject to solicitor-client privilege, because they were created outside of the professional relationship. A search warrant executed on the lawyer's office thus cannot be resisted on the basis of the privilege.[92]

2) Communications and Observations concerning Pre-existing Physical Evidence

Statements made to a lawyer by a client while exhibiting or handing over physical evidence relevant to a crime will ordinarily be privileged, for they constitute confidential communications made for the purpose of obtaining legal advice.[93] Moreover, there is a strong argument that

---

90   See *British Columbia (Securities Commission) v Branch* (1995), 97 CCC (3d) 505 at para 43 (SCC) [*Branch*]; *R v Colvin* (1970), 1 CCC (2d) 8 at 13 [para 12] (Ont HCJ); *Keefer Laundry Ltd v Pellerin Milnor Corp*, 2006 BCSC 1180 at para 61; *United States of America v Berke*, 2013 BCSC 619 at paras 17–27; *Kilbreath v Saskatchewan (AG)*, 2004 SKQB 489 at paras 11–16 [*Kilbreath*].

91   *Murray*, above note 7 at para 115, cited with approval on this point in *R v National Post*, 2010 SCC 16 at para 65.

92   The facts and result are based on the decision in *Kilbreath*, above note 90.

93   See *Murray*, above note 7 at para 115.

a lawyer's *observations* of the physical evidence will also be covered by solicitor-client privilege. This is so because Canadian courts have been reluctant to draw a sharp distinction between an event occurring within the professional relationship and a client-lawyer communication in determining whether the privilege applies.[94] The jurisprudential focus has instead been on ascertaining whether affording the protection of privilege to the event will advance the policies that the privilege is designed to promote, which in the criminal context include the need to facilitate the client's exercise of her constitutional rights.[95] Where a lawyer's observations of a physical object are inextricably linked to the legal advice provided, they should therefore be treated as presumptively covered by solicitor-client privilege. This conclusion is supported by American caselaw directly on point,[96] but a close analogy can also be drawn to Canadian authority extending the privilege to a client's identity where such is closely connected to the nature of the retainer.[97]

Although a lawyer's observations of physical evidence relevant to a crime are likely covered by solicitor-client privilege where made in connection with the giving of legal advice, the object itself will not be privileged, as explained in Section F(1), above in this chapter. Furthermore, the lawyer's observations will not be privileged if unconnected to the giving of legal advice.[98]

Sometimes, instead of receiving physical evidence relevant to a crime, counsel obtains information from the client as to the location of such evidence. This information, though pertaining to evidence that

---

94   See *Maranda v Richer*, 2003 SCC 67 at paras 30–31 [*Maranda*]; *Federation of Law Societies of Canada*, above note 49 at para 72; *R v Li*, 2013 ONCA 81 at para 61, leave to appeal to SCC refused, [2013] SCCA No 142.

95   See *Maranda*, above note 94 at paras 28–29. See also Chapter 4, Section F.

96   See Layton, above note 11 at 83; *State ex rel Sowers v Olwell*, 394 P2d 681 at 685 (Wash 1964) [*Olwell*]; *People v Meredith*, 631 P2d 46 at 52–53 (Cal 1981) [*Meredith*]; *People v Investigation into a Certain Weapon*, 448 NYS 2d 950 at 954–55 (1982); *People v Nash*, 341 NW2d 439 (Mich 1983), aff'd 341 NW 2d 439 at 448 (1983) [*Nash*]; *Hitch v Pima County Superior Court*, 708 P2d 72 at 79 (Ariz 1985) [*Hitch*]; *Commonwealth v Stenhach*, 514 A2d 114 at 123 (Pa Super 1986), appeal denied 534 A2d 769 (1987) [*Stenhach*]; *State v Green*, 493 So 2d 1178 at 1184 (La 1986) [*Green*]; *Rubin v State*, 602 A2d 677 at 687–88 (Md 1992) [*Rubin*]; *Dean v Dean*, 607 So 2d 494 at 499 (Fla Dist Ct App 1992); *Sanford v State*, 21 SW3d 337 at 344 (Tex App El Paso 2000) [*Sanford*].

97   See Chapter 4, Section L. Further support lies in caselaw holding that the privilege *prima facie* extends to fee payments made in the criminal context, at least where information about the payments might harm the client's legal interests if disclosed: *Maranda*, above note 94 at paras 33–34; *R v Cunningham*, 2010 SCC 10 at paras 28–30.

98   See *Foster Wheeler Power Co v SIGED Inc*, 2004 SCC 18 at para 39.

is not in itself privileged, is provided to counsel as part and parcel of a communication made in the course of the professional relationship. Privilege therefore applies to the communication.[99] Solicitor-client privilege or litigation privilege will likely also cover any information obtained by counsel as a direct result of the client's communication. For example, in the famous case of *People v Belge*,[100] also known as the Lake Pleasant Bodies Case, a client charged with murder told his lawyers that he had killed other victims and divulged the location of the corpses. The lawyers went to the site and photographed the bodies but did not disclose this information to the authorities until their client's testimony at trial.[101] The lawyers faced public criticism for not divulging the information sooner, and one of them was charged with interfering with burial rights and failing to give notice of death without medical assistance. The charges were dismissed, however, on the grounds that the knowledge acquired by the lawyer from his client, as well as his observations at the burial site, fell within the attorney-client privilege.[102]

3) Items Created as Part of a Client-Lawyer Communication

Items created as part of a client-lawyer communication will usually be subject to solicitor-client privilege.[103] A common example would be a summary of pertinent events written by the client for use by a lawyer. As already noted, privileged items are not covered by the criminal and ethical rules restricting lawyers in their handling of physical evidence of a crime.[104]

4) Litigation Privilege

Litigation privilege encompasses communications that pass between the lawyer or client and third parties for the dominant purpose of existing

---

99 See, for example, *Sanford*, above note 96: defence counsel improperly breached privilege by revealing the location of physical evidence to the authorities.

100 372 NYS2d 798 (Co Ct 1975), aff'd 376 NYS2d 771 (App Div 1975), aff'd 359 NE2d 377 (1976) [*Belge*].

101 The accused revealed the information during his testimony-in-chief, in advancing an insanity defence.

102 See *Belge*, above note 100.

103 See *Branch*, above note 90 at para 43: privilege applies to documents created for the purpose of obtaining advice from a lawyer; *Murray*, above note 7 at para 115: privilege applies to a map or sketch prepared for counsel.

104 See the text associated with note 88, above in this chapter.

or anticipated litigation, as well as materials prepared by counsel or an agent for the dominant purpose of such litigation.[105] Corporeal items will often be covered by litigation privilege, such as a lawyer's note to file outlining strategy for the case or a videotaped witness statement prepared by a private investigator. Their disclosure cannot be compelled as long as the privilege persists.[106]

5) The Crime-Fraud and Other Exceptions to Solicitor-Client Privilege

Where a client asks counsel to handle physical evidence in a manner that would constitute a criminal offence, solicitor-client privilege does not apply.[107] This result is dictated by the crime-fraud exception to the privilege, which applies to communications that are in themselves criminal or are made with the purpose of obtaining legal advice to facilitate the commission of a crime.[108] However, the crime-fraud exception applies only if the client knew or should have known that the intended conduct was unlawful.[109] Thus, good-faith consultations with a lawyer for the purpose of finding out whether a proposed action is legal will not run afoul of the crime-fraud exception.

Other exceptions may also operate to render solicitor-client privilege inapplicable in the physical-evidence context. For instance, the public-safety exception might apply to displace the privilege where a client-lawyer communication — for instance, the client's stated intention to use the gun he is holding to kill a Crown witness — leads counsel reasonably to fear that disclosure is necessary to prevent death or serious bodily harm.[110]

G. TYPES OF PHYSICAL EVIDENCE COVERED BY THE ETHICAL RULES

The question sometimes arises as to precisely what types of physical evidence are subject to ethical or legal restrictions when handled by law-

---

105 See Chapter 4, Section D.
106 See Third Restatement § 119, comment "a."
107 See *State v Taylor*, 502 So 2d 537 at 539 (La 1987) [*Taylor*]: communications will fall within the crime-fraud exception if made with the aim of concealing a weapon from the authorities; *Clark*, above note 85 at 346–47 (same as *Taylor*).
108 See Chapter 5, Section K(1).
109 See *R v Campbell* (1999), 133 CCC (3d) 257 at paras 57–61 (SCC).
110 See Chapter 5, Section I(2).

yers. In this section, we will examine the wording of the ethical rules to ascertain the scope of the physical evidence they purport to cover. The focus will be on two questions. First, do the ethical rules cover only the handling of "fruits or instrumentalities" of crime? Second, do the rules exclude documents from their purview? A third, more controversial question — whether the ethical rules apply to physical evidence that is wholly or predominantly exculpatory — is discussed in Section I(10), below in this chapter.

1) Fruits or Instrumentalities of Crime

Some commentators argue that the rules pertaining to physical evidence, and most particularly the obligation to turn such evidence over to the authorities, should be restricted to the "fruits or instrumentalities" of a crime, that is, items used to commit an offence or obtained during the course of the crime.[111] However, none of the ethical codes that address the physical-evidence problem limits counsel's ethical obligations to fruits or instrumentalities,[112] and several leading American cases appear to eschew such a restriction.[113] Nor is there any principled reason for constraining counsel's obligations in this way.[114] Physical evidence that reveals a damning motive, connects the client to the victim in a material way, or constitutes inculpatory postoffence

---

111   See Gavin MacKenzie, *Lawyers and Ethics: Professional Responsibility and Discipline* (Toronto: Carswell, 1993) (loose-leaf 2012 supplement) § 7.3 at 7–12; Rachel Fogl, "Sex, Lies and Videotape: The Ambit of Solicitor-Client Privilege in Canadian Criminal Law as Illuminated in *R v. Murray*" (2001) 50 UNBLJ 187 at 200; Allan C Hutchinson, *Legal Ethics and Professional Responsibility*, 2d ed (Toronto: Irwin Law, 2006) at 166; Brian Gover & Luisa Ritacca, "Carrying Out Instructions" in Adam Dodek, *Canadian Legal Practice: A Guide for the 21st Century* (Markham, ON: LexisNexis, 2012) ch 9 at § 9.126.

112   See Alta r 4.01(9) & (commentary): obligation to turn over applies to "inculpatory" physical evidence; Sask r 2.05(6) (commentary); Man, NS, NL r 3.5-7, commentary 2: lawyers should generally turn over "property relevant to a crime"; BC, Ont r 5.1-2(e): lawyers should not "suppress what ought to be disclosed"; FLSC Code r 5.1-2A, commentary 1: rule applies to incriminating physical evidence not covered by solicitor-client privilege not otherwise available to the authorities; CBA Code ch IX, commentary 2(e); ABA Model Rule 3.4(a): lawyer should not conceal "material having potential evidentiary value"; Third Restatement § 119: obligation to turn over applies to evidence of "client crimes"; ABA Defense Standard 4-4.6: restrictions apply to any physical item received in "circumstances implicating a client in criminal conduct."

113   See, for example, *Morrell v State*, 575 P2d 1200 (Alaska 1978) [*Morrell*]; *State v Carlin*, 640 P2d 324 at 328 (Kan Ct App 1982) [*Carlin*].

114   See MacDonald & Pink, above note 11 at 124.

conduct is often *not* an instrument or product of a crime. Yet destroying or concealing such evidence to prevent its use by the prosecution is just as damaging to the administration of justice[115] and undoubtedly leaves counsel open to a charge of obstructing justice.[116]

2) Documentary Evidence

Pre-existing documents that constitute evidence of a crime should attract the same ethical and legal obligations as apply to any other kind of physical evidence. There is no reason to afford lawyers dispensation from their usual responsibilities simply because they are handling documents,[117] and neither the caselaw[118] nor the ethical rules[119] suggest otherwise. A document can be integrally related to the commission of a crime, for instance a cheque forged by the client to defraud his employer. Counsel who destroys or conceals such a document to prevent its use by the prosecution, or who advises a client to do so, has obstructed justice just as surely as if the same steps were taken with respect to a knife used in a robbery.

There *is* one very important regard, however, in which documents may be analytically different from other types of physical evidence relevant to a crime: they usually can be or have been copied. If counsel knows that an identical version of a client's document is available to police from other obvious and readily accessible sources, such as a complainant, bank, employer, Internet service provider, or the Canada

---

115 See Section C(2), above in this chapter.

116 See Section E(2), above in this chapter.

117 See Third Restatement § 119, comment "a"; Geoffrey Hazard, "Quis custodiet ipsos custodes?" (1986) 95 Yale LJ 1523 at 1532; Norman Lefstein, "Incriminating Physical Evidence, the Defense Attorney's Dilemma, and the Need for Rules" (1986) 64 NCL Rev 897 at 898 and 926; Ian D Scott, "Can Documents Smoke? The *R v Murray* Decision and Documents Characterized as Evidence of Crime" (2003) 47 Crim LQ 157 at 160–62 and 167–69.

118 Cases that extend restrictions regarding the handling of physical evidence relevant to a crime to documents include *Clutchette v Rushen*, 770 F2d 1469 at 1472–73 (9th Cir 1985) [*Clutchette*] (cleaning receipts); *Morrell*, above note 113 at 1210–11 (written plan); *State v Guthrie*, 631 NW2d 190 at 194 (SD 2001) (purported suicide note); *People v Sanchez*, 24 Cal App 4th 1012 at 1019–20 (1994) (personal writings revealing motive) [*Sanchez*].

119 See the rules referenced at note 112, above in this chapter, none of which excludes documents from its scope. Indeed, documents are expressly encompassed by the definition of physical evidence set out in FLSC Code r 5.1-2A, commentary 1. See also *Special Committee Report*, above note 14 at appendix C, Commentary C (rule said to cover all types of property including "original documents and documents that are electronically stored or formatted").

Revenue Agency, there is a good argument that she should be permitted to take and retain the document for a purpose legitimately related to preparing the client's defence.[120] The same argument applies with even greater force where the client makes a copy of a document for counsel's use and keeps the original, as explained in Section H, further below in this chapter. The reason that the usual restrictions imposed by the criminal law and ethical rules should not apply on these scenarios is simple: in neither instance is there any real risk that the authorities will be deprived of the document or that the administration of justice will otherwise suffer because of counsel's possession. Nonetheless, if possession of the document is itself illegal, a copy made for counsel will probably constitute property obtained by crime, and so neither the client's version nor a reproduction can be accepted by counsel.[121]

Example 1: A client is charged with sexual assault. He informs counsel that he has retained a number of emails on his computer sent to him by the complainant, which will show that the sex was consensual. The client provides printouts of the emails to counsel. These printouts should not be seen to fall within any criminal law or ethical prohibition against counsel's handling physical evidence relevant to a crime, because the same information is available to police from the complainant, the client's computer, and probably the complainant's and client's Internet service providers as well.[122]

Example 2: The facts in the previous example are changed so that the client has obtained the potentially exculpatory information through the unauthorized use of the complainant's computer and email password. In doing so, the client has committed the criminal offence of unauthorized use of a computer.[123] All printouts and any electronic copies of the emails will constitute property obtained by crime and so cannot be accepted by counsel.

---

120 FLSC Code r 5.1-2A, commentary 1, excludes from the ambit of the restrictions on handling incriminating physical evidence "documents . . . that the lawyer reasonably believes are otherwise available to the authorities." See also Scott, above note 117 at 172–73.

121 See Section I(3), below in this chapter.

122 Additionally, the printouts are likely privileged, having been created by the client for the purpose of obtaining legal advice: see Section H, below in this chapter.

123 *Criminal Code*, above note 37, s 342.1.

H. USING PHYSICAL EVIDENCE WITHOUT TAKING POSSESSION

The thorniest ethical problems in this area occur where a lawyer actually takes possession of physical evidence of a crime. Counsel who reasonably believes that an item may assist in making full answer and defence should therefore begin by ascertaining whether his representational duties can adequately be carried out *without* taking possession. For instance, as mentioned in Section G, above in this chapter, documents, whether hard-copy or electronic, as well as audio or video recordings, can be copied by the client, and the reproductions provided to counsel.[124] These copies will be covered by solicitor-client or litigation privilege and do not qualify as "evidence,"[125] and in any event their possession by the lawyer in no way jeopardizes the ability of the authorities to access the versions retained by the client.[126] The legal and ethical restrictions concerning the handling of physical evidence are therefore not engaged, provided the act of copying does not alter the item's evidentiary value.[127]

Another viable alternative to taking possession may be for counsel to view the physical evidence at the client's premises, or any other location where the property is normally kept. An example of counsel's viewing physical evidence *in situ* is found in the *Belge* case, discussed above,[128] where lawyers learned of the location of two of the client's murder victims and attended at the burial site to view and photograph the remains. Much less dramatically, where a client brings an item to a lawyer's office, the lawyer may be able to conduct an adequate examination without taking possession.

If counsel can examine the physical evidence without taking possession and determines it will be useful to the defence at trial, the original item can be brought to court by the client or whoever else has

---

124 Having the client make the copies avoids the need for counsel to take possession of the client's versions for the purpose of doing so. Yet there is a good argument that counsel should be permitted to take temporary possession to make copies: see Peter Brauti & Gena Argitis, "Possession of Evidence by Counsel: Ontario's Proposed Solution" (2003) 47 Crim LQ 211 at 217.

125 See sections F(3) & F(4), above in this chapter.

126 See Scott, above note 117 at 171–72; David Layton, "Handling Physical Evidence of a Crime: What's Happened since *Murray*" *The Verdict* (December 2005) at 16.

127 See FLSC Code r 5.1-2A, commentary 6. An analogous point is made in section I(4), below in this chapter.

128 Section F(2), above in this chapter.

possession at the appropriate time. The lawyer can take possession at the last minute for the purpose of using the item at trial.

The option of using or examining an item without taking possession will not always be available. The physical evidence may not be amenable to copying, or copying may create a material risk of altering its evidentiary value. Or a proper forensic examination may require that the lawyer take possession, as opposed to viewing the item *in situ*. Problems may also arise where possession by the lawyer is necessary to preserve the evidentiary integrity of the item. Finally, as explained in Section G, above in this chapter, a lawyer will also face difficulties — often insurmountable — where the physical evidence is contraband.

I. HANDLING PHYSICAL EVIDENCE RELEVANT TO A CRIME

While solicitor-client privilege rarely extends to physical evidence, it does not necessarily follow that counsel's ethical duty of confidentiality has no application.[129] It is indisputable, for instance, that the ethical duty prevents counsel from discussing the physical evidence with friends, family, or non-firm colleagues. Ordinarily, the same duty, along with the duty of loyalty, would prevent counsel from disclosing the evidence or information about it to the police or prosecution. But when the physical evidence is relevant to a crime, the duties counsel owes to the administration of justice may also be engaged. The question becomes, when do these latter duties preclude taking possession of the item? The answer depends on the facts of each case, including counsel's purpose and manner in handling the evidence, and the nature of the ethical rules operative in the jurisdiction.

In this section, we will review several situations where counsel is presented with an opportunity to handle physical evidence relevant to a crime, the aim being to determine whether taking possession is permitted under the legal and ethical rules. Some scenarios engender considerable debate. But many can be resolved fairly easily by applying the following guidelines:

1) Counsel should *never* voluntarily take possession of physical evidence relevant to a crime unless she reasonably believes there is a good justification for doing so.[130]

---

129 See Chapter 4, Section D.
130 As Uphoff, above note 25 at 1203, observes, in most of the American physical-evidence cases there was absolutely no strategic reason for counsel to take

2) In some cases, there will be disagreement as to what constitutes a good justification for taking possession. It is nonetheless clear that no such justification will exist where handling the item will neither help with the proper conduct of the defence nor advance an important public interest such as preventing the improper destruction of the item or protecting the public from physical harm.

3) Even where taking possession will further legitimate representational aims, counsel should always consider whether these same aims could be achieved in other ways, such as by using copies or viewing the item *in situ*, as explained in Section H, above in this chapter.

1) Prohibition against Possession for Purpose of Destruction

Lawyers are prohibited both ethically and legally from destroying physical evidence of a crime. As we have seen, such action constitutes a criminal offence and also violates the rules of professional conduct.[131]

2) Prohibition against Possession for Purpose of Concealment

Counsel cannot be a depository for incriminating physical evidence that the client seeks to hide from the authorities. Taking possession to impair the authorities' access in a pending investigation or criminal case is illegal and unethical.[132] Nor can counsel aid another to conceal such an item, not even where doing so does not involve taking possession.[133]

3) Counsel Should Usually (But Not Always) Refuse Possession of Contraband

As discussed earlier, a lawyer should usually refuse to handle physical evidence the possession of which is itself illegal.[134] There are, however, some exceptions. Counsel may have contraband foisted upon him.[135]

---

possession of the item.

131 See Section E, above in this chapter. See also *Olwell*, above note 96 at 685; *Stenhach*, above note 96 at 123.

132 See Section E, above in this chapter. See also *Murray*, above note 7 at para 123; *Olwell*, above note 96 at 685; *Stenhach*, above note 96 at 123.

133 See Section E(5), above in this chapter.

134 See Section E(4), above in this chapter.

135 Section I(6), below in this chapter

And it is proper to accept contraband to prevent physical harm to a person[136] or where the client wishes to have it delivered to the authorities.[137] In all these cases, counsel should almost always arrange prompt delivery of the evidence to the authorities in a manner that protects the client's identity from being disclosed.[138]

4) Prohibition against Interfering with Evidentiary Value

Counsel cannot handle physical evidence relevant to a crime so as to alter its evidentiary value, for instance, by wiping a client's DNA or fingerprints from the surface of a murder weapon. To do so is akin to destroying an aspect of the evidence.

Going further still, it has been argued that counsel should not act so as to deprive the prosecution of the opportunity to observe the evidence in its original location when to do so might impede the prosecution case. This position is examined in the well-known California case of *People v Meredith*.[139] There, the client had been charged with first-degree murder and robbery. He informed his initial counsel that the victim's wallet was in a trash can behind his home. This counsel retained a private investigator to find and retrieve the wallet, which was then examined and provided to the authorities. At trial, the prosecutor wanted to establish that the wallet had been found behind the defendant's home, a fact that would be highly damaging to the defence, and to this end called the private investigator as a witness.

The court in *Meredith* recognized that attorney-client privilege ordinarily covers observations made by a lawyer or the lawyer's agent in the course of investigating information provided by the client.[140] To hold otherwise would have the pernicious effect of inferentially revealing the initial communication between counsel and client. On the other hand, if such observations are always protected by privilege and if counsel is permitted to remove or alter the condition of physical evidence, the prosecution will effectively be barred from access to the item's full evidential import. Such a result might even encourage defence counsel to race the police to seize critical evidence.

---

136 See Section I(5), below in this chapter.

137 See Section I(8), below in this chapter.

138 See Section K, below in this chapter. Handling contraband for this limited purpose is permitted under the doctrine of innocent possession: see Section E(4), above in this chapter. For a rare case where destruction of contraband by counsel appears justified, see Section J(2), below in this chapter.

139 Above note 96.

140 *Ibid* at 51. See also Section F(2), above in this chapter.

Meredith resolved these conflicting policy concerns by holding that where a lawyer removes physical evidence, the client forfeits the protection of privilege regarding its original location or condition. The court also observed that counsel should not, as a general rule, remove evidence but recognized that in some instances examination or testing may be important to the competent preparation of the defence case.[141] Counsel who removes evidence for this purpose must therefore understand that in doing so an element of solicitor-client privilege is sacrificed and that she also risks becoming a witness.[142]

5) Possession Permitted to Prevent Serious Physical Harm

There is a well-recognized exception to the duty of confidentiality that applies where disclosure of otherwise confidential information is necessary to prevent serious future harm.[143] For the same reason that a lawyer's duties to the client may require modification where the spectre of future harm arises, counsel should be permitted to take possession of physical evidence relevant to a crime where he reasonably believes that not doing so will result in physical harm to a person.[144] Taking possession is justified even where the physical evidence is contraband, as in the case of a loaded restricted weapon.[145] Upon acquiring the item, counsel should promptly arrange to turn it over to the authorities.[146]

6) Possession Permitted Where Counsel Given No Choice

A lawyer cannot be faulted ethically or under the criminal law for possessing physical evidence relevant to a crime that is forced on her without any choice. To hold otherwise would be to ignore practical realities and impose an ethical responsibility for events that are truly beyond counsel's control.

---

141 *Ibid* at 53, n 7.
142 A possible solution is for the defence to stipulate the facts concerning the item's original location. The prohibition against counsel being a witness is discussed in Chapter 6, Section L.
143 See Chapter 5, Section I.
144 See ABA Defense Standard 4-4.6(c)(3); *Special Committee Report*, above note 14, appendix C, r 4.01(11)(b).
145 See Section I(3), above in this chapter.
146 See Section K, below in this chapter.

7) Possession Permitted to Prevent Destruction, Loss, or Alteration

Counsel should be allowed — but not required — to take possession of physical evidence relevant to a crime in order to prevent its reasonably anticipated destruction, loss, or alteration.[147] This approach encourages preservation of the item's evidentiary integrity and may also avoid any suggestion of counsel's complicity in an illegal act of destruction or concealment.

The lawyer who chooses not to take possession of physical evidence despite reasonably fearing that it will be destroyed, lost, or altered must *genuinely* advise the client or other source against taking any action that would contravene the law. A nudge or a wink designed to let the client know that the "advice" should be ignored is unprofessional and possibly criminal. Counsel should also document the advice, in writing signed by the client or other source if possible.

8) Possession Permitted Where Counsel Instructed to Deliver Evidence to the Authorities

Counsel is legally and ethically permitted to accept physical evidence relevant to a crime for the purpose of delivering it to the authorities, even where the evidence is contraband.[148] A very public example of a lawyer's doing so occurred in 2004 after thieves had stolen ivory statuettes worth $1.5 million from the Art Gallery of Ontario. Two weeks later, a lawyer turned the statuettes over to police but refused to reveal how they had come into his possession. In our view, the lawyer acted properly in taking possession of the statuettes for the purpose of having them returned to their rightful owner.

---

147 See ABA Defense Standard 4-4.6(c)(2); *Special Committee Report*, above note 14, appendix C, r 4.01(11)(a); Stephen Gillers, "Guns, Fruits, Drugs, and Documents: A Criminal Defense Lawyer's Responsibility for Real Evidence" (2011) 63 Stan L Rev 813 at 855–56.

148 This justification is implicitly accepted by Alta r 4.01(9) (commentary); Sask r 2.05 (commentary); Man, NS, NL 3.5-7, commentary 2; FLSC Code r 5.1-2A, commentary 3; and expressly recognized in *Special Committee Report*, above note 14, appendix C, r 4.01(11)(c).

9) Possession Should Be Permitted for Examination or Testing

On occasion, counsel may wish to examine physical evidence relevant to a crime, or perhaps have an expert conduct testing, based on a reasonable expectation that the item might be helpful to the defence case. The main argument against allowing possession for this purpose is that lawyers will enter into unseemly races with police to obtain evidence and end up as repositories for incriminating items.[149] Deprived of such evidence, the police and Crown will be unduly hampered in investigating and prosecuting crime. If examination or testing is required, so the argument goes, the better approach is for counsel to accept possession and then promptly deliver the item to the authorities or court. Suitable testing can be carried out by the Crown or if the Crown refuses to do so by the defence on application to the court. Or if the aim is not to test but rather to examine, defence counsel can do so as part of the *Stinchcombe* disclosure process once the item is in the possession or control of the Crown.[150]

Yet there are strong arguments going the other way. Permitting counsel to retain physical evidence for examination or testing where there is a reasonable possibility that doing so will assist the defence at trial furthers the client's constitutional right to make full answer and defence. Indeed, in such circumstances counsel arguably has a positive ethical duty to examine or test the evidence.[151] Examination or testing *after* counsel has turned the evidence over to the authorities or court is unsatisfactory because the ultimate determination may be that the evidence harms the client's cause. Forced turnover as a precondition to examination or testing will thus lead many counsel to decline possession altogether, at least where the usefulness of the evidence to the defence is not certain.[152] It may also discourage clients from seeking legal advice, making them more likely to keep the evidence and never show it to counsel.[153] Either way, the client's right to make full answer and defence suffers.

It is also important to remember that the client typically has no legal duty to disclose the physical evidence to the authorities while it

---

149 See, for example, Scott, above note 117 at 160.

150 See *Stinchcombe*, above note 33, and Chapter 12, Section G.

151 See *Re Olson*, 222 P3d 632 at 638 (Mont 2009) [*Olson*]; Lefstein, above note 117 at 931.

152 See Kent Roach, "Smoking Guns: Beyond the *Murray* Case" (2000) 43 Crim LQ 409 at 409; Layton, above note 11 at 90–91; Gillers, above note 147 at 852.

153 See Lefstein, above note 117 at 927.

remains in her possession.[154] Why, then, should this duty arise simply because a lawyer takes possession of the item for a purpose that lies at the very core of the defence function — to determine its utility to the defence? Such a result penalizes the client for bringing the item to counsel to obtain legal advice. But more than this, it undermines the principle against self-incrimination by making the obtainment of legal advice and the exercise of the right to full answer and defence contingent on disclosing the evidence to the authorities. Transfer to a lawyer for the purpose of exercising legitimate constitutional rights should not operate to create an automatic defence disclosure obligation.[155]

As for the contention that allowing a lawyer to take possession for examination or testing will lead to an unseemly race with the police for evidence, in the vast preponderance of cases the police will have completed their search of targeted people and places for physical evidence before counsel is retained.[156] And permitting a lawyer to take possession for examination or testing will not be tantamount to making him a repository for incriminating evidence. As elaborated on below, sensible limits placed on a lawyer's ability to accept items for this purpose can guard against such an outcome. The spectre of lawyers racing after and warehousing incriminating physical evidence is only convincing if one assumes that there will be no constraints on when and how examination and testing can be conducted. For some or all of these reasons, a number of American cases,[157] as well as commentators,[158] accept that counsel may on occasion legitimately take possession of physical evidence relevant to a crime for examination or testing. Several Canadian commentators agree.[159]

---

154 See Section D, above in this chapter.

155 See Layton, above note 11 at 90–91; Wayne Renke, "Real Evidence, Disclosure and the Plight of Counsel" (2003) 47 Crim LQ 175 at 199–200; Gillers, above note 147 at 829.

156 See Uphoff, above note 25 at 1208.

157 *Meredith*, *Olwell*, and *Stenhach*, all above note 96; *Ryder*, above note 75; *Clutchette*, above note 118; *Olson*, above note 151 at 638.

158 Gillers, above note 147 at 857; Uphoff, above note 25 at 1205–9; Sisk, above note 80, part IV(B)(1); Lefstein, above note 117 at 931–32; John Wesley Hall, Jr, *Professional Responsibility in Criminal Defense Practice* (St Paul, MN:Thomson/West, 2005) (loose-leaf September 2012 supplement) § 28:60 at 992, point 2 (albeit expressing discomfort with the notion of testing in note 8).

159 Roach, above note 152 at 409; Renke, above note 155 at 199–200; Austin Cooper, "The Ken Murray Case: Defence Counsel's Dilemma" (2003) 47 Crim LQ 141 at 154. The same view is implicitly taken by Code, above note 38 at 472–73, and by Alice Woolley, *Understanding Lawyers' Ethics in Canada* (Markham, ON: LexisNexis, 2011) at 140–41, who refers to Code's position with apparent approval. Others recognize the possible legitimacy of possession to examine or

The propriety of a lawyer's taking possession of physical evidence for examination or testing also finds some support in *R v Murray*. Justice Gravely held that Murray's retention of the videotapes *prima facie* tended to obstruct justice but that the *actus reus* of the offence could only be satisfied if he had no legal justification for doing so.[160] In discussing whether a legal justification existed, the judge noted, without adverse comment, that the ABA Defense Standards permit counsel to retain physical evidence of a crime for a reasonable time for examination and testing. Justice Gravely held that this justification did not apply to Murray, because he had never intended to test the tapes and kept possession of them long after his examination had been completed.[161] The judgment appears to conclude that only upon examining the tapes and discovering they were overwhelmingly incriminating could Murray be said to have lacked legal justification for keeping them, at which point his continued retention met the *actus reus* for obstructing justice.[162]

What do the ethical codes say? The ABA Defense Standards, referenced in *Murray*, allow counsel to retain physical evidence that implicates the client in a crime for a reasonable period of time where defense counsel "intends to test, examine, inspect, or use the item in any way as part of defense counsel's representation of the client."[163] Similarly, the Third Restatement permits a lawyer to retain physical evidence of a client crime for the time reasonably necessary to conduct examination or testing "where reasonably necessary for the purposes of the representation."[164]

In Alberta, the relevant ethical rule states that the prohibition against altering physical evidence so as to affect its evidentiary value "is not intended to interfere with the testing of evidence as contemplated by the Rules of the Court."[165] This appears to be a reference to

---

test but would thereafter require counsel to deliver the item to the authorities or inform them of counsel's possession: G Arthur Martin, "The Role and Responsibility of the Defence Advocate" (1970) 12 Crim LQ 376 at 392; MacDonald & Pink, above note 11 at 132; Brauti & Argitis, above note 124 at 218–22.

160   *Murray*, above note 7 at para 112.

161   *Ibid* at para 117.

162   *Ibid* at paras 124–25.

163   ABA Defense Standard 4-4.6(c)(4). This provision was relied on by the majority in *Olson*, above note 151 at 638, to condone counsel's removing physical evidence from a client's residence following execution of a search warrant.

164   Third Restatement § 119(1). However, unlike with ABA Defense Standard 4-4.6(c)(4), counsel must turn the item over to the authorities once the examination or testing is complete: Third Restatement § 119(2).

165   Alta r 4.01(9)(c) (commentary).

the process of testing exhibits by bringing an application under section 605 of the *Criminal Code*,[166] as opposed to testing conducted by the defence without the involvement or knowledge of the police or Crown. The Alberta rule further provides that counsel must deliver *inculpatory* physical evidence to the authorities.[167] Arguably, Alberta lawyers are therefore not prohibited from taking possession of physical evidence relevant to a crime for examination or testing, without notifying the authorities, provided they do not alter its evidentiary value and deliver the evidence to the authorities if examination or testing shows that it incriminates the client.

The ethical code commentaries currently operating in Saskatchewan, Manitoba, Nova Scotia, and Newfoundland provide several options for a lawyer who comes into possession of physical evidence relevant to a crime, one of which is to deposit the property with the court to facilitate access by the Crown or defence for examination or testing.[168] Yet these options are said to apply "generally," as opposed to constituting the entire universe of acceptable responses. Consequently, there appears to be room for lawyers in these provinces to take possession of physical evidence for examination or testing without first delivering the evidence to the authorities or the court.

A commentary to the FLSC Code rule introduced in October 2014 somewhat similarly states that a lawyer's options on coming into possession of incriminating physical evidence include delivering the evidence to the court to permit testing or examination.[169] But a subsequent commentary expressly envisions testing or examination by the lawyer provided care is taken to ensure the physical evidence is not thereby concealed, destroyed or altered.[170] This commentary adds that a lawyer who has decided to test or examine evidence before delivery or disclosure should do so without delay.[171]

Also of interest is the draft rule recommended by the majority of the Ontario law society's Special Committee on Lawyers' Duties with respect to Property Relevant to a Crime or Offence. Though never adopted, this rule would have allowed a lawyer to take possession of

---

166 Above note 37.

167 Alta r 4.01(9)(c) (commentary).

168 Sask r 2.05(6) (commentary); Man, NS, NL r 3.5-7, commentary 2.

169 FLSC Code r 5.1-2A, commentary 3(b).

170 FLSC Code r 5.1-2A, commentary 6.

171 See *ibid*. Whether these words import a duty always to deliver or disclose the evidence to the authorities after testing or examination is unclear, but such a reading is not unreasonable and would be in line with the approach taken by the Third Restatement, as described in note 164, above in this chapter.

property relevant to a crime for examination or testing provided three preconditions were met. First, the lawyer had to reasonably believe that examining or testing the item before disclosing it to the authorities was "in the interests of justice." Second, the examination or testing could not alter or destroy the essential characteristics of the item. And third, the lawyer had to obtain advance approval from a committee of the law society.[172]

The arguments in favour of allowing defence lawyers to retain physical evidence relevant to a crime for examination or testing are persuasive and find some support in the caselaw and various ethical codes. We therefore believe that counsel should be permitted to take possession for this purpose subject to the following conditions and guidelines:

1) Examination or testing must be reasonably necessary for the purposes of the client's proper representation, that is, to prepare the defence.[173]

2) A lawyer must never accede to a client's request to hold but not examine or wait to examine property that the lawyer suspects may be relevant to a crime.[174]

3) Counsel cannot accept contraband for examination or testing, not even where doing so would clearly benefit the defence.[175]

4) Counsel must not handle, examine, or test the item in a manner that alters or destroys its material characteristics.[176] Counsel should also keep careful records of the item's continuity.[177]

5) Counsel should retain the physical evidence only for the time reasonably necessary to complete the examination or testing[178] absent the emergence of another legitimate basis for keeping possession.

6) Counsel who removes physical evidence from its original location for a legitimate examination or testing purpose risks losing the protection of solicitor-client privilege, at least with respect to the

---

172 *Special Committee Report*, above note 14, appendix C, r 4.01(11)(d) and (12). It is not clear whether these provisions, read in conjunction with r 4.01(14)–(16), require turnover to the authorities after examination or testing is complete.

173 See Third Restatement § 119.

174 See Roach, above note 152 at 409.

175 See Section I(3), above in this chapter.

176 See Third Restatement § 119(1); FLSC Code r 5.1-2A, commentary 6.

177 See *Olson*, above note 151 at 634: items bagged, tagged, sealed as evidence, inventoried, and stored under lock and key in counsel's office.

178 See Third Restatement § 119; ABA Defense Standard 4-4.6(c)(4); FLSC Code r 5.1-2A, commentary 6.

facts surrounding the item's location and condition.[179] She additionally risks becoming a witness.[180]

7) Given the debate in this area regarding counsel's proper legal and ethical obligations, before or immediately on taking possession for examination or testing, counsel should obtain a supportive opinion from his governing body or, at the very least, an experienced and highly respected senior criminal law practitioner.[181] It is imperative that counsel make full and fair disclosure of all salient facts in seeking this option.[182]

8) The fact that examination or testing has occurred if properly conducted is covered by solicitor-client or litigation privilege,[183] and there is no general defence obligation to make disclosure of this information to the authorities.[184]

9) As in any ethically sensitive area, counsel should fully document all steps taken.

10) Possession of Wholly or Predominantly Exculpatory Evidence Should Be Permitted to Make Full Answer and Defence at Trial

In the preceding section, we argue that a lawyer should be permitted to examine or test physical evidence relevant to a crime to ascertain whether it may be helpful in making full answer and defence. If the lawyer concludes that the evidence will not assist in this regard, she must give up possession, a topic that is addressed in sections J and K, below in this chapter. But what if the lawyer determines that the evidence is wholly or predominantly exculpatory and wishes to use it to advance the defence at trial? Can the lawyer keep possession for this purpose? It is instructive to begin by examining what the various ethical rules say about the treatment of incriminating versus exculpatory physical evidence.

The rule in Alberta provides that a lawyer must not conceal "property having potential evidentiary value in a criminal proceeding,"[185]

---

179 See Section I(4), above in this chapter.

180 See *ibid*.

181 This precondition is similar to that stipulated in the *Special Committee Report*, above note 14, appendix C, r 4.01(12), and reflects the approach taken by Austin Cooper in *Murray*, above note 7 at para 70.

182 For an example of counsel's failing to do so, see *Murray*, above note 7 at paras 32–33.

183 See Section F, above in this chapter.

184 See Uphoff, above note 25 at 1221; Section D, above in this chapter.

185 Alta r 4.01(9)(d).

and the commentary adds that "evidence in a criminal matter" should not be concealed or destroyed.[186] No distinction is thus drawn between incriminating and exculpatory evidence when it comes to prohibiting concealment or destruction. The Alberta rule *used to* take the same approach with respect to its mandatory "turnover" obligation, the commentary stating that where a lawyer comes into possession of "potential evidence" in a criminal matter, "it will be necessary to turn the evidence over to the appropriate authorities."[187] However, the turnover obligation was amended in 2011 to state as follows: "it will be necessary to turn *inculpatory* evidence over to the appropriate authorities."[188] Consequently, lawyers in Alberta are not required to deliver *exculpatory* physical evidence to the police, Crown, or court.

The physical-evidence commentaries currently operating in Saskatchewan, Manitoba, Nova Scotia, and Newfoundland apply to "property relevant to a crime or offence."[189] Unlike the Alberta rule, they at no point draw a distinction between incriminating and non-incriminating property. However, these commentaries further differ from Alberta's in that they do not contain a mandatory turnover obligation. Instead, they provide that "generally" a lawyer possessing property relevant to a crime should as soon as reasonably possible deliver the property to the authorities or court or inform the authorities that it is in the lawyer's possession.[190] Turnover is clearly not required in every case, and there appears to be no reason why in deciding whether to do so lawyers in these provinces cannot legitimately consider whether or not the evidence exculpates the client.

The provisions adopted by the FLSC in October 2014 are yet again different. The basic rule states that the restriction against concealment, destruction, or alteration applies only to "incriminating physical evidence."[191] A commentary adds that the rule does not apply to evidence tending to establish a client's innocence, such as an alibi, but stresses that "a lawyer must exercise prudent judgment in determining whether such evidence is wholly exculpatory, and thus falls outside

---

186 Alta r 4.01(9)(d) (commentary).

187 The Law Society of Alberta, *Code of Professional Conduct* (Calgary: Law Society of Alberta, 1995) ch 10, r 20, commentary 20, set out in full in Michel Proulx & David Layton, *Ethics and Canadian Criminal Law* (Toronto: Irwin Law, 2001) at 485–86.

188 Alta r 4.01(9)(d) (commentary) [emphasis added].

189 Sask r 2.05(6) (commentary); Man, NS, NL r 3.5-7, commentary 2.

190 *Ibid.*

191 FLSC Code r 5.1-2A, commentary 2.

the rule."[192] The commentary goes on to caution that "if the evidence is both incriminating and exculpatory, improperly dealing with it may result in a breach of the rule and also expose the lawyer to criminal charges."[193]

In the United States, the approach taken by the Third Restatement is reminiscent of that in Alberta and under the new FLSC provisions insofar as a distinction is made between evidence of a *"client* crime" and non-incriminating physical evidence.[194] Only the former is subject to the rule that limits a lawyer to taking possession of physical evidence for the time reasonably necessary to conduct examination or testing, after which the evidence or its existence must be disclosed to the authorities.[195] Exculpatory evidence is therefore not captured by the Third Restatement rule. The same can be said for ABA Defense Standard 4-4.6, which applies only to evidence received by a lawyer "under circumstances implicating a *client* in criminal conduct."[196]

Several arguments support always prohibiting a lawyer from keeping possession of physical evidence relevant to a crime for use at trial, even where it is exculpatory, and instead requiring that the evidence or its existence be disclosed to the authorities. First, the police duty to investigate is not limited to searching for evidence that incriminates their prime suspect.[197] The criminal justice system has a need for *all* material evidence, of whatever type. Second, it can be difficult to determine whether evidence is inculpatory or exculpatory. In many instances, the same evidence may have uses for both the prosecution and the defence. In this vein, concern has been expressed that defence lawyers, by definition zealous advocates for their clients, are ill-suited to make the determination as to whether the evidence is truly exculpatory.[198] A rule encompassing all relevant evidence addresses these concerns and is easy to apply to boot.[199] Third, the police and Crown may make decisions materially impacting the course of the investigation and prosecution while the evidence is in defence counsel's possession, decisions that would have been different had they known about

---

192 *Ibid.*

193 *Ibid.*

194 Third Restatement § 119 [emphasis added].

195 *Ibid.*

196 ABA Defense Standard 4-4.6(a) [emphasis added].

197 See *Hill v Hamilton-Wentworth Regional Police Services Board*, 2007 SCC 41 at para 84; *Canadianoxy Chemical Ltd v Canada (AG)* (1999), 133 CCC (3d) 426 at para 24 (SCC).

198 See Scott, above note 117 at 165.

199 See Scott, *ibid* at 163–65; *Special Committee Report*, above note 14, appendix A at 22–23 (minority position).

the evidence.[200] This possibility exists regardless of whether, or how much, the evidence exculpates the accused. Finally, little or no prejudice will accrue to the client if exculpatory physical evidence is subject to a mandatory turnover obligation, because such evidence can only benefit the defence.[201]

On the other hand, defence counsel who retains exculpatory physical evidence for use at trial furthers the client's constitutional right to make full answer and defence. The arguments already made regarding the propriety of retaining items for examination or testing apply equally in this context but with even greater force because counsel has determined that the evidence is exculpatory.[202] So do the arguments based on the accused's constitutional right against having to disclose evidence to the Crown in advance of trial.[203] Moreover, the physical evidence is kept by counsel only until trial, at which point it will be used in court. The policy concerns related to the potential for negative impact on the administration of justice are consequentially less prominent, leaving the accused's constitutional rights to prevail. Worries about possible adverse affect on investigative or prosecutorial decisions while the evidence is in defence counsel's possession are mitigated by the fact that an inability to access exculpatory evidence is unlikely to cause the police or Crown to take action unduly favourable to the accused. As for concern about lack of oversight for defence counsel's determination that the evidence is exculpatory, the answer is to encourage or even require counsel to obtain a supportive opinion from the law society or an experienced and highly respected senior counsel.

It is true that exculpatory physical evidence may retain its full power to advance the defence position even where disclosed to the authorities before trial. If so, the client will usually instruct counsel to make immediate disclosure in an effort to have the charges withdrawn or stayed as soon as possible. Yet delivering exculpatory evidence to the authorities may materially risk diluting its impact when used by the defence at trial. This is especially so where the item contradicts a key Crown witness on a material point. Disclosing the item to the police or Crown may create a real risk that the witness will learn of its planned

---

200 See Brauti & Argitis, above note 124 at 219–20; *Special Committee Report*, above note 14, appendix A at 21–22 (minority position).

201 See Roach, above note 152 at 410; *Special Committee Report*, above note 14, appendix A at 23 (minority position).

202 See the paragraph associated with notes 151–53, above in this chapter.

203 See the paragraph associated with notes 154–55, above in this chapter.

use by the defence and adjust his trial testimony accordingly.[204] Losing the element of surprise can seriously detract from the probative force of such evidence in advancing the defence.

Tellingly, no judicial precedent in Canada or the United States suggests that counsel cannot accept and retain possession of *exculpatory* physical evidence for use in advancing the defence at trial. It has been argued that *Murray* holds that counsel cannot retain such evidence,[205] yet this reading of the case is unpersuasive. Justice Gravely held that the *actus reus* for obstructing justice is not satisfied merely because the police or Crown might have conducted the investigation or prosecution differently had they known about the physical evidence. Rather, the trier of fact must *also* find that defence counsel had no legal justification for taking possession of the evidence.[206] The defence argued that Ken Murray was legally justified in retaining the tapes because they had some exculpatory value and because he intended to use them to make full answer and defence at trial.[207] Justice Gravely rejected this argument, not because retaining an item to make full answer and defence can never constitute legal justification, but rather because the tapes were "overwhelmingly inculpatory."[208] The requirement that Murray give up possession — that is, the cessation of any legal justification for continued retention — crystallized once he discovered that the tapes were highly damaging to his client's defence.[209] Had the tapes been exculpatory rather than highly incriminating, Murray would have had legal justification to keep them for use at trial, and the *actus reus* of obstructing justice would not have been met.

Based on this reading of *Murray*, the policy arguments canvassed above, and the tendency of most ethical codes to exclude exculpatory evidence from the ambit of any turnover obligation,[210] we believe that lawyers should be permitted to retain wholly or predominantly exculpa-

---

204 See *Special Committee Report*, above note 14 at para 39(b); Gillers, above note 147 at 858–59. Regarding the propriety of Crown counsel's informing the witness of the physical evidence's existence, see Chapter 8, Section G(3)(j).

205 See *Special Committee Report*, above note 14 at 14, para 38, & 15, para 40 (minority position).

206 *Murray*, above note 7 at para 112.

207 *Ibid* at para 114.

208 *Ibid* at para 117. Similar comments are made at *ibid*, paras 109, 134(10), & 134(11).

209 *Ibid* at paras 124–25.

210 Or, in the case of the commentaries currently in use in Saskatchewan, Manitoba, Nova Scotia, and Newfoundland, to provide room for counsel to forgo the "general" turnover rule in relation to exculpatory physical evidence.

tory physical evidence for use in making full answer and defence at trial. However, before doing so counsel must

1) reasonably conclude that
   a) the evidence is wholly or predominantly exculpatory;
   b) the evidence is not contraband, such as a controlled substance or property obtained by crime;[211]
   c) turning the evidence over to the authorities will have a material negative impact on its usefulness to the defence at trial; and
   d) alternatives to retaining possession, such as copying the evidence or documenting it *in situ* or having the client keep the evidence until needed for court,[212] are unavailable or will have a material negative impact on the usefulness of the evidence to the defence at trial;
2) and immediately obtain a supportive opinion from her governing body or, at the very least, an experienced and highly respected senior criminal law practitioner.[213] This opinion must be based on a full disclosure of all material facts.

Our view, or one similar to it, is shared by several Canadian commentators.[214] Other Canadian writers take a position that while conceptually very different is mostly the same in effect: they would limit the mandatory turnover obligation to fruits or instrumentalities of a crime.[215] The effect would mostly be the same as under our approach because fruits or instrumentalities brought to counsel by a client will usually fail to meet our list of preconditions.

A compromise between keeping possession for use at trial and mandatory turnover would be for defence counsel to apply to the court

---

211 See Section I(3), above in this chapter.

212 See Section H, above in this chapter.

213 For a somewhat similar requirement, see *Special Committee Report*, above note 14, appendix C, r 4.01(12). Code, above note 38 at 472, recommends this step where the exculpatory uses of the evidence are not plain and obvious or are not clearly the predominant uses of the material.

214 Code, *ibid* at 472–73; Woolley, above note 159 at 140–41; Renke, above note 155 at 208–10. See also *Special Committee Report*, above note 14, appendix C, r 4.01(11)(e) and (12): retention is permitted where (1) the lawyer reasonably believes that a wrongful conviction may be prevented if the item is first disclosed at trial, (2) this use will be significantly diminished if the item is disclosed before trial, and (3) retention is authorized by a governing body committee. American commentators who take a similar view include Gillers, above note 147 at 858–59; Lefstein, above note 117 at 933; Uphoff, above note 25.

215 See the authors cited at note 117, above in this chapter.

for an order permitting retention of the item until trial.[216] Of some relevance in this regard, many Canadian ethical codes contain a rule stating that if a lawyer is unsure of the proper person to receive a client's property, he must apply to the court for directions.[217] Applying to the court has the benefit of ensuring independent oversight of counsel's decision and reduces the risk of counsel later being charged with a criminal offence.

It has been suggested that the court application be brought without notice,[218] which makes some sense given that the point of the exercise is to ascertain whether the physical evidence or its existence must be disclosed to the police or Crown. Others have argued that the benefits of judicial oversight require that the application be made with notice to the Crown of particulars sufficient to permit responding argument.[219] It is difficult, however, to imagine what those particulars would be, short of full disclosure as to the nature of the evidence and its relevance to the extant proceeding. The better approach might therefore be for the court to appoint an *amicus curiae* to assist it on the without notice application.[220] Or Crown counsel could receive full disclosure on an undertaking to keep it strictly confidential apart from use on the extant application, or at the very least not to share it with a particular witness, absent consent of the accused or leave of the court.

A different sort of compromise, arguably falling closer on the spectrum to mandatory turnover, would be for defence counsel simply to advise the Crown that she possesses physical evidence relevant to a crime and reasonably believes that retaining the evidence until trial is necessary to ensure that it can be used to full effect by the defence.[221] The Crown could respond by applying to the court for production of the evidence, or could do nothing. Presumably, on bringing an application, the Crown would seek full or near-full disclosure from the

---

216 A prime proponent of this approach is Roach, above note 11 at 122–23 and above note 152 at 410. See also Proulx & Layton, above note 187 at 515; Renke, above note 155 at 210.

217 Alta, Sask r 2.05(6); BC, Man, Ont, NS, NL r 3.5-7.

218 See Roach, above note 152 at 410; Proulx & Layton, above note 187 at 515. Compare *Olson*, above note 151: counsel obtained an *ex parte* order permitting him to handle contraband evidence for the purpose of advancing the defence.

219 See Renke, above note 155 at 210.

220 The proper role of an *amicus curiae* is addressed generally in *Ontario v Criminal Lawyers' Association of Ontario*, 2013 SCC 43.

221 This option finds support in *Murray*, above note 7 at para 124(c); Sask r 2.05(6); Man, NS, NL r 3.5-7, commentary 2(d); FLSC Code r 5.1-2A, commentary 3(c). It is discussed in some detail and promoted by Brauti & Argitis, above note 124 at 221–22.

defence so that the court could make its decision based on a complete record and argument. The result would likely be the same as if defence counsel simply brought an application with notice to the Crown.

J. RELINQUISHING POSSESSION OF PHYSICAL EVIDENCE RELEVANT TO A CRIME

Where counsel legitimately takes possession of physical evidence relevant to a crime, whether willingly or not, there will usually come a time when he can no longer keep the item. That is to say, excessive retention will constitute illegal and unethical concealment and cannot be countenanced. The question becomes, what options are available to counsel who must divest himself of the evidence?

1) Return to Client or Other Source

One possibility is to return the item to its source — usually, but not always, the client. This option can be controversial and is sometimes rejected in favour of a rule mandating prompt delivery to the authorities once any reasonable justification for possession has ended. One argument against permitting source return is that the source may respond by improperly hiding or destroying the item.[222] Another is that the only way to compensate for the possibility that the lawyer's possession has deprived the authorities of access to the evidence is to mandate disclosure once the possession ends.[223] A bright-line rule requiring turnover to the authorities in every instance also protects lawyers against allegations of misconduct.[224] Finally, privilege will often operate to prevent the Crown from linking the accused to physical evidence delivered by a lawyer,[225] which should minimize the harm caused to clients by adopting a mandatory turnover rule.

The argument against a mandatory turnover rule should be familiar by now, having been made in addressing the propriety of a lawyer's taking possession of physical evidence for examination or testing.[226] The

---

222 See Third Restatement § 119(1), comment "c."

223 This point is noted, though not endorsed in, Layton, above note 11 at 88.

224 See *ibid* at 88–89.

225 See Section F(2), above in this chapter, and Section K, below in this chapter.

226 See in particular the paragraphs associated with notes 151–55, above in this chapter.

same argument militates in favour of a limited source-return option. Its dominant components are the importance of facilitating the ability of clients to obtain legal advice and the need to protect other fundamental constitutional rights such as the principle against self-incrimination and the right to make full answer and defence.

Moreover, while in some cases there may be a realistic possibility that the lawyer's possession of physical evidence has deprived the police of items they might otherwise have located during the criminal investigation, this will often not be so, because the authorities' active search for evidence will have concluded by the time counsel is retained.[227] Allowing source return in carefully circumscribed cases is thus unlikely to make it any less probable that the evidence will see the light of day, while having the advantage of ensuring that the client receives proper legal advice as to the exercise of her constitutional rights.[228]

Finally, it is true that solicitor-client privilege may afford some clients considerable protection from harm to their legal interests caused by a mandatory turnover rule. But this will not be so where the item's probative value does not depend on proof that the lawyer received it from the client. Because the privilege does not apply to the item itself, the turnover option may supply the authorities with compelling incriminating evidence against the client.[229]

What do the ethical rules, cases, and commentators say about source return versus mandatory turnover? Most American cases prefer the latter over the former where the evidence is incriminating.[230] The Alberta ethical code is to the same effect, requiring mandatory turnover for inculpatory physical evidence.[231] Several Canadian commentators support mandatory turnover where the evidence is a fruit or instrumentality of crime.[232]

But other commentators advocate for source return in broader circumstances and would not mandate turnover simply because the item

---

227 See also the text associated with note 156, above in this chapter.
228 See Lefstein, above note 117 at 929; Layton, above note 11 at 91.
229 See Layton, *ibid* at 89.
230 Leading cases include *Olwell*, above note 96 at 684–85; *Morrell*, above note 113 at 1210; *People v Lee*, 3 Cal App 3d 514 at 526 (1970). See also *Rubin*, above note 96 at 686–87; *Green*, above note 96 at 1182; *Sanchez*, above note 118 at 1019–20; *Carlin*, above note 113 at 328; *Nash*, above note 96 at 314; *Taylor*, above note 107 at 539; *Clutchette*, above note 118 at para 23. Cases condoning source return albeit in *obiter* include *Hitch*, above note 96 at 78; *Stenhach*, above note 96 at 123.
231 Alta r 4.01(9)(d) (commentary).
232 See the authors cited at note 111, above in this chapter. MacDonald & Pink, above note 11 at 130–31, support mandatory turnover for fruits or instrumentalities *plus* any other physical evidence that incriminates the client.

is incriminating or a fruit or instrumentality.[233] Moreover, the physical-evidence commentaries currently in use in Saskatchewan, Manitoba, Nova Scotia, and Newfoundland state only that a lawyer who comes into possession of physical evidence relevant to a crime should "generally" turn it over to the authorities.[234] These codes do not, therefore, contain a blanket prohibition on lawyers' returning evidence to its source.

The FLSC rule and commentaries adopted in October 2014 appear even more open to the possibility of source return. As in the just-mentioned provinces, the only options expressly noted for a lawyer in possession of incriminating physical evidence involve prompt turnover to the authorities.[235] But nothing is said to suggest that turnover is the mandated, preferred, or even usual choice, and the wording in the relevant commentary clearly allows the lawyer to explore other options provided they are "carefully considered," presumably meaning that they do not involve breaching the law or participating in the concealment, destruction, or alteration of the evidence.[236]

The rule proposed by the majority of the Ontario law society's Special Committee on Lawyers' Duties with respect to Property Relevant to a Crime or Offence, had it been adopted, would have permitted a lawyer to return physical evidence relevant to a crime to its source provided the lawyer was satisfied on reasonable grounds that the evidence would not be altered, concealed, lost, destroyed, or used to cause physical harm to any person.[237] A minority of the committee took the polar opposite view, arguing for a mandatory turnover obligation for all such evidence in all cases, regardless of whether it was incriminatory or a fruit or instrumentality.[238]

The disagreement as to whether source return should ever be permitted is also reflected in the leading American ethical codes. The Third Restatement endorses a mandatory turnover rule for physical evidence of a client crime, although as we have seen it allows lawyers to retain temporary possession for a period reasonably necessary to permit examination or testing.[239] In sharp contrast, ABA Defense Standard

---

233 See, for example, Renke, above note 155 at 200–2. American commentators who favour source return include Lefstein, above note 117 at 928–29 and 937–38; Uphoff, above note 25 at 1198–203; Gillers, above note 147 at 857; Sisk, above note 80, part IV(B)(2); Hall Jr, above note 158, § 28:60 at 992, point 4.

234 Sask r 2.05(6) (commentary); Man, NS, NL r 3.5-7, commentary 2.

235 FLSC Code r 5.1-2A, commentaries 3(a)–(c).

236 *Ibid.*

237 *Special Committee Report*, above note 14, appendix C, r 4.01(15).

238 *Special Committee Report*, *ibid*, appendix A.

239 Third Restatement § 119.

4-4.6, triggered when counsel receives physical evidence in circumstances implicating the client in a crime, endorses source return as the default option, precluded only where contraband is involved, return to the source would cause physical harm to a person, or turnover to the authorities is mandated by law or court order.[240] ABA Model Rule 3.4(a) includes a commentary stating that the law may require counsel to deliver physical evidence of client crimes to the authorities, but otherwise offers no guidance.[241]

The source return versus turnover debate is also addressed in *Murray*. Justice Gravely recognized that some American cases impose an obligatory turnover duty where physical evidence is incriminating and that most Canadian commentators do the same for fruits or instrumentalities.[242] But he questioned whether this position is truly warranted, stating:

> I am not entirely clear why there exists this almost universal view that incriminating physical evidence must go to the prosecution. In my opinion it does not follow that because concealment of incriminating physical evidence is forbidden there is always a corresponding positive obligation to disclose. In *R. v. P. (M.B.)* (1994), 89 C.C.C. (3d) 289 (S.C.C.), Lamer C.J.C., said at page 304:
>
> > With respect to disclosure, the defence in Canada is under no legal obligation to cooperate with or assist the Crown by announcing any special defence such as an alibi, or by producing documentary or *physical evidence*.[243]

Justice Gravely posited that the attraction of mandatory turnover lies in the difficulty in identifying other acceptable options where counsel is "*improperly* in possession of incriminating physical evidence."[244] He gave the example of a lawyer presented with a murder weapon by a confessing client who is about to be arrested for the crime.[245] This scenario, as presented, does not involve the lawyer actually taking possession of the weapon, nor in our opinion could the lawyer properly do so except for the purpose of promptly delivering it to the authorities.[246] In any event, Gravely J noted that ABA Defense Standard 4-4.6 *does*

---

240 ABA Defense Standard 4-4.6(a) & (b).
241 ABA Model Rule 3.4(a), comment 2.
242 *Murray*, above note 7 at paras 118–19.
243 *Ibid* at para 120 [emphasis in original].
244 *Ibid* at para 121 [emphasis added].
245 *Ibid*, quoting from Martin, above note 159 at 392. The same scenario is analyzed in great detail in Hall, Jr, above note 158, § 28:61 at 1009–12.
246 See sections I(5) and I(8), above in this chapter.

permit source return after counsel has finished examining or testing the item.[247] He concluded that even if permissible this option was unavailable to Ken Murray because "[w]hile he had no obligation to assist the police in their investigation or the Crown in its prosecution, Murray could not be a party to concealing this evidence. Having removed the tapes from their hiding place, he could not hide them again. Nor could he implement any instructions from Bernardo that would result in their continued concealment."[248] Source return having been ruled out, Gravely J held that Murray had but three permissible options: (1) turn the videotapes over to the prosecution, either directly or anonymously, (2) deposit the tapes with the trial judge, or (3) disclose their existence to the prosecution "and prepare to do battle to retain them."[249]

We do not read *Murray* as foreclosing lawyers from ever engaging in source return. And in our view the policy reasons for permitting counsel to do so in limited circumstances are compelling. Accordingly, unless the client instructs counsel to deliver physical evidence relevant to a crime to the authorities, we believe a lawyer should be allowed to return it to the client or other source provided she is reasonably satisfied that[250]

1) the item is not contraband;[251]
2) source return is possible, which will usually not be the case if the client is the source and has disappeared or is in custody; and
3) source return will not cause the item to be destroyed, concealed or reconcealed, altered, lost, or used to cause physical harm to anyone.[252]

In returning physical evidence to its source, the lawyer should advise the client, or anyone else to whom the evidence is returned, of the legal consequences pertaining to concealment or destruction of the item.[253] Counsel should also keep a written record of all communica-

---

247 *Murray*, above note 7 at para 122.
248 *Ibid* at para 123.
249 *Ibid* at para 124.
250 A further condition, recommended by Gillers, above note 147 at 854–55, is that the lawyer must have taken possession for a proper purpose in the first place. The aim is to discourage improper possession and to reduce the risk of harm to state interests where such occurs. We prefer to rely on lawyers following the cardinal rule that possession should not be taken without a good justification: see the text associated with note 130, above in this chapter.
251 See *Hitch*, above note 96 at 78. Counsel can only accept contraband for the purpose of turning it over to the authorities: see Section I(3), above in this chapter.
252 We agree with *Murray*, above note 7 at para 123, that counsel should not return an item to the place where the client hid it from the authorities.
253 See *Hitch*, above note 96 at 78.

tions and actions taken respecting the item. Ideally, a signed receipt, including an acknowledgement of the legal advice provided, will be obtained from the source.

2) Delivery or Notice to Police, Crown, or Court

Where source return is not prudent or possible, counsel usually has an ethical obligation to deliver the item to the police, Crown, or court, or to inform the authorities that she has possession.[254] Justifications for taking this step can include the need to follow the client's instructions, the prohibition against lawyers' being complicit in the concealment or destruction of physical evidence, and the duty not to take action that risks causing physical harm.

We believe that turnover to or notification of the authorities should almost always be mandated where the preconditions necessary for source return are not met, namely, where

1) the client instructs counsel to deliver the item to the authorities or to notify them that counsel has possession;[255]
2) source return is not possible, for instance where the client has been taken into custody or where the item cannot be returned without risk that it will be destroyed, concealed or reconcealed, altered, lost, or used to cause physical harm to anyone;[256] or
3) the item is contraband.

Very rarely, a lawyer may find herself in a situation that falls within one or more of the above categories yet be justified in not turning the item over to the authorities. Suppose, for example, that counsel receives an email and attachment from her client. The client says that the attachment contains emails exchanged between the two complainants in the

---

254 These turnover options are set out in *Murray*, above note 7 at para 124, and replicated in Sask r 2.05(6) (commentary); Man, NS, NL r 3.5-7, commentary 2; FLSC Code r 5.1-2A, commentary 3.

255 It will sometimes be in the client's best interests to do so: see Section L, below in this chapter.

256 By contrast, ABA Defense Standard 4-4.6 would allow counsel to retain the item indefinitely in such cases unless prohibited from doing so by law. Gillers, above note 147 at 855–56 & 857–59, agrees where turnover would harm the client's interests. But he goes on to propose the creation of a physical-evidence registry, to which the lawyer would immediately on taking possession provide the client's name, plus the source of the item if not the client. Provided the police had sufficient basis to obtain a search warrant directed at the source, they could query the registry to see whether the target was listed, in which case the warrant could be directed at the lawyer's office (*ibid* at 859–63).

case against him, in which they discuss their proposed evidence. The client admits that he obtained these communications by improperly accessing one of the complainant's email accounts.

The attachment is property obtained by crime, because it derives directly or indirectly from the client's crime of unauthorized use of a computer.[257] Possession of the attachment is thus illegal. The attachment is also physical evidence of a crime. There is no suggestion that the police are investigating this computer-data crime. But even if they were, counsel merely has an electronic copy of the attachment. Her possession does nothing to prevent the authorities from obtaining the same evidence from the client, and probably other readily accessible sources as well. The usual restrictions surrounding the handling of physical evidence are thus arguably inapplicable, including the requirement that contraband be turned over to the authorities.[258] Continued possession of the attachment is of course illegal. Yet a recipient of contraband does not commit an offence by acting promptly to turn the item over to the authorities or *destroy it*.[259] Counsel can thus delete the client's email and the attachment without breaking any law or acting unethically.[260]

K. MODE OF DELIVERY TO THE AUTHORITIES

Delivering physical evidence relevant to a crime to the police, Crown, or court can cause obvious harm to the client. For example, if counsel provides a murder weapon to the police and if the client's DNA or fingerprint is on the weapon, this fact will likely be important to the prosecution case. Such damage to the client's interests may be unavoidable; certainly, counsel cannot wipe the weapon clean before turning it over to the authorities. On the other hand, there are rules of law and practical steps that can minimize the deleterious effects to the client.

In particular, delivering physical evidence to the authorities does not totally extinguish the application of solicitor-client privilege. The source of the item and the circumstances by which it came into counsel's possession will often remain privileged.[261] The lawyer's ethical duty of confidentiality also continues to apply with full force. Coun-

257 See Example 2 in Section G(2), above in this chapter.
258 See Section G(2), above in this chapter.
259 See Section E(4), above in this chapter.
260 Counsel must also advise the client as to what he should do with the emails: see Section E(4), above in this chapter.
261 See Section F(2), above in this chapter.

sel's obligation to maintain the privilege and honour the ethical duty usually requires that the item be provided to the authorities without revealing any more information than is necessary. Counsel must also oppose any efforts by the Crown to obtain information surrounding the item if that information can be reasonably seen as privileged.[262]

The best way to protect the privilege and the duty of confidentiality when delivering physical evidence to the authorities is to retain another lawyer to turn over the evidence. This lawyer will be provided with only the bare essentials necessary to permit physical delivery. She will not know the client's identity or anything about the case and will be instructed to withhold the identity of instructing counsel.[263] This approach minimizes the possibility of accidental disclosure of privileged or confidential information and also makes clear that privilege is not being waived.

Another delivery option is to provide the item to the police, Crown, or court by means of a completely anonymous delivery. This approach should be avoided however, for it may prevent the court from determining whether privilege properly applies and if so to what extent, and it may also stymie an otherwise legitimate judicial inquiry into whether counsel acted properly in handling the evidence.[264]

Finally, it will sometimes be in the client's best interests to have his identity revealed when delivering physical evidence to the authorities, for instance where the aim is to return stolen property to make a victim whole and express remorse before a guilty plea.[265]

L. PROVIDING ADVICE TO THE CLIENT

When presented with physical evidence relevant to a crime, counsel should advise the client as to the applicable ethical duties and legal rules and how they may affect the client's interests. Among other things, the client should be informed of many or all of the following points:

1) On no account can counsel accept possession of physical evidence without examining or reviewing it.

---

262 See Chapter 4, Section J.
263 This manner of proceeding is recommended in Sask r 2.05(6) (commentary); Man, NS, NL r 3.5-7, commentary 3; FLSC Code r 5.1-2A, commentary 4.
264 See Lefstein, above note 117 at 936–37; Layton, above note 11 at 89–90.
265 See Peter Joy & Kevin McMunigal, "Incriminating Evidence: Too Hot to Handle?" (2009) 24 Criminal Justice 42 at 44.

2) Counsel cannot help destroy or conceal the evidence, nor can counsel alter or in any way tamper with its evidentiary integrity.

3) Counsel can take possession of physical evidence only in limited circumstances and even then only temporarily.

4) The police or the Crown can successfully seize the evidence by means of a valid search warrant, regardless of whether the evidence is held by the client or lawyer.

5) If the evidence is left with counsel, she may ultimately be required to turn it over to the authorities. The advantages and disadvantages of leaving the evidence with counsel should be canvassed.

6) Counsel should be alert to and discuss the possibility that the client wants the item delivered to the authorities. After all, the operation of solicitor-client privilege may provide significant protection when compared with the downside of later being found in possession of the evidence. Or the client may decide to turn over the item in an attempt to obtain leniency where a plea is likely.

7) If the client chooses to keep the evidence, he cannot alter or tamper with it in any way. Doing so risks attracting separate criminal charges and may also constitute evidence against the client in the predicate prosecution. It is true that the client may destroy or hide the evidence in any event, but the system is probably no worse off than would be the case if he did not consult with the lawyer in the first place.

In dealing with a physical-evidence problem, a lawyer should be aware of the possibility that the client will later inform the police of the matter or that the police will otherwise discover some or all of the facts regarding the lawyer's involvement. To protect against allegations of impropriety, including those made by a client, the lawyer should scrupulously avoid any conduct that might be viewed as untoward and fully document all events as they occur.

CHAPTER 11

TERMINATION OF THE CLIENT-LAWYER RELATIONSHIP

A. INTRODUCTION

Termination of a client-lawyer relationship can occur in a number of ways. The most usual is where the purpose for which the relationship was created has ended, for instance when charges are stayed or a trial matter concluded. The focus of this chapter, however, is on termination that occurs while the client's matter is ongoing. This kind of termination is most likely to occur because the client discharges the lawyer or because the lawyer withdraws from the case. Of these two scenarios, withdrawal throws up the more contentious issues, in particular concerning the circumstances where a lawyer can properly withdraw from a case and the duties associated with withdrawal.

Ideally, a number of different interests should be accommodated by the rules of ethics that govern withdrawal. First, the fiduciary nature of the client-lawyer relationship, with attendant duties of competence, loyalty, and communication, requires that counsel act in the client's best interests. As far as possible, the client should receive competent and continuing representation, without undue delay or excessive cost occasioned by termination. Second, lawyers are bound by demanding professional standards in the conduct of the client's defence. There are ethical obligations not to breach the law, mislead the court, or otherwise undermine the administration of justice in representing a client. Sometimes, withdrawal will be the only method by which these obligations can be met. Third, society at large and participants in the criminal justice process other than the accused and defence counsel have an interest in ensuring reasonably efficient and prompt proceedings that promote a fair and just outcome.

In light of these diverse but interconnected interests, counsel is not permitted to terminate the client-lawyer relationship at will. Withdrawal must be for good cause with appropriate notice to the client. And where withdrawal is justified, the lawyer must extricate herself from the case with a minimum of prejudice to the client. Lawyers would therefore do well to think ahead by considering difficulties that might lead to or arise on withdrawal before accepting a case in the first place.[1]

Lawyers are not often exposed to complaint or censure for inappropriately withdrawing from a case. It is possible, however, for a dissatisfied former client to launch a disciplinary complaint or sue the lawyer civilly for negligence, breach of fiduciary duty, or breach of contract. The issue of the former lawyer's conduct may also be raised by the abandoned client in seeking an adjournment or basing an appeal on a denial of the right to the effective assistance of counsel. Finally, a lawyer who disobeys a court order to continue with a case may be cited for contempt. The prospect of being subjected to such inquires or challenges provides an incentive for lawyers to exercise the withdrawal option with appropriate care and caution.

B. SPECIAL RULES OF PROFESSIONAL CONDUCT FOR WITHDRAWAL IN CRIMINAL CASES

Most Canadian law societies provide members with rules applicable specifically to withdrawal in criminal proceedings, which show substantial appreciation for the particular problems that can arise in the criminal context.[2] Typical are the Ontario rules and associated commentary, which state as follows:

> 3.7-4 A lawyer who has agreed to act in a criminal case may withdraw because the client has not paid the agreed fee or for other adequate cause if the interval between a withdrawal and the date set for the trial of the case is sufficient to enable the client to obtain another

---

1   This point is closely related to the question of whether a lawyer is obliged to accept, or refuse, a proffered retainer: see Chapter 2.

2   Alta r 2.07(4); Sask r 2.07(4)–(6); BC, Ont, NS, NL r 3.7-4 to 3.7-6. See also NB ch 10, commentary 4(b).

licensee to act in the case and to allow such other licensee adequate time for preparation, and the lawyer

(a) notifies the client, preferably in writing, that the lawyer is with-drawing because the fees have not been paid or for other ad-equate cause;

(b) accounts to the client for any monies received on account of fees and disbursements;

(c) notifies Crown counsel in writing that the lawyer is no longer acting;

(d) in a case when the lawyer's name appears on the records of the court as acting for the accused, notifies the clerk or registrar of the appropriate court in writing that the lawyer is no longer act-ing; and

(e) complies with the applicable rules of court.

Commentary

[1] A lawyer who has withdrawn because of conflict with the client should not indicate in the notice addressed to the court or Crown counsel the cause of the conflict or make reference to any matter that would violate the privilege that exists between lawyer and client. The notice should merely state that the lawyer is no longer acting and has withdrawn.[3]

3.7-5 A lawyer who has agreed to act in a criminal case may not with-draw because of non-payment of fees if the date set for trial is not far enough removed to enable the client to obtain another licensee or to enable another licensee to prepare adequately for trial and an adjournment of the trial date cannot be obtained without adversely affecting the client's interests.[4]

3.7-6 In circumstances where a lawyer is justified in withdrawing from a criminal case for reasons other than non-payment of fees, and there is not sufficient time between a notice to the client of the law-yer's intention to withdraw and the date set for trial to enable the client to obtain another licensee and to enable such licensee to pre-pare adequately for trial:

---

3   Ont r 3.7-4. Very similar are Alta r 2.07(4); Sask r 2.07(4)–(6); BC, NS, Nfld r 3.7-4, although subparagraph (d) is not included in the Alta rule, and the commentary is not included in the BC rule.

4   Ont r 3.7-5. Very similar are Sask r 2.07(5); BC, NS, NL r 3.7-5; NB ch 10, com-mentary 4(b).

(a) the lawyer should, unless instructed otherwise by the client, attempt to have the trial date adjourned;

(b) the lawyer may withdraw from the case only with the permission of the court before which the case is to be tried.

Commentary

[1] If circumstances arise that, in the opinion of the lawyer, require an application to the court for leave to withdraw, the lawyer should promptly inform Crown counsel and the court of the intention to apply for leave in order to avoid or minimize any inconvenience to the court and witnesses.[5]

Some governing bodies have only general withdrawal rules that apply to both civil and criminal matters. The special rules pertaining to criminal matters reproduced above nonetheless provide an excellent guide for counsel in these other jurisdictions, assuming the applicable governing body has not adopted rules that are inconsistent.

C. RULES OF THE COURT

Some courts have rules of criminal procedure that bear on the withdrawal issue, providing yet another layer of potential obligations for counsel. A lawyer who is considering withdrawal must determine whether any rules of the court apply, and make sure to comply with them in bringing the client-lawyer relationship to an end.[6]

For instance, rule 25 of the *Criminal Proceedings Rules for the Superior Court of Justice (Ontario)* provides guidelines for counsel seeking to get off the record in a criminal matter.[7] Among other things, rule 25 stipulates that an application for withdrawal must be made "as soon as is reasonably practicable and sufficiently in advance of the scheduled date of trial to ensure that no adjournment of the proceedings will be required for such purpose."[8] Rule 25 also sets out requirements pertaining to notice to the prosecutor and court and to the contents of

---

5   Ont r 3.7-6. Very similar are Sask r 2.07(6); BC, NS, NL r 3.7-6.

6   The obligation to comply with the rules of the court is confirmed in subparagraph (e) of the ethical rules cited at note 3, above in this chapter, plus Alta r 2.07(7)(g); Sask r 2.07(9)(h); BC, Man, Ont, NS, NL r 3.7-9(g); CBA Code ch XII, commentary 3.

7   SI/2012-7.

8   *Ibid*, r 25.02.

the affidavit filed by or on behalf of the applicant lawyer.[9] Slightly less detailed, though to similar effect, are the *Rules of Practice of the Superior Court of the Province of Quebec, Criminal Division, 2002*, requiring leave of the court if withdrawal is sought during the court term or within fourteen days preceding the opening of term.[10]

D. DISCHARGE BY THE CLIENT

The client has an absolute and unreviewable power to discharge counsel at any time and for any reason.[11] The rationale behind this power is that the client-lawyer relationship is based on confidence and trust and has a significant impact on the ability to make full answer and defence. If the client loses confidence in counsel, for whatever reason, his representation is likely to suffer. Moreover, the client's rights to autonomy and dignity in conducting the defence demand respect for the decision to reject a particular lawyer in favour of retaining new counsel or going it alone.[12] In short, the client must have unfettered freedom to discharge counsel.[13]

What is more, a lawyer cannot be forced on a reluctant accused. Once it is clear the accused has discharged counsel,[14] the court cannot insist that counsel nevertheless continue with the representation.[15]

---

9   *Ibid*, r 25.03 & 25.04, respectively.
10   SI/2002-46, r 10.
11   See *R v Cunningham*, 2010 SCC 10 at para 9 [*Cunningham*]; *R v Amos*, 2012 ONCA 334 at para 19 [*Amos*]; *R v Vachon*, 2011 QCCA 2103 at para 39 [*Vachon*]; *R v Deschamps*, 2003 MBCA 116 at para 19 [*Deschamps*]; *R v DDC* (1996), 110 CCC (3d) 323 at 325 [para 8] (Alta CA), leave to appeal to SCC refused, [1996] SCCA No 453 [*DDC*]. See also Alta, Sask r 2.07(1) (commentary); BC, Man, Ont, NS, NL r 3.7-1, commentary 1; NB ch 10, commentary 1(a); CBA Code ch XII, commentary 1.
12   See *R v Swain* (1991), 63 CCC (3d) 481 at 504–6 [paras 33–36] (SCC) [*Swain*]; *R v McCallen* (1999), 131 CCC (3d) 518 [paras 32–37] (Ont CA) [*McCallen*].
13   This freedom cannot be unduly constrained by agreement: see Third Restatement § 31, comment "d": retainer cannot forbid client from discharging lawyer.
14   See, for example, *R v Szostak*, 2012 ONCA 503 at para 67: the fact that the client has applied to legal aid to authorize a change of counsel does not, without more, constitute a discharge; *R v Bottyan*, 2013 ABCA 150 at para 5: a request to discharge counsel must be clear and unequivocal.
15   See *Cunningham*, above note 11 at para 9; *Swain*, above note 12 at 505–6 [para 36]; *R v Vescio* (1948), 92 CCC 161 at 164 (SCC); *R v Ryan*, 2012 NLCA 9 at para 99 [*Ryan*]; *Vachon*, above note 11 at para 39; *R v OFB*, 2006 ABCA 130 at para 9; *R v Huber*, 2004 BCCA 43 at paras 79, 100, and 140 [*Huber*]; *R v Romanowicz* (1999), 138 CCC (3d) 225 at para 28 (Ont CA); *R v Bowles* (1985), 21 CCC (3d)

Nor can the lawyer continue to act of her own accord.[16] It matters not that the trial is under way or that the client has no articulable reason for firing counsel or may suffer prejudice as a result. In some circumstances, however, the court may decide to appoint an *amicus curiae* to ensure that justice is done,[17] and on occasion this will be the accused's discharged counsel.[18]

Where a client informs counsel that the latter is discharged and where the trial is imminent or under way, counsel should make sure the client understands that the matter may proceed as scheduled. The client should be under no illusion that an adjournment is automatic[19] and should also know that where the circumstances suggest an intent to delay, the judge may have some leeway to question her about why counsel was fired in determining whether an adjournment should be granted to obtain new counsel.[20] If, despite these warnings, the client is adamant about effecting a discharge, counsel has no choice but to accede.

Once fired, counsel should confirm in writing the fact of the discharge, the client's reasons if any,[21] and that the trial should be expected to proceed as scheduled and new counsel thus promptly retained.[22] The

---

540 at 543 [para 7] (Alta CA); *R v Fabrikant* (1995), 97 CCC (3d) 544 at 555 [paras 44–45] (Que CA), leave to appeal to SCC refused, [1995] SCCA No 211; *R v Mian* (1998), 133 CCC (3d) 573 at paras 5–9 (NSCA).

16   See *Lovin v State*, 286 SW3d 275 at 284–88 (Tenn 2009), criticizing counsel for continuing to act after being discharged and failing to inform the court that he had been fired.

17   See *Cunningham*, above note 11 at para 9; *Ryan*, above note 15 at paras 118–20 and 156; *R v Bitternose*, 2009 SKCA 54 at paras 6–13.

18   See *Amos*, above note 11 at paras 24–29; *R v Samra* (1998), 129 CCC (3d) 144 at paras 10–25 (Ont CA), leave to appeal to SCC refused, [1998] SCCA No 558; *R v MS* (1996), 111 CCC (3d) 467 at paras 18–20 (BCCA), leave to appeal to SCC refused, [1997] SCCA No 62; *R v Irving*, 2013 SKPC 101 at paras 6–8. The proper role of *amicus curiae* is addressed in *Ontario v Criminal Lawyers' Association of Ontario*, 2013 SCC 43.

19   For cases where a client discharged counsel just before or during trial and then was refused an adjournment, see *Amos*, above note 11 at paras 7 and 12–22; *R v Phung*, 2012 ONCA 720 [*Phung*]; *R v Maitland Capital Ltd*, 2008 ONCJ 523 at paras 11–13; *R v Pomeroy* (1984), 15 CCC (3d) 193 at 194 [paras 4–6] (Alta CA); *R v Mitchell* (1981), 28 CR (3d) 112 at 115 [paras 18–24] (BCCA); *R v MacDonald* (1981), 50 NSR (2d) 207 (SCAD), leave to appeal to SCC refused, [1982] SCCA No 389; *R v Richard* (1992), 55 OAC 43 at paras 6–7 (CA). See also the general comments in *R v McGibbon* (1988), 45 CCC (3d) 334 at 346 (Ont CA); *Huber*, above note 15 at para 114.

20   See *Phung, ibid* at para 34.

21   See Alta r 2.07(6)(a)(i) & (ii); Sask r 2.07(9)(a)(i) & (ii); BC, Man, Ont, NS, NL r 3.7-9(i) & (ii); NB ch 10, commentary.

22   Alta r 2.07(7)(a)(iii); Sask r 2.07(9)(a)(iii); BC, Man, Ont, NS, NL r 3.7-9(iii).

purpose of this letter is not to disparage the client's decision but to set out fairly the circumstances to prevent misunderstanding and avoid future harm. Counsel must refrain from seeking revenge for a discharge and should take reasonable measures to mitigate any adverse impact on the client.[23] Generally speaking, the same duty to mitigate prejudice that applies on withdrawal by counsel operates in the case of discharge by the client.[24]

E. GENERAL PROHIBITION AGAINST WITHDRAWAL

Lawyers do not have the same untrammelled freedom as clients in ending the professional relationship.[25] Most Canadian rules of professional conduct dealing with withdrawal adopt the proposition that a lawyer owes the client a general duty *not* to withdraw services absent good cause and reasonable notice.[26] This starting point is justified by the lawyer's fiduciary duty to the client.[27] Loyalty demands that the lawyer be restricted from taking any action that will harm the client's interests absent good cause. Consequently, even though there is substantial leeway in choosing whether to represent a client in the first place,[28] a lawyer's control over the continuation of the relationship is significantly curtailed once retained. For example, a lawyer's knowledge that a client is guilty does not justify putting an end to the retainer.[29] Nor can counsel end the professional relationship because she feels the accused is destined to lose or because doing so will allow her to take on a new client whose representation would otherwise be precluded because of

---

23   See ABA Model Rule 1.16, comment 9.
24   See ABA Model Rule 1.16(d). Most Canadian codes of professional conduct impose the same duties on departing counsel whether he withdraws or has been discharged: Alta r 2.07(7); Sask r 2.07(9); BC, Man, Ont, NS, NL r 3.7-9; NB ch 10, commentary 5; CBA Code ch XII, commentary 8. These duties are discussed in sections J–N, below in this chapter.
25   See *Cunningham*, above note 11 at para 9; Alta, Sask r 2.07(1) (commentary); BC, Man, Ont, NS, NL r 3.7-1, commentary 1; Que s 3.03.04; NB ch 10, commentary 1(a); CBA Code ch XII, commentary 1.
26   Alta, Sask r 2.07(1); BC, Man, Ont, NS, NL r 3.7-1; NB ch 10, rule; CBA Code ch XII, rule. See also *R v Kong*, 2003 ABQB 192 at para 3 [*Kong*].
27   See *Cunningham*, above note 11 at para 9.
28   See Chapter 2.
29   See Chapter 1, Section G.

conflict of interest rules.[30] It is also improper for a lawyer to withdraw because of dissatisfaction or frustration with a judge's ruling.[31] Nevertheless, it has been suggested that withdrawal in reaction to an adverse ruling may be acceptable in the rare and extreme case where the ruling prevents a fair trial and interferes with counsel's ability to represent the client.[32]

At the beginning of the client-lawyer relationship, counsel may wish to consider expressly identifying in the retainer agreement those conditions under which withdrawal will be permitted. Given the fiduciary nature of the relationship and the duty to act in the client's best interests, it is unlikely that the client can contract out of all protections otherwise provided by the law.[33] It would, for instance, be unethical to provide for unilateral withdrawal by the lawyer at any time without cause. But a lawyer can surely lay out the groundwork for a reasonable right to terminate and include provisions covering notice.

Another matter counsel should consider covering in a written retainer agreement is the natural end point of the relationship.[34] Since ambiguous contracts are construed to the advantage of the client, clearly demarcating the end point of the retainer is a good idea.[35] Most clients realize that the trial lawyer is not bound to continue with an appeal, but such is not always the case. A trickier area concerns post-trial matters with respect to which the client could frequently benefit from a lawyer's help. Criminal lawyers are sometimes requested to assist clients in working out problems at penal institutions or following up on rehabilitation efforts. Some counsel refuse to accept any responsibility for undertaking this "postretainer" work, at least absent additional payment. Others aid the client without giving much thought to

---

30   See *Canadian National Railway Co v McKercher LLP*, 2013 SCC 39 at paras 44 and 55 [*McKercher*]; FLSC r 3.4-1, commentary 8.

31   See *R v Swartz* (1977), 34 CCC (2d) 477 at 481–82 [paras 10–13] (Man CA) [*Swartz*]; *R v Gillespie*, 2000 MBQB 57 at paras 8 and 12 [*Gillespie*]: application to withdraw following an adverse ruling was termed "suspicious." For an atrocious example of counsel's leaving a client in the lurch by withdrawing in response to a clash with the trial judge, in a murder trial at that, see *Dunkley v R*, [1994] UKPC 32 [*Dunkley*].

32   See *Swartz*, above note 31 at 482 [para 13].

33   See Third Restatement § 32, comments "h(i)" and "i," permitting agreement on withdrawal where the client's consent is informed, but the arrangement cannot work to impair the quality of representation.

34   See *R v Williams* (1897), 3 CCC 9 (Ont Div Ct): the authority of a lawyer to act is *prima facie* terminated following an accused's acquittal.

35   See Third Restatement § 31, comment "h."

whether a formal retainer continues to exist, and charge nothing for their assistance.

When the relationship does come to an end, a reporting letter to the client is always a good idea. If the client is expressly told that the relationship has ended, the possibility of misunderstanding and continued reliance, to the detriment of the client and counsel, is alleviated.

F. MANDATORY WITHDRAWAL BY THE LAWYER

While Canadian lawyers have a duty to continue acting for a client absent good justification for termination, there are instances where withdrawal is mandated. Most governing bodies purport to itemize all of the grounds that impose on a lawyer the duty to end the relationship. The trend is to limit mandatory withdrawal to three situations, namely, where the lawyer is discharged by the client,[36] where the client persists in instructing the lawyer to act contrary to professional ethics,[37] or where the lawyer is incompetent to continue to handle the matter.[38] Some ethical codes list a few other instances where lawyers must withdraw, which mostly fall within the broad obligation to withdraw where a client instructs counsel to act unethically.[39] Ultimately, the fundamental guiding principle is straightforward: a lawyer must withdraw where continued representation will necessarily compromise service to the client or involve the lawyer in violating legal or ethical duties. Once the standard for mandatory withdrawal is met, the

---

36 Alta r 2.07(5)(a); Sask r 2.07(7)(a); BC, Man, Ont, NS, NL r 3.7-7(a); CBA Code ch XII, commentary 4.

37 Alta r 2.07(5)(b); Sask r 2.07(7)(b); BC, Man, Ont, NS, NL r 3.7-7(b); NB ch 10, commentary 3(a)(v); CBA Code ch XII, commentary 4(c).

38 Alta r 2.07(5)(c); Sask r 2.07(7)(c); BC, Man, Ont, NS, NL r 3.7-7(c); NB ch 10, commentary 3(a)(vi); CBA Code ch XII, commentary 4(d). The Quebec code only mandates withdrawal where the client has induced the lawyer to commit an illegal or fraudulent act and persists after being advised of such by the lawyer: Que s 3.03.04.

39 For instance, where the client is guilty of dishonourable conduct or takes a position solely to harass or maliciously injure another: NB ch 10, commentary 3(a)(ii) and (iv); CBA Code ch XII, commentary 4(a); where the client instructs the lawyer to do something inconsistent with his duty to the court: NB ch 10, commentary 3(a)(i); CBA Code ch XII, commentary 4(a); or where the client has induced a lawyer to commit an illegal or fraudulent act and persists after being advised of such by the lawyer: Que s 3.03.04.

fact that the client will suffer prejudice because of termination of the retainer becomes irrelevant.

In considering whether withdrawal is obligatory, counsel must carefully assess the circumstances. Because the consequences of withdrawal can be severe for the client, such action should not be taken lightly. The lawyer who apprehends a possible duty to end the relationship must ensure she is in possession of all relevant facts. There is also an issue relating to the precise nature of a lawyer's knowledge regarding anticipated client misbehaviour. What standard must be met to mandate withdrawal, or, to put it conversely, what degree of uncertainty will justify staying on the case?[40] Is it sufficient the lawyer reasonably believes that instructions will involve illegal or otherwise unethical conduct, or must the lawyer "irresistibly know" that such will be the case? The latter standard has been discussed in the context of the client known to be guilty and the client intending to commit perjury[41] and in our view may be usefully employed in other situations as well.

Assuming counsel knows that carrying out the client's instructions will result in unethical conduct on his part, if the client cannot be persuaded to abandon the plan, can counsel simply refuse to carry out the offending instructions and thereby avoid having to withdraw? Refusing to carry out the offending instructions ensures that the unethical conduct does not occur and spares the client any hardship that may accompany a loss of counsel. As explained elsewhere, however, the better view is that counsel must withdraw rather than override the client's improper instructions and continue with the case.[42]

It is imperative that the matter be discussed with the client before withdrawing where at all possible. On learning of the problem, the client might readily agree to abandon the troublesome instructions. Yet counsel must never forget that the grounds mandating withdrawal generally involve a substantial threat to the administration of justice and perhaps also to the best interests of the client, as where counsel is not competent to conduct the case. The lawyer's interest in self-protection may also be implicated, for example where remaining on the case may invite allegations of complicity in client fraud. On occasion, for these reasons, the lawyer may have to act quickly, in extreme cases perhaps even withdrawing absent notice to the client, to avoid knowingly violating the ethical rules.

---

40   These issues are addressed in Geoffrey Hazard & W William Hodes, *The Law of Lawyering*, 3d ed (Gaithersburg, MD: Aspen Law & Business, 2001) (loose-leaf 2013 supplement) at § 20.7.

41   See Chapter 1, Section F, and Chapter 7, Section F(1).

42   See Chapter 3, Section J.

G. OPTIONAL WITHDRAWAL BY THE LAWYER

Many Canadian ethical codes state that a lawyer may withdraw from the representation where there has been "a serious loss of confidence between the lawyer and the client."[43] The commentary to this rule gives some examples as to when such a loss of confidence may arise, including when the lawyer has been deceived by the client, when the client refuses to accept and act on the lawyer's advice on a significant point, when the client is persistently unreasonable and uncooperative in a material respect, or when the lawyer is facing difficulty in obtaining adequate instructions.[44] Other Canadian ethical codes are more or less to the same effect.[45]

As the examples just given illustrate, the threshold for discretionary withdrawal is typically met where the central components of trust and confidence that are so essential to an effective client-lawyer relationship have substantially eroded and where the relationship is possibly dysfunctional. There may also be an element of self-protection evident in the decision to withdraw, the lawyer legitimately desiring to terminate the relationship to avert a real possibility of being blamed for past or future illegality. This concern would be evident, for example, if the lawyer discovered that she had been the unknowing dupe of the client in tracking down a Crown witness for the purpose of intimidation or attempted bribery.

While the trend in Canada is for the rules dealing with optional withdrawal to focus on a serious loss of confidence, there may be other circumstances where withdrawal is possible, despite the absence of any distrust or disagreement between lawyer and client. In particular, counsel should be allowed to withdraw where granted informed permission to do so by the client.[46]

In exercising the discretion inherent in the ethical rules that address optional withdrawal, counsel should consider the following factors:

1) It is necessary to determine the extent to which the problem fundamentally undermines the professional relationship. The lawyer and client may have a huge disagreement regarding a matter relevant to the case but without any continued adverse impact on the integrity of the relationship. The lawyer must ascertain whether the relationship can properly function to the continued benefit of the client.

---

43   Alta, Sask r 2.07(2); BC, Man, Ont, NS, NL r 3.7-2.
44   Alta, Sask r 2.07(2) (commentary); BC, Man, Ont, NS, NL r 3.7-2, commentary 1.
45   Que s 3.03.04; NB ch 10, commentary 4(a); CBA Code ch XII, commentary 5.
46   See Third Restatement § 32(3)(c).

2) If there is a serious rift, counsel should consider whether the problem can be repaired. However, sometimes the effort and time required to do so will be impractical, or there will be little chance of permanent success.

3) The prejudicial impact that termination of the retainer will have on the client must be taken into account.[47] In some circumstances, withdrawal may implicitly suggest to outsiders that the client has done or is going to do something improper.[48] In other instances, the client will be unable to obtain a new lawyer by virtue of an ongoing trial or prohibitive cost. In almost every case, withdrawal will cause the client some harm in the form of time lost, added cost, or stress. It may be that the withdrawing lawyer can mitigate such harm by refunding fees or helping to find a new lawyer, but such is not always possible.

4) The temptation to terminate the retainer must be avoided where, though perhaps justified on the facts, the real reason for wishing to end the relationship is extraneous to any proper consideration. A desire to escape from what appears to be an insurmountable Crown case, to ease the pressures of a busy practice, or to attend an important social engagement is not a valid reason.

As in the case where withdrawal is mandatory, the lawyer considering optional withdrawal has a duty to discuss the matter with the client in an effort to repair the damaged relationship and in any event to inform the client of the decision to withdraw.[49] Moreover, given that withdrawal is permitted, not required, where feasible the proper course

---

47   See Alta, Sask r 2.07(1) (commentary); BC, Man, Ont, NS, NL r 3.7-1, commentary 2; NB ch 10, commentary 2(b); CBA Code ch XII, commentary 7, stating that the lawyer "should not desert the client at a critical stage of a matter or at a time when withdrawal would put the client in a position of disadvantage or peril." See also the Third Restatement § 32(4), providing that a lawyer may not exercise his discretion to withdraw if the harm thereby caused will significantly exceed the harm to the lawyer or others in not withdrawing. This restriction applies only to certain specified grounds of optional withdrawal (client insists on repugnant or imprudent action, breach of contract including failure to pay fees, irreparable breakdown, and "other good cause").

48   For instance, withdrawal just before the client testifies may cause some outsiders to wonder, rightly or wrongly, whether the client plans to commit perjury: see Chapter 7, Section F(4)(a).

49   See Alta, Sask r 2.07(1) (commentary); BC, Man, Ont, NS, NL r 3.7-1, commentary 2; NB ch 10, commentary 2(b); CBA Code ch XII, commentary 7.

in mitigating prejudice to the client may be to continue to act until new counsel is retained.[50]

Prohibition: Counsel should never threaten withdrawal as a means of forcing the client to make a "hasty decision on a difficult question."[51] Granted, there will be instances where a quick decision is needed and the client must be told that withdrawal may be the lawyer's response. But ending the professional relationship should not be used as a brickbat to improperly make the client bow to counsel's dictates.

As a last point, we believe that in some or even most cases where the client-lawyer relationship has totally broken down, leading to an utter and irreconcilable lack of trust, the discretion to withdraw begins to shade into a mandatory duty to terminate. Surely, counsel cannot be expected or allowed to continue acting in such circumstances, given the detrimental effect on the client's constitutional rights and the administration of justice. Undoubtedly, a terribly malfunctioning client-lawyer relationship will quite often cause the client to discharge the lawyer. But where this step is not taken, there is a good argument that the lawyer must withdraw, especially where any resulting adverse impact to the client is manageable. Indeed, an excellent case can be made that a total and irremediable rupture to the client-lawyer relationship makes pursuing the representation improper under various rules of professional conduct — pertaining to loyalty, competence, integrity, and so on — and hence mandates withdrawal because continued employment will clearly lead to a breach of the rules.[52]

The potential for a blurring of the line between mandatory and optional withdrawal can be seen in the discussion in *R v Cunningham*,[53] the leading Canadian case on withdrawal in criminal matters. In considering applications to the court for leave to withdraw based on "ethical reasons," Rothstein J defined this term as encompassing instances where "an issue has arisen in the solicitor-client relationship where it is now *impossible* for counsel to continue in good conscience to represent the accused."[54] He gave as an example of an "ethical reason" the situation where an accused instructs counsel to act unethically,[55] which as

---

50   "As a general rule, the client should be given sufficient time to retain and instruct replacement counsel": Alta, Sask r 2.07(1) (commentary); BC, Man, NS, NL r 3.7-1, commentary 2; NB ch 10, commentary 2(b).

51   See Alta, Sask r 2.07(2) (commentary); BC, Man, Ont, NS, NL r 3.7-2, commentary 1; CBA Code ch XII, commentary 5.

52   See the rules cited at note 37, above in this chapter, and accompanying text.

53   *Cunningham*, above note 11.

54   *Ibid* at para 48 [emphasis added].

55   *Ibid*.

552 ETHICS AND CRIMINAL LAW

we have seen would mandate withdrawal under all Canadian ethical codes.[56] But he went on to offer, as a second example, the case of a client who refuses to accept counsel's advice on an important trial matter.[57] In our view, such a refusal does not *necessarily* constitute a serious loss of confidence between counsel and client so as to trigger the optional withdrawal provisions in the Canadian ethical codes. But where it *does* amount to a serious loss of confidence *and* where counsel concludes that as a result it is "impossible to continue in good conscience to represent the accused," the only viable option is to withdraw, seeking leave of the court to do so if necessary in the circumstances.[58] Of course, in determining whether it is impossible to continue, counsel must consider all of the circumstances, including the four points set out above.

Example 1: Part way through the trial, the accused absconds. Counsel applies to withdraw. This course of action is justified, and perhaps even mandated, because the lawyer is unable to obtain instructions.[59] Nonetheless, where a client goes missing, the lawyer should take reasonable steps to attempt to locate her.[60]

Example 2: A client relentlessly insists from the start of the retainer that he testify at trial. Counsel eventually concludes that testifying will undermine any prospect of acquittal and following the close of the Crown case strongly advises against the client's taking the stand. The client nonetheless persists in the desire to testify. If the difference of opinion between counsel and client is so severe that the integrity of the client-lawyer relationship has been destroyed, counsel may seek leave of the court to withdraw.[61] But this step should not be lightly taken, given the difficulty the client will likely have in completing the case

---

56 See the rules cited at note 37, above in this chapter, and accompanying text.

57 *Cunningham*, above note 11 at para 48.

58 See Section L, below in this chapter.

59 See Alta r 2.02(4) (commentary): the lawyer may be forced to withdraw if implied authority does not extend to the tasks necessary to continue with the representation; Alta, Sask r 2.07(2) (commentary); BC, Man, Ont, NS, NL r 3.7-2, commentary 1: difficulty obtaining adequate instructions may justify optional withdrawal; *R v Garofoli* (1988), 41 CCC (3d) 97 at 143 (Ont CA), rev'd on other grounds (1990), 60 CCC (3d) 161 (SCC): court comes close to saying that a lawyer for an absconding accused has a right to withdraw; *R v Dillon*, [1996] OJ No 4014 at paras 51–52 (Gen Div): court grants application to withdraw but only after counsel finishes examining a defence witness in chief.

60 See Chapter 3, Section M.

61 See *R v Brigham* (1992), 79 CCC (3d) 365 at 380–83 (Que CA), upon which this example is loosely based. See also *R v Steele* (1991), 63 CCC (3d) 149 at 160 (Que CA); "Panel Discussion: Problems in Ethics and Advocacy" in Law Society of Upper Canada, *Defending a Criminal Case* (Toronto: R De Boo, 1969) 279 at 284.

without the help of counsel. The much better approach on these facts would be to end the retainer well before trial or accede to the client's wishes but obtain written instructions setting out counsel's firm advice to the contrary.

H. A LIMITED RESIDUAL RIGHT TO WITHDRAW

It is possible to conceive of a residual right to withdraw, pursuant to which a lawyer can unilaterally end a retainer provided that the client suffers no harm and that termination is not effected for an improper purpose such as to delay the proceedings. In this vein, ABA Model Rule 1.16(b) and the Third Restatement § 32(3)(a) both allow an attorney to withdraw for any reason whatsoever where there is no "material adverse effect on the interests of the client."

Canadian codes of professional conduct contain nothing approaching such a broad-based residual right to withdraw, which serves to emphasize the seriousness of counsel's professional obligations once a retainer is accepted. Yet many codes do provide lawyers with a general power to withdraw provided that they have "good cause" and give the client reasonable notice.[62] Most of these codes also contain a further rule applicable only in criminal matters that permits counsel to withdraw for "adequate cause" provided that the client has time to retain new counsel to prepare for the scheduled trial and that certain notifications are made.[63] To this limited extent, lawyers in Canada are arguably permitted to withdraw for reasons not listed in the mandatory or optional withdrawal provisions in their codes. Although, as explained in Section J, below in this chapter, the "reasonable notice" requirement can operate to prevent withdrawal where it will cause prejudice to the client. Moreover, some bases for withdrawing can never constitute good or adequate cause, usually because they necessarily violate the duty of loyalty owed to the client.[64]

---

62   Alta, Sask r 2.07(1); BC, Man, Ont, NS, NL r 3.7-1. See also NB ch 10, rule; CBA Code ch XII, rule.

63   Alta, Sask r 2.07(4); BC, Ont, NS, NL r 3.7-4.

64   See, for example, the text associated with notes 29–31, above in this chapter.

I. NON-PAYMENT OF FEES OR UNREASONABLE FINANCIAL BURDEN

Non-payment of fees is frequently a major concern for criminal lawyers, whose clients are often unemployed or underemployed, incarcerated, or otherwise financially disadvantaged. Complete payment at the beginning of the relationship is nothing more than an unattainable aspiration in many cases. Counsel is left with no alternative but to accept partial payments of a piecemeal nature, the client agreeing to pay the full amount before the trial commences. Where, for any one of a number of reasons, the client substantially defaults in paying the agreed-upon amounts before trial, the issue of prematurely ending the retainer arises.

Yet withdrawal is not always the proper response. Most Canadian ethical codes state that if after reasonable notice the client fails to provide a retainer or funds on account of disbursements or fees, a lawyer may withdraw "unless serious prejudice to the client would result."[65] Several of these codes go on to comment that a lawyer who withdraws because of non-payment of fees should ensure that the client has sufficient time to retain another lawyer and for that lawyer to prepare adequately for trial.[66]

Many Canadian codes provide additional guidance specific to the criminal context. These codes state that where a lawyer acts in a criminal case and where there is sufficient time to enable the client to retain another lawyer to prepare for trial, the lawyer can withdraw for non-payment of the agreed fee provided that

1) the client is notified in writing that the lawyer is withdrawing for this reason;
2) the lawyer accounts to the client for monies received;
3) the Crown is notified in writing that the lawyer is no longer acting;
4) if the lawyer is formally on the record, she notifies the clerk or registrar of the court of the withdrawal; and
5) the lawyer complies with any court rules applicable in the circumstances.[67]

---

65   Alta, Sask r 2.07(3); Man, Ont, NS, NL r 3.7-3; NB ch 10, commentary 4(a)(vi); CBA Code ch XII, commentary 6. The British Columbia rule does not include the emphasized words, but the accompanying commentary is arguably of the same import: BC r 3.7-3, commentary 1. See also Third Restatement § 32(3)(g), permitting withdrawal for non-payment of fees provided undue prejudice does not occur.

66   Alta, Sask r 2.07(3) (commentary); BC, NS, NL r 3.7-3, commentary 1.

67   Alta, Sask r 2.07(4); BC, Ont, NS, NL r 3.7-4.

However, most of these same codes add that if there is inadequate time to hire a new lawyer to conduct the scheduled trial and if an adjournment cannot be obtained without adversely affecting the client's interests, counsel must remain on the case.[68]

The typical instance where unacceptable prejudice would result, and where withdrawal is therefore improper, sees counsel wait until the trial is about to begin or has already started before attempting to extricate himself from the retainer. The client will usually be unable to retain and instruct replacement counsel on such short notice. An adjournment might be a satisfactory answer but only where permitted by the court and not adverse to the client's interests.[69] The bottom line is that failure to pay fees justifies withdrawal under most Canadian ethical rules only where the client will not suffer substantial adverse impact.

Example: Counsel is retained privately under a flat-fee arrangement to defend the client on a fraud charge, with the trial expected to last two weeks. The case is fairly complex, and the prosecution evidence involves substantial documentation. Defence counsel realizes that the retainer provides insufficient compensation for the work required. The day before the trial is to commence, he asks for further funds, telling the client that the trial "will go badly" otherwise. On this scenario, counsel has only himself to blame for underestimating the fee required and especially for leaving the matter of an extra payment to the last minute. The late request puts improper pressure on the client, who will almost certainly fear a substandard performance absent an infusion of funds. On these facts, counsel was wrong to make the request.[70]

Even where the accused will suffer no real prejudice, the failure to pay fees need not always trigger immediate withdrawal. Counsel should ensure the client understands that a breach has occurred before rushing to the worst conclusions and taking action to end the relationship. The client may quite legitimately have forgotten about a payment deadline or reasonably misunderstood the lawyer's expectations. In any event, the lawyer should warn of a possible withdrawal to allow the client an opportunity to correct the failure to pay. Where the client still fails to pay and where counsel is with good reason determined to do no more work on the case, the proper course is to make a definitive break. Simply failing to provide any further service, without notice to the client, is unacceptable. This sloppy response may cause serious

---

68 Sask r 2.07(5); BC, Ont, NS, NL r 3.7-5; NB ch 10, commentary 4(b).
69 See the rules cited in notes 65 and 68, above in this chapter.
70 See *Vachon*, above note 11 at para 65.

harm to the client, and the lawyer could end up being forced to act in the case because the trial date, initially well in the future, is allowed to become imminent.

In the United States, the ABA Model Rules allow withdrawal not only because the client has failed to live up to her end of the retainer agreement but also where continued representation "will result in an unreasonable financial burden on the lawyer."[71] Thus, counsel can conceivably withdraw where the problem stems from an unexpected turn of events that increases the work required or where the lawyer has simply made a significant mistake in estimating the proper fees. Canadian rules do not expressly provide for withdrawal based on a lawyer's financial miscalculation,[72] and in most instances counsel should bear the brunt of a failure to estimate properly the work required to conduct a case. There is nothing wrong with asking the client to amend the agreement or, better yet, with drafting the original agreement so that subsequent events will trigger adjustments to the payment amount and schedule. But the lawyer cannot unilaterally shirk his duties to the client by breaching the contract and ignoring the obligations of a fiduciary.

J. NOTICE TO CLIENT OF WITHDRAWAL

The lead rule found in the termination section of most Canadian ethical codes prohibits withdrawal absent good cause and "reasonable"[73] or "appropriate"[74] notice to the client. This notice obligation is part and parcel of the broader duty to keep the client informed regarding all matters relevant to the representation.[75] It also flows from the duty of loyalty, which requires counsel to act with the best interests of the client in mind. Withdrawal can have a devastating impact on the client, including a negative effect on the ability to make full answer and defence, so counsel must take reasonable measures to avoid prejudice to the client. In particular, notice allows the client to act expeditiously in arranging for new counsel.

---

71   ABA Model Rule 1.16(b)(6).
72   The residual power to withdraw may, however, be engaged in such circumstances: see Section H, above in this chapter.
73   Alta, Sask r 2.07(1); BC, Man, Ont, NS, NL r 3.7-1. See also *Gillespie*, above note 31 at paras 9–10.
74   NB ch 10, rule and commentary 2(b); CBA Code ch XII, rule and commentary 7.
75   See Chapter 3, Section E.

In line with this rationale, Canadian codes typically elaborate on the concept of reasonable or appropriate notice, stating:

> No hard and fast rules can be laid down as to what will constitute reasonable notice prior to withdrawal. Where the matter is covered by statutory provisions or rules of court, these will govern. In other situations the governing principle is that the lawyer should protect the client's interests so far as possible and should not desert the client at a critical stage of a matter or at a time when withdrawal would put the client in a position of disadvantage or peril.[76]

The absence of "hard and fast rules" regarding what is "reasonable" supports the sensible view that in rare instances notice may not be required at all, such as where the client cannot be located despite counsel's diligent efforts to make contact.

Most rules of professional conduct contain additional provisions bearing on the need for notice. First, in criminal matters where the lawyer wishes to withdraw for non-payment or other adequate cause and where the client has time to engage new counsel to prepare for the scheduled trial, the lawyer must notify the client in writing that the lawyer is withdrawing and set out the reason why.[77] Second, there is a general, somewhat overlapping notice requirement applicable in all cases that states that on discharge or withdrawal a lawyer must notify the client in writing setting out

1) the fact that the lawyer has withdrawn;
2) the reasons, if any, for the withdrawal; and
3) in the case of litigation that the client should expect that the hearing or trial will proceed on the date scheduled and that the client should retain new counsel promptly.[78]

The benefits of written notice are worth accentuating. It reduces the possibility of misunderstanding and protects both the client and the lawyer if a dispute later arises as to the circumstances surrounding withdrawal. Plus, written notice of the sort required by the rules helps ensure the client knows that she should retain replacement counsel promptly and must not assume that an adjournment will be granted.

---

76 Alta, Sask r 2.07(1) (commentary); BC, Man, Ont, NS, NL r 3.7-1, commentary 2; NB ch 10, commentary 2(b); CBA Code ch XII, commentary 7. See also *R v Brundia*, 2007 ONCA 725 at para 48 [*Brundia*].
77 Alta, Sask r 2.07(4); BC, Ont, NS, NL r 3.7-4.
78 Alta r 2.07(7)(a); Sask r 2.07(9)(a); BC, Man, Ont, NS, NL r 3.7-9(a). The first commentary to this rule states that where the lawyer is in a firm, the client should be told that neither the lawyer nor the firm is acting.

K. NOTICE TO THE COURT AND CROWN OF WITHDRAWAL

Newer Canadian ethical codes contain a general obligation to notify the court, opposing parties, and others directly affected of counsel's withdrawal.[79] Most of these codes additionally stipulate that counsel notify the court and Crown in writing of his withdrawal in a criminal matter.[80] This obligation is warranted as a means of minimizing systemic disruption and as a professional courtesy to the court and prosecutors. There is often an appreciable benefit to the client as well. For example, the Crown lawyer who knows about a withdrawal will not mistakenly send new disclosure or application materials to the former lawyer.

In some instances, the applicable jurisprudence or rules of the court require that defence counsel seek leave of the court to withdraw. Bringing an application to withdraw necessarily involves providing the Crown and court with timely notification. A number of ethical codes make this point expressly, stating that prompt notice to the Crown and court of an application for leave is required to minimize inconvenience to the court and witnesses.[81]

There may be instances, however, where notice to the court or Crown is not required, and the ethical codes to varying degrees recognize this possibility. Thus, where the lawyer's name does not appear on the court records as representing the accused, the rules do not require that counsel give notice to the court.[82] Also, a defence lawyer who withdraws before any court appearance or interaction with a prosecutor can surely dispense with notice to the Crown, especially where new counsel is promptly retained. To hold otherwise would impose a needless burden on counsel and in some cases might reveal information rightly considered by the client to be confidential, namely, that she has retained a lawyer in connection with the matter.

Caution: Notice to the Crown or court must never reveal solicitor-client confidences, absent the client's consent or the application of a recognized exception to the duty of confidentiality.[83]

---

79   Alta, Sask r 2.07(1) (commentary); BC, Man, Ont, NS, NL r 3.7-1, commentary 3.

80   Sask r 2.07(4)(c) & (d); BC, Ont, NS, NL r 3.7-4(c) & (d). Alta r 2.07(4)(c) provides only for notice to the Crown, presumably because, as mentioned in the accompanying commentary, the usual practice in Alberta when withdrawing from a criminal case is to seek leave in open court.

81   Sask r 2.07(6) (commentary); BC, Ont, NS, NL r 3.7-6, commentary 1.

82   Sask r 2.07(4)(d); BC, Ont, NS, NL r 3.7-4(d).

83   See Section M, below in this chapter.

L. LEAVE OF THE COURT TO WITHDRAW

A hotly debated issue in Canada used to be whether criminal defence counsel had to obtain leave of the court before terminating the client-lawyer relationship. Until a few years ago, most ethical codes did not contain such a requirement, Ontario being the notable exception, and the caselaw in British Columbia and Yukon clashed with that from most of the rest of the country on this point.[84] But the debate in this area has now mostly been settled by the Supreme Court of Canada's decision in *R v Cunningham*.[85]

1) Jurisdiction of Court to Regulate Counsel's Withdrawal

Cunningham holds that courts have the inherent or statutorily implied power to regulate the withdrawal of criminal defence counsel.[86] The rationale behind affording courts this jurisdiction is that lawyers are "key actors in the administration of justice" and that courts must therefore have the power to regulate their conduct where required to safeguard the integrity of the justice system.[87]

More particularly, the withdrawal of counsel has the potential to cause considerable harm to the judicial process, in which case there may be good reason for the court to intervene to prevent a lawyer from getting off the record. An obvious injury that can flow from withdrawal of counsel is prejudice to the accused caused by being forced on to trial without a lawyer. But harm can also arise where the proceeding is delayed so that the accused can attempt to retain new counsel, including

- prejudice to the accused in the form of the ongoing stigmatization that arises from criminal charges and, if he does not have bail, prolonged pre-trial custody;
- prejudice to the Crown case if witnesses become unavailable or their memories fade;
- inconvenience or stress caused to complainants, other witnesses, and jurors; and
- the deleterious impact on society's interest in having criminal matters resolved in an expedient manner.[88]

---

84   For a discussion of how things used to be, see Michel Proulx & David Layton, *Ethics and Canadian Criminal Law* (Toronto: Irwin Law, 2001) at 615–20.

85   *Cunningham*, above note 11. See also *R v Anderson*, 2014 SCC 41 at para 58.

86   *Cunningham*, above note 11 at paras 18–20.

87   *Ibid* at para 18.

88   *Ibid* at para 22.

This judicial power to regulate criminal defence counsel's withdrawal does not, however, supplant each law society's ability to do so as well. Courts must sometimes intervene to prevent harm to the administration of justice, and so act to prevent future harm. Law societies tend to act reactively, becoming involved after the fact if a lawyer has withdrawn without good cause. As noted in *Cunningham*, both the judicial and governing-body roles are important in helping to regulate the legal profession and protect the proper operation of the justice system.[89]

2) Operation of Privilege and Confidentiality in relation to Non-payment of Fees

Cunningham holds that requiring a lawyer to inform the court that the client has failed to pay agreed-upon fees as a precondition to obtaining leave to withdraw does not violate solicitor-client privilege. This is so because the privilege does not cover fee information that is unrelated to the merits of the case and will not prejudice the client's interests regarding the merits if released. The "sliver of information" that the accused has failed to pay or will not be paying his fees will rarely be of any use to the prosecution in proving guilt.[90]

Granted, the ethical duty of confidentiality continues to apply to all fee information, including whether or not the client has paid or will be paying his fees.[91] But *Cunningham* permits counsel to release this information, as an exception to the ethical duty, where necessary to bring an application for leave to withdraw.[92]

3) Outer Limit of Court's Jurisdiction: No Threat to Scheduled Hearing Date

According to *Cunningham*, where a lawyer wishes to withdraw far enough ahead of a scheduled proceeding that an adjournment will be unnecessary, the court must allow withdrawal, and there is no need to inquire into counsel's reasons for seeking to get off the record.[93] This limit on the court's jurisdiction to refuse leave to withdraw or delve into the reasons behind counsel's decision makes sense given that the power to intervene is based on the need to prevent the harm that can arise

---

89 *Ibid* at para 35.
90 *Ibid* at paras 28–31.
91 *Ibid* at para 31. See also Example 3 in Chapter 4, Section D.
92 *Cunningham*, above note 11 at paras 31 and 48. See also Chapter 5, Section F.
93 *Cunningham, ibid* at paras 47 and 59.

where an accused is forced on without counsel or where withdrawal leads to the trial being delayed. The spectre of these harms does not arise where counsel gets off the record in sufficient time for the client to retain and instruct a new lawyer to appear at the scheduled hearing.

4) Court's Jurisdiction Where Withdrawal Jeopardizes Scheduled Hearing Date

Where the trial date is close enough that withdrawal may result in the need for an adjournment, counsel must seek leave of the court to get off the record. Counsel should inform the court that she seeks leave to withdraw for "ethical reasons," non-payment of fees, or another specific reason if solicitor-client privilege is not engaged.[94]

a) Ethical Reasons
Cunningham defines "ethical reasons" as encompassing those cases where "an issue has arisen in the solicitor-client relationship where it is now impossible for counsel to continue in good conscience to represent the accused."[95] Examples given of "ethical reasons" include where the client instructs counsel to act unethically or where the client has refused counsel's advice on an important trial issue.[96] "Ethical reasons" does *not* include non-payment of fees.[97]

Two important consequences flow from counsel's statement to the court that withdrawal is being sought for ethical reasons. First, the court must accept this explanation at face value and cannot inquire further as to specifics; to hold otherwise would impermissibly risk violating solicitor-client privilege.[98] Second, the court must grant a request to withdraw for ethical reasons because it would be inappropriate to force counsel to continue with the retainer when to do so would mean acting unethically.[99]

---

94   *Ibid* at para 48.
95   *Ibid*.
96   *Ibid*. See also *R v Abada*, 2011 ONSC 2803 at paras 24–27.
97   *Cunningham*, above note 11 at para 48. See also *R v Cartolano*, [2012] OJ No 6319 at para 3 (SCJ) [*Cartolano*]; *Deschamps*, above note 11 at para 24.
98   *Cunningham*, above note 11 at para 48. But see *R v Leask*, 2012 BCSC 1416 at para 3 [*Leask*]: where counsel seeks to withdraw for ethical reasons, the court should allow withdrawal "after inquiring sufficiently to ascertain the general basis of the application"; *R v Wilson*, 2012 SKQB 339 at para 4 (QB) [*Wilson*]: court can make limited inquiries not intruding on solicitor-client privilege to clarify whether leave is sought for non-payment of fees or ethical reasons.
99   *Cunningham*, above note 11 at paras 49 and 59.

It has been argued that, by requiring the court to accept counsel's explanation at face value, *Cunningham* precludes the client from challenging the assertion that withdrawal is required for ethical reasons, as opposed to some other motive, such as a failure to pay legal fees.[100] This interpretation of *Cunningham* cannot be accurate. The client is always free to reveal privileged and confidential information, and if he does so, the court will rule on defence counsel's application based on whatever findings of fact are justified.[101] Of course, unless the lawyer is misleading the court, it will almost always be in the client's best interests that nothing more be said. The rationale behind the "ethical reasons" category is to protect the client's confidences, unless waived, while recognizing that lawyers should not be forced to act unethically in putting forward a defence.

A second, more valid complaint is that in uttering the phrase "ethical reasons" the lawyer is implicitly stating, "My client insists that the defence be conducted in an illegal or unethical way." The concern is that harmful privileged and confidential information is being released by implication. The "ethical reasons" phrase is most redolent of client impropriety where counsel seeks to withdraw just after the Crown has closed its case or during the defence case, for the inference will often be available that the client is insisting that counsel lead false evidence. This problem has been discussed in Chapter 7.[102] Suffice it here to say that the term "ethical reasons" is not restricted to instances where the client wants to act or has acted improperly, and its adoption in *Cunningham* is a considerable improvement on the sorts of things that lawyers have in the past said to courts while withdrawing. Unless and until courts and law societies endorse criminal defence counsel's continuing to act in knowing breach of the ethical codes, the "ethical reasons" solution in *Cunningham* is the best response available to an admittedly difficult problem.

b) Non-payment of Fees

Where the lawyer seeks to withdraw for non-payment of fees, the need to protect solicitor-client privilege prohibits the court from inquiring

---

100 See Annalise Acorn, "Jumping Ship: *R v Cunningham* and the Lawyer's Right to Withdraw" (2011) 44 UBC L Rev 381 at 397–98.

101 This approximates what occurred in *R v Potts*, 2009 ABPC 281, although counsel there initially revealed much, much more information than would be permitted under *Cunningham*. See also *Leask* and *Wilson*, both above note 98, which suggest that courts are prepared to make some further inquiries of defence counsel to ensure that the term "ethical reasons" is being used properly.

102 See, in particular, Chapter 7, Section F(4)(a).

to obtain further details.[103] Nonetheless and in sharp contrast to where the lawyer's application is based on ethical reasons, *Cunningham* holds that a court has the power to refuse leave for non-payment where "necessary to prevent serious harm to the administration of justice."[104] Still, this standard is demanding: the discretion to refuse leave to withdraw will be exercised only in the most serious of circumstances, exceedingly sparingly, and as a last resort.[105] Moreover, a decision to force counsel on requires a proper basis in the record.[106]

Cunningham states that in determining whether to grant leave to withdraw for non-payment of fees the court should consider the following non-exhaustive list of factors:[107]

- whether it is feasible for the accused to represent herself;
- other means of obtaining representation;
- impact on the accused from delay in proceedings, particularly if the accused is in custody;
- conduct of counsel, for example whether counsel gave reasonable notice to the accused to allow the accused to seek other means of representation or whether counsel sought leave of the court to withdraw at the earliest possible time;
- impact on the Crown and any co-accused;
- impact on complainants, witnesses, and jurors;
- fairness to defence counsel, including consideration of the expected length and complexity of the proceedings;
- history of the proceedings, for example whether the accused has changed lawyers repeatedly.

Whether the allotted court time can otherwise be usefully filled is *not*, however, a proper consideration in determining whether leave to withdraw should be granted.[108]

---

103 *Cunningham*, above note 11 at para 48.

104 *Ibid* at paras 1, 45, 50, and 59.

105 *Ibid* at paras 45 and 54. Query whether or not this high standard retreats somewhat from the position, taken in some earlier decisions, that leave to withdraw will generally be refused where the result would be to cause serious prejudice to the client: see, for example, *R v Peterman* (2004), 70 OR (3d) 481 at para 38 (CA) [*Peterman*]; *Deschamps*, above note 11 at paras 17 and 25; *R v Cai*, 2002 ABCA 299 at para 51, leave to appeal to SCC refused, [2003] SCCA No 360; *Kong*, above note 26 at para 8.

106 *Cunningham*, above note 11 at para 54.

107 *Ibid* at para 50, adding that all of these factors are independent of the solicitor-client relationship, and so their revelation does not threaten a breach of solicitor-client privilege.

108 *Ibid* at para 51.

c) Other Reasons

Cunningham recognizes that counsel may seek to withdraw for reasons other than non-payment of fees or ethical reasons. Examples given are requests to get off the record because counsel has an interesting new file requiring immediate attention, has vacation plans that conflict with the scheduled hearing date, or is facing an unmanageable workload.[109] Whatever the reason, the application for leave must set out the basis on which withdrawal is sought provided that doing so does not violate solicitor-client privilege.[110]

5) Counsel's Obligations If Leave Is Refused and Avoiding Problems in Advance

If the court refuses to allow a lawyer to terminate the relationship, there may be room to seek review from a higher court on a correctness standard.[111] But unless the court's order is overturned, counsel must remain on the case — refusing to do so may lead to a contempt citation[112] and will amount to a breach of the ethical rules governing withdrawal.[113]

In continuing on with the case, counsel must not eschew the duty to defend the client competently, resolutely, and loyally. Doing so may call for extraordinary patience and understanding, but the client should not be made to suffer simply because counsel is unhappy with the court's decision. On the other hand, counsel who is forced to continue with a case does not thereby acquire a licence to conduct the defence in a manner that violates the rules of professional conduct.

Caution: Counsel should anticipate and react to ethical problems that raise the spectre of withdrawal well in advance of the trial if reasonably

---

109 *Ibid* at paras 40 and 48. The last of these examples arguably implicates the issue of competence and may oblige counsel to apply to withdraw: see Section F, above in this chapter; American Bar Association, Standing Committee on Ethics and Professional Responsibility, Formal Opinion 06-441, "Ethical Obligations of Lawyers Who Represent Indigent Criminal Defendants When Excessive Caseloads Interfere with Competent and Diligent Representation" (13 May 2006).

110 *Cunningham*, above note 11 at para 48.

111 See *ibid* at paras 55–58. See also *Wilson*, above note 98 at para 3.

112 See *Cunningham*, above note 11 at para 50.

113 ABA Model Rule 1.16(c) states that a lawyer must continue to act where so ordered by the court, despite having valid reason to withdraw. The Third Restatement § 31, comment "c," & § 32, comment "d," suggest that counsel who is wrongly denied leave to withdraw can do no more than seek to overturn the decision on appeal.

possible. Doing so lessens the chance that leave of the court to with-draw will be required or that where required it will be denied.[114]

Advice: A lawyer who fears well before trial that the client may be un-able to fulfill a contractual obligation to provide payment may reason-ably wish to avoid later having to bring an application to withdraw or to minimize the danger of leave to withdraw being denied. One option is to appear on a limited scope retainer and not commit to act at trial until sufficient payment is received. Yet in doing so the lawyer must expressly articulate to the court and Crown the limited nature of the retainer at the time of counsel's first appearance and continue to do so on each subsequent appearance unless and until the status of the retainer changes.[115]

6) Relationship between *Cunningham*, Ethical Code Rules, and Rules of the Court

The ethical rules in several Canadian jurisdictions echo the decision in *Cunningham* insofar as they require counsel to bring an application for leave to withdraw where there is insufficient time for the client to retain new counsel who can prepare for the scheduled trial date.[116] They also provide that counsel who believes that leave of the court is required to withdraw should promptly inform the Crown and court of the intention to apply for leave so as to minimize inconvenience to the court and witnesses.[117]

Yet these same governing bodies prohibit counsel from withdrawing for non-payment of fees where the client does not have time to find a new lawyer who can prepare for the scheduled hearing and where an adjournment of the case is not possible without adversely affecting the

---

114 Cases where counsel waited too long to withdraw based on non-payment of fees and was denied leave include *R v Okafor*, 2009 ONCA 672 at para 11; *Brundia*, above note 76 at paras 46–52; *Cartolano*, above note 97 at para 7. Delay in bringing the application also appears to have occurred in *R v Montgomery*, 2013 BCSC 1007. Contrast *R v RND*, 2010 MBQB 252 at para 13, where counsel acted promptly to bring the application.

115 See *Cunningham*, above note 11 at para 13; *Deschamps*, above note 11 at para 22; *DDC*, above note 11 at 329 & 330 [paras 23–24 and 27]. See also Alta, Sask r 2.02(1.1); BC, NL r 3.2-1.1; Man, NS r 3.2-1A; Ont r 3.2-1A & 3.2-1A.1, which address limited scope retainers and among other things require that the client be fully informed as to the restricted scope of representation, that the nature of the retainer be confirmed with the client in writing, and that the lawyer be careful not to mislead the court as to the scope of the retainer.

116 Sask r 2.07(6); BC, NS, Ont, NL r 3.7-6.

117 Sask r 2.07(6) (commentary); BC, Ont, NS, NL r 3.7-6, commentary 1.

client's interests.[118] By contrast, *Cunningham* envisions the possibility that counsel will be allowed to withdraw for non-payment even though the client is forced on to trial on the scheduled date, with or without counsel, or even though an adjournment to retain new counsel will cause the client prejudice. The restrictions imposed under these ethical rules are thus more demanding than is the threshold for obtaining leave to withdraw under *Cunningham*.[119]

As noted in Section L(3), above in this chapter, pursuant to *Cunningham* the court has no jurisdiction to prevent counsel from withdrawing or to inquire of counsel as to the reasons why the retainer is being terminated where getting off the record does not put the scheduled trial date at risk. Absent a realistic risk that withdrawal will delay a scheduled proceeding, *Cunningham* thus appears not to require leave of the court to withdraw, a conclusion that finds support in a number of ethical codes.[120] Nonetheless, in some jurisdictions the rules of the court will require an application to withdraw once counsel has gone on the record, even where terminating the retainer poses no risk to the scheduled trial date.[121]

M. CONFIDENTIALITY

Some duties owed by a lawyer to the client survive the end of the client-lawyer relationship and most certainly persist during the withdrawal process, such as the duty to avoid conflicts of interest.[122] Prime among these persisting duties is the lawyer's obligation concerning confidentiality. Maintaining confidences despite the retainer's termination encourages the client to be candid with counsel during the life of the relationship, secure in the knowledge that the confidences will never be revealed. Both ethical rules and caselaw indicate that counsel must

---

118 Sask r 2.07(5); BC, Ont, NS, NL r 3.7-5.

119 Indeed, there is a good argument that pre-*Cunningham* authorities suggesting that the test for granting leave to withdraw for non-payment is coterminous with that imposed by the ethical codes are no longer good law (for example, *Peterman*, above note 105 at para 38; *R v Clement* (2002), 166 CCC (3d) 219 at para 16 (Ont CA); *Brundia*, above note 76 at para 47; *R v Middaugh*, [2007] OJ No 2347 at para 9 (SCJ)).

120 Alta, Sask r 2.07(4); BC, NS, Ont, NL r 3.7-4. Counsel will nonetheless be required to notify the Crown and court in writing that he is getting off the record: see Section K, above in this chapter.

121 See Section C, above in this chapter.

122 This duty applies to former clients too: see Chapter 6, Section I(1).

keep a client's confidences not only during the course of the retainer but also after counsel's employment has terminated.[123]

It is thus axiomatic that counsel must not reveal confidential information out of spite or revenge where the relationship has dissolved into acrimony. However, on occasion, counsel's duty to maintain confidences in the course of withdrawing presents a real challenge and is not so quickly amenable to a straightforward solution.

1) Providing Reasons for Withdrawal

Keeping the client's confidences can be difficult where counsel is seeking leave of the court to withdraw from a case. The challenge is to remain loyal to the client, respecting the secrets with which counsel has been entrusted, but at the same time to convince the court that withdrawal is warranted. In particular, some grounds for withdrawal are not valid or could be the subject of disagreement among reasonable people. Other grounds clearly warrant or mandate termination of the retainer.

Cunningham makes clear that where counsel is withdrawing for ethical reasons or non-payment, no other information as to the reasons for the application can be required by the court, for to do so would create an unacceptable risk of eroding solicitor-client privilege.[124] The court may nonetheless require that counsel provide information as to the general background of the matter and the potential for harm if leave is or is not granted where such matters do not involve privileged information.[125]

A number of rules of professional conduct dealing with withdrawal address the issue of confidentiality. In British Columbia, the code forbids the withdrawing lawyer from disclosing any confidential information as to the reason for withdrawal unless the client consents or unless counsel is permitted by an exception at law, such as the recognition in *Cunningham* permitting disclosure of non-payment of fees.[126] Other Canadian codes state that a lawyer who has withdrawn because of a conflict with the client should not reveal the cause of the dispute in

---

123 See Chapter 4, Section H(7). In the particular context of withdrawal, see also BC r 3.7-9.1; Alta, Sask r 2.07(4) (commentary); Man r 3.7-9, commentary 1; Ont, NS, NL 3.7-4, commentary 1; *Cunningham*, above note 11 at paras 26, 31–34, 48, and 50.

124 *Cunningham, ibid* at para 48. See also *DDC*, above note 11 at 330 [para 26]; *R v Downey*, [2002] OJ No 1524 at para 85 (SCJ); *R v Golding*, 2007 NBQB 320 at para 13.

125 *Cunningham*, above note 11 at para 50.

126 BC r 3.7-9.1 & commentary 1.

addressing the Crown or court or make reference to any matter that would violate solicitor-client privilege.[127]

Example 1: Counsel decides to withdraw from a joint retainer based on the belief that his clients have misled the court in an attempt to obtain an adjournment. In applying to withdraw, he expresses this belief to the judge, mentioning that he has absolutely no confidence in anything his clients tell him and does not want to be part of what might be perceived as a fraud on the court. These comments are highly improper, even if fully justified. Counsel should have said no more than that he was applying to withdraw for ethical reasons.[128]

Example 2: A lawyer applies to withdraw during the trial. The court asks for an explanation and is obviously not satisfied with counsel's rote comment that confidentiality mandates silence. The judge accordingly turns her attention to the accused and strongly pressures him to waive confidentiality. At this point, the client and counsel are in a difficult bind. The client essentially lacks representation, even though leave to withdraw has not yet been granted, and is probably unfamiliar with the law. Counsel seeking to withdraw does not necessarily have the same interests as the client and may in fact prefer that confidentiality be waived to provide a stronger basis for the application for leave to withdraw. For these reasons, counsel should attempt to intervene where the court persists in questioning the client and, if appropriate, suggest that the client receive independent legal advice.[129]

Cross-reference: One of the most difficult challenges to counsel's duty to maintain confidentiality occurs where the client persists in a plan to act illegally in conducting the defence. The applicable considerations are discussed in detail in Chapter 1, Section H, and Chapter 7, sections F(4)(a) and G(3)(a).

As a final point, defence lawyers should not jump to the conclusion that the reasons for withdrawal are confidential in every case. In some instances, the reasons may not involve confidential information, for example where counsel formerly represented a Crown witness in

---

127 Sask r 2.07(4) (commentary); Ont, NS, NL r 3.7-4, commentary 1. To roughly similar effect, see Alta r 2.07(4) (commentary); Man r 3.7-9, commentary 1.

128 This example is based on the facts in *R v Bolianatz*, 2012 ABCA 238 at paras 14–15.

129 See *Leask v Cronin* (1985), 18 CCC (3d) 315 at 326 [para 14] (BCSC), discussed in *Cunningham*, above note 11 at paras 32–33 (criticizing the trial judge's pressuring the accused to waive confidentiality).

a related matter.[130] It may also be that the confidences will not, if disclosed, cause any material harm to the client, and the client is happy to consent to their revelation. Very occasionally, disclosure against the client's wishes will be permitted, for instance where the client responds to counsel's application for leave to withdraw by alleging professional misconduct and has thereby waived confidentiality to the limited extent necessary to enable counsel to defend herself.[131]

2) Withdrawal as Implied Disclosure of Confidential Information

Sometimes counsel can withdraw without arousing any suspicion as to the reason for terminating the retainer. Take the example where the lawyer discovers very early on in the matter that the client has fraudulently obtained legal aid.[132] The lawyer can terminate the relationship without providing any explanation whatsoever to the Crown or court,[133] and in the circumstances the act of withdrawal will provide no basis for anyone to know or even suspect the real reason.

However, the mere act of withdrawal may threaten the implied disclosure of confidences, no matter how little counsel says in seeking leave to terminate the retainer. Such is often the case where the client-lawyer relationship abruptly ruptures in the middle of a trial, and the context of the request to withdraw suggests that the client has acted improperly or plans to do so.[134] Sometimes there is no way to avoid the possibility that outsiders may suspect, perhaps correctly, the reason for counsel's application to withdraw. Counsel's use of the term "ethical reasons" in bringing the application, endorsed in *Cunningham*, lessens the risk of harm in this respect.[135] Nonetheless, the resulting potential for harm to the client is a legitimate factor to take into account where counsel has discretion in deciding whether to seek leave to withdraw.[136]

---

130 See also Section L(4)(c), above in this chapter, providing other examples that clearly do not involve confidential client information.

131 See Chapter 5, Section E.

132 A lawyer must surely withdraw in such circumstances, for continuing to work on the case and collect from the legal aid plan would constitute knowing participation in the fraud.

133 See Section L(3), above in this chapter.

134 See, for example, Chapter 7, Section F(4)(a).

135 *Cunningham*, above note 11. See the discussion in the paragraph associated with note 102, above in this chapter.

136 See Section G, above in this chapter.

A very different approach is for counsel intentionally to utilize a "noisy" withdrawal to disavow any connection to fraudulent acts unknowingly committed on behalf of the client during the course of legal representation. In the United States, the American Bar Association (ABA) used to condone lawyers' withdrawing in a manner that alerted an opponent to the possibility that the client had used counsel's services to commit an ongoing or future fraud.[137] An example of a noisy withdrawal would be counsel's notifying a third party that a letter or document previously prepared by counsel should not be relied upon. As noted elsewhere, the distinction between an impermissible disclosure of confidences and a noisy withdrawal is not always transparent.[138] In any event, the ABA's noisy withdrawal option has been replaced by an expanded future-harm exception that permits disclosure of otherwise confidential information to prevent substantial injury to property or financial interests caused by client crime involving a lawyer's services.[139] More importantly, noisy withdrawal is likely forbidden by Canadian rules of professional conduct, even where the client has implicated counsel in illegality.[140]

3) Successor Lawyers

A separate matter concerns confidentiality vis-à-vis the successor lawyer. It has been suggested that counsel cannot provide the new lawyer with confidential information except as instructed to do so by the former client.[141] Yet it usually makes sense for the lawyer to assume that the client consents to passing on information regarding matters pertinent to the case. A rule found in most Canadian ethical codes states that on new counsel being retained former counsel must "co-operate with the successor lawyer in the transfer of the file so as to minimize expense and avoid prejudice to the client."[142] The commentary to this

---

137 See American Bar Association, Standing Committee on Ethics and Professional Responsibility, Formal Opinion 92-366, "Withdrawal When a Lawyer's Services Will Otherwise Be Used to Perpetrate a Fraud" (8 August 1992); American Bar Association, Standing Committee on Ethics and Professional Responsibility, Formal Opinion 93-375, "The Lawyer's Obligation to Disclose Information Adverse to the Client in the Context of Bank Examination" (6 August 1993).
138 See Chapter 5, Section L(4).
139 See Chapter 5, Section L(6).
140 See Chapter 5, Section K, and in particular the discussion of the ethical rules in Section K(3).
141 See Mark Orkin, *Legal Ethics*, 2d ed (Toronto: Canada Law Book, 2011) at 95.
142 Alta r 2.07(7)(f); Sask r 2.07(9)(f); BC, Man, Ont, NL r 3.7-9(f); NS r 3.7-9(h); NB ch 10, commentary 5(a)(v); CBA Code ch XII, commentary 8(e).

rule precludes the conveyance of "confidential information not clearly related to the matter" absent the client's express written consent.[143] This rule and commentary appear to recognize an implicit authority to reveal confidential information clearly related to the matter to the successor lawyer.[144] Yet in our view former counsel must not do so where expressly forbidden by the client barring the application of an exception to the ethical duty of confidentiality.

Practice observation: Many criminal lawyers who have withdrawn from a matter or been discharged require a signed direction from the client before releasing the file or relevant confidential information to successor counsel, and successor counsel typically comply with these requests.

N. OTHER DUTIES UPON TERMINATION

While confidentiality and notice are especially important duties associated with the termination of a client-lawyer relationship, there are other obligations that fall upon the lawyer who has withdrawn or been discharged. Many codes of professional conduct state that withdrawing or former counsel must "try to minimize expense and avoid prejudice to the client" and "do all that can reasonably be done to facilitate the orderly transfer of the matter to the successor lawyer."[145] More specifically, the codes provide that a lawyer whose retainer has been terminated should

1) deliver to or to the order of the client all papers and property to which the client is entitled;[146]

---

143 Alta r 2.07(7) (commentary); Sask r 2.07(9) (commentary); BC, Man, Ont, NS, NL r 3.7-9, commentary 4; NB ch 10, commentary 5(a). CBA Code ch XII, commentary 9, is to the same effect, but consent does not have to be in writing.

144 By contrast, until 2011 Alberta forbade the disclosure of confidential information to successor counsel unless expressly or impliedly authorized by the client, and until 2012 Nova Scotia prohibited such disclosure absent the client's express instructions: see Proulx & Layton, above note 84 at 624–25.

145 Alta r 2.07(6); Sask r 2.07(8); BC, Man, Ont, NS, NL r 3.7-8. Almost identical language is used in NB ch 10, commentary 1(b); CBA Code ch XII, commentary 2. See also ABA Model Rule 1.16(d); Third Restatement § 33: counsel must act "to the extent reasonably practicable to protect the client's interests."

146 Alta r 2.07(7)(b); Sask r 2.07(9)(b); NS r 3.7-9(d); BC, Man, Ont, NL r 3.7-9(b); NB ch 10, commentary 5(a)(i); CBA Code ch XII, commentary 8(a). See *In re Anonymous*, 914 NE2d 265 (Ind 2009); *In re Peterson*, 725 SE2d 252 (Ga 2012).

2) subject to any applicable trust conditions give the client all information that may be required in connection with the case or matter;[147]
3) account for all funds of the client then held or previously dealt with, including the refunding of any remuneration not earned during the representation;[148]
4) promptly render an account for outstanding fees and disbursements;[149]
5) co-operate with the successor lawyer in the transfer of the file so as to minimize expense and avoid prejudice to the client;[150] and
6) comply with the applicable rules of the court.[151]

Caveat: The duty to deliver file materials to or to the order of a former client only applies to those materials to which the client is entitled.[152] This duty is thus subject to (1) any undertakings that apply to disclosure materials received from the Crown and (2) counsel's duty to scrupulously avoid any conduct that he reasonably suspects would aid a client or third party in committing a crime.[153]

Most governing bodies also include a commentary stating that where the withdrawing lawyer formerly acted for two or more clients and ceases to act for any of them, she "should co-operate with the successor lawyer or lawyers to the extent required by the rules and should seek to avoid unseemly rivalry, whether real or apparent."[154] In Alberta, this commentary is made subject to the rules on confidentiality and conflict of interest.[155] The central concerns thus appear to be that confidential information not be shared with the successor lawyer if pre-

---

147 Alta r 2.07(7)(c); Sask r 2.07(9)(c); NS r 3.7-9(e); BC, Man, Ont, NL r 3.7-9(c); NB ch 10, commentary 5(a)(ii); CBA Code ch XII, commentary 8(b).
148 Alta r 2.07(7)(d); Sask r 2.07(9)(d); NS r 3.7-9(f); BC, Man, Ont, NL r 3.7-9(d); NB ch 10, commentary 5(a)(iii); CBA Code ch XII, commentary 8(c).
149 Alta r 2.07(7)(e); Sask r 2.07(9)(e); NS r 3.7-9(g); BC, Man, Ont, NL r 3.7-9(e); NB ch 10, commentary 5(a)(iv); CBA Code ch XII, commentary 8(d).
150 Alta r 2.07(7)(f); Sask r 2.07(9)(f); NS r 3.7-9 (h); BC, Man, Ont, NL r 3.7-9(f); NB ch 10, commentary 5(a)(v); CBA Code ch XII, commentary 8(e). This duty includes providing the successor lawyer with any memoranda of fact or law prepared for the matter: see Alta r 2.07(7) (commentary); Sask r 2.07(9) (commentary); BC, Man, Ont, NS, NL r 3.7-9, commentary 4; NB ch 10, commentary 5(a); CBA Code ch XII, commentary 9.
151 Alta r 2.07(7)(g); Sask r 2.07(9)(h); Man r 3.7-9(h); NS r 3.7-9(i); BC, Ont, NL r 3.7-9(g).
152 See the rules and commentaries cited at note 146, above in this chapter.
153 See the discussion in Chapter 4, Section R.
154 Alta r 2.07(7) (commentary); Sask r 2.07(9) (commentary); BC, Ont, NS, NL r 3.7-9, commentary 5; NB ch 10, commentary 5(b); CBA Code ch XII, commentary 10.
155 Alta r 2.07(7) (commentary).

cluded by these other rules and that withdrawing counsel strive not to favour one former client's interest over another's in dealing with successor counsel.

We believe that counsel though not explicitly required by Canadian rules has an obligation to pass on to the client, or successor lawyer, all material communications received from third parties following termination where related to the case and reasonable to do so. For instance, disclosure materials or a resolution offer mistakenly sent to counsel after withdrawal or discharge should be conveyed to the former client, or successor counsel. The Third Restatement is one of the few codes of professional responsibility that specifically imposes this requirement.[156] Yet the general obligation to mitigate prejudice on withdrawing, imposed by most Canadian codes, surely embraces a duty to pass on material communications related to the matter in question.[157]

Where termination occurs because of conflict of interest or concerns regarding competence and where the client appears to require help finding new representation, counsel has a duty to provide reasonable assistance.[158] Where termination occurs for other reasons, especially where counsel has withdrawn owing to a serious deception by the client or been discharged without valid cause, we do not believe that such a duty applies. This is especially so where the lawyer reasonably believes that the client will attempt to dupe the new lawyer into unknowingly assisting with an illegal aim. To help search for a new lawyer in such circumstances would be to further the client's illegal purpose and so violate the prohibition against conduct that assists in dishonesty, fraud, or illegality.[159]

O. DUTIES OF A POTENTIAL SUCCESSOR LAWYER AND A SUCCESSOR LAWYER

The lawyer who takes over a case from a colleague whose retainer has terminated or who is asked to consider doing so by a prospective client should be guided by a number of considerations and duties. A distinction in this regard can be made between the lawyer who is approached while another lawyer is, or may be, currently acting (the potential successor-lawyer situation) and the lawyer who is formally retained

---

156 Third Restatement § 33(2)(c).
157 See the rules referred to at note 145, above in this chapter.
158 See the related discussion in Chapter 2, Section J.
159 The rules setting out this prohibition are discussed in Chapter 2, Section B(1).

following the termination of a retainer with a previous lawyer (the successor-lawyer situation).

1) Potential Successor Lawyer

Let us begin with a fairly common scenario. A lawyer is approached by an individual who is, or may be, currently represented by another counsel. This individual is not happy with the existing representation and wishes to switch to new counsel. Under these circumstances, the rules of professional conduct require that the potential successor counsel satisfy himself that the other lawyer has already withdrawn or been discharged.[160] We do not disagree but prefer the following, more nuanced, approach:

1) Counsel must first attempt to determine the exact status of the client's legal representation. Some clients may be mistaken, confused, or unclear regarding this point, yet the matter can be clarified with a few simple questions. If uncertainty in this regard cannot be resolved, the interview should go no further absent communication with the other counsel (see point 3, below).

2) If there is any question whether the individual is currently represented by another lawyer, counsel should generally decline to discuss the case, because to do so is prohibited by the no-contact rule.[161] It is nonetheless permissible to communicate with an already represented individual without obtaining the permission of, or even notifying, existing counsel for the limited purpose of providing a second opinion regarding a matter.[162]

3) Counsel may wish to inform the other lawyer that she has been approached, so that a frayed professional relationship can be patched up, but can do so only if the prospective client does not object.[163] There is no duty, however, to advise the prospective client to maintain the professional relationship. Indeed, it may be improper to

---

160 Alta r 2.07(8); Sask r 2.07(10); BC, Man, NS, NL r 3.7-10. Other rules are to the same effect but also permit the potential successor lawyer to take on the case if satisfied that the other lawyer approves: Ont r 3.7-10; CBA Code ch XII, commentary 12. See also American Bar Association, Standing Committee on Ethics and Professional Responsibility, Formal Opinion 95-396, "Communications with Represented Persons" (28 July 1995), part VIII.

161 See Chapter 8, Section C(1).

162 See Chapter 8, Section C(1)(h).

163 A potential client's consultation with a lawyer whom he is contemplating retaining is covered by solicitor-client privilege and the ethical duty of confidentiality: see Chapter 4, Section H(6).

pressure the individual unduly in this regard, given the freedom of choice that all accused must have in deciding whom to retain as counsel.[164]

4) If counsel is satisfied that the other lawyer has withdrawn or been discharged, it is permissible to discuss the matter with the prospective client and seriously consider taking on the case.

5) The fact that the individual has failed to pay an outstanding account from former counsel may justify refusing to take on the case provided the individual is not unduly prejudiced as a result.[165]

These guidelines strive to avoid rash meddling in a pre-existing professional relationship but also recognize that a client must be free to obtain a second opinion and to discharge a lawyer and hire new counsel, if that is her wish.

2) Successor Lawyer

Once the successor lawyer is properly retained, he should represent the client in the normal course like any other. An issue sometimes arises, however, regarding an outstanding account from the former lawyer. Canadian rules of professional conduct state that successor counsel may properly urge the client to satisfy any such account, especially if the former lawyer withdrew for good cause or was capriciously discharged.[166] But where the trial is imminent or in progress, the successor lawyer should not allow an outstanding debt to former counsel to interfere with the current representation.[167]

A lawyer should exercise caution in taking on a case for a client who has discharged former counsel or whose former counsel has withdrawn owing to allegations of client impropriety or for any reason that is not immediately apparent. The circumstances that led to the termination of the previous client-lawyer relationship may identify the client as difficult and foretell a similar end to any subsequent relationship. The successor lawyer should consider adopting protective measures where necessary and possible, including a written agreement and advance

---

164   See *McCallen*, above note 12 at paras 32–40; *R v Le* (2011), 275 CCC (3d) 427 at para 41 (Man CA), leave to appeal to SCC refused, [2011] SCCA No 526; *R v Racine*, [2011] QJ No 15861 at para 31 (CA).

165   See Section O(2), below in this chapter.

166   Alta r 2.07(8) (commentary); Sask r 2.07(10) (commentary); BC, Man, Ont, NS, NL r 3.7-10, commentary 1; CBA Code ch XII, commentary 12.

167   See rules and commentaries cited at the preceding note except for Man r 3.7-10, which does not reference this point; J Morden, "A Succeeding Solicitor's Duty to Protect the Account of the Former Solicitor" (1971) 5 L Soc'y Gaz 257 at 259.

payment in full. By the same token, counsel should take special care to monitor the relationship and communicate fully with the client on an ongoing basis, the better to avoid repetition of a previous breakdown.

P. DISSOLUTION OF A LAW FIRM OR LAWYER LEAVING A FIRM

When a law firm dissolves, the contracts between the clients and at least some of the firm's lawyers will be frustrated. An individual lawyer handling a client's file does not automatically continue with the case. Granted, in most instances the client will prefer to retain the services of the lawyer whom she regards as being in charge of their matter.[168] But the final decision rests with the client, whose choice must be respected.

Lawyers whose retainers end because of the dissolution of a firm are required to adhere to the ethical rules applicable in all cases of withdrawal.[169] The same guidelines should apply when a lawyer leaves a firm.[170]

Q. TERMINATION FOR OTHER CAUSES

Sometimes events will transpire to end the relationship absent any intentional impetus from client or lawyer. A client or lawyer may die. The lawyer may be disbarred or suspended or ordered off the case by the court owing to conflict of interest alleged by a third party. Most commonly, the representation may run its natural course, leaving no further need for professional services.[171] In each of these examples, the lawyer's authority to continue acting for the client is terminated, and the duties normally attendant upon termination apply to the extent reasonably applicable in the circumstances.

---

168 See Alta, Sask r 2.07(1) (commentary); BC, Man, Ont, NS, NL r 3.7-1, commentary 4; NB ch 10, commentary 8; CBA Code ch XII, commentary 13.

169 See the commentaries mentioned in the preceding note except for NB ch 10, commentary 8, which does not reference this point.

170 See Alta, Sask r 2.07(1) (commentary); BC, Man, Ont, NS, NL 3.7-1, commentary 4. See also Third Restatement § 31, comment "f."

171 As to which, see notes 34–35, above in this chapter, plus the associated text.

THE PROSECUTOR

A. INTRODUCTION

The proper analysis of a prosecutor's ethical obligations begins with the recognition that the Crown occupies a unique role as a party in criminal litigation, seeking justice in the form of a reliable result reached through a fair process. Consequently, though in many ways the standards of conduct for prosecutors are similar to those for defence lawyers, a prosecutor cannot be guided by the exact same principles as govern a lawyer appearing for the accused. There are particular constraints imposed on prosecutors on account of their mission as advocates committed to truth seeking and fairness, constraints that do not apply to defence counsel. Granted, defence lawyers also owe an allegiance to a greater good in the sense that as officers of the court they cannot be purely adversarial and exclusively committed to their clients at the expense, for instance, of misleading the court. But defence counsel's obligations to the court are not nearly as extensive as the prosecutor's broad duties to the public interest.

Setting high ethical standards is consistent with the tradition of Crown counsel in this country, who generally carry out their role in an exemplary way.[1] Still, the amount of scrutiny levelled at prosecutors by the public, judiciary, and government has increased over the

---

1   See *R v Stinchcombe* (1991), 68 CCC (3d) 1 at 12 [para 23] (SCC) [*Stinchcombe*]; *R v Bain* (1992), 69 CCC (3d) 481 at 511 [para 2] (SCC).

past twenty-five years. Conviction appeals frequently include grounds attacking the propriety of prosecutorial conduct, for example an assertion that the cross-examination of an accused was abusive. More generally, post-mortems conducted on many wrongful convictions have reviewed Crown counsel's function at various stages of the criminal process,[2] and public inquiries have also probed the exercise of prosecutorial discretion following public criticism of charging decisions or plea resolutions.[3] Prosecution services have responded by formulating and making public comprehensive policy manuals that set standards regarding many aspects of the Crown function[4] and by endeavouring to ensure that prosecutions are carried out in a fair manner that achieves accurate results.[5]

---

2   See, for example, Nova Scotia, *Royal Commission on the Donald Marshall, Jr., Prosecution: Findings and Recommendations*, vol 1 (Halifax: The Commission, 1989) [*Marshall Inquiry Report*]; Ontario, *Report of the Commission on Proceedings Involving Guy Paul Morin* (Toronto: Ministry of the Attorney General, 1998) (Chair Fred Kaufman) [*Morin Inquiry Report*]; Manitoba, *The Inquiry regarding Thomas Sophonow: The Investigation, Prosecution and Consideration of Entitlement to Compensation* (Winnipeg: Attorney General, 2001) (Commissioner P Cory); Manitoba, *Report of the Commission of Inquiry into Certain Aspects of the Trial and Conviction of James Driskell* (Winnipeg: The Commission, 2007) (Commissioner Patrick J LeSage, QC) [*Driskell Inquiry Report*]; Newfoundland, *The Lamer Commission of Inquiry pertaining to the Cases of: Ronald Dalton, Gregory Parsons, and Randy Druken — Report and Annexes* (St John's: Government of Newfoundland and Labrador, 2006) (Commissioner Antonio Lamer) [*Lamer Inquiry Report*]; *Inquiry into Pediatric Forensic Pathology in Ontario: Report* (Toronto: Attorney General of Ontario, 2008) (Commissioner Hon Stephen T Goudge).

3   See, for example, British Columbia, *Forsaken: The Report of the Missing Women Commission of Inquiry* (Vancouver: The Commission, 2012) (Commissioner Wally T Oppal, QC) vol 2A at 26–80: decision to stay charge against Robert Pickton; Manitoba, *Report of the Taman Inquiry into the Investigation and Prosecution of Derek Harvey-Zenk* (Winnipeg: The Inquiry, 2008) (Commissioner Roger Salhany, QC) at 85–109: plea resolution involving police officer charged with serious off-duty offence.

4   See Section B, below in this chapter.

5   See, for example, the Canada, FPT Heads of Prosecutions Committee Working Group, *Report on the Prevention of Miscarriages of Justice* (Ottawa: Department of Justice, 2004) [FPT Heads of Prosecutions 2004 Report]; Canada, FPT Heads of Prosecutions Subcommittee on the Prevention of Wrongful Convictions, *The Path to Justice: Preventing Wrongful Convictions* (Ottawa: Public Prosecution Service of Canada, 2011) [FPT Heads of Prosecutions 2011 Report].

B. RULES OF PROFESSIONAL CONDUCT AND PROSECUTION SERVICE POLICY MANUALS

Canadian codes of professional conduct devote only modest space to the role of a prosecutor but nonetheless manage to succinctly encapsulate Crown counsel's singular justice-seeking function as an advocate. The relevant rule and commentary found in most codes states as follows:

> When acting as a prosecutor, a lawyer must act for the public and the administration of justice resolutely and honourably within the limits of the law while treating the tribunal with candour, fairness, courtesy, and respect.
>
> Commentary
>
> When engaged as a prosecutor, the lawyer's prime duty is not to seek to convict but to see that justice is done through a fair trial on the merits. The prosecutor exercises a public function involving much discretion and power and must act fairly and dispassionately. The prosecutor should not do anything that might prevent the accused from being represented by counsel or communicating with counsel and, to the extent required by law and accepted practice, should make timely disclosure to defence counsel or directly to an unrepresented accused of all relevant and known facts and witnesses, whether tending to show guilt or innocence.[6]

Much more detailed expositions of the proper function of a prosecutor can be found in the various Crown counsel policy manuals promulgated by Canadian prosecution services. These manuals provide guidance regarding a myriad of topics, from very general matters such as Crown counsel's duty to seek justice in the public interest and the importance of prosecutorial independence to extremely narrow and specific aspects of the prosecution function such as how to handle a domestic assault bail matter and when it is permissible to renege on a plea agreement. Traditionally unavailable to the public,[7] most Crown

---

6   Alta r 4.01(4) & commentary; Sask r 4.01(3) & commentary; BC, Man, NS, NL r 5.1-3 & commentary 1. Ont r 5.1-3 & commentary is the same except the rule uses "shall" instead of "must." To similar effect are CBA Code ch IX, commentary 9, and NB ch 8, commentary 13.

7   See John Edwards, "The Attorney General and the *Charter of Rights*" in Robert Sharpe, ed, *Charter Litigation* (Toronto: Butterworths, 1987) at 66: manuals were not public documents at that time; *R v Power* (1994), 89 CCC (3d) 1 at 17–18 [para 39] (SCC) [*Power*]: suggesting that prosecutorial charging decision guidelines should remain confidential.

policy manuals are now easily accessible on the Internet. This welcome development fosters a better understanding of the prosecution function among other actors in the justice system as well as the public.[8]

Prosecution service policy manuals do not constitute law and so are not binding on the courts.[9] Nor are they tantamount to rules of professional conduct enforced by the law societies, although breach of a manual guideline may lead to disciplinary action where also violating a governing body's own standards. Rather, the manuals are produced largely for the in-house management purpose of providing direction and guidance for Crown prosecutors.[10] They nonetheless constitute an important source of information regarding the principles and practice that inform prosecution work. It is therefore unsurprising that prosecution service manuals are sometimes given weight by courts in ascertaining Crown counsel's proper role in conducting a criminal prosecution.[11]

As a final point, many rules of professional conduct apply to both defence and Crown counsel. The prosecutor's special role as minister of justice may impact the way in which the particular rule affects Crown counsel. The same is true regarding defence counsel's special role as zealous advocate. But it is wrong to say that Crown lawyers are somehow held to a higher standard of ethical conduct.[12] The same level of

---

8   See *Public Prosecution Service of Canada Deskbook* (Ottawa: PPSC, 2014) ch 2.1, section 3 (Accountability), online: www.ppsc.gc.ca/eng/pub/fpsd-sfpg/index.html [*PPSC Deskbook*]: making such directives and guidelines public increases the accountability of Crown prosecutors. See also Hon Marc Rosenberg, "The Attorney General and the Administration of Criminal Justice" (2009) 34 Queen's LJ 813 at 848–51; Adam Dodek, "Lawyering at the Intersection of Public Law and Legal Ethics: Government Lawyers as Custodians of the Rule of Law" (2010) 33 Dal LJ 1 at 43–44.

9   See *R v Stobbe*, 2011 MBQB 280 at para 47; *R v Van Bibber*, 2010 YKTC 49 at para 76; *R v Wilder*, 2001 BCSC 1634 at para 8; *R v Atomic Energy of Canada Ltd*, [2001] OJ No 1580 at para 18 (SCJ) [*Atomic Energy*]; *R v Blencowe* (1997), 118 CCC (3d) 529 at paras 54–55 (Ont Ct Gen Div).

10 See *Atomic Energy*, above note 9.

11 See, for example, *R v Anderson*, 2014 SCC 41 at para 56 [*Anderson*]; *R v Spiers*, 2012 ONCA 798 at paras 47 and 87(a); *R v Gill*, 2012 ONCA 607 at para 67; *R v Dudley*, 2009 SCC 58 at para 55; *R v SJL*, 2009 SCC 14 at paras 38–39; *Miazga v Kvello Estate*, 2009 SCC 51 at para 64 [*Miazga*]; *R v Tshiamala*, 2011 QCCA 439 at para 110, leave to appeal to SCC refused, [2011] SCCA No 220 [*Tshiamala*]; *R v Duhamel*, 2012 ONSC 6449 at para 95; *R v Mohla*, 2012 ONSC 30 at para 127; *R v McFarlane*, [2006] OJ No 4857 at para 28 (SCJ); *R v Dosanjh*, 2002 BCSC 25 at para 10. See also Robert J Frater, *Prosecutorial Misconduct* (Aurora, ON: Canada Law Book, 2009) at 259.

12 See *Everingham v Ontario* (1992), 88 DLR (4th) 755 at 761 at paras 20–22 (Ont Div Ct).

professionalism is expected of all lawyers, whether they appear for the Crown, or they are members of the defence bar.

C. THE PROSECUTOR'S DUAL ROLE: MINISTER OF JUSTICE AND ADVOCATE

The Canadian tradition, consistent with other Anglo-American countries, sees the prosecutor occupying a dual role as minister of justice and advocate. Our constitution has long granted prosecutors a special status, distinct from that of a mere opponent at trial. The office of the attorney general, which has its beginnings in thirteenth-century England and was adopted in Canada in the late 1700s, exercises powers derived from the royal prerogative, defined as the residue of discretionary or arbitrary authority residing in the hands of the Crown at any given time.[13] As chief law officer of the Crown, each provincial attorney general heads the ministry of the executive branch of government that assumes primary responsibility for the administration of the criminal law. At the federal level, the minister of justice is *ex officio* Her Majesty's attorney general.[14] At the same time, the attorney general acts as prosecutor in individual cases through Crown counsel who are appointed as agents to prosecute on his behalf.

These Crown counsel are accountable to their attorney general, who in turn is responsible to the legislature and so to the public. Granted, the nature of accountability is somewhat different federally and in Quebec and Nova Scotia, where quasi-independent prosecution services have been established.[15] And finding a happy balance between political accountability and independence from partisan political meddling is an ongoing topic of discussion.[16] What is indisputable, however, is that

---

13 See *Power*, above note 7 at 14 [para 30]; *Krieger v Law Society of Alberta*, 2002 SCC 65 at para 24 [*Krieger*]; *Ontario v Criminal Lawyers' Association of Ontario*, 2013 SCC 43 at para 34 [*Criminal Lawyers' Association of Ontario*].

14 See *Department of Justice Act*, RSC 1985, c J-2, s 2(2).

15 See *Director of Public Prosecutions Act*, SC 2006, c 9, s 121; *United States of America v Adam*, 2014 BCCA 136 at paras 62–65 [*Adam*]; *An Act Respecting the Director of Criminal and Penal Prosecutions*, CQLR c D-9.1.1; *Public Prosecutions Act*, SNS 1990, c 21 [NS *Public Prosecutions Act*]. The situation in British Columbia is somewhat similar, for as with the quasi-independent model any instructions from the attorney general to the prosecution service regarding a specific case must be in writing and gazetted: see *Crown Counsel Act*, RSBC 1996, c 87, s 5.

16 See, for example, Philip Stenning, "Independence and the Director of Public Prosecutions: The Marshall Inquiry and Beyond" (2000) 23 Dal LJ 385; Bruce A MacFarlane, "Sunlight and Disinfectants: Prosecutorial Accountability and

Crown counsel are part of an institution that is answerable to the public and must always act in the public interest.

1) Role as Minister of Justice

Because the attorney general is ultimately responsible to the public and plays a special constitutional role, the lawyers who carry out the day-to-day function of prosecuting cases have an overarching duty to achieve justice by exercising their powers fairly.[17] The leading jurisprudential exposition of this sentiment remains the classic statement of Rand J in *R v Boucher*:

> It cannot be over-emphasized that the purpose of a criminal prosecution is not to obtain a conviction, it is to lay before a jury what the Crown considers to be credible evidence relevant to what is alleged to be a crime. Counsel have a duty to see that all available legal proof of the facts is presented: it should be done firmly and pressed to its legitimate strength, but it must also be done fairly. The role of the prosecutor excludes any notion of winning or losing; his function is a matter of public duty than which in civil life there can be none charged with greater personal responsibility. It is to be efficiently performed with an ingrained sense of the dignity, the seriousness and the justness of judicial proceedings.[18]

In short, the prosecutor does not act in the heightened partisan sense usually required of defence counsel but as a promoter of the public interest in achieving justice who "represents the collective interest in the just and correct outcome of the case."[19]

Independence through Public Transparency" (2001) 45 Crim LQ 272; Rosenberg, above note 8; Philip C Stenning, "Prosecutions, Politics and the Public Interest: Some Recent Developments in the United Kingdom, Canada and Elsewhere" (2010) 55 Crim LQ 449; Kent Roach, "Prosecutorial Independence and Accountability in Terrorism Prosecutions" (2010) 55 Crim LQ 486.

17 See *R v Morneau*, [2004] JQ No 1234 at para 44 (CA), quoting the first edition of this text.

18 *R v Boucher* (1954), 110 CCC 263 at 270 (SCC) [*Boucher*]. These sentiments have been repeatedly affirmed in subsequent Supreme Court of Canada cases, including *R v Cook* (1997), 114 CCC (3d) 481 at para 21 (SCC) [*Cook*]; *Proulx v Quebec (AG)*, 2001 SCC 66 at para 41 [*Proulx*]; *R v Regan*, 2002 SCC 12 at para 65 [*Regan*]; *R v Taillefer*, 2003 SCC 70 at para 68 [*Taillefer*]; *R v Trochym*, 2007 SCC 6 at para 79 [*Trochym*]; *Criminal Lawyers' Association of Ontario*, above note 13 at para 37.

19 *Toronto (City) v CUPE Local 79*, 2003 SCC 63 at para 31 [*Toronto (City)*].

This notion that prosecutors must temper partisanship has been expressed by stating that counsel appearing for the prosecution should regard themselves as "ministers of justice."[20] Our Supreme Court has taken up this language stating that "the Crown is not an ordinary litigant. As a minister of justice, the Crown's undivided loyalty is to the proper administration of justice."[21] Similarly, it has been said that prosecutors are "quasi-judicial officers."[22] Others, seeking to emphasize the role and responsibility of the prosecutor as a decision maker on a broad policy level whose actions shape the character, quality, and efficiency of the criminal justice system, have called the prosecutor an "administrator."[23] Still other formulations refer to the prosecutor as "assistant to the Court in the furtherance of justice"[24] and a "symbol of authority and as a spokesperson for the community in criminal matters."[25] These monikers incorporate several aspects of the prosecutor's role. All are accurate insofar as they accord great importance to the linchpin obligation to advance the public interest by seeking a fair and just result in the prosecution of criminal matters.

The public interest in achieving justice demands unwavering fidelity to the truth-seeking function of the criminal justice system. It also necessitates respect for the constitutional rights of the accused, as promoted by our due-process model of justice, allegiance to the concept of equality of application, and a keen sense of proportion and substantive justice in pursuing a course of action that can have a significant impact on the liberty and reputation of the accused.[26] The idea that the rights of the accused should somehow bear on the duties of the Crown is worth stressing. A prosecutor must assiduously avoid doing

---

20 *R v Puddick* (1865), 176 ER 662.

21 *R v McNeil*, 2009 SCC 3 at para 49 [*McNeil*]. Other decisions referring to the prosecutor as a "minister of justice" include *Nelles v Ontario*, [1989] 2 SCR 170 at 191 [para 39]; *Stinchcombe*, above note 1 at 12 [para 23]; *Regan*, above note 18 at paras 151 and 155–56, Binnie J, dissenting but not on this point; *Toronto (City)*, above note 19 at para 31; *Miazga*, above note 11 at paras 47, 49, 51, and 88–89; *R v Davey*, 2012 SCC 75 at para 32 [*Davey*]; *R v Quesnelle*, 2014 SCC 46 at para 18 [*Quesnelle*].

22 *Boucher*, above note 18 at 267; *Regan*, above note 18 at para 66; *Miazga*, above note 11 at para 66; *Krieger*, above note 13 at para 32; *R v Babos*, 2014 SCC 16 at para 61 [*Babos*]; *R v Elliott* (2003), 181 CCC (3d) 118 at para 152 (Ont CA) [*Elliott*]; *R v Mitchell* (2006), 212 CCC (3d) 258 at para 18 (Ont CA); *Marshall Inquiry Report*, above note 2 at 227–28.

23 ABA Prosecution Standard 3-1.2(b).

24 *Babos*, above note 22 at para 61.

25 *R v Logiacco* (1984), 11 CCC (3d) 374 at 379 (Ont CA) [*Logiacco*].

26 See Stanley Fisher, "In Search of the Virtuous Prosecutor: A Conceptual Framework" (1988) 15 Am J Crim L 197 at 236–37.

anything that might subvert the accused's fair trial rights. Indeed, in some respects she has an affirmative duty to further those rights, for instance by complying with extensive pre-trial disclosure obligations.[27] Prosecutors must never forget that those they prosecute may be innocent and should be allowed a fair opportunity to answer the case against them.[28]

Another aspect of the prosecutor's role as "minister of justice" that deserves special emphasis is the need for independence.[29] Though accountable to Parliament and the courts, the attorney general and his agents are permitted liberal discretion in making decisions affecting the prosecution of criminal cases, and they must be secure from political or social pressures in this regard. A guarantee of independence encourages courageous decisions where needed and thus works to safeguard the public interest. This guarantee is an essential check on the overweening use of power and influence, whether intentional or not, on the part of other government actors including but by no means limited to the police.[30] For this reason, independence in exercising the prosecution function has been recognized as an important constitutional principle that infuses the office of attorney general.[31]

This is not to dispute that a prosecutor must consider public needs and community concerns in reaching a decision as to the best course of action to take in any given circumstance. But in some matters the prosecutor's duty will lie in defying intemperate community pressures, though always within the confines of the law. Since the Crown is charged with the broad duty to ensure that every accused person is treated fairly, it is "especially in high profile cases, where the justice system will be on display, that counsel must do their utmost to ensure that any resultant convictions are based on facts and not on emotions. When the Crown allows its actions to be influenced by public pressure the essential fairness and legitimacy of our system is lost."[32] The truly

---

27   See Section G, below in this chapter.

28   See Ken Crispin, "Prosecutorial Ethics" in Stephen Parker & Charles Sampford, eds, *Legal Ethics and Legal Practice: Contemporary Issues* (Oxford: Clarendon Press, 1995) at 189.

29   See *Regan*, above note 18 at paras 157–58, Binnie J, dissenting but not on this point; *Krieger*, above note 13 at paras 29–30.

30   Michael Code, "Judicial Review of Prosecutorial Decisions: A Short History of Costs and Benefits, in Response to Justice Rosenberg" (2009) 34 Queen's LJ 863 at 872.

31   See *Krieger*, above note 13 at paras 30–32; *R v Beaudry*, 2007 SCC 5 at para 48 [*Beaudry*]; *Miazga*, above note 11 at para 46; *R v Nixon*, 2011 SCC 34 at para 20 [*Nixon*]; *Anderson*, above note 11 at para 37.

32   *R v Curragh Inc* (1997), 113 CCC (3d) 481 at para 120 (SCC), McLachlin and Cory JJ, dissenting but not on this point.

independent Crown counsel is thus able to bring critical thinking to bear in approaching a case and exercises "not only professional skills and judgment but also courage."[33]

Observation: Decisions whether or how to proceed with a charge sometimes occur in a context where there is a legitimate concern as to the appearance of prosecution service independence. Examples include matters involving politicians or high-ranking police officers. In these situations, prosecution services frequently look to outside lawyers to take carriage of the file, be they ad hoc prosecutors selected from the private bar, so-called special prosecutors appointed under a statutory scheme, or counsel employed by a prosecution service from another province.[34]

Canadian rules of professional conduct affirm that prosecutors play a special justice-seeking role in the adversarial justice system, among other things stating that a prosecutor "exercises a public function . . . and must act fairly and dispassionately" and that her "prime duty is not to seek to convict but to see that justice is done through a fair trial on the merits."[35] The policy manuals issued by the various prosecution services contain similar language. For instance, the *Public Prosecution Service of Canada Deskbook*, applicable to all federal prosecutors including those working for the Public Prosecution Service of Canada, states the following:

> Public interest considerations require Crown counsel to exercise judgment and discretion which go beyond functioning simply as advocates. Counsel appearing for the DPP are considered "ministers of justice", more part of the court than proponents of a cause . . . . Fairness, moderation, and dignity should characterize Crown counsel's conduct during criminal litigation.[36]

In summary, the prosecutor's overriding duty is to seek justice in the public interest, which encapsulates several related principles:

1) A prosecutor's goal is not to win the case but rather to pursue a just result, which involves not only fidelity to the truth-seeking function of the criminal justice system but also respect for the fair trial rights of the accused.

---

33   *Lamer Inquiry Report*, above note 2 at 136–37.
34   See MacFarlane, above note 16 at 294–97.
35   See the rules & commentaries cited at note 6, above in this chapter.
36   *PPSC Deskbook*, above note 8, ch 2.2, section 2 (The Conduct of Criminal Litigation) [notes omitted].

2) Carrying out the prosecutorial role requires independence from partisan influences that might divert counsel from his mission as minister of justice.

3) Crown counsel must be accountable to the public in a way that finds form in unwavering adherence to the minister of justice role and, more concretely perhaps, in the attorney general's responsibility to the legislature.

4) A prosecutor must carry out her duties in an objective and impartial way.

2) Role as Advocate

The flip side of the prosecutor's responsibility as minister of justice is the necessary tempering of the partisan function undertaken by most other lawyers. Thus, while Canadian ethical codes note that the lawyer's role as advocate is "openly and necessarily partisan" so that "the lawyer is not obliged to assist an adversary or advance matters harmful to the client's case," they contain the caveat that such partisanship is "subject to the duties of a prosecutor."[37] In other words, while a lawyer is not normally obliged to assist his adversary, the prosecutor as minister of justice cannot wholeheartedly embrace partisanship.[38]

The role as minister of justice does not, however, prevent a prosecutor from legitimately striving to seek a just conviction.[39] In *R v Cook*, the Supreme Court of Canada affirmed that Crown counsel can act as a "strong advocate" and that it is permissible and desirable that prosecutors vigorously pursue a legitimate result to the best of their ability.[40] As *Cook* quite rightly recognizes, the prosecutor as strong advocate is a critical element of this country's criminal law mechanism.[41] To argue otherwise is to lose sight of the adversarial nature of our justice system and to unduly handicap Crown counsel's ability to put forward the state's position at trial.[42] Consequently, there is nothing wrong with Crown counsel's adopting adversarial strategies and tactics best calculated to advance the state's case,[43] asking the trier of fact to convict

---

37 Alta, Sask, Man r 4.01(1) (commentary); BC, Ont, NS, NL r 5.1-1, commentary 3.

38 See *Cook*, above note 18 at para 21.

39 See *Elliott*, above note 22 at paras 152–53.

40 *Cook*, above note 18 at para 21. See also *R v Hurd*, 2014 ONCA 554 at para 32.

41 *Cook*, above note 18 at para 21. See also *R v Assoun*, 2006 NSCA 47 at paras 227–28, leave to appeal to SCC refused, [2006] SCCA No 233.

42 *Cook*, above note 18 at para 39.

43 See *R v Jolivet*, 2000 SCC 29 at para 21 [*Jolivet*]; *Anderson*, above note 11 at para 60; *R v Ng*, 2003 ABCA 1 at para 140.

where such a result is justified on the evidence,[44] or declining to act so as to assist the accused in presenting the best possible defence.[45] The prosecutor's distinct mission requires competent, vigorous, and thorough advocacy[46] provided nothing is done to undermine the truth-seeking and fairness functions of the criminal justice process. One should perhaps therefore speak of a prosecutor as exercising "controlled zeal," a modified version of the traditional advocate's zeal.

This view of Crown counsel's legitimate role as resolute advocate fits well with the state's expansive duty to make full disclosure to the defence.[47] The duty to disclose, recognized in its contemporary form by the Supreme Court of Canada in the 1991 case of *R v Stinchcombe*, is discussed more fully below.[48] For now, suffice it to say that pre-*Stinchcombe* the defence was not necessarily privy to all relevant information gathered by the police in investigating the charged offence. This lack of knowledge could represent a significant disadvantage and cause unfairness. Imposing greater limits on Crown counsel's ability to act as a resolute advocate — or, to put it conversely, a greater obligation to assist the defence — ameliorated resulting harm to the defence. *Stinchcombe's* endorsement of a demanding prosecutorial disclosure obligation has arguably lessened concerns about unfairness to the defence resulting from firm and determined Crown advocacy.[49]

Nonetheless, real tension can arise between a prosecutor's role as advocate and the non-adversarial aspects of her duty as minister of justice. This tension is fomented where a prosecution service pressures its members to win cases as a means of securing career advancement.[50] A special strength of character is required if Crown counsel is to resist getting caught up in a "culture of winning" or a "conviction psychology" and is not to lose sight of the need to make sure the accused is treated

---

44   See *Boucher*, above note 18 at 265; *R v Felderhof*, [2002] OJ No 4103 at paras 20–33 (SCJ), aff'd (2003), 180 CCC (3d) 498 at para 79 (Ont CA) [*Felderhof* CA].

45   See *R v Ford* (1993), 78 CCC (3d) 481 at 499 [paras 71–72] (BCCA).

46   See *PPSC Deskbook*, above note 8, ch 2.2, section 2 (The Conduct of Criminal Litigation).

47   See Michael Code, "Ethics and Criminal Law Practice" in Alice Woolley et al, *Lawyers' Ethics and Professional Regulation*, 2d ed (Markham, ON: LexisNexis, 2012) at 447–48 and 451 (comment 4). A somewhat similar point is made in Alice Woolley, *Understanding Lawyers' Ethics in Canada* (Markham, ON: LexisNexis, 2011) at 300.

48   See Section G, below in this chapter.

49   This sort of logic is embraced in *Cook*, above note 18 at paras 33–37.

50   Concern that such pressures may cause a prosecutor to deviate from his proper role as minister of justice is expressed in the *Lamer Inquiry Report*, above note 2 at 135.

fairly. To the extent the notion of winning has any proper place in Crown counsel's mindset, the victory lies in doing justice, not simply in gaining a conviction.[51]

Prosecutors must also take care not to push the outer limits of zealousness in response to perceived truth-defeating tactics employed by defence counsel. If an accused obtains an advantage because of basic constitutional guarantees, then the criminal justice system is operating as intended. Defence counsel has done nothing wrong by relying on such guarantees. Even where defence counsel acts improperly, the idea that unethical retaliation by the prosecutor is justified should be rejected. An "eye for an eye" response risks fatally undermining trial fairness and will often lead to an escalating series of ethical improprieties.[52] While the prosecutor can certainly respond to improper defence actions, for instance by seeking a remedy from the court, the public interest does not allow a departure from normal ethical standards in doing so.

In a perfect world, the boundary between acceptably resolute advocacy by the Crown and impermissible prosecutorial abuse would be easily discerned and never give rise to disagreement. But drawing clear lines is sometimes very difficult. What is more, and importantly, the extent to which a prosecutor's role as minister of justice should temper her function as advocate may wax and wane with the circumstances.[53] For example, the adversarial role essentially disappears when Crown counsel is considering whether to proceed with a charge but justifiably takes on greater prominence when she is cross-examining a defence witness. Ultimately, the debate over the acceptable degree of advocacy practised by Crown counsel will probably never cease given the dynamics of the adversarial system and the inherent tension between a prosecutor's dual roles as minister of justice and forceful advocate.

3) Preventing Tunnel Vision and Wrongful Convictions

Advocacy untempered by Crown counsel's concomitant duties of fairness, objectivity, and independence can lead to the wrongful conviction of an innocent person, one of the greatest failures possible in our criminal justice system. Wrongful convictions are often caused, at least in part, by tunnel vision on the part of the police or Crown counsel.

---

51   See Robert H Jackson, "The Federal Prosecutor" (1940) 31 J Crim L & Criminology 3 at 4.
52   See David Pannick, *Advocates* (Oxford: Oxford University Press, 1993) at 114–19.
53   See Graeme Mitchell, "'No Joy in This for Anyone': Reflections on the Exercise of Prosecutorial Discretion in *R v Latimer*" (2001) 64 Sask L Rev 491 at 497–99.

Tunnel vision has been defined as "the single minded and overly narrow focus on an investigation or prosecution theory so as to unreasonably colour the evaluation of information received and one's conduct in response to the information."[54] A prosecutor can fall victim to tunnel vision for any number of reasons including an unchecked desire to win as a means of attaining personal satisfaction or promoting career advancement, undue identification with the police or a victim, an inability to withstand media or special interest group pressure, isolation from alternative perspectives, or a lack of critical thinking borne of overwork, indolence, or inexperience.[55]

There is no single, simple antidote for ridding prosecutorial services of tunnel vision. Yet the ongoing education of Crown lawyers is a valuable means of guarding against a loss of objectivity not only with respect to matters of ethics but also regarding areas of the criminal law that have often contributed to wrongful convictions such as unreliable eyewitness testimony, false confessions, jailhouse informants, junk science, and guilty pleas by the factually innocent. Institutionalizing the importance of a prosecutor's examining a case critically, with an eye to challenging the police outlook and considering the defence perspective, is also extremely important.[56] So too is the development and implementation of policies that protect against a loss of independence and objectivity vis-à-vis the police, such as generally not assigning carriage of a prosecution to Crown counsel who has played a significant pre-charge role in advising police.[57] Crown lawyers should also be encouraged to seek second opinions or case reviews within their office or service, not only while handling a matter but after the case has concluded as well.[58] Prosecutors must be constantly vigilant to ensure that strong feelings about a case do not undermine the duties of objectivity and fairness.[59]

---

54 *Morin Inquiry Report*, above note 2 at 1136 (Recommendation 74); FPT Heads of Prosecutions 2004 Report, above note 5 at 35; FPT Heads of Prosecutions 2011 Report, above note 5 at 43; *PPSC Deskbook*, above note 8, ch 2.4, section 2 (Tunnel Vision).

55 See FPT Heads of Prosecutions 2004 Report, above note 5 at 36; FPT Heads of Prosecutions 2011 Report, above note 5 at 43.

56 See FPT Heads of Prosecutions 2004 Report, above note 5 at 39–40; FPT Heads of Prosecutions 2011 Report, above note 5 at 53.

57 See FPT Heads of Prosecutions 2004 Report, above note 5 at 39; FPT Heads of Prosecutions 2011 Report, above note 5 at 54. See also Section F(2), below in this chapter.

58 See FPT Heads of Prosecutions 2004 Report, above note 5 at 39. See also *R v Henry*, 2010 BCCA 462 at para 27: a highly problematic conviction was uncovered by a prosecutor over twenty years after the appellant had been convicted.

59 See *Regan*, above note 18 at para 89.

Combatting tunnel vision involves much more than serving up platitudes at the occasional session at a Crown counsel conference. Preventing biased thinking and avoiding wrongful convictions is grounded in the foundational principles that underlie the proper role of the Crown. The anti-tunnel-vision mindset must be ingrained in the culture and policies of every office in every prosecution service so that it is respected and fostered in everything the members of that service do.[60] Given Crown counsel's broad duty to avoid wrongful convictions,[61] there can be no doubt that the prosecutorial function must never be clouded by tunnel vision.

4) Crown Counsel's Dual Role Reflected in Prosecutorial Service Guidelines

As noted, the codes of professional conduct in Canada devote limited attention to the role of the prosecutor whereas most prosecution service manuals address the topic comprehensively and in great detail.[62] Illustrative of the approach taken in these policy manuals is the *Public Prosecution Service of Canada Deskbook* (*PPSC Deskbook*), which articulates the general principles that we have already discussed: public interest considerations that limit the ordinary function of advocates require Crown counsel to exercise judgment and discretion as ministers of justice; fairness, moderation, and dignity should characterize the conduct of Crown counsel during criminal litigation; and the trial process should not become a personal contest of skill or professional pre-eminence, although prosecutors are not prevented from conducting trials with vigour and thoroughness.[63]

The *PPSC Deskbook* also gives more detailed standards for prosecutors, which provide good guidance as to the ways in which a prosecutor's duties as a minister of justice should operate to temper the zealousness of his advocacy, for example:

---

60   See Bruce MacFarlane, "Convicting the Innocent: A Triple Failure of the Justice System" (2006) 31 Man LJ 403 at 441–44; Melvyn Green, "Crown Culture and Wrongful Convictions: A Beginning" (2005) 29 CR (6th) 262; *PPSC Deskbook*, above note 8, ch 2.4, section 2 (Tunnel Vision).

61   See *Quesnelle*, above note 21 at para 18.

62   See Section B, above in this chapter.

63   *PPSC Deskbook*, above note 8, ch 2.2, section 2 (The Conduct of Criminal Litigation).

2.1. The duty to ensure that the mandate of the Director is carried out with integrity and dignity

Counsel fulfill this duty by:

- complying with their bar association's applicable rules of ethics;
- complying with the Public Prosecution Service of Canada (PPSC) Code of Conduct;
- exercising careful judgment in presenting the case for the Crown, in deciding whether or not to oppose bail, in deciding what witnesses to call, and what evidence to tender;
- acting with moderation, fairness, and impartiality;
- conducting oneself with civility;
- not discriminating on any basis prohibited by s. 15 of the *Canadian Charter of Rights and Freedoms* (Charter);
- adequately preparing for each case;
- remaining independent of the police or investigative agency while working closely with it; and
- conducting resolution discussions in a manner consistent with the DPP guideline.

2.2. The duty to maintain judicial independence

Counsel fulfill this duty by:

- not discussing matters relating to a case with the presiding judge without the participation of defence counsel unless there is a legal justification for such *ex parte* discussions such as portions of an application under s. 37 of the *Canada Evidence Act* or in addressing common law informer privilege;
- not dealing with matters in chambers that should properly be dealt with in open court;
- avoiding personal or private discussions with a judge in chambers while presenting a case before that judge; and
- refraining from appearing before a judge on a contentious matter when a personal connection exists between Crown counsel and the judge that would compromise the independent function of either role.

2.3. The duty to be fair and to maintain public confidence in prosecutorial fairness

In order to maintain public confidence in the administration of justice, Crown counsel must not only act fairly; their conduct must be seen to be fair. One can act fairly while unintentionally leaving an impression of secrecy, bias or unfairness.

Counsel fulfill this duty by:

- making disclosure in accordance with the law;
- bringing all relevant cases and authorities known to counsel to the attention of the court, even if they may be contrary to the Crown's position;
- not misleading the court;
- not expressing personal opinions on the evidence, including the credibility of witnesses or on the guilt or innocence of the accused in court or in public. Such expressions of opinion are improper;
- not adverting to any unproven facts, even if they are material and could have been admitted as evidence;
- asking relevant and proper questions during the examination of a witness and not asking questions designed solely to embarrass, insult, abuse, belittle, or demean the witness. Cross examination can be skilful and probing, yet still show respect for the witness. The law distinguishes between a cross-examination that is "persistent and exhaustive", which is proper, and a cross-examination that is "abusive";
- stating the law accurately in oral pleadings;
- respecting defence counsel, the accused, and the proceedings while vigorously asserting the Crown's position, and not publicly and improperly criticizing defence strategy;
- respecting the court and judicial decisions and not publicly disparaging judgments; and
- avoiding themselves engaging in active "judge shopping".

2.4. The duty to maintain objectivity

Counsel fulfill this duty by:

- being aware of the dangers of tunnel vision and ensure they review the evidence in an objective, rigorous and thorough manner in assessing the strength of the evidence emanating from the police investigation throughout the proceedings;
- exercising particular care regarding actual and perceived objectivity when involved in an investigation at the pre-charge stage;
- making all necessary inquiries regarding potentially relevant evidence;
- never permitting personal interests or partisan political considerations to interfere with the proper exercise of prosecutorial discretion; and

- not exceeding the scope of appropriate opening remarks, for example elevating the role of Crown counsel in the eyes of the jury to the custodian of the public interest.[64]

D. THE PRINCIPLE OF PROSECUTORIAL DISCRETION

Many decisions concerning the operation of the criminal justice system involve the exercise of discretion by the prosecutor. It can also be said that many of defence counsel's decisions in conducting a client's case or a police officer's decisions in investigating a crime involve the exercise of discretion. The prominence and importance of discretion in our system is substantial: a system without discretion would be "unworkably complex and rigid."[65] There is thus no doubt that the prosecutor's discretion is an essential feature of the administration of justice.

1) Limited Judicial Review of Prosecutorial Discretion

The Supreme Court of Canada has affirmed that the existence of prosecutorial discretion does not offend the principles of fundamental justice.[66] But more than this, the Court has recognized that the Crown's independence in exercising prosecutorial discretion is constitutionally enshrined.[67] Granted, the exercise of a discretionary power is not absolute and can sometimes be reviewed by the courts.[68] But the prosecutor's broad discretion is afforded considerable deference.[69] It can be interfered with only to remedy an abuse of the court's process in the clearest of cases.[70] To hold otherwise would undermine prosecutorial independence, erode the separation of powers between the executive

---

64 *Ibid*, ch 2.2 [notes omitted].
65 *R v Beare* (1988), 45 CCC (3d) 57 at 76 [para 51] (SCC) [*Beare*]. See also *Anderson*, above note 11 at para 37.
66 See *Beare*, above note 65; *R v VT* (1992), 71 CCC (3d) 32 at 39 [para 13] (SCC) [*VT*]; *Cook*, above note 18 at para 19; *Srisjkandarajah v United States of America*, 2012 SCC 70 at para 27; *Anderson*, above note 11 at para 32.
67 See the cases cited at note 31, above in this chapter.
68 See *VT*, above note 66 at 41–42 [paras 19–21]; *Krieger*, above note 13 at para 32.
69 See *Krieger*, above note 13 at paras 45 and 48; *Miazga*, above note 11 at paras 46–47; *Anderson*, above note 11 at paras 46–47.
70 See *R v O'Connor* (1995), 103 CCC (3d) 1 at paras 59 and 68 (SCC) [*O'Connor*]; *R v Neil*, 2002 SCC 70 at para 40; *Miazga*, above note 11 at para 48; *Nixon*, above note 31 at para 37; *R v Ryan*, 2013 SCC 3 at para 35; *Anderson*, above note 11 at paras 48 and 51.

and judiciary, and create significant inefficiencies in the proper working of the justice system.[71]

An abuse of process exists where the exercise of the prosecutorial discretion in question will, if left unchecked, undermine the fairness of the trial or the integrity of the criminal justice process.[72] A finding of abuse can involve misconduct or improper motive by the prosecutor but is not limited to such cases.[73] Because there is a presumption that the Crown has exercised its discretion properly, the court will allow an abuse of process application to proceed only where the accused establishes a proper evidentiary foundation to conclude that there is a reasonable likelihood an abuse has occurred.[74] If this threshold is not met, the Crown will not be required to provide reasons for the impugned decision, and the accused's application will be dismissed without need for a full-fledged hearing.[75]

In *Krieger v Law Society of Alberta*, the Supreme Court affirmed both the importance of prosecutorial discretion in the operation of the criminal justice system and the limited power that courts have to review its exercise.[76] The Court also stated that the term "prosecutorial discretion," used to describe the sphere of constitutional independence within which Crown counsel's decisions are immune from judicial review absent a showing of abuse of process, has a special and limited meaning:

> "Prosecutorial discretion" is a term of art. It does not simply refer to any discretionary decisions made by a Crown prosecutor. Prosecutorial discretion refers to the use of those powers that constitute the core of the Attorney General's office and which are protected from the influence of improper political and other vitiating factors by the principle of independence.[77]

Krieger and the Court's subsequent decision in *R v Anderson* hold that decisions falling within this definition of prosecutorial discretion share an important commonality: "they involve the ultimate decisions as to *whether* a prosecution should be brought, continued or ceased, and

---

71   See *Anderson, ibid* at paras 46–47.

72   See *Nixon*, above note 31 at paras 33–42; *Krieger*, above note 13 at paras 48–49; *Miazga*, above note 11; *Anderson*, above note 11 at paras 49–50. Regarding the test for abuse of process more generally, see *Babos*, above note 22 at paras 31–47.

73   See *Nixon*, above note 31 at paras 39–40; *Babos*, above note 22 at para 37; *R v Pietrangelo*, 2008 ONCA 449 at para 66.

74   See *Anderson*, above note 11 at paras 52–56.

75   *Ibid.*

76   *Krieger*, above note 13 at paras 29–32.

77   *Ibid* at para 43.

what the prosecution ought to be for."[78] To put it another way, "prosecutorial discretion refers to decisions regarding the nature and extent of the prosecution and the Attorney General's participation in it."[79]

Krieger and *Anderson* each provide non-exhaustive lists of the sorts of decisions that fall within this definition of prosecutorial discretion. *Krieger* mentions the decisions whether to prosecute a charge laid by the police, enter a stay of proceedings, accept a guilty plea to a lesser charge, withdraw from criminal proceedings altogether, and take over a private prosecution.[80] *Anderson* includes within the rubric of prosecutorial discretion the decisions whether to negotiate a plea, repudiate a plea agreement, pursue a dangerous offender application, proceed by direct indictment, charge multiple offences, tender statutory notice of intention to seek a greater punishment because of previous convictions, proceed summarily or by indictment on a hybrid offence, and launch an appeal.[81]

2) Tactics or Conduct before the Court and Constitutional Obligations

Krieger draws an important distinction between decisions falling within the definition of "prosecutorial discretion," which as noted attract very high deference from the courts, and Crown counsel's decisions governing tactics or conduct before the court, which do not fall within this definition and so are subject to judicial oversight as part of the inherent jurisdiction of the court to control its own processes.[82]

This distinction is fleshed out in *Anderson*, which in particular considers the category of decisions relating to "tactics or conduct before the court." *Anderson* states that the court's inherent jurisdiction to regulate such matters derives from the need to ensure that the machinery of the courts functions in an orderly and effective manner.[83] A judge can therefore penalize counsel for ignoring rulings and orders or for inappropriate behaviour such as being tardy or uncivil, conducting an

---

78   *Ibid* at para 47 [emphasis in original].

79   *Ibid.* See *Anderson*, above note 11 at paras 40–41 and 44.

80   *Krieger*, above note 13 at para 46.

81   *Anderson*, above note 11 at paras 44 and 62–63.

82   *Krieger*, above note 13 at para 47. See also *Miazga*, above note 11 at para 45; *Nixon*, above note 31 at paras 18–21.

83   *Anderson*, above note 11 at para 58. This power overlaps considerably with, and indeed may in essence be the same as, the trial management power recognized in *Felderhof* CA, above note 44 at paras 37–57; *R v Auclair*, 2013 QCCA 671 at paras 46, 52–57, and 109, aff'd 2014 SCC 6.

abusive cross-examination, making improper comments in opening or closing address, or wearing inappropriate attire.[84] Such matters, says *Anderson*, relate to "the conduct of the *litigants*" and so fall within the court's jurisdiction to intervene.[85]

As for Crown counsel's tactical decisions, that is, decisions regarding "the conduct of the *litigation* itself," *Anderson* recognizes that these usually deserve a high degree of deference from the court.[86] This has little if anything to do with Crown counsel's unique role as minister of justice. Rather, it arises from the nature of our adversarial system, which itself constitutes a fundamental principle of justice and in which courts generally defer to counsel regarding the conduct of the case.[87] A system in which tactical decisions made by the Crown, or any other litigant, were automatically subject to judicial review at the opponent's behest on a standard of correctness, or even reasonableness, would erode the foundations of the adversarial system and seriously undermine trial efficiency. Accordingly, the deference afforded tactical decisions made by the Crown is probably no different from that granted defence counsel in the same or comparable matters.[88]

This is not to say that tactical decisions are immune from review absent a showing of abuse of process. We do not have a purely adversarial system, where lawyers have absolute freedom in presenting their cases.[89] The court can therefore intervene to override a tactical decision that threatens trial fairness or is otherwise contrary to law,[90] or would prevent the trial from proceeding in an orderly manner.[91] And so the court can override Crown counsel's decision on a matter of trial tactics to prevent unfairness to the accused, for instance where the result would be to violate a constitutional right.[92] Likewise, a Crown decision to lead a piece of evidence at trial will be rebuffed by the court if the evidence is inadmissible according to established rules of law. In short, a prosecutor's tactical decisions — the way she chooses to run the case — are accorded significant deference, but judicial intervention

---

84   See *Anderson*, above note 11 at para 58.
85   *Ibid* at para 59 [emphasis in original].
86   *Ibid* [emphasis in original].
87   See Code, above note 30 at 883–84; *R v SGT*, 2010 SCC 20 at paras 36–37 [*SGT*].
88   See, for example, *R v Rybak*, 2008 ONCA 354 at para 172, leave to appeal to SCC refused, [2008] SCCA No 311 [*Rybak*]: Crown is treated the same as defence regarding judicial deference accorded the decision as to what witnesses to call.
89   See *Felderhof* CA, above note 44 at paras 45 and 53–55.
90   See *SGT*, above note 87 at para 37.
91   See *Felderhof* CA, above note 44 at paras 37–57; *R v Spackman*, 2012 ONCA 905 at para 104 [*Spackman*].
92   See *Anderson*, above note 11 at paras 59–60.

is not limited to those instances where a decision constitutes an abuse of process.[93]

On a different but related point, *Krieger* and *Anderson* both note that the Crown may be subject to constitutional obligations that take a particular decision outside the ambit of prosecutorial discretion, a prime example being the duty to disclose all relevant information to the defence.[94] The same rationale arguably applies to any legal duty, whether statutory, common law, or constitutional, that requires the Crown to conduct litigation in a particular way, with the obvious caveat that courts will not lightly recognize or create legal duties that trench on what would otherwise be areas of prosecutorial discretion. Doing so would undermine the policies that justify affording discretionary decisions considerable deference and might even amount to an unconstitutional interference with the attorney general's independence.

3) Guidelines for Exercise of Prosecutorial Discretion

In making discretionary decisions, Crown counsel should be guided by the principles that inform his role as minister of justice in an adversarial legal system. Further guidance may come from policy statements, directives, or considerations found in prosecution service policy manuals. Indeed, a Crown policy or guideline may be ascribed weight by a court in determining whether prosecutorial discretion was exercised in an abusive manner. For example, Crown counsel's failure to follow a policy or guideline may help an accused meet the threshold evidentiary burden necessary to embark on an inquiry into the reasons behind the impugned decision.[95]

On the other hand, blindly following a flawed policy manual provision regarding a matter of prosecutorial discretion might conceivably amount to an abuse of process. For instance, in *R v MK* the prosecution service was seen to have adopted a "zero-tolerance" policy in charging domestic violence cases.[96] The Manitoba Court of Appeal held that this policy was objectionable and so subject to judicial review because it

---

93   *Ibid* at para 61.
94   *Krieger*, above note 13 at para 54; *Anderson*, above note 11 at para 45. See Section G, below in this chapter.
95   See *Anderson*, above note 11 at para 56.
96   (1992), 74 CCC (3d) 108 (Man CA), leave to appeal to SCC refused, [1992] SCCA No 415. A number of commentators have criticized this decision: see, for example, Woolley, *Understanding Lawyers' Ethics in Canada*, above note 47 at 295; Anne McGillivray, "*R v K.(M.)*: Legitimating Brutality" (1992) 16 CR (4th) 125.

nullified prosecutorial discretion.[97] Somewhat similarly, in *R v Catagas* the same court accepted that the Crown has the ability in the exercise of prosecutorial discretion to stay proceedings in an individual case but has no right to grant a particular group or race blanket dispensation against application of a statute.[98]

E. CHARGING AND STAYING DECISIONS

In this section, we will examine the prosecutor's exercise of the discretion whether to proceed with a case, focusing primarily on the factors that should and should not be taken into account in making the decision. It is helpful to begin by reviewing the role of the police in investigating crime, the better to understand the context in which a prosecutor's charging decision is made and to provide a foundation for later discussions regarding the propriety of Crown counsel's getting involved in a criminal matter during the investigatory phase.

1) Independence of the Police in Investigating Crime

By constitutional convention, a police officer engaged in a criminal investigation is independent of the direction and control of the executive branch and does not act as the agent or servant of any external institution or individual, including Crown counsel.[99] This independence promotes the rule of law and composes part of the system of checks and balances helping to guarantee that criminal prosecutions are carried out where justified but not otherwise.[100]

The police nonetheless have an affirmative duty to investigate crime in a diligent and proper manner; they cannot use their independence

---

97 A similar sentiment regarding the exercise of Crown discretion and zero tolerance in the context of bail policies is expressed in *R v Villota* (2002), 163 CCC (3d) 507 at para 70 (Ont SCJ).

98 (1977), 38 CCC (2d) 296 (Man CA).

99 See *R v Campbell* (1999), 133 CCC (3d) 257 at paras 28–29 (SCC) [*Campbell*]; *Regan*, above note 18 at paras 66–71 and 159–60; *Beaudry*, above note 31 at para 48; *McNeil*, above note 21 at para 23.

100 See Ontario, *Report of the Attorney General's Advisory Committee on Charge Screening, Disclosure, and Resolution Discussions* (Toronto: Attorney General of Ontario, 1993) (Chair: G Arthur Martin) at 39 [Martin Committee Report]; Michael Code, "Crown Counsel's Responsibilities When Advising the Police at the Pre-charge Stage" (1998) 40 Crim LQ 326 at 333–37; Rosenberg, above note 8 at 830; *Regan*, above note 18 at paras 159–60, Binnie J, dissenting but not on this point.

as justification for acting negligently, irresponsibly, or with bias in a criminal investigation.[101] Moreover, while police enjoy a discretion in deciding whether to conduct an investigation, this discretion must be exercised honestly, transparently, and in the public interest, based on grounds that are valid and reasonable in light of the seriousness of the conduct in question.[102]

2) Involvement of Crown Counsel in Approving or Screening a Charge: Two Different Models

Throughout Canada, criminal charges are almost always laid by the police. Yet two different approaches are employed regarding Crown counsel's involvement in the police's charging decision. In British Columbia, Quebec, and New Brunswick, approval by Crown counsel is typically obtained before a charge is laid by a police officer.[103] This pre-charge approval function is best viewed as a screening process intended to safeguard against ill-founded charges. True, a peace officer can ignore a prosecutor's advice and proceed to lay the charge before a justice of the peace.[104] Yet police in these jurisdictions almost always follow the advice of Crown counsel.[105] This is not surprising because a charge, once laid, remains subject to prosecutorial screening, and Crown counsel will stay any count that does not meet the applicable standard.

In the remaining Canadian jurisdictions, the police do not routinely seek prosecutorial approval before charging, and most informations are

---

101 See *Beaudry*, above note 31 at para 35; *Hill v Hamilton-Wentworth Regional Police Services Board*, 2007 SCC 41 at paras 1, 41, 115–16, and 138; Martin Committee Report, above note 100 at 35 and 117; Code, above note 100 at 331–32.

102 See *Beaudry*, above note 31 at paras 37–40.

103 See *Regan*, above note 18 at paras 72, 76, & 77; *Beaudry*, above note 31 at para 47; *Adam*, above note 15 at para 61.

104 Section 504 of the *Criminal Code*, RSC 1985, c C-46, provides that "anyone" can lay a charge. There are, however, a few instances where the *Criminal Code* requires the attorney general's consent, for example, s 83.24 (terrorism offences), s 251(3) (unsafe vessel, aircraft, railway equipment), s 319(6) (hate propaganda), s 318(3) (advocating genocide), and s 477.2 (offences in territorial seas).

105 In British Columbia, it appears that the police have never laid a charge against the advice of the Crown under the current system: see Gary McCuaig, QC, "British Columbia Charge Assessment Review" in BC Justice Reform Initiative, *A Criminal Justice System for the 21st Century: Final Report to the Minister of Justice and Attorney General Honourable Shirley Bond* (Vancouver: British Columbia Ministry of Justice, 2012) (Chair: D Geoffrey Cowper, QC) schedule 11 at 25 [BC Charge Assessment Review].

laid without prior input from a Crown lawyer.[106] Crown counsel in these jurisdictions nonetheless screen charges once laid, at which point they, and not the police, have the power to decide whether the prosecution should proceed. Moreover, in serious or complex cases the police sometimes consult Crown counsel in advance as to whether the screening standard is satisfied and for what charges. Knowing that the Crown has the power to stay the charges after a court information is laid, police are unlikely to proceed against the prosecutor's considered advice.

These two models regarding the prosecutor's involvement in the decision whether to charge reflect differing views as to the best way to ensure an effective and constitutionally sound relationship between the police and Crown.[107] We will not delve into the merits of the competing approaches here for two reasons. First, at the end of the day, under either approach Crown counsel assesses whether the charging standard is met and will not proceed with the matter where a negative conclusion is reached. Second, it seems clear that both models are constitutionally acceptable provided the mutual independence and objectivity of the police and Crown are preserved.[108]

3) Applying the Discretion: Sufficiency of Evidence and Public Interest

Our common law tradition does not require the automatic prosecution of a charge every time an allegation of criminal conduct is made. Rather, the decision whether to prosecute requires the exercise of a discretion. This decision becomes a pivotal event that "prevents the process of the criminal law from being used oppressively."[109] Given the substantial consequences that a charge can have for the liberty, security, and reputation of an accused, even if eventually exonerated, as well as for the public interest and victims, the fact and appearance of objectivity, independence, and fairness is crucial.[110] Exercising the discre-

---

106 See, for example, the Martin Committee Report, above note 100 at 37, describing the operation of the charge-laying process in Ontario.

107 For discussions of the strengths and weaknesses of the two models, see Stephen Owen, *Report of the Discretion to Prosecute Inquiry* (Vancouver: British Columbia Ministry of the Attorney General, 1990) at 20–27; Law Reform Commission of Canada, *Controlling Criminal Prosecutions: The Attorney General and the Crown Prosecutor* (Working Paper 62) (Ottawa: The Commission, 1990) at 69–76; BC Charge Assessment Review, above note 105 at 26–36.

108 Support for this view can be found in *Regan*, above note 18 at paras 71–91.

109 Martin Committee Report, above note 100 at 51.

110 See *British Columbia (AG) v Davies*, 2009 BCCA 337 at para 30, leave to appeal to SCC refused, [2009] SCCA No 421 [*Davies*].

tion whether to proceed with a prosecution is thus vital to the integrity of the system and the rights of those individuals who are or may be accused of a criminal offence.

Courts afford Crown counsel considerable deference regarding the determination whether to prosecute, for the decision involves the exercise of prosecutorial discretion.[111] Absent a showing of abuse of process, "a judge does not have the authority to tell prosecutors which crimes to prosecute or when to prosecute them."[112] As we have seen, establishing an abuse is extremely difficult.[113] Applying this high standard of review reduces the external pressures on prosecutors when making charging decisions and so promotes independence, and also preserves the constitutional separation of powers between the executive and judicial branches.[114]

Not only is a prosecutor's charging decision almost never subject to review as part of the adversarial process, but it is not made in a public forum such as a courtroom. Nor is a prosecutor immediately accountable to a tangible client for the decision, unlike defence lawyers with respect to important decisions. It is therefore especially important that Crown lawyers adhere to their *Boucher* duties of fairness, independence, and objectivity in exercising this important discretion. Crown counsel's role as minister of justice should be superordinate. The adversarial component of the prosecutorial function, which is usually strongest during the trial after full disclosure has been provided, has no real part to play.[115] As stated in *R v Regan*, the Crown must be an "ardent prosecutor once charges have been laid, but also objective defender of the general public interest in determining *whether* to prosecute the charges recommended by police."[116]

What then are the factors to consider in exercising the discretion? The *Criminal Code* provides no guidance, nor do Canadian rules of professional conduct have anything specific to say. The Supreme Court of Canada has noted a number of considerations that can properly bear on the decision to prosecute, including the strength of the case, the

---

111 See Section D(1), above in this chapter; *Krieger*, above note 13 at paras 46–49; *Nixon*, above note 31 at paras 18–21; *Regan*, above note 18 at paras 166 and 168, Binnie J, dissenting but not on this point.

112 *Power*, above note 7 at 19 [para 41].

113 See the paragraph associated with notes 72–75, above in this chapter, as well as David Layton, "The Prosecutorial Charging Decision" (2002) 46 Crim LQ 447 at 453–57.

114 See *Davies*, above note 110 at paras 38–42.

115 See Layton, above note 113 at 450–51.

116 *Regan*, above note 18 at para 62 [emphasis in original].

general deterrence value of proceeding with the charge, and the government's enforcement priorities.[117] But the most extensive source of guidance is found in policies adopted by the various Canadian prosecution services. These policies invariably set out two prongs that determine whether a prosecution will be launched or continued: first, the evidence must be sufficient to warrant proceeding, and, second, the public interest must otherwise justify prosecuting the charge.

a) The Evidentiary Prong

Canadian prosecution services employ somewhat different evidentiary standards in determining whether to proceed with a charge. In British Columbia, a charge will not be approved unless there exists a "substantial likelihood of conviction."[118] This standard will be met where Crown counsel "is satisfied that there is a strong, solid case of substance to present to the Court." The policies in Alberta, Saskatchewan, Manitoba, Prince Edward Island, and Newfoundland all require there to be a "reasonable likelihood of conviction," which appears to equate with a determination that a conviction is more probable than not.[119] Ontario and the PPSC use the "reasonable prospect of conviction" standard, which notably does *not* require that a conviction be more probable than not.[120] New Brunswick and Nova Scotia prosecutors must assess whether there is a "realistic prospect of conviction," which in the former jurisdiction at least is said to require that a conviction be

---

117 See *VT*, above note 66 at 40–41 [para 18], quoting from *Wayte v United States*, 470 US 598 (1985).

118 British Columbia Criminal Justice Branch, Ministry of Justice, *Crown Counsel Policy Manual* [*BC Crown Policy Manual*], CHA 1, "Charge Assessment Guidelines" (2 October 2009).

119 Alberta Crown Prosecution Service, *Crown Prosecutors' Manual*, "Decision to Prosecute" (20 May 2008); Saskatchewan Public Prosecutions Division, *Public Prosecution Policies* [*Sask Crown Policy Manual*], "Prosecutions — Proceeding with Charges" at 1; Manitoba Prosecution Service, Manitoba Justice, "Prosecutions: Role of the Manitoba Prosecution Service — Deciding to Prosecute," online: Manitoba Justice www.gov.mb.ca/justice/prosecutions/mbprosecutionservice. html. The Prince Edward Island and Newfoundland policies, though not available online, are set out in BC Charge Assessment Review, above note 105 at 19.

120 Ministry of Attorney General, Province of Ontario, *Crown Policy Manual* [*Ont Crown Policy Manual*], "Charge Screening" (21 March 2005) at 1–2. See Martin Committee Report, above note 100 at 66; *PPSC Deskbook*, above note 8, ch 2.3, section 3.1 (Reasonable Prospect of Conviction).

more likely than an acquittal.[121] Finally, Crown counsel in Quebec must be "reasonably satisfied" that guilt can be established.[122]

Some of these standards appear more demanding than others. Yet in every case the exercise involves an objective assessment.[123] The need for objectivity is part and parcel of the prosecutor's general *Boucher* duties, but it is also promoted by the requirement in many of the policies that the prospect or likelihood of conviction be "reasonable" or "realistic." Factors to consider in undertaking this objective evaluation of the evidence include the apparent credibility of the witnesses, the inherent frailties of certain types of evidence, whether evidence is admissible, and any reasonably anticipated defences. In applying these factors, Crown counsel must assess the strength of the case on the assumption that the fact-finder will perform its duties competently, dispassionately, and in accordance with the evidence and the law.[124]

The prosecutor's application of the evidentiary prong of the charging decision also has a subjective element: she must believe that the applicable evidentiary standard has been met.[125] It is nonetheless *not* a precondition that Crown counsel personally believe the accused is guilty beyond a reasonable doubt.[126] The rationale for not imposing such a requirement is that provided the basic evidentiary standard has been met a determination of guilt should be made by the judge or jury after a public trial. A prosecutor who refuses to proceed merely because she entertains a reasonable doubt supplants the trial process and does damage to the principles of openness and community involvement that infuse the criminal justice system. After all, the defence will have a full opportunity to obtain an acquittal at trial based on full disclosure

121 Office of the Attorney General, New Brunswick, *Public Prosecution Operational Manual*, "Attorney General's Policy — Public Prosecutions" at 3; Nova Scotia Public Prosecution Service, *Crown Attorney Manual — Prosecution and Administrative Policies for the PPS* [*NS Crown Attorney Manual*], "The Decision to Prosecute (Charge Screening)" (1 February 2011) at 3–7. The Nova Scotia policy states that this standard cannot be expressed in mathematical terms but offers that the "prospect of displacing the presumption of innocence must be real" and allows that in "borderline" cases a prosecutor may properly decide to proceed despite being unable to determine whether a conviction is more likely than not (*ibid* at 3–4).

122 Directeur des poursuites criminelles et pénales, *Directives du Directeur*, ACC-3, "Accusation — Poursuite des procédures" (9 April 2014) at §6.

123 See *Regan*, above note 18 at paras 62, 69–70, 83, 155–56, and 166–68.

124 See Martin Committee Report, above note 100 at 67.

125 See *Miazga*, above note 11 at para 58.

126 See *ibid* at paras 65–67; *Proulx*, above note 18 at para 31; Martin Committee Report, above note 100 at 69–72; John Pearson, "*Proulx* and Reasonable and Probable Cause to Prosecute" (2002) 46 CR (5th) 156. Arguments going the other way are discussed in Layton, above note 113 at 472–73.

received from the state, including all of the facts and information that ground Crown counsel's personal doubt.

Nonetheless, Crown counsel who reasonably believes an accused is not guilty should be permitted to pass the case on to another prosecutor if she so desires.[127] Moreover, the significant discretion associated with the charging decision means that, in reality, an individual prosecutor's reasonable doubt as to whether the accused is guilty may end up tipping the balance when it comes to determining whether the evidentiary standard is met.[128] It has also been suggested that a decision not to proceed may be justified, even when the evidentiary standard is met, where any responsible prosecutor would hold a subjective reasonable doubt on the issue of guilt.[129]

b) The Public Interest Prong

Even when the evidentiary standard is satisfied, a prosecutor has the discretion not to proceed with a charge if he concludes that doing so is not in the public interest. The Ontario Attorney General's Advisory Committee on Charge Screening, Disclosure, and Resolution Discussions has suggested that where the evidentiary standard is met, the prosecution will typically proceed,[130] which amounts to a presumption of sorts that the public interest favours prosecution in such cases. While this presumption may exist in theory, its strength is impossible to assess in a vacuum. A minor breach of the law causing no harm, committed by an individual with no prior record, will usually not require prosecution. Commission of a serious offence resulting in real harm to a complainant will, by contrast, very often tilt the public interest strongly in favour of proceeding with the charge.[131] In other words, the strength of the presumption will ebb and flow depending on how various factors bearing on the public interest are engaged.

Prosecution services provide their lawyers with valuable guidance by setting these factors out in the policy manual. Typical is the *PPSC Deskbook*, which states that matters bearing on the assessment of the public interest may include the following:

---

127 See ABA Prosecution Standard 3-3.9.
128 See Martin Committee Report, above note 100 at 73–74.
129 See *ibid* at 72–73.
130 *Ibid* at 76–77. To similar effect, see *PPSC Deskbook*, above note 8, ch 2.3, section 3.2 (The Public Interest).
131 See, for example, *PPSC Deskbook*, *ibid*, ch 2.3, section 3.2(1)(a), which is reproduced in the next paragraph.

1) **The nature of the alleged offence**

a. Its seriousness or triviality. The more serious the alleged offence, the more likely the public interest will require that a prosecution be pursued. However, where the alleged offence is not so serious as to plainly require a prosecution, Crown counsel must consider their duty to uphold the law enacted by Parliament and any important public interest served by conducting a prosecution, for example ensuring compliance with a regulatory regime through prosecution;

b. Significant mitigating or aggravating circumstances relating to the underlying conduct, for example those set out in the *Criminal Code* or other acts of Parliament;

c. The prevalence and impact of the alleged offence in the community and the need for general and specific deterrence;

d. The likely sentence in the event of a conviction;

e. The delay between the commission of the alleged offence and the time of the charging decision. Considerations relevant to the impact of any delay include the responsibility of the accused for the delay, the discoverability of the alleged offence by the police or investigative agency, and the complexity and length of the investigation; or

f. The law that is alleged to have been breached is obsolete or obscure.

2) **The nature of the harm caused by or the consequences of the alleged offence**

a. The nature of the harm includes loss or injury caused by the alleged offence and relevant consequences to the victim, the community, the environment, natural resources, safety, public health, public welfare or societal, economic, cultural or other public interests;

b. Whether the alleged offence engenders considerable concern in the community;

c. The entitlement of any person to criminal compensation, reparation or forfeiture if a prosecution occurs; or

d. The availability of civil remedies is not a factor that militates against a prosecution.

3) **The circumstances, consequences to and attitude of victims**

Although Crown counsel do not act as lawyers for victims, the effect of the alleged offence on victims is relevant to the public interest.

a. The attitude of the victim of the alleged offence to a prosecution. This may include the attitude of the victim's family members;

b.   The impact of the alleged offence on the victim and their family including any loss, injury or harm suffered;

c.   The youth, age, intelligence, vulnerability, disability, dependence, physical health, mental health, and other personal circumstances of the victim;

d.   Whether the victim was serving the public or was a public official; or

e.   Whether a prosecution is likely to have an adverse effect on the victim's physical or mental health.

4)   **The level of culpability and circumstances of the accused**

a.   The accused's degree of responsibility, level of involvement and whether they were in a position of authority or trust;

b.   The harm the accused caused, especially to vulnerable victims or persons;

c.   The accused's motivation, and in particular any bias, prejudice or hate based on race, national or ethnic origin, language, religion, gender, age, mental or physical disability, sexual orientation, or any other similar factor;

d.   The accused's agreed upon co-operation with the investigation or prosecution of others, or the extent to which they have already done so;

e.   The accused's age, intelligence, physical or mental health or infirmity; or

f.   The accused's background, including their antecedents and the likelihood of future illegal conduct.

5)   **The need to protect sources of information**

Whether prosecuting would require or cause the disclosure of information that should not be disclosed in the public interest, for example it would be injurious to:

a.   Confidential informants;

b.   Ongoing investigations;

c.   International relations;

d.   National defence; or

e.   National security.

6)   **Confidence in the administration of justice**

a.   Whether a prosecution would maintain public confidence in the government, courts, a regulatory regime, and the administration of justice or have the opposite effect;

b.   The likelihood of achieving the desired result and requisite level of specific and general deterrence and denunciation without a prosecution through available alternative measures, non-criminal processes or a prosecution by a provincial prosecution service;

c.   The effect on the administration of justice of committing resources to conduct the proceedings when considered in relation to the seriousness or triviality of the alleged offence, the likely sentence that would result from a conviction, and the attendant public benefit(s); or

d.   Whether the consequences of a prosecution or conviction would be disproportionately harsh or oppressive.[132]

As the *PPSC Deskbook* observes, the application of these and any other relevant factors will depend on the circumstances of the case.[133]

There are also a number of factors that Crown counsel must *not* take into account in deciding whether to proceed or continue with a criminal charge. For example, the *PPSC Deskbook* sets out the following irrelevant criteria:

a.   The race, national or ethnic origin, colour, religion, sex, sexual orientation, political associations, activities or beliefs of the accused or any other person involved in the investigation;

b.   Crown counsel's personal feelings about the accused or the victim;

c.   Possible political advantage or disadvantage to the government or any political group or party; or

d.   The possible effect of the decision on the personal or professional circumstances of those responsible for the prosecution decision.[134]

Relying on any of these inappropriate considerations constitutes a serious breach of the prosecutor's fundamental duty to act with fairness and impartiality. Even where a prosecution is clearly justified, reliance on an irrelevant or improper factor in launching or continuing with a case seriously detracts from the appearance of justice.[135] On the other hand, selective prosecution is not, without more, unethical. Impropriety arises only where the selection is based on impermissible factors such as a *Charter*-prohibited ground of discrimination,[136] and it does not, for example, preclude the Crown from bringing a test case for the

---

132 *Ibid*, ch 2.3, section 3.2 (The Public Interest) [notes omitted].

133 *Ibid*.

134 *Ibid*, ch 2.3, section 3.3 (Irrelevant Criteria).

135 See Layton, above note 113 at 479.

136 See, for example, *Yick Wo v Hopkins*, 118 US 256 (1886): prosecution for bylaw infractions was brought only against Chinese-owned laundries.

purpose of assessing the constitutionality of a law or sending a message of general deterrence.[137]

4) Applying the Discretion throughout the Entire Matter: Staying or Withdrawing a Charge

Crown counsel has an ethical duty to remain cognizant of the factors bearing on the charge approval or screening decision throughout the currency of the matter. As the case wends its way through the criminal justice process, events may occur or information come to light that the prosecutor reasonably views as impacting on the charging decision. For instance, a viable defence may emerge, or the reliability of a key Crown witness may be seriously undermined by further police investigation. If the standard necessary to justify proceeding is no longer met, the prosecutor must stay or withdraw the charge.

As with the decision to proceed with a charge, Crown counsel's decision to stay a matter under section 579 of the *Criminal Code* involves an exercise of prosecutorial discretion and is therefore accorded substantial judicial deference.[138] A court will intervene only where the decision amounts to an abuse of process.[139] This high degree of deference operates not only where an accused attacks a Crown decision to stay[140] but also where a private prosecutor challenges the Crown's ability to take over the prosecution and either proceed with it or stay it.[141]

The same level of judicial deference applies to the Crown's decision whether to withdraw a charge as permitted at common law, at least before the entering of a plea, and it matters not whether the information was sworn by a private individual or a peace officer.[142] It has been suggested that leave of the court is required to withdraw a charge once a plea has been entered.[143] Yet given the conclusion in *Krieger* that

---

137 See, generally, Frater, above note 11 at 33–35; Robert W Hubbard, Peter Brauti, & Candice Welsch, "Selective Prosecutions and the *Stinchcombe* Model for Disclosure" (1999) 42 Crim LQ 338; Robert K Allen, "Selective Prosecution: A Viable Defence in Canada?" (1992) 34 Crim LQ 414.

138 *Criminal Code*, above note 104. See *Krieger*, above note 13 at para 46.

139 See Section D(1), above in this chapter.

140 See, for example, *R v DN*, 2004 NLCA 44 at paras 11–29.

141 See, for example, *Steele v Alberta*, 2014 ABQB 124 at para 37; *Ahmadoun v Ontario (AG)*, 2012 ONSC 955 at paras 13–14.

142 See *Krieger*, above note 13 at para 46; *McHale v Ontario (AG)*, 2010 ONCA 361 at paras 32–42 and 53–77, leave to appeal to SCC refused, [2010] SCCA No 290 [*McHale*]; *R v Phillion*, 2010 ONSC 1604 at paras 89–98, 114, and 123 [*Phillion*].

143 See *R v Blasko* (1975), 29 CCC (2d) 321 at 322 [para 6] (Ont HCJ); *R v Forrester* (1976), 33 CCC (2d) 221 (Alta SC). See also the authorities discussed in *R v Carr*

the decision to withdraw engages prosecutorial discretion, it is highly doubtful that a court can refuse leave, postplea or not, absent a finding of abuse of process.[144]

F. PRE-CHARGE INVOLVEMENT IN A MATTER, THE DUTY TO INVESTIGATE, AND ADVISING THE POLICE

The mutual independence of the police and Crown functions is a well-established principle of our criminal justice system.[145] Yet mutual independence does not mean that police and Crown counsel cannot work together at the investigative and prosecutorial stages. To the contrary, as stated in the *PPSC Deskbook*:

> Administration of criminal justice is a continuum. At the one end, the police investigate criminal offences and arrange for suspected offenders to appear in court. At the other, Crown counsel are responsible for presenting the Crown's case in court. Their roles are interdependent. While both have separate responsibilities in the criminal justice system, they must inevitably work together in cooperation to administer and enforce criminal laws effectively.[146]

These sentiments reflect the jurisprudence, which, as we will see, recognizes that the police and Crown must interact if the criminal justice system is to operate effectually. Interaction is unproblematic provided that the mutual independence of the investigative and prosecutorial functions is not compromised.

1) Duty to Request That Police Take Investigative Steps

A prosecutor may conclude that further police investigation is needed before she can fulfill the charge approval function. If so, the prosecutor has a duty to identify the deficiency and request that police conduct whatever additional investigation is needed to permit a decision as to

---

(1984), 54 NBR (2d) 138 at 140–43 [paras 7–15] (QB), aff'd (1984), 58 NBR (2d) 99 (CA).

144 See *Phillion*, above note 142 at paras 89–133: not guilty plea had been entered, yet court applied *Krieger* standard in determining whether the decision to withdraw should be allowed to stand.

145 See *Regan*, above note 18 at para 71.

146 *PPSC Deskbook*, above note 8, ch 2.7, section 1 (Introduction).

whether charges should proceed.[147] An analogous duty applies where a prosecutor determines that further investigation is needed to properly prosecute an ongoing case or to ascertain whether the Crown's evidence or theory of the case is truly accurate.[148]

As minister of justice, Crown counsel cannot shirk from requesting additional police investigation merely because it might undermine the prosecution case.[149] Prosecution services may even be duty bound to review whole categories of cases, for instance convictions relying on subsequently discredited expert evidence, for the purpose of identifying any wrongful convictions.[150] The duty to investigate is not, however, so broad as to require Crown counsel to make inquiries at the behest of the accused simply because the investigation may yield information helpful in advancing a defence.[151]

Example 1: The disclosure brief in a robbery case reveals that the complainant has provided no identification evidence implicating the accused. No other admissible evidence links the accused to the crime. Despite repeated requests from defence counsel, the prosecutor refuses to ask police to conduct a proper photo lineup or pursue other investigative avenues to determine whether the charge-screening standard is met. Instead, Crown counsel insists that a trial date be set and suggests that the accused plead guilty to promote "economies of scale." This conduct falls short of that reasonably expected of a prosecutor.[152]

Example 2: A complainant reports a sexual assault that occurred in her bedroom. Her male roommate, with whom she had previously had a sexual relationship, at first tells police he was the man in her bedroom but later says no one went into the room. The police charge the accused

---

147 See Martin Committee Report, above note 100 at 134–35.

148 See also Section H(8)(d), below in this chapter.

149 See, for example, *R v Ahluwalia* (2000), 149 CCC (3d) 193 at paras 71–72 (Ont CA) [*Ahluwalia*]; *McNeil*, above note 21 at paras 49–50; ABA Prosecution Standard 3-3.11(c).

150 See Bruce A MacFarlane, "Wrongful Convictions: Is It Proper for the Crown to Root Around, Looking for Miscarriages of Justice?" (2012) 36 Man LJ 1; FPT Heads of Prosecutions 2011 Report, above note 5 at 153–54.

151 See *R v Darwish*, 2010 ONCA 124 at paras 26–40 [*Darwish*], leave to appeal to SCC refused, [2010] SCCA No 124; *Spackman*, above note 91 at paras 108–9; *R v Dias*, 2010 ABCA 382 at para 38; *R v Levin*, 2014 ABCA 142 at paras 44–47 [*Levin*]. To somewhat similar effect, in an analogous context, see *Canada (Citizenship and Immigration) v Harkat*, 2014 SCC 37 at para 103 [*Harkat*].

152 This example is based on *R v BM* (2003), 64 OR (3d) 299 (SCJ), where costs were awarded against the Crown on the basis that its handling of the file constituted an abuse of process.

based on the complainant's identification evidence. They seize clean underwear she put on immediately after the sexual assault but do not submit it for testing. They also seize male underwear apparently left in her bed by the assailant. Testing reveals semen on this underwear, but the accused is excluded as the source. On these facts, Crown counsel should ask the police to conduct further investigation, first, to compare the DNA profile found on the male underwear with the roommate's DNA profile and, second, to determine whether semen is located on the complainant's underwear and if so whether the DNA profile matches that of the accused or the roommate.[153]

Even where Crown counsel has an ethical duty to request further investigation by the police, he cannot *force* compliance, because the independence of the police in performing the investigatory function is constitutionally protected.[154] Yet police services usually accede to reasonable prosecution requests for further investigation. Indeed, a police officer's refusal may constitute a breach of her duty to investigate crime in a diligent and competent manner.[155]

2) Limits on Crown Counsel's Involvement at the Investigative Phase

Crown prosecutors frequently have contact with and assist the police during the investigative phase of a criminal matter, especially in larger and more complex cases. Examples include acting as agent on an application to obtain an authorization to intercept private communications, interviewing prospective witnesses, interacting with police regarding witness immunity agreements, and providing advice to police on matters as diverse as

- how to structure the investigation to ensure a sustainable prosecution,
- novel or complex search warrant applications,
- disclosure obligations and management,
- how to structure the case brief,
- handling agents and informers,
- whether certain steps should be taken to obtain information from a witness such as a *KGB* interview,

---

153 This example is based on *R v Folland* (1999), 132 CCC (3d) 14 at para 35 (Ont CA), in which the court criticized Crown counsel, albeit "in hindsight," for failing to conduct such testing before trial.

154 See Section E(1), above in this chapter.

155 See the text associated with note 101, above in this chapter.

- the strength of the case and the form and content of proposed charges, and
- whether it is proper to obtain advice on a particular matter in the first place.[156]

The ability of the police to obtain assistance of this sort from the prosecution branch is often necessary for the proper operation of the administration of justice.[157] Yet Crown and police interactions at this or any other stage of the criminal justice process must not operate to blur either's independence or objectivity because "separating the investigative and prosecutorial powers of the state is an important safeguard against the misuse of both."[158]

The leading case in this area is the Supreme Court of Canada's decision in *R v Regan*.[159] There, the accused obtained a stay of proceedings at trial for abuse of process based in part on a senior Crown counsel's role in joining the police in conducting pre-charge re-interviews of many sexual-assault complainants in a high-profile case. The prosecutor had participated in the re-interviews for the purposes of making credibility assessments, preparing for the preliminary hearing, and providing the complainants with information about the court process so they could make informed decisions about their involvement.

The majority in *Regan* disagreed with the trial judge's view that prosecutors should be precluded from conducting pre-charge interviews except for the limited purpose of protecting an accused by screening out unsupportable charges. The majority recognized that the separation of police and Crown functions is an important guard against a prosecutor's losing objectivity[160] but was not about to micromanage the police-Crown relationship by adopting a bright-line rule specifying how that separation should be maintained.[161] Rather, the important question is whether a particular action taken by the Crown has undermined prosecutorial objectivity or independence or is otherwise improper in the circumstances. *Regan* makes clear that interaction between police and Crown, or other involvement by Crown counsel at the investigatory stage, is not *per se* prohibited. The laying of charges is not a milestone

---

156 These and other examples are mentioned in the *PPSC Deskbook*, above note 8, ch 2.7, section 3 (Role of Crown Counsel Before and After Charges Are Laid). See also Code, above note 100 at 357–58.

157 See *Campbell*, above note 99 at para 49.

158 *Davey*, above note 21 at para 37, quoting from the Martin Committee Report, above note 100 at 39.

159 *Regan*, above note 18.

160 *Ibid* at paras 65–66 and 71.

161 *Ibid* at para 64. See also *R v Bagri*, 2004 SCC 42 at para 94 [*Bagri*].

point before which the Crown is precluded from involvement in a criminal matter.[162]

Regan thus rejects the notion that pre-charge interviews by a prosecutor are necessarily or even usually improper and recognizes that there are valid reasons to carry them out, including to inform potential witnesses of the legal process, to test the resolve of a complainant to pursue a matter, to assess witness credibility, for efficiency in the administration of justice, and for the sake of the appearance of decisive action in a highly public and controversial case.[163] On the facts, the majority in *Regan* saw nothing wrong with Crown counsel's decision to re-interview the complainants and refused to view her conduct as abusive.[164]

Recommendation: Crown counsel can properly play a role at the investigative phase for the purpose of providing the police with legal advice and other assistance, as well as to carry out prosecution function tasks. But prosecutors should take care not to assume the role of investigator and must scrupulously maintain independence from the police. The more extensive Crown counsel's participation at the pre-charge stage, the greater the risk of eroding the appearance of objectivity. If Crown counsel's pre-charge role is such that a reasonable person would view prosecutorial objectivity as being threatened, Crown counsel should play no role in the charge approval or screening function or the conduct of the prosecution, or measures should be taken sufficient to alleviate such concerns.[165]

---

162 *Regan*, above note 18 at para 87.
163 *Ibid* at paras 73, 81, 84–86, and 103. The minority dissented on the facts but did not disagree with the law as set out by the majority (*ibid* at paras 137, 151–60, and 182–83).
164 *Ibid* at paras 87–91 and 100–4. Compare *R v Trang*, 2002 ABQB 286 at paras 74–75 [*Trang*]: a prosecutor providing dedicated legal advice to a large and ongoing police investigation was held not to have lost her objectivity; *Bagri*, above note 161 at paras 93–95: Crown counsel does not lose objectivity merely by participating in an anti-terrorism judicial investigative hearing; *R v Atatise*, 2011 MBQB 82 at paras 33–36 (QB): prosecutor did not act improperly in making direct contact with prospective witnesses; *Lamer Inquiry Report*, above note 2 at 129–31, 137–39, and 141: prosecutor was criticized for losing objectivity in the course of working with police before and shortly after the laying of charges.
165 See, for example, *PPSC Deskbook*, above note 8, ch 2.7, section 3.4 (Charge Review): factors to consider in determining whether counsel who provides the police with pre-charge advice should participate further in the matter include "the effective and efficient prosecution of the matter, the orderly transition of the file, the length of time and involvement of the pre-charge Crown counsel, the need to avoid preconceived notions, exclusion if called as a witness, and the value of fresh eyes assessing the case."

3) Crown Counsel Does Not Take Instructions from the Police

Crown counsel does not stand in an ordinary client-lawyer relationship with the police officer to whom legal advice is provided. The officer receiving the advice and Crown counsel giving it are not in an agency relationship.[166] And the police cannot direct Crown counsel as would a private client his lawyer.[167] In other words, just as the Crown has no power to dictate the course of a criminal investigation to the police, so too are the police unable to direct Crown counsel regarding the conduct of a prosecution. Any other view would undermine Crown counsel's role as minister of justice, including the sacrosanct duties of independence and objectivity.

G. DISCLOSURE OF INVESTIGATIVE MATERIALS TO THE DEFENCE

In 1969, Brian A Grosman, in his book *The Prosecutor: An Inquiry into the Exercise of Discretion*,[168] denounced the lack of transparency, consistency, and coherence on the part of Canadian prosecutors in making pre-trial disclosure. Grosman concluded that prosecutors frequently viewed pre-trial disclosure as a favour exchanged with certain defence lawyers. By 1977, the situation had not changed appreciably, leading Stanley Cohen to wonder whether the Crown's attitude towards disclosure had not become "truly anathema to the rule of law."[169]

This is not to deny that by the mid-1970s and into the 1980s many prosecutors co-operated with defence counsel in making disclosure available before trial.[170] There was even some caselaw, including from the Supreme Court of Canada, that recognized an obligation to make disclosure of some sort to the defence.[171] And in 1974 a new Canadian

---

166 See *Campbell*, above note 99 at para 54.

167 See *ibid* at para 51; *Trang*, above note 164 at para 58.

168 Brian A Grosman, *The Prosecutor: An Inquiry into the Exercise of Discretion* (Toronto: University of Toronto Press, 1969).

169 Stanley Cohen, *Due Process of Law: The Canadian System of Criminal Justice* (Toronto: Carswell, 1977) at 139.

170 This rather haphazard approach was acknowledged by the Law Reform Commission of Canada in *Disclosure by the Prosecution* (Report 22) (Ottawa: The Commission, 1984).

171 See the cases discussed in *Taillefer*, above note 18 at paras 63–70; David Tanovich, "*Taillefer*: Disclosure, Guilty Pleas and Ethics" (2004) 17 CR (6th) 149 at 149–51.

Bar Association code was adopted, which provided that a prosecutor "should make timely disclosure to the accused or his counsel of all relevant facts and witnesses known to him, whether tending towards guilt or innocence."[172] Yet the practice of making disclosure varied from one province to another and also depended on the nature of the case and the individual prosecutor involved. While ethical and legal duties to disclose existed, their parameters were most definitely subject to disagreement.[173]

Then came the seminal 1991 judgment of the Supreme Court of Canada in *Stinchcombe*.[174] *Stinchcombe* marked a sea change by recognizing a robust ethical and constitutional prosecutorial duty to make disclosure to the defence.

1) Crown Disclosure Obligation after *Stinchcombe*

Stinchcombe and its progeny provide that the Crown has an obligation to disclose relevant police investigative materials to the accused, who enjoys a constitutional right to disclosure protected by section 7 of the *Charter of Rights and Freedoms*.[175] This disclosure obligation is expansive. The Crown must disclose all relevant information under its control, whether inculpatory or exculpatory, regardless of whether the information pertains to evidence that the prosecution intends to adduce or that would be admissible for the defence at trial.[176] The concept of relevance is defined broadly, extending to materials in the possession or control of the Crown where there is a reasonable possibility that the information contained therein will be useful to the accused in making full answer and defence.[177] A discretion is nonetheless left to

---

172 Canadian Bar Association, *Code of Professional Conduct* (Ottawa: CBA, 1974) ch VIII, commentary 7. This rule was used in part to justify a finding of professional misconduct against a prosecutor in *Bledsoe v Law Society of British Columbia* (1984), 13 CCC (3d) 560 at 569 [para 35] (BCCA) [*Bledsoe*].

173 See *Taillefer*, above note 18 at para 64; Tanovich, above note 171 at 151.

174 *Stinchcombe*, above note 1.

175 Part I of the *Constitution Act, 1982*, being Schedule B to the *Canada Act 1982* (UK), 1982, c 11 [*Charter*]. See *R v La* (1997), 116 CCC (3d) 97 at para 23 (SCC) [*La*]; *Taillefer*, above note 18 at para 61; *McNeil*, above note 21 at para 14; *Quesnelle*, above note 21 at para 11.

176 See *Taillefer*, above note 18 at paras 59–60; *McNeil*, above note 21 at paras 17 and 44.

177 *Taillefer*, above note 18 at paras 59–60. A statutory exception to this rule applies where the Crown has possession of non-investigatory records containing the personal information of a witness in sexual offence matters: see *McNeil*, above note 21 at para 21.

the Crown on certain issues.[178] For instance, the timing and manner of disclosure remain a matter of discretion, albeit subject to review by the courts. The Crown also has leeway in excluding what is clearly irrelevant, withholding the identity of a person to afford protection from harassment or injury, and enforcing a legal privilege.

Because the Crown's obligation to disclose is a continuing one,[179] new information may have to be provided to defence counsel during the trial and sometimes even after conviction.[180] Thus, the expression "pre-trial disclosure" is a less than totally accurate reflection of the real scope of the disclosure duty. Moreover, though the obligation prevails for any material in the possession or control of the Crown, the police have a concomitant duty to provide all relevant investigatory materials to the prosecution; non-fulfillment of the Crown's disclosure obligation cannot be justified by police failure to comply with this duty.[181]

Inherent in the obligation to disclose is the duty to preserve the fruits of the investigation.[182] Where evidence goes missing, the Crown will have to show that the loss or destruction was not owing to unacceptable negligence. Whether reasonable steps have been taken will, in many cases, require the Crown to establish good faith. A knowing participation in the destruction of evidence or even failure by a prosecutor to inform the court of her knowledge that the police have destroyed relevant materials makes more likely a holding that loss or destruction has breached the accused's constitutional right to disclosure.

These aspects of the disclosure obligation flow naturally from the overarching principle that lies at its core, namely, that investigative materials are not the Crown's to be employed in securing a conviction but rather belong to "the public to be used to ensure that justice is done."[183] This central principle is closely aligned with the Crown's ethical duty to seek justice in the public interest.

178　See *Stinchcombe*, above note 1 at 9 [paras 16 and 20]; *R v Egger* (1993), 82 CCC (3d) 193 at 203 [para 19] (SCC) [*Egger*]; *Krieger*, above note 13 at para 54; *Mc-Neil*, above note 21 at para 18.

179　See *Stinchcombe*, above note 1 at 14 [para 28]; *R v Chaplin* (1995), 96 CCC (3d) 225 at para 21 (SCC) [*Chaplin*]; Martin Committee Report, above note 100 at 206.

180　See *McNeil*, above note 21 at para 17; *R v Trotta* (2004), 23 CR (6th) 261 at paras 22–26 (Ont CA); Martin Committee Report, above note 100 at 207–8; ABA Model Rule 3.8(g) & (h).

181　See *R v Illes*, 2008 SCC 57 at para 63; *McNeil*, above note 21 at paras 14 and 23–24; *Quesnelle*, above note 21 at para 12.

182　See *La*, above note 175 at para 17; *Re Charkaoui*, 2008 SCC 38 at para 49.

183　*Stinchcombe*, above note 1 at 7 [para 12].

2) Ethical Components of Crown Disclosure Obligation

The constitutional disclosure obligations incumbent on the Crown are heavily influenced by the prosecutor's role as a minister of justice who has a responsibility to ensure that the accused is treated fairly and is not denied the ability to make full answer and defence. In *R v Chaplin*,[184] the Supreme Court of Canada held that the Crown must exercise the utmost good faith in determining which information must be disclosed and in providing ongoing disclosure.[185] The Court added that a departure from the disclosure obligation may constitute a serious breach of professional ethics,[186] echoing similar comments previously made in *Stinchcombe*.[187]

Canadian codes of professional conduct also recognize that a failure to disclose may violate a prosecutor's ethical responsibilities. Most codes state that "a prosecutor . . . , to the extent required by law and accepted practice, should make timely disclosure to defence counsel or directly to an unrepresented accused of all relevant and known facts and witnesses, whether tending to show guilt or innocence."[188] Crown counsel's ethical duties in relation to disclosure are likewise affirmed in the highly influential Martin Committee Report.[189] The report opines that it is "very serious professional misconduct" for Crown counsel to fail to disclose to the defence as required[190] and that it is also inappropriate for a prosecutor to make disclosure contingent on defence counsel's waiving or limiting a preliminary inquiry[191] or to withhold disclosure unless defence counsel undertakes not to share the information with the client.[192]

Not every breach of the constitutional duty to disclose will constitute unethical conduct by the prosecutor, at least not in the sense of professional misconduct sufficient to trigger disciplinary action by a law society. Professional misconduct occurs where a lawyer's act or omission is a marked departure from the conduct expected of a reasonable and competent lawyer. While not requiring proof of intentional

---

184 *Chaplin*, above note 179.
185 *Ibid* at para 21.
186 *Ibid*.
187 *Stinchcombe*, above note 1 at 11 [para 20]. See also *Krieger*, above note 13 at para 54.
188 See the provisions set out at note 6, above in this chapter.
189 Martin Committee Report, above note 100 at 170–75.
190 *Ibid* at 170.
191 *Ibid* at 171–73.
192 *Ibid* at 173–75. This prohibition may not apply, however, where the undertaking is sought for a proper purpose and is limited to discrete items: see Chapter 4, Section R(3).

wrongdoing or bad faith, this standard needs at least a showing of gross culpable neglect.[193] Most instances of non-disclosure will therefore fall short of professional misconduct, for instance, where the police have failed to pass relevant materials on to the Crown, where the Crown's refusal to disclose is based on a non-frivolous but ultimately incorrect view of the law, or where the lack of disclosure is attributable to standard as opposed to gross negligence. These sorts of lapses will breach the accused's constitutional rights but will not make the prosecutor guilty of professional misconduct.[194] Similarly, a prosecution service administrative determination that its disclosure guidelines have been breached does not by definition mean that Crown counsel has committed professional misconduct.[195]

A law society should be able to discipline a prosecutor for failure to disclose where the omission constitutes professional misconduct. This view jibes with the Supreme Court of Canada's holdings in *Krieger* and *Anderson* that the duty to disclose does not fall within the definition of prosecutorial discretion.[196] These holdings square nicely with the law that allows courts to review a failure to disclose on a correctness standard, as opposed to the much more demanding test for abuse of process.[197] By parity of reasoning, a law society should be able to conduct a review of a failure to disclose using the professional misconduct standard. Yet at several points *Krieger* seems to say that a law society can only discipline a prosecutor where the lapse amounts to dishonesty or bad faith.[198] This position is extremely hard to reconcile with the analysis in *Krieger* and *Anderson* as to why and when certain prosecutorial decisions are accorded a highly deferential standard of review. A possible explanation for the apparently incongruent comments in *Krieger* is that the ethical code under consideration, as it read at the time, permitted the law society to discipline a prosecutor for only a bad faith failure to disclose.[199]

---

193 See Gavin MacKenzie, *Lawyers and Ethics: Professional Responsibility and Discipline* (Scarborough, ON: Carswell, 1993) (loose-leaf March 2013 supplement) at § 26.7; Stephen Grant, Linda Rothstein, & Sean Campbell, *Lawyers' Professional Liability*, 3d ed (Markham, ON: LexisNexis 2013) at § 1.36.

194 See *Krieger*, above note 13 at para 59 (quoting first edition of this text).

195 See *ibid* at paras 57–58.

196 *Krieger, ibid* at para 54; *Anderson*, above note 11 at para 45. See also Section D(2), above in this chapter.

197 *Ibid.*

198 *Krieger*, above note 13 at paras 4–5, 51–55, and 60.

199 *Ibid* at paras 15 and 38(3). The current provision, Alta r 4.01(4), no longer contains this qualification.

3) Protecting Third-Party Privacy and Security Interests

Police investigative files often contain information over which third parties hold a privacy interest.[200] These interests must to a considerable extent give way so that disclosure can be made to the accused for the purpose of making full answer and defence at trial. Yet in some circumstances disclosing the materials in the usual way risks undue harm to a third party's privacy and perhaps to his physical security as well. If so, the Crown will generally be under a duty, as minister of justice acting in the pubic interest, to ensure that only relevant information is produced and to prevent an unwarranted intrusion on the third party's legitimate interests.[201] This duty can usually be carried out by redacting irrelevant portions of the disclosure, such as witness contact information, where there is a specific and real concern about safety or security[202] or by imposing restrictions on handling disclosure, such as a prohibition against allowing a complainant's video statement to leave defence counsel's possession.[203] Crown counsel must not, however, take steps that meaningfully impinge on the accused's right to make full answer and defence.

Observation: The need for the Crown to seek an express undertaking restricting the ability of defence counsel to disseminate portions of disclosure materials is much reduced in jurisdictions where an implied undertaking has been recognized as applying to the disclosure brief.[204]

4) Witness Interviews Conducted by the Crown in Preparing for Trial

Crown counsel does not have to disclose her work product, for instance notes made in preparation for leading a witness's evidence at trial, because such information is ordinarily covered by litigation privilege.[205]

---

200 See Chapter 4, Section R(1).
201 See *McNeil*, above note 21 at paras 43–45, discussing third-party production but drawing on principles said to apply in the *Stinchcombe* disclosure context; *Stinchcombe*, above note 1 at 12 [para 22].
202 See Martin Committee Report, above note 100 at 227–28; *R v Brown*, [1997] OJ No 6165 (Gen Div); *R v Mitchell*, 2013 ONSC 1865. Sometimes, however, witness contact information must be disclosed: see *R v Pickton*, 2005 BCSC 967; *R v Charlery*, 2011 ONSC 2952.
203 See Chapter 4, Section R(3).
204 See Chapter 4, Section R(2).
205 See *O'Connor*, above note 70 at para 87; *R v Swearengen* (2003), 68 OR (3d) 24 at paras 6–7 (SCJ); *R v Mullin*, 2011 ONSC 6251 at paras 24–34 (SCJ); *R v Lalo*, 2002 NSSC 169 [*Lalo*]; *R v Giroux*, [2001] OJ No 5495 at paras 22–26 (SCJ);

However, if new relevant information is revealed to Crown counsel during a witness's trial preparation interview, it must be disclosed pursuant to *Stinchcombe*.[206]

5) Plea Discussions and Sentencing

Crown counsel's *Stinchcombe* duty to disclose encompasses information that is relevant to plea discussions or might otherwise impact the accused's sentence after a guilty plea or conviction at trial.

Example 1: During plea discussions, the prosecutor learns that the star Crown witness has just testified in another proceeding in a different country and has contradicted testimony given at the preliminary hearing in Canada. The prosecutor is almost certain that counsel for the accused is not aware of this development. Disclosure must be made because a substantial inconsistency provided under oath is relevant to the witness's credibility. Disclosure may weaken the prosecutor's case and cause the defence to withdraw from plea discussions or insist on a more favourable resolution, but such a result is commensurate with the Crown's overriding duty to seek justice.

Example 2: Defence counsel and the prosecutor have finalized a plea resolution. A few days before the guilty plea is to be entered, Crown counsel discovers that the key Crown witness has died. The witness neither testified at a preliminary inquiry nor provided a statement meeting the requirements of the principled exception to the hearsay rule. The information that the witness has died falls within the ambit of the ethical duty to disclose. It affects the accused's potential punishment and his adherence to the plea bargain because knowledge of the death may lead the accused to withdraw consent to the bargain.[207] In fact, if there is no realistic prospect of conviction absent the testimony of the witness, Crown counsel must withdraw or stay the charges.

6) Bridging the Gap between First-Party Disclosure and Third-Party Production

Materials that may be useful to the accused in making full answer and defence but are in the hands of a third party other than the investi-

---

R v Johal, [1995] BCJ No 1271 at para 15 (SC); Martin Committee Report, above note 100 at 251–53.

206 See the authorities cited in the preceding note, as well as R v Logan (2002), 159 OAC 165 at para 4 (CA); *PPSC Deskbook*, above note 8, ch 2.5, Part 3.17.

207 The accused can almost certainly do so: see Chapter 9, Section Q.

gative agency do not fall within the Crown's *Stinchcombe* duty.[208] The defence if it wishes to obtain production of such third-party materials must bring what is known as an *"O'Connor"* application.[209] An *O'Connor* application will succeed where the accused is able to meet a two-stage test. First, she must establish that the sought-after materials are "likely relevant" to the proceedings, meaning that there is a reasonable possibility the information contained therein is logically probative to an issue at trial.[210] If this first stage is met, the court will review the materials to determine whether they are indeed likely relevant. If so, they will be produced to the defence where the court determines that if the materials were in the hands of the Crown, such would be the result under *Stinchcombe*.[211]

It sometimes occurs that Crown counsel learns of the possible existence of third-party records held by other government departments or agencies that are potentially relevant to the defence and so could be the subject of a viable *O'Connor* application. Unless the existence or relevance of the records appears unfounded, the prosecutor's special role as minister of justice obliges him to make reasonable inquiries and obtain the information from the third-party department or agency if feasible. If the third party declines to provide the records to the prosecutor, disclosure of their existence and/or the third party's position must be made to the defence so the accused can bring an *O'Connor* application if deemed appropriate.[212]

H. ETHICAL RESTRAINTS ON ADVOCACY

The distinctive feature of the prosecutor's role as advocate is zealousness tempered by the general duty to seek justice, not simply convictions. As already mentioned, Crown counsel's obligations as minister of justice do not require her to abjure advocacy.[213] Crown lawyers are

---

208 See *McNeil*, above note 21 at para 22.
209 Named after *O'Connor*, above note 70. If the accused is charged with a sexual offence, the application is instead governed by ss 278.1–278.91 of the *Criminal Code*, above note 104: see *McNeil*, above note 21 at paras 21 and 30–32; *Quesnelle*, above note 21 at paras 14–17.
210 See *McNeil*, above note 21 at para 33; *Quesnelle*, above note 21 at para 13.
211 *McNeil*, above note 21 at paras 34–42 and 47; *Quesnelle*, above note 21 at para 13.
212 See *McNeil*, above note 21 at paras 48–51; *Quesnelle*, above note 21 at para 12; *Levin*, above note 151 at para 44.
213 Section C(2), above in this chapter.

expected to be adversarial provided they are ethical as well.[214] A fair and ethical prosecutor can thus advance strong and determined positions and employ favourable trial strategy and tactics. In this section, we examine some of the dilemmas a prosecutor can face in exercising the adversarial function as a minister of justice.

1) Judge Shopping

In *Regan*,[215] Crown counsel had advised the police to wait before laying charges against a former politician in a high-profile case to avoid the matter going before a particular judge who she believed might be sympathetic to the accused. She had also offered to monitor the court docket to look for a more favourable judge.[216] The Supreme Court of Canada held that Crown counsel had engaged in improper judge shopping. It is overzealous, said the Court, for a prosecutor to manipulate a power not available to the defence — in *Regan*, to advise the police when to lay charges based on access to scheduling information — to select a favourable judge.[217] Such conduct creates an inequality between Crown and defence that is unfair to the accused and tarnishes the reputation of the justice system.[218]

2) Bail Hearings

In *R v Brooks*,[219] Hill J offered the following astute observations regarding Crown counsel's obligations concerning bail hearings:

> Crown counsel are expected to exercise discretion to consent to bail in appropriate cases and to oppose release where justified. That discretion must be informed, fairly exercised, and respectful of prevailing jurisprudential authorities. Opposing bail in every case, or without exception where a particular crime is charged, or because of a victim's wishes without regard to individual liberty concerns of the arrestee, derogates from the prosecutor's role as a minister of justice and as a guardian of the civil rights of all persons.
>
> Because the police and the prosecution have significant discretion to exercise respecting the release of accused persons, the admin-

---

214 See *R v Rose* (1998), 129 CCC (3d) 449 at para 22 (SCC) [*Rose* SCC].
215 *Regan*, above note 18.
216 There was no evidence as to whether the prosecutor had followed up on this offer (*ibid* at paras 59 and 181).
217 *Ibid* at paras 59–61.
218 *Ibid* at para 61.
219 (2001), 153 CCC (3d) 533 (Ont SCJ).

istration of criminal justice logically expects that these parties will not simply dump all bail decisions into contested hearings before the courts. Not only does this serve to choke the operation of the bail courts but, as said, the statutory and constitutional regime demands otherwise.[220]

These sentiments reflect the basic duties of Crown counsel in exercising prosecutorial discretion. The bail context does not somehow justify aberrant Crown conduct.

3) Prospective Jurors: Improper Contact and Background Inquiries

In *R v Kirkham*,[221] a Crown lawyer was charged with two counts of attempting to obstruct justice in connection with the original Robert Latimer murder trial. The first count alleged that the prosecutor had authorized police officers to collect personal information about potential jurors in an attempt to obtain an unfair advantage over the defence. The second count alleged that despite knowing potential jurors had been directly contacted by police he had failed to promptly advise defence counsel and the court of such contacts.

The prosecutor was acquitted on both counts. With respect to the first, the court concluded that he had not intended that the police contact any of the prospective jurors. As for the second, the court held that the failure to disclose did not meet the *mens rea* requirement for attempting to obstruct justice, largely because there was no policy in place to provide professional guidance regarding contact with prospective jurors. Nor was it obvious to counsel that his failure to disclose would result in an obstruction of justice since he believed that he would be able to keep the "tainted" jurors off the actual jury. The trial judge nonetheless had some harsh words for the prosecutor's failure to disclose, holding that on a principled basis he should have promptly informed the court on learning of the direct contact with the prospective jurors.[222]

---

220 *Ibid* at paras 22–23.
221 *R v Kirkham* (1998), 126 CCC (3d) 397 (Sask QB) [*Kirkham*].
222 *Ibid* at paras 21–22 and 29. The Supreme Court of Canada had earlier termed the prosecutor's actions a "flagrant abuse of process and interference with the administration of justice" (*R v Latimer* (1997), 112 CCC (3d) 193 at para 43 (SCC) [*Latimer*]). He was later suspended for six months for not promptly informing the court that the police had been in direct contact with prospective jurors: see *Law Society of Saskatchewan v Kirkham*, [1999] LSDD No 19. More recently, in *R v Emms*, 2012 SCC 74 at para 46 [*Emms*], the Court noted that the

At the time *Kirkham* was decided, in 1998, a number of Canadian ethical codes expressly permitted counsel to investigate a prospective juror for the purpose of ascertaining any basis for challenge but prohibited direct or indirect contact with the individual in question.[223] There was, it has been observed, some uncertainty as to how far Crown counsel could go in conducting vetting investigations.[224] However, in a trilogy of 2012 cases, the Supreme Court of Canada clarified the acceptable bounds of jury vetting, at least on the part of the Crown and police.[225] The Court was particularly concerned about the negative impact on actual and perceived fairness that can occur where the Crown investigates prospective jurors' backgrounds by accessing police databases. Police-database vetting risks unjustified state intrusion into prospective jurors' privacy and raises the spectre of the prosecution's seeking to exclude certain classes of people from juries based on stereotype or discrimination. The Crown's use of police-database information creates a further concern that the state is seeking to engineer a selection process favourable to it but not the accused.[226]

For these reasons, the trilogy restricts police-database vetting to ascertaining whether an individual is eligible to serve on a jury. Crown counsel can thus properly obtain police assistance to perform database checks limited to identifying potential jurors who because of criminal conduct are ineligible to serve on a jury under applicable provincial law or section 638(1)(c) of the *Criminal Code*, provided all information thereby obtained is disclosed to the defence.[227] The trilogy further holds that information obtained purely as a by-product of such legitimate vetting and relevant to other aspects of the selection process — for instance, on

---

state actors in *Latimer* knew or should have known that contacting the prospective jurors and obtaining their views on various issues was "off-limits and completely unacceptable."

223 See, for example, what is now CBA Code ch IX, commentary 21.

224 See *Emms*, above note 222 at paras 45–47.

225 *R v Yumnu*, 2012 SCC 73 [*Yumnu*]; *Emms*, *ibid*; *Davey*, above note 21. *Emms* appears to leave open the possibility that the same restrictions apply to the defence (*Emms*, above in this note at para 47), as perhaps do comments in *Yumnu* stating that the jury selection process "is not governed by the strictures of the adversarial process" (*ibid* at para 71).

226 See *Yumnu*, *ibid* at paras 36–43.

227 See *Yumnu*, above note 225 at paras 50–51 and 63; *Emms*, above note 222 at para 25. Provincial legislation differs in terms of the circumstances that may render an individual ineligible to serve as a juror. Section 638(1)(c) of the *Criminal Code*, above note 104, provides that an individual cannot serve if convicted of an offence resulting in a term of imprisonment exceeding twelve months.

the issue of whether an individual would be impartial — can be used by the Crown and defence to inform their selection strategies.[228]

Finally, the trilogy concludes that Crown counsel should not systematically distribute jury panel lists to local police services to collect opinions from member officers as to the suitability of listed individuals' serving on a jury. Such opinion gathering is tantamount to accessing an informal police database and so engages the concerns mentioned above.[229] The Crown may, however, partake in targeted consultation with a limited number of individuals working on the prosecution case, including police officers, to discuss concerns relating to the eligibility or suitability of a prospective juror.[230] This more confined canvassing for information is of lesser concern in terms of creating an imbalance between Crown and defence or intruding upon juror privacy.[231] Information thereby obtained that is relevant to the selection process must be disclosed to the defence, including where derived from an officer's involvement in law enforcement.[232] By contrast, the Crown need not disclose general impressions, personal or public knowledge in the community, rumours, or hunches.[233] But the Crown has a duty to ascertain the basis for an officer's opinion to determine whether it derives from information that falls within the disclosure obligation.[234] If Crown counsel is uncertain on this score, the opinion itself should be disclosed.[235]

Ethical codes and the trilogy: Most Canadian ethical codes prohibit counsel from having direct or indirect contact with a prospective juror or her family,[236] which is in keeping with the jurisprudence.[237] But the codes appear to provide broader scope for the Crown to engage in vetting prospective jurors than does the Supreme Court of Canada trilogy,

---

228 *Yumnu*, above note 225 at paras 53–55 and 63. As for the difficulties in limiting the search to information directly relevant to the eligibility issue, see the comments in *Yumnu, ibid* at paras 56–61.

229 See the text associated with notes 225–26, above in this chapter, as well as *Davey*, above note 21 at paras 34–37.

230 *Davey, ibid* at paras 9 and 38.

231 *Ibid* at paras 38–40.

232 *Ibid* at para 41.

233 *Ibid* at para 46.

234 *Ibid* at para 47.

235 *Ibid* at paras 9 and 59. Otherwise, it appears that the opinion, as opposed to the information on which it is based, need not be disclosed to the defence: *ibid* at para 48.

236 Alta, Sask r 4.05(1); BC, Man, Ont, NS, NL r 5.5-1; CBA Code ch IX, commentary 21.

237 See *Kirkham*, above note 221; *Latimer*, above note 222 at para 43; *Emms*, above note 222 at para 46.

for they state that "a lawyer may investigate a prospective juror to ascertain any basis for challenge."[238] Prosecutors must nonetheless abide by the restrictions imposed by the trilogy to ensure trial fairness and public confidence in the administration of justice.

4) Jury Selection in Court

A prosecutor cannot dispense with the public interest and violate fundamental principles of justice in the jury selection process. Seeking to exclude individuals from the jury on the basis of race or ethnicity is especially pernicious and would almost certainly constitute a breach of the equality guarantee enshrined in section 15 of the *Charter*.[239] This point is made in *R v Gayle*, where Sharpe J reviewed the law on point and concluded as follows:

> In my view, it follows from the quasi-judicial nature of the Crown's discretionary powers and from the overriding values of the *Charter* that there are circumstances where a court will review and constrain the exercise of the Crown's right of peremptory challenge. It seems to me that if the exercise of the power is at odds with the quasi-judicial nature of the Crown's duty, or at odds with the basic rights and freedoms guaranteed by the *Charter*, a court can and should intervene as has been done in relation to other discretionary Crown powers. In particular, it is my view that public confidence in the administration of justice would be seriously undermined if Crown counsel were permitted to exercise the power of peremptory challenge on racial or ethnic grounds. The rationale for peremptory challenges is to foster confidence in the fairness and impartiality of jury trials. The Crown should not be permitted to subvert that rationale by using peremptory challenges to achieve precisely the opposite result.[240]

On the facts in *Gayle*, however, the appellant failed to make out a case that the trial Crown had improperly utilized the peremptory challenge power.[241]

---

238 See the rules cited at note 236, above in this chapter.
239 *Charter*, above note 175.
240 (2001), 154 CCC (3d) 221 at para 66 (Ont CA) [citation omitted], leave to appeal to SCC refused, [2001] SCCA No 359 [*Gayle*].
241 *Ibid* at paras 68–71. A similar result was reached in *R v Amos*, 2007 ONCA 672.

5) Opening Statement to the Jury

Improper opening statements rarely occur in Canada. Prosecutors usually respect the narrow purpose of the opening statement, which is to introduce the parties, explain the process, and state the evidence expected during the trial — *not* to present argument, invective, or opinion.[242] The restraint demanded of the Crown is thus greater than that which applies to a closing address.[243] Where a prosecutor does make an inappropriate comment during an opening,[244] it will often be possible to alleviate any resulting prejudice through a prompt correcting instruction from the court.[245]

The potential for harm arising from an opening statement is exemplified by the facts in the Supreme Court of Canada case of *R v Jolivet*.[246] Crown counsel's opening mentioned that he would call witness "B" to corroborate the main prosecution witness, who was an unsavoury informer. Later, he advised that witness "B" would no longer be called. The Supreme Court held that any unfairness created by the Crown's change of position, and the trial judge's refusal to allow defence counsel to attack the change in closing submissions, did not warrant a new trial. Nevertheless, *Jolivet* should serve to remind prosecutors of the significance that may attach to an apparently inoffensive opening statement, owing to later unforeseen events.

Recommendation: Crown counsel should consider whether there is a reasonable possibility that evidence she wishes to call will be successfully challenged by the defence during the trial. If so, the safest course is to avoid mentioning the evidence in the opening or to request a pre-trial ruling regarding its admissibility.[247]

---

242   See *R v Mallory*, 2007 ONCA 46 at para 338 [*Mallory*].

243   *Ibid* at paras 338–39.

244   See, for example, *Mallory, ibid* at paras 331, 338, and 342–43: comments demeaning the defence; *R v Barnes* (1997), 117 OAC 371 at paras 2–4 (CA) [*Barnes*]: suggestion that pre-trial rulings would deprive the jury of evidence; *R v Carrière* (2004), 190 CCC (3d) 164 at paras 48–50 and 79 (Ont CA) [*Carrière*]: expression of personal opinion about the case; *R v Bradbury*, 2004 NLCA 82 at paras 22 and 25: overfamiliar comments termed "gauche" by appeal court; *R v LL*, 2009 ONCA 413 at paras 63–64 and 72 [*LL*]: overstatement of import of evidence; *R v Brown*, 2009 BCSC 1870 [*Brown*]: jury told that prosecution only occurs after Crown determines that there is a substantial likelihood of conviction.

245   See, for example, most of the cases cited in the preceding note, *Brown* being a notable exception. Other exceptions include *R v DAH*, 2000 BCCA 688 at paras 8–12 and 15 [*DAH*]; *R v Simard* (1995), 39 CR (4th) 131 (Que CA).

246   *Jolivet*, above note 43.

247   See *DAH*, above note 245 at para 10.

6) Calling and Interacting with Witnesses

This section discusses Crown counsel's ethical obligations in calling and interacting with witnesses, the aim being to ascertain the extent to which a prosecutor's role as lawyer in an adversarial system should be tempered by the overarching duty to seek the truth within a fair trial process.

a) No General Obligation to Call Witnesses

The Crown has no general obligation to call a witness as part of its case.[248] Given that all relevant information must be disclosed to the defence before the trial, a prosecution duty to call a material witness, even one said to be "essential to the narrative" such as a complainant, is not needed to ensure trial fairness. The Crown is thus afforded considerable discretion in calling witnesses; only an improper or oblique motive in refusing to do so will justify judicial intervention.[249] Such a motive will exist where the Crown declines to call a witness to avoid disclosing relevant information or where the decision not to call the witness amounts to an abuse of process.[250]

Although the prosecution has no general duty to call witnesses, the failure to do so may have a negative impact on the Crown case. Without the witness's testimony, the Crown may be unable to establish an essential element of the charged offence.[251] Or the failure to call the witness may entitle the fact-finder to draw an inference adverse to the prosecution.[252]

While the Crown's decision not to call a witness is usually unassailable, the accused may nonetheless be able to apply to have that witness called by the court.[253] Or Crown counsel may agree to call a witness solely for the purpose of making him available for cross-examination by the defence.[254]

---

248 See *Cook*, above note 18 at paras 17–58; *Jolivet*, above note 43 at paras 14–21; *R v Darrach*, 2000 SCC 46 at para 69; *Rybak*, above note 88 at paras 171–73. Comments to the contrary in older authorities are no longer good law.

249 See *Cook*, above note 18 at paras 57–58; *Jolivet*, above note 43 at paras 18–21.

250 See *Cook*, above note 18 at paras 57–58; *Jolivet*, above note 43 at para 20.

251 See *Cook*, above note 18 at paras 30–31 and 50–51; *R v Rudge*, 2011 ONCA 791 at para 82, leave to appeal to SCC refused, [2012] SCCA No 64 [*Rudge*].

252 See *Jolivet*, above note 43 at paras 22–30 and 39; *Rudge*, above note 251 at para 78.

253 See *R v Finta* (1994), 88 CCC (3d) 417 at 529–33 [paras 295–304] (SCC) [*Finta* SCC]; *Cook*, above note 18 at para 58.

254 See *Cook, ibid* at para 56.

b) Duty Not to Call a Witness Believed to Be Unreliable

Crown counsel is usually prohibited from calling a witness to elicit testimony that she has determined is unreliable. In *R v Lane*,[255] for example, the accused was charged with a murder that the Crown alleged had been witnessed by two unsavoury associates. One of the associates was the star Crown witness, but the other, named Campbell, was not called by the Crown to testify after having provided dramatically inconsistent statements regarding the events, including testimony at the preliminary inquiry that led to his being charged with perjury. At trial, Crown counsel advised the court that he was not using Campbell as a witness because he was ethically forbidden from calling a witness who he believed would lie.[256] While addressing a related evidentiary issue on appeal, the Ontario Court of Appeal agreed that, given counsel's view that Campbell would mislead the court if called, his decision not to have Campbell testify was entirely proper.[257]

Yet there are caveats to the general interdiction against a prosecutor's calling evidence she believes is unreliable. For instance, sometimes Crown counsel will call a witness who it is anticipated may be hostile and therefore recant an earlier statement. If counsel's fears are realized and the witness recants, portions of the examination-in-chief, and the Crown's cross-examination too if the witness is declared hostile at common law or if a successful application is brought under sections 9(1) or 9(2) of the *Canada Evidence Act*,[258] may involve putting questions to the witness that counsel believes will elicit false evidence. Or consider the scenario where a Crown eyewitness is clearly mistaken about some aspects of the viewed incident but not others. The prosecutor can properly elicit both the testimony believed to be true, such as the actions of the perpetrator and the perpetrator's distinctive tattoo, and the testimony thought to be inaccurate, such as the description of the perpetrator's clothing or estimated weight and height.

The conduct described in the preceding paragraph is perfectly acceptable because the prosecutor is not eliciting the unreliable testimony to help prove guilt or mislead the court. To the contrary, he will almost certainly be leading other evidence to show that the testimony is inaccurate and will make submissions to this effect in closing. In this respect, it is worth remembering that neither the Crown nor the defence is precluded from calling evidence inconsistent with the testimony of

---

255 *R v Lane*, 2008 ONCA 841.
256 *Ibid* at para 56.
257 *Ibid* at paras 74–75.
258 RSC 1985, c C-5.

one of its witnesses.[259] To hold otherwise would undermine the truth-finding function of the justice system and lead to the nonsensical result that a party might be saddled with one view of events as opposed to another depending simply upon the order in which the witnesses were called.

c) Out-of-Court Contact with and Preparation of Witnesses

The ethical obligations engaged when a lawyer interacts with a witness outside of court are discussed in Chapter 8.[260] These obligations apply to prosecutors, and Crown counsel's role as minister of justice requires that she be especially careful to avoid taking any steps that risk distorting a witness's memory.[261]

7) Cross-examination of Defence Witnesses (Especially the Accused)

Cross-examining a defence witness, and most especially the accused, can present a particularly difficult challenge in terms of Crown counsel's reconciling his dual role as advocate and minister of justice.[262] A prosecutor is certainly entitled to attack the credibility of the accused or any other defence witness,[263] and there is nothing wrong with launching a skilful, probing, and devastating cross-examination.[264] But where cross-examination becomes unfair, an ethical line has been crossed. The result may be a serious violation of the accused's legal and constitutional rights, not to mention harm to the administration of justice and the prosecutor's professional reputation.

Improper cross-examination by Canadian prosecutors while not endemic is far from uncommon and has led to sharp rebukes from appel-

---

259 See *R v Precourt* (1976), 39 CCC (2d) 311 at 325 [para 60] (Ont CA), leave to appeal to SCC refused, [1977] 1 SCR xi; *R v Benji*, 2012 BCCA 55 at paras 29–31 and 155–63; *R v Ryan*, 2014 ABCA 85 at paras 42–45.

260 See, for example, Chapter 8, Sections C, G, I, & J.

261 See Bennett Gershman, "Witness Coaching by Prosecutors" (2002) 23 Cardozo L Rev 829 at 851.

262 See *R v Henderson* (1999), 134 CCC (3d) 131 at para 28 (Ont CA) [*Henderson*].

263 See *R v Krause* (1986), 29 CCC (3d) 385 at 391 [para 17] (SCC).

264 See *Logiacco*, above note 25 at 383–84; *Henderson*, above note 262 at para 28; *R v AJR* (1994), 94 CCC (3d) 168 at 176 [para 22] (Ont CA) [*AJR*]; *R v Clark* (2004), 182 CCC (3d) 1 at para 122 (Ont CA); *R v Dalen*, 2008 BCCA 530 at para 55.

late courts,[265] as well as from prosecutors themselves.[266] It is therefore worth examining in detail how Crown counsel can run into trouble when conducting a cross-examination.

a) Abusive and Unfair Cross-examination

There are a myriad of ways in which Crown counsel can engage in abusive and unfair cross-examination. It is unprofessional to cross-examine an accused in a manner that insults, belittles, and demeans;[267] to adopt a sarcastic tone and repeatedly insert editorial commentary calculated to humiliate;[268] or to be flippant and disrespectful.[269] It is also wrong for Crown counsel to express her personal opinion in cross-examination[270] or to adopt the persona of spokesperson for the jury.[271] Nor should a prosecutor cross-examine so as to unduly stress the prejudicial aspects of bad character evidence that is properly before the court.[272]

---

265 See, for example, *AJR*, above note 264 at 176 [para 21], and the cases cited therein; *R v Rose* (2001), 153 CCC (3d) 225 at paras 26–27 (Ont CA) [*Rose CA*]; *R v Robinson* (2001), 153 CCC (3d) 398 at paras 42–46 (Ont CA) [*Robinson*]; *R v White* (1999), 132 CCC (3d) 373 at para 6 (Ont CA) [*White*]; *Henderson*, above note 262 at para 26.

266 See, for example, John Walsh, "Cross-examination by the Prosecutor: Stopping Transgressions" (2007) 11 Can Crim L Rev 301; Suhail Akhtar, "Improprieties in Cross-examination" (2004) 15 CR (6th) 236; Robert J Frater, "The Seven Deadly Prosecutorial Sins" (2002) 7 Crim L Rev 209.

267 See *Logiacco*, above note 25 at 379; *Robinson*, above note 265 at para 35; *R v Bouhsass* (2002), 169 CCC (3d) 444 at paras 8 and 12(16) (Ont CA) [*Bouhsass*]; *LL*, above note 244 at para 65.

268 See *AJR*, above note 264 at 177 [para 26]; *R v Singh*, 2010 ONCA 808 at para 42 [*Singh*], leave to appeal to SCC refused, [2011] SCCA No 48.

269 See *R v FS* (2000), 144 CCC (3d) 466 at para 17 (Ont CA) [*FS*].

270 See *LL*, above note 244 at paras 67, 69, & 70; *R v RSL*, 2006 NBCA 64 at para 80; *Bouhsass*, above note 267 at para 12(4); *R v Kaufman* (2000), 151 CCC (3d) 566 at paras 16 and 38–39 (Que CA) [*Kaufman*]; *R v EMW*, 2011 SCC 31 at para 8. See also Alta, Sask r 4.01(1) (commentary); BC, Man, Ont, NS, NL r 5.1-1, commentary 5; CBA Code ch IX, commentary 5: advocate shall refrain from expressing personal opinion on merits to the tribunal.

271 See *Singh*, above note 268 at para 43; *LL*, above note 244 at para 67; *R v Khan* (1998), 126 CCC (3d) 523 at para 23 (BCCA), leave to appeal to SCC refused, [2001] SCCA No 126.

272 See *R v Walker* (1994), 90 CCC (3d) 144 at 150–53 [paras 19–23] (Ont CA) [*Walker*]; *Bouhsass*, above note 267 at paras 10–11.

b) Cross-examination on Inadmissible Matters

There are many subject areas on which Crown counsel is generally pre-cluded from cross-examining an accused or another defence witness by virtue of one or more rules of evidence:

- *Irrelevant matters*: It is improper to cross-examine on irrelevant mat-ters.[273] For instance, it is wrong for Crown counsel to cross-examine in an attempt to establish that a defence witness's testimony was rejected in an unrelated trial; such evidence is irrelevant and hence inadmissible.[274] For essentially the same reason, it is improper to ask the accused to provide an opinion on the law.[275]

- *Bad character*: An accused cannot be cross-examined on his bad character unless one of a very limited number of exceptions applies, such as the statutory rule permitting cross-examination on prior criminal convictions[276] or the common law doctrine that allows the introduction of bad character evidence where the accused has put character in issue.[277] Thus, an accused cannot be questioned about a tattoo simply to suggest that he subscribes to an unsavoury lifestyle so as to encourage improper propensity reasoning by the jury.[278] It is also improper for Crown counsel to cross-examine an accused so as to compel him to assert good character in an effort to force open the door allowing cross-examination on bad character.[279]

- *Access to disclosure*: A prosecutor should not cross-examine an accused to suggest that the latter's testimony is suspect because she has re-ceived disclosure of the Crown case.[280] The inference may be logical,

---

273 See *R v FEE*, 2011 ONCA 783 at para 68 [*FEE*]; *Brownell v Brownell* (1909), 42 SCR 368 at 374.

274 See *R v Karaibrahimovic*, 2002 ABCA 102 at paras 7–12 [*Karaibrahimovic*].

275 See *R v Rochon* (2003), 173 CCC (3d) 321 at paras 45–47 (Ont CA), leave to ap-peal to SCC refused, [2004] SCCA No 230.

276 See *Canada Evidence Act*, above note 258, s 12, which is nonetheless subject to limitations where the prejudicial impact of the questioning exceeds its proba-tive value: see *R v Corbett* (1988), 41 CCC (3d) 385 (SCC). Also, s 12 does not extend to permit cross-examination on the details of the accused's record: see *R v Bricker* (1994), 90 CCC (3d) 268 at 278–79 [para 20] (Ont CA) [*Bricker*], leave to appeal to SCC refused, [1994] SCCA No 331.

277 See, for example, *R v Arcangioli* (1994), 87 CCC (3d) 289 at 296 [para 26] (SCC); *R v GM*, 2011 ONCA 503 at paras 64–65.

278 See *R v Tash*, 2013 ONCA 380 at paras 48–62.

279 See *Bricker*, above note 276 at 278 [para 18]; *R v WAA* (1996), 112 CCC (3d) 83 at 88 [para 18] (Man CA).

280 See *White*, above note 265 at paras 15–23; *Bouhsass*, above note 267 at para 12(3); *R v Gahan*, 2014 NBCA 18 at para 21 [*Gahan*]; *R v Marshall* (2005), 200 CCC (3d) 179 at para 71 (Ont CA) [*Marshall*], leave to appeal to SCC refused, [2006] SCCA No 105.

but permitting it to be drawn unfairly penalizes an accused for exercising a fundamental constitutional right. Such cross-examination may be permitted, however, where the accused raises the issue of having reviewed disclosure materials in a manner that is relevant to a live trial issue[281] or where there is a legitimate basis to assert that a defence alibi was concocted to jibe with details in the disclosure.[282]

- *Right to silence*: The Crown is usually prohibited from cross-examining an accused on his exercise of the right to silence, for it would be a "snare and a delusion" were the state permitted to use the exercise of a constitutional right to assist in proving guilt.[283] Yet such cross-examination may be allowed where the exercise of the right is inextricably bound up in the narrative and cannot easily be extracted[284] or for the limited purpose of assessing credibility where the defence has been conducted so as to make silence a relevant issue.[285]

- *Right against self-incrimination*: Section 13 of the *Charter* prevents a prosecutor from cross-examining an accused on incriminating testimony compelled at a prior proceeding, even for the limited purpose of attacking credibility based on inconsistency.[286] Cross-examination is thus precluded on incriminating testimony given by the accused as a witness under subpoena at another individual's trial. But the prohibition does not extend to incriminating testimony given by the accused at her earlier trial in the same matter[287] or at the bail hearing[288] because in neither instance was the prior evidence compelled. Moreover, the protection in section 13 extends only to testimony that is incriminating in the sense that it could be used to help prove an essential element of the offence for which the accused is later tried.[289]

---

281 See *R v Cavan* (1999), 139 CCC (3d) 449 at paras 28–49 (Ont CA), leave to appeal to SCC refused, [2000] SCCA No 600; *Marshall*, above note 280 at paras 74–75; *R v Kokotailo*, 2008 BCCA 168 at paras 56–58 [*Kokotailo*].

282 *FEE*, above note 273 at paras 71 and 76.

283 *R v Turcotte*, 2005 SCC 50 at paras 41–46 [*Turcotte*]; *R v Wojcik*, 2002 MBCA 82 at paras 9–17 [*Wojcik*]; *R v Poirier* (2000), 146 CCC (3d) 436 at paras 17–23 (Ont CA); *R v Paris* (2000), 150 CCC (3d) 162 at para 43 (Ont CA), leave to appeal to SCC refused, [2001] SCCA No 124; *R v Schell* (2000), 148 CCC (3d) 219 at para 56 (Ont CA).

284 See *Turcotte*, above note 283 at para 50.

285 See *ibid* at paras 47–50; *R v GAO* (1997), 119 CCC (3d) 30 at 36–38 [paras 10–17] (Alta CA) [*GAO*].

286 *Charter*, above note 175. See *R v Henry*, 2005 SCC 76 at paras 49–50 [*Henry*]; *R v Nedelcu*, 2012 SCC 59 at paras 5–9 and 90–96 [*Nedelcu*].

287 See *Henry*, above note 286 at paras 41–47; *Nedelcu*, above note 286 at paras 1 and 89–92.

288 See *Mallory*, above note 242 at paras 157–71.

289 See *Nedelcu*, above note 286 at paras 1–43.

- *Case-splitting*: A prosecutor must not cross-examine the accused on subject matter that should have been led during the Crown's own case, for to do so unfairly splits the case against the accused.[290]
- *Assessing another witness's credibility*: It is improper for Crown counsel when cross-examining an accused to demand an assessment of the credibility of another witness. Such questioning implies that the accused bears an onus to explain why the Crown witness would lie, which impermissibly undermines the presumption of innocence.[291] Where the accused proffers the view that another witness has a motive to fabricate, however, the Crown can properly cross-examine on this testimony.[292]
- *Defence failure to cross-examine a witness*: The accused should not be cross-examined regarding a failure by the defence to question a Crown witness on a material point. The failure may justify a jury instruction that is favourable to the Crown, but the accused should not himself be confronted, because the failure may have been the result of a tactical decision or oversight on the part of defence counsel.[293]
- *Defence failure to call a witness*: Somewhat similarly, a prosecutor should not cross-examine an accused as to why the defence has not called a particular witness or on the absence of any independent evidence corroborating her version of events.[294] These subject areas are better left for comment in closing submissions to the trier of fact.
- *Excluded or presumptively inadmissible material*: It is improper for a prosecutor to question an accused on evidence that has been excluded.[295] Crown counsel should also refrain from cross-examining to elicit evidence that is presumptively inadmissible, such as a state-

---

290 See *R v Khan*, 2011 BCCA 382 at paras 93–102; *Mallory*, above note 242 at para 233.
291 See *Rose CA*, above note 265 at para 37; *Wojcik*, above note 283 at paras 9 and 20–21; *R v Ellard*, 2003 BCCA 68 at paras 21–24 [*Ellard*]; *R v Beare*, 2008 SKCA 172 at paras 23–25, leave to appeal to SCC refused, [2009] SCCA No 76.
292 See *Ellard*, above note 291 at para 24; *LL*, above note 244 at para 33.
293 See *R v McNeill* (2000), 144 CCC (3d) 551 at paras 39–42 (Ont CA) [*McNeill* Ont CA].
294 See *Bouhsass*, above note 267 at para 12(2); *AJR*, above note 264 at 180 [para 38]. It may nonetheless be permissible to cross-examine the accused as to the names of people who could have supported an alibi (*R v Alphonso*, 2008 ONCA 238 at paras 7–10), which will by implication raise the issue of why they were not called as witnesses.
295 See the discussion and cases cited in Chapter 8, Section H(2). In this regard, prosecutors should note that cross-examination on evidence excluded under the *Charter* is permitted only in "very limited circumstances": see *R v Calder* (1996), 105 CCC (3d) 1 at para 35 (SCC).

ment made to a person in authority[296] or hearsay evidence,[297] without first obtaining a permissive ruling from the court. A prosecutor should likewise not ask a question the effect of which would be to encourage the accused to reveal solicitor-client privileged information.[298]

- *Defence attack on admissibility of evidence*: Crown counsel must not cross-examine an accused to bring out the fact that the defence unsuccessfully opposed the admission of a particular piece of evidence at trial. Eliciting such testimony improperly transforms the right to bring a non-frivolous challenge to the admissibility of evidence into an indicator of guilt, and may also cloak the evidence in question with undue import.[299]

Where there is reason to believe that the defence may raise a viable objection to the propriety of cross-examining on these or other issues, Crown counsel should canvass the matter with the court in advance.[300] Doing so dramatically decreases the risk of an improper cross-examination occurring.

c) Good-Faith Basis and Avoiding Speculation

It is unacceptable for a prosecutor to cross-examine to discredit a witness known to be truthful.[301] This prohibition is dictated by the truth-seeking aspect of Crown counsel's role as minister of justice. It is thus no surprise to find that courts have criticized Crown counsel for putting an inaccurate factual assertion to a witness[302] or cross-examining a witness based on information obtained from a source the prosecutor has concluded is unreliable.[303]

Some of the guiding principles in this regard can be found in the Supreme Court of Canada's decision in *R v Lyttle*.[304] *Lyttle* holds that a lawyer must have a "good-faith basis" for putting a question to a witness

---

296 See *R v DWN*, 2009 BCCA 317; *R v Bradley*, 2007 ONCA 181.

297 See *R v Hofung* (2001), 154 CCC (3d) 257 at paras 26–34 (Ont CA).

298 See *R v Nealy* (1986), 30 CCC (3d) 460 at 464 (Ont CA) [*Nealy*]; *AJR*, above note 264 at 180 [para 38].

299 See *R v GC* (1996), 110 CCC (3d) 233 at 249–50 [para 35] (Nfld CA).

300 See Chapter 8, Section H(2), as well as *Kokotailo*, above note 281 at para 52.

301 See ABA Prosecution Standard 3-5.7(b).

302 See, for example, *R v Takacs* (1982), 1 CCC (3d) 351 at 352 [paras 1–2] (Alta CA), and *Wojcik*, above note 283 at para 9, although both deal with erroneous facts inadvertently put to the accused.

303 See *R v Wilson* (1983), 5 CCC (3d) 61 at 77 and 83–87 [paras 74–87 and 101–2] (BCCA) [*Wilson*]; *Mallory*, above note 242 at paras 253–55.

304 2004 SCC 5 [*Lyttle*].

in cross-examination. A good-faith basis does not require that counsel have at his disposal other admissible evidence in support of the assertion contained in the question.[305] Rather, a good-faith basis is "a function of the information available to the cross-examiner, his or her belief in its likely accuracy, and the purpose for which it is used."[306] It may be grounded merely on reasonable inference, experience, or intuition.[307] The good-faith basis threshold is not met, however, where counsel puts suggestions to a witness knowing them to be false, is reckless as to whether such is the case, or poses a question that asserts or implies in a manner calculated to mislead.[308]

Although *Lyttle* addressed the propriety of a cross-examination by the defence, the same limitations undoubtedly apply to a prosecutor.[309] If anything, they operate with *more* force because a prosecutor, unlike defence counsel, has a duty as minister of justice to seek the truth in a manner that is fair to the accused.[310] Cross-examining a witness so as to assert or imply a fact where Crown counsel knows or is reckless as to whether the fact is false is completely inconsistent with this duty. It is also improper for Crown counsel to put an assertion to a witness in cross-examination based on mere speculation.[311]

Example: A defence witness testifies that, from what he heard through a bedroom door, the complainant in a sexual-assault case appeared to be having consensual sex with the accused. Crown counsel cross-examines the witness to suggest that, for various reasons, the complainant was unlikely to have had consensual sex with anyone. However, based on reliable but excluded evidence, Crown counsel knows that the complainant had consensual sex with the defence witness very shortly afterwards. Crown counsel thus lacked a good-faith basis for her questions, and so they should not have been put to the witness.[312]

---

305   *Ibid* at para 48.
306   *Ibid.*
307   *Ibid.*
308   *Ibid.*
309   See *Mallory*, above note 242 at paras 225, 233, and 247–49.
310   See *ibid* at para 249.
311   See *Nealy*, above note 298 at 465; *Logiacco*, above note 25 at 381–82; *R v Tom-bran* (2000), 142 CCC (3d) 380 at para 42 (Ont CA), leave to appeal to SCC refused, [2000] SCCA No 294 [*Tombran*]; *Bouhsass*, above note 267 at para 12(5); *R v Luciano*, [2004] OJ No 4613 at para 12 (SCJ).
312   The facts and analysis in this example are derived from *R v Butts*, 2012 ONCA 24 [*Butts*].

Even where a good-faith basis for a question exists, a prosecutor must take care that the prejudicial effect of putting it to the accused does not outweigh the attendant probative value.[313] In particular, a prosecutor should be slow to put a highly incriminating assertion to the accused where there is no prospect of its ever being proven.[314] Suppose, for example, that Crown counsel decides not to call an unsavoury witness who would testify to having received a confession to the charged murder from the accused. The accused takes the stand and denies the crime. Provided that the decision not to call the witness was unrelated to reliability issues, a good-faith basis for cross-examining on the alleged confession likely exists. The cross-examination may nonetheless be precluded, even with a limiting jury instruction, if the probative value to be gleaned from the accused's denial of the alleged confession is outweighed by the prejudicial impact that hearing about it will have on the jury.[315]

Advance rulings: If there is a real issue as to whether the good-faith basis standard is met or if so whether the prejudicial impact of the cross-examination might exceed its probative value, Crown counsel should ask for an advance ruling from the court.[316]

8) Duty of Candour

Canadian ethical codes require all lawyers to treat the tribunal with candour when acting as advocates.[317] Most repeat the same admonition in the rule dealing specifically with prosecutors.[318] An advocate's duty of candour is also firmly established in the jurisprudence.[319] Furthermore, the rules of professional conduct require lawyers to exhibit good

---

313 See *Mallory*, above note 242 at para 233.

314 *Ibid* at paras 228, 233, and 257–71.

315 This example is based on *Mallory*, *ibid*, which at paras 256–69 identifies the factors that a trial judge should consider in deciding whether such questioning will be permitted. See also *R v Mullins-Johnson* (1996), 112 CCC (3d) 117 at 124 [paras 15–16] (Ont CA), aff'd (1998), 124 CCC (3d) 381 (SCC): Crown improperly suggested to the accused that he had made an incriminating statement regarding the charged murder.

316 See *Wilson*, above note 303 at 77 and 89 [paras 96 and 104]; *Mallory*, above note 242 at paras 248–52; *R v Sidhu*, 2014 ONSC 732 at paras 1–4 and 19. More generally, see the sources cited at note 300, above in this chapter.

317 Alta, Sask r 4.01(1); BC, Man, Ont, NS, NL r 5.1-1; NB ch 8, rule (a); CBA Code ch IX, commentary 1.

318 See the rules cited at note 6, above in this chapter.

319 See Chapter 1, Section E.

faith in their professional dealings with opposing counsel, court staff, witnesses, and members of the public.[320]

The duty of candour means that a prosecutor must act truthfully and with integrity in her dealings with the administration of justice. Not only the courts but many other participants in the criminal justice system as well depend on Crown counsel's honesty at every stage of the process. Candour requires that Crown counsel scrupulously avoid misleading the court on the facts and the law and take curative steps to investigate, and if necessary remedy, possible falsehoods perpetrated against the court.

What is more — and this is a crucial point that does not apply to defence counsel — prosecutors have a general duty to take action to prevent the court from being misled, regardless of the source of the threat or the fact that no Crown lawyer, agent, or witness is implicated. Defence counsel can sometimes rely on the principle against self-incrimination and an especially strong partisan role to remain silent in the face of falsehood provided he is not complicit in misleading the court.[321] But Crown counsel is not resolutely partisan in this way and has a broad obligation to seek justice and preserve the truth-finding function of the criminal process.

We have already reviewed several instances of Crown counsel's duty of candour in action, such as the obligation not to knowingly call an unreliable witness[322] and the prohibition against putting inaccurate factual assertions to a witness in cross-examination.[323] In this section of the chapter, we consider other concrete situations that illustrate the prosecutor's duty of candour.

a) Advising the Police regarding Deceptive but Lawful Investigative Practices

Given the prosecutor's duty to be candid with the court and to act in good faith in professional dealings with others, the question arises whether Crown counsel should provide legal advice to the police regarding investigative techniques that involve lying to a target or suspect. Examples include advice regarding carrying out a "Mr Big" operation, in which undercover officers pretend to be criminals to obtain a confes-

---

320 Alta, Sask r 6.02(1); BC, Man, Ont, NS, NL r 7.2-1; NB ch 15, rule; CBA Code ch XVI, rule.
321 See, for example, the discussion of defence counsel's role in defending a client known to be guilty in Chapter 1.
322 Section H(6)(b), above in this chapter.
323 Section H(7)(c), above in this chapter.

sion from a target,[324] or input on the extent to which police can lie to a suspect during a formal interview without undermining the voluntariness of any ensuing statement.[325]

There is nothing unethical about Crown counsel's providing legal advice to police regarding lawful investigatory steps that involve deceiving a target or suspect. Enabling police to obtain such advice facilitates the proper administration of justice.[326] Crown counsel cannot be said to have engaged in bad faith dealings with the deceived target or suspect, because in carrying out an investigation the police do not act as prosecution agents but rather are constitutionally independent.[327] And the deception will be revealed if charges are later laid, as part of *Stinchcombe* disclosure. Nonetheless, in providing advice, Crown counsel must not lose the objectivity and independence that is a hallmark of the prosecutorial function.[328] Crown counsel must also avoid suggesting or condoning any police conduct that would breach the law or an individual's constitutional rights.

b) Without Notice Applications

Canadian codes of professional conduct require that lawyers be candid and make full disclosure to the court in bringing a without notice application. Specifically, most codes provide that

> [w]hen opposing interests are not represented, for example, in without notice or uncontested matters or in other situations in which the full proof and argument inherent in the adversarial system cannot be achieved, the lawyer must take particular care to be accurate, candid and comprehensive in presenting the client's case so as to ensure that the tribunal is not misled.[329]

---

324 Mr Big operations are discussed in many cases including *R v Hart*, 2014 SCC 52; *R v Grandinetti*, 2005 SCC 5; *R v Osmar*, 2007 ONCA 50, leave to appeal to SCC refused, [2007] SCCA No 157; *R v Earhart*, 2011 BCCA 490.

325 See *R v Oickle*, 2000 SCC 38 at paras 61, 65–67, and 100: in interviewing a suspect, the police can resort to deception that does not shock the conscience of the community or create oppression.

326 See Section F(2), above in this chapter.

327 See Section E(1), above in this chapter; *Campbell*, above note 99 at para 54. Contrast the position of defence counsel who engages in similar conduct, which is discussed in Chapter 8, Section C(3).

328 See Section F, above in this chapter.

329 Alta, Sask r 4.01(1) (commentary); BC, Man, Ont, NS, NL r 5.1-1, commentary 6. See also NB ch 8, commentary 3(c); CBA Code ch IX, commentary 15. These ethical code provisions mirror the duties imposed at common law: see *Ruby v Canada (Solicitor General)*, 2002 SCC 75 at para 27; *Harkat*, above note 151 at para 101.

The rationale for this rule is that the adversarial process usually relied on to sort out the truth and ensure fairness in litigation is much reduced on a without notice application, and so counsel is obliged to make full disclosure of material facts to avoid an unjust result.[330]

The need for prosecutors to be candid with the court in making without notice applications is well-established in the caselaw.[331] The ethical imperative is especially important for Crown lawyers for two reasons. First, as ministers of justice, their duty of candour is particularly strong. And second, they are much more likely than defence counsel to appear on without notice applications, for example on applications to intercept private communications, to restrain or seize suspected proceeds of crime, or to conduct a terrorism investigatory hearing under section 83.28(2) of the *Criminal Code*.[332]

A prosecutor's duty to make full, frank, and fair disclosure to the tribunal on a without notice application does not, however, equate with an obligation to conduct an independent investigation or audit the entire police file for the purpose of ensuring completeness and accuracy.[333] This is so for several reasons. First, requiring Crown counsel to audit the police investigation risks interfering with the independence of the police in the investigative sphere. Second, becoming too involved in the police investigation may lead Crown counsel to lose objectivity as prosecutor. Third, Crown counsel may lack the expertise and resources to audit the police investigation. Fourth, the police affiant on a without notice application is a professional who has a duty to make full, frank, and fair disclosure of material information[334] as does Crown counsel with respect to any factual information and jurisprudence reviewed in the course of advising the police.[335] Absolving Crown counsel of the obligation to conduct an independent investigation or audit the police file thus does not detract from the duty of the state to make proper disclosure to the court on the application.

330 See Alta r 4.01(1) (commentary).
331 See *Bagri*, above note 161 at para 98; *R v Pilarinos*, 2001 BCSC 1690 at para 157; *R v Land* (1990), 55 CCC (3d) 382 at 398 (Ont HCJ); *R v Nguyen*, 2005 ABQB 506 at para 10; *R v Higgins*, 2009 ABQB 147 at paras 31 and 65.
332 *Criminal Code*, above note 104.
333 See Martin Committee Report, above note 100 at 39; *R v Ebanks*, 2009 ONCA 851 at para 49, leave to appeal to SCC refused, [2010] SCCA No 84.
334 See, for example, *R v Morelli*, 2010 SCC 8 at para 44; *R v Araujo*, 2000 SCC 65 at paras 46–47.
335 See the cases cited at note 331, above in this chapter.

c) Misleading the Court for a Laudable Ulterior Motive

A very different twist on Crown counsel's duty of candour to the court is seen in *In Re Friedman*,[336] which involved disciplinary proceedings brought against an Illinois prosecutor. To obtain proof of bribery by defence lawyers in two different cases, the prosecutor authorized police officers to accept bribes from the lawyers and give false testimony as requested. The prosecutor also arranged for police witnesses to be absent from court proceedings in accordance with the defence lawyers' illegal plans. The sham proceedings were dismissed, following which the lawyers were arrested.

An Illinois disciplinary board recommended that the prosecutor be censured for having misled the court. But the Supreme Court of Illinois, in a majority decision, overturned the board's sanction. Two of the majority judges held that the prosecutor's temporary deception of the court was for a laudable purpose and thus violated no ethical prescriptions. The other two members of the majority concluded that the prosecutor's conduct was unethical but ruled that no sanction should be imposed because there was no precedent on point, and the expert consensus was that he had acted properly. The two dissenters held that lawyers cannot be excused for conduct that deceives the court, regardless of a valid ulterior motive or the limited impact of the deception, and would have censured the prosecutor regardless of his motive.

We favour the view that a laudable motive on the part of a prosecutor does not excuse a breach of the duty of candour, a view shared by four of the six judges in *Friedman* and supported by subsequent American jurisprudence.[337] Were the *Friedman* scenario to arise in Canada, the proper approach would therefore be for Crown counsel to advise police to conclude the investigation before the presentation of fabricated evidence or to obtain immunity in advance from the courts via a without notice application.[338]

---

336 392 NE2d 1333 (Ill 1979) [*Friedman*].

337 *In re Malone*, 105 AD2d 455 (NY App Div 1984): prosecutor advised informant to lie to tribunal to protect informant from retribution; *People v Reichman*, 819 P2d 1035 (Colo 1991): prosecutor filed sham charges against undercover officer to bolster officer's credibility with criminals; *In re Pautler*, 47 P3d 1175 (Colo 2002): prosecutor posed as defence counsel to facilitate murder suspect's surrender.

338 Compare *R v Thomson*, 2006 BCCA 392, where an information to obtain (ITO) referred to the same person as though he were three different individuals to better conceal his identity as a confidential informant. The ITO was held not to be improper, because the ruse had been revealed to the authorizing judge and carried no risk of misleading the accused on any material issue (*ibid* at paras 42–60).

Compare the Canadian disciplinary case of *Law Society of Alberta v Piragoff*.[339] An accused was charged with murder, and one of the witnesses against him was a jailhouse informant. The prosecutor assigned to the case, Piragoff, knew that the police had fabricated a letter purporting to be from the informant to the accused in the hope that on receiving the letter the accused would take action or make comments indicative of guilt. Instead, the accused gave the letter to his defence counsel, who produced it at the bail hearing arguing that the accused's decision to reveal the item to counsel constituted the actions of an innocent man. Piragoff suspected the letter was the product of the police ruse, but instead of asking for an adjournment to clarify, he made submissions in favour of denying bail and referred to the letter as though genuine. After the hearing, a police officer told Piragoff the letter was a fake and expressed concern regarding Piragoff's submissions. Piragoff failed to take prompt remedial action, believing the letter's authenticity had not been material to the court's bail decision, and waited eleven months to disclose the truth to the defence.

The disciplinary panel found that Piragoff had committed professional misconduct in being reckless and making gross errors in judgment in two regards: first, as to whether his submissions about the letter would mislead the court and defence counsel, which they clearly did,[340] and, second, in failing to correct his misstatements promptly on being told by police that the letter was not genuine.[341] He was fined $15,000 and avoided a suspension only because of a number of mitigating factors including his otherwise clean professional conduct record and the fact that his actions had resulted in a demotion.

Example: Crown counsel knows the police are conducting an undercover operation seeking evidence that the accused bribed a key prosecution witness to recant. The witness is about to be cross-examined by the Crown as an adverse witness. Crown counsel wishes to obtain an adjournment to provide more time for the undercover operation, but revealing the true reason for the request will scupper the investigation. It is nonetheless improper for Crown counsel to provide a false basis for requiring an adjournment. The only acceptable options are to forgo the adjournment or disclose the real reason for the request in camera.[342]

---

339 [2005] LSDD No 47.

340 *Ibid* at paras 12–29.

341 *Ibid* at paras 30–37.

342 This example is based on the facts and analysis in *Tshiamala*, above note 11 at paras 59–67, 74–77, and 152–54.

d) Prosecutor Learns That a Crown Witness Has Testified Falsely

Crown counsel who learns that a prosecution witness has testified falsely must immediately disclose the perjury to the accused and court.[343] It does not matter whether the falsehood occurs in examination-in-chief, cross-examination, or re-direct. Mere inconsistency by a witness does not equate with misleading testimony and hence does not on its own require remedial action. Yet, whenever the Crown comes by information suggesting a reasonable possibility the court has been or will be misled, action must be taken.[344]

In *R v Ahluwalia*,[345] for example, the appellant had pleaded guilty to drug-related offences and then sought to stay the proceedings based on entrapment. A key Crown witness on the entrapment application was an American police agent, handled by FBI officers, who repeatedly testified to having a single criminal conviction. The entrapment argument was rejected, but following sentencing defence counsel learned that the agent had several convictions. He asked the Crown for an explanation. The Crown lawyer confirmed the more extensive criminal record, and hence the agent's perjury, and added that neither the Crown law office nor the Canadian police were aware of this information before defence counsel's post-trial request. But the Crown refused to make inquiries of the FBI as to why the agent's criminal record and the trial perjury had not been disclosed.

The Ontario Court of Appeal was disturbed by the nature of the perjury, observing that the Crown disclosure provided to trial counsel perfectly matched the lie told by the agent at trial. It thus appeared, though no finding could be made on the point, that the state may have been complicit in misleading the court and denying the accused his rights. Indeed, it seemed that the agent's FBI handler, who was aware of the truth, had been in court when the perjury had occurred yet had said nothing. The Court of Appeal was thus unimpressed with the Crown's failure to investigate further, holding as follows:

> The Crown has obligations to the administration of justice that do not burden other litigants. Faced with its own witness's perjury and the fact that the perjured evidence coincided with the incomplete disclosure that the Crown says it innocently passed to the defence, the Crown was obliged to take all reasonable steps to find out what had

---

343 See "Panel Discussion: Problems in Advocacy and Ethics" in Law Society of Upper Canada, *Defending a Criminal Case* (Toronto: R De Boo, 1969) 279 at 335. See also *R v Kozar*, 2000 SKQB 221 at paras 14–15.

344 *Driskell Inquiry Report*, above note 2 at 105; *Phillion*, above note 142 at paras 57–58.

345 *Ahluwalia*, above note 149.

happened and to share the results of those inquiries with the defence. In my view, the Crown did not fulfill its obligations to the administration of justice by acknowledging the incomplete disclosure discovered by the defence, and after making limited inquiries, professing neither a responsibility for the incomplete disclosure nor an ability to provide any explanation for it. The Crown owed both the appellant and the court a fuller explanation than it chose to provide.[346]

There can thus be a positive obligation on the Crown to investigate material and meritorious allegations of state misconduct,[347] not only as a means of exposing a falsehood, but also to uncover the reason for the court's having been misled. As *Ahluwalia* shows, this obligation continues after the conclusion of trial, at least where the state misconduct, if made out, stands any possibility of meeting the test for the admission of fresh evidence on appeal.[348]

e)   Court or Defence Makes an Error Favouring the Prosecution
Crown counsel may learn of an error or misapprehension by the judge or defence counsel that inures to the prosecution's advantage. The duty of candour to the court in tandem with the prosecutor's special duties as minister of justice obliges Crown counsel to promptly disclose the mistake to the court and defence counsel.[349]

f)   Raising a Theory Inconsistent with Facts Not in Evidence
Sometimes Crown counsel has access to information that, for a valid reason, cannot be disclosed to the accused. For instance, the Crown might have possession of private counselling records that a complainant successfully argues should not be produced to the defence.[350] Or perhaps information pertaining to a confidential informant is kept secret because the innocence-at-stake exception does not apply.[351] The prosecutor cannot present an argument or invoke a theory that to her

---

346   *Ibid* at para 72, quoted with approval in *McNeil*, above note 21 at para 50.
347   See also *Darwish*, above note 151 at para 38; *Spackman*, above note 91 at para 109; David Tanovich, "Judicial and Prosecutorial Control of Lying by the Police" (2013) 100 CR (6th) 322 at 330–34.
348   See also the authorities cited at note 180, above in this chapter, regarding the Crown's post-conviction disclosure obligation.
349   See, for example, *R v Rafferty* (1983), 6 CCC (3d) 72 at 75 [para 4] (Alta CA): Crown counsel has a duty to bring any errors of fact to the attention of the court. See also *R v DK*, 2009 QCCA 987 at paras 52–57: Crown counsel made an incomplete statement of law, which the defence relied on to its detriment.
350   See *Criminal Code*, above note 104, ss 278.2–278.91; *R v Mills* (1999), 139 CCC (3d) 321 (SCC).
351   The parameters of the privilege are discussed in Chapter 8, Section C(4).

knowledge is inconsistent with such information. To do so would be unfair to the accused and mislead the court.[352]

Example: Police find narcotics in a car driven by the accused. The defence is that the registered owner of the car may have secreted the contraband in the vehicle without the accused's knowledge. In closing submissions, Crown counsel suggests that the accused may have registered the vehicle in a fake name despite counsel's being aware of reliable evidence, uncalled at trial, suggesting the accused and the registered owner are not one and the same person. This submission, though available on the trial record, is improper because the effect is to mislead the fact-finder.[353]

Example: Crown counsel elicits evidence of a letter to suggest that a bribe caused a witness to recant testimony favourable to the prosecution. Yet Crown counsel knows of other information, covered by confidential informant privilege and so not disclosable to the defence, that weakens considerably the probative value of this letter in supporting the bribery theory. In these circumstances, Crown counsel should have forgone any mention of the letter or, at the very least, should have disclosed the confidential information to the court at an in camera hearing for the purpose of obtaining directions before mentioning the letter.[354]

The same principle applies where the information is known to the defence but has been excluded from evidence for reasons that do not in any way undermine its reliability[355] or where the information has not been called by the defence because the accused has absconded and defence counsel has successfully applied to be removed from the record.[356]

9) Dealing with the Self-Represented Accused

Accused persons who are without counsel, whether by choice or because they lack funds and do not qualify for legal aid, are generally at a distinct disadvantage in criminal proceedings. In such instances, the prosecutor's role as minister of justice will often oblige him to take

---

352 See *R v Hay* (1982), 70 CCC (2d) 286 at 290 [para 14] (Sask CA) [*Hay*].

353 This scenario is based on the facts and reasoning in *Hay*, *ibid*.

354 This scenario is based on the facts and reasoning in *Tshiamala*, above note 11 at paras 10, 80(104), 87–93, and 103–15.

355 See *Butts*, above note 312 at paras 18–24; *R v Patterson* (2006), 205 CCC (3d) 171 at paras 12–30 (Ont CA); *R v Clark* (1981), 63 CCC (2d) 224 at 237–38 [paras 20–24] (Alta CA), leave to appeal to SCC refused, [1981] SCCA No 345 [*Clark*].

356 See *R v Udy*, 2006 BCCA 174 at para 24.

measures to help ensure a fair trial that would not be necessary were the accused represented by competent counsel.[357]

Perhaps most obviously, Crown counsel must ensure that the accused knows about the right to disclosure.[358] But more than this, a prosecutor should be open to providing reasonable support to a trial judge who is attempting to satisfy the court's duty to assist the self-represented accused.[359] Other areas of assistance might include explaining procedural matters to the accused, tailoring submissions to the court in language the accused can understand, suggesting or supporting reasonable adjournment applications so the accused has time to prepare, asking for an order excluding Crown witnesses at the start of the trial, making available to the accused excerpts from legal texts bearing on points in dispute, assisting with the subpoenaing of defence witnesses, and so on.[360]

Yet the mere fact that an accused is self-represented does not prevent Crown counsel from seeking a conviction. Moreover, a prosecutor must not assist an accused in ways tantamount to taking on the role of defence counsel — the rationale for providing assistance is based solely on counsel's duties as minister of justice. Finally, Crown counsel should proactively guard against any allegations of impropriety that might be levelled by a self-represented accused regarding out-of-court interactions. The danger of such allegations will be low or negligible with many self-represented individuals. But where the accused is mercurial or prone to making unfounded claims of wrongdoing, the prudent course will be to ensure that most or all interactions occur or are promptly confirmed on the record.

Ethical code rules: Crown counsel must adhere to the rules of professional conduct in dealing with a self-represented accused, in particular ensuring that the accused understands that a prosecutor acts solely for the Crown and not as counsel for the accused.[361] It may also be necessary to urge the accused to retain counsel, especially where the accused is

---

357 See *R v Sykes*, 2014 NSCA 4 at paras 26–27; *R v Kankis*, 2012 ONSC 378 at para 39; *R v Fontaine* (1930), 53 CCC 164 at 165 [para 5] (Ont CA).

358 See *Stinchcombe*, above note 1 at 14 [para 28]; *R v Stilla*, 2013 ONSC 2197 at para 43.

359 The trial judge's duty in this regard is discussed in various cases including *R v Phillips*, 2003 ABCA 4 at paras 16–28, aff'd 2003 SCC 57; *R v Sullivan*, 2013 BCCA 32 at para 40; *R v Ryan*, 2012 NLCA 9 at paras 128–32. See also *R v Mian*, 2014 SCC 54 at para 44.

360 See Frater, above note 11 at 137; *R v CM*, 2005 SKCA 124 at para 16.

361 See Chapter 8, Section C(2)(b); Ben Kempinen, "The Ethics of Prosecutor Contact with the Unrepresented Defendant" (2006) 19 Geo J Legal Ethics 1147 at 1153–54 and 1180–81.

self-represented by choice, and not because of a lack of resources, and is seeking legal advice from the prosecutor or seems clearly out of his depth.[362] Finally, Crown counsel must avoid giving the self-represented accused legal advice (as opposed to information); doing so would conflict with her duty as lawyer for the Crown.[363]

If it becomes apparent that a self-represented accused cannot have a fair trial absent assistance going beyond what Crown counsel or the trial judge is able to provide, it may be necessary to bring an application for the appointment of a lawyer as *amicus curiae*.[364] An *amicus curiae* will be appointed where necessary to permit the proceeding to be successfully and justly adjudicated.[365] Such appointments are made sparingly and with caution in response to specific and exceptional circumstances.[366] While *amicus curiae* may be asked by the trial judge to take a position commensurate with the accused's best interests, she does not play the role of defence counsel but rather assists the court in providing a perspective that is otherwise lacking.[367]

10) Closing Address to the Jury

Crown counsel can never be faulted for making firm and effective closing submissions based on the evidence led at trial; as minister of justice, he has a duty to do so.[368] Still, since *Boucher* was decided, almost fifty years ago, courts have not infrequently expressed disapproval of inflammatory or irregular summations given by prosecutors, mainly because of the serious consequences for trial fairness and the criminal justice system as a whole. Improper and prejudicial closing addresses by Crown counsel run a real risk of requiring a new trial, with great attendant expense to the emotional well-being of complainants, accused persons, and the administration of justice more generally.[369]

---

362 See Chapter 8, Section C(2)(b); Kempinen, above note 361 at 1156–57 and 1183–84.

363 See Chapter 8, Section C(2)(b); Kempinen, above note 361 at 1154–56 and 1181–82.

364 See, for example, *R v Hart*, 2009 NLCA 10.

365 See *Criminal Lawyers' Association of Ontario*, above note 13 at paras 44 and 87.

366 See *ibid* at paras 47 and 115.

367 See *ibid* at paras 47–56 and 115–21; David Berg, "The Limits of Friendship: the *Amicus Curiae* in Criminal Trial Courts" (2012) 59 Crim LQ 67.

368 See *Karaibrahimovic*, above note 274 at paras 50–51; *R v Usereau*, 2010 QCCA 894 at paras 111–12 [*Usereau*], leave to appeal to SCC refused, [2010] SCCA No 253; *R v GS*, 2009 NBCA 82 at para 75; *R v Boudreau*, 2012 ONCA 830 at para 15, leave to appeal to SCC refused, [2013] SCCA No 330 [*Boudreau*]; *R v Daly* (1992), 57 OAC 70 at 76 (CA).

369 See *R v AF* (1996), 30 OR (3d) 470 at 472 (Ont CA); *R v Tremblay* (1963), 40 CR 303 at 309 [para 24] (Que QB).

a) Inflammatory Language regarding Trial Issues, Witness Credibility, and Conduct of Defence Counsel

Inflammatory speeches must be avoided.[370] Addresses calculated to appeal to the emotions of the jury instead of reason and common sense are unethical.[371] Thus, prosecutors must not launch diatribes against the accused, be disrespectful and sarcastic,[372] employ invective,[373] urge the jury to convict to do justice to a victim,[374] or make wholly inappropriate and irrelevant remarks such as comparing the defendant's group home to a Nazi death camp.[375] The types of comments that improperly appeal to jury emotions instead of a reasoned review of the evidence are endless, but common categories of excessive rhetoric include suggestions that a guilty verdict is needed to protect society, that a conviction will give voice to the interests of the victim, and that the jury should join Crown counsel in the common cause of ensuring justice.[376]

A prosecutor should also avoid making derogatory comments about defence counsel, for instance by suggesting that she has acted unethically or contrary to the rules of evidence or is not to be trusted.[377] If defence counsel has truly acted improperly, Crown counsel should raise the matter with the trial judge and ask for a remedy, as opposed to taking matters into his own hands.[378]

This last point leads us to a related observation. An inflammatory closing is not justified even where preceded by defence counsel's own

---

370 See *PPSC Deskbook*, above note 8, ch 2.2, Part 2.4.1.

371 See *R v Romeo* (1991), 62 CCC (3d) 1 at 7 [paras 17–18] (SCC) [*Romeo*]; *Kaufman*, above note 270 at paras 15–40; *R v Charest* (1990), 57 CCC (3d) 312 at 324–33 (Que CA) [*Charest*]; *R v RBB*, 2001 BCCA 14 at paras 12–15; *R v Ballony-Reeder*, 2001 BCCA 293 at paras 6 and 15–16; *R v RC*, 1999 BCCA 411 at paras 9 and 17; *Karaibrahimovic*, above note 274 at para 54; *R v Sheri* (2004), 185 CCC (3d) 155 at paras 130–34 (Ont CA); *Kokotailo*, above note 281 at paras 60–61.

372 See *R v Dupuis* (1967), 3 CRNS 75 at 83 (Que CA).

373 See *ibid*; *FS*, above note 269 at paras 23–24.

374 See *Re LSJPA - 1037*, 2010 QCCA 1627 at para 178 [*LSJPA - 1037*], leave to appeal to SCC refused, [2010] SCCA No 440.

375 See *R v Therrien*, [1990] JQ No 921 (CA), leave to appeal to SCC refused, [1990] SCCA No 124.

376 See Frater, above note 11 at 177–78.

377 See *R v CD* (2000), 145 CCC (3d) 290 at paras 102–4 (Ont CA) [*CD*]; *R v Siu* (1998), 124 CCC (3d) 301 at paras 37–38 and 68–71 (BCCA); *Mallory*, above note 242 at paras 334 and 344. But see *R v Khatchatourov*, 2014 ONCA 464 at paras 30–36: calling the defence theory "sleight of hand," because it attempted to distract the jury from the real issue of whether the accused was guilty, was held to be reasonable adversarial rhetoric.

378 See *CD*, above note 377 at para 103.

excesses.[379] Ethical duties do not recede in proportion to the improprieties of opposing counsel. Simplistic "tit for tat" reasoning cannot discount the ethical duties ordinarily demanded of a prosecutor.[380] Once again, the proper response where defence counsel has acted inappropriately is to ask the trial judge for a corrective instruction, or perhaps permission to counter the improper comments in the Crown closing.[381]

b) Expressing a Personal Opinion or Referring to the Crown's Charge-Screening Role

Neither a prosecutor[382] nor defence counsel for that matter[383] is entitled to express a personal opinion about a witness, an issue, or the case in general.[384] This is so for several reasons. First, counsel's personal opinion is not relevant. Second, such an opinion may contaminate the jury's reasoning, leading to a decision based on an assumed verification of facts that is extraneous to the evidence. Third, allowing an advocate to assert a personal belief puts the opponent who properly refrains from doing so at a disadvantage. It is no answer to allow both counsel to express their personal opinions, one in response to the other, for the one who is more renowned or more talented will possess an advantage.

It is also improper for Crown counsel to inform the jury that her prosecution service proceeds with a case only if it has concluded that a demanding charge-screening standard has been met. Such information is completely irrelevant to the jury's task and risks unfairness to the accused because the jury may conclude that a case meeting the screening threshold should end in a conviction.[385] The same goes for comments by Crown counsel to the effect that he is honest and just and that if the

---

379 See *Henderson*, above note 262 at para 24. The import of *R v Peruta* (1992), 78 CCC (3d) 350 at 375–79 (Que CA) [*Peruta*], is to the same effect.

380 See Pannick, above note 52 at 118–19. See also *CD*, above note 377 at para 103.

381 Correcting defence counsel without clearing the proposed language with the court in advance can be perilous: see *CD*, ibid at paras 102–4.

382 See *R v Chambers* (1990), 59 CCC (3d) 321 at 335 [paras 33–34] (SCC); *Robinson*, above note 265 at paras 40 and 45–46; *Kaufman*, above note 270 at paras 33 and 38–40; *Carrière*, above note 244 at paras 49–50; *LL*, above note 244 at para 71; *R v Sutherland*, 2011 ABCA 319 at para 16.

383 See *R v Finta* (1992), 73 CCC (3d) 65 at 182 (Ont CA), aff'd without addressing this point, *Finta* SCC, above note 253; *Peruta*, above note 379 at 377–79; *R v Shchavinsky* (2000), 148 CCC (3d) 400 at paras 79 and 83–84 (Ont CA).

384 This prohibition is set out not only in the caselaw cited in the preceding two notes but also in many ethical codes: Alta, Sask r 4.01(1) (commentary); BC, Man, Ont, NS, NL r 5.1-1, commentary 5.

385 See *R v Dorion*, 2007 NBCA 41 at paras 120–21, leave to appeal to SCC refused, [2007] SCCA No 413 [*Dorion*]; *Barnes*, above note 244 at paras 14–15.

jury is not convinced of the accused's guilt, it is because he has failed to do his job successfully.[386]

c) Alluding to Facts Not Properly in Evidence

As explained by the Supreme Court of Canada in *R v Rose*, Crown counsel's closing address should not refer to facts for which there is no evidence in the record or make assertions based on counsel's personal observations or experiences.[387] Many other cases hold to the same effect. References to facts not in evidence that have attracted judicial rebuke include the

- allusion to possible reprisals by fellow inmates in an attempt to explain a Crown witness's testimony;[388]
- suggestion that the evidence had established the blood types of the accused and the victim, thus tending to prove the prosecution theory;[389]
- explanation as to why the prosecutor did not call a witness;[390]
- comments as to events that occurred during a *voir dire*;[391]
- rebuttal of a hostile prosecution witness's allegations of prosecutorial misconduct by referring to out-of-court events to which Crown counsel had been privy;[392]
- reference to the date the disclosure was provided to the defence and the benefits provided to an unsavoury prosecution witness;[393] and
- assertion that a disputed fact had been proven against the accused in an earlier trial.[394]

---

386 See *FS*, above note 269 at paras 16 and 18.

387 See *Rose* SCC, above note 214 at para 107. The same prohibition applies to defence counsel too: see *R v Williams*, 2008 ONCA 413 at para 82; *R v Tomlinson*, 2014 ONCA 158 at para 96.

388 See *Clark*, above note 355 at 235–36.

389 See *R v St-Laurent* (1990), 57 CCC (3d) 564 at 567 (Que CA).

390 See *R v Yaari* (1995), 101 CCC (3d) 401 at 403–5 [paras 3 and 6–8] (Ont CA), leave to appeal to SCC refused, [1998] SCCA No 274. Compare *R v Stymiest* (1993), 79 CCC (3d) 408 at 433 [para 93(1)] (BCCA), discussed in Frater, above note 11 at 176.

391 See *R v Neaves* (1992), 75 CCC (3d) 201 at 207–9 (NSCA), leave to appeal to SCC refused, [1992] SCCA No 344.

392 See *Dorion*, above note 385 at paras 120 and 124.

393 See *R v Klatt* (1994), 94 CCC (3d) 147 at 156 [paras 34–36] (Alta CA).

394 See *Carrière*, above note 244 at paras 49 and 54.

d) Misstating the Evidence, Unwarranted Speculation, Improper Inferences, and Asking the Jury to Use Evidence for an Impermissible Purpose

There is nothing wrong with a prosecutor's asking the jury to draw a reasonable inference from the evidence led at trial.[395] But it is improper for Crown counsel to contend that a fact has been established when the evidence does not reasonably support such a conclusion or to otherwise misstate the evidence.[396] It is also inappropriate for a prosecutor to urge the jury to reach a factual conclusion based on unwarranted speculation[397] or to ask the jury to draw an inference that, while available on the evidence, Crown counsel knows is inaccurate.[398]

Furthermore, Crown counsel must not ask the jury to employ evidence for a purpose not countenanced at law. For example, prosecutors have been criticized for

- suggesting that evidence of prior misconduct admitted for a limited narrative purpose be used to infer that the accused is the type of person to commit the offence,[399]
- adverting to the accused's unremarkable demeanour when confronted by police during an interview as evidence of guilt,[400]
- asking the jury to draw an inference that the trial judge had earlier ruled was prohibited,[401]
- submitting that an accused's refusal to admit wrongdoing in response to a police question is indicative of guilt,[402]

---

395 See *R v Hawkins*, 2011 NSCA 6 at paras 127–30, leave to appeal to SCC refused, [2011] SCCA No 102; *R v Mitchell* (2006), 212 CCC (3d) 258 at para 29 (Ont CA) [*Mitchell*].

396 See *LL*, above note 244 at paras 42–46; *R v MB*, 2011 ONCA 76 at paras 30–31; *R v Angelis*, 2013 ONCA 70 at para 39; *LSJPA - 1037*, above note 374 at para 175; *R v Adams*, 2012 NLCA 40 at para 19 [*Adams*]; *Usereau*, above note 368 at paras 117 and 124–25; *Mitchell*, above note 395 at paras 18 and 22–23; *R v West*, 2010 NSCA 16 at para 249; *R v Quinn*, 2009 BCCA 267 at paras 99–106; *FS*, above note 269 at paras 24–25.

397 See *Walker*, above note 272 at 153–54 [paras 24–25]; *McNeill* Ont CA, above note 293 at paras 54–60; *Tombran*, above note 311 at para 42; *Boudreau*, above note 368 at para 16; *Adams*, above note 396 at paras 15 and 19; *R v James*, 2013 BCCA 11 at paras 71–77, leave to appeal to SCC refused, [2013] SCCA No 87.

398 See Section H(8)(f), above in this chapter.

399 See *Robinson*, above note 265 at paras 38–39. See also *R v Precup*, 2013 ONCA 411 at paras 58–66: improperly relying on hearsay for its truth and for impermissible propensity purpose.

400 See *Adams*, above note 396 at para 17.

401 See *R v Kociukic*, 2011 MBCA 85 at paras 59–66, aff'd 2012 SCC 15.

402 See *Adams*, above note 396 at para 18. See also *GAO*, above note 285 at paras 14–17; *R v Gilling* (1997), 117 CCC (3d) 444 at paras 17–19 (Ont CA); *Turcotte*, above note 283 at paras 57–59.

- asserting that the failure of the accused to testify can be considered in deciding whether to convict,[403] and
- portraying a defence failure to subject a Crown exhibit to DNA testing as probative of guilt.[404]

These sorts of comments often operate to undermine the accused's constitutionally guaranteed rights, such as the right to be presumed innocent,[405] the right to silence,[406] the right to disclosure,[407] the right not to take the stand at trial,[408] and so on.

e) Discrediting the Legal System

In *R v Swietlinski*,[409] it was held to be unacceptable for a prosecutor conducting a parole eligibility hearing with a jury, under what is now section 745.6 of the *Criminal Code*,[410] to urge the jurors not to make a decision in accordance with the law if they felt that the law was bad. The effect of Crown counsel's remarks to the jury was to imply that the procedure set out in the *Criminal Code* was unduly favourable to the applicant and to urge the subversion of Parliament's intent regarding early parole. Addresses that support this sort of nullification of the law are at odds with the ethical duties to respect the rights of the accused and strive to achieve justice in the public interest.

---

403 See *R v Biladeau*, 2008 ONCA 833 at paras 25–34 [*Biladeau*]. It is not improper, however, for the prosecutor to simply state that the Crown case stands uncontradicted: *LSJPA - 1037*, above note 374 at paras 180–89.

404 See *Usereau*, above note 368 at paras 128–31.

405 See *R v Parsons* (1996), 146 Nfld & PEIR 210 at paras 60–64 (Nfld CA), leave to appeal to SCC refused, [1997] SCCA No 43: comments regarding failure to point to an alternative suspect (but contrast *R v Perlett* (2006), 212 CCC (3d) 11 at paras 87–93 (Ont CA), leave to appeal to SCC refused, [2007] SCCA No 96; *R v Czibulka* (2004), 189 CCC (3d) 199 at paras 73–75 (Ont CA), leave to appeal to SCC refused, [2004] SCCA No 502); *Biladeau*, above note 403 at para 33: comment undermines concept of reasonable doubt. See also *R v Laboucan*, 2010 SCC 12 at paras 11–14: deals with comments by trial judge but nonetheless supports proposition that the Crown closing should refrain from suggesting that avoiding conviction provides the accused with a motive to lie.

406 See the authorities cited at note 402, above in this chapter. See also *Adams*, above note 396 at para 18.

407 See *R v Peavoy* (1997), 117 CCC (3d) 226 at paras 10–15 (Ont CA).

408 See the authorities cited at note 403, above in this chapter.

409 (1994), 92 CCC (3d) 449 at 458–60 [paras 16–22] (SCC).

410 *Criminal Code*, above note 104.

f) Conclusion: The Duty to Be Accurate and Dispassionate

In *R v Charest*,[411] Fish J wrote that the Crown should press fully all proper arguments supporting guilt but must be "accurate, fair and dispassionate" in addressing the jury.[412] More recently, in *R v Trochym*, Deschamps J referred to Crown counsel's *Boucher* duties then stated that "rhetorical techniques that distort the fact-finding process, and misleading and highly prejudicial statements, have no place in a criminal prosecution."[413] Personalizing a closing or using it to launch excessive attacks against the accused denigrates Crown counsel's role as minister of justice. Tempered advocacy, not unbridled partisanship, must guide the prosecutor's actions and words.

I. PLEA DISCUSSIONS AND SENTENCING

Chapter 9 focuses on the ethical duties of defence counsel regarding plea discussions but has much to say that applies equally to prosecutors. In this section, we will briefly examine some of the duties that pertain in particular to Crown counsel.

1) A Principled Approach

The *PPSC Deskbook* sets out several principles that should guide a prosecutor's approach to plea negotiations: fairness, openness in soliciting and weighing the views of those involved in the Crown case such as a complainant and the police, accuracy for the development of a consistent and informed practice, and the interest of the public in the effective and consistent enforcement of the criminal law.[414] Crown counsel can only hope to fulfill these duties if she is properly prepared before engaging in meaningful plea discussions, in the sense of being familiar with the facts of the case and any relevant legal principles.[415]

---

411 *Charest*, above note 371.

412 *Ibid* at 330, quoting from *R v Pisani* (1970), 1 CCC (2d) 477 (SCC). To similar effect, see *Rose* SCC, above note 214 at 494 [para 107].

413 *Trochym*, above note 18 at para 79.

414 *PPSC Deskbook*, above note 8, ch 3.7, section 2 (Principles Guiding Resolution Discussions).

415 See Mary Lou Dickie, "Through the Looking Glass — Ethical Responsibilities of the Crown in Resolution Discussions" (2005) 50 Crim LQ 128 at 132–33.

2) Duty Not to Delay Resolution Discussions

Crown counsel should act expeditiously in responding to a plea-resolution initiative proposed by the defence. It is often advisable for prosecutors to take the initiative themselves by contacting defence counsel regarding the possibility of a plea resolution. One way or another, Crown counsel should engage in resolution discussions where the defence is amenable and where doing so is in the public interest.

3) Overcharging and Improper Threats

It is wrong for Crown counsel to proceed with more charges than are justified on the evidence or in the public interest, merely as a means of providing extra bargaining power during plea discussions.[416] It is especially improper for a prosecutor to offer to drop a charge in exchange for a concession by the accused where the charge is not justified in the first place. Nor should a more serious charge than is warranted be laid to pressure the accused to plead guilty to a less serious offence arising out of the same transaction. It is not, however, improper to lay overlapping charges where all are justified by the evidence, for instance, charges of "over 80" and impaired driving or of theft and possession of proceeds.

It is acceptable for a prosecutor to offer to withdraw or stay a charge in exchange for the accused's pleading guilty to an offence.[417] Crown counsel is also free to tell defence counsel that if the matter proceeds and evidence supporting additional charges emerges at the preliminary inquiry, a request will be made to commit the accused on the additional charges.[418] But using threatening language to pressure defence counsel to accept a plea offer early in the case or else face additional charges after a preliminary inquiry where the disclosure is not yet sufficient to permit an informed decision by the accused is improper.[419] Not surprisingly, it is also unacceptable to threaten sexual violence at the hands of prison inmates unless the accused agrees to waive the right to contest a criminal proceeding.[420]

---

416 See *PPSC Deskbook*, above note 8, ch 3.7, section 3.2 (Charge Discussions).
417 See *Babos*, above note 22 at para 59.
418 See *ibid*.
419 See *ibid* at paras 10, 59–61, and 71–72.
420 See *ibid* at para 70.

4) Misrepresentations Made to the Accused

Crown counsel must avoid the use of deception in dealing with defence counsel during plea discussions. Extensive disclosure obligations drastically reduce the possibility of this occurring. Nevertheless, prosecutors must take care to conduct discussions in good faith and without knowingly misleading the defence lawyer.[421]

5) Charge Pleaded to Must Be Reasonably Supported on the Facts

A prosecutor must not agree to a plea of guilty to an offence that is not justified on the evidence.[422] Rather, where Crown counsel realizes that the charge cannot be supported by the facts, it must be stayed or withdrawn. By the same token, it is improper for a prosecutor to accept a plea to a lesser offence that cannot be made out on the evidence in an effort to reach a plea resolution acceptable to the accused.

Example: The accused is charged with a number of counts, including possession of a restricted weapon contrary to section 91(2) of the *Criminal Code*,[423] in relation to his being found with a loaded handgun. Crown counsel agrees to a resolution under which the accused will plead guilty to the section 91(2) offence but later realizes that the definition of "restricted weapon" excludes a firearm. Having become aware that the facts do not permit a conviction under section 91(2), Crown counsel is ethically precluded from proceeding with the plea resolution agreement.[424]

6) Misleading the Court

Crown counsel can negotiate with defence counsel regarding the facts to be relied on for the purposes of sentencing. It is not acceptable, however, to reach an agreement respecting facts that cannot be supported on any reasonable view of the evidence.[425] Knowingly putting inaccurate

---

421 Crown counsel are subject to the duty to bargain in good faith discussed in Chapter 9, Section O. See also ABA Prosecution Standard 3-4.1 (comment).

422 See *PPSC Deskbook*, above note 8, ch 3.7, section 3.2 (Charge Discussions).

423 *Criminal Code*, above note 104.

424 This example is based on the facts and reasoning in *R v Bérubé*, 2012 BCCA 345 at para 30 [*Bérubé*].

425 See Martin Committee Report, above note 100 at 325; *PPSC Deskbook*, above note 8, ch 3.7, section 3.5 (Agreements as to the Facts of the Offence); *Nixon*, above note 31 at para 53; *R v Beswick*, [1996] 1 Cr App R 427 at 430 (CA).

facts before the judge at a sentence hearing not only breaches counsel's duty of candour to the court but also runs contrary to the public's interest in a reliable result.

7) Aggregate Plea Offers in Joint Trials

The prosecution sometimes makes plea resolution offers to all of the accused in a joint criminal proceeding with the offer to each being conditional on all of the others also accepting the proposed resolution. There is nothing unethical in Crown counsel's making an aggregate offer of this sort,[426] and there is usually very good reason to do so. Often, it is only if all accused accept the offer that the expenditure of substantial trial resources can be avoided. Crown counsel may also have a legitimate concern that one of the accused will accept a certain level of responsibility on a plea only to testify to having played a much more prominent role if called by the defence at the trial of an accused who did not accept the resolution offer.

8) Duty to Honour Plea Agreement

In *R v Nixon*, the Supreme Court of Canada ruled that the Crown's decision to repudiate a plea agreement constitutes an exercise of prosecutorial discretion[427] and so is subject to judicial review only for abuse of process.[428] *Nixon* thus pours cold water on the argument that a plea agreement can be enforced against the Crown like a contractual term or lawyer's undertaking.[429] *Nixon* also rejected the contention, which had attracted support in earlier jurisprudence, that a court can hold the Crown to a repudiated plea agreement where the agreement, if enforced, could not reasonably be said to bring the administration of justice into disrepute.[430]

Nixon nonetheless recognizes that honouring resolution agreements is an ethical imperative for Crown counsel and is necessary if the crim-

---

426 See *R v Pawliuk*, 2001 BCCA 13 at paras 53–56; *United States of America v Prudenza* (2006), 213 CCC (3d) 312 at para 29 (Ont CA), leave to appeal to SCC refused, [2006] SCCA No 418.

427 *Nixon*, above note 31 at para 30. See also *Anderson*, above note 11 at para 44. Prosecutorial discretion is discussed more generally in Section D, above in this chapter.

428 *Nixon*, above note 31 at para 31; *Bérubé*, above note 424 at paras 23–35. The test for establishing an abuse of process is discussed in the paragraph associated with notes 72–75, above in this chapter.

429 *Nixon*, above note 31 at paras 44–45.

430 *Ibid* at paras 50–53.

inal justice system is to operate properly, given that the great bulk of criminal cases are resolved through such agreements.[431] If defence counsel were unable to rely on prosecutors fulfilling the terms of plea agreements, the significant benefits that such agreements bring to defendants and the justice system more generally would be lost. *Nixon* thus concludes that the vital importance of upholding plea resolutions means that in some instances Crown counsel may simply have to live with a completed agreement that, on further reflection, appears less than ideal.[432]

Good ethical practice need not be coterminous with legal duty. There is thus no contradiction in *Nixon*'s emphasizing that proper ethics militates strongly against prosecutors' reneging on plea agreements without good justification while at the same time imposing a demanding standard for judicial review of a decision to repudiate. Nor is there any reason to believe that Crown counsel in Canada will repudiate plea agreements with any greater frequency in the wake of *Nixon*. The many attorneys general who made submissions on the appeal unanimously accepted that honouring plea agreements is important to the justice system and that repudiating a plea agreement should occur only in exceptional cases.[433] The policy guidelines adopted by many Canadian prosecution services expressly state the same thing, typically providing that repudiation is justified only where clearly in the public interest and approved by a senior regional prosecutor.[434]

In fact, the forceful holding in *Nixon* that it is of "crucial importance to the proper and fair administration of criminal justice that plea agreements be honoured" by Crown counsel[435] informs the application of the abuse of process test in a highly material way. In an ordinary case involving an attack on the exercise of prosecutorial discretion, an accused is not allowed to proceed with her challenge without meeting the threshold standard of showing an evidentiary record capable of supporting the claim.[436] But *Nixon* holds that honouring a plea agreement is so important and repudiation so rare and exceptional that the accused will meet the threshold for embarking on a review merely by showing that the Crown has reneged. The evidentiary burden then shifts to the Crown to explain the circumstances and reasons for repudiation.

431 *Ibid* at paras 46–47 and 63.
432 *Ibid* at para 48.
433 *Ibid* at para 49.
434 See, for example, *PPSC Deskbook*, above note 8, ch 3.7, section 2.2 (Fairness).
435 *Nixon*, above note 31 at para 63.
436 *Nixon*, *ibid* at paras 27 and 60–62. See also the text associated with notes 74–75, above in this chapter.

While the onus of establishing an abuse remains on the accused, minimal or no explanation from the Crown as to why the agreement was breached will weigh heavily in favour of finding that an abuse has occurred.[437]

At the end of the day, it is probably safe to say that Crown counsel in Canada will renege on a plea resolution only where to do otherwise would be clearly against the public interest, in the sense that carrying out the agreement would bring the administration of justice into disrepute.[438] This standard will usually if not always be met where the agreement has been obtained by fraud or misrepresentation or has been materially breached by the accused.[439]

Undertaking not to appeal: Pre-*Nixon* caselaw provides that Crown counsel at trial cannot extinguish the attorney general's statutory discretion to appeal a sentence with an undertaking given to the defence.[440] It has thus been suggested that Crown counsel should avoid agreeing to a plea resolution term that attempts to restrict the appeal rights of either side.[441]

9) Direct Communication with Accused

The ethical rule restricting contact with a person who is represented by a lawyer in the matter applies equally to prosecutors.[442] This means that Crown counsel cannot bypass defence counsel and negotiate a plea

---

437 *Nixon, ibid* at paras 63–64.

438 See, for example, *BC Crown Policy Manual*, above note 118, RES 1, "Resolution Discussions and Stays of Proceedings" (2 October 2009) at 3; *NS Crown Attorney Manual*, above note 121, "Resolution Discussions and Agreements" (20 November 2013) at 2.

439 See *R v Obadia* (1998), 20 CR (5th) 162 (Que CA); *R v MacDonald* (1990), 54 CCC (3d) 97 (Ont CA).

440 See *R v Ryazanov*, 2008 ONCA 667 at paras 40–49 [*Ryazanov*]; *R v Dubien* (1982), 67 CCC (2d) 341 at 346 [para 19] (Ont CA); *R v Wood* (1988), 43 CCC (3d) 570 at 574 (Ont CA). Such an undertaking would nonetheless be enforced if the repudiation would constitute an abuse of process: see *Ryazanov, ibid* at paras 50–55. See also *Anderson*, above note 11 at para 44: decision whether to appeal is a matter of prosecutorial discretion.

441 See *Ryazanov*, above note 440 at para 49; Dickie, above note 415 at 13; *Ont Crown Policy Manual*, above note 120, "Resolution Discussions" (21 March 2005) at 2; *Sask Crown Policy Manual*, above note 119, "Resolution Discussions Policy" at 1; *NS Crown Attorney Manual*, above note 121, "Resolution Discussions and Agreements" (20 November 2013) at 3.

442 See Chapter 8, Section C(1).

resolution directly with an accused unless defence counsel consents.[443] It matters not that the communication originates with the accused or that the accused expresses a desire to waive his right to counsel.[444] There are a number of reasons for applying the no-contact rule here, including concerns that the accused's best interests will not be protected and that his relationship with defence counsel will be seriously undermined.[445]

However, in exceedingly rare cases the interests of justice may favour a represented accused's being able to negotiate a plea agreement without the involvement or knowledge of his current counsel.[446] Suppose that an accused in a multi-accused prosecution approaches the police or Crown counsel with credible allegations that his defence lawyer is being paid for by a criminal organization. He wants to explore cooperating with the prosecution in exchange for leniency in sentencing. But he adds that the criminal organization would view even the mere discharge of his current lawyer as a sign that he has broken with the group and could no longer be trusted, hence putting his life in jeopardy.

In such a case, it may be appropriate for Crown counsel to take the extraordinary measure of bringing the accused before a judge in camera to obtain an order appointing "shadow" counsel to act for the accused in plea negotiations.[447] Another option, at first blush sensible given that the accused may be fabricating the allegations, would be for Crown counsel to provide the accused with the names of several reputable defence lawyers for the purpose of obtaining advice.[448] Yet even this modest step arguably violates the no-contact rule, at least absent a court order. And any defence counsel approached by the accused will be subject to the rule as well.[449]

---

443 See *R v Newsham*, [2002] OJ No 2739 (Ct J); *US v Lopez*, 4 F3d 1455 at 1458–61 (9th Cir 1993) [*Lopez*]; ABA Prosecution Standard 3-4.1(b).

444 See Chapter 8, Section C(1)(e).

445 See Chapter 8, Section C(1)(a), discussing the rationale for the no-contact rule in the context of represented witnesses. The rationale is heightened for a represented accused, given what is at stake in a criminal matter.

446 See ABA Model Rule 4.2, comment 6: in exceptional circumstances, a lawyer may seek a court order to engage in conduct otherwise in breach of the no-contact rule, for example where necessary to avoid reasonably certain injury. See also *Lopez*, above note 443 at 1461–62; Daniel C Richman, "Cooperating Clients" (1995) 56 Ohio St LJ 69 at 148–50.

447 Such an approach is condoned by the majority in *People v Stewart*, 230 AD2d 116 at 118 and 123–25 (NY App Div 1997), but subject to condemnation by the dissent (*ibid* at 130–48 and 155–56).

448 See Geoffrey C Hazard & W William Hodes, *The Law of Lawyering*, 3d ed (Gaithersburg, MD: Aspen Publishers, 2001) (loose-leaf 2013 supplement) at § 38.9.

449 See Chapter 9, Section I(1).

Some argue that the best solution to this problem is to reject the paternalistic notion that the no-contact rule can never be waived by the client.[450] A different resolution would be to read into the rule an exception applicable where necessary to prevent reasonably anticipated wrongdoing by the person's lawyer.[451] Neither option is particularly attractive for Crown counsel in our scenario given the absence of supporting language in Canadian no-contact rules.

The no-contact rule does not, however, prohibit a lawyer from communicating with a represented person whose counsel is acting under a limited scope retainer provided the communications are restricted to matters outside the scope of that retainer.[452] It is thus permissible for a prosecutor to deal directly with an accused who wants to negotiate a co-operation agreement as long as defence counsel's retainer is limited to exclude such matters. Crown counsel will nonetheless be bound by the rules governing communications with an unrepresented person.[453] And because this issue will almost always arise in the context of complex and serious proceedings, she should ordinarily insist that the accused retain new counsel to handle the negotiations.[454]

---

450 See Geoffrey C Hazard & Dana Remus Irwin, "Toward a Revised 4.2 No-Contact Rule" (2009) 60 Hastings Law J 797 at 825–28.

451 See *US v Talao*, 222 F3d 1133 at 1140–41 (9th Cir 2000).

452 See Chapter 8, Section C(1)(i).

453 See Chapter 8, Section C(2)(b).

454 The ability of defence counsel to act in such circumstances is discussed in Chapter 9, Section I(1).

TABLE OF CASES

INDEX

ABOUT THE AUTHORS

David Layton obtained his LLB from Dalhousie Law School in 1987 and a master's degree in law from Oxford University in 1989. He clerked for the late Chief Justice Brian Dickson at the Supreme Court of Canada in 1990. David worked as defence counsel for over twenty years in Toronto and Vancouver before joining the British Columbia Ministry of Justice as an appeals prosecutor in 2014. He has taught courses at the University of British Columbia and the University of Victoria faculties of law on ethics and criminal law, and wrongful convictions. He is currently a member of the Law Society of British Columbia's disciplinary hearing panel pool.

Hon. Mr. Justice Michel Proulx (1939–2007) was a member of the Court of Appeal of Quebec from 1989 until 2004. Prior to his appointment, he had a distinguished litigation practice, mainly in criminal law, from 1963 to 1989. He also served as an adjunct professor of law at McGill University from 1967 to 1989. After leaving the bench, Michel was a partner at Davies Ward Phillips & Vineberg.